THE S. MARK TAPER FOUNDATION

IMPRINT IN JEWISH STUDIES

BY THIS ENDOWMENT
THE S. MARK TAPER FOUNDATION SUPPORTS
THE APPRECIATION AND UNDERSTANDING
OF THE RICHNESS AND DIVERSITY OF
JEWISH LIFE AND CULTURE

*The publisher gratefully acknowledges the generous support of the Jewish Studies Endowment Fund of the University of California Press Foundation, which was established by a major gift from the S. Mark Taper Foundation.*

THE NEW
*Mediterranean*
*Jewish Table*

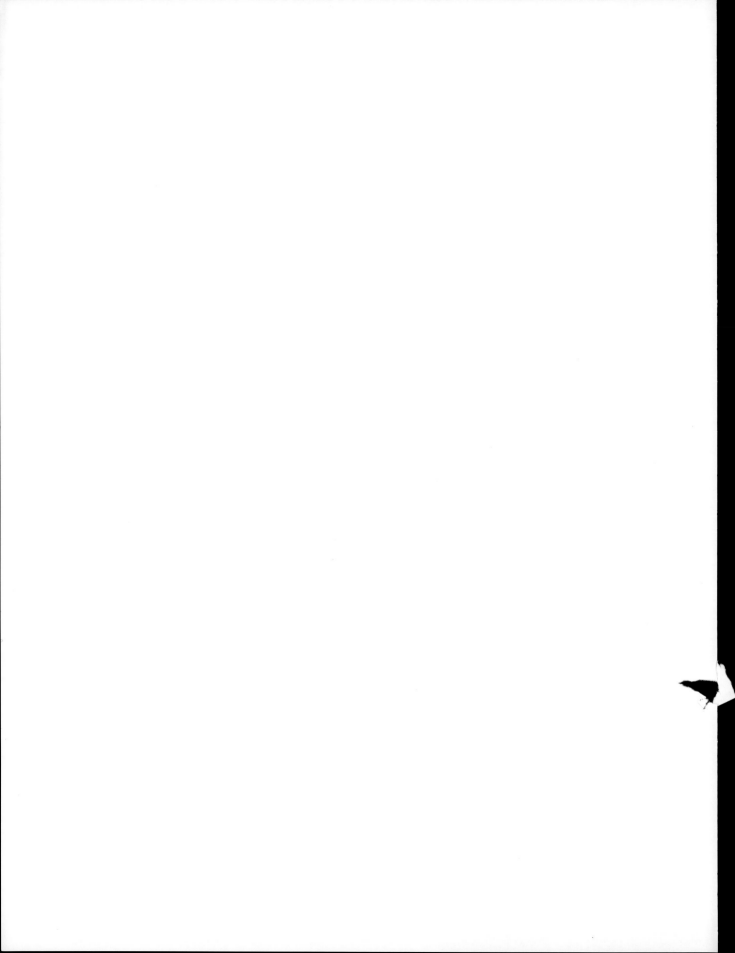

# THE NEW
# *Mediterranean*
# *Jewish Table*

## OLD WORLD RECIPES

### FOR THE

## MODERN HOME

### *Joyce Goldstein*

*Illustrations by Hugh D'Andrade*

UNIVERSITY OF CALIFORNIA PRESS

University of California Press, one of the most distinguished university presses in the United States, enriches lives around the world by advancing scholarship in the humanities, social sciences, and natural sciences. Its activities are supported by the UC Press Foundation and by philanthropic contributions from individuals and institutions. For more information, visit www.ucpress.edu.

University of California Press
Oakland, California

Library of Congress Cataloging-in-Publication Data

Names: Goldstein, Joyce Esersky, author.
Title: The new Mediterranean Jewish table : Old World recipes for the
    modern home / Joyce Goldstein.
Description: Oakland, California : University of California Press, [2016] |
    2016 | Includes bibliographical references and index.
Identifiers: LCCN 2015043306 | ISBN 9780520284999 (cloth : alk. paper)
    | ISBN 9780520960619 (ebook)
Subjects: LCSH: Jewish cooking. | Cooking, Mediterranean. | LCGFT:
    Cookbooks.
Classification: LCC TX724 .G657224 2016 | DDC 641.5/676—dc23

LC record available at http://lccn.loc.gov/2015043306

Manufactured in the United States of America

24   23   22   21   20   19   18   17   16
10   9   8   7   6   5   4   3   2   1

The paper used in this publication meets the minimum requirements of
ANSI/NISO Z39.48–1992 (R 2002) (*Permanence of Paper*).

# Contents

Introduction

## JEWS IN AMERICA

In the early 1900s, waves of Ashkenazi Jews came to America from Russia, Poland, Romania, and Germany. Most settled on the East Coast, where they maintained their religious and culinary culture. Their communities were large enough to sustain neighborhood delicatessens, appetizer stores, bakeries, and kosher meat and poultry markets. Brisket, borscht, matzo ball soup, chopped liver, pickled herring, gefilte fish, bagels and lox, latkes, blintzes, kugel, knishes, kasha, challah, and rye bread—these Ashkenazi staples became the cornerstone of Jewish food in America. This is not the healthiest or most varied diet, especially because the only green on the plate might be a token sprig of parsley, but it is a cuisine that has a strong emotional pull on Jewish Americans who want to hold on to their eastern European heritage.

Many early Jewish households in America were observant and kept kosher kitchens. When not cooking traditional family recipes from memory, they relied on a few basic Jewish cookbooks recommended by friends and relatives. These no-nonsense volumes offered practical advice to the housewife, or *balaboosta,* on shopping, kosher cooking, and preparations for holiday celebrations.

In time, more modern Jewish cookbooks were published, as families looked for a broader range of recipes and for time-saving shortcuts. Food processors replaced hand graters for making latkes, and shredded carrots or sweet potatoes were mixed with the traditional russet potatoes for a new taste. Clever recipes for gefilte fish loaves and savory layered kugels appeared, and Lipton soup mix, cranberry sauce, Coca-Cola, and canned beef broth turned up in recipes for braised brisket. Despite these "creative and modern innovations," the recipe repertoire remained basically Ashkenazi. At the same time, enterprising kosher food companies began selling food products nationwide that echoed and thus enforced Ashkenazi traditions. Every year at Rosh Hashanah and Hanukkah, my local supermarket brings out the gefilte fish and matzo meal, even though these foods have no specific relevance to these holidays. Given this scenario, it is not surprising that most Americans think all Jewish food is brisket, chopped liver, bagels and lox, and gefilte fish.

But not all Jewish cooking traditions come from eastern Europe. For centuries, Jewish people lived and cooked in southern Europe, North Africa, and the Middle East—what is thought of as the Mediterranean. Because Mediterranean Jews did not immigrate to the United States in large numbers, their delicious and varied cuisines have been nearly unknown here until recently.

Today, many American diners have enthusiastically embraced the Mediterranean diet, seeing it as both a healthful and a flavorful way to eat. It offers a diverse range of recipes from the kitchens of Spain, Portugal, Italy, Greece, Turkey, North Africa, and the Middle East. But even though many Americans, including American Jews, know and enjoy Mediterranean food, relatively few have made the connection between Mediterranean cuisine and its Jewish culinary traditions. This book will enable readers to make that connection by bringing the delicious and varied foods of the Mediterranean Jews into their kitchens and their family traditions.

## MEDITERRANEAN JEWISH COMMUNITIES

Large communities of Jews have lived in the Middle East since biblical times, and they have been at home in Italy, Spain, Portugal, and North Africa for centuries. Due to the climate, agricultural possibilities, and local culinary traditions, Jews of the Mediterranean were not dining on borscht, bagels, or brisket. They cooked the traditional recipes of the region in which they lived while observing the kosher laws. That meant a Mediterranean diet filled with seasonal fresh vegetables and fruits, legumes, grains, and small portions of meat, poultry, or fish. Abundant use of spices and fresh herbs and a pantry of homemade condiments made simple foods taste more complex and interesting.

Many people lump Jewish food that is not Ashkenazi under the broad term *Sephardic*, but this blanket designation is inaccurate from both a culinary and a cultural point of view. I prefer to differentiate between Sephardic and Mediterranean Jews. In ancient times, Sepharad was the Hebrew name given to the Iberian Peninsula, and Jews who were forced to flee Spain and Portugal after the Spanish Inquisition and settled in other countries were called Sephardim. The term *Sephardic* does not encompass many of the Jews who lived in Italy, the Maghrebi Jews in North Africa, or the Mizrahi, or Oriental Jews, in the Muslim lands of the Middle East. These Jews and their recipes are Mediterranean and not necessarily Sephardic.

Cultural differences distinguish the Ashkenazim and the Mediterranean Jews. The former maintained a rather closed community to ensure their continued survival. In contrast, even though Mediterranean Jews and Sephardim suffered persecution, their communities, often along the Silk Road, were more integrated with the larger society. They shared recipes and culinary traditions with their non-Jewish neighbors and were open to new ingredients and spices that did not break the kosher laws.

## OLD WORLD FOOD IN A NEW WORLD KITCHEN

In the United States, over the last fifty years, major demographic and societal changes have transformed the Jewish home and kitchen. Intermarriage and assimilation have resulted in fewer traditional observant Jewish households. Today, many Jews do not keep kosher homes or regularly attend synagogue. Yet they still identify with being Jewish. American secular Jews celebrate Jewish holidays and keep an emotional and cultural connection to their heritage. Along with this cultural change, our country is undergoing a culinary revolution fueled by a deep, new interest in food culture. Younger generations of Jewish home cooks are looking for contemporary ideas to match their evolving palates. No matter how many ways one can be innovative with brisket or latkes, these are still brisket and latkes. Rather than stay attached to the predictable and old-fashioned Ashkenazi recipes, these young cooks want to broaden their culinary horizons and eat a more varied and healthful diet. They want to move from heavy, limited cold-weather foods into the sunlight of the Mediterranean and its abundant culinary possibilities.

This does not mean that we are never to cook brisket and latkes again. But it does mean that we need to expand our concept of Jewish cooking to reflect today's greater cultural diversity and broader palate. People are dining out more often and sampling many different ethnic cuisines, so greater variety, innovation, and bolder flavors are in. This increased interest in ethnic food is a big part of why Jewish cuisine is now approached with a fresh eye and open mouth. Jews and non-Jews alike are enjoying Jewish food at restaurants, most of which are not kosher. Even new hip delis like Mile End in New York and Wise Sons in San Francisco are adding Middle Eastern Jewish dishes such as hummus, falafel, *shakshuka,* and preserved-lemon aioli. Today, many Americans attend Passover dinners at restaurants like Perbacco and Delfina in San Francisco, Spago in Los Angeles, and Lumière in Boston, often in place of a Seder at home. Secular and contemporary Jews feel a subliminal cultural connection to Israel and proudly patronize restaurants like Zahav in Philadelphia and Balaboosta in New York, which are run by Israeli chefs who serve food that is neither kosher nor necessarily traditionally Jewish. Indeed, much of it is clearly Arab in inspiration. Despite shellfish stews and meatballs with yogurt sauce, if an Israeli chef is cooking it, the food is "Jewish" by osmosis.

"Old World food in a New World kitchen" is a phrase that has come to define my culinary path. For as long as I have been cooking, at home or at my former San Francisco restaurant, Square One, my passion has been to take traditional recipes and make them enticing to contemporary diners. It is not enough for recipes to be true to their country of origin; they need to satisfy and reflect the flavor qualities and foods that are enjoyed today. In the past, restaurants and cooks prided themselves on culinary "authenticity" and sought to re-create traditional recipes. To mess with a time-honored dish was sacrilege and cause for criticism and kvetching. Not so today. Contemporary cooks and diners value creativity and innovation. They recognize that our palates change as we discover new foods, new flavors, and new cuisines. We can now buy ingredients like *za'atar, ras el hanout,* sumac, pomegranate molasses, Aleppo and Maras peppers, and all manner of fresh fruits, vegetables, and herbs that were not readily available when I first started writing cookbooks.

It's not often that one gets the chance to revisit his or her early work with a fresh eye, an open mind, and a newly sharpened palate. This Mediterranean Jewish cookbook for the modern kitchen will build and expand on carefully selected recipes from many of my cookbooks. I have focused on dishes that I still cook today because they continue to please everyone who has eaten them at my table. I have updated recipes to reflect my evolving palate and trends in American dining. I have expanded my definition of Mediterranean cuisine to include my growing interest in Middle Eastern flavors. The recipes in this new book show how to recognize and integrate the signature flavors of the Mediterranean regions—the Sephardic foods of Spain, Portugal, parts of Italy, Greece, and Turkey; the foods of the Middle Eastern countries of Iran, Iraq, Jordan, Syria, and Lebanon; and the North African countries of Morocco, Tunisia, Algeria, Egypt, and Libya—into your cooking so that you can delight in diverse and adventurous flavors at the Jewish family table.

It is both possible and desirable for Jewish cooking to evolve—to go beyond the Ashkenazi table—as the varied, seasonal, and healthful Mediterranean dishes that follow illustrate. My hope is that you will find yourself making the recipes again and again for family and friends, as the goal of this book is not only to demonstrate the dynamic, creative elements of a culinary heritage but also to influence future generations of cooks.

## ABOUT THE RECIPES

The recipes in this book are based on, or inspired by, dishes from three Mediterranean Jewish cultures: the Sephardic, the Maghrebi, and the Mizrahi. In Israel today, for political expediency, all three identify themselves as Sephardic because they follow the traditions of the Sephardic Jews as opposed to the Ashkenazi Jews and come under the jurisdiction of the Sephardic rabbi. As a group, they represent 70 percent of the Jews in the country. But their culinary heritages and cuisines are not the same.

The Sephardim were western European Jews from the Iberian Peninsula who were expelled after the Spanish Inquisition and found new homes in other parts of the Mediterranean. They spoke a language called Ladino. Maghrebi Jews lived in the North African countries of Morocco, Tunisia, Algeria, Libya, and Egypt. The term *Mizrahi* translates as "Eastern" or "Oriental" and is the label applied to Jews who had been living in Muslim lands since biblical times. I often refer to the food of Mizrahi Jews as Judeo-Arabic. The cuisines of all three populations were influenced by the local culinary traditions and agricultural possibilities of their homelands. One important element that unites these groups is their ability to adapt local recipes while observing kosher law.

Jews have a long history of intermittent religious persecution and were often forced to move from their homelands. As they roamed from country to country, their recipes changed and were adjusted to reflect local ingredients and traditions. Some recipes evolved so much that it is hard to discern their true origin. For example, the food of the

Sephardic Jews who moved to Italy looks and tastes Italian, and the food of the Sephardic Jews who went to Turkey mirrors Turkish cuisine. In Mediterranean countries, Jews and non-Jews prepare similar recipes in the same manner. You can sometimes identify a recipe as Jewish by the title, such as the inclusion of a biblical figure like Rachel, Rebecca, Ezekiel, or Moses. Or the dish might be described as *all'ebraica* or *alla giudia* in Italy, or as *a la djudia* in the Middle East. But another tip-off is seeing how the traditional recipes have been adapted to conform to the kosher laws. The lamb and eggplant moussaka of Greece and Turkey has a dairy topping, but the Jewish version does not. Observant Jews do not soak bread in milk for their meatballs and do not spoon yogurt sauces on cooked lamb or add a cheese component to pasta with meat sauce. Because of the kosher laws, fish soups do not include shellfish, and sausages are made with beef or lamb rather than pork.

Traditionally, a family's recipe collection was not extensive, and the ingredients available were limited by transportation and region. Unlike today, novelty and constant change were not a priority. The same dishes were prepared over and over again, so recipes were committed to memory and passed on from generation to generation, from mother to daughter. If they were written down, they were "sketches," with just enough information to jog the memory of someone who had made the dish before or had seen it prepared. Measurements were vague—an eggshell of this, a small mustard glass of that—and cooking directions were obtuse—"roast until done," or "fold dough in the usual manner."

Kitchens were nothing like the equipment-enhanced marvels they are today. There were no food processors, blenders, or electric mixers. Before World War II, few homes had refrigerators, and many kitchens had burners but no oven. Traditional cooking methods were not always the most efficient, but they were familiar, the way things had been done for generations. That meant that technique was not challenged and efficiency was not important. It also meant that there was time for cooking. Women fed the immediate family or guests and extended family in a hospitable and generous manner. They went to the market daily and prepared lunch as well as dinner. They preserved food for future meals when certain ingredients might not be available or in season. They cooked special foods for weddings, circumcisions, holidays, and the Sabbath. Most women did not work outside the home, which meant that they did not usually have to rush to get a meal together for a family that might eat in haste because of computer classes, soccer practice, or a full social or business calendar attached to the end of the workday.

Most of the recipes I have collected and cooked over the years are for everyday home cooking and holiday or celebratory meals, much as in the past. I have relied on a variety of sources: a family's stained recipe cards, conversations with home cooks and restaurant chefs, and recipes found in scores of regional cookbooks.

Most of the historic recipes in these books have been transcribed based on oral description. When asked how a dish was prepared, people would give measurements and directions from memory. Few recipes were recorded as cooks worked in the kitchen. No one followed grandma around with a pad and pencil or a video recorder. So when I began testing old recipes, I often found errors in procedure, missing steps and ingredients, or inaccurate timing. These were not significant impediments to cooking the recipes at the time, because they were part of everyday life, the dishes were familiar, and cooks had seen them prepared many times. But for those of us cooking today, accuracy is important because the recipes are not part of our tradition or our daily routine and fewer people have as much kitchen experience as home cooks did in the past. Nowadays, the goal is to encourage and support home cooking, which means that recipes are typically written in great detail, with every grain of salt, every pan size, every heat level, and every minute precisely recorded to prevent wasting time, effort, and ingredients.

The recipes in this book are not museum pieces. Recipes must be alive, open to change, adaptation, and personal interpretation. Although I respect tradition and believe that cultural authenticity is important, I want a recipe to be efficient and to produce truly flavorful food. To meet those goals, I've reorganized some of the older traditional recipes, primarily revising the order in which the steps are performed or grouped.

During my research, I found many interesting old recipes that would intrigue food historians, but the ingredients would be difficult for contemporary home cooks to find, and even if they could be tracked down, few cooks would take the time to work with them. So in this book I opted for practicality and deliciousness. Most of the recipes are based on traditional dishes that I have updated for today's eclectic palates. Others have been modernized to make them more appealing and relevant to the way we now eat. And some are my own creations, based on traditional ideas.

More often than not, I've increased the amount of herbs, spices, garlic, and other seasonings to bring the recipes more in line with the modern palate, which is accustomed to bolder tastes acquired from eating in diverse ethnic restaurants. I have also adjusted cooking times to accommodate contemporary tastes and schedules. Cooking times were excessively long in some of the recipes. Modern stoves are more powerful than old-time burners, so I do not call for boiling soup noodles for two hours or fish for over an hour. But whenever a long simmer resulted in a delicious dish with melting textures, I preserved the recommended cooking time. I also kept cooking times longer than is currently in vogue for some vegetables if improved flavor was worth the loss of crunch.

After you have cooked a recipe a few times, you will adjust the seasoning to bring out the best in your ingredients and to suit your palate and sense of flavor balance. I tested the recipes using the best ingredients and without much technical sleight of hand. Most are not overly time-consuming and many are economical. Although prosperous Jewish families lived in some major cities, most Mediterranean and Sephardic Jews were not wealthy, so the recipes reflect a sense of thriftiness. They also display creativity in the way that a few humble ingredients or leftovers are transformed into something special.

Finally, I have given preference to recipes that mesh with my palate, dishes I want to eat over and over again. They represent the comfort of home and hearth, simple celebrations, a sense of cultural and culinary continuity with our ancestors as viewed through a contemporary mind-set. It is thrilling for me to see my grandchildren eat these dishes with delight because it gives me hope that perhaps they will continue to cook them long after I have given up my place at the stove.

## The Ingredients

Although cooking with seasonal, local food is often characterized as a new trend, in the Mediterranean kitchens of generations past, ingredients were always locally grown, seasonal, and unadulterated. Everything was newly harvested, either from a home garden or from a neighboring farm, and then sold in a nearby market. There were no refrigerated trucks and airfreight. With no deterioration from time and travel, flavors were clean and vibrant. Thus seasoning was kept to a minimum, used to enhance the flavor of truly fresh, seasonal ingredients. Cooks used just a bit of salt and pepper; a pinch of a spice, such as cinnamon, nutmeg, cardamom, or cumin; or a good squeeze of lemon juice. Parsley, thyme, and bay were the most common herbs, with oregano, mint, cilantro, and dill used occasionally. Today, large-scale food manufacturing and farming and long-distance shipping have made many ingredients readily available, but they have suffered a loss of flavor and are not as vibrant as in the past. Taste the average supermarket tomato or apple and you'll know what I'm talking about. Who knows when that tomato or apple was harvested?

Plus, manufacturers have laced many prepared foods and condiments with excessive salt and sweeteners (as well as with preservatives and additives) that our palates have inadvertently come to accept as part of the flavor profile. Given such manipulation, it is not surprising that many of the original Mediterranean and Sephardic recipes seem flat and stripped down. This is where careful shopping comes in, because shopping is just as important as cooking.

Dazzling culinary technique and the finest equipment cannot make up for poor ingredients. I am lucky because I live in San Francisco, which has abundant fresh, organic produce at farmers' markets, nearby farming areas with long growing seasons, and people raising poultry, lamb, and beef responsibly. Of course, not everyone has easy access to ideal ingredients. If possible, seek out a butcher and a fishmonger to avoid prepackaged meats and fish and encourage your local markets to stock organic ingredients. For the best seasonal produce, shop at a farmers' market or sign up for a CSA (community-supported agriculture) delivery.

If your community does not have specialty markets, look to online sources for quality oils, spices, and other ingredients, such as vinegars, tahini, and pomegranate molasses. Herbs, except for oregano and bay, which are traditionally used dried, should be fresh. I recommend kosher salt and sea salt, as the best brands do not contain additives, and unsalted butter and good-quality olive oil. For frying and sautéing, use olive oil (sometimes labeled "pure olive oil") or sunflower or canola oil. Although extra virgin olive oil is traditional even for deep-frying, it can be costly, so use it when you can taste it. Toss out any old spices and then buy new ones in small batches from a company dedicated to spices or from another source with high turnover. Whenever possible, grind pepper and spices as you need them for greater pungency. Taste and adjust the seasoning as you cook, not only at the end.

### The Mediterranean Flavor Palate

As noted earlier, I distinguish the cuisines of Sephardic and Mediterranean Jews, dividing them into Sephardic, Maghrebi, and Mizrahi kitchens. Following years of research and recipe testing, I have identified the traditional spices and other ingredients that create the signature flavor profile of each group. So when I speak of the Mediterranean flavor palate, I am speaking of the traditional flavor combinations, spice medleys, or groups of ingredients that appear often in that region or country's cooking, such as tomatoes and cinnamon in Greece; rose water and cardamom in Iran; pine nuts and raisins or tahini, garlic, and lemon in Arab countries; and cumin, coriander, caraway, garlic, and hot pepper in Tunisia. When I see these flavor combinations in a recipe, I know where I am.

Compared with North Africa and the Middle East, the Italian Jewish palate is most restrained—almost austere—in seasoning. Because the Italians had, and still have for the most part, stellar raw materials, Italian Jewish cooks don't rely on exotic spices and herbs to achieve full-flavored dishes. They are ingredient focused. They use salt, a bit of pepper, and a few grains of nutmeg, though they can't resist a squeeze of lemon on near-ly everything. Their herb of choice is parsley, followed by thyme and basil. Their prefer-ence for clean flavors resulted in an uncomplicated cuisine, even when the foods of the New World were added to their larder. Keep in mind that the simpler the cooking style, the more attention you need to pay to every detail. The margin for error is smaller, which means ingredients must be chosen with great care.

The Sephardim of Spain and Portugal who settled in the Ottoman Empire and Greece already had a Moorish, or Arabized, palate. Theirs was a cuisine with vivid spices, like cinnamon, allspice, cumin, and paprika, and mint, dill, and bay leaves joined parsley in the herb bouquet. They ate rice, spinach, and artichokes and gradually embraced the foods of the New World, such as tomatoes, peppers, pumpkins, vanilla, and chocolate. They brought with them nut-and-bread-thickened sauces, saffron, a love of citrus, a penchant for sweet-and-sour combinations, and a sweet tooth for desserts.

Judeo-Arabic cooks, the southern Mediterranean Jews living in Iraq, Syria, Iran, and Lebanon, share much of the Ottoman flavor profile, but add sumac, tamarind, pomegran-ate, and sesame to their pantry, as well as dates, figs, and apricots. The Jews of North Af-rica play with an even fuller spice spectrum, using ginger, cumin, coriander, and cayenne, along with cinnamon, pepper, and elaborate homemade spice mixtures. Cilantro (fresh coriander) joined mint, dill, and parsley in the herb garden. Flower petals coupled with orange flower water and rose water add scent and sweetness. Preserved lemons, tangy ol-ives, and spicy *harissa* join the dried fruits and nuts for a complex and sensual cuisine.

Although Israel does not represent a distinct culture covered in this book, I would be remiss if I did not mention the Israeli flavor palate here. Israel is a Mediterranean country, but it is a melting pot of diverse cultures and has a gradually evolving cuisine of its own. Like the food of the United States, Israel's food reflects all of the immigrants who have settled there. You can find Ashkenazic dishes of Russian, German, and Polish Jews; foods of the Yemenites, Ethiopians, Moroccans, and Arabs; and now, contemporary restaurant cuisine with some chefs cooking Asian-inspired dishes. Like here in the States, trendiness and fusion have also become part of the country's current food scene. Instead of trying to narrowly define a true Israeli cuisine, I have chosen to base my Sephardic, Maghrebi, and Mizrahi dishes on original sources, rather than filter them through the eclectic Israeli kitchen.

## Sephardic Recipe Sources

Although it would be wonderful to discover a cookbook of classic Spanish and Portuguese Sephardic recipes from pre-Inquisition days, I do not believe one exists. Yes, there are Jewish recipes documented from the medieval period in Spain, and recipes from Arab cookbooks from the period before Columbus and before the introduction of foods from the New World. They are, like many recipes of that period, seasoned with far too many spices in what today would be considered unconventional and not always palate-pleasing combinations, or they are excessively laced with sugar or honey in the Arab fashion. Some of these recipes are loosely described in medieval texts, such as the thirteenth-century *La cocina hispano-magrebi al-Andaluz,* the fourteenth-century *Libre de Sent Soví,* and Roberto de Nola's *Libre del coch* from 1520. Other Sephardic recipes are referred to obliquely in the transcripts of Inquisition trials, where people testified as to what was cooked in the converso household, to reveal their covert adherence to Jewish life. Preparing a stew on Friday afternoon to be served as Sabbath lunch certainly put a family in danger, because it showed that they had not given up observing Jewish law, which did not allow work on the Sabbath. A most interesting book that attempts to re-create and guesstimate some of these early Sephardic recipes is *A Drizzle of Honey: The Lives and Recipes of Spain's Secret Jews,* prodigiously researched by David Gitlitz and Linda Kay Davidson, fine scholars but not accomplished culinary professionals, which they readily admit. The stories are fascinating but most of the food is unappealing to the contemporary cook.

Different cooking styles existed in northern and southern Iberia. The north preserved the culinary customs of the Roman Empire, while the south was more heavily Islamized. The Romans planted vineyards, olive trees, and wheat. The Arabs established the cultivation of rice in Valencia and updated Roman irrigation systems. In the Levant, on the Spanish Mediterranean coast, they planted sugarcane. In Andalusia and the Algarve in Portugal, they cultivated almonds, citrus fruits (including oranges and lemons from China), eggplants, spinach, and artichokes. The quince may have come with the Romans or the Arabs, from its original home in Iran. The Arabs also introduced the use of such spices as cumin, nutmeg, saffron, and black pepper. The custom of double cooking—that is, frying and then stewing or baking—is an Arabic culinary practice. Their mark is everywhere, from bread-based soups to egg-based sweets to the nut- or bread-thickened sauces that are now a signature of Portugal and Spain and continue to manifest themselves in the Sephardic kitchen.

The medieval manner of seasoning and food preservation, which involved an excessive use of spices, herbs, and sweeteners, was not retained in the Sephardic kitchens of Spain and Portugal, except in the case of highly sweetened desserts. Once the Sephardim emigrated to Italy and the Ottoman Empire, where they learned local styles of cuisine and became familiar with the foods from the New World, they dropped their old culinary ways, adopting new ingredients and Turkish and Greek recipes in their place. (The flow of Iberian Jews to the Ottoman Empire was not a single late-fifteenth-century event but continued well into the sixteenth century, along with the dispersal of foods from the New World.) True, some older terms like *almodrote* (garlic, oil, and cheese sauce) and *albóndigas* (meatballs) and Arab ingredients such as *alcachofas* (artichokes), *arroz* (rice), *almendras* (almonds), *azafrán* (saffron), and *naranjas* (oranges), as well as eggplant and chickpeas and other beans, were still employed, along with a stray sprinkle of cinnamon or sugar on fried eggplant, or a nut-thickened sauce in the Arab manner (probably already in use in the Arabized Ottoman Empire), but that is about as far as the medieval Arab-inspired cuisine was carried. Gone are the various *almori,* thick pastes made from rotting and fermented grains, salt, spices tempered with water, and cilantro juice. (Cilantro is used now primarily in Portugal and North Africa but not in Spain or Greece and only rarely in Turkey.) Saffron, cinnamon, and cumin were retained on the spice shelf, but they were typically joined by allspice, paprika, and hot pepper. Arab egg-based sauces, with the egg-and-lemon *agristada* and *ajada* or *allioli* (garlic mayonnaise), were kept on, as well. In the estimable *Eat and Be Satisfied: A Social History of Jewish Food,* John Cooper also notes that Sephardic Jews were used to cooking with lots of onions and garlic in Spain but cut back on garlic when they moved to Turkey, as they sensed that Muslim Turks had an aversion to the pungent bulb.

The recipes of the Sephardim in Turkey bear a great resemblance to the cuisines of Andalusia, Valencia, and the Balearic Islands. Méri Badi's *250 recettes de cuisine juive espagnole* is a valuable source of Spanish-inspired recipes that appear similar to many Sephardic Turkish recipes found in *Sefarad Yemekleri: Sephardic Cooking Book,* a collection of recipes edited by Viki Koronyo and Sima Ovadya. Many of these recipes are derived from the oral tradition and have vague or nonexistent cooking instructions. For the Greek table, I am indebted to Nicholas Stavroulakis's *Cookbook of the Jews of Greece,* a thorough compilation of recipes by this multitalented historian, artist, and scholar. He also helped to put together *Salonika: A Family Cookbook,* an interesting volume of recipes from the family of a woman named Esin Eden. Her family members were Ma'amin, Muslimized Jews who emigrated to Salonika from Turkey. Although over the years their recipes had drifted away from the kosher laws and mixed dairy with meat, I have brought them back to their Jewish roots and made the readjustments. Eden's family recipes are outstanding in flavor and have become some of my favorites. Both volumes of *La table juive* by Martine Chiche-Yana revealed traditions and holiday specialties from Greece and Turkey and other parts of the Mediterranean. *The Book of Jewish Food,* a masterpiece by my friend Claudia Roden, proved both helpful and inspiring. We have used many of the same original sources for recipes and share a certain predilection for similar flavors. But Claudia also has an extraordinary family history to tell, and she generously shares many of her family's recipes and traditions.

In doing my research, I have looked at classic Greek, Turkish, Spanish, and Portuguese cookbooks in search of ancestors of, and variations on, the recipes. I needed to see what remains from the Spanish legacy, or was derived from it, and how the recipes have changed and evolved as the Sephardim moved to new locales. These points of comparison often reveal minor variations or surprising historic origins of dishes. The titles of the recipes may vary from Ladino to Turkish to French to Greek. I have tried to keep them in the language of my original sources. It follows that many of the same recipes appear under different names.

*Maghrebi and Mizrahi Recipe Sources*

Most of the source cookbooks for the Maghrebi and Mizrahi recipes have been written by women, who did all of the cooking, working together as families: grandmothers, aunts and cousins, mother and daughter teams, mothers-in-law and daughters-in-law teams—and neighbors, too. Thanks to Fortunée Hazan-Arama, Andrée Zana-Murat, Simy Danan, Hélène Gans Perez, Daisy Taieb, Maguy Kakon, Jeanne Ifergan, Jacqueline Cohen-Azuelos, Léone Jaffin, Zette Guinaudeau, Poopa Dweck, Jennifer Abadi, Stella Cohen, Suzy David, Lisa Elmaleh Craig, and Viviane Moryoussef and her mother, Nina, for taking the time to transcribe the recipes as they prepared them in their homes and thus keeping these flavors and memories alive. I have also relied on cookbook authors who are experts in the traditional cuisines of North Africa and the Middle East to see what non-Jews were cooking and evaluate the differences.

In *The Architecture of Memory,* Joëlle Bahloul traces her Algerian family's cuisine and notes that while taste memories and home traditions were important to the men, their remembrances were focused primarily on public ritual, on the gatherings at the synagogue, and on the community at large. The women's memories revolved around "ritual gestures and foods that embody the slowing of the domestic pace and the strengthening of family ties." Their community was more intimate. Marketing and cooking filled up their days and brought their families pleasure, treasured traditions, and long-lasting memories.

Life is easier now with refrigerators and freezers, stoves with ovens, blenders and food processors. But today as we work—often alone—in our appliance-laden modern kitchens, what we miss is the joy of team effort, with lots of nimble, experienced hands gathered around the kitchen table folding intricate pastries, rolling grape leaves and stuffing vegetables, grinding nuts and spices, and trimming fruits for preserves, all the while discussing flavor balance and the news of the day. Television newscasts and food processors are not worthy substitutes for those communal times in the kitchen.

Many of the traditional pastries, sweets, and preserves are rarely made at home these days. Instead, they are purchased from stores, anonymous and compromised in flavor, less personal and idiosyncratic. Although it is true that they are time-consuming for the single cook, if some of the more intricate recipes tempt you, I recommend that you invite a friend, daughter, son, or other family member to join you. It promises to be one of the best times you will have spent together. And it will create taste memories and traditions that your family will never forget.

## THE KOSHER LAWS

You may wonder what makes the recipes in this book Jewish. At first glance, they don't appear different from similar Mediterranean recipes. What distinguishes them is that they follow kashrut, the dietary laws that govern the kosher kitchen.

Many still believe the old story that these laws came about as a health measure, to prevent the Jews from eating foods that were more likely to transmit disease. It is true, for example, that pigs were known to pass along trichinosis. But there is another explanation. The rabbis of the Talmudic period cite the Torah when explaining the dietary regulations, and while the book does detail the restrictions, it offers no explanation for them. However, such laws were holy, to be obeyed, not questioned. The rabbis also believed that the secret of Jewish survival was separatism. By limiting contact with non-Jews, the religion and culture would be preserved.

The twelfth-century philosopher Maimonides, seeking a rationale for the dietary laws, surmised that they "train us to master our appetites, to accustom us to restrain our desires; and to avoid considering the pleasure of eating and drinking as the goal of man's existence." While those of us who are used to total culinary freedom might feel a bit stifled by the restrictive kosher diet, the laws inspired great creativity in observant Jewish cooks. Over time, Mediterranean Jews adapted regional cuisine for the kosher home, joyfully embracing both the local flavors and the traditional boundaries of kashrut.

Kosher laws are set forth in the Torah's books of Leviticus and Deuteronomy, which specify which animals are kosher and which are not. The word *kosher* (derived from *kasher*) did not originally refer to food. It means "good" and "proper" and was used for ritual objects. Foods that are not kosher are considered *treyf* or *treyfe*.

Many of the most important kosher laws describe what kinds of meats can be consumed. Only animals with split hooves and who chew their cud are kosher (thus the absence of the pig). Animals must be slaughtered in a ritual manner by a *shochet*, or trained ritual butcher; beasts killed by hunters, for example, are forbidden. The *shochet* must sever the jugular vein in one clean cut and drain all of the blood from the animal, as blood is the essence and symbol of life. To remove all signs of blood, the meat must then be salted and soaked, unless it is slated to be broiled or flame cooked. Liver cannot be drained of blood, so it must be broiled, and only after it has been broiled can it be sautéed. Before the hindquarter of an animal can be eaten, the sciatic nerve and the blood vessels attached to it must be removed. Expert butchers can remove the nerve, but it is a time-consuming process, so many kosher butchers prefer to sell this part to non-kosher butchers, or to halal butchers who do not share the same restriction. Now you know why there are so few kosher recipes for steak or leg of lamb. In Israel today, some butchers are learning how to remove this nerve, a technique called *traibering*, thus broadening the kosher cuts available. All meats must be koshered before they can be frozen.

Kosher law also extends to fish and fowl. Only fish with scales and fins are permitted. Some fish are born with fins and scales but lose them at some point in their development. Such fish, including swordfish and sturgeon, are controversial for observant Jews, and not all authorities permit their consumption. Unlike cows or sheep, a fish does not have to be slaughtered in a prescribed manner, as it is considered to die a natural death when removed from the water. According to Deuteronomy, all shellfish, because they lack fins and scales, are non-kosher. A kosher fowl is a domesticated bird such as a chicken, turkey, game hen, duck, or goose. A wild fowl killed by a hunter is non-kosher because, as with meats, it has not been killed in the prescribed manner. Only eggs from kosher birds may be eaten.

Additional laws govern what foods may be eaten or prepared together. For this purpose, foods are categorized as meat (*fleishig*) or dairy (*milchig*). Other foods are designated neutral (pareve) and can be served at both meat and dairy meals. Fish is pareve, as are eggs, spices, grains, fruits, and vegetables. In Deuteronomy, it is written that Jews shall not cook a kid in its mother's milk, and thus kosher law prohibits eating meat and milk at the same meal. Additionally, many observant Jews will not eat cheeses made with animal rennet, perceiving them as a combination of meat and dairy. The length of separation between eating meat and dairy can range from one to six hours, depending on the orthodoxy of the community and local rabbinical views. Many observant families keep different sets of dishes for meat meals and dairy meals, as well as two sets of pots and pans.

The holiday of Passover adds yet another layer of kosher laws. Products that contain wheat, barley, rye, oats, or spelt and have come into contact with any kind of moisture for more than eighteen minutes are considered fermented or leavened foods, or *hametz*, and thus forbidden. This is why matzo, which is made from wheat but whose production falls under the eighteen-minute rule, replaces bread on the Passover table. The Ashkenazim, though not the Sephardim, also abstain from eating rice, millet, corn, and legumes during Passover.

## THE FOOD OF JEWISH HOLIDAYS

Throughout this book, I have noted certain dishes that are ideal for serving, or are traditionally served, on one or more of the Jewish holidays. Holiday foods are also listed in the index. Here are brief descriptions of the major holidays on the Jewish calendar and, with the exception of those holidays that are fast days, the dishes or foods that are associated with them.

## The Sabbath

The Sabbath (or Shabbat) is the Jewish day of rest and spiritual rejuvenation. It begins every Friday before sundown; is ushered into the home with the lighting of candles and the kiddush, a blessing recited over wine or bread; and ends at sundown on Saturday. The Sabbath dinner is a festive meal, but because this is a holy day, orthodox law prohibits work or business of any kind, including cooking, until the Sabbath has ended. That means the Saturday midday meal must be prepared before sunset on Friday. In the days before refrigeration and modern appliances, observing the Sabbath inspired great ingenuity in the kitchen. Cooks prepared dishes over very low heat, or they buried them in the *hamin* (oven) for many hours or sometimes overnight. This type of cooking was regarded as a passive activity, thereby escaping the no-working rule. Cooked vegetables and marinated fish that tasted good served at room temperature were also on the Sabbath table. Today, many of these vegetable and fish dishes would be called meze, the small dishes commonly found on the menus of Mediterranean restaurants.

## Rosh Hashanah: The Jewish New Year

Rosh Hashanah marks the start of the New Year. A two-day celebration that begins on the first day of the month of Tishri, usually in late September or early October, it is a joyful holiday for the most part, with people wishing one another good luck, happiness, and health in the coming year. It is the beginning of the Days of Awe, a ten-day period of introspection, which culminates on Yom Kippur.

Many symbolic foods appear on the Rosh Hashanah table. Among them are apples with honey, which symbolize the wish that the New Year will be sweet. The many seeds of the pomegranate signify the many good deeds to be performed in the coming year. Black-eyed peas characterize abundance and fertility, and pumpkin or winter squash with its hard covering symbolizes the desire for protection from harmful and oppressive decrees, and the hope to be remembered for good deeds. Leeks represent the wish for all enemies to be cut off. Spinach and chard represent the hope that all enemies will be removed from the community. Dates signify the wish that our enemies cease harassment. For Moroccan Jews, the couscous with seven vegetables represents the seven days it took for God to create the world. A whole fish is often served, its head representing the head—the beginning—of the New Year.

## Yom Kippur

Yom Kippur, which falls on the tenth day of Tishri, is the most solemn day of the year—a day when you seek forgiveness from God for your sins, so you can start the New Year with a clean slate. As on the Sabbath, you must do no work. You must also fast for twenty-five hours, consuming neither food nor water or other liquid. The meal before the fast must be filling, simple, and not highly seasoned, to avoid making the diners thirsty during their fast.

## Sukkoth: The Feast of the Tabernacles

Sukkoth begins on the evening of the fifteenth day of Tishri, usually in October, and lasts for seven days. It is an autumn harvest festival during which celebrants construct a temporary straw or wood shelter, or *sukkah* (*sukkoth* is the plural) outdoors, in memory of the forty years the Jews spent wandering in the desert living in temporary shelters after their exodus from slavery. The four important plants carried and waved during this holiday are a citron (*etrog*), a palm branch (*lulav*), three myrtle branches (*hadasim*), and two willow branches (the *aravot*). The last day of Sukkoth is known as Simchat Torah, or "joy of the Torah," because it is the final day of the annual cycle of Torah reading. Stuffed vegetables might be served along with nut-filled pastries.

## Hanukkah: The Festival of Lights

Hanukkah begins on the twenty-fifth day of the month of Kislev, which usually falls in December, and lasts eight days and nights. It celebrates the recapture of Jerusalem and the rededication of the Temple. The story of Hanukkah is a recounting of a miraculous event and of triumph over adversity. The victors were determined to purify the newly won Temple by burning oil in its lamp for eight days. Although in the Temple they found only enough oil for one night, it inexplicably lasted for the full eight days. To celebrate this miracle, it is customary to light one candle on the menorah on the first night of Hanukkah, two candles on the second night, and so on for eight consecutive evenings. The miracle of the oil is also celebrated with the serving of fried foods, such as fried chicken, sweet and savory fritters, and doughnuts, throughout the holiday.

## Tu B'Shevat: The New Year for Trees

Tu B'Shevat, which falls in late January or early February, is a one-day holiday that is celebrated by planting trees to commemorate the time of year in the Mediterranean when trees are just starting to bloom, signaling the beginning of a new fruiting cycle. Fresh and dried fruits, especially those mentioned in the Torah—dates, pomegranates, figs, grapes—are eaten on this holiday.

## Purim: The Festival of Queen Esther

This joyful holiday, also called the Festival of Lots, is celebrated on the fourteenth day of the month of Adar, usually in March, and commemorates the triumph of Queen Esther, aided by her cousin Mordecai, in outwitting the evil minister Haman, who had advised King Ahasuerus to kill all of the Jews in a single day. Many of the dishes are sweet-and-sour to recall how sweet it was to conquer the sourness of adversity.

## Pesach: Passover

This holiday, which celebrates the Exodus of the Jews from Egypt, begins on the fifteenth day of the month of Nisan, usually in April, and lasts for eight days in the

Diaspora or seven days in Israel. Cooking practices change dramatically when Passover begins. The Jews reportedly fled Egypt in such haste that their bread dough did not have time to rise. To commemorate this story, no leavened foods (*hametz*) may be eaten during Passover, which is why matzo is served during the holiday. Rigorously observant Orthodox Jews eat only handmade *shemura* matzo, or "watched" matzo, which is under rabbinical supervision from the moment the wheat is harvested through the milling of the grain to the baking of the matzo to ensure no fermentation, and thus leavening, takes place.

Just before the first day of Passover, households are given a thorough spring cleaning to rid them of any traces of *hametz,* and many observant Jews bring in special plates and silverware to use during the holiday. Ritual dinners called Seders are held the first and second nights of Passover. At the Seder, participants read from a book called the Haggadah and retell the story of Exodus. Four glasses of wine are drunk in memory of God's four promises of freedom in Israel. The centerpiece of the table is the Seder plate, which is divided into sections to hold the ritual foods: *karpas,* a mild herb or green such as parsley or romaine, represents new growth and is dipped into salt water to symbolize the tears of the slaves; *maror* and *hazeret,* or bitter herbs, such as horseradish or chicory, recall the bitter times of slavery; *beitzah,* or roasted egg, symbolizes the sacrificial offering in the Temple and the cycle of life; *zeroah,* or roasted lamb, goat, or poultry bone, represents the sacrifice of a lamb by the slaves on the eve of the Exodus and symbolizes religious freedom; and finally, *haroset,* a fruit-and-nut paste, signifies the mortar used by the Jews to construct the pyramids.

### Shavuot: Festival of the Giving of the Torah

Shavuot, which falls fifty days (seven weeks) after the second night of Passover, usually in late May or early June, celebrates the anniversary of the Revelation on Mount Sinai and the giving of the Torah to the Jewish people. Synagogues are traditionally decorated with flowers, leaves, and tree branches to recall the flowers that bloomed on Mount Sinai the day the Torah was presented and because Shavuot was once a harvest holiday. (It is also known as the Festival of First Fruits, commemorating the first day that *bikkurim,* or "first fruits," could be brought to the Temple in Jerusalem.) A dairy and vegetable meal is traditionally served.

### Tisha B'Av: Fast of the Ninth of Av, or Commemoration of the Fall of the First and Second Temples

Tisha B'Av falls on the ninth day of Av, in mid-July to early August, and commemorates the fall of the First Temple in Jerusalem in 586 BCE and the fall of the Second Temple in 70 CE. It is also a time to reflect on other communal tragedies that have befallen the Jews, many of which occurred on or around the ninth of Av, such as the expulsion of the Jews from Spain. Beginning on the seventeenth day of Tammuz, which is a fast day, observant Jews enter a three-week period of mourning that ends on Tisha B'Av. During this time, no weddings are performed, no music is played, and no new clothing may be worn. Beginning on the first day of Av, observant Jews refrain from consuming meat or wine except on the Sabbath. Symbolic foods of mourning, such as legume soups and stews, are often served, along with mainly vegetarian and dairy meals. Tisha B'Av is a fast day—from both food and liquid—among the orthodox.

Appetizers,
Spreads,
and Salads

I N THE MEDITERRANEAN JEWISH HOME, hospitality is of prime importance, and there is no better way to welcome family and friends than with something to eat. In Italy, the small bites to whet your appetite before the meal are called antipasti, in Spain they are tapas, and in Morocco and the Middle East the meal begins with an assortment of small plates called mezes. In Algeria, the mezes are called *kemia,* and in Tunisia, they are *aadu.* These might include a bowl of olives, stuffed grape leaves, or spreads such as hummus or chopped eggplant served with warm pita bread. Hot fritters such as falafel or small savory pastries are sometimes added to enrich the assortment of room-temperature dishes.

Leafy salads are a recent development in the history of Mediterranean Jewish cooking. Recipes for greens tossed in vinaigrette are relatively rare in older cookbooks, though these salads are popular today. The term *salad* in Sephardic and Mediterranean kitchens usually refers to dishes of cooked vegetables served at room temperature, and some that in contemporary terms would be dips or spreads.

I have found the vinaigrettes in Sephardic recipes from Greece and Turkey to be unusual. In the Mediterranean, in Spain and Portugal, in Italy and France, the ratio of oil to vinegar is usually three to one. But in many of the Sephardic Turkish recipes, the ratio is one to one—a very tart palate. I cannot say why this is the case. Excess acidity can act as a preservative and brighten dishes served at room temperature, but this would be true all over the Mediterranean. Vinegar is not the only acid used, either. Lemon is popular, too, with most dishes arriving with a side plate of lemon wedges. I have a natural predilection for acidic foods, so these dishes don't pucker my palate, but you will have to play with these recipes until you reach your desired tartness level.

## Moroccan Marinated Olives   OLIVES MARINÉES

A bowl of olives is always part of the meze table, and in Morocco, cooks like to treat the olives to a pungent marinade. In most recipes, they are soaked in cold water for an hour to remove the excess brine before the marinade is added, after which they are left to sit for at least a couple of days before serving. If you need to get them on the table quickly, however, you can rinse, drain, and dry them well and then add the marinade and serve them later the same day. Olives that are slightly cracked will absorb the marinade more easily. SERVES 6

1⅔ cups drained brined black or green olives

6 tablespoons chopped fresh flat-leaf parsley

6 tablespoons chopped fresh cilantro

3 cloves garlic, chopped

1 teaspoon red pepper flakes, or 2 fresh red chiles, slivered lengthwise

½ teaspoon ground cumin

½ cup extra virgin olive oil

2 teaspoons fresh lemon juice

3 or 4 thin strips lemon or orange zest, or peel of ½ preserved lemon, homemade (page 356) or store-bought, rinsed and cut into strips, with some of its juice

Using a meat pounder or the side of a heavy cleaver, crack the olives. Put the olives in a bowl, add water to cover, and let stand for about 1 hour. Drain well, pat dry, and return to the bowl.

Add the parsley, cilantro, garlic, pepper flakes, cumin, oil, lemon juice, and lemon zest and toss well to coat evenly. Transfer to a jar or other container, cap tightly, and refrigerate for 2 days before serving. They will keep for up to 7 days.

VARIATION: *Black Olives with Bitter Orange (Olives Noires à l'Orange):* Use brined pitted black olives. Proceed as directed, adding the chopped pulp of 2 small bitter or blood oranges along with the other ingredients. If only sweet oranges are available, increase the lemon juice to 2 to 3 tablespoons.

## Braised Green Olives with Anchovies   OLIVES VERTES AUX ANCHOIS

Olives are typically served at room temperature, but this Algerian recipe proves they can be a revelation when they are eaten warm: creamy, juicy, and more aromatic. SERVES 6

8 ounces drained brined green olives

2 tablespoons extra virgin olive oil

3 cloves garlic, minced

3 olive oil–packed anchovy fillets, chopped

¼ cup water

1 lemon, peeled and cut into small pieces

½ teaspoon sweet paprika

½ teaspoon ground cumin

1 fresh chile, crushed, or pinch of cayenne pepper

Using a meat pounder or the side of a heavy cleaver, crack the olives. Warm the oil in a sauté pan over low heat. Add the garlic and anchovies and cook, stirring occasionally, for a few minutes, until fragrant. Add the olives, water, lemon, paprika, cumin, and chile and cook over low heat, stirring occasionally, until the olives have softened, about 10 minutes. Serve warm.

## Persian Olives with Pomegranate and Walnuts   ZEYTUN-E PARVARDEH

Olives grow in abundance in Gilan Province, in northwestern Iran. This dish, which originates in the region, is served all over the country to welcome friends and family for dinner. SERVES 4 TO 6

| | |
|---|---|
| 12 ounces brined green olives, drained | ¼ cup finely chopped fresh mint, or 2 tablespoons dried mint |
| ½ cup grated walnuts | |
| ¼ cup pomegranate molasses | 1 small clove garlic, finely minced |
| 3 tablespoons extra virgin olive oil | Salt |

Put the olives in a bowl, add water to cover, and let stand for 30 minutes. Drain well, pat dry, and return to the bowl.

In a small bowl, stir together the walnuts, pomegranate molasses, oil, mint, and garlic. Add to the olives and toss to mix well, then taste and adjust the seasoning. You may want a bit of salt or a bit more pomegranate molasses. Let marinate for at least 1 hour or up to 6 hours before serving.

## Rice-Stuffed Vine Leaves   YAPRAKES DE PARRA

Throughout Greece, Turkey, and most of the Middle East, stuffed grape leaves, commonly called dolmas, are a mainstay of the meze table. They are ideal for the Sabbath meal, as they can be prepared in advance and keep well for a few days in the refrigerator. These Sephardic Greek *yaprakes* stuffed with rice are served at room temperature or lightly chilled, while most meat-filled dolmas are served warm. In some parts of the Middle East, cooked lentils are added to the rice. If you like, line the pan with tomato slices or grape leaves before adding the dolmas. MAKES ABOUT 36 PIECES

| | |
|---|---|
| FILLING | 2 yellow onions, chopped |
| 1 cup basmati or other long-grain white rice | 3 cloves garlic, minced |
| 3 tablespoons extra virgin olive oil | 2 or 3 tomatoes, peeled, seeded, and diced (fresh or canned; about 1 cup) |

¼ cup finely chopped fennel fronds or fresh dill

6 tablespoons chopped fresh mint

¼ cup chopped fresh flat-leaf parsley

¼ cup pine nuts, toasted (optional)

¼ cup dried currants, plumped in hot water and drained (optional)

2 teaspoons salt

1 teaspoon freshly ground black pepper

36 to 40 jarred grape leaves, well rinsed and patted dry

1 cup extra virgin olive oil

Juice of 2 lemons

Lemon wedges and plain yogurt for serving

---

To make the filling, in a bowl, soak the rice in water to cover for 1 hour, then drain.

While the rice is soaking, warm the oil in a sauté pan over medium heat. Add the onions and cook, stirring occasionally, until translucent and tender, 8 to 10 minutes. Add the garlic and cook for a few minutes more. Add the drained rice, stir well, and remove from the heat. (You do not need to precook the rice, as the rice will be submerged in the cooking liquid and will expand as it absorbs the liquid through the grape leaves.)

Transfer the rice mixture to a bowl. Add the tomatoes, fennel fronds, mint, parsley, pine nuts, currants, salt, and pepper and mix well.

Lay the grape leaves, smooth side down, on a work surface. Snip off the stems with scissors. Place a teaspoon or so of the rice mixture near the stem end of a leaf. Fold the stem end over the filling, fold in the sides, and then roll toward the top of the leaf, forming a cylinder. Do not roll too tightly, as the rice will expand as it cooks. Repeat with the remaining leaves and filling.

Place the filled leaves, seam side down and close together, in a single layer in a wide saucepan. Pour in the oil and lemon juice. Place an ovenproof plate or other weight on the filled leaves so they don't unroll during cooking. Add very hot water just to cover the filled leaves and bring the liquid to a boil over medium-high heat. Cover, turn down the heat to low, and simmer for 35 to 40 minutes. To test for doneness, sample a dolma; the rice should be tender. (Alternatively, cook the filled leaves in a preheated 350°F oven for 35 to 40 minutes.)

Remove the pan from the heat and uncover so the filled leaves will cool quickly. Let them rest for about 15 minutes; then, using a spatula, carefully transfer them to a platter and let cool completely before serving. Garnish with the lemon wedges and accompany with a bowl of yogurt. Or, transfer the filled leaves to a shallow container, let cool, cover, and refrigerate for up to 1 week, then bring to room temperature before serving.

VARIATIONS: This same rice filling can be used for *reynadas* or *rellenos* (stuffed vegetables), but the rice must be precooked for 10 to 15 minutes before it is combined with the other filling ingredients because the stuffed vegetables are not submerged in liquid during cooking. Stuff the filling into 3 pounds assorted vegetables, prepared as directed (see following), being careful not to pack it too tightly, as the rice will continue to expand in the oven. Arrange the vegetables in a baking dish. Pour water to a depth of 1 inch into the dish, then mix together ½ cup extra virgin olive oil and 3 tablespoons fresh lemon juice and add to the dish. Cover with aluminum foil and bake in a preheated 350°F oven until the vegetables and rice are tender, about 45 minutes. Serve at room temperature garnished with yogurt or dressed with extra virgin olive oil and lemon juice.

For stuffed sweet peppers *(reynadas de pipirushkas):* Cut the top off of each pepper and set the tops aside. Scoop out and discard the seeds and thick ribs. Bring a large saucepan filled with water to a boil and parboil the peppers for 4 to 5 minutes. Drain well, then fill the peppers with the rice filling, replace the tops, and bake as directed.

For stuffed eggplants *(reynadas de berenjena):* Use small globe or Italian eggplants. Cut in half lengthwise and scoop out the pulp, leaving a ¼-inch-thick wall. Chop the pulp, discarding as many seeds as possible. Sauté the chopped pulp with the onions. Sauté the eggplant cases in olive oil for about 5 minutes to soften. Fill the eggplant cases with the rice filling and bake as directed.

For stuffed zucchini *(reynadas de kalavasas):* If using large zucchini, halve lengthwise and scoop out and discard the seeds. If necessary, enlarge the cavity by cutting out enough pulp to leave a ¼-inch-thick wall. Chop any removed pulp, then sauté the pulp with the onions. Bring a large saucepan filled with water to a boil and parboil the zucchini cases for 3 minutes. Drain well, then fill the zucchini cases with the rice filling and bake as directed.

For stuffed tomatoes *(reynadas de tomat):* Tomatoes are handled a little differently than the peppers, eggplants, and zucchini. Cut the top off of 12 firm ripe tomatoes and scoop out the pulp, leaving a ¼-inch-thick wall. Reserve the tomato pulp and its juices and the tops. Sprinkle the inside of each tomato with salt and a little sugar. Set the tomato cases aside. In a blender or food processor, purée the tomato pulp and juices until smooth, then add to the rice filling and mix well. Spoon the filling into the tomatoes, being careful not to pack it too tightly. Place in a baking dish and replace the tops. Pour about ⅓ cup hot water into the dish and spoon ½ cup extra virgin olive oil over the tomatoes. Cover and bake as directed, basting the tomatoes a few times with the pan juices and reducing the cooking time to 30 minutes if the tomatoes are small or very ripe.

# Tuna Spread for Toasted or Grilled Bread
## SPUMA DI TONNO CON CROSTINI

In Italy and in all parts of the Mediterranean, most recipes that call for tuna are referring to canned tuna packed in olive oil. These crostini can be part of an antipasto assortment at a dairy-based meal. If served before a meat meal, you can bind the tuna with mayonnaise instead of butter, though the result will not have the same unctuous texture. SERVES 6

1 can (8 ounces) olive oil–packed tuna, preferably Italian or Spanish, drained

5 to 6 tablespoons unsalted butter, at room temperature

Grated zest of 1 lemon

2 olive oil–packed anchovy fillets, finely minced (optional)

Fresh lemon juice for seasoning

Salt and freshly ground black pepper

12 small slices coarse country bread, toasted or grilled

3 tablespoons brined capers, rinsed and coarsely chopped

3 tablespoons coarsely chopped pitted green olives

Put the tuna in a food processor and pulse to break it up. Add the butter, lemon zest, and anchovies and process until a smooth, creamy purée forms. Season with lemon juice and pepper. If using the anchovies, no salt should be needed. If not, season to taste with salt.

Spread the mixture on the bread slices, dividing it evenly, and top with the capers and olives.

## Red Pepper, Walnut, and Pomegranate Spread  MUHAMMARA

Peppers, both hot and sweet, are native to the New World and were carried by Spanish and Portuguese explorers to the Old World in the 1500s, from which they were fairly quickly disseminated globally. Each country now cultivates sweet and hot varieties to suit the local taste. You need red bell peppers to make this Syrian and Turkish spread, which is usually served with pita bread but is also a delicious spicy condiment for cooked meats. Make a little extra to spoon over grilled or broiled fish or even simple roasted potatoes. MAKES ABOUT 1¾ CUPS

2 large red bell peppers

1¼ cups (about 6 ounces) walnuts, toasted

½ cup fine dried bread crumbs

¼ cup extra virgin olive oil

¼ cup tomato purée

1 tablespoon coarsely ground red pepper flakes or crushed Aleppo or Maras pepper flakes

1 teaspoon ground toasted cumin

½ teaspoon ground allspice

Pinch of sugar

2 to 3 tablespoons pomegranate molasses or fresh lemon juice, or a mixture

Salt

Finely chopped fresh flat-leaf parsley for garnish

To roast the bell peppers, hold them directly over the flame on a gas stove top or place on a sheet pan under a preheated broiler and turn them as needed until the skin is blistered and charred on all sides. Transfer to a closed plastic container or a bowl covered with plastic wrap and let stand for 20 minutes. Peel or rub off the skin from each pepper, then stem, halve lengthwise, remove and discard the seeds and thick ribs, and chop coarsely.

In a food processor or blender, combine the roasted peppers, walnuts, bread crumbs, oil, tomato purée, pepper flakes, cumin, allspice, sugar, 2 tablespoons pomegranate molasses, and a pinch of salt and process until a smooth purée forms. Taste and adjust the seasoning with pomegranate molasses or salt if needed. Spoon the purée into a small bowl, cover, and chill until serving. Garnish with the parsley just before serving.

## Cooked Pepper and Tomato Salad  MISHWIYA

Called *choukchouka* in Algeria and *mishwiya* in Morocco and Tunisia, this classic salad is traditionally served as a first course but would make a fine accompaniment or sauce to a main course of fish or meat. It is a staple in the North African pantry and is often served at Rosh Hashanah. The Algerian version is much milder, with no heat and no lemon. I prefer the Moroccan version, which is fairly piquant with spice and lemon. Tunisian cooks sometimes turn this into a niçoise-like salad by garnishing it with canned tuna, olives, and hard-boiled eggs. You can also combine the roasted peppers and tomatoes with all of the remaining ingredients except the parsley, skip the simmering step, and garnish the salad with strips of preserved lemon. SERVES 8

4 pounds firm ripe tomatoes

2 pounds green bell peppers

5 cloves garlic, minced

1 small fresh chile, seeded and finely minced (optional)

¼ to ½ teaspoon cayenne pepper

Peel of ½ preserved lemon, homemade (page 356) or store-bought, rinsed and finely diced, or pulp of ½ fresh lemon, finely chopped (optional)

1 tablespoon salt

1 tablespoon sweet paprika

½ teaspoon ground cumin (optional)

½ teaspoon freshly ground black pepper

6 tablespoons extra virgin olive oil

3 to 4 tablespoons chopped fresh flat-leaf parsley or cilantro

To roast the tomatoes and bell peppers, preheat the broiler and arrange them on a sheet pan (work in batches if necessary). Place under the broiler and turn them as needed until the skin is blistered and charred on all sides. Transfer to a closed plastic container or a bowl covered with plastic wrap and let stand for 20 minutes. Peel or rub off the skin from each tomato and pepper. Stem the peppers, halve lengthwise, remove and discard the seeds and thick ribs, and chop the flesh. Core the tomatoes, halve crosswise, ease the seeds out of the seed sacs, and chop the flesh.

Combine the roasted tomatoes and peppers, garlic, chile, cayenne to taste, preserved lemon, salt, paprika, cumin, black pepper, and oil. You can serve it immediately or place over medium-low heat, bring to a simmer, and simmer until all of the liquid released by the tomatoes has evaporated and the mixture is as thick as marmalade, about 30 minutes.

Transfer to a serving dish and serve warm or at room temperature, sprinkled with the parsley.

## *Israeli Cooked Pepper and Tomato Salad*   MATBUCHA

*Matbucha,* sometimes spelled *matboukha,* means "cooked" in Arabic. The origin of this Israeli dish is North Africa, and it is closely related to the Moroccan and Tunisian dish known as *mishwiya* (page 25). If you cannot find ripe, flavorful fresh tomatoes, canned can be substituted. As the mixture cooks, be sure to stir it from time to time to avoid scorching. This salsa-like salad is delicious spread on bread and is a good accompaniment to meat or fish. It can also be used as the base for *shakshuka* (page 99), replacing the traditional spicy tomato sauce in which the eggs are cooked.   SERVES 8 TO 10

3 red bell peppers

1 poblano or other mild green chile

8 or 9 ripe tomatoes, peeled, seeded, and chopped (about 6 pounds)

8 to 10 cloves garlic, crushed

1 tablespoon sweet paprika

1 teaspoon cayenne pepper or harissa, homemade (page 355) or store-bought

1 teaspoon salt

To roast the bell peppers and chile, hold them directly over the flame on a gas stove top or place on a sheet pan under a preheated broiler and turn them as needed until the skin is blistered and charred on all sides. Transfer to a closed plastic container or a bowl covered with plastic wrap and let stand for 20 minutes. Peel or rub off the skin from each pepper and the chile, then stem, halve lengthwise, remove and discard the seeds and thick ribs, and chop.

In a large sauté pan, cook the tomatoes over medium heat, stirring occasionally, until all of the liquid they release evaporates, 8 to 12 minutes; the timing depends on the juiciness of the tomatoes. Add the roasted peppers and chile, garlic, paprika, cayenne, and salt, mix well, turn down the heat to low, and cook until the mixture is shiny and very thick, about 1 hour.

Taste and adjust the seasoning with salt and cayenne. Transfer to a serving dish and serve at room temperature.

# Chopped Tomato Salad  ARMIKO DE TOMAT

This cooked tomato spread is based on a recipe from *Sefarad Yemekleri,* a book compiled by the Istanbul-based Subat, the Society for the Assistance of Old People. It is similar to the Spanish *salmorejo,* a tomato-based, bread-thickened spread, but unlike *salmorejo, armiko* is thickened with rice and served warm. Esin Eden, coauthor of *Salonika: A Family Cookbook,* calls it a salad and serves it chilled, garnished with mint, basil, or parsley. She adds quite a bit of chopped garlic and lemon juice to the mixture, and because I share her palate, I have included those ingredients here. *Armiko di tomat* can also be served warm as a sauce for fish.  SERVES 6 TO 8

4 to 5 tablespoons extra virgin olive oil

2 yellow onions, chopped

3 or 4 pounds tomatoes, peeled, seeded, and coarsely chopped

2 green bell peppers, seeded and finely chopped

3 tablespoons long-grain white rice, soaked in water to cover for 1 hour and drained

¼ cup chopped fresh flat-leaf parsley

3 to 5 cloves garlic, minced (optional)

¼ cup fresh lemon juice (optional)

1 tablespoon sugar

Salt and freshly ground black pepper

Chopped fresh mint, flat-leaf parsley, or basil for garnish

Warm the oil in a large sauté pan over medium heat. Add the onions and cook, stirring occasionally, until translucent and tender, 8 to 10 minutes. Add the tomatoes, bell peppers, rice, parsley, garlic, lemon juice, and sugar, stir well, and simmer until the liquid has been absorbed and the rice is tender, about 20 minutes.

Season with salt and pepper and remove from the heat. Serve chilled as a spread or warm as a side dish. Garnish with the mint just before serving.

# Master Recipe for Roasted Eggplant

When a recipe calls for roasting eggplant, you can roast it in the oven or, for a smoky taste, char it directly over the flame on a gas stove top, on a grill over a charcoal fire, on a stove-top grill pan or griddle, or under the broiler.

To roast the eggplants in the oven, preheat the oven to 400°F. Prick the eggplants with a fork in a few places so they don't burst, then put them on a sheet pan and slip the pan into the oven. Roast the eggplants, turning them a few times to ensure even cooking, until they are soft throughout when pierced with a knife and have collapsed, 45 to 60 minutes.

For a smoky flavor, turn the burner of a gas stove to medium. Do not prick the eggplants, as you do for oven roasting. Put an eggplant directly on the grate of the burner and leave it undisturbed until it begins to smoke and sputter a bit. Then, using tongs, rotate the eggplant about a quarter turn, so the blackened, charred skin becomes visible and a new portion of the skin is exposed directly to the flame. Continue in this way until all of the skin is blackened and charred and the eggplant is soft throughout and has collapsed. Repeat with the remaining eggplants. Follow this same technique if using a stove-top grill pan or griddle, a charcoal grill, or a broiler.

When the eggplants are ready, transfer them to a colander to drain and cool until just warm or until fully cooled. One at a time, put them on a cutting board, strip away the charred skin, and discard any large seed pockets. Transfer all of the pulp to a colander and let drain for about 30 minutes to rid it of excess water, then proceed as directed in individual recipes.

## *Sephardic Roasted Eggplant Salad* SALATA DE BERENJENA ASADA

This Turkish salad is sometimes called "eggplant caviar," I suspect because many seeds become visible when the eggplants are cooked. After you have peeled away the skin from the eggplants, be sure to remove and discard any large pockets of hard seeds, even though doing so will reduce your yield. The seeds are bitter and add an unpleasant texture to a dish that should be creamy and tender. To keep the eggplant white, a point of pride in Turkey, briefly soak the cooked pulp in acidulated water or squeeze lemon juice over it. This dish is often served at Sukkoth. SERVES 6 TO 8

---

3 or 4 globe eggplants (about 3 pounds total weight)

4 to 6 tablespoons extra virgin olive oil

Juice of 2 to 3 lemons

4 cloves garlic, minced (optional)

Salt and freshly ground black pepper

¼ cup finely chopped fresh flat-leaf parsley

Warmed pita bread (see note) for serving

---

Roast the eggplants as directed in Master Recipe for Roasted Eggplant (page 27). After draining the pulp, transfer it to a bowl and mash with a fork. You should have about 3 cups. Alternatively, pulse the pulp in a food processor, being careful not to get carried away and reduce it to baby food. Add 4 tablespoons of the oil, the juice of 2 lemons, the garlic, and salt and pepper and mix well. Taste and adjust the seasoning with more oil, lemon juice, salt, and pepper if needed.

Serve at once, or cover and refrigerate for up to 3 days and then bring to room temperature before serving. Garnish with the parsley and accompany with the pita.

NOTE: The easiest way to warm pita bread is in a microwave oven. Cover the breads with a glass lid and heat for 30 to 40 seconds. Alternatively, wrap the pita breads tightly in foil and steam in the top of a double boiler until warm, about 5 minutes. If the pita is accompanying spreads or salads, cut into quarters or eighths before serving.

If you prefer pita chips, cut the breads into serving pieces, arrange on a baking sheet, and heat in a 350°F oven until crisp, 15 to 20 minutes.

VARIATIONS: For a simple Middle Eastern touch, add 1 to 2 teaspoons ground toasted cumin with the salt and pepper. Or, top the salad with crumbled feta cheese along with the parsley. An ancient Arabic version adds finely chopped walnuts and ground toasted caraway to the eggplant and uses a little vinegar in place of the lemon juice.

## Italian Eggplant Spread on Toasted Bread
### CROSTINI DI MELANZANE ARROSTE

This spread works well as an appetizer to accompany drinks or as part of an antipasto assortment. SERVES 6

| | |
|---|---|
| 3 large globe eggplants (about 3 pounds total weight) | 2 tablespoons brined capers, rinsed, plus more for garnish (optional) |
| ½ cup extra virgin olive oil, plus more if needed | Salt and freshly ground black pepper |
| 3 cloves garlic, finely minced | 12 to 18 slices coarse country bread, toasted |
| ¼ cup red wine vinegar | Finely chopped fresh flat-leaf parsley for garnish |

Roast the eggplants as directed in Master Recipe for Roasted Eggplant (page 27). After draining the pulp, chop it coarsely and set aside in a bowl.

Warm about 2 tablespoons of the oil in a sauté pan over low heat. Add the garlic and cook for a minute or two just until soft. Do not allow it to color. Add the garlic to the eggplant and then fold in the remaining 6 tablespoons oil along with the vinegar. Fold in the capers and season with salt and pepper. If the mixture seems too firm, add a little more oil.

Spread the eggplant on the bread and garnish with the parsley and a few more capers if you like. Arrange on a platter to serve.

## Eggplant Purée with Tahini    BABA GHANOUJ

For this recipe, a favorite throughout the Levant, you want the smokiness that results from cooking directly over a flame (on a gas-stove burner grate, heavy griddle, or charcoal grill), as it will balance the flavors of the tahini and lemon. Tahini brands vary, so it is important to add the tahini in increments. Start with ¼ cup and add more to taste. Sometimes I add the garlic uncooked, but it can be "hot" on the tongue when very fresh and cooking it briefly tames the heat. MAKES ABOUT 3 CUPS

3 large globe eggplants (about 3 pounds total weight)

3 cloves garlic, very finely minced

2 to 4 tablespoons extra virgin olive oil

¼ cup tahini, stirred well before use, plus more if needed

¼ cup fresh lemon juice, plus more if needed

Salt

2 to 3 tablespoons water, if needed

¼ cup pine nuts, toasted

2 tablespoons chopped fresh flat-leaf parsley

Warmed pita bread (see note, page 28) or raw vegetables (trimmed radishes, cucumber and carrot batons) for serving

Roast the eggplants as directed in Master Recipe for Roasted Eggplant (page 27). After draining the pulp, chop it coarsely and set aside.

Taste the garlic, and if it is "hot" on your tongue, warm 2 tablespoons of the oil in a small sauté pan over low heat. Add the garlic and cook for a minute or two just until soft. Do not allow it to color.

Transfer the eggplant to a food processor, add the tahini, lemon juice, and garlic and use 1-second pulses to combine the ingredients just until blended and the mixture is smooth. Alternatively, transfer the eggplant to a bowl and use a whisk to beat in the ingredients just until blended. Season with salt. If the mixture seems too thick, whisk in the remaining 2 tablespoons oil and/or the water as needed. Taste and adjust the seasoning with more tahini, lemon juice, and salt if needed.

Spoon into a shallow serving bowl and sprinkle with the pine nuts and parsley. Serve with the pita.

## Turkish Nine-Ingredient Eggplant Salad

DOKUZ TÜRLÜ PATLICAN TARATOR

This recipe takes the basic eggplant salad and enriches it with bitter peppers and nuts, salty cheese, tart, creamy yogurt, and a bit of heat. Although less familiar than baba ghanouj (page 29), it may become your favorite spread, as it offers many diverse textures with every bite. SERVES 8

3 large globe eggplants (about 3 pounds total weight)

2 green bell peppers

½ cup finely chopped toasted walnuts

4 ounces feta cheese, crumbled

½ cup plain Greek yogurt

4 or 5 cloves garlic, smashed or minced

1 fresh hot chile, seeded and finely minced

4 to 6 tablespoons extra virgin olive oil

Juice of 2 to 3 lemons

Salt

Warmed pita bread (see note, page 28) for serving

Roast the eggplants as directed in Master Recipe for Roasted Eggplant (page 27). After draining the pulp, chop coarsely and set aside in a bowl.

To roast the bell peppers, hold them directly over the flame on a gas stove top or place on a sheet pan under the broiler and turn them as needed until the skin is blistered and charred on all sides. Transfer to a closed plastic container or a bowl covered with plastic wrap and let stand for 20 minutes. Peel or rub off the skin from each pepper, then stem, halve lengthwise, remove and discard the seeds and thick ribs, and chop.

Add the bell peppers, walnuts, feta, yogurt, garlic, chile, 4 tablespoons of the oil, and the juice of 2 lemons to the eggplant and mix well. Taste and adjust the seasoning with more oil and lemon juice if needed and with salt if the feta does not provide enough. Serve at room temperature with the pita.

## Tunisian Spicy Chopped Eggplant Salad  AJLOUK D'AUBERGINE

Salads of mashed or chopped cooked vegetables are called *ajlouk* in Tunisia and *zahlouk* in Morocco. This recipe is reminiscent of one I cooked with Tunisian chef Abderrazak Haouari, who lives on the island of Djerba. Although he is not Jewish, he is well acquainted with Tunisian Jewish food because Djerba is home to a Jewish colony that dates back twenty-five hundred years and is the site of one of the oldest synagogues in the world. I have been happy to act as his sous-chef at many Mediterranean conferences sponsored by the Culinary Institute of America and the American Institute of Wine and Food. Here, he uses a head of garlic, but you may want to cut back to 6 cloves, as raw garlic and *harissa* deliver quite a kick.  SERVES 6

3 large globe eggplants (about 3 pounds total weight)

1 fresh hot red chile, such as serrano, or 2 to 3 milder red chiles, such as jalapeño

1 small head garlic, cloves separated, peeled, and chopped

Juice of 1 large lemon

2 to 3 teaspoons harissa, homemade (page 355) or store-bought

1 teaspoon ground caraway

½ cup extra virgin olive oil

Salt

Roast the eggplants as directed in Master Recipe for Roasted Eggplant (page 27). After draining the pulp, chop it finely and set aside in a bowl.

To roast the chile, hold it directly over the flame on a gas stove top (or place on a wire baking rack atop the burner) or place on a sheet pan under the broiler and turn it as needed until the skin is blistered and charred on all sides. Transfer to a closed plastic container or a bowl covered with plastic wrap and let stand for 20 minutes. Peel or rub off the skin from the chile, then stem, halve lengthwise, remove and discard the seeds, and finely chop.

Add the chile, garlic, lemon juice, 2 teaspoons of the harissa, and the caraway to the eggplant and mix well. Stir in the oil, then season with salt. Taste and adjust the seasoning with the remaining 1 teaspoon harissa if needed. Serve at room temperature.

## Moroccan Chopped Eggplant Salad ZAHLOUK

*Zahlouk* appears on both Muslim and Jewish tables in Morocco. This version is based on one from cookbook author Simy Danan, whose family lived in Fez after emigrating from Andalusia. Other cooks add 3 large tomatoes, peeled and seeded, in place of, or in addition to, the roasted peppers, along with a few tablespoons of grated onion. Although the use of preserved lemon is a signature of Fez, fresh lemon juice or chopped fresh lemon pulp can be substituted. If using preserved lemon, add it gradually, as its flavor can be intense. This salad, or one of its many variations, is traditionally served to break the fast after Yom Kippur. SERVES 4 TO 6

3 large globe eggplants (about 3 pounds total weight)

2 red bell peppers

3 cloves garlic, minced

Peel of ½ preserved lemon, homemade (page 356) or store-bought, rinsed and minced, or pulp of ½ fresh lemon, finely chopped

1 to 2 teaspoons ground toasted cumin

1 to 2 teaspoons sweet paprika

1 teaspoon salt

½ to ⅔ cup extra virgin olive oil

3 large ripe tomatoes, peeled, if desired, and cut into ½-inch dice (optional)

¼ cup chopped fresh flat-leaf parsley and/or cilantro

Freshly ground black pepper

Roast the eggplants as directed in Master Recipe for Roasted Eggplant (page 27). After draining the pulp, chop it coarsely and set aside in a bowl.

To roast the bell peppers, hold them directly over the flame on a gas stove top or place on a sheet pan under the broiler and turn them as needed until the skin is blistered and charred on all sides. Transfer to a closed plastic container or a bowl covered with plastic wrap and let stand for 20 minutes. Peel or rub off the skin from each pepper, then stem, halve lengthwise, remove and discard the seeds and thick ribs, and chop.

In a small bowl, stir together the garlic, preserved lemon, cumin and paprika to taste, and salt and then beat in ½ cup of the oil to make a dressing. Pour the dressing over the eggplant, add the bell peppers, tomatoes, and parsley, season with a few grinds of pepper, and mix well. Mix in additional oil if needed for a good consistency. Taste and adjust the seasoning with salt, pepper, or other spices and lemon if needed. Serve at room temperature.

## Cucumber and Yogurt Salad   CACIK

This Turkish salad would also be at home in the Balkans, Lebanon, and Iran. In Greece, this same mixture is called *tzatziki* and is used as a dip for pita bread or as a sauce for fried eggplant, zucchini, or fish. In Bulgaria, walnuts are added and it is called *tarator*. In Iran, raisins and walnuts are added and it is known as *khiar bil laban*. In summer, Iranian cooks thin it with ice water and serve it as a soup, which they top with chopped dill and mint and garnish with an ice cube and rose petals.

Minus the cucumbers, this recipe becomes a versatile, tart, and creamy dressing for beets and carrots, eggplant, and zucchini. In Greece and Turkey, it is used to dress a salad of purslane. In Iran, it is mixed with cooked spinach, beets, mushrooms, eggplant, and carrots, as well as cucumbers, in salads called *borani* (page 34). The most common additions to the basic yogurt mixture are chopped fresh mint or dill and minced garlic. SERVES 4

---

2 cucumbers, peeled, halved lengthwise, seeded, and cut into small dice

Salt

2 cloves garlic, finely minced

3 to 4 tablespoons extra virgin olive oil, plus 2 teaspoons for sautéing the garlic if needed

2 cups plain Greek yogurt, or 4 cups plain regular yogurt, drained in a cheesecloth-lined sieve for at least 6 to 8 hours or up to 1 day

4 to 6 tablespoons chopped fresh mint or dill

---

Put the cucumbers in a colander in the sink or over a bowl, sprinkle with salt, and let drain for 30 minutes. This will draw out some of their excess moisture, which can thin the yogurt. Pat the cucumbers dry. If the garlic is sharp flavored, sauté it in a small pan in the 2 teaspoons oil over low heat for a minute or two to soften its bite.

In a bowl, combine the cucumbers, garlic, yogurt, 3 tablespoons of the oil, and 4 tablespoons of the mint and mix well. Add the remaining 1 tablespoon oil if needed for a good consistency, then taste and adjust the seasoning with more mint if desired. Cover and refrigerate until serving.

VARIATION:  *Turkish Yogurt and Chile Dip (Haydari):* Omit the cucumbers. Add 1 fresh hot chile, seeded and minced, to the yogurt and garlic and use dill instead of mint.

# Three Persian Salads with Yogurt    BORANI

*Borani* is the Persian name for cold dishes that combine cooked vegetables with a yogurt sauce. They were a great favorite of Queen Poorandokht (known also as Queen Boran), who, in 630 CE, became the first woman to rule Persia. According to legend, these salads were called *poorani* after the queen because of her love of yogurt, but following the Arab conquest of her one-time empire, they became known as *borani* because the new rulers did not have the soft letter *p* in their language. Who knows if this is true, but it does make for a good story. EACH RECIPE SERVES 4 TO 6

## Mushroom Salad    BORANI-E GHARCH

| | |
|---|---|
| 3 tablespoons unsalted butter | Salt |
| 1 small yellow onion, chopped | Yogurt Sauce (page 36) |
| 1 pound cremini or white mushrooms, coarsely chopped or cut into small pieces | 2 tablespoons chopped fresh mint |
| | Warmed pita bread (see note, page 28) for serving |

Melt the butter in a medium sauté pan over medium heat. Add the onion and cook, stirring occasionally, until translucent and tender, 5 to 8 minutes. Add the mushrooms and cook, stirring occasionally, until tender, 4 to 6 minutes. Season lightly with salt, then remove from the heat and let cool.

In a bowl, toss the cooled mushroom mixture with the sauce and top with the mint. Serve with the pita.

## Spinach Salad    BORANI-E ESFENAJ

| | |
|---|---|
| 3 tablespoons unsalted butter | Yogurt Sauce (page 36), made without garlic |
| 1 small yellow onion, minced | |
| 2 cloves garlic, minced | Salt and freshly ground black pepper |
| ½ teaspoon ground cinnamon (optional) | 1 tablespoon finely shredded fresh mint |
| ½ teaspoon ground turmeric (optional) | 3 tablespoons chopped toasted walnuts (optional) |
| 1 pound spinach, stemmed and coarsely chopped | Warmed pita bread (see note, page 28) for serving |

Melt the butter in a large sauté pan over medium heat. Add the onion and cook, stirring occasionally, until translucent, about 5 minutes. Add the garlic and cook briefly to soften, then stir in the cinnamon and turmeric. Add the spinach and cook, tossing and stirring often, just until wilted, a few minutes. Remove from the heat, drain well in a colander, and let cool.

In a bowl, toss the cooled spinach mixture with the sauce. Taste and adjust the seasoning with salt and pepper. Sprinkle with the mint and walnuts. Serve with the pita.

## *Beets with Yogurt*   BORANI-E LABU

If you use red beets for this salad (also known as *borani chogondar*), they will tint the yogurt an electric pink. Small beets—red, golden, or red-and-white-striped Chioggia— are best for this salad, though large beets can be used.

| | |
|---|---|
| 2 bunches beets, red, yellow, or Chioggia (8 to 10 small beets or 4 to 5 large beets) | Salt |
| | 1 bunch watercress, mâche, or purslane, coarsely chopped |
| Yogurt Sauce (page 36), made with garlic | 2 tablespoons chopped fresh dill |
| 2 tablespoons chopped fresh mint | 3 tablespoons chopped toasted walnuts (optional) |
| ¼ teaspoon ground cinnamon | Crumbled feta cheese for garnish |

Trim the tops from the beets, leaving about ½ inch of the stem attached to prevent the beets from bleeding color. Reserve the tops for another use. Put the beets in a pot, add salted water to cover, and bring to a boil over high heat. Turn down the heat to a simmer and cook, uncovered, until tender, about 30 minutes for small beets and about 50 minutes for large beets. Pour off most of the hot water, add cold water to cover, and let sit for about 1 minute (the cold-water bath makes the beets easier to peel), then peel the beets while they are still warm. Alternatively, trim the beets as directed, rub them with a little oil, place in a baking pan, add water to a depth of ½ inch, and cover the pan with foil. Bake in a preheated 350°F oven until tender, about 40 minutes for small beets and about 1 hour for large beets. Peel while still warm.

Make the sauce as directed, stirring in the mint and cinnamon along with the garlic. Season with salt.

If the beets are large, cut them into ¼-inch-thick slices or into ¼-inch dice. If they are small, cut each beet into 4 or 8 wedges. Place the beets and watercress in a large bowl. Add the sauce and toss to coat evenly. Top with the dill, walnuts, and feta.

# Yogurt Sauce

This versatile sauce is used to dress not only Persian *borani* but also roasted and stuffed vegetables and other dishes throughout the Mediterranean Jewish world. MAKES ABOUT 1¼ CUPS

1 cup plain Greek yogurt, or 2 cups plain regular yogurt, drained in a cheesecloth-lined sieve for at least 6 to 8 hours or up to 1 day

3 tablespoons extra virgin olive oil

2 tablespoons fresh lemon juice

1 to 2 teaspoons minced garlic (optional)

Salt

In a bowl, stir together the yogurt, oil, lemon juice, and garlic to taste. Season with salt.

# Master Recipe for Winter Squash Purée

1 or 2 yellow winter squashes, such as butternut, banana, or kabocha (about 3 pounds total weight)

You can peel and dice the squash(es) and cook them on the stove top in simmering water until soft. But the flavor will be fuller if you roast them. Preheat the oven to 375°F. Prick the squash(es) with the tip of a knife and place in a baking pan. Alternatively, cut the squash(es) in half, scoop out the seeds, and place the halves, cut side down, on an oiled sheet pan. Halving the squash(es) will speed up the cooking but you may need to scrape away any hardened or burned edges.

Bake the squashes until tender when pierced with a skewer, 45 to 60 minutes, or longer depending on size. If baking whole squash, remove from the oven and, when cool enough to handle, cut in half, scoop out the seeds and fibers and discard, and then peel the halves. If baking squash halves, peel when cool enough to handle. Pass the squash flesh through a food mill placed over a bowl, or mash the flesh in a bowl with a potato masher. You should have about 3 cups purée. If the puréed squash has a lot of moisture, drain it in a sieve placed over a bowl for 1 hour.

# Three Winter Squash Spreads

We don't usually associate winter squash with spreads, probably because it is dense, starchy, and sweet. These recipes show how it seems lighter when highly spiced, made tart with yogurt and lemon, or tempered with creamy tahini.

## Spicy Squash Spread  THURSHI

This spread, also known as *chirshi,* is of North African origin. Some say it is from Libya, but it also could be from Tunisia because it calls for caraway, a signature spice in *tābil,* the classic Tunisian seasoning mixture. I was surprised to find a version of this recipe in Edda Servi Machlin's *The Classic Cuisine of the Italian Jews.* She recommends serving it as an accompaniment to couscous, so it is likely that the recipe made its way into the Italian Jewish kitchen in Livorno, where many North African Jews settled. It is more typically served as a spread on bread.  SERVES 6 TO 8

½ cup extra virgin olive oil

6 cloves garlic, finely minced

1 tablespoon caraway seeds, toasted in a dry pan until fragrant and lightly crushed

½ teaspoon cayenne pepper, or 1 teaspoon harissa, homemade (page 355) or store-bought, plus more if needed

2 to 3 cups squash purée (see master recipe, page 36)

½ cup fresh lemon juice

Grated zest of 2 lemons

Salt and freshly ground black pepper

Warmed pita bread (see note, page 28) for serving

Warm the olive oil in a sauté pan over low heat. Add the garlic, caraway, and cayenne and cook for a minute or two until fragrant. Add the squash and lemon juice and zest, mix well, and warm gently, stirring often, until the flavors are blended and the mixture is heated through. Remove from the heat and season with salt and pepper. If using harissa, taste and add more if needed.

Serve warm with the pita. Alternatively, prepare the spread up to two days in advance, let cool, cover, and refrigerate, then reheat gently and adjust the seasoning before serving.

## Turkish Pumpkin Squash Dip  KABAK SALATASI

I have suggested pita for serving, but *lavash,* the thin, clay oven–baked flatbread enjoyed in much of West Asia, or even nontraditional naan would be good here, as well.  SERVES 6 TO 8

2 to 3 cups squash purée (see master recipe, page 36)

½ cup plain Greek yogurt, or 1 cup plain regular yogurt, drained in a cheesecloth-lined sieve for at least 6 to 8 hours or up to 1 day

1 to 2 cloves garlic, minced

1 tablespoon fresh lemon juice

1 tablespoon extra virgin olive oil

1 small fresh hot chile, seeded and minced, or 1 teaspoon crushed Maras pepper flakes

Salt

Warmed pita bread (see note, page 28) for serving

In a bowl, combine the squash, yogurt, garlic, lemon juice, oil, and chile and mix well. Season with salt. Serve with the pita bread.

## *Pumpkin Squash Hummus*   QARA' BIL TAHINI

This tahini-enriched Levantine squash spread is popular in Syria and Lebanon, where *za'atar* or nigella seeds are sometimes used in place of the pomegranate seeds. SERVES 6 TO 8

2 to 3 cups squash purée (see master recipe, page 36)

½ cup tahini, stirred well before use

4 cloves garlic, minced

⅓ cup fresh lemon juice

3 tablespoons chopped fresh flat-leaf parsley or dill

Salt and freshly ground black pepper

Extra virgin olive oil for garnish

Pomegranate seeds or ground sumac for garnish

Warmed pita bread (see note, page 28) for serving

In a bowl, combine the squash, tahini, garlic, lemon juice, and parsley and mix well. Season with salt and pepper. Garnish with a drizzle of oil and a scattering of pomegranate seeds. Serve with the pita bread.

## *Chickpea Purée with Tahini Dressing*   HUMMUS BA TAHINI

Favas and chickpeas are indigenous Mediterranean pulses and are widely eaten all over the Middle East. They have been cultivated in the area since ancient times, and remnants of them have been discovered in the remains of mummies.

Hummus is so widely known, you may wonder why I have included a recipe here. It is actually worthy of a dissertation, as there are so many variations and so many different peoples—Israeli Jews and Arabs from Syria, Egypt, Lebanon, and Palestine—who claim it as their own. This classic chickpea spread, popular as a meze, has become a staple on supermarket food-to-go shelves, often "enhanced" with other ingredients, such as roasted peppers, spinach, and tomatoes. I prefer to make my own so I can control the texture and the amount of tartness and garlic.

Tahini brands vary in quality, flavor, and consistency (see Pantry). I prefer Al Wadi brand from Lebanon, but you may find others that you like better. Before using tahini, always stir it well, as the sesame paste settles to the bottom and the oil rises to the top. Also, add it gradually and taste as you go, as some brands are stronger flavored than others. SERVES 6 TO 8

1 cup dried chickpeas

Salt

6 to 8 tablespoons tahini, stirred well before use

2 to 3 cloves garlic, finely minced

½ cup fresh lemon juice, plus more if needed

1 teaspoon ground toasted cumin (optional)

2 tablespoons extra virgin olive oil

Generous pinch of sweet paprika or Aleppo pepper flakes (optional)

3 tablespoons chopped fresh flat-leaf parsley

2 tablespoons pine nuts, toasted

Warmed pita bread (see note, page 28) for serving

Pick over the chickpeas, then place in a bowl, add water to cover, and let soak in the refrigerator overnight. Drain, rinse well, and transfer to a 2-quart saucepan. Add water to cover by 3 inches and bring to a boil over high heat. Turn down the heat to low, cover, and simmer until very soft, 1 to 1½ hours. The timing will depend on the age of the beans. After the first 30 minutes of cooking, add 2 teaspoons salt. (Some cooks add 1 teaspoon baking soda to the cooking water to soften them more quickly, but I detect a soapy aftertaste.) If you have the patience, you can remove the loose skins from the cooked chickpeas.

Drain the chickpeas, reserving the cooking liquid. If you like, set aside a couple of tablespoons of chickpeas for garnish. Transfer the remaining chickpeas to a food processor and pulse until puréed. Add 6 tablespoons of the tahini, the garlic to taste, and the lemon juice and pulse again until puréed. Pulse in enough of the reserved cooking liquid (or cold water) to achieve a creamy and spreadable consistency, then season with salt. Taste and adjust the flavor balance with the cumin and additional tahini and lemon juice if needed. If not serving immediately, cover and set aside at room temperature for up to 2 hours. The hummus will thicken as it stands. Just before serving, thin with more cooking liquid or with water to achieve the correct consistency. It can also be refrigerated for a day or two and then brought to room temperature for serving. Thin if necessary and adjust the seasoning, as flavors may have faded.

To serve, spoon the hummus onto a shallow plate and smooth the surface with the back of a spoon or with a spatula. Drizzle with the oil and then garnish with the paprika, parsley, pine nuts, and reserved whole chickpeas, if using. Serve with the pita.

# Greek Parsley Salad with Tahini Dressing *TAHINI SALATA*

Although this recipe is called a salad, it is a chunky meze spread for accompanying pita. I sometimes add toasted pine nuts to the parsley and tahini mixture for both texture and sweetness. If you don't have green onions on hand, substitute ¼ cup chopped fresh chives. SERVES 4 TO 6

½ cup tahini, stirred well before use

2 to 3 cloves garlic, finely minced

½ cup fresh lemon juice, plus more if needed

6 to 8 tablespoons water

Salt and freshly ground black pepper

1½ to 2 cups chopped fresh flat-leaf parsley

3 green onions, including green tops, finely chopped

2 tablespoons pine nuts, toasted and coarsely chopped (optional)

Warmed pita bread (see note, page 28) for serving

In a blender or small food processor, combine the tahini, garlic, and lemon juice and process until smooth. With the machine running, slowly add the water as needed until the mixture is thin enough to coat a parsley leaf lightly. Salt is crucial for the correct balance of flavor, so dip a parsley leaf into the dressing, then taste and season with salt and pepper and with more lemon juice if needed.

In a bowl, toss together the parsley, green onions, and pine nuts. Drizzle with the dressing and toss to coat evenly. Serve with the pita for scooping.

# Bean Purée with Toasted Cumin *BESSARA*

Hummus is the best known of the many bean-based spreads and dips enjoyed around the Mediterranean. Dried fava beans or white beans are a good choice for this simple North African bean dip. If using fava beans, look for peeled favas, which will save you time. In Greece, a similar bean spread known as *fava* calls for simmering yellow split peas until soft, then puréeing them and serving them topped with a drizzle of olive oil, a scattering of shaved red onions, and maybe some chopped dill and accompanied with lemon wedges. SERVES 6 TO 8

1½ cups dried fava beans or large white beans

Few cloves garlic, peeled, plus 1 clove, minced (optional)

1 tablespoon ground toasted cumin

½ cup mild, fruity extra virgin olive oil

3 tablespoons fresh lemon juice

Salt and freshly ground black pepper

Za'atar for garnish (optional)

Warmed pita bread (see note, page 28) or crackers for serving

Pick over the beans, then place in a bowl, add water to cover, and let soak in the refrigerator overnight. Drain and rinse well. If using unpeeled fava beans, rub the beans with your fingers to remove the wrinkly skins. In a saucepan, combine the beans, whole garlic cloves, and water to cover by 3 inches and bring to a boil over high heat. Turn down the heat to low, cover, and simmer until the beans are very soft, 1 to 1 ½ hours. The timing will depend on the type and age of the beans. Drain well and mash the beans and garlic cloves in a bowl with a potato masher or fork until smooth, or pulse in a food processor until mashed but not too puréed, then transfer to a bowl.

In a small bowl, whisk together the cumin, oil, and lemon juice. Gradually stir the cumin mixture into the beans, mixing well. Season with salt and pepper. Transfer to a serving bowl and top with the za'atar. Serve with the pita.

## Turkish Lentil Salad   ADAS SALATASI

Lentils are used in salads and soups all over the Mediterranean. When they are cooked for salads, they must keep their shape and some texture, so I recommend against brown or red lentils, which soften and lose their contours too easily. The best lentils to use for salads are deep green lentils from Le Puy in France, the brownish green Pardina variety from Castile and León in Spain, or the speckled green to brown Castelluccio lentils from Umbria in Italy. Some excellent green lentils are also being cultivated in the United States, with Zürsun Idaho Heirloom Beans a good example of a high-quality supplier. I also like black lentils, which are occasionally labeled "beluga" lentils because of their resemblance to caviar.

Some salads are good the day you make them but are better on the second day. Lentil salads are like that. They need time for the flavors to marry, so make them a day ahead of serving. Just remember to bring them to room temperature and adjust the salt if needed before serving. This salad is of Turkish origin, but a similar salad, *salata bil adas,* is served in Lebanon. For a general Middle Eastern version, replace the mint vinaigrette with a dressing of mild, fruity extra virgin olive oil, lemon juice, and ground toasted cumin and garnish the salad with tomato wedges, oil-cured black olives, and crumbled feta. SERVES 4 TO 6

2 cups green lentils, picked over and rinsed

Salt

3 tablespoons extra virgin olive oil

1½ cups diced yellow onion

| ½ cup peeled and diced carrot | 1 cup Mint Vinaigrette (recipe follows) |
|---|---|
| ⅓ cup diced celery | Freshly ground black pepper |
| 1 teaspoon minced garlic | 4 ounces fresh goat cheese or feta cheese, crumbled (optional) |

In a saucepan, combine the lentils with water to cover by 2 inches and bring to a boil over high heat. Turn down the heat to low and simmer gently until tender but not soft, 20 to 35 minutes. The timing will vary depending on the age of the lentils. After the lentils have simmered for about 15 minutes, add 2 teaspoons salt.

While the lentils are cooking, warm the oil in a sauté pan over medium heat. Add the onion, carrot, and celery and cook, stirring occasionally, until all the vegetables are tender, 10 to 15 minutes. Add the garlic and cook for a minute or two longer. Remove from the heat and let cool.

Drain the lentils, transfer to a bowl, and let cool until warm. Add the onion mixture and toss to combine, then drizzle with the dressing and toss again. Taste and adjust the seasoning with salt and pepper. Serve at room temperature, topped with the cheese.

## Mint Vinaigrette

In Italy, Greece, Turkey, Morocco, and the countries of the Arab world, mint dressing is ubiquitous. Starting with an infusion of mint and lemon juice intensifies the mint flavor. This dressing is excellent on spinach salads, bean and grain salads, citrus salads, and on cooked carrots, beets, asparagus, and potatoes, and it can be substituted for the preserved lemon dressing used for the Moroccan lentil salad on page 43. It is also delicious spooned over cooked fish. MAKES ABOUT 2 CUPS

| INFUSION | ¼ cup red wine vinegar |
|---|---|
| ¼ cup fresh lemon juice | 2 tablespoons fresh lemon juice |
| ¼ cup chopped fresh mint | ½ cup packed chopped fresh mint |
| | 1 teaspoon honey |
| 1¼ cups mild, fruity extra virgin olive oil | ½ teaspoon salt |

To make the infusion, combine the lemon juice and mint in a small saucepan. Bring to a boil over high heat and remove from the heat. Let steep for about 10 minutes. Strain through a fine-mesh sieve into a small bowl, pressing against the mint to extract all of the liquid. You should have about ¼ cup. It will no longer be green because of the lemon juice, but it will be intensely minty.

To finish the vinaigrette, whisk the oil, vinegar, lemon juice, mint, honey, and salt into the infusion. Leftover vinaigrette can be stored in a covered container in the refrigerator for 2 to 3 days. Bring to room temperature, then whisk in a little fresh mint and taste for salt and acidity and adjust if needed.

# Moroccan-Inspired Lentil Salad with Carrots, Dates, and Mint

Sometimes an unusual combination of tastes catches my attention. At his San Francisco restaurant, Aziza, chef Mourad Lahlou served a wonderful lentil soup garnished with dates and a celery salad. When I asked about this surprising pairing, he explained that after breaking the Ramadan fast, Moroccans start their evening meal with a bite of a sweet date and then eat a bowl of the hearty lentil soup called *harira*. This striking mix of sweet and earthy flavors was on my mind when I decided to make a new lentil salad for my family.

The carrots can be prepared two different ways. If the carrots at your market are just average in flavor and appearance, dice them and cook them along with the onions, as instructed in the recipe. They will provide texture and some mild sweetness. If the carrots are small, young, and delicate, roast them separately. (Stay away from bagged "baby carrots," which are actually large, starchy carrots cut by machine to look adorable.) Buy about 8 ounces (2 small bunches), peel them, and toss them with a little olive oil to coat evenly. Spread them on a sheet pan, sprinkle lightly with kosher salt, and roast in a preheated 450°F oven until tender, 20 to 25 minutes. Their sweetness will intensify during roasting. Let cool, then slice on the diagonal into 1- to 1 ½-inch pieces and toss with the lentils along with the dates and mint.

You can make this salad many hours or even a day ahead of serving and the flavors will improve. If it has been refrigerated, bring it to room temperature and adjust the salt if needed before serving. SERVES 4 TO 6

---

2 cups green lentils, picked over and rinsed

Salt

¼ cup mild, fruity extra virgin olive oil, plus more for tossing with lentils

1½ cups diced yellow onion

2½ cups peeled and diced carrots

¾ to 1 cup Preserved Lemon Citrus Dressing (recipe follows)

20 dates, pitted and sliced crosswise

½ cup fresh mint or anise hyssop leaves, cut into very narrow strips (chiffonade)

---

In a saucepan, combine the lentils with water to cover by 2 inches and bring to a boil over high heat. Turn down the heat to low and simmer gently until tender but not soft, 20 to 35 minutes. The timing will vary depending on the age of the lentils. After the lentils have simmered for about 15 minutes, add 2 teaspoons salt.

While the lentils are cooking, warm the oil in a sauté pan over medium heat. Add the onion and carrot and cook, stirring occasionally, until they are tender, 10 to 15 minutes. Remove from the heat and let cool.

Drain the lentils, transfer to a bowl, toss with a little oil, and let cool until warm. Add the onion mixture and toss to combine. Drizzle with the dressing and toss well. Let cool completely, then fold in the dates and mint and toss again. Taste and adjust the seasoning with salt. Serve at room temperature.

## Preserved Lemon Citrus Dressing

Here, preserved lemon adds pungency to a mildly spiced vinaigrette. MAKES ABOUT 1¾ cups

½ cup fresh lemon juice

1 teaspoon sweet paprika

1 teaspoon ground toasted cumin

1¼ cups extra virgin olive oil, plus more if needed

Peel of 1 preserved lemon, homemade (page 356) or store-bought, rinsed and finely chopped

Salt and freshly ground black pepper

In a small bowl, whisk together the lemon juice, paprika, and cumin. Whisk in the oil, stir in the preserved lemon, and then whisk in more oil if needed for good balance. Season with salt and pepper. Leftover dressing can be stored in a covered container in the refrigerator for 2 to 3 days. Bring to room temperature, then taste for salt and acidity and adjust if needed.

## Sephardic Chickpea Salad    SALATA DE GARBANZOS

White beans, favas, lentils, black-eyed peas, and all manner of other legumes always have a place on the meze or salad table. Here's a Hispano-Turkish salad of chickpeas dressed in the Sephardic manner, using a double ratio of vinegar to oil. If you find it too sharply flavored, add more oil for balance. SERVES 4 TO 6

1 rounded cup dried chickpeas

Salt

¼ cup extra virgin olive oil

½ teaspoon dried oregano

2 cloves garlic, minced

½ cup red or white wine vinegar

1 small yellow onion, finely chopped

½ cup chopped red bell pepper

½ cup chopped green bell pepper

½ teaspoon freshly ground black pepper

Pick over the chickpeas, then place in a bowl, add water to cover, and let soak in the refrigerator overnight. Drain, rinse well, and transfer to a 2-quart saucepan. Add water to cover by 3 inches and bring to a boil over high heat. Turn down the heat to low, cover, and simmer until tender, 40 to 60 minutes. The cooking time will depend on the age of the chickpeas. During the last 10 minutes of cooking, add 2 teaspoons salt.

While the chickpeas are cooking, warm the oil in a small saucepan over very low heat. Add the oregano and garlic and warm for 2 minutes. Remove from the heat and let steep until the chickpeas are ready.

Drain the chickpeas, transfer to a bowl, and let cool until warm. Meanwhile, whisk the vinegar into the oil. Drizzle the oil mixture over the warm chickpeas and toss to coat evenly. Let cool completely, then stir in the onion, bell peppers, 1 teaspoon salt, and the pepper. Taste and adjust the seasoning with salt and pepper. Serve at room temperature.

## Turkish Onion Salad with Sumac   SOĞAN SALATASI

This is not a salad to eat on its own. It is a condiment salad to accompany kebabs and other cooked dishes. Like *tzatziki* or tahini, it is a standby on the Mediterranean table. Some Turkish cooks might add a bit of chopped mint or omit the sumac. The Iraqis call it *salatat basal wa summaq*.  SERVES 8

---

3 large red onions, thinly sliced

1 cup water

½ cup wine vinegar, any kind

2 teaspoons salt

2 tablespoons ground sumac

---

In a bowl, combine the onions, water, vinegar, and salt and mix gently. Let stand for 2 hours, stirring from time to time. Just before serving, drain well and sprinkle with the sumac.

## Lebanese Bulgur and Parsley Salad   TABBOULEH

Tabbouleh is served all over the Middle East, and every country wants to claim it. This is a popular Lebanese version. The success of this grain-based salad depends on good tomatoes, so it is best in the summer. The technique for softening the grain varies: some cooks pour boiling salted water over the bulgur, others soak it in salted cold water, and still others use salted warm water. If all the water has not been absorbed but the grain is tender and still a bit crunchy, drain the grain in a sieve. Measurements for this salad need not be exact. More tomato, less parsley—it will still be delicious and refreshing.  SERVES 6

1 to 1½ cups fine-grind bulgur, rinsed

2 to 3 cups finely chopped fresh flat-leaf parsley

2 to 3 cups chopped ripe tomatoes

1 cup chopped fresh mint

½ cup chopped green onions, including green tops

½ cup mild, fruity extra virgin olive oil

¼ cup fresh lemon juice, plus more if needed

Salt and freshly ground black pepper

Romaine lettuce leaves for serving

In a bowl, soak the bulgur in warm salted water to cover (use about twice as much water as bulgur) until tender yet still slightly crunchy, 20 to 30 minutes. Pour into a sieve to drain off any excess water, then transfer to a large bowl.

Add the parsley, tomatoes, mint, and green onions to the bulgur and toss to mix. In a small bowl, whisk together the oil and lemon juice. Drizzle over the bulgur mixture and toss to coat evenly. Season with salt and pepper, taste, and adjust with more lemon juice if needed.

Serve the salad with the romaine leaves for scooping.

## Turkish Spicy Bulgur Salad    KISIR

This salad is a bit like tabbouleh but with cucumber, bell pepper, and a kick of heat and with lettuce folded in instead of served on the side. The salad minus the lettuce and dressed with a tahini and walnut dressing is called *batırık*.    SERVES 6

1 to 1½ cups fine-grind bulgur

2 to 3 cups chopped ripe tomatoes

1 cup chopped cucumber

1 green bell pepper, seeded and finely chopped

1 small head romaine lettuce, leaves separated and finely shredded

1 bunch fresh flat-leaf parsley, chopped

6 green onions, including green tops, chopped

½ cup mild, fruity extra virgin olive oil

¼ cup fresh lemon juice, plus more if needed

1 teaspoon each sweet paprika and hot paprika, or 2 teaspoons crushed Aleppo or Maras pepper flakes

Salt and freshly ground black pepper

In a bowl, soak the bulgur in warm salted water to cover (use about twice as much water as bulgur) until tender yet still slightly crunchy, 20 to 30 minutes. Pour into a sieve to drain off any excess water, then transfer to a large bowl.

Add the tomatoes, cucumber, bell pepper, lettuce, parsley, and green onions and stir gently to mix well. In a small bowl, whisk together the oil, lemon juice, and sweet and hot paprika and season with salt and pepper. Taste and adjust the seasoning with more lemon juice, salt, and pepper if needed. Drizzle the dressing over the bulgur mixture, toss to coat evenly, and serve.

## Syrian Bulgur and Nut Salad  BAZERGAN

*Bazergan*—literally "of the bazaar"—is a Syrian Jewish version of tabbouleh. Some recipes add chopped hazelnuts or pine nuts to the mix, but walnuts are typical. Grated onion is an occasional addition. The dressing is enhanced with tamarind paste or pomegranate molasses; I have used the latter here, as it is easier to find at the market. Both ingredients have a tart-sweet quality that, along with the lemon juice, accents the spices. Let the completed salad marinate for a few hours or as long as overnight for the flavors to develop. At serving time, adjust the seasoning with salt and the tartness with lemon juice if needed.

Although adding fruit other than pomegranate seeds is not traditional, I think the sweetness helps balance the salad. In winter I use diced apples. When cherries are in season, pit and halve them and use them in place of the pomegranate seeds. They pair well with the walnuts and the pomegranate dressing. I served the cherry version at a Zinfandel festival and it was a perfect match for the wine. SERVES 6 TO 8

2 cups fine-grind bulgur

1 tablespoon ground toasted cumin

2 teaspoons ground coriander

½ teaspoon ground allspice

¼ teaspoon cayenne pepper

3 tablespoons tomato paste

5 tablespoons fresh lemon juice, plus more if needed

6 tablespoons pomegranate molasses

½ cup mild, fruity extra virgin olive oil, plus more if needed

Salt

2 cups pitted cherries, halved, in spring, or 2 cups diced apple in winter (optional)

1 cup diced fennel (optional)

1 cup walnuts, toasted and coarsely chopped

¼ cup pine nuts, toasted (optional)

¼ cup chopped fresh flat-leaf parsley

¼ cup fresh mint leaves, cut into very narrow strips (chiffonade)

Seeds of 1 pomegranate (optional)

Romaine lettuce leaves for serving (optional)

In a bowl, soak the bulgur in warm salted water to cover (use about twice as much water as bulgur) until tender yet still slightly crunchy, 20 to 30 minutes. Pour into a sieve to drain off any excess water, then transfer to a large bowl.

In a small bowl, whisk together the cumin, coriander, allspice, cayenne, tomato paste, and lemon juice, then whisk in the pomegranate molasses and oil. Season with salt, taste, and adjust with more lemon juice or oil, if needed. Drizzle the dressing over the bulgur and toss to coat evenly. Fold in the cherries, fennel, walnuts, pine nuts, parsley, and mint, mixing well. Top with the pomegranate seeds and serve at room temperature with the romaine leaves for scooping.

## Lebanese Toasted Pita Bread Salad    FATTOUSH

As soon as we introduced *fattoush* to our diners at Square One in 1984, it became the most requested summer salad. *Fatta* means "torn into pieces," so be sure to tear the pita, rather than cut it into neat little squares. Such precision is antithetical to the dish.

For maximum crunch, dress the salad just before serving so the bread does not become soggy. A lemon and olive oil dressing enhanced with tart sumac is typical, along with lots of fresh mint and parsley. The addition of fleshy purslane is optional, as it is not readily found in most markets. A search of farmers' markets is worth the effort. Although not traditional, crumbled feta cheese is a tasty addition. SERVES 4 TO 6

---

4 large or 8 small pita breads

About ½ cup extra virgin olive oil

Juice of 2 lemons

2 teaspoons ground sumac

Salt and freshly ground pepper

2½ to 3 cups diced tomatoes (½-inch dice)

2 cups diced cucumber (peeled and seeded if necessary; ½-inch dice)

½ cup finely diced red onion

6 tablespoons finely chopped green onions, including green tops

½ cup chopped fresh mint

1 cup chopped fresh flat-leaf parsley

4 cups loosely packed romaine lettuce strips (1 inch wide)

2 cups stemmed purslane (optional)

---

Preheat the oven to 350°F. Place the pita breads in a single layer on a sheet pan and bake until dry, about 15 minutes. Remove from the oven and, when cool enough to handle, break into large bite-size pieces.

In a small bowl, whisk together the oil, lemon juice, and sumac, then season with salt and pepper.

In a large bowl, combine the tomatoes, cucumber, red onion, green onions, mint, and parsley and toss gently to mix. Add half of the dressing and toss to coat evenly. Add the pita pieces, romaine, and purslane, drizzle the remaining dressing over the top, and toss once again. Serve immediately.

## Shepherd's Salad    SALADE PASTORALE

This chopped salad, which is known as *salata djoban* in Ladino, is ubiquitous throughout the Mediterranean. Its name is related to the classic Greek salad known as *horiatiki salata,* which means "country salad," though the pieces are larger in the Greek version. It also resembles the Spanish chopped salad from Jaén called *pipirrana,* the classic Turkish chopped salad known as *çoban salatası,* and Iran's *salad e Shirazi.* In Tunisia, *slata jida,* a similar chopped salad, includes tomatoes, cucumbers, peppers, spring onions, lemon, and olive oil. The garlic is not traditional here, but I think it adds a welcome lively flavor. The mint is also my addition. Note the high proportion of vinegar to oil, the Sephardic signature for salad dressings.

If you would like to assemble this salad a few hours ahead of serving, keep in mind that the tomatoes will continue to give off their liquid. You can add them just before serving, or you can drain off the excess liquid from the assembled salad and then adjust the seasoning with oil, vinegar, salt, and pepper before serving.  SERVES 6 TO 8

3 large tomatoes, peeled, seeded, and chopped

2 small cucumbers, peeled, halved, seeded, and chopped, or 1 English cucumber, halved, seeded, and chopped

1 small bell pepper, seeded and chopped (green, red, or yellow)

1 red onion, finely minced

2 cloves garlic, minced (optional)

½ cup chopped fresh flat-leaf parsley

¼ cup chopped fresh mint

4 to 6 tablespoons extra virgin olive oil

½ cup wine vinegar, plus more if needed

Salt and freshly ground black pepper

Oil-cured black olives for garnish

4 to 8 olive oil–packed anchovy fillets (optional)

In a large bowl, combine the tomatoes, cucumbers, bell pepper, onion, garlic, parsley, and mint and toss gently to mix. In a small bowl, whisk together 4 tablespoons of the oil and the vinegar, pour over the salad, and toss to coat evenly. Season with salt and pepper, then taste and adjust with more oil, salt, and pepper if needed.

Transfer to a serving bowl and top with the olives and anchovies.

## Greek Spinach and Mushroom Salad    SALATA DE SPINAKA

This Greek Sephardic salad from Thrace is unusual in that it is made with uncooked spinach. Most Mediterranean spinach "salads" are cooked spinach dressed with oil and vinegar or lemon juice. The recipe comes from my friend Nicholas Stavroulakis, author of *Cookbook of the Jews of Greece* and former director of the Jewish Museum in Salonika. If you have concerns about using raw egg yolks to make the dressing, you can use a few tablespoons of commercial mayonnaise instead. The mixture of two acids, lemon juice and vinegar, balances the bitter walnuts and spinach with the earthy mushrooms perfectly. SERVES 4

---

1 pound baby spinach, or 2 bunches regular spinach, stemmed

5 to 6 ounces white or cremini mushrooms, thinly sliced

½ cup walnut halves, toasted and coarsely chopped or broken into large pieces by hand

¼ cup extra virgin olive oil

1 tablespoon white wine vinegar, plus more if needed

1 tablespoon fresh lemon juice, plus more if needed

2 egg yolks

½ teaspoon dry mustard

Salt and freshly ground black pepper

---

Rinse the spinach well and drain dry. If using large spinach leaves, tear into smaller pieces. If using baby spinach, leave whole. In a large bowl, combine the spinach, mushrooms, and walnuts and toss to mix.

In a small bowl, whisk together the oil, vinegar, lemon juice, egg yolks, and mustard, then season with salt and pepper. Taste and adjust with more vinegar or lemon juice if needed. Drizzle the dressing over the spinach mixture and toss to coat evenly. Serve immediately.

## *Zucchini with Mint and Vinegar* CONCIA

Although this dish is popular in the Roman Jewish community, it is of Sicilian origin. In the Veneto, it is called *zuchete in aseo* and *zucchini all'aceto,* and it is known as *zucchini all'agro* elsewhere. Eggplant is prepared the same way and called *concia di malignane* or *melanzane all'aceto. Concia* is served as part of an antipasto spread or as an accompaniment to meat dishes, especially *bollito* (boiled beef). It can also be made into a wonderful snack by sandwiching it between two pieces of bread or using it as a topping for crostini. SERVES 4

---

4 to 6 small zucchini (about 1½ pounds total weight)

Salt

3 tablespoons chopped fresh mint or basil

2 tablespoons chopped fresh flat-leaf parsley

2 large cloves garlic, minced

6 tablespoons extra virgin olive oil

¼ cup red or white wine vinegar

---

Cut the zucchini into ¼-inch-thick slices. Put the slices in a colander in the sink or over a bowl, sprinkle with salt, and let drain for 30 minutes. This will draw out any bitter juices. Rinse and pat dry. In a small bowl, stir together the mint, parsley, and garlic.

Warm the oil in a sauté pan over medium-high heat. In batches, add the zucchini in a single layer and cook, turning as needed, until golden on both sides, 4 to 5 minutes for each batch. Using a slotted spoon, transfer the slices to a shallow serving dish and sprinkle with half of the mint mixture and half of the vinegar. Repeat with the remaining zucchini, mint mixture, and vinegar.

Let stand at room temperature for 1 to 2 hours, basting occasionally with the vinegar in the dish, before serving.

## Eggplant with Vinegar   MELANZANE ALL'ACETO

This is a variation on *concia* (page 50) made with eggplant, but here the eggplant slices are grilled or broiled instead of sautéed. If grilling, cut the slices a little thicker than for frying, as eggplant shrinks in cooking and the slices need to be substantial enough to turn easily on the grill.   SERVES 6

---

| | |
|---|---|
| 2 globe eggplants, peeled and cut lengthwise into ½-inch-thick slices | ¼ cup red wine vinegar |
| ½ cup olive oil, plus more if needed | Chopped fresh mint or flat-leaf parsley for garnish |
| Salt and freshly ground black pepper | 2 cloves garlic, minced |

---

Prepare a fire in a charcoal grill or preheat the broiler. Brush the eggplant slices on both sides with the oil and sprinkle on both sides with salt and pepper. Place directly over the coals or slip under the broiler and cook, turning once, until golden on both sides and tender and translucent, 4 to 5 minutes total.

Transfer to 1 or 2 platters and drizzle evenly with the vinegar, then sprinkle with the mint and garlic. Let stand at room temperature for an hour or two to allow the eggplant to absorb the dressing before serving.

## Sweet-and-Sour Eggplant, Jewish Style   CAPONATA ALLA GIUDIA

Eggplants came to Spain with the Arabs, and the Jews took to the new vegetable right away. When the Inquisition banned the Jews from Spain and Spanish settlements in southern Italy, the Italian Jews fled north, bringing with them a repertoire of eggplant dishes. It's not surprising that many of the best eggplant recipes are from Sicily, as that is where the Arabic influence was the greatest. They are often served at room temperature, which means they are ideal for preparing late on Friday for serving at Sabbath lunch.

The variations on Sicilian caponata are almost as numerous as the families on the island. In *The Classic Cuisine of the Italian Jews,* Edda Servi Machlin offers a particularly unusual version that adds peppers and carrots and is baked in the oven. Caponata is served at room temperature as part of an antipasto assortment or as an accompaniment to cooked meats or fish and is also tasty with grilled or toasted bread. Make it a day in advance so that the flavors can marry. Readjust the vinegar and salt at serving time, as they have a tendency to fade. Serve garnished with quartered hard-boiled eggs, if you like. SERVES 6 TO 8

---

2 large globe eggplants (about 1 pound each)

Salt and freshly ground black pepper

1 to 1½ cups extra virgin olive oil, or as needed

1 cup sliced or diced celery (½ inch thick)

2 yellow onions, chopped or sliced ¼ inch thick

3 cloves garlic, minced

1½ pounds tomatoes, peeled, seeded, and diced, or 1 cup tomato purée

½ cup red wine vinegar

2 to 3 tablespoons sugar

3 tablespoons brined capers, rinsed

24 Mediterranean-style green olives, pitted and coarsely chopped

¼ cup pine nuts or blanched slivered almonds, toasted

---

Peel the eggplants and cut into 1-inch cubes. Put the cubes in a colander in the sink or over a bowl, sprinkle with salt, and let drain for about 1 hour. This will draw out any bitter juices. Rinse and pat dry.

Pour the oil to a depth of ¼ inch into a large, wide, preferably nonstick sauté pan and warm over medium-high heat. In batches, add the eggplant cubes and cook, turning often and adding oil as needed, until the eggplant is golden and cooked through, 8 to 10 minutes for each batch. Using a slotted spatula, transfer to paper towels to drain. Set aside.

Add oil to the pan as needed to measure 2 tablespoons and warm over medium heat. Add the celery and sauté briefly. It should still be crisp. Using the slotted spoon, transfer to a plate.

Add oil to the pan as needed to measure 2 to 3 tablespoons and warm over medium heat. Add the onions and cook, stirring occasionally, until tender but not brown, about 8 minutes. Add the garlic and tomatoes and return the celery to the pan. Stir well and simmer uncovered, stirring occasionally, for 10 minutes. Return the eggplant to the pan and add the vinegar, sugar, capers, olives, and pine nuts. Turn down the heat to low and continue to simmer, uncovered, until the mixture has thickened and you can taste the vinegar when you bite into a piece of eggplant, about 20 minutes. Season with salt and pepper.

Transfer to a serving dish and let stand for at least several hours or refrigerate overnight. Taste and adjust the seasoning before serving. Serve at room temperature.

## Tunisian Roasted Pepper Salad   SLATA FILFIL

Plates of roasted peppers are often on the appetizer table, but leave it to the Tunisians to add the heat. Of course, you can make this dish without the hot chiles and with less garlic, but you'd be missing the touch that distinguishes this salad from the pack. Keep in mind, too, that the garlic loses some of its bite when it is cooked. Also known as *fefla*, this pepper salad is garnished with anchovy fillets along with olives, as pepper salads are in Italy, but the Italians hold back on the heat. SERVES 6 TO 8

2 red bell peppers

2 yellow bell peppers

2 fresh hot red chiles

7 tablespoons extra virgin olive oil

1 head garlic, cloves separated, peeled, and thinly sliced

1 teaspoon ground caraway

1 teaspoon ground fennel

Juice of 1 lemon

Salt and freshly ground black pepper

¾ cup oil-cured black olives

Thin strips preserved lemon peel, homemade (page 356) or store-bought, rinsed, for garnish

Olive oil–packed anchovy fillets for garnish (optional)

To roast the bell peppers and chiles, hold them directly over the flame on a gas stove top or place on a sheet pan under the broiler and turn them as needed until the skin is blistered and charred on all sides. Transfer to a closed plastic container or a bowl covered with plastic wrap and let stand for 20 minutes. Peel or rub off the skin from each pepper and chile, then stem, halve lengthwise, and remove and discard the seeds and thick ribs. Cut the bell peppers lengthwise into strips ¾ inch wide, and cut the chiles lengthwise into thin strips. Transfer the peppers and chiles to a bowl.

Warm 2 to 3 tablespoons of the oil in a small sauté pan over medium heat. Add the garlic and sauté briefly just until fragrant. Do not allow the garlic to color. Add the garlic and its oil, caraway, and fennel to the peppers and chiles and toss to mix well. Drizzle with the remaining oil and lemon juice and toss to coat evenly, then season with salt and pepper. Garnish with the olives, preserved lemon, and anchovy fillets. Serve at room temperature.

## Sweet Moroccan Carrot Salad   SALATA DE SEFANORYA

Serve this sweet salad, also known as *salade de carottes,* alongside a tart or hot one for a pleasing contrast. It also makes a nice accompaniment to grilled or roasted chicken. The dressing complements roasted or boiled beets, as well.   SERVES 4 TO 6

| | |
|---|---|
| **1 pound carrots** | **⅛ teaspoon cayenne pepper** |
| **¼ cup fresh lemon juice** | **3 tablespoons sugar** |
| **½ teaspoon ground cinnamon** | **2 tablespoons extra virgin olive oil** |
| **½ teaspoon ground cumin** | **Salt** |
| **½ teaspoon sweet paprika** | **Chopped fresh mint or cilantro or chopped pistachios for garnish** |

Peel the carrots, then thinly slice or cut into julienne. Bring a large saucepan filled with salted water to a boil, add the carrots, and cook until the carrots are tender, 5 to 8 minutes. Remove from the heat, drain well, and transfer to a bowl.

In a small bowl, stir together the lemon juice, cinnamon, cumin, paprika, cayenne, and sugar. While the carrots are still warm, drizzle with the lemon juice mixture and toss to coat evenly. Add the oil, season with salt, and stir to mix. Garnish with the mint.

## Tunisian Carrot Salad   MZOURA

Tunisians have a propensity for spicy dishes, so it is not surprising that they like their carrot salad spicy hot. They use their signature *harissa* to add the heat.   SERVES 4 TO 6

| | |
|---|---|
| **1 pound carrots, peeled and thinly sliced** | **5 cloves garlic, finely minced** |
| **1 to 2 teaspoons harissa, homemade (page 355) or store-bought** | **1 teaspoon ground caraway** |
| **6 tablespoons water** | **1 teaspoon ground cumin** |
| **5 tablespoons extra virgin olive oil** | **1 teaspoon salt** |
| **¼ cup white wine vinegar** | **Chopped fresh flat-leaf parsley or cilantro for garnish** |

Bring a large saucepan filled with salted water to a boil, add the carrots, and parboil for 4 to 5 minutes. Remove from the heat and drain well.

In a small bowl, stir together the harissa to taste and the water. Combine the harissa mixture, oil, vinegar, garlic, caraway, cumin, and salt in a saucepan, stir well, and place over medium-low heat until hot. Add the carrots and heat until the carrots have absorbed most of the liquid and are hot throughout, about 5 minutes.

Remove from the heat, transfer to a serving dish, and garnish with the parsley. Serve warm or at room temperature.

## Moroccan Orange Salad with Olives   SALADE D'ORANGES

Refreshing, colorful, and a perfect foil for spicy foods, orange salads are popular throughout Morocco. This one pairs oranges and olives with sweet spices. Others include thinly sliced radishes for a subtle hint of heat, or they are dressed with sugar and lemon juice and then finished with a sprinkle of cinnamon or cayenne. SERVES 6 TO 8

2 pounds blood oranges and 1 pound bitter oranges, or 3 pounds sweet oranges

1 teaspoon ground cumin

1 teaspoon sweet paprika

1 teaspoon ground cinnamon

2 cloves garlic, chopped (optional)

Salt and freshly ground black pepper

Juice of 2 lemons

¼ cup extra virgin olive oil

8 ounces black olives, pitted (about 1⅔ cups)

Leaves from 1 bunch fresh cilantro

Peel the oranges, removing all the white pith, and cut into segments or crosswise into rounds. Transfer to a terra-cotta dish or stoneware salad bowl. Sprinkle the oranges with the cumin, paprika, cinnamon, garlic, salt, and pepper. Sprinkle with the lemon juice and oil and top with the olives. Mix briefly.

Let rest for 30 minutes to allow the flavors to mingle and penetrate the oranges, then mix again. Decorate with the cilantro just before serving.

## Artichokes Cooked with Orange   SALADE D'ARTICHAUTS CUITS À L'ORANGE

In this Algerian recipe, artichokes are cooked with tangy citrus slices, which provide bright contrast to their slightly bitter flesh. The artichoke hearts can be cut into slices ⅓ inch thick, rather than cooked whole (reduce the cooking time to 12 to 15 minutes), and orange segments can be added for a colorful garnish. This is an ideal dish for the Tu B'Shevat table. SERVES 6

Juice of 1 lemon

6 large artichokes

1 orange

1 lemon

2 tablespoons extra virgin olive oil

3 cloves garlic, minced

| | |
|---|---|
| Pinch of saffron threads | Salt and freshly ground black |
| ¼ cup water | pepper |

Have ready a large bowl of water to which you have added the lemon juice. Working with 1 artichoke at a time, trim off the stem flush with the bottom, then remove all of the leaves until you reach the heart. Remove and discard the choke with a small pointed spoon or a paring knife. Pare away the dark green areas from the base. As each artichoke heart is trimmed, slip it into the lemon water.

Peel the orange and lemon, removing all the white pith, and thinly slice crosswise. Drain the artichoke hearts. In a saucepan, combine the artichokes, orange and lemon slices, oil, garlic, saffron, and water. Season with salt and pepper, bring to a gentle simmer over low heat, cover, and cook until the artichoke hearts are tender and are infused with the other flavors, 15 to 25 minutes. The timing depends on the size of the artichokes. Check the water level from time to time and add more water as needed to prevent scorching, though a little caramelization will make the artichokes tasty.

Transfer to a serving dish and serve warm or at room temperature.

## *Artichokes Braised in Citrus Juices*   CARCIOFI AI QUATTRO SUCCHI

This Sicilian artichoke classic combines three citrus juices and vinegar, adds salt in the form of anchovies, and brings in sugar for sweetness and flavor balance. These spectacular artichokes are best served at room temperature. They are stellar in an antipasto assortment. SERVES 6

| | |
|---|---|
| Juice of 1 lemon | ¼ cup white wine vinegar |
| 6 artichokes | 2 cups water |
| ½ cup extra virgin olive oil, plus 1 tablespoon | 1 teaspoon salt |
| 3 yellow onions, halved through the stem end and thinly sliced | 2 tablespoons salt-packed capers, well rinsed |
| ½ cup fresh orange juice | 4 olive oil–packed anchovy fillets, finely minced |
| ½ cup fresh tangerine juice | 2 tablespoons sugar, plus more if needed |
| ¼ cup fresh lemon juice | Chopped fresh mint for garnish (optional) |

Have ready a large bowl of water to which you have added the lemon juice. Working with 1 artichoke at a time, trim the stem to 2 inches if it is tender, then peel away the dark green fibrous outer layer. If the stem is tough, trim it off flush with the bottom. Pull off and discard all of the tough outer leaves until you reach a small cone of pale green, tender leaves. Cut off the top 1 inch of the leaves to remove the thorn-like tips (or, if you prefer, you can remove all of the leaves). Pare away the dark green areas from the base. Cut the artichokes in half lengthwise and carefully remove the choke from each half with a small pointed spoon or a paring knife. As each artichoke is trimmed, slip the halves into the lemon water.

Drain the artichoke halves. Pour ½ cup of the oil into a Dutch oven or similar pot over low heat and add the artichokes, onions, citrus juices, vinegar, water, and salt. Cover and cook very slowly until the artichokes are tender when pierced with a knife, 35 to 40 minutes.

Using a slotted spoon, transfer the artichokes to a serving dish. Add the capers to the onions and liquid remaining in the pan, bring to a boil over high heat, and cook until reduced and thickened to a good sauce consistency, 10 to 15 minutes.

In a small sauté pan or saucepan, warm the anchovies in the remaining 1 tablespoon oil over low heat. When the anchovies have dissolved into the oil, add the anchovy oil and the sugar to the reduced pan juices and cook over low heat, stirring occasionally, for 5 minutes to blend the flavors. Taste and adjust the balance with more sugar if needed.

Spoon the sauce over the artichokes and let cool. Serve at room temperature, garnished with the mint.

Savory
Pastries

SAVORY PASTRIES FORM A LARGE AND IMPORTANT category in Sephardic and Mediterranean cooking. More than just food, they are symbols of hospitality and celebration. In the past, the women of an extended family worked together as a team. Gathered around a table, they would drink tea, chat, and make dozens of elegant little pastries for special holidays, weddings, or bar mitzvahs.

With more and more women working outside the home, these handmade pastries are an endangered species. It would be a shame to lose them forever. Some of the small pastries are a bit of work for one person, but if you do them on an afternoon when you are not pressed for time, you will find that working with your hands has a calming and meditative effect. Or invite a friend to make them with you and then split the bounty. You have a big advantage over the women of days gone by. Contemporary equipment such as food processors and electric mixers speed up mixing, and refrigerators and freezers allow you to make the pastries in advance and store them to have on hand for festive meals.

With pastries, the name game is confusing. Depending on where people live or family traditions, the identical recipe can go under a variety of titles. A *tapada* is a double-crusted pie. Its name likely comes from the Spanish verb *tapar,* which means "to cover" and is also the origin of the term *tapas.* A double-crusted pie is sometimes called an *inchusa* and smaller single-crusted tarts are *kezadas.* In Italy, it is a *torta* or pizza, from the Greek *pitta.* Small cup-shaped pastries filled with cheese are called *kassates* in Ioannina and a larger cheese-filled tart is a *kassata* in Salonika.

*Borekas* are small pastries served on holidays and the Sabbath by Turkish Jews. They can have a savory or a sweet filling and resemble Spanish empanadas in concept. Their name comes from the Turkish *boerek,* meaning "pie," and you can make them with the oil-based *boreka* dough on page 70 or with the margarine-and-oil-based dough used for the *tapada* recipe on page 60.

Some Sephardic families call these smaller pastries *boyos* (from the Spanish *bolo,* for "cake") and make them with strudel-type dough. Others use the term *boyos* for cheese pastries rolled up like pinwheels, with cheese incorporated into both the dough and the filling. The diminutive form, *boyikos,* can also refer to cheese biscuits. During Passover, pastries are made with matzo or matzo meal. A *mina* is a Sephardic matzo pie layered with vegetables or cheese, and a *megina* is a meat-filled one. In Italy, these pies are called *scacchi.*

*Bulemas* are Sephardic filo pastries, popular in Greece and Turkey, especially on the Sabbath and on holidays. When coiled or rolled, they are also called *tsaizika* in the regions of Larissa and Trikala in Greece and are a variation of the Greek *rodanches* (roses) or the Turkish *kol böreği.* As if all of these terms are not confusing enough, when the filo pastries are formed into triangles rather than rolled, they are called *holjadres, rojaldes,* or *filas.* It is the same filo and the same filling but a different shape, which means a different name. These filo pastries can be baked or deep-fried.

In North Africa, these same pastries are called *bestels* (from the Sephardic *pastel,* for "pie"), *b'stilla, briouats,* and *briks.* In Syria, Lebanon, and Iraq, they are *sambousak* or *sbanikh.* Some of them are stuffed with spiced meat or chicken; others are filled with an assortment of cheeses or with greens, such as spinach or chard enhanced with pine nuts and raisins or tangy olives. The dough can be shortcrust pastry, yeast-raised dough, flaky filo, or the paper-thin semolina pastry called *ouarka* in Morocco, *malsouka* in Tunisia, and *feuille de brik* in French, all of them translated as "leaf" because the pastry is so thin. Some pastries are baked; some are fried for extra crunch. A *brik* is filled with tuna or spiced potatoes and a whole egg, posing a challenge on how to take a bite without the egg dribbling down your chin. The most spectacular North African pie is the *b'stilla,* which is served at weddings and other family celebrations and is filled with chicken or squab, sweetened almonds, and a savory egg mixture.

The stuffed pastries are an example of the thriftiness of the Mediterranean Jewish kitchen, where bits of leftovers are transformed into something special. Leftover cooked meat, poultry, fish, and mashed cooked eggplant seasoned with onion and tomato are all possibilities. Other savory fillings made from scratch are called *gomos* and can be potato and cheese, leeks and cheese, spinach and cheese, eggplant and cheese, or just cheese. (These fillings are similar to the gratin mixtures—*quajado, fritada,* and *almodrote*—minus the bread, in the Eggs and Fritters chapter.) Keep in mind that all fillings should have a more intense flavor than if you were eating them as is, because the relatively bland pastry crust dulls their impact. My advice is to taste for balance and then amp up the salt, pepper, spices, and herbs so the fillings do not vanish on the palate.

## Sephardic Potato and Cheese Pie    TAPADA DE PATATA KON KEZO

A *tapada* is a double-crusted pie, here filled with a mixture of potatoes and cheese. For added texture, mix in ½ cup chopped walnuts with the eggs and cheese. According to Martine Chiche-Yana in *La table juive,* this pie is served on Shavuot in Turkey. SERVES 10

## FILLING

3 large russet potatoes, peeled and quartered

2 tablespoons olive oil

6 green onions, including green tops, chopped, or 1 yellow onion, chopped

2 eggs, lightly beaten

8 ounces feta or other soft white cheese, crumbled (about 1¼ cups)

1 cup grated kashkaval or Gruyère cheese

½ cup chopped fresh dill

1½ teaspoons salt

1 teaspoon freshly ground black pepper

½ teaspoon freshly grated nutmeg

## PASTRY

3½ cups all-purpose flour

1 teaspoon salt

½ cup sunflower oil

½ cup margarine or butter, melted and cooled

½ cup lukewarm water

1 egg yolk, lightly beaten

To make the filling, combine the potatoes with salted water to cover in a saucepan and bring to a boil over high heat. Turn down the heat to medium and simmer until the potatoes are easily pierced with a fork, 20 to 30 minutes. Drain well, transfer to a bowl, and then mash until lump-free. You should have 2 to 2½ cups.

Warm the oil in a small sauté pan over medium heat. Add the green onions and sauté until softened, 2 to 3 minutes. Add the onions to the potatoes and mix well. Fold in the eggs, cheeses, and dill, distributing them evenly. Add the salt, pepper, and nutmeg and mix well. You should have 4 to 4½ cups filling.

Preheat the oven to 400°F.

To make the pastry, in a bowl, stir together the flour and salt. Gradually add the oil, margarine, and water, stirring and tossing with a fork until the mixture comes together in a rough mass. Alternatively, combine the flour and salt in a food processor and pulse briefly to mix. Add the oil, margarine, and water and process until the mixture comes together in a rough mass.

Turn out the dough onto a lightly floured work surface and knead until cohesive and smooth. Divide the dough into 2 portions, one slightly larger than the other. Clean the work surface, lightly dust again with flour, and roll out the larger portion into a 13-inch round about ⅛ inch thick. Carefully transfer the dough round to a deep 10-inch pie pan or an 11-inch pie pan, pressing it gently onto the bottom and up the sides of the pan. Trim the dough, leaving a ¾-inch overhang, then turn the edge under and press to seal.

Line the dough-lined pan with foil and fill with pie weights. Bake until the crust is set and dry, about 10 minutes. Transfer the pan to a wire rack, remove the weights and foil, and let cool for 20 minutes. Leave the oven on.

Spoon the filling into the cooled crust. Roll out the second portion of dough into a 12-inch round about ⅛ inch thick. Carefully place the second round over the filling, trim the overhang to about ¾ inch, turn under the pastry edges to create an attractive rim, and press to seal. Cut a few steam vents in the top crust and brush the crust with the egg yolk wash.

Bake the pie until the crust is golden, 25 to 30 minutes. Transfer to a wire rack and let cool for 10 to 15 minutes. Serve hot or warm.

VARIATIONS: *All-Oil Pastry:* If you do not have margarine, you can use all oil. Mix together 3½ cups all-purpose flour, 1 teaspoon salt, ¾ cup sunflower oil, and ¾ cup warm water in a bowl or food processor as directed.

*Spinach Pie (Tapada de Espinaka):* In a bowl, combine 2 pounds spinach, cooked, well drained, and chopped, or 2 packages (10 ounces each) frozen chopped spinach, thawed and squeezed dry; 4 eggs, lightly beaten; 1 pound feta cheese, crumbled; and 1 cup grated kashkaval, Gruyère, or Monterey Jack cheese and mix well. Season liberally with salt and freshly ground black pepper and with freshly grated nutmeg, if you like. You should have 3½ to 4 cups filling. Bake as directed for potato and cheese pie.

*Cheese Pie (Tapada de Kezo):* In a bowl, combine 1 pound feta cheese, crumbled, and 1 pound ricotta or cottage cheese or part ricotta and part grated Monterey Jack or Gruyère cheese and mix well. Add 4 eggs, lightly beaten; ½ cup chopped fresh flat-leaf parsley; ½ cup chopped fresh dill; and ½ teaspoon freshly grated nutmeg. Season liberally with salt and freshly ground black pepper. You should have about 4 cups filling. Bake as directed for potato and cheese pie.

## *Double-Crusted Vegetable Pie*   PIZZA EBRAICA DI ERBE

This vegetable-filled pie resembles many of the double-crusted vegetable and cheese *torte* eaten today in Liguria. The term *pizza* here is an old one and is related to the Greek *pitta,* a layered filo pie, a name still in use in Puglia, where many dishes reflect a Greek heritage. This recipe calls for *pasta frolla salata,* a shortcrust pastry that gives the pie a wonderful richness. SERVES 8

PASTRY

2½ cups all-purpose flour

½ teaspoon salt

8 to 10 tablespoons cold unsalted butter or margarine, cut into ¾-inch cubes

1 egg, lightly beaten

2 to 4 tablespoons ice water, or as needed

FILLING

Juice of 1 lemon

3 large or 5 medium artichokes

Olive oil for sautéing

| | |
|---|---|
| 1 large yellow onion, diced | 1 tablespoon salt |
| ½ cup water | ½ teaspoon freshly ground black pepper |
| 1 large bunch fresh flat-leaf parsley, chopped (about ⅓ cup) | ½ teaspoon freshly grated nutmeg, or to taste |
| 1 pound beet greens or spinach, coarsely chopped | 2 eggs, lightly beaten |
| 2 pounds English peas, shelled (about 2 cups shelled) | Olive oil or lightly beaten egg for coating pastry |

To make the pastry, in a bowl, stir together the flour and salt. Scatter the butter over the flour mixture and, using a pastry blender, cut in the butter until the mixture resembles coarse meal. Add the egg and 2 tablespoons of the water and stir and toss with a fork until the mixture is evenly moist. If the dough seems too crumbly, drizzle in more water, a little at a time, and toss to mix. Alternatively, combine the flour and salt in a food processor and pulse briefly to mix. Scatter the butter over the flour and pulse until most of the butter is the size of peas. Add the egg and 2 tablespoons of the water and pulse until the mixture comes together in a rough mass, adding more water, a little at a time, if the mixture is too crumbly. Gather the dough into a rough ball and divide the dough into 2 portions, one slightly larger than the other. Flatten each portion into a disk, place the disks in a plastic bag, and refrigerate for 1 hour.

To make the filling, have ready a large bowl of water to which you have added the lemon juice. Working with 1 artichoke at a time, trim off the stem flush with the bottom, then remove all of the leaves until you reach the heart. Pare away the dark green areas from the base. Cut the artichoke heart in half and scoop out and discard the choke from each half with a small pointed spoon or a paring knife. Cut each half into ¼-inch-thick slices and slip the slices into the lemon water.

Pour enough oil into a large sauté pan to form a film on the bottom and place over medium heat. Add the onion and sauté until softened, 3 to 4 minutes. Drain the artichokes and add them to the pan along with the water, parsley, greens, and peas. Turn down the heat to low, cover, and cook until the mixture is almost dry, 10 to 15 minutes. Remove from the heat and let cool completely. Season with the salt, pepper, and nutmeg, add the eggs, and mix well (see note).

Preheat the oven to 375°F.

On a lightly floured work surface, roll out the larger pastry disk into an 11-inch round about ⅛ inch thick. Carefully transfer the dough round to a 9-inch tart pan with a removable bottom or a 9-inch springform pan, pressing it gently onto the bottom and up the sides of the pan. Spoon the filling into the pastry-lined pan.

Roll out the second pastry disk into a 10-inch round about ⅛ inch thick. Carefully place the second round over the filling, trim the overhang to about ¾ inch, turn under the pastry edges to create an attractive rim, and press to seal. Cut a few steam vents in the top crust and brush the crust with the oil.

Bake the pie until the crust is golden, 30 to 40 minutes. Transfer to a wire rack to cool. Remove the pan sides, slide onto a serving plate, and serve warm or at room temperature.

NOTE: If the filling seems a bit wet and you are worried about the bottom crust becoming soggy, sprinkle a thin layer of fine dried bread crumbs over the pastry before adding the filling. Alternatively, line the bottom crust with foil and fill it with pie weights, then blind bake it at 400°F until set and dry, 10 to 15 minutes. Remove the weights and foil and let cool completely before adding the filling.

## Ricotta Pie with Potato Crust   PIZZA DI RICOTTA

*La cucina nella tradizione ebraica* is a seminal reference cookbook assembled by a branch of ADEI WIZO, a Jewish Italian women's group, in Padua in 1987. While leafing through the book, I found this delicious recipe for ricotta pie, which closely resembles a classic dish from Puglia, *pitta di patate*. I prefer baking the potatoes, rather than boiling them, as I think they result in a firmer crust. It will not, however, become fully crisp in either case. The chewy potato character will always dominate. This pie is typically served as an appetizer at a dairy-based meal, though it also makes a fine main dish.   SERVES 8

---

| | |
|---|---|
| 1 tub (14 or 15 ounces) ricotta cheese (about 1¾ cups) | ½ cup pitted and sliced green olives |
| 1 pound potatoes (russet if baking, Yukon Gold if boiling) | Freshly ground black pepper |
| 1⅔ cups all-purpose flour, or as needed | ¼ cup grated Parmesan cheese |
| 1 teaspoon salt | 1 to 2 tablespoons chopped fresh marjoram or summer savory |

---

Spoon the ricotta cheese into a sieve placed over a bowl and refrigerate for 2 hours to drain off the excess liquid.

Meanwhile, if baking the potatoes, poke them once or twice with a fork, place in a preheated 400°F oven, and bake until very soft, about 1 hour. Let cool until they can be handled, cut in half, scoop out the flesh into a ricer or food mill held over a bowl, or place in a bowl and mash with a potato masher. While the potatoes are still warm, add the flour and salt, turn the mixture out onto a lightly floured work surface, and knead until a firm, smooth dough forms, similar to gnocchi dough, adding more flour if needed to achieve the correct consistency. Alternatively, if boiling the potatoes, peel them and place in a saucepan with salted water to cover generously. Bring to a boil and cook until tender, about 30 minutes. Drain well, pass through a ricer or food mill or mash in a bowl, and add the flour and salt as directed above.

Preheat the oven to 375°F. Lightly oil a 10-inch pie dish.

On a lightly floured work surface, roll out the dough into an 11-inch round about ¼ inch thick. Carefully transfer the dough round to the prepared pie dish, pressing it gently onto the bottom and up the sides of the dish. Turn under the edges and press onto the rim. Alternatively, oil a sheet pan, transfer the dough round to the prepared pan, and fold up the edges like a pizza crust.

Spread the ricotta evenly over the crust, then distribute the olives evenly over the ricotta. Sprinkle with the pepper, Parmesan, and marjoram.

Bake the pie until golden, 30 to 45 minutes. Transfer to a wire rack to cool slightly. Serve warm.

## Leek and Cheese Matzo Pie    MINA DI PRASA KON KESO

A *mina* is a Passover pie that is layered like lasagna, using soaked matzo in place of the pasta. It can be filled with vegetables, cheeses, or meat. The handmade matzos of Greece and Italy were often round and were thicker than today's delicate and crisp factory-made matzos. Early recipes advise a soaking time that would be too long for our contemporary cracker-like matzos, which take no more than a minute or two to soften. Some recipes call for soaking the matzos in water and then dipping them in egg, so be careful not to soak them in water too long or they will fall apart in the egg step. The filling for Double-Crusted Vegetable Pie (page 62) will also work well in this recipe. SERVES 4 AS A MAIN COURSE, OR 6 TO 8 AS A SIDE DISH

| | |
|---|---|
| 5 leeks | ¼ cup chopped fresh dill |
| 3 tablespoons unsalted butter, olive oil, or margarine | 1½ teaspoons salt |
| | ½ teaspoon freshly ground black pepper |
| 1 yellow onion, chopped | Few gratings nutmeg |
| 1 cup (8 ounces) ricotta or farmer cheese | 4 matzos |
| 3 eggs | 1⅓ cups grated kashkaval or Gruyère cheese |

Remove all but 1 to 2 inches of the green from each leek, then halve the leeks lengthwise and thinly slice crosswise. (If the leeks are very fat, coarsely chop them.) Immerse in a sink filled with cold water, then lift out and drain well. You should have about 3½ cups.

Warm the butter in a large sauté pan over medium heat. Add the leeks and onion and sauté, adding water ¼ cup at a time and allowing it to evaporate before adding more, until the leeks are very tender and all of the water has evaporated, about 20 minutes. Remove from the heat, drain well in a sieve to remove any lingering moisture, and transfer to a bowl. Let cool, then add the ricotta, 2 of the eggs, and the dill, salt, pepper, and nutmeg.

Preheat the oven to 375°F. Oil an 8-inch square baking pan.

Beat the remaining egg in a shallow pan large enough to hold a matzo. Pour water into a second shallow pan large enough to hold the matzo. Soak a matzo in the water for 1 to 2 minutes, then drain. Dip the matzo into the egg, coating evenly and allowing the excess to drip off, and place in the prepared baking pan. Repeat until you have enough matzo to fill in any gaps in the pan. Sprinkle evenly with two-thirds of the grated cheese and all of the leek and onion mixture. Top with a layer of egg-coated matzo and then the remaining cheese.

Bake the pie until browned, 30 to 40 minutes. Let rest for 10 minutes, then cut into squares with a serrated knife and serve.

## Passover Cheese Pie from Chania   PESAH MINA

Using just *mizithra* cheese, feta and Parmesan, or feta and Monterey Jack or Gruyère for this Passover pie (known as *tyropita yia Pesah* in Greece) makes for a tasty but dry filling, despite the half dozen eggs. So I added 1 cup ricotta cheese to the mix to contribute some welcome moisture. You may top this with a bit of tomato sauce or serve it with a bowl of tomato soup (page 133). SERVES 8 AS A MAIN DISH, OR 12 AS A SIDE DISH

---

1 pound mizithra cheese, grated;
8 ounces each feta cheese, crumbled,
and Parmesan cheese, grated; or
8 ounces each feta cheese, crumbled,
and Monterey Jack or Gruyère cheese,
grated

1 cup ricotta cheese

¼ cup olive oil, plus more for drizzling

½ cup chopped fresh dill

¼ cup chopped fresh mint

6 eggs, separated

8 matzos, or as needed to cover

---

Preheat the oven to 375°F. Oil a 10-by-14-by-2-inch baking pan.

In a large bowl, combine the mizithra cheese, ricotta cheese, oil, dill, and mint and mix well. In a medium bowl, beat the egg yolks until creamy, then fold them into the cheese. In a separate bowl, whisk the egg whites until stiff peaks form, then fold them into the cheese mixture. You will probably not need any salt, as the cheese is rather salty.

Pour water into a shallow pan large enough to hold the matzo. Soak a matzo in the water for 1 to 2 minutes, then drain and place in the prepared pan. Repeat with more matzos as needed to cover the bottom of the pan. Drizzle the matzo layer with oil. Spoon the cheese mixture evenly over the matzo layer and drizzle with oil. Top with a layer of water-softened matzos and then a final drizzle of olive oil.

Bake the pie until browned, 30 to 45 minutes. Let rest for 10 minutes, then cut into squares with a serrated knife and serve.

## Meat and Matzo Pie from Rhodes   MEGINA

I discovered recipes for this meat-filled matzo pie in a trio of cookbooks and have fashioned my own from them. Occasionally, mashed potato is added to the ground meat filling, but the primary variables are the number of eggs and matzo. I found the seasoning rather bland, so I have added cinnamon. Tomato sauce or sautéed mushrooms would enliven this pie considerably. You might otherwise find it too dry. SERVES 8

| | |
|---|---|
| 2 tablespoons olive oil | ½ teaspoon freshly ground black pepper |
| 2 yellow onions, chopped | 8 or 9 eggs |
| 2 pounds ground beef (not too lean) | ½ cup chopped fresh flat-leaf parsley |
| 2 teaspoons salt | ½ cup chopped fresh dill |
| 1 teaspoon ground cinnamon | 8 to 10 matzos, or as needed to cover |

Warm the oil in a large sauté pan over medium heat. Add the onions and cook, stirring occasionally, until translucent and tender, 8 to 10 minutes. Add the beef and cook, breaking up any lumps with a wooden spoon, until browned, 8 to 10 minutes. Season with the salt, cinnamon, and pepper, mixing well, and remove from the heat. Let cool for 5 minutes. In a small bowl, lightly beat 4 of the eggs, then fold them into the beef mixture along with the parsley and dill.

Preheat the oven to 375°F. Oil a 10-by-13-by-2-inch baking dish.

Beat 2 of the remaining eggs in a shallow pan large enough to hold a matzo. Pour water into a second shallow pan large enough to hold the matzo. Soak a matzo in the water for 1 to 2 minutes, then drain. Dip the matzo into the egg, coating evenly and allowing the excess to drip off, and place in the prepared baking dish. Repeat with more matzos as needed to cover the bottom of the baking dish. Spoon the meat mixture evenly over the matzo layer. Beat the remaining 2 or 3 eggs in the same shallow pan, then top the meat mixture with a layer of egg-coated matzo. Pour any leftover egg over the top.

Bake the pie until golden, about 45 minutes. Let rest for 10 minutes and then cut into squares with a serrated knife and serve hot or warm.

## Peppery Cheese Biscuits    BOYIKOS DE KAŞER

This recipe is adapted from one that appeared in an Istanbul-published collection. I find it appealing because the *boyikos* are spicy as well as cheesy. These festive pastries are traditionally served at Shavuot and Tisha B'Av, but I like to offer them to guests as an accompaniment to a glass of wine. The more assertive the cheese, the tastier the biscuit, so look for a robustly flavored cheese. If you do not like peppery foods, omit the pepper flakes in the dough and sprinkle the egg yolk–washed biscuit tops with cumin, nigella seeds, or *dukkah* before baking.    MAKES ABOUT TWENTY 2-INCH ROUND BISCUITS

2½ cups all-purpose flour, plus more if needed

2 teaspoons salt

1 teaspoon Maras or Aleppo pepper flakes, or ½ teaspoon red pepper flakes

1 cup grated kasseri, Parmesan, or full-flavored Cheddar cheese, plus more for sprinkling (optional)

¾ cup sunflower or canola oil

¼ cup water

1 egg yolk, lightly beaten

Preheat the oven to 350°F. Line a large sheet pan with parchment paper or oil lightly.

In a bowl, stir together the flour, salt, pepper flakes, and cheese. Gradually add the oil and water, stirring and tossing with a fork until the mixture comes together in a rough mass and adding more flour if needed for a workable dough. Alternatively, combine the dry ingredients in a food processor and pulse briefly to mix. Add the oil and water and process until the mixture comes together in a rough mass, adding more flour if needed for a workable dough.

Transfer the dough to a lightly floured surface, flatten into a disk, and roll or pat out into a ¼-inch-thick round. Using a 2-inch round biscuit cutter or an overturned glass, cut out as many biscuits as possible and transfer to the prepared pan, spacing them about ½ inch apart. (They do not spread in the oven.) Gather up the scraps and reroll to cut out more biscuits. Brush the tops with the egg yolk, then sprinkle lightly with the cheese.

Bake the biscuits until golden, about 25 minutes. Transfer to a wire rack to cool. The biscuits can be served warm, or they can be cooled completely, stored in an airtight container at room temperature for up to several days, and then reheated in a low oven before serving.

# Cheese Pinwheels  BOYOS DE KEZO

In *Sephardic Holiday Cooking,* Gilda Angel offers a recipe for cheese pinwheels for serving during Tisha B'Av, perhaps to accompany her red lentil soup (page 120). I have based this recipe on hers, with the notable addition of a minced herb. To give the pastries a more colorful appearance, use golden Cheddar cheese, first making sure that it is flavorful and not just salty. You can also use Parmesan, or a mixture of golden Cheddar and Parmesan, *kashkaval,* or Gruyère. These pastries do not keep well, so it is best to enjoy them freshly baked. MAKES 36 TO 44 PASTRIES

| | |
|---|---|
| 4½ cups all-purpose flour | 1 cup sunflower or canola oil |
| 1 tablespoon salt | ⅔ cup water or milk |
| Generous pinch of freshly ground black pepper | ¼ cup minced fresh chives or dill |
| 2½ cups grated full-flavored Cheddar or Parmesan cheese, or a mixture | 1 egg or egg yolk, lightly beaten |

Preheat the oven to 400°F. Line 2 sheet pans with parchment paper.

To make the dough, in a bowl, stir together the flour, salt, pepper, and ⅔ cup of the cheese. Add the oil and water, stirring and tossing with a fork until the mixture comes together in a rough mass. Alternatively, combine the dry ingredients, including ⅔ cup of the cheese, in a food processor and pulse briefly to mix. Add the oil and water and process until the mixture comes together in a rough mass. The dough will be soft. If it is too soft to work with, cover and refrigerate for 20 minutes.

Divide the dough in half. Lay a sheet of plastic wrap or parchment paper about 15 inches long on a work surface. Place half of the dough on the sheet and roll out into a rectangle about 6 inches wide, 12 inches long, and ¼ inch thick. In a bowl, combine 1⅓ cups of the cheese and the chives and toss and stir to mix well. Sprinkle ⅔ cup of the cheese mixture evenly over the dough rectangle. Starting from a long side, and using the plastic wrap or parchment as an aid, roll up the dough into a cylinder. Cut the cylinder crosswise into ½-inch-thick slices and transfer to a prepared pan. Press down gently on each slice with the flat of your hand to flatten slightly. Repeat with the remaining dough and remaining cheese mixture.

Brush the top of each pinwheel with the egg and then sprinkle the tops with the remaining ½ cup cheese. Bake the pastries, rotating the pans back to front halfway through the baking, until golden, 25 to 30 minutes. Let cool on the pans on wire racks (or transfer to the racks) for 10 minutes and serve warm.

# *Small Stuffed Pastries* BOREKAS

The outer crust of these classic Sephardic pastries, known as *burriche* in Italy, can be either a simple tart dough or a dough that is folded many times to create a rich, layered flaky pastry. Because you can buy good-quality puff pastry, I have included only the recipe for the plain oil-based dough. Three different fillings are given here, each of them sufficient to fill half of the pastry recipe. The chicken filling, which is in the style of Ferrara, is possibly the one that was stuffed into the *burriche* fashioned in the famed kosher shop Signora Betsabea in Giorgio Bassani's *The Garden of the Finzi-Continis*. MAKES ABOUT 48 SMALL TURNOVERS

### BEEF FILLING

2 tablespoons rendered chicken fat or olive oil

1 yellow onion, finely chopped

¼ cup chopped fresh flat-leaf parsley

2 teaspoons minced garlic

12 ounces ground beef (not too lean)

½ teaspoon ground cinnamon (optional)

¼ teaspoon freshly grated nutmeg

Salt and freshly ground black pepper

⅓ cup pine nuts, toasted

⅓ cup raisins, plumped in hot water and drained

1 egg, lightly beaten

3 to 4 tablespoons fine dried bread crumbs

### CHICKEN FILLING

3 tablespoons rendered chicken fat

1 yellow onion, finely chopped

12 ounces ground raw chicken or turkey, or 2 cups chopped leftover roast chicken

¼ cup chopped fresh flat-leaf parsley or thyme

¼ cup water or chicken broth

3 slices bread, soaked in chicken broth and squeezed dry

⅓ cup raisins, plumped in hot water and drained (optional)

1 egg, lightly beaten

Salt and freshly ground black pepper

Freshly grated nutmeg

### FISH FILLING

2 tablespoons canola or sunflower oil

1 large yellow onion, chopped

2 cups flaked cooked fish, such as salmon, mackerel, or tuna

½ cup cooked white rice or mashed potato

¼ cup chopped fresh flat-leaf parsley

½ cup chopped fresh dill

¼ cup chopped walnuts or almonds (optional)

1 to 2 teaspoons grated lemon zest

1 egg, lightly beaten

Salt and freshly ground black pepper

### PASTRY

1 cup sunflower or mild olive oil

1 cup warm water

1 teaspoon salt

5 to 6 cups all-purpose flour, or as needed

TOPPING

1 egg yolk, lightly beaten with a little water

Sesame seeds for sprinkling (optional)

As noted in the headnote, each filling recipe will fill half of the pastry dough recipe, so select just 2 fillings to make. To make the beef filling, melt the chicken fat in a large sauté pan over medium heat. Add the onion and sauté until softened, about 8 minutes. Add the parsley garlic, beef, cinnamon, and nutmeg, season with salt and pepper, and cook, breaking up any lumps of beef with a wooden spoon and stirring occasionally, until the beef is cooked through, about 10 minutes. Remove from the heat and add the pine nuts, raisins, egg, and enough bread crumbs to bind the mixture, mixing well. Let cool for at least 30 minutes, then use immediately or cover and refrigerate for up to 8 hours.

To make the chicken filling, melt the chicken fat in a large sauté pan over medium heat. Add the onion and cook, stirring occasionally, until translucent and tender, 8 to 10 minutes. Add the raw chicken and parsley, stir well, and sauté, breaking up any lumps of chicken with a wooden spoon and stirring occasionally, for 5 minutes. Add the water and cook, stirring occasionally, until the water has evaporated and the chicken is tender, about 8 minutes longer. If using cooked chicken, cook the onion as directed, then add the chicken, parsley, and water and cook, stirring occasionally, just until the water has evaporated. Remove from the heat and add the bread, raisins, and egg, mixing well. Season highly with the salt, pepper, and nutmeg, as the chicken (or turkey) can be bland. Let cool for at least 30 minutes, then use immediately or cover and refrigerate for up to 8 hours.

To make the fish filling, warm the oil in a sauté pan over medium heat. Add the onion and cook, stirring occasionally, until soft and golden, about 10 minutes. Remove from the heat, transfer to a bowl, and add the fish, rice, parsley, dill, walnuts, lemon zest to taste, and egg, mixing well. Season with salt and liberally with pepper.

To make the pastry, in a large bowl, stir together the oil, warm water, salt, and as much of the flour as is needed for the mixture to come together in a smooth, workable dough. Cover with a kitchen towel and let stand at room temperature for about 20 minutes. (You do not have to chill this dough.) The dough will be rather springy. Once all of the dough is rolled out, cut out, filled, and sealed, any dough scraps can be gathered up, rerolled, and filled, but the dough will need to rest between the rollings.

Preheat the oven to 350°F. Lightly oil 2 sheet pans or line them with parchment paper.

Divide the dough into 3 or 4 equal portions, keeping the dough you are not working with covered with the towel. On a lightly floured work surface, roll out 1 portion of the dough about ⅛ inch thick. Using a 3-inch round biscuit cutter or an overturned glass, cut out as many rounds as possible. Place about 1 tablespoon of the filling in the center of each round. With your fingertip, lightly moisten the edge of the round with water, then fold the round over the filling to form a half-moon, pressing the edges to seal. Place the half-moons on a prepared pan, spacing them well apart. Repeat with the remaining dough and filling. (The pastries can be assembled up to 1 day in advance and refrigerated until baking. Or, they can be frozen on the sheet pans, transferred to lock-top bags, and then kept in the freezer for up to 3 months. Bake without thawing, increasing the baking time to about 40 minutes.)

Brush the pastries with the egg yolk–water mixture and sprinkle with the sesame seeds. Bake the pastries, rotating the pans back to front halfway through the baking, until golden, about 30 minutes. Remove from the oven and serve warm.

## *Meat-Stuffed Potato Pastries* BOREKAS DI KARTOF

This Sephardic pastry is similar to that used for *pizza di ricotta,* a ricotta-topped open-faced pizza made with a potato crust (page 64). Here the dough is rolled or patted out, rounds are cut, a meat filling is added, the dough is folded over, and the pastries are fried. Yes, they can be baked, and I provide directions for baking, but frying makes the dough more tender and the filling juicier. Plus, if they are fried, they are perfect to serve for Hanukkah. Although the original recipe calls for boiling the potatoes for the dough, I prefer to bake them, as the dough will be less moist, making shaping easier. Iraqi cooks flavor the meat filling with *baharāt,* a versatile spice mixture popular throughout the region. MAKES 18 TO 20 PASTRIES; SERVES 8 TO 10

---

POTATO DOUGH

2 pounds potatoes (russet if baking, Yukon Gold if boiling)

2 eggs, lightly beaten

1 tablespoon salt

½ teaspoon freshly ground black pepper

1½ cups all-purpose flour, or a bit more if needed

MEAT FILLING

2 tablespoons olive oil

1 yellow onion, minced

2 cloves garlic, minced

8 ounces ground beef (not too lean)

1 teaspoon salt

½ teaspoon freshly ground black pepper

½ teaspoon ground cinnamon

2 tablespoons chopped flat-leaf parsley

1 egg, lightly beaten

Fine dried bread crumbs, if needed

1 egg white, lightly beaten

Canola, sunflower, or olive oil, if deep-frying

1 egg yolk, lightly beaten, or olive oil for brushing, if baking

---

To make the dough, if baking the potatoes, poke them once or twice with a fork, place in a preheated 400°F oven, and bake until very soft, about 1 hour. Let cool until they can be handled, cut in half, scoop out the flesh into a ricer or food mill held over a bowl, or place in a bowl and mash with a potato masher. While the potatoes are still warm, add the eggs, salt, pepper, and enough flour to make a smooth gnocchi-like dough that holds together. Start with 1½ cups flour and knead in more if the dough is too wet. Alternatively, if boiling the potatoes, peel them and place in a saucepan with salted water to cover generously. Bring to a boil and cook until tender, about 30 minutes. Drain well and pass through a ricer or food mill or mash in a bowl, then add the eggs, salt, pepper, and flour as directed above. On a lightly floured work surface, knead the dough for a few minutes until it holds together and feels a bit elastic but not wet.

While the potatoes are cooking, make the filling. Warm the oil in a sauté pan over medium heat. Add the onion and cook, stirring occasionally, until translucent and tender, 8 to 10 minutes. Add the garlic and beef and cook, breaking up any lumps of beef with a wooden spoon and stirring occasionally, until the meat is no longer pink, 5 to 8 minutes. Add the salt, pepper, cinnamon, and parsley and stir well. Continue to cook, stirring occasionally, until the meat is browned, about 10 minutes. Taste and adjust the seasoning with more salt, pepper, and cinnamon if needed. Remove from the heat, stir in the whole egg, and then stir in some bread crumbs if needed to absorb excess juices. Let the filling cool completely.

On a lightly floured work surface, roll out the dough ⅓ inch thick. Using a 3-inch round biscuit cutter or an overturned glass, cut out as many rounds as possible. Place a heaping teaspoon of the meat mixture in the center of each round. With your fingertip, lightly moisten the edge of the round with egg white, then fold the round over the filling to form a half-moon, pressing the edges to seal. Gather up the scraps, reroll to cut out more rounds, and then fill and seal.

To deep-fry the pastries, pour the oil to a depth of 3 inches into a deep, heavy saucepan or a deep fryer and heat to 350°F. In batches, add the pastries and fry, turning once, until golden, about 6 minutes total. Using a slotted spoon or tongs, transfer the pastries to paper towels to drain. Serve hot.

Alternatively, to bake the pastries, preheat the oven to 400°F and oil 1 or 2 sheet pans. Arrange the pastries on the prepared pan(s), brush the top of each pastry with the egg yolk, and bake until golden, about 30 minutes. Serve hot.

## *Arabic Cheese-Filled Pastries*   SAMBUSAK BIL JIBNEH

Savory pastries filled with cheese or meat are a holiday staple of Iraqi, Syrian, and Egyptian Jews. The cheese versions use a butter-based pastry, but the meat-filled ones use margarine in the dough. Here, feta is the filling, but some cooks prefer part feta and part *kasseri*. If folded into a half-moon, the pastries are called *sambusak,* a name of Persian origin. Triangular pastries are called *sbanikh* or *fatayer.* Some families use a yeast dough for *sambusak* (see page 75). MAKES 24 TO 36 PASTRIES

**CHEESE FILLING**

1 pound feta cheese, mashed or crumbled

2 eggs, lightly beaten

6 tablespoons chopped fresh mint, or 3 tablespoons dried mint

¼ cup za'atar

Freshly ground white or black pepper

**DOUGH**

½ cup unsalted butter

½ cup olive oil

½ cup warm water

1 teaspoon salt

1 pound all-purpose flour (about 3⅔ cups)

1 egg, lightly beaten

6 tablespoons sesame seeds

To make the filling, combine the cheese, eggs, mint, and za'atar, season with pepper, and mix well. Set aside.

To make the dough, melt the butter in a small saucepan over low heat. Do not allow it to bubble. Remove from the heat and add the oil, warm water, and salt. Transfer to a food processor and pulse once to combine. Gradually add the flour, pulsing after each addition. The dough will be very soft and should not stick to the sides of the bowl.

Preheat the oven to 400°F. Have ready ungreased sheet pans.

Transfer the dough to a lightly floured work surface and divide it into 8 equal portions. Roll out each portion about ⅛ inch thick. Using a 3-inch cookie cutter or an overturned glass, cut out as many rounds as possible. Place a heaping teaspoon of the filling on the center of each round, then fold the round over the filling to form a half-moon. Seal the edges with fork tines and place the pastries on a sheet pan, spacing them about ½ inch apart. Repeat with the remaining dough portions and filling. Gather up the scraps, reroll to cut out more rounds, and then fill and seal.

Brush the pastries with the egg, then sprinkle with the sesame seeds. Bake until golden, about 20 minutes. Serve hot.

VARIATION: You can also deep-fry the pastries. Pour canola oil to a depth of 3 inches into a deep, heavy saucepan or a deep fryer and heat to 365°F. Omit the egg wash. In batches, dip the pastries into the sesame seeds and fry until the pastries are golden, about 4 minutes. Using a slotted spoon or wire skimmer, transfer to paper towels to drain. Serve at once.

## *Iraqi Chicken-and-Chickpea-Filled Pastries* SAMBUSAK B'TAWAH

Although Iraq is not directly on the Mediterranean, it once had a large Jewish population, so I have included this recipe, which is closely related to the Arabic pastries on page 73. Some versions omit the chicken and just use mashed chickpeas. MAKES ABOUT 36 PASTRIES

**FILLING**

2¾ cups drained cooked chickpeas (home cooked or canned)

¼ cup olive oil

2 yellow onions, chopped

1 small green bell pepper, seeded and chopped (optional)

2 teaspoons ground toasted cumin

½ teaspoon ground turmeric

Salt and freshly ground black pepper

2 cups chopped cooked chicken

2 eggs, lightly beaten

Dough for Arabic Cheese-Filled Pastries (page 73), with margarine substituted for the butter

Canola, sunflower, or olive oil for deep-frying

To make the filling, put the chickpeas in a bowl and mash coarsely with a fork. Do not make them too smooth, as you want some texture.

Warm the oil in a sauté pan over medium heat. Add the onions and bell pepper and cook, stirring occasionally, until almost tender, about 8 minutes. Add the cumin and turmeric, season with salt and pepper, and cook for 3 minutes longer. Add the chicken and the chickpeas and cook, stirring often, for a few minutes to blend the flavors. Stir in the eggs and cook, stirring, just to set the eggs, 1 to 2 minutes. Remove from the heat and let cool completely.

Make the dough as directed. To shape each pastry, pinch off a walnut-size ball of the dough and roll it out on a lightly floured work surface into a 3-inch round. Place a generous spoonful of the filling in the center of the round, fold the round over the filling to form a half-moon, and seal the edges with fork tines.

Pour the oil to a depth of 3 inches into a deep, heavy saucepan or a deep fryer and heat to 365°F. In batches, add the pastries and fry, turning once, until golden, 4 to 5 minutes total. Using a slotted spoon or wire skimmer, transfer the pastries to paper towels to drain. Serve hot.

## *Lebanese Spinach Pastries* SBANIKH BIL AJEEN

Made with a yeast-raised pastry rather than a shortcrust pastry (like the one used for the *sambusak* on page 73), these Lebanese spinach pastries can be made a few hours ahead of time and reheated. Sometimes the filling also calls for ½ cup raisins or pomegranate seeds. The same dough is used to make *lahm bil ajeen,* the lamb-topped pizza that is popular all over Turkey, Lebanon, and Syria (page 77). The filling for *sambusak* can be substituted for the spinach filling. MAKES 12 PIES

DOUGH

1 envelope (2½ teaspoons) active dry yeast

¾ cup lukewarm water

3 cups all-purpose flour

1½ teaspoons salt

2 tablespoons olive oil

SPINACH FILLING

1 pound spinach

Salt

2 tablespoons olive oil

1 cup chopped yellow onion or green onion, including green tops

1 teaspoon ground allspice

1 tablespoon ground sumac

6 tablespoons pine nuts or coarsely chopped walnuts, toasted

2 to 4 tablespoons fresh lemon juice

3 tablespoons chopped fresh mint

½ teaspoon freshly ground black pepper

Olive oil for brushing

To make the dough, in a small bowl, sprinkle the yeast over the lukewarm water and let stand until bubbling and foamy, 5 to 10 minutes. In a large bowl, stir together the flour and salt. Add the yeast mixture and oil and stir until the mixture comes together in a rough mass. Transfer to a lightly floured work surface, knead briefly until smooth, and shape into a ball. Place in a large oiled bowl, turn the dough to coat evenly with oil, cover the bowl with a kitchen towel, and let the dough rise in a warm place until doubled in size, about 1½ hours.

To make the filling, remove the stems from the spinach, chop the leaves coarsely, then rinse and drain well. Place in a colander in the sink, sprinkle with 1 teaspoon salt, and let stand for 1 hour. Squeeze the moisture out of the spinach and chop it finely.

Warm the oil in a large sauté pan over medium heat. Add the onion and cook, stirring occasionally, until translucent and tender, 8 to 10 minutes. Add the allspice and sumac and cook for 1 minute longer. Stir in the spinach and cook, stirring occasionally, until the spinach wilts, 2 to 3 minutes. Stir in the pine nuts, lemon juice to taste, mint, and pepper and season with salt. Return the mixture to the colander and drain for twenty minutes if it seems wet.

Preheat the oven to 400°F. Lightly oil a large sheet pan.

Punch down the dough and turn out onto a lightly floured work surface. Divide the dough into 12 equal portions and shape each portion into a ball. On the floured surface, flatten a ball into a disk and roll out into a 6-inch round. Spoon about ⅓ cup of the spinach mixture into the center of the round. Bring up the three edges of the pastry and press together to seal. The pastry will be triangular, reminiscent of hamantaschen in shape. Repeat with the remaining dough and filling. As the pastries are shaped, transfer them to the prepared pan, spacing them ½ inch apart.

Bake the pastries until golden, 15 to 20 minutes. Remove from the oven, brush the tops with oil, and serve warm.

# Middle Eastern Lamb Flatbread  LAHM BIL AJEEN

This spiced lamb flatbread is popular in Lebanon, Turkey, and Syria. For its hallmark sweet-and-sour tang, some Syrian Jews prefer tamarind while others, along with the Lebanese and Turkish Jews, prefer pomegranate molasses. In winter, canned tomatoes or tomato paste can be used.  MAKES TWELVE 6-INCH FLATBREADS

**Dough for Lebanese Spinach Pastries (page 75)**

**LAMB TOPPING**

2 tablespoons olive oil

2 yellow onions, finely chopped

2 cloves garlic, minced

1 teaspoon ground cinnamon

1 teaspoon ground cumin or coriander (optional)

½ teaspoon ground allspice

1 pound ground lamb

¾ cup peeled, seeded, and chopped plum tomatoes

¼ cup pine nuts, toasted

2 tablespoons fresh lemon juice or pomegranate molasses, or more to taste

Salt and freshly ground black pepper

Make the dough as directed and set aside to rise.

To make the topping, warm the oil in a large sauté pan over medium heat. Add the onions and cook, stirring occasionally, until translucent and tender, 8 to 10 minutes. Add the garlic, cinnamon, cumin, and allspice and cook for 2 minutes longer. Add the lamb and cook, breaking up any lumps with a wooden spoon and stirring occasionally, until it is no longer pink, 8 to 10 minutes. Add the tomatoes and cook for a few minutes longer. Stir in the pine nuts and lemon juice and season with salt and pepper. Remove from the heat and let cool completely.

Preheat the oven to 400°F. Lightly oil 2 large sheet pans.

Punch down the dough and turn out onto a lightly floured work surface. Divide the dough into 12 equal portions and shape each portion into a ball. On the floured surface, flatten a ball into a disk and roll out into a 6-inch round. Spread one-twelfth of the lamb mixture evenly over the round, leaving a ½-inch rim uncovered. Repeat with the remaining dough and topping. As the flatbreads are topped, transfer them to the prepared pans, spacing them ½ inch apart.

Bake the flatbreads until the pastry is golden brown, about 20 minutes. Serve warm or at room temperature.

# Turkish Stuffed Bread Dough Pastries  MANTIKOS

Traditional Turkish *mantı* are made with a tender pasta dough and are usually dressed with paprika butter and a yogurt and garlic sauce. The Sephardic *mantikos* pastry from

Çanakkale is a yeast-raised dough. These meat-filled pastries might accompany a bowl of soup for supper. In Izmir, this same dough was used for *boyos* (half-moon pastries). Each filling is sufficient to fill one batch of dough.  MAKES 18 TO 24 PASTRIES

**STARTER**

1 teaspoon active dry yeast

½ teaspoon sugar

1 cup warm water

2 tablespoons all-purpose flour

**DOUGH**

3 cups all-purpose flour

1 teaspoon salt

6 tablespoons safflower or olive oil

**MEAT FILLING**

2 to 3 tablespoons olive oil

2 yellow onions, chopped

2 cloves garlic, minced

12 ounces ground beef (not too lean)

2 teaspoons salt

1 teaspoon freshly ground black pepper

¼ cup chopped flat-leaf parsley

**SPINACH FILLING**

1 pound spinach, stemmed, cooked, squeezed dry, and chopped

2 eggs, lightly beaten

1 cup feta cheese, crumbled

1½ cups grated kashkaval or other grating cheese

1 teaspoon ground sumac

Few gratings nutmeg

Salt and freshly ground black pepper

**CHEESE FILLING**

1½ cups grated Parmesan cheese

1½ cups farmer or ricotta cheese

2 eggs, lightly beaten

2 fresh red chiles, chopped

¼ cup chopped fresh mint

2 to 3 tablespoons plain yogurt

**ONION AND CHEESE FILLING**

3 tablespoons olive oil or margarine

3 yellow onions, chopped

1 cup crumbled feta cheese

1 cup ricotta cheese, fromage blanc, or cottage cheese

2 eggs, lightly beaten

¼ cup chopped fresh dill

Freshly ground black pepper

Freshly grated nutmeg (optional)

Ground sumac (optional)

1 egg, lightly beaten with a little water

To make the starter, in a small bowl, dissolve the yeast and sugar in the warm water, then stir in the flour. Let stand until bubbling and foamy, 5 to 10 minutes.

To make the dough, in the bowl of a stand mixer fitted with the dough hook, combine the flour, salt, 4 tablespoons of the oil, and the starter and beat on medium speed until a soft dough forms, about 10 minutes. Turn the dough out onto a lightly floured work surface, divide it into 18 to 24 equal portions, and form each portion into a ball. Place the balls in a large bowl, drizzle with the remaining 2 tablespoons oil, and turn the dough to coat evenly with oil. Cover the bowl with a kitchen towel and let the dough rise in a warm place until almost doubled in size, about 30 minutes.

Meanwhile, select a filling and prepare it. To make the meat filling, warm the oil in a sauté pan over medium heat. Add the onions and cook, stirring occasionally, until translucent and tender, 8 to 10 minutes. Add the garlic and beef and cook, breaking up any lumps in the beef with a wooden spoon and stirring occasionally, until the meat is no longer pink, 5 to 8 minutes. Add the salt, pepper, and parsley and cook, stirring occasionally, until the meat is browned, about 10 minutes. Let cool completely.

To make the spinach filling, in a bowl, combine the spinach, eggs, cheeses, sumac, and nutmeg and mix well. Season with salt and pepper.

To make the cheese filling, in a bowl, combine the cheeses, eggs, chiles, mint, and only enough yogurt to hold the cheeses together and make the mixture creamy.

To make the onion and cheese filling, warm the oil in a sauté pan over medium heat. Add the onions and cook, stirring occasionally, until soft and golden, about 15 minutes. Transfer to a bowl, let cool completely, and fold in the cheeses, eggs, and dill. Season with pepper, nutmeg, and sumac.

Preheat the oven to 350°F. Line 2 large sheet pans with parchment paper.

One at a time, flatten each dough ball into a disk on a lightly floured work surface and roll out into a rectangle or square about ⅓ inch thick. Place a generous tablespoon of the filling on the center of the dough, then fold in the sides, fold up the bottom, and fold down the top over the bottom. Pinch the seam tightly to seal. As the pastries are shaped, transfer them, seam side down, to a prepared pan, spacing them about 1½ inches apart.

Brush the tops of the pastries with the egg wash. Bake until golden, 25 to 30 minutes. Serve hot or warm.

## North African Filo Pastries   BESTELS

*Bestels* resemble *borekas:* thin layers of dough wrapped around a savory filling. But instead of a shortcrust or flaky pastry, Moroccan *bestels* are traditionally made with *ouarka,* which means "leaf" in Arabic. The same pastry is known as *malsouka* in Tunisia and as *feuilles* (leaves) *de brik* in France. The pastry is made from a rather springy semolina dough that is pressed in an overlapping circular pattern onto a hot flat pan called a *tobsil* and then peeled off when the paper-thin film of dough has set. Because the process is so time-consuming, most North African home cooks buy *ouarka* from those who specialize in making it. *Feuilles de brik* can be purchased from restaurant-food wholesalers, but first you must find a source and then the minimum order is typically quite large, usually about 250 sheets, which are difficult to store. (Some online sources have more reasonably-sized packages, but the pastry ends up costing about a dollar a sheet, which is insane, and it is likely not to arrive in the best condition because of the rigors of transit.) The good news is that you can make these pastries with filo, which is widely available.

Traditionally served during Rosh Hashanah and at special dinners, *bestels* come in two shapes, triangular and cylindrical; the latter are also called *cigares* or *briouats*. As evidence of the Spanish roots of these pastries, both Maguy Kakon in *La cuisine juive du Maroc de mère en fille* and Viviane and Nina Moryoussef in *Moroccan Jewish Cookery* call the meat filling *migas,* a Spanish term for bread crumbs enriched with meat juices. To ensure moisture, some cooks add a little tomato juice or some chopped tomatoes to the filling. Every family seasons the meat mixture in a different way. Some use quite a lot of garlic, others add onion, and still others favor ginger and turmeric along with, or in place of, the cinnamon. In *Marrakech la Rouge,* Hélène Gans Perez includes the juice of a lemon, and I have followed her lead. In *150 recettes et mille et un souvenirs d'une juive d'Algérie,* Léone Jaffin offers an Algerian *bestel* filling that calls for a trio of large onions and nutmeg instead of cinnamon. MAKES ABOUT 24 SMALL PASTRIES

MEAT FILLING

8 ounces ground beef or lamb

4 to 6 cloves garlic, chopped

1 small yellow onion, grated (optional)

1 teaspoon ground cumin

1 teaspoon ground cinnamon

1 teaspoon ground turmeric (optional)

½ teaspoon ground ginger

½ teaspoon cayenne pepper (optional)

4 tablespoons olive oil, or as needed

Salt and freshly ground black pepper

3 tablespoons chopped fresh cilantro

Juice of 1 lemon (optional)

1 egg, lightly beaten

POTATO FILLING

2 russet potatoes, peeled and cubed

2 tablespoons olive oil

1 yellow onion, finely chopped

3 cloves garlic, finely minced

2 teaspoons ground toasted cumin

1 teaspoon salt

½ teaspoon freshly ground black pepper

¼ cup chopped fresh flat-leaf parsley

¼ cup chopped fresh mint or cilantro

1 egg, lightly beaten

1 or 2 hard-boiled eggs, peeled and coarsely chopped (optional)

12 feuilles de brik, or 8 to 12 filo sheets

1 egg lightly beaten with a bit of water, if using feuilles de brik

½ cup unsalted butter or margarine, melted, if using filo

Canola, safflower, or olive oil, if deep-frying

First, prepare both fillings. To make the meat filling, in a bowl, combine the meat, garlic, onion, cumin, cinnamon, turmeric, ginger, cayenne, and 2 tablespoons of the oil and mix well. Season with salt and pepper.

Warm the remaining 2 tablespoons oil in a large sauté pan over medium heat. Add the seasoned meat and cook, breaking up any lumps with a wooden spoon and stirring occasionally, until no longer pink, about 5 minutes. Add a little more oil if needed and continue to cook, stirring occasionally, until the meat is browned, 5 to 8 minutes. Remove from the heat, stir in the cilantro, and season with salt and pepper. Taste and add the lemon juice if you like. Stir in the egg to bind the mixture. Let cool completely.

To make the potato filling, combine the potatoes with salted water to cover in a saucepan and bring to a boil over high heat. Turn down the heat to medium and simmer until the potatoes are easily pierced with a fork, 15 to 20 minutes. Drain well, transfer to a bowl, and mash with a potato masher until smooth. Set aside.

Warm the oil in a small sauté pan over medium heat. Add the onion and cook, stirring occasionally, until translucent and tender, about 7 minutes. Add the garlic, cumin, salt, and pepper and cook for 2 minutes. Stir in the parsley and mint and remove from the heat. Add the onion mixture to the potatoes, mix well, then taste and adjust the seasoning with salt and pepper. Add the raw egg, stirring well to bind the mixture, and then stir in the hard-boiled eggs. Let cool completely.

To assemble the pastries, if using feuilles de brik, cut the circles in half. Place a generous tablespoon of the filling in the center of the lower half of each semicircle, moisten the edges of the pastry with the egg wash, and then fold over to cover the filling and create a triangle with a rounded bottom. Lightly pat the pastry down and press the edges to seal.

Filo usually comes in sheets that measure about 12 by 18 inches. If that is the size of your sheets, you will need only 8 sheets, which you will cut into rectangles that measure 12 by 6 inches. If your filo sheets are smaller, cut them in half. You want 24 rectangles total. Keep the filo you are not immediately using covered with a damp kitchen towel to prevent drying.

To make cigar-shaped pastries, brush a filo rectangle with butter (or margarine if you are using the meat filling). Put a strip of the filling on a short edge of the rectangle, placing it about 1 inch in from the edge and the sides. Fold the bottom edge over the filling, fold in the sides, and then roll up the pastry until you reach the far end. The finished pastry will be about 1½ inches in diameter and 4 inches long. (If you want a crunchier pastry, you can stack 2 strips of filo for each pastry, brushing each one with butter.) Brush with butter to seal.

To make triangular filo pastries, cut the 6-by-12-inch strips in half so you have 3-by-12-inch strips. Place a strip on the work surface, with a short edge facing you. Brush the strip with butter and then top with a second strip and brush it with butter. Place 1 tablespoon of the filling about 1½ inches from the short edge nearest you. Fold the filo over the filling on the diagonal so the corner meets the opposite edge, and then fold the triangle up, so the long side is flush with the straight edge of the strip. Continue to fold in this manner—as if folding a flag—until you reach the far end of the strip.

The pastries can be arranged in a single layer on a sheet pan, covered loosely with a foil tent, and refrigerated for up to 24 hours before cooking. Do not press the foil (or plastic wrap) directly onto pastries made with filo, as dough can tear easily.

To deep-fry the pastries, pour the oil to a depth of 3 inches into a deep, heavy saucepan or a deep fryer and heat to 365°F. In batches, add the pastries and fry, turning once, until golden, 3 to 4 minutes total. Using a slotted spoon or wire skimmer, transfer the pastries to paper towels to drain. Serve hot.

Alternatively, to bake the pastries, preheat the oven to 400°F and line sheet pans with parchment paper. Brush the pastries with melted butter and arrange them on the prepared pans, spacing them about 1 inch apart. Bake until golden, about 25 minutes. Serve hot.

VARIATIONS: *Algerian Potato-and-Cheese Filling (Bestels aux Pommes de Terre et Fromage):* Combine 3 large potatoes, peeled, boiled in salted water until tender, drained, and mashed, with 2 tablespoons milk; ⅔ cup grated Gruyère cheese; 2 cloves garlic, minced; 2 tablespoons chopped fresh flat-leaf parsley; and 1 egg yolk, lightly beaten, and mix well. Season with salt, freshly ground black pepper, and freshly grated nutmeg.

*Cheese Filling (Bestels de Fromage):* Combine 3 cups grated Gruyère cheese, ½ cup fromage blanc or cottage or farmer cheese, and 2 eggs, lightly beaten, and mix well. Stir in finely chopped fresh mint leaves (1 small whole leaf per pastry).

# Moroccan Chicken and Almond Filo Pie   B'STILLA

*B'stilla* is a dish of celebration, served at weddings, bar mitzvahs, and other festive occasions. The origin of this dish is hotly debated. Was it an Arabic dish brought to Spain or a Hispano-Arabic dish brought to Morocco from Andalusia? Perhaps it was a Spanish dish that came to the Ottoman Empire with the Jews. At this point, the source remains speculative, so it is best just to enjoy it as a masterpiece of Moroccan cuisine. *B'stilla* is traditionally made with *ouarka* and fried. Filo sheets are a good substitute for the *ouarka,* and the pie is more easily baked than fried. Although squab is the deluxe traditional filling, young chicken works as well. SERVES 8 AS A MAIN COURSE, 12 TO 16 AS AN APPETIZER

FILLING

4 pounds squabs or poussins, or 2 pounds bone-in chicken breasts (about 2 whole)

Salt and freshly ground black pepper

¼ cup canola oil, or as needed

2 large yellow onions, chopped

¼ cup chopped fresh cilantro

2 tablespoons chopped fresh flat-leaf parsley

1 teaspoon ground ginger

1 teaspoon ground cumin

½ teaspoon cayenne pepper

½ teaspoon ground turmeric

½ teaspoon ground cinnamon

½ teaspoon saffron threads

1 cup water

2 tablespoons fresh lemon juice (optional)

8 eggs, lightly beaten

ALMOND LAYER

2 tablespoons olive oil

1½ cups slivered blanched almonds

2 tablespoons sugar

½ teaspoon ground cinnamon

1 box (1 pound) filo sheets

½ cup margarine, melted and cooled

3 tablespoons confectioners' sugar

1 tablespoon ground cinnamon

Whole blanched almonds for garnish (optional)

Cut the whole birds into quarters or cut the whole breasts into halves and sprinkle with salt and pepper. Warm the oil in a large, heavy sauté pan over medium heat. Add the poultry pieces and brown evenly on all sides, turning often. Using tongs, transfer the pieces to a platter. Add the onions to the fat remaining in the pan and cook over medium heat, stirring occasionally, until the onions are translucent and tender, about 10 minutes. Add the cilantro, parsley, ginger, cumin, cayenne, turmeric, cinnamon, saffron, and water and bring to a boil. Return the poultry pieces to the pan, turn down the heat to low, cover, and simmer until the meat is tender, about 30 minutes.

Using the tongs, transfer the poultry pieces to a clean platter. When cool enough to handle, remove all of the meat from the bones, discard the bones, and shred the meat into strips. You should have about 4 cups shredded meat. (You can use the skin too, if you like.)

Reduce the liquid in the sauté pan over high heat until you have about 1¾ cups. Turn down the heat to very low, add the lemon juice, and then add the eggs and stir constantly and gently either with a silicone spatula or wooden spoon until very soft curds form, 6 to 8 minutes. Remove from the heat, season with salt and pepper, and set aside.

To make the almond layer, warm the oil in a sauté pan over medium heat. Add the almonds and sauté, stirring occasionally, until golden brown, about 5 minutes. Using a slotted spoon, transfer to paper towels to drain. (Alternatively, to reduce the oil in the recipe, spread the almonds on a sheet pan and toast in a preheated 350°F oven until golden, about 8 minutes.) Chop coarsely, transfer to a bowl, add the sugar and cinnamon, and toss to coat the nuts evenly. Set aside.

To assemble the pie, preheat the oven to 400°F. Brush a 10- or 12-inch round pie dish or a 14-inch pizza pan with margarine. Place the filo sheets on a work surface and immediately cover the sheets with a damp kitchen towel or plastic wrap to prevent drying, removing 1 sheet at a time as needed.

Arrange 6 filo sheets in the prepared pie dish, brushing each sheet with margarine, arranging the sheets like the spokes of a wheel, and overlapping the sheets so the pie dish is completely covered and the filo is overhanging the sides. Be sure to brush the overhang with margarine. Sprinkle one-third of the almond mixture in an even 10-inch circle in the center of the dish. Spoon the egg mixture over the almond layer. Top the egg layer with the shredded meat. Sprinkle the remaining almond mixture over the meat. Fold the overhanging filo over the layered filling. Top the pie with 6 to 8 more filo sheets, again brushing each one with margarine, arranging them like the spokes of a wheel, and being careful to brush the overhang. Carefully tuck the overhang under the pie. (At this point, the pie can be loosely covered with a foil tent and refrigerated for up to 8 hours before baking.)

Bake the pie until golden on top, about 20 minutes. Remove from the oven and carefully drain off any excess oil. Lift up the edge of the pie to peek at the underside. The odds are it is starting to brown nicely. Continue to bake until golden brown, 15 to 20 minutes longer. However, if the bottom looks pale and has not begun to brown, invert another pie dish or a pizza pan over the pie and carefully flip the pie into a second pie dish (or pan). Return the pie to the oven and bake until the top is browned, about 10 minutes longer. Invert the pie one more time and bake for 5 minutes longer. Remove from the oven and let rest for 10 minutes.

Slide the pie out of the dish onto a platter or serve directly from the cooking vessel. In a small bowl, stir together the confectioners' sugar and cinnamon. Sprinkle the cinnamon sugar in crisscrossing lines over the top of the warm pie. Top with the whole almonds in a decorative pattern. Using a sharp serrated knife, cut into wedges and serve warm.

## Pumpkin-Filled Filo Roses   RODANCHES DE KALAVASA

These coiled pastries were traditionally made with paper-thin pastry dough that was difficult to handle. Some cooks gave up and made them as small turnovers (*borekas de calabasa*), abandoning their unique shape. Cookbook author Nicholas Stavroulakis decided to make the pastries with filo, which is easier to handle, and I have followed him. *Rodanches* are called "roses" because when these Greek pastries are traditionally made, they resemble the flowers. (If one is less poetically inclined, the image of snails or coiled snakes may come to mind.) Sephardic Turkish pastries with this shape are called *bulemas* or *kol böreği* and are filled with spinach, eggplant, or just cheese. The pumpkin filling here is a specialty served for Rosh Hashanah and Sukkoth. It is also used to fill the large Greek filo pie known as *kolokithopita* (see variation).

Pumpkin *rodanches* walk a fine line between being a savory pastry and a dessert. (The sweet versions in Turkey are called *bulemas dulses de balkabak* and are a tradition of the Georgian Jews who settled in Istanbul.) You can reduce the amount of sugar and add some salty cheese to make the filling more savory or, conversely, you can increase the sugar to make it a dessert pastry.

Mediterranean pumpkin-type squash is much redder than our pumpkin. It is quite large and is often sold by the piece. The closest in texture and taste is our butternut squash, or the Japanese kabocha squash, which has a bit looser texture. If you cannot find butternut squash, canned pumpkin can be used (it is often actually butternut squash). Some versions of this recipe even use zucchini and sweeten it the same way. MAKES 12 PASTRIES

---

2 cups squash purée (see master recipe, page 36), or 1 can (16 ounces) solid-pack pumpkin purée, drained

½ to 1 cup sugar

1 teaspoon ground cinnamon

2 tablespoons olive oil

1 cup walnuts, toasted and chopped (optional)

Salt

½ cup crumbled feta or other salty soft white cheese, if making a savory version (optional)

¼ cup chopped fresh mint or flat-leaf parsley, if making a savory version (optional)

8 filo sheets

½ cup unsalted butter or margarine, melted, or olive oil

---

In a saucepan, combine the squash purée, sugar (use the smaller amount—or even less—if you want a more savory filling and the entire cup for a sweet version), cinnamon, and oil, stir well, and place over low heat. Cook, stirring often, until any moisture has cooked away and the mixture is thick, which should happen fairly quickly. Remove from the heat. At this point, I recommend that you drain the purée in a colander for a few hours to ensure the filling is not too wet, especially if you plan to make the pastries ahead of time.

Transfer the purée to a bowl, fold in the walnuts, and season with a little salt, especially if you are accenting the savory rather than the sweet in the filling. If you are making a savory filling, stir in the cheese and mint.

Preheat the oven to 350°F. Oil a sheet pan or line it with parchment paper.

Cut the filo sheets into thirds to create rectangles measuring about 6 by 12 inches. Cover the rectangles you are not using immediately with a damp kitchen towel to prevent drying, removing 2 rectangles at a time as needed.

Brush 1 filo rectangle with butter. Top with a second rectangle and brush with butter. Place a thin line of squash filling just inside one long edge. Fold over the edge to cover the filling and continue to roll, lightly brushing with butter as you roll, until you have a long, snake-like cylinder. Do not roll too tightly or the cylinder may crack when you try to coil it. Coil the cylinder into a spiral, being careful not to coil the spiral too tightly or the filo may crack, and transfer to the prepared pan. Repeat until all of the filling and filo are used. (At this point, the spirals can be loosely covered with a foil tent and refrigerated for up to 6 hours. Just before baking, brush with butter, then increase the baking time by about 10 minutes.)

Bake the pastries until golden, 30 to 45 minutes. Serve hot or warm.

VARIATION: *Kolokithopita:* You can use the same filling to make a Greek baklava-like dish, or pan *börek*. Layer 8 filo sheets, brushing each one with melted butter, in a baking dish. Add the squash filling, spreading it in an even layer. Top with 8 more filo sheets, brushing each one with melted butter. Refrigerate for 1 hour to firm up the butter; then, using a sharp serrated knife, precut into serving portions, cutting all the way through to the bottom of the dish. Bake in a preheated 350°F oven until golden brown, 25 to 40 minutes. Serve hot or warm.

## *Eggplant Filo Rolls*   BULEMAS DE BERENJENA

To liven up the flavor of these Sephardic Sabbath pastries, popular in Greece and Turkey, I am including the option of adding nutmeg and/or dill to the filling. Some Greek cooks mix in chopped walnuts, as well. A fresh sheep or goat cheese or even ricotta is a good stand-in for the feta. MAKES 10 TO 12 PASTRIES

---

2 large globe eggplants (about 1 pound each)

8 ounces feta or other soft white cheese, crumbled

1 cup grated kashkaval, Gruyère, or Parmesan cheese

2 eggs, lightly beaten

3 tablespoons chopped fresh dill (optional)

Salt and freshly ground black pepper

Freshly grated nutmeg (optional)

¼ to ½ cup fine dried bread crumbs, if needed

8 to 10 filo sheets

½ cup unsalted butter or margarine, melted, or olive oil

1 egg yolk, lightly beaten and grated kashkaval cheese for topping, if making Turkish version

---

Roast the eggplants as directed in Master Recipe for Roasted Eggplant (page 27). After draining the pulp, pulse briefly in a food processor or finely chop by hand. You should have 1½ to 2 cups eggplant. Return the pulp to the colander and drain again for 20 minutes.

Transfer the eggplant pulp to a bowl, add the cheeses, eggs, and dill and mix well. Season with salt, pepper, and nutmeg. If the filling seems too wet, add the bread crumbs as needed to absorb the excess moisture.

Preheat the oven to 375°F. Oil a sheet pan or line it with parchment paper.

Cut the filo sheets into thirds to create rectangles measuring about 6 by 12 inches. Cover the rectangles you are not using immediately with a damp kitchen towel to prevent drying, removing 2 rectangles at a time as needed.

Brush 1 filo rectangle with butter. Top with a second rectangle and brush with butter. Using 2 layers is enough, but if you like, you can add a third filo layer, and brush it with butter, to ensure against leaking. Place a thin line of eggplant filling just inside one long edge. Fold over the edge to cover the filling and continue to roll, lightly brushing with butter as you roll, until you have a long, snake-like cylinder. Do not roll too tightly or the cylinder may crack when you try to coil it. Coil the cylinder into a spiral, being careful not to coil the spiral too tightly or the filo may crack, and transfer to the prepared pan. Repeat until all of the filling and filo are used. (At this point, the spirals can be loosely covered with a foil tent and refrigerated for up to 8 hours. Just before baking, brush with butter, then increase the baking time by about 10 minutes.) If making Turkish pastries, brush the tops of the pastries with the egg yolk and sprinkle with the cheese.

Bake the pastries until golden, about 30 minutes. Serve hot or warm.

## *Smoky Eggplant Börek*   MELITZANOPITA

After testing many eggplant filo recipes, I created this layered *börek,* which can also be called *pastel de berenjena.* It makes a great first course, or a main course with a salad. I once served it to eighty guests at a fund-raising dinner to great acclaim. If green garlic is in season, you can use 6 stalks in place of the green onions and garlic. This recipe is easily halved and assembled in a 7-by-12-by-2-inch baking dish, or in a 9-by-12-by-2-inch baking dish for a *börek* of less height. SERVES 12 TO 16

8 large or 12 medium eggplants

3 tablespoons olive oil

1½ cups chopped green onions, including the green tops

2 tablespoons finely minced garlic

1 tablespoon ground toasted cumin

2 teaspoons Aleppo pepper flakes

1½ teaspoons ground sumac

1 cup walnuts, toasted and chopped

1½ pounds feta cheese, crumbled

¼ cup chopped fresh dill

2 teaspoons freshly ground black pepper

Salt

3 eggs, lightly beaten

1 box (1 pound) filo sheets

Fine dried bread crumbs, for sprinking, plus more, if needed, to absorb moisture

1 pound unsalted butter, melted and cooled

Roast the eggplants as directed in Master Recipe for Roasted Eggplant (page 27). After draining the pulp, pulse briefly in a food processor or finely chop by hand. You should have about 12 cups eggplant. Return the pulp to the colander and drain again for 20 minutes. Transfer the eggplant to a large bowl.

Warm the oil in a sauté pan over medium heat. Add the green onions and cook, stirring occasionally, until soft, 3 to 4 minutes. Add the garlic, cumin, Aleppo pepper, and sumac and cook, stirring occasionally, for 1 to 2 minutes longer. Remove from the heat and let cool for a few minutes.

Add the green onion mixture to the eggplant and stir to mix. Fold in the walnuts, feta, dill, black pepper, and a generous measure of salt. Stir in the eggs. Cover and chill well for a few hours or up to overnight.

Preheat the oven to 375°F. Brush a shallow 12-by-20-inch hotel pan or a 13-by-19-inch lasagna pan with butter. Unroll the stack of filo sheets and cover with a damp kitchen towel to prevent drying, removing one sheet at a time as needed. (You can also use two 7-by-12-by-2-inch baking dishes and cut the filo sheets to fit.)

Look at the chilled filling. If you see pockets of liquid, stir in a few spoons of bread crumbs to absorb some of the moisture. The mixture should be loose but not wet.

Layer about half of the filo sheets in the prepared pan, brushing each sheet with butter. Sprinkle the final layer lightly and evenly with bread crumbs. Add the eggplant filling, spreading it in an even layer. Top with the remaining filo sheets, brushing each sheet with butter. Refrigerate for 1 hour to firm up the butter; then, using a sharp serrated knife, precut into serving portions, cutting all the way through to the bottom of the baking dish.

Bake until golden, 45 to 60 minutes. Serve hot or warm.

## Tunisian Fried Pastries with Egg BRIKS À L'OEUF

The small savory pastry called *bestel* or *briouat* in Morocco and *burak* in Algeria is called *brik* in Tunisia. According to food scholar Clifford Wright in *A Mediterranean Feast,* the name *brik* comes from the Turkish term *börek,* called *boreka* by the Jews. *Briks,* which are deep-fried, are made with sheets of *malsouka,* which is, as noted earlier, the Tunisian name for Moroccan *ouarka.* You can instead use filo or even Chinese egg roll wrappers. You will need small eggs for these pastries, which are nearly impossible to find in markets, so choose the smallest eggs available to you.

These Tunisian pastries can be filled with cooked meat or poultry, mashed potatoes, or canned tuna. A raw egg is usually nested on top of the filling, and the pastry is carefully sealed without breaking the egg. A meat filling is usually lamb seasoned with onion, cumin, paprika, cayenne, and parsley or cilantro; a mashed potato filling is flavored with onion, garlic, and parsley; and a chicken filling often calls for cooked potatoes and onion. These egg-filled pastries must be eaten very carefully to avoid dripping egg yolk on your shirt front.

At an American Institute of Wine and Food dinner, I fried one hundred egg-filled *briks,* two at a time, for Tunisian guest chef Abderrazak Haouari. We were told not to add the raw egg because everyone was dressed up, but Haouari insisted and I agreed that we had to do it the right way. We received no complaints—and no dry-cleaning bills. SERVES 8

1 tablespoon peanut or canola oil, plus more for deep-frying

1 small yellow onion, chopped

2 cans (6 ounces each) olive oil–packed tuna, drained and mashed

2 tablespoons brined capers, rinsed and chopped (optional)

3 tablespoons chopped fresh flat-leaf parsley

1 to 2 tablespoons fresh lemon juice

Salt and freshly ground black pepper

Harissa, homemade (page 355) or store-bought, for seasoning (optional)

8 feuilles de brik, egg roll wrappers, or filo sheets

8 small eggs

1 large egg white, lightly beaten

Canola or safflower oil for deep-frying

Warm the 1 tablespoon oil in a sauté pan over medium heat. Add the onion and cook, stirring occasionally, until translucent and tender, 8 to 10 minutes. Remove from the heat and let cool for a few minutes. In a bowl, combine the onion, tuna, and capers and mix well. Add the parsley and the lemon juice to taste, then season with salt, pepper, and harissa.

If using feuilles de brik or egg roll wrappers, lay the wrappers in a single layer on a work surface and divide the tuna filling evenly among the wrappers, mounding it in the center of each wrapper. Using the back of a spoon, make a depression in the center of each mound of filling, and break an egg into each depression. Brush the edge of each wrapper with the egg white and fold the wrapper in half, covering the filling completely. Press the edges together to seal, then fold over the edge to make a ½-inch-wide rim. It will look like a half moon.

If using filo, cover the filo sheets you are not using immediately with a damp kitchen towel to prevent drying, removing 1 sheet at a time as needed. To shape each pastry, lay 1 filo sheet on a work surface, brush with oil, and fold in half crosswise so you have two layers. Place one-eighth of the filling in the center of the folded sheet, positioning it about 2 inches from the top edge and leaving 1 inch uncovered on each side. Using the back of a spoon, make a depression in the center of the mound of filling, and break an egg into the depression. Fold in the left side and then the right side of the filo to cover the filling. Brush the top and bottom edges of the pastry with egg white, then fold up the bottom to join the top. Press the top and bottom edges gently to seal.

Pour the oil to a depth of 3 inches into a deep, heavy saucepan or a deep fryer and heat to 365°F. In batches, add the pastries and fry, turning once, until crisp and golden, 5 to 7 minutes. Using a slotted spoon or wire skimmer, transfer to paper towels to drain. Serve hot and eat carefully.

VARIATION: *Potato Filling:* Sauté 1 yellow onion, finely chopped, and 3 cloves garlic, minced, in 2 tablespoons olive oil until tender, about 10 minutes. Let cool slightly, then combine with 2 potatoes, peeled, cooked, and mashed; 1 teaspoon salt; ½ teaspoon freshly ground black pepper; ¼ cup chopped fresh flat-leaf parsley; 2 tablespoons chopped fresh cilantro; and 1 egg, lightly beaten. A few spoons of brined capers, rinsed, are an optional addition.

Eggs
and
Fritters

CHICKENS WERE VALUED MORE FOR THEIR EGGS than for their meat in the traditional Mediterranean Jewish kitchen, as the sizable selection of delicious egg dishes that follows illustrates. As with the savory pastries in chapter 2, different names are used for similar preparations—*sfongo, quajado, fritada, inchusa, almodrote*—and how they are made varies from country to country and even from family to family. Not surprisingly, crafting a clear description of many of the egg dishes is a nearly impossible task. Some are vegetable gratins, others are vegetable bread puddings, and still others incorporate meat and poultry. Potatoes, bread, matzo, or cheese might be used as a thickener. The only constant is the presence of eggs. Even a dish we would typically call an omelet has different names. It can be an *egga, ojja, kuku, marcoude,* or *fritada.* Plus, the same dish can have one name if the eggs are beaten and added to the ingredients and another if the eggs are poached on top.

Eggs are also essential in the preparation of fritters, those irresistible fried tidbits that whet the appetite before the meal or might even be a simple main dish. I like to use a deep, heavy saucepan (or even a wok, which uses less oil than a saucepan) for deep-frying, but if you have a deep fryer, by all means use it. A Chinese wire skimmer, a flat slotted spoon, or even long cooking chopsticks, if you are adept at their use, are ideal for removing delicate fritters from hot oil. I avoid metal tongs, as the fritters are more likely to break. Olive oil—pure rather than extra virgin—is a good frying oil if the oil temperature does not exceed 375°F. Canola or safflower oil is also excellent.

Some fritters are accompanied by a dipping sauce made from tahini or yogurt that sets up a delicious contrast of crunch and creaminess. Others may need only a sprinkle of flaky sea salt. All of them will be warmly received by everyone at your table.

## Long-Cooked Onion Skin Eggs   HUEVOS HAMINADOS

Often served at the Sabbath meal and during Passover, *huevos haminados* have long been part of Mediterranean Jewish cuisine. Cooks save brown onion skins during the week, then cook eggs under a bed of the skins, sometimes along with coffee grounds or tea leaves to ensure the eggs turn a rich brown. A dash of wine vinegar or a few whole spices are sometimes added to the cooking water along with the olive oil. The word *hamin* means "oven," and traditionally the eggs were cooked in the oven of the local baker. Nowadays, they are easily prepared on the stove top. The eggs pick up a slight onion perfume and a creamy texture during the long cooking. Italians call these eggs *uova turche* (Turkish eggs), or if coffee grounds have been added to the pan, they call them *uova inhaminade al caffè* (eggs baked with coffee). Greeks call them *Selanlik yamurta* (Salonika eggs) or *Yahudi yamurta* (Jewish eggs). Eat them plain or serve them with sliced cucumbers and radishes or bread and goat cheese. SERVES 8

3 to 4 cups brown or red onion skins

8 eggs

1 bay leaf (optional)

4 whole cloves (optional)

8 black peppercorns (optional)

¼ cup black tea leaves, or 1½ cups coffee grounds

¼ cup olive oil

1 tablespoon red wine vinegar

Layer about half of the onion skins on the bottom of a heavy pot and place the eggs on the onion skins. Add the bay leaf, cloves, and peppercorns, then add the remaining onion skins and the tea leaves. Pour in cold water to cover, add the oil and vinegar, and cover the pot tightly.

Place the pot over very low heat and cook at a bare simmer for 6 hours. Check the pot occasionally and add water as needed to keep the eggs covered. Alternatively, put the pot in a 250°F oven for the same amount of time, checking the water level occasionally.

When the eggs are done, have ready a bowl of cold water in the sink. Scoop the eggs out of the pot and plunge them into the bowl of water, then let them sit under running cold water until they are cold. Peel just before serving.

## Sephardic Eggs Baked with Cheese and Tomatoes   KEZO KOTCHO

This simple recipe, which is adapted from one in Méri Badi's *250 recettes de cuisine juive espagnole,* is not earthshaking, but it is one you will make again and again if you love eggs and cheese. SERVES 2

2 tablespoons extra virgin olive oil

2 large tomatoes, grated on the large holes of a box grater and skin discarded

Salt and freshly ground black pepper

2 thin slices kashkaval, Gruyère, or mozzarella cheese

2 eggs

Warm the oil over medium heat in a sauté pan large enough to hold the cheese slices in a single layer. Add the tomatoes and sauté until almost melted, about 8 minutes. Season lightly with salt and pepper. Add the cheese slices in a single layer, then carefully crack an egg onto each slice. Cover and cook until the whites are set and the yolks are still soft, 5 to 6 minutes, or until done to your liking. Serve warm.

## Chickpea and Chicken Omelet    MERTZEL

Moroccan families serve this hearty omelet to break the Yom Kippur fast. *Mertzel* resembles a Spanish tortilla but is made with chickpeas instead of potatoes. It is part of a long Mediterranean Jewish omelet tradition that includes the Algerian *meguina,* made with vegetables, chicken, and eggs, the *marcoude* of Tunisia, and the *almodrote, fritada,* and *quajado* of the Greek and Turkish Jews. This version is a combination of recipes from two books, one by Martine Chiche-Yana and a second by Jeanne Ifergan and Marek Lebkowski. If you prefer to bake the omelet and do not have an ovenproof sauté pan, combine all of the ingredients as directed, then transfer the mixture to an oiled baking dish and bake the omelet in a 350°F oven for 20 to 30 minutes. SERVES 6

| | |
|---|---|
| 1 cup dried chickpeas | Freshly ground black pepper |
| 3 tablespoons extra virgin olive oil, plus more for drizzling | 1 bone-in whole chicken breast, cooked just until tender, boned, and diced |
| 2 or 3 cloves garlic, minced | 8 eggs, lightly beaten |
| 2 teaspoons sweet paprika | Generous grating of freshly grated nutmeg, or pinch of saffron threads (optional) |
| 1 teaspoon salt | |

Pick over the chickpeas, then place in a bowl, add water to cover, and let soak in the refrigerator overnight. Drain, rinse well, and transfer to a 2-quart saucepan. Add water to cover by 3 inches and bring to a boil over high heat. Turn down the heat to low, cover, and simmer until almost tender, about 30 minutes. The timing will depend on the age of the beans. Remove from the heat.

Warm the oil in a deep nonstick sauté pan over medium-low heat. Add the garlic, paprika, salt, pepper to taste, and the chickpeas and their liquid and simmer, stirring occasionally, for 30 minutes, adding a bit of water if the mixture is too dry. The chickpeas will have further softened and will have absorbed the spices. Just a little liquid should remain in the pan.

Add the chicken, eggs, and nutmeg to the chickpeas and mix well, then drizzle some oil over the surface. Cover, turn down the heat to low, and cook until the eggs are set and the sides are golden when gently pulled away from the pan, about 30 minutes. Unmold the omelet onto a serving plate and serve warm.

## Potato and Egg Cake   MARCOUDE

*Marcoude* is a North African version of the well-known tapas bar staple, the Spanish potato tortilla. It is sometimes called a *cuajado,* derived from the Arabic term *qaş'ah,* which is also the source of the term *cazuela* (*cassola* in Catalan), the popular Spanish clay cooking vessel. This Algerian recipe calls for "old" potatoes, or russets, rather than boiling potatoes. Some Tunisian cooks include ground chicken with the potato and offer the enriched dish at Passover. If you use only half of the eggs, this dish becomes a gratin or potato cake. Serve as a main dish or as a side dish.  SERVES 8

---

2½ pounds russet potatoes, peeled and cubed

4 to 6 cloves garlic, peeled but left whole

8 eggs, lightly beaten

3 spring onions, minced, or 6 green onions, including the green tops, minced

3 tablespoons chopped fresh flat-leaf parsley

½ teaspoon ground toasted cumin (optional)

Pinch of freshly grated nutmeg

Salt and freshly ground black pepper

Olive oil for brushing

---

Combine the potatoes and garlic with salted water to cover in a saucepan and bring to a boil over high heat. Turn down the heat to medium and simmer until the potatoes are easily pierced with a fork, 15 to 20 minutes. Drain well, transfer to a bowl, and mash the potatoes and garlic with a fork. Stir in the eggs, onions, parsley, cumin, and nutmeg, mixing well. Season with salt and pepper.

Preheat the oven to 400°F. Brush a 10-inch round pie dish or gratin dish liberally with oil.

Spread the potato mixture evenly in the dish. Place in the oven and bake the cake until golden, about 30 minutes. Serve hot or warm.

## Persian Potato Omelet   KUKU-YE SIBZAMINI

*Sibzamini* translates to "apple of the earth," a charming nickname for the modest potato. A *kuku* (sometimes spelled *kookoo*) traditionally combines eggs and vegetables. This combination of eggs and potatoes is particularly popular in eastern Iran. SERVES 4

1 pound boiling potatoes

¼ cup olive oil, plus more for brushing

1 yellow onion, finely chopped

½ teaspoon sweet paprika

½ teaspoon ground toasted cumin

½ teaspoon ground turmeric

Salt and freshly ground pepper

6 eggs, lightly beaten

Combine the potatoes with salted water to cover in a saucepan and bring to a boil over high heat. Turn down the heat to medium and simmer until the potatoes are easily pierced with a fork, about 30 minutes. Drain the potatoes well. When cool enough to handle, peel and grate them on the large holes of a box grater.

Preheat the oven to 400°F. Oil a 10-inch pie dish or round gratin dish.

While the oven heats, warm the oil in a sauté pan over medium heat. Add the onion, paprika, cumin, turmeric, and salt and pepper to taste and cook, stirring occasionally, until the onion is translucent and tender, 8 to 10 minutes. Let cool slightly, then combine with the potatoes and the eggs, mixing well.

Spread the potato mixture evenly in the oiled dish. Place in the oven and bake the omelet until golden, about 30 minutes. Serve hot or warm.

## *Moroccan Layered Potato Cake*   PASTELA

In *Moroccan Jewish Cookery,* Viviane and Nina Moryoussef call the meat filling in this layered potato cake *migas,* a classic Iberian term for crumbs. If you like, after brushing the top with egg, use fork tines to create a decorative pattern. SERVES 6

FILLING

8 ounces ground beef or lamb (not too lean)

1 yellow onion, chopped

¼ cup rendered chicken fat

1 bunch fresh flat-leaf parsley, chopped

½ teaspoon saffron threads

1 cup water

½ teaspoon salt

½ teaspoon freshly ground pepper

½ teaspoon freshly grated nutmeg

½ teaspoon ground cinnamon

2 tablespoons red or white wine vinegar

Juice of 1 lemon

3 pounds russet potatoes, peeled and cut into 1½-inch pieces

7 to 8 eggs

1 teaspoon salt

2 hard-boiled eggs, peeled and sliced crosswise

¼ cup extra virgin olive oil

To make the filling, combine the meat, onion, chicken fat, parsley, saffron, and water in a sauté pan and bring to a simmer over medium heat. Cook until the liquid has evaporated, about 20 minutes. Add the salt, pepper, nutmeg, cinnamon, vinegar, and lemon juice, stir well, and continue to cook until the meat mixture is dry, 5 to 7 minutes longer. Set aside.

Preheat the oven to 400°F. Oil a 1½-quart baking dish with 2-inch sides or a 9-inch square baking pan or dish.

Combine the potatoes with salted water to cover in a saucepan and bring to a boil over high heat. Turn down the heat to medium and simmer until the potatoes are easily pierced with a fork, 20 to 30 minutes. Drain well, transfer to a bowl, and then mash with a potato masher until smooth. Beat in 5 or 6 of the raw eggs, one at a time, until a smooth purée forms, and then add the salt. Reserve a little beaten egg for the final glaze. Spread half of the potato purée in the prepared baking dish.

Lightly beat the 2 remaining raw eggs and stir them into the filling. Spread the filling evenly over the potato layer in the baking dish and top with the hard-boiled eggs. Spoon the remaining potato purée evenly over the egg layer. Brush the top with the reserved beaten egg, decorate the top with fork tines, if you like, and then drizzle the oil over the top.

Bake the cake until golden, about 45 minutes. Serve hot or at room temperature.

## Tunisian Omelet with Tomatoes, Peppers, and Merguez

OJJA BIL MERGUEZ

The primary difference between an *ojja* (or *egga,* as it is sometimes called) and a *shakshuka* (see page 99) is that the eggs are stirred into the filling for an *ojja* and are cooked whole on top of a *shakshuka*. (*Shakshuka* is not to be confused with *choukchouka,* a salad of roasted peppers and tomatoes, also known as *mishwiya* in Morocco and Tunisia.) You may also make this without the *merguez* for a meatless omelet. SERVES 8

¼ cup olive oil

1 pound merguez, homemade (page 351) or store-bought, cut into 1-inch pieces

3 green bell peppers, seeded and sliced lengthwise into ¼-inch-wide strips

4 cloves garlic, finely minced

½ teaspoon harissa, homemade (page 355) or store-bought, dissolved in 2 tablespoons water

1 teaspoon ground caraway

2 teaspoons sweet paprika

6 ripe tomatoes, peeled, seeded, and coarsely chopped (about 3 cups)

4 boiling potatoes, peeled, boiled until tender-firm, and cubed

¼ cup water

10 eggs, lightly beaten

Salt and freshly ground black pepper

Warm the oil in a large sauté pan over high heat. Add the merguez and fry, turning once, until browned on both sides. Add the bell peppers and garlic and cook, stirring often, for 5 minutes. Lower the heat to medium, add the diluted harissa, caraway, paprika, tomatoes, potatoes, and water, and stir well. Simmer, stirring occasionally, until thickened, about 15 minutes.

Add the eggs to the sausage mixture and stir over medium heat until the eggs have thickened and are creamy, 10 to 15 minutes. Sprinkle with salt and pepper and serve at once.

## *Poached Eggs in Spicy Tomato Sauce*  SHAKSHUKA

The Tunisian *shakshuka* (sometimes spelled *shakshouka*) has been adopted by the Israelis in a big way. Jaffa even boasts a restaurant called Dr. Shakshuka. Whereas in the *ojja* (page 98) the eggs are beaten and mixed in, here whole eggs are poached in the sauce. To reduce the possibility of breaking an egg yolk as the egg is added to the pan, each egg is cracked into a cup and then carefully slid into the simmering sauce. SERVES 4

¼ cup extra virgin olive oil

2 cloves garlic, minced

5 or 6 large ripe tomatoes, peeled, seeded, and diced, or 1½ cups crushed canned tomatoes

2 to 3 tablespoons tomato paste, if needed to enhance tomato flavor

1 tablespoon harissa, homemade (page 355) or store-bought, or more to taste

½ teaspoon ground cumin or caraway (optional)

Salt and freshly ground black pepper

8 eggs

Select a wide, deep sauté pan large enough to accommodate all of the eggs side by side and warm the oil over low heat. Add the garlic and cook for 1 to 2 minutes to flavor the oil. Do not allow the garlic to brown. Add the tomatoes, raise the heat to medium, and cook, stirring occasionally, until they break down and form a sauce, 10 to 15 minutes. Taste the sauce and add some tomato paste if needed to boost the flavor, then stir in the harissa and cumin and season with salt and pepper. Taste again to make sure the sauce is to your liking, as once the eggs are dropped into it, you cannot make seasoning adjustments.

One at a time, crack each egg into a cup or ramekin and slide it into the sauce. Turn down the heat to low and, if you like, partially cover the pan. Cook the eggs until the whites are set and yolks are still soft, 5 to 6 minutes, or until done to your liking. Serve hot, using a large spoon to transfer the unbroken eggs along with sauce to each individual serving plate.

## Summer Squash Frittata  FRITADA DE KALAVASA

Yes, that word is familiar. The Sephardic *fritada* is related in name and style to the better-known Italian frittata. While this version adds bread for thickening, other recipes add mashed potatoes or matzos (during Passover). Still others simply add cheese to firm up the mixture, in the style of the *inchusa* or *almodrote*. To make the nomenclature even more confusing, some recipes call this a *quajado*. And some call for only eggs to bind, as in a classic omelet. I have taken the liberty of adding dill to the basic recipe, as it fits with the flavor profile of another zucchini *almodrote* recipe. Mint would also be a nice contrast. The original Turkish recipe called for peeling the squash, but I don't find it necessary if you salt the squash to remove any bitterness. SERVES 6

2 pounds zucchini or summer squash, grated on the large holes of a box grater (about 6 cups loosely packed)

Salt

2 firm ripe tomatoes, peeled, seeded, and chopped

6 tablespoons chopped fresh flat-leaf parsley

¼ cup chopped fresh dill

4 slices bread, crusts removed, soaked in water, and squeezed dry

6 green onions, including green tops, minced

8 eggs, lightly beaten

½ teaspoon freshly ground black pepper

Plain yogurt for serving

Place the grated zucchini in a colander in the sink, sprinkling it with salt as you go, and let it drain for 30 minutes. Rinse and squeeze dry and transfer to a large bowl. Add the tomatoes, parsley, dill, bread, onions, eggs, 1½ teaspoons salt, and the pepper and mix well.

Preheat the oven to 350°F. Oil a 9-by-12-by-2-inch baking dish and place it in the preheated oven to warm.

Remove the dish from the oven and pour in the egg mixture. Bake the frittata until set and golden, 30 to 40 minutes. Serve warm or at room temperature. Accompany with the yogurt.

## Baked Spinach with Eggs  INCHUSA DE ESPINAKA

This *inchusa* has no potatoes and is thickened with bread (though during Passover, matzo could be used). One recipe I found called for blanching the spinach and gave a choice of potatoes or bread. Another used finely chopped raw spinach. I have found it is best to blanch the spinach and drain it well so that it doesn't give off too much liquid when it is mixed and then baked with the eggs. I know that four pounds of spinach seems like a lot of greens, but it shrinks considerably when it is cooked. SERVES 6 TO 8

4 pounds spinach

8 eggs, lightly beaten

4 slices coarse country bread, crusts removed, soaked in water, and squeezed almost dry

6 tablespoons extra virgin olive oil

½ cup ricotta or soft white cheese, such as fromage blanc

1 cup grated kashkaval cheese

Salt

Freshly grated nutmeg

1 hard-boiled egg, peeled and sliced

Stem the spinach, rinse well, and then place in a large pot with just the rinsing water clinging to the leaves. Cook over medium-low heat until wilted and tender, about 5 minutes. Drain well and chop finely, then transfer to a sieve and press out the excess moisture with the back of a spoon. You should have about 4 cups.

Preheat the oven to 350°F. Oil a 9-by-12-by-2-inch baking dish.

In a bowl, combine the spinach, eggs, bread, oil, and cheeses and mix well. Season with salt and nutmeg. Transfer to the prepared baking dish.

Bake until set, 20 to 30 minutes. Serve hot or warm, cut into squares and topped with slices of hard-boiled egg.

## Persian Spinach and Herb Omelet  KUKU-YE SABZI

How the Persians love mixed greens! They eat them raw with feta and bread, add herbs to their green salads, and take every opportunity to add *sabzi* (greens) to their cooked dishes, including to this simple omelet, which can be cooked on the stove top or in the oven. Some recipes call for adding ⅓ cup chopped walnuts or 1 cup cooked English peas or fresh fava beans to the mixture. SERVES 4 TO 6

4 tablespoons unsalted butter or olive oil

1 cup chopped yellow onion

1 cup chopped leek, white and a little green

1 teaspoon salt

½ cup chopped fresh cilantro

½ cup chopped fresh flat-leaf parsley

½ cup chopped fresh dill

½ teaspoon ground turmeric

½ teaspoon freshly ground black pepper

2 cups chopped spinach

6 to 8 eggs

1½ tablespoons all-purpose flour

Plain yogurt for serving

Warm 2 tablespoons of the butter in a large sauté pan over medium heat. Add the onion and leek, sprinkle with the salt, and cook, stirring occasionally, until they are tender, about 10 minutes. Add the cilantro, parsley, dill, turmeric, and pepper and stir well. Add the spinach and cook, stirring, just until the spinach wilts. Remove from the heat, drain in a sieve if very wet, and then transfer to a large bowl.

In a separate bowl, combine the eggs and flour and beat lightly just until blended. Add the eggs to the spinach mixture and mix well. Warm the remaining 2 tablespoons butter in a large nonstick frying pan over medium heat. Add the egg mixture and cook until the eggs are just set and the sides are golden when gently pulled away from the pan, about 10 minutes. Slide the omelet onto a plate and return it to the pan, browned side up. Continue to cook until the bottom is set and golden. Slide onto a serving plate and serve hot or warm. Pass the yogurt at the table.

## Sephardic Spinach Omelet for Passover    FRITADA DE ESPINAKA

Here is a basic vegetable omelet made with matzo for Passover that can be easily adapted to other vegetables (see variations). SERVES 6

---

2 pounds fresh spinach, stemmed and chopped, or 2 packages (10 ounces each) frozen spinach, thawed

4 matzos, soaked in warm water for 1 to 2 minutes and squeezed dry

8 eggs, lightly beaten

1½ teaspoons salt

½ teaspoon freshly ground black pepper

3 tablespoons olive oil

1 cup grated kashkaval cheese or ricotta or farmer cheese (optional)

---

Preheat the oven to 350°F. Oil a 2-quart or a 9-by-12-by-2-inch baking dish.

In a large bowl, combine the spinach, matzos, eggs, salt, pepper, oil, and cheese and mix well. Spoon the mixture into the prepared baking dish.

Bake the omelet until set, 30 to 45 minutes. Serve hot or warm.

VARIATIONS:   *Leek Passover Omelet (Fritada de Prasa):* Substitute 2 pounds leeks, white parts and a little green, chopped and sautéed in unsalted butter or olive oil until tender, for the spinach.

*Swiss Chard Passover Omelet (Fritada de Pazi):* Substitute 2 pounds Swiss chard, tough stems removed, blanched, and chopped, for the spinach.

*Eggplant Passover Omelet (Fritada de Berenjena):* Substitute 2 large globe eggplants (about 1 pound each), roasted as directed in Master Recipe for Roasted Eggplant (page 27), for the spinach. Drain the eggplant pulp as directed, then mash well.

## Algerian Passover Matzo and Pea Omelet   DJIADJIA TAIRAT

This Passover omelet is cooked in full-flavored meat drippings rather than oil. Chicken fat can be used as well. Garlic and chile make this a lively Mediterranean version of *matzo brei,* the classic Ashkenazi dish of scrambled eggs with matzo.   SERVES 4

5 tablespoons meat drippings, rendered chicken fat, or olive oil

6 to 8 cloves garlic, coarsely chopped

2 cups water

1 teaspoon sweet paprika

1 bay leaf

1 small dried hot chile, crushed, or ½ teaspoon red pepper flakes

1 teaspoon ground caraway or cumin

Salt and freshly ground black pepper

4 matzos, broken into small pieces

1 cup English peas, blanched

6 eggs, lightly beaten

Warm the drippings in a sauté pan over medium heat. Add the garlic and sauté until fragrant and softened, about 2 minutes. Add the water, paprika, bay leaf, chile, and caraway, season with salt and pepper, and bring to a boil over high heat. Add the matzos and the peas and cook until most of the water has been absorbed, about 10 minutes.

Reduce the heat to medium and pour the eggs over the matzo mixture. Using a fork, pull the edge of the omelet away from the pan sides so the uncooked egg will run down the sides. Continue to cook until the omelet is set but still quite moist, 3 to 5 minutes. Slide the omelet onto a plate and serve at once.

## Leek and Potato Gratin   QUAJADO DE PRASA

In the community cookbook from the Sephardic Temple Bikur Holim congregation in Seattle, the word *quajado* is translated as "quiche," which this dish resembles, though minus a crust. As noted earlier, the Arabic word for an earthenware cooking vessel is *qaṣ'ah,* so *quajado* has a logical historical origin. It might also be related to *quesada,* a type of Spanish cheesecake or cheese custard (or to *queijada,* which is Portuguese for "cheesecake"). The same term is used for the bread-based pudding on page 104, as well. This recipe is from Rhodes and is ideal for Passover. I like it rather peppery, and the dill is a nice addition.   SERVES 8

3 pounds leeks (about 12 small, 8 medium, or 4 very large)

4 matzos (optional)

2 cups mashed cooked potatoes

1 cup farmer, cottage, or ricotta cheese

1 cup grated Cheddar, Gruyère, or kashkaval cheese

6 eggs, lightly beaten

¼ cup chopped fresh dill (optional)

2 tablespoons olive oil

2 teaspoons salt

1 teaspoon freshly ground black pepper

Use the white and only a little of the green of the leeks. Halve the leeks lengthwise, then cut crosswise ½ inch thick. You should have about 6 cups. Immerse in a sink filled with cold water, then lift out and drain. Boil the leeks in lightly salted water in a saucepan until very tender, 20 to 30 minutes. Drain well, let cool, and squeeze dry. You should have about 2½ cups. Transfer to a bowl.

Preheat the oven to 350°F. Oil a 9-by-12-by-2-inch baking dish.

If using the matzos, soak in warm water for a minute or two until soft, then squeeze dry. Add the matzos, potatoes, cheeses, eggs, dill, oil, salt, and pepper to the leeks and mix well. Spoon the mixture into the prepared baking dish.

Bake the gratin until set and the top is golden, 35 to 45 minutes. Serve warm, cut into squares.

## Tomato Bread Pudding   QUAJADO DE TOMATE

This recipe is a delectable cross between an omelet and a bread pudding and is one of the joys of the summer tomato season. The term *quajado,* like the term *cuajado* (page 96), is related to the Spanish *cazuela.* In her award-winning book *Traditional Spanish Cooking,* Janet Mendel includes a recipe for *cuajado de almendra,* an almond bread pudding, so the word is still in use in Spain. For this wonderful dish, only full-flavored seasonal tomatoes need apply. SERVES 6 TO 8

3 pounds ripe tomatoes, peeled, seeded and chopped (about 6 cups)

Salt and freshly ground black pepper

Sugar, as needed

4 slices coarse country bread, crusts removed, soaked in water, and squeezed dry

6 to 8 eggs, lightly beaten

4 to 6 tablespoons chopped fresh flat-leaf parsley

8 ounces kashkaval cheese or 4 ounces each Gruyère and Parmesan cheese, grated

Preheat the oven to 350°F. Oil a 9-by-12-by-2-inch baking dish.

Place the tomatoes in a colander in the sink, sprinkling them with salt and a bit of sugar to draw out the excess moisture as you go. Let drain for 1 hour.

Transfer the tomatoes to a bowl and add the bread, eggs, parsley, and all but about ⅓ cup of the cheese. Season with salt and pepper and mix well. Spoon into the prepared baking dish and top with the remaining cheese.

Bake the pudding until golden, about 30 minutes. Serve hot or warm.

## Eggplant Gratin   ALMODROTE DE BERENJENA

The word *almodrote* is of Arabic origin. This recipe appears in nearly every Sephardic cookbook and dates back to Moorish Spain. In medieval Catalonia, *almodroc* referred to a dish with garlic, eggs, and cheese. Somewhere along the way the garlic disappeared, but the cheese and eggs remained. The variables that I find with this recipe have to do with proportions: more or fewer eggplants, more or less cheese, more or fewer eggs. Some recipes include bread as a thickener; others are lighter with no bread at all. If you want to return the garlic to the concept, add a clove or two, well minced, to the mashed eggplant. Some chopped fresh flat-leaf parsley or dill would also be a good addition. SERVES 8

3 large globe eggplants (about 3 pounds total weight)

4 slices coarse country bread, crusts removed, soaked in water, and squeezed dry

8 eggs, lightly beaten

1 cup ricotta or other fresh white cheese, or 6 ounces not-too-salty feta cheese, crumbled

8 ounces kashkaval or Gruyère cheese, grated

5 tablespoons extra virgin olive oil

1½ to 2 teaspoons salt

½ teaspoon freshly ground pepper

Roast the eggplants as directed in Master Recipe for Roasted Eggplant (page 27). After draining the pulp, transfer it to a large bowl. You should have 2 to 2½ cups pulp.

Preheat the oven to 350°F. Oil a 9-by-12-by-2-inch baking dish.

Mash the eggplant well. Add the bread, eggs, ricotta cheese, all but ⅓ cup of the grated cheese, 2 tablespoons of the oil, and the salt and pepper, and mix well. Spoon the mixture into the prepared baking dish, top with the remaining ⅓ cup grated cheese, and drizzle evenly with the remaining 3 tablespoons oil.

Bake the gratin until set and golden, 30 to 40 minutes. Serve hot or warm.

VARIATION:   *Summer Squash Gratin (Almodrote de Kalavasa):* Substitute 2½ to 3 pounds summer squash or zucchini, grated on the large holes of a box grater and squeezed dry, for the eggplant. Proceed as directed, adding ½ cup chopped fresh dill with the eggs, cheese, and bread.

## Lebanese Cauliflower Fritters with Yogurt Dipping Sauce
QARNABEET MAKLI

Although these fritters are delicious on their own, dressed with just a squeeze of lemon, they are even better accompanied with the yogurt sauce included here. Or, if you want to serve the fritters for a meat meal, accompany them with a tahini dip (page 112). SERVES 4 TO 6

**FRITTERS**

1 cauliflower, cut into 1- to 1½-inch florets

4 eggs

¾ cup all-purpose flour

⅓ cup water, plus more if needed

½ cup finely minced yellow onion or green onion, including green tops

½ cup chopped fresh flat-leaf parsley

½ cup chopped fresh mint

½ teaspoon ground cinnamon

½ teaspoon ground cumin

1 teaspoon salt

½ teaspoon freshly ground black pepper

Canola, safflower, or olive oil for deep-frying

**YOGURT DIPPING SAUCE**

2 cups plain Greek yogurt

¼ cup extra virgin olive oil

Grated zest of 1 lemon or 2 small limes

¼ cup fresh lemon or lime juice

Salt

2 teaspoons minced garlic (optional)

2 tablespoons chopped fresh mint, dill, or cilantro (optional)

Lemon wedges for serving

To make the fritters, simmer the cauliflower florets in salted water to cover (or steam over boiling water) until tender, about 8 minutes, then drain well and let cool. You should have 2 cups florets.

To assemble the fritter batter, in a bowl, whisk together the eggs, flour, and water until smooth and creamy and the consistency of crepe or pancake batter, adding a little more water if it is too thick to flow easily off a spoon. (Or, process in a blender or food processor until smooth and transfer to a bowl.) Add the onion, parsley, mint, cinnamon, cumin, salt, and pepper and mix well, then stir in the cauliflower.

Pour the oil to a depth of 3 inches into a deep, heavy saucepan or a deep fryer and heat to 365° to 375°F.

While the oil is heating, make the dipping sauce. In a bowl, whisk together the yogurt, oil, and lemon zest and juice, then season with salt. You can serve as is, or you can whisk in either the garlic or the herb.

When the oil is ready, in batches and using a soupspoon, drop in the batter by the spoonful and fry, turning once, until golden, 3 to 5 minutes. Using a slotted spoon or wire skimmer, transfer the fritters to paper towels to drain. Serve hot, accompanied with the lemon wedges and the dipping sauce.

## Turkish Zucchini Fritters   KABAK MÜCVERİ

Although fritters taste best when they are hot, in Turkey *mücveri* are also served at room temperature as part of the meze course. They could be a side dish for fish, as well, and keep them in mind for Hanukkah. SERVES 8 AS A MEZE, OR 4 AS A SIDE DISH

1 pound zucchini (6 to 8 small), grated on the large holes of a box grater

Salt and freshly ground black pepper

½ cup or more crumbled feta cheese, or part feta and part ricotta, or grated kasseri cheese

6 green onions, including green tops, minced

½ cup chopped fresh dill

¼ cup chopped fresh mint

¼ cup chopped fresh flat-leaf parsley

3 or 4 eggs, lightly beaten

¾ to 1 cup all-purpose flour

Canola, safflower, or olive oil for deep-frying

Plain yogurt for dipping (optional)

Place the grated zucchini in a colander in the sink, sprinkling with salt as you go. Let drain for 30 minutes, then squeeze dry. Transfer to a bowl and add the cheese, green onions, dill, mint, parsley, and 3 eggs and mix well. Stir in the ¾ cup flour and season with salt and pepper. If the mixture seems too wet, add a bit more flour. If it looks too dry, add the remaining egg.

Preheat the oven to 200°F. Line a sheet pan with paper towels. Pour the oil to a depth of about 1 inch into a large sauté pan and heat to 360°F. In batches, drop in 2 to 3 tablespoons batter for each fritter and fry, turning once, until browned on both sides, about 5 minutes total. Using a slotted metal spatula, transfer the fritters to the towel-lined pan and place in the oven to keep warm until all of the fritters are cooked. Serve hot with the yogurt.

VARIATION: *Turkish Carrot Fritters (Havuç Mücveri):* Combine 2 cups firmly packed grated carrots; ½ cup crumbled feta cheese; 4 to 6 green onions, including green tops, chopped; ¼ cup each chopped fresh dill and flat-leaf parsley; 1 teaspoon each ground toasted cumin and coriander; grated zest of 1 lemon; 3 eggs, lightly beaten; and about 1 cup all-purpose flour. Mix well and season with salt and pepper. Fry as directed. You can substitute 2 cups grated butternut squash for the carrots.

## *Sephardic Leek Fritters*   KEFTES DE PRASA

Many Jewish cooks suggest serving leek fritters at Rosh Hashanah. The matzos and matzo meal in the recipe make them a good choice for Passover, as well. And, of course, because they are fried, they would be ideal for Hanukkah. You can't miss serving these fritters at all three holidays! You can also bake this mixture as a gratin. The Leek and Potato Gratin on page 103 is similar to this mixture, with mashed potatoes replacing the matzos or bread. The walnuts are a wonderful addition, adding a pleasant bitterness and a nice crunch. These fritters can be fried ahead of time and held in a 200°F oven for up to 30 minutes. They can also be reheated in a light tomato sauce. MAKES ABOUT 16 FRITTERS; SERVES 6 TO 8

| | |
|---|---|
| 3 pounds leeks (about 12 small, 8 medium, or 4 very large) | Salt |
| 4 matzos or slices coarse country bread | ½ teaspoon freshly ground black pepper |
| 3 eggs, lightly beaten | Matzo meal for coating |
| ½ cup chopped toasted walnuts or pine nuts (optional) | Canola, safflower, or olive oil for deep-frying, plus more if needed for binding |
| ⅓ cup grated Parmesan cheese (optional) | Lemon wedges for serving |

Use the white and only a little of the green of the leeks. Halve the leeks lengthwise, then cut crosswise ½ inch thick. You should have about 6 cups. Immerse in a sink filled with cold water, then lift out and drain. Boil the leeks in lightly salted water in a saucepan until very tender, 20 to 30 minutes. Drain well, let cool, and squeeze dry. You should have about 2½ cups cooked leeks.

If using bread, remove the crusts, then soak the matzos or bread in water until soft and squeeze dry. In a large bowl, combine the leeks, soaked matzos or bread, eggs, walnuts, cheese, 1½ teaspoons salt, and the pepper and mix well. Form the mixture into patties about 2 inches in diameter and ½ to ¾ inch thick. If the mixture seems too moist, add matzo meal as needed to bind along with a pinch of salt.

Preheat the oven to 200°F. Line a sheet pan with paper towels. Pour the oil to a depth of about 1 inch into a large sauté pan and heat to 350°F. While the oil is heating, spread some matzo meal on a plate and dip the patties, one at a time, into the meal, coating both sides and tapping off the excess.

When the oil is hot, in batches, add the patties and fry, turning once, until golden on both sides, 6 to 8 minutes total. Using a slotted metal spatula, transfer the fritters to the towel-lined pan and place in the oven to keep warm until all of the fritters are cooked. Sprinkle with salt and serve piping hot, accompanied with the lemon wedges.

## *Potato Croquettes* CROCCHETTE DI PATATE

This recipe is from Giuseppe Maffioli's *La cucina padovana,* but in a Roman cookbook by Donatella Pavoncello, a similar recipe calls for chicken fat instead of butter. These delicious potato croquettes are traditionally served as an appetizer or as an accompaniment to cooked fish and would be a perfect addition to the Hanukkah table. Similar croquettes are known as *bimuelos de patata* in the Balkans, *keftikes de patata* in Greece, *fritas de patata kon kezo* among Ladino speakers, and *patates topları* in Turkey. The word *toplar* means "cannonball," which describes the shape, not the heft, of the fritters. Unlike their counterparts elsewhere, they are dipped in broken pasta, rather than bread crumbs, before frying. You can also use baked russet potatoes for the croquettes, scooping the cooked flesh from the skins into a ricer or food mill held over a bowl, or scooping it directly into a bowl and then mashing it. SERVES 4 TO 6

| | |
|---|---|
| 1½ pounds boiling potatoes, peeled and quartered | Salt and freshly ground black pepper |
| 2 whole eggs, plus 2 eggs, separated | Freshly grated nutmeg or ground mace |
| 4 tablespoons unsalted butter or rendered chicken fat | Canola, sunflower, or olive oil for deep-frying |
| ¾ cup grated Parmesan cheese | Fine dried bread crumbs for coating |

Place the potatoes in a saucepan with salted water to cover generously, bring to a boil, and cook until tender, 15 to 20 minutes. Drain the potatoes well and, while they are still warm, pass them through a ricer or food mill held over a bowl, or place them in a bowl and mash with a potato masher. Add the whole eggs, egg yolks, butter, and cheese and mix well. Season generously with salt, pepper, and nutmeg. Shape the mixture into ovals about the length of your thumb (about 3 inches long) and about 1 inch thick.

Preheat the oven to 200°F. Line a sheet pan with paper towels. Pour the oil to a depth of 3 inches into a deep, heavy saucepan or a deep fryer and heat to 375°F. Meanwhile, in a bowl, beat the egg whites until soft peaks form. Spread the bread crumbs on a plate.

When the oil is ready, dip the croquettes, one at a time, first into the beaten egg whites and then into the crumbs, coating evenly and tapping off the excess. In batches, slip them into the hot oil and fry until golden, about 5 minutes. Using a slotted spoon or wire skimmer, transfer the croquettes to the towel-lined pan to drain and place in the oven to keep warm until all of them are cooked. Serve hot.

## Salt Cod Fritters  FRITTELLE DI BACCALÀ

Versions of this recipe, also known as *cotolette di baccalà,* appear in Giuliana Ascoli Vitali-Norsa's *La cucina nella tradizione ebraica* and in the second volume of Edda Servi Machlin's *The Classic Cuisine of the Italian Jews.* The fritters are held together with eggs and softened bread, unlike Spanish *buñuelos* and Portuguese *pastéis,* which are bound with potatoes. If you are not sure of the quality of the salt cod, cook it as directed, pick through it for the whitest and most tender pieces, and discard the rest. You can also omit the coating of beaten egg and bread crumbs and spoon the mixture into the hot oil as if making pancakes. SERVES 8

1 pound salt cod fillet

2 cups water, or 1 cup each water and milk, or as needed

3 slices day-old coarse country bread, 1 inch thick, crusts removed, soaked in water, and squeezed dry

4 olive oil–packed anchovy fillets, finely chopped

¼ cup chopped fresh flat-leaf parsley

3 tablespoons grated Parmesan cheese

Pinch of cayenne pepper, or few grinds freshly ground black pepper

2 to 3 eggs, plus 1 egg for coating

Salt

All-purpose flour for binding, if needed

Fine dried bread crumbs for coating

Olive oil for frying

Lemon wedges or garlic mayonnaise (page 231) for serving

Place the cod in a bowl with cold water to cover and refrigerate for 24 to 36 hours, changing the water three times. Drain, transfer to a saucepan, add the water, and bring to a simmer over medium heat. Turn down the heat to low and simmer gently until the cod is very tender, 10 to 20 minutes. The timing will depend on the thickness of the fillet. Drain the cod, let cool, then flake with a fork or your fingers, removing and discarding any tough pieces or errant bones. Transfer the cod to a food processor and pulse until very finely chopped.

In a bowl, combine the cod, bread, anchovies, parsley, cheese, cayenne, and 2 of the eggs and mix well. Fry a small patty of the mixture in a little oil and taste to check the seasoning and texture. Adjust the seasoning with salt and cayenne if needed. The mixture may also need another egg or a bit of flour to bind it.

Line 1 or 2 sheet pans with parchment paper. Spread the bread crumbs on a plate. Lightly beat the egg for coating in a shallow bowl. Shape the cod mixture into small balls or flattened cakes. Dip each fritter in the beaten egg and then coat with the bread crumbs, tapping off the excess. As the fritters are coated, place them on the sheet pan(s).

Preheat the oven to 200°F. Line 1 or 2 sheet pans with paper towels. Pour the oil to a depth of ½ inch into a large, deep sauté pan and heat over medium-high heat. When the oil is hot, in batches, add the fritters and fry, turning once, until golden on both sides, about 6 minutes total. Using a slotted spatula, transfer the fritters to a towel-lined pan to drain and place in the oven to keep warm until all of them are cooked. Serve hot, accompanied with the lemon wedges.

## *Chickpea Croquettes*  FALAFEL

Falafel originated in Egypt, but today these croquettes are also popular street food in Lebanon, Syria, and Israel. Tuck these crunchy spheres into warm pita bread along with chopped tomato and cucumber and add a good drizzle of tahini sauce. Most recipes call for soaking the chickpeas overnight but do not cook them. Others instruct to cook them briefly until they have softened a bit. MAKES ABOUT 16 CROQUETTES, OR 8 SANDWICHES

CROQUETTES

1 cup dried chickpeas

1 small yellow onion, minced

4 cloves garlic, finely minced

1 slice coarse country bread, crust removed and crumbled

1 egg, lightly beaten

¼ cup chopped fresh flat-leaf parsley

½ teaspoon freshly ground black pepper

½ teaspoon cayenne pepper, or 1 teaspoon Aleppo pepper flakes

1 teaspoon ground toasted cumin

½ teaspoon ground turmeric

2 tablespoons all-purpose flour, plus more for coating

1 teaspoon baking soda

Salt

Canola, sunflower, or olive oil for deep-frying

8 small rounds pita bread, warmed (see note, page 28) and halved crosswise

Chopped tomato and cucumber (½-inch dice) for serving

Tahini sauce for serving (recipe follows)

Pick over the chickpeas, then place in a bowl, add water to cover, and let soak in the refrigerator overnight. Drain and rinse well. You should have about 2 cups soaked chickpeas. Although it is not traditional, at this point, you can simmer the chickpeas in water to cover for about 15 minutes to soften them a bit, then drain well. This step makes the falafel texture a bit less granular.

Pass the chickpeas and onion through a meat grinder fitted with the coarse blade into a bowl. Add the garlic, bread, egg, parsley, black and cayenne peppers, cumin, turmeric, flour, and baking soda and mix well, adding a little water as needed to bind the mixture. Season with salt. Alternatively, in a food processor, pulse the chickpeas and onion until coarsely ground. Add the garlic, bread, egg, parsley, black and cayenne peppers, cumin, turmeric, flour, and baking soda and pulse until well mixed, adding a little water as needed to bind the mixture. Transfer to a bowl and season with salt.

Line a sheet pan with parchment paper. Shape the chickpea mixture into balls 1½ inches in diameter, flatten each ball slightly between your palms, and set aside on the prepared pan.

Preheat the oven to 200°F. Line a sheet pan with paper towels and a second sheet pan with parchment paper. Pour the oil to a depth of 3 inches into a deep, heavy saucepan or a deep fryer and heat to 365°F. Spread the flour on a plate. One at a time, coat the croquettes with the flour, tapping off the excess, and set aside on the parchment-lined pan.

When the oil is hot, in batches, add the croquettes to the oil and fry until golden and crunchy on both sides, 3 to 5 minutes. Using a slotted spoon or wire skimmer, transfer the croquettes to the towel-lined pan to drain and place in the oven to keep warm until all of the croquettes are cooked.

To serve, push a finger gently into each pita half to open the pocket. Spoon about 2 tablespoons each tomato and cucumber into each pocket, add some tahini sauce, and then insert a croquette. Spoon in a little more sauce, if you like. Serve right away.

EGYPTIAN VARIATION: Increase the onion to 2 onions and the garlic to 10 cloves and add ½ cup each chopped fresh cilantro and dill to the mixture.

## Tahini Sauce or Dip

Sauces and dips made from tahini are popular everywhere from North Africa and Iran to Turkey and Greece. This versatile recipe pairs well with fritters, roasted vegetables, and other dishes. MAKES ABOUT 1¼ CUPS SAUCE OR ¾ TO 1 CUP DIP

---

½ cup tahini, stirred well before use

¼ cup fresh lemon juice

1 to 2 cloves garlic, finely minced

½ cup water, or more as needed

Salt and freshly ground black pepper

Pinch of cayenne pepper (optional)

½ teaspoon ground toasted cumin (optional)

Chopped fresh flat-leaf parsley for garnish, if making a dip

---

In a blender or food processor, combine the tahini, lemon juice, and garlic and process until smooth. To use as a dressing, add the water and process until you have a good salad dressing consistency, adding more water as needed. Transfer to a bowl and season with salt, black and cayenne peppers, and cumin. To use as a dip, make as directed but use less water for a thicker consistency. Transfer to a bowl, season as directed, and either sprinkle with the parsley or stir in the parsley.

## Polenta and Anchovy Fritters    REBECCHINE DI GERUSALEMME

Versions of these anchovy-filled polenta sandwiches appear in almost every book on the cuisine of Italian Jews. The name suggests that these fritters were popular in Jerusalem, though I doubt they were ever served there. Instead, the name Gerusalemme, like the name Rebecca, or in this case the diminutive Rebecchine, indicates a Jewish origin. Today in Trieste, which was once home to a sizable Jewish population, the term *rebecchini* is still used to refer to a snack served at midmorning. SERVES 6 TO 8

| | |
|---|---|
| 1 cup polenta | 2 tablespoons olive oil |
| 4 cups water | Canola, safflower, or olive oil for deep-frying |
| 1 teaspoon salt | |
| ¼ pound salt-packed anchovies (about 12 anchovies) | 1 to 2 eggs |
| | All-purpose flour for dusting |

Combine the polenta, water, and teaspoon salt in a heavy saucepan and place over medium-high heat. Bring to a boil, whisking occasionally. Turn down the heat to a simmer and cook, stirring often, until very thick and no longer grainy on the tongue, about 30 minutes. If the polenta thickens too quickly but still feels undercooked and grainy, stir in some hot water and continue to cook until it is cooked through and soft. Taste and adjust the seasoning with salt.

Butter or oil a 9-by-12-by-2-inch baking pan, pour the hot polenta into the pan, let cool until just set, and then cover with plastic wrap and refrigerate until chilled and fully set.

Fillet and rinse the anchovies and then chop coarsely. Put them in a sauté pan with the olive oil, place over low heat, and cook, stirring often with a fork, until they soften and melt, about 5 minutes. It is imperative that they do not burn. Remove from the heat.

Using a 2½- to 3-inch cookie or biscuit cutter or an overturned glass, cut the chilled polenta into rounds. Spread half of the rounds with the anchovy purée, then top them with the remaining rounds.

Preheat the oven to 200°F. Line a sheet pan with paper towels. Pour the canola oil to a depth of 3 inches into a deep, heavy saucepan or a deep fryer and heat to 375°F. Meanwhile, break 1 egg into a shallow bowl and beat until blended (add the second egg later if needed). Spread the flour on a plate.

One at a time, dip the polenta sandwiches into the beaten egg and then into the flour, tapping off the excess flour (some cooks reverse the order, dipping them first in flour and then in egg) and slip them into the hot oil, being careful not to crowd the pan. Fry, turning once, until golden, about 4 minutes total. Using a slotted spoon or wire skimmer, transfer the sandwiches to the towel-lined pan to drain and keep warm in the oven until all of the sandwiches are cooked. Serve warm.

VARIATION: If you don't like anchovies, omit them, cut the chilled polenta into fingers, dredge the fingers lightly in flour, and deep-fry them as directed. Or, place a slice of Fontina or mozzarella cheese between each pair of polenta rounds, dip the sandwiches in egg and then flour, and deep-fry as directed.

Soups

IN THE SEPHARDIC AND MEDITERRANEAN JEWISH KITCHENS, soup was such an everyday affair that recipes were rarely commemorated in text. Many soups call for legumes and meat or vegetables, the better to fill you up. Cooks often made use of leftover bits and pieces of meat and poultry, too, which sometimes turned the dish into a complete meal.

In this chapter, you will find bean and lentil soups, vegetable soups and vegetable purées, and simple broths enriched with rice or matzo and sometimes embellished with beef or chicken meatballs or thickened with egg and lemon. Many of these recipes are easy to assemble, often requiring little more than a long simmer on the stove top, and all are highly satisfying at the table.

## Soup with Chickpeas, Pumpkin, and Cilantro
SOUPE AUX POIS CHICHES, LA COURGE ROUGE, ET CORIANDRE

You will find numerous versions of this hearty classic in Moroccan and Tunisian Jewish kitchens. Some cooks use dried favas or white beans instead of chickpeas, some omit the greens, and still others add bits of cooked meat. This is a stick-to-your-ribs dish and is a full meal when paired with bread or a salad. SERVES 6 TO 8

2¼ cups (1 pound) dried chickpeas

1 large or 2 medium yellow onions, chopped

1 carrot, peeled and chopped

2 pounds butternut squash or pumpkin, peeled, seeded, and cut into 1-inch cubes

6 to 8 cups vegetable or chicken broth or water, plus more if needed

¼ cup chopped fresh cilantro

1 to 2 bunches Swiss chard, stemmed and leaves cut into narrow strips

½ teaspoon ground cinnamon

Salt and freshly ground black pepper

Sugar, if needed

Pick over the chickpeas, then place in a bowl, add water to cover, and let soak in the refrigerator overnight. Drain, rinse well, and transfer to a soup pot. Add the onions, carrot, squash, broth to cover, and half of the cilantro and bring to a boil over high heat. Turn down the heat to low, cover, and simmer until the chickpeas and squash are tender, 45 to 60 minutes. Remove from the heat, pass the contents of the pot through a food mill, and return the purée to the pot.

In a saucepan, combine the chard and a little water over medium heat and cook until wilted and tender, about 5 minutes. Drain well and add to the puréed soup.

Reheat the soup over medium-low heat, adding water if needed to thin to a good consistency and stirring often to prevent scorching. Add the cinnamon and season with salt and pepper and with a little sugar to pick up on the sweetness of the squash if needed. Serve hot, sprinkled with the remaining cilantro.

## *Syrian Lentil Soup*    SHOURABA IL ADDIS

Syrian and Lebanese Jews like lentil soup with wilted greens and a squeeze of lemon juice. The soup is typically made with lamb broth or water and seasoned with cinnamon or cumin and is occasionally enriched with rice or noodles. Sometimes a stalk or two of chopped rhubarb or a few tablespoons of pomegranate molasses are used in place of, or in addition to, the lemon juice.  SERVES 6

| | |
|---|---|
| 5 tablespoons olive oil | 2 cloves garlic, minced (optional) |
| 1 large yellow onion, chopped (about 1½ cups) | 2 small stalks rhubarb, cut into ½-inch pieces (optional) |
| 1 carrot, peeled and chopped | 1 teaspoon ground cumin |
| 1 rib celery with leaves, chopped | 1 teaspoon ground coriander |
| 1⅓ cups (12 ounces) green or brown lentils, picked over and rinsed | Generous pinch of ground allspice or cinnamon |
| 8 cups lamb broth or water | 2 tablespoons fresh lemon juice |
| 1 bunch spinach or Swiss chard | Salt and freshly ground black pepper |

Warm 3 tablespoons of the oil in a heavy saucepan over medium heat. Add the onion, carrot, and celery and cook, stirring occasionally, until tender and pale gold, 8 to 10 minutes. Add the lentils and broth and bring to a boil. Turn down the heat to low, cover, and simmer until the lentils are very soft, about 45 minutes.

While the lentils are cooking, rinse the spinach or chard. If using chard, separate the leaves and stems, and if using spinach, discard the stems. Cut the spinach or chard and chard stems into narrow strips. Warm the remaining 2 tablespoons oil in a large sauté pan over medium heat. Add the garlic, rhubarb, cumin, coriander, allspice, and the spinach or chard with just the rinsing water clinging to the leaves and stir to mix well. Turn down the heat to low and cook, stirring occasionally, until the greens wilt, 8 to 10 minutes. Remove from the heat.

When the lentils are tender, add the seasoned greens and simmer over low heat for 10 to 15 minutes to combine the flavors. Season the soup with the lemon juice, salt, and pepper. Serve hot.

## Moroccan Fava or Lentil Soup   BESSARA

In the Moroccan cities of Fez and Meknes, fava and lentil soups are served during Passover and also at times of mourning. Both legumes are used to make this simple yet flavorful soup known as *bessara,* which is also the name of a bean purée served as a dip with pita bread. Some cooks garnish the soup with strips of barely cooked celery for a contrasting crunch, while others simmer pieces of cooked beef or lamb sausage along with the beans for a more filling soup. SERVES 6

---

1 pound dried fava beans or green lentils (about 1¾ cups lentils or 3 cups favas)

2 large cloves garlic, halved lengthwise and any green sprouts removed

1 tablespoon sweet paprika

2 teaspoons ground toasted cumin

½ teaspoon ground turmeric (optional)

Salt

½ teaspoon freshly ground black pepper

½ cup tomato purée (optional)

1 bunch fresh cilantro, chopped (about ⅓ cup)

Fried croutons, fried onions, or chopped fresh mint for garnish

---

If using fava beans, pick over the beans, then place in a bowl, add water to cover, and let soak overnight. Drain and rinse well. If using unpeeled favas, rub the beans with your fingers to remove the wrinkly skins. If using lentils, pick over and rinse well.

In a saucepan, combine the favas or lentils, garlic, and water to cover by 3 inches and bring to a boil over high heat. Turn down the heat to low and simmer until tender, 45 to 60 minutes for the favas and 30 to 40 minutes for the lentils. Midway through the cooking, add the paprika, cumin, turmeric, salt to taste, and pepper and then stir in the tomato purée, mixing well. Discard the garlic or mash it into the soup.

Continue to simmer as directed until the beans or lentils are tender, stirring in the cilantro during the last few minutes. Serve hot, garnished with the croutons.

# Persian Yogurt Soup with Chickpeas, Lentils, and Spinach

ASH-E MAST

This creamy soup starts with yogurt stabilized with egg and flour to prevent it from breaking. Usually the legumes, rice, and broth are added at the same time and cooked in the soup. Because I am a fiend for texture, I cook the chickpeas, lentils, and rice separately, as their cooking times are different, and then add them at the same time and cook them briefly to blend their flavors. Never let the soup boil or the yogurt will curdle. The jewel-like pomegranate seeds, the yellow turmeric tint to the yogurt, and the green of the herbs and spinach make this soup visually a stunner. SERVES 6

½ cup dried chickpeas

½ cup green lentils

½ cup basmati rice, rinsed, soaked in water to cover for 1 hour, and drained

5 cups vegetable broth or water, or as needed

3 to 4 cups plain Greek yogurt

1 egg, lightly beaten

2 tablespoons all-purpose flour

½ teaspoon ground turmeric

½ teaspoon ground cinnamon

¼ cup chopped fresh flat-leaf parsley

¼ cups chopped green onions, including green tops

1 pound spinach, stemmed and chopped

5 tablespoons chopped fresh mint

2 tablespoons unsalted butter

2 cloves garlic, finely minced

Salt and freshly ground black pepper

Pomegranate seeds for garnish

Pick over the chickpeas, then place in a bowl, add water to cover, and let soak in the refrigerator overnight. Drain, rinse well, and transfer to a saucepan. Add water to cover by 3 inches and bring to a boil. Turn down the heat to low and simmer until tender, 45 to 60 minutes. Pick over and rinse the lentils, then transfer to a saucepan, add water to cover by 2 to 3 inches, and cook until tender but still slightly firm, 25 to 35 minutes. Drain the chickpeas and lentils and set aside. Cook the rice in 2 cups of the broth or water until the rice is tender but still slightly firm, 10 to 12 minutes. If the rice is ready and there is liquid left in the pan, do not drain the liquid off.

Spoon the yogurt into a large saucepan, using the larger amount if you prefer a creamier soup. Add the egg, flour, turmeric, and cinnamon and whisk together until smooth. Add the rice and the remaining 3 cups broth and bring to a simmer over medium-low heat, stirring occasionally. Add the cooked chickpeas and lentils, parsley, green onions, spinach, and 3 tablespoons of the mint, stir well, and simmer gently, stirring occasionally, for 10 to 15 minutes to blend the flavors. Add more broth if the soup is too thick.

Meanwhile, in a small sauté pan, melt the butter over low heat. Add the garlic and sauté until soft but not colored, 1 to 2 minutes. When the soup is ready, add the garlic to the soup, taste and adjust the seasoning with salt and pepper, and sprinkle with the remaining 2 tablespoons mint. Serve hot, garnished with the pomegranate seeds.

## *Chickpea and Spinach Soup*   SOPA DE GARVANSOS KON ESPINAKA

Spanish Christians adopted this classic Sephardic soup of chickpeas and spinach after the Inquisition and embellished it with ham or, during Lent, with salt cod. I have taken the liberty of enriching it with a Spanish *picada,* a mixture of fried bread and garlic, to thicken the broth. If you prefer it soupier, you can thin it with broth or water after adding the *picada.*

The Portuguese prepare a similar soup called *sopa de grão com espinafres,* but it does not include a *picada* for thickening. Instead, it is thickened by puréeing half of the cooked chickpeas and then returning the purée to the pot. The soup is garnished with chopped cilantro. SERVES 6 TO 8

---

2 cups (14 ounces) dried chickpeas

7 cloves garlic, peeled and left whole

2 yellow onions, peeled and left whole

1 bay leaf

Salt

1½ pounds spinach, stemmed, rinsed, and coarsely chopped (5 to 6 cups)

3 tablespoons olive oil

2 slices coarse country bread, crusts removed

Pinch of saffron threads

Vegetable broth or water, if needed

Freshly ground black pepper

8 ounces salt cod fillet, soaked in water for 24 to 36 hours in the refrigerator, changing the water three times, then cooked and broken up into bite-size pieces (optional)

2 hard-boiled eggs, peeled and chopped

---

Pick over the chickpeas, then place in a bowl, add water to cover, and let soak in the refrigerator overnight. Drain, rinse well, transfer to a soup pot, and add water to cover by 3 inches, 4 of the garlic cloves, the onions, and the bay leaf. Bring to a boil over high heat, turn down the heat to low, and simmer until tender, 45 to 60 minutes. Add 2 teaspoons salt after the first 15 minutes of cooking.

When the chickpeas are tender, remove from the heat, then remove and reserve the onions and garlic and remove and discard the bay leaf. Pour off 1 cup of the cooking liquid and reserve. Leave the remaining liquid in the pot with the chickpeas.

Put the spinach in a large saucepan with only the rinsing water clinging to the leaves, place over medium-low heat, and cook until wilted and tender, 3 to 4 minutes. Drain well and set aside.

To make the picada, warm the oil in a small sauté pan over medium heat. Add the bread and the remaining 3 garlic cloves and fry, turning as needed, until the bread is golden on both sides, about 5 minutes total. Break up the bread, add the bread, garlic, and saffron to a blender or food processor, and process until smooth. Add the reserved cooked onions and garlic cloves and the reserved 1 cup cooking liquid and purée until smooth.

Add the purée and the spinach to the pot holding the chickpeas, stir well, and bring to a simmer over medium heat. If the mixture is too thick, thin with the broth as needed. Season to taste with salt and with lots of pepper. Add the salt cod and warm through. Serve hot, garnished with the eggs.

## *Red Lentil Soup*   SOPA DE LENTEJA KOLORADA

When served during the nine days of Tisha B'Av, this Sephardic lentil soup is traditionally accompanied with *boyos de kezo* (page 69) or other small cheese pastries for a complete meal. But you don't need a holiday to serve this soup. The original Sephardic recipe is rather plain, so I like to add a little ground cumin, a small pinch of hot pepper, and some lemon juice to brighten it. You have other options, as well. Greek Jews pass oil and vinegar at the table for diners to add as they wish. At a dairy meal, Turkish Jews might thin the soup with milk and garnish it with croutons and mint, or they might finish it with hot melted butter, Aleppo pepper flakes, and dried mint. Syrian Jews ladle the soup over a spoonful of cooked rice placed in the bottom of each bowl and set out a plate of lemon wedges. SERVES 6

---

1½ cups red lentils

¼ cup olive oil

2 yellow onions, chopped

3 ribs celery, chopped

4 carrots, peeled and chopped

1 to 2 ripe tomatoes, peeled, seeded, and finely chopped, or
2 tablespoon tomato paste (optional)

½ cup chopped fresh flat-leaf parsley

1 bay leaf

8 cups water

2 teaspoons salt

1 to 2 teaspoons ground toasted cumin

1 to 2 pinches of Aleppo or Maras pepper flakes

Freshly ground black pepper

Fresh lemon juice for seasoning

---

Pick over the lentils, then place in a bowl, add water to cover, and let soak for a few hours. Drain and rinse well.

Warm the oil in a large saucepan over medium heat. Add the onions and cook, stirring occasionally, until translucent and tender, 8 to 10 minutes. Add the celery, carrots, tomatoes, lentils, parsley, bay leaf, and water and bring to a boil. Turn down the heat to low, cover, and simmer until the lentils are tender, about 1 hour.

Remove and discard the bay leaf. Add the salt and the cumin, pepper flakes, black pepper, and lemon juice to taste. Serve hot.

## Lentil Soup with Meatballs   MINESTRA DI ESAU

In Italy, Esau's biblical "mess of pottage" is a delicious lentil soup enriched with little meatballs. You can use brown or green lentils. The brown variety is more readily available and cooks and breaks down more quickly, but if you want the lentils to hold their texture, use green lentils from Italy, France, or Spain.   SERVES 8

2 cups (about 1 pound) green or brown lentils, picked over and rinsed

3 large yellow onions, finely chopped

2 carrots, peeled and finely chopped

2 ribs celery, finely chopped

1 cup tomato purée or sauce

⅓ cup chopped fresh flat-leaf parsley

1 pound ground beef (not too lean)

Salt and freshly ground black pepper

5 tablespoons rendered chicken or goose fat or margarine

In a large saucepan, combine the lentils, onions, carrots, celery, tomato purée, parsley, and water to cover by about 2 inches and bring to a boil over high heat. Turn down the heat to medium-low, cover, and cook until the lentils are firm-tender, about 25 minutes.

Meanwhile, season the beef with salt and pepper and shape into marble-size meatballs. Melt the fat in a large sauté pan over medium-high heat. Add the meatballs and brown on all sides, 3 to 5 minutes. Remove from the heat. The meatballs should still be raw in the center.

When the lentils are ready, add the meatballs and the fat from the pan to the soup and simmer until the lentils are tender and the meatballs are cooked through, 15 to 20 minutes longer. Season with salt and pepper and serve hot.

ROMAN VARIATION: Roman cooks insert a tiny piece of beef marrow into the center of each meatball; simmer the meatballs in meat broth until cooked through, about 15 minutes; and then add them and their broth to the finished lentil soup and simmer for 5 minutes to meld the flavors.

## Venetian Bean Soup with Pasta and Meatballs
PASTA E FAGIOLI ALLA VENETA

Here's a Venetian version of *pasta e fagioli*, called *fasoi co la luganega* in dialect, that calls for fresh pasta and for homemade beef sausage shaped into meatballs. It is an interpretation of a recipe in *La cucina nella tradizione ebraica* and is a wonderfully homey and filling bean soup that can be a meal-in-a-bowl. If you like, add 2 cups chopped cooked Swiss chard, escarole, or frisée during the last 10 minutes of cooking.  SERVES 6 TO 8

1¾ cups (about 14 ounces) dried borlotti or white beans, picked over and rinsed

7 tablespoons extra virgin olive oil

2 yellow onions, finely chopped

2 ribs celery, finely chopped

2 carrots, peeled and finely chopped

Beef Sausage (page 350)

12 ounces fresh fettuccine, cut into maltagliati (irregular 1½-inch pieces)

About 2 cups meat broth

1 tablespoon salt

1 teaspoon freshly ground black pepper

Place the beans in a saucepan with cold water to cover generously and bring to a boil. Boil for 2 minutes. Remove from the heat, cover, and let stand for 1 hour. Drain the beans well, return them to the pan, add fresh water to cover, and again bring to a boil.

While the beans are heating, warm 4 tablespoons of the oil in a sauté pan over medium heat. Add the onions, celery, and carrots and cook, stirring occasionally, until softened, about 10 minutes. Add the vegetables and oil to the beans, return the beans to a boil, turn down the heat to low, cover, and simmer until the beans are very tender, about 1½ hours.

Meanwhile, make the sausage mixture, shape into tiny meatballs about ¾ inch in diameter, and cover and refrigerate until needed.

When the beans are ready, remove them from the heat. Scoop out and reserve about 2 cups beans. Let the remaining beans cool slightly; then, in batches, transfer them to a blender or food processor and process until smooth. Transfer the purée, the reserved whole beans, and any cooking liquid to a large saucepan and bring to a boil. If the mixture is too thick, thin with hot water.

While the soup is reheating, cook the pasta in boiling water until al dente, then drain. At the same time, in a saucepan, bring the broth to a gentle boil over medium heat, add the meatballs, and poach until cooked through, about 15 minutes. Add the pasta, the meatballs and their broth, and the salt and pepper to the soup and simmer gently for 10 minutes to blend the flavors, stirring with a wooden spoon to prevent scorching. If the soup begins to thicken too much, add a little hot water from time to time.

Just before serving, taste and adjust the seasoning. Ladle into bowls, drizzle with the remaining 3 tablespoons oil, and finish with a grind of pepper.

## White Bean Soup   SOPA DE AVIKAS

A soupy version of a classic one-pot Spanish Sabbath dish, this recipe from Salonika uses beef and white beans and is part of the *cocido* (stew) or *adafina* (bean-and-meat stew) tradition. It can be quite thick and stew-like or thinned and served as a filling soup. After the Inquisition, pork was substituted for beef in the recipe as a test for conversos. If they would not eat it, it was obvious that they had not converted. The Greeks serve this soup with lemon wedges, as the acidity cuts the richness. I sometimes add a pinch of ground cinnamon with the tomatoes. SERVES 6

1 pound stewing beef, chuck, or meat from the shank or brisket, cut into 1-inch pieces

1 cup dried white beans, picked over, rinsed, and soaked in water to cover overnight

3 tablespoons olive oil

2 yellow onions, chopped

3 cloves garlic, minced

3 large ripe tomatoes, peeled, seeded, and chopped, or 3 cups drained, seeded, and chopped canned tomatoes

¼ cup chopped fresh flat-leaf parsley

Salt and freshly ground black pepper

Lemon wedges for finishing (optional)

In a saucepan, combine the beef with water to cover and bring to a boil over high heat. Cook, skimming off any scum that forms on the surface, for 10 minutes. Turn down the heat to low, cover, and simmer until the meat is cooked through and starting to soften, 30 to 40 minutes.

Drain the beans, transfer to a saucepan, and add water to cover. Bring to a boil and cook for 15 minutes, then drain and add to the meat.

Warm the oil in a sauté pan over medium heat. Add the onions and cook, stirring occasionally, until translucent and tender, 8 to 10 minutes. Add the garlic and tomatoes and cook until the tomatoes break down and form a sauce, about 10 minutes. Add the tomato mixture to the beans and meat, stir well, cover, and simmer over low heat until the meat and beans are tender, 45 to 60 minutes.

If you like, thin the soup with water, then stir in the parsley and season with salt and pepper. Ladle into bowls and finish with a squeeze of lemon juice.

## Lemony Bean and Rice Soup for Yom Kippur HARIRA DE KIPPOUR

*Harira,* also spelled *h'rira* and *h'riba,* is the traditional Moroccan soup served by Muslims and Jews alike to break a fast, whether it be Ramadan or Yom Kippur. The variables are the amount of lentils, chickpeas, and rice or pasta and the choice of beef, lamb, or chicken. The soup is thickened at the end with flour and its flavor is brightened with lemon juice. Some versions call for eggs mixed with lemon juice for thickening rather than flour. In Morocco, the fast is ended with a bite of a sweet date and then the soup. Although you can put all of the ingredients into the pot and cook them together, I like to prepare the chickpeas and lentils separately to control their texture. Dried fava beans (look for peeled ones) can be used in place of the chickpeas. SERVES 8

1 cup dried chickpeas

Salt and freshly ground black pepper

3 to 4 tablespoons olive oil

8 ounces beef or lamb shank meat, cut into ½-inch pieces

2 yellow onions, chopped

2 ribs celery, chopped

1 teaspoon ground cinnamon

½ teaspoon ground turmeric

½ teaspoon ground ginger

¼ teaspoon saffron threads, steeped in 2 tablespoons hot water

3 cups water

1½ cups brown lentils, picked over and rinsed

½ cup white rice, orzo, pastina, or broken spaghetti

4 tomatoes, peeled, seeded, and chopped (fresh or canned)

1 bunch fresh cilantro, chopped (about ⅓ cup)

1 bunch fresh flat-leaf parsley, chopped, (about ⅓ cup)

2 tablespoons all-purpose flour, dissolved in ¼ cup water (optional)

Juice of 1 or 2 lemons

Pick over the chickpeas, then place in a bowl, add water to cover, and let soak in the refrigerator overnight. Drain, rinse well, and transfer to a 1-quart saucepan. Add water to cover by 3 inches and bring to a boil over high heat. Turn down the heat to low, cover, and simmer until tender but not falling apart, about 1 hour. Remove from the heat, salt lightly, and set aside. You should have about 1½ cups beans and not too much liquid.

While the chickpeas are cooking, warm the oil in a large sauté pan over high heat. Add the meat and brown on all sides. Add the onions, celery, cinnamon, turmeric, ginger, and saffron infusion and stir for 1 minute. Add water to cover and simmer over low heat for 30 minutes.

Meanwhile, in a 3-quart soup pot, bring the water to a boil over high heat. Add the lentils, turn down the heat to medium-low, and simmer for 20 minutes, then add the rice and cook for 10 minutes longer.

Transfer the meat and onion mixture and its cooking juices to the lentils, then add the cooked chickpeas, tomatoes, and half each of the cilantro and parsley. Simmer gently, uncovered, until the rice is tender, about 15 minutes longer. If you want to thicken the soup, gradually stir in the flour paste and then whisk continuously over low heat until absorbed. Add the lemon juice and the rest of the cilantro and parsley and season to taste with salt and with lots of pepper. (The soup should be peppery.) Ladle into bowls and serve hot.

## Rosh Hashanah Seven-Vegetable Soup  SOPA DE LA SIETE VERDURAS

In *Marrakech la Rouge,* Hélène Gans Perez reminisces about the *soupe aux sept légumes* that was part of her family's Rosh Hashanah tradition. The seven vegetables are onion, pumpkin, gourd, zucchini, Swiss chard, chickpeas, and quince. I could not get over how closely it resembles the Andalusian soup called *olla gitana,* or "gypsy stew," which uses pears instead of quinces. I suspect that the gypsy title was added after the Inquisition to conceal the soup's Jewish origin. The recipe has remained in the culinary pipeline. Today in Spain, ham is added to flavor the broth, but before the Inquisition, the soup was most likely made with beef. If you cannot find a vegetable marrow (large summer squash), turnip or rutabaga would be a good substitute. You can add diced cooked brisket to the basic vegetable soup for a more filling dish. In Tétouan, Moroccan cooks add greens along with the pumpkin and use white beans instead of chickpeas. SERVES 6 TO 8

---

⅔ cup dried chickpeas

3 yellow onions, chopped

8 cups beef or vegetable broth

2 pounds pumpkin or butternut squash, peeled and seeded

3 zucchini

1 small vegetable marrow

2 apples, quinces, or pears, peeled, cored, and diced

1 bunch Swiss chard, stemmed and greens cut into strips

1 teaspoon freshly ground black pepper

1 teaspoon ground cumin (optional)

½ teaspoon ground cinnamon

Salt

Sugar, if needed

---

Pick over the chickpeas, then place in a bowl, add water to cover, and let soak in the refrigerator overnight. Drain, rinse well, and transfer to a saucepan. Add the onions and broth and bring to a boil over high heat. Turn down the heat to low, and simmer until the chickpeas are almost tender, about 45 minutes.

Meanwhile, cut the pumpkin, zucchini, marrow, and apples into rounds, quarter rounds, or large dice, depending on their size and shape. When the chickpeas are ready, add the freshly cut vegetables, the apples, and the chard to the pan and season with the pepper, cumin, cinnamon, and salt. Simmer until the vegetables and chickpeas are tender, 25 to 30 minutes. Taste and adjust the seasoning with salt and spices and add a little sugar to balance the flavors if needed. Serve hot.

## Meat and Vegetable Soup with Plums, Georgian Style  MIJAVYANI

I discovered this deliciously lively Georgian-style soup in a Sephardic Turkish cookbook. *Mijavyani* is the Georgian name, but in Turkish it is called *erikli sebze çorbası.* Greengage plums add both sweetness and tartness to the herb-scented beef, onion, and rice soup, though in true Turkish Sephardic tradition, lemon juice is also added. If you don't have any leftover cooked stewing beef, you can gently simmer 1 pound beef chuck or brisket, cut into 1-inch pieces, in broth or water to cover for about 1½ hours and then add the meat and cooking liquid to the soup. And if you cannot find greengage plums, any tart plum will do. SERVES 6

3 tablespoons olive oil

2 yellow onions, chopped, or 2 bunches green onions, including green tops, chopped

½ pound greengage plums, pitted and chopped

1 bunch fresh dill, chopped (about ⅓ cup)

1 medium-large bunch fresh flat-leaf parsley, chopped (about ½ cup)

3 tablespoons chopped fresh mint

¼ cup long-grain white rice

4 to 6 tablespoons fresh lemon juice

1 teaspoon sugar

2 teaspoons tomato paste

3 cups cooked stewing beef, in bite-size pieces

Beef broth or water to cover

Salt and freshly ground black pepper

Warm the oil in a large saucepan over medium heat. Add the onions and sauté until translucent and tender, 8 to 10 minutes. Add the plums, half each of the dill and parsley, the mint, the rice, lemon juice to taste, sugar, tomato paste, beef, and broth to cover. Bring to a boil over medium-high heat, turn down the heat to medium-low, and simmer until the rice is tender, about 20 minutes.

Season to taste with salt and pepper. Ladle into bowls and garnish with the remaining dill and parsley.

## Leek Soup with Mushrooms  SOPA DE PRASA

This Sephardic soup from Rhodes, which is traditionally thickened with egg and lemon and is often served at Passover, is very much like *purrusalda,* a popular Spanish leek soup seasoned with paprika and occasionally garnished with salt cod. SERVES 4 TO 6

6 leeks

¼ cup olive oil

Salt and freshly ground black pepper

8 ounces white mushrooms, sliced

4 large boiling potatoes, peeled and diced

8 cups chicken or vegetable broth or water

½ cup chopped fresh dill

2 eggs

2 to 3 tablespoons fresh lemon juice

Remove most of the green from the leeks, then halve lengthwise and cut crosswise into pieces about ¾ inch thick. Immerse in a sink filled with cold water, then lift out and drain well.

Warm the oil in a wide 2-quart saucepan over medium heat. Add the leeks and cook, salting once and stirring often, until they have lost most of their sour root flavor, about 15 minutes. Add the mushrooms and sauté for 5 minutes. Then add the potatoes and broth, raise the heat to high, and bring to a boil. Turn down the heat to low and simmer for about 20 minutes. Add half of the dill, season with salt and pepper, and mix well. The soup can be prepared up to this point, cooled, and refrigerated for up to 1 day. It should be chunky and a bit brothy. If it thickens while sitting, thin it with more broth or water.

If the soup has been refrigerated, bring it to a boil and then lower the heat to a simmer. Taste the soup. If it is slightly sour, you will want to use the smaller amount of lemon juice and omit the remaining dill. Beat the eggs and lemon juice until very frothy. Gradually beat about 1 cup of the hot soup into the egg mixture to temper and warm the eggs, then slowly add the egg mixture to the simmering soup while whisking constantly.

Remove from the heat, add the remaining dill, if using, and serve hot. Once the eggs have been added, the soup cannot be reheated.

## Leek and Potato Soup with Almonds and Mint

My inspiration for this soup was the Sephardic leek and potato soup on page 126, minus the earthy mushrooms and egg-lemon tartness. I wanted to take the soup in a sweeter direction by adding almonds, a classic Hispano-Arabic accent, to counteract the natural sourness of the leeks. You have two options for incorporating the almond flavor. You can use the nuts as a garnish or you can steep them in the cream and then purée the cream along with the soup. When used only as a garnish, they add a nice surface sweetness and keep their toasty character. But when the nuts are steeped in the cream, the sweetness they add is more intense. The nutmeg and mint are also welcome sweet accents. SERVES 6 TO 8

½ cup almonds, toasted, if making almond cream, plus more for garnish

1 cup heavy cream

8 large leeks

4 tablespoons unsalted butter

4 boiling potatoes, peeled and diced

4 cups vegetable broth

Pinch of freshly grated nutmeg

Salt and freshly ground black pepper

¼ cup chopped fresh mint

If making the almond cream, in a small saucepan, combine the almonds and cream and bring to a boil over medium-high heat. Remove from the heat and steep for 1 hour.

Meanwhile, remove most of the green from the leeks, then halve lengthwise and cut crosswise into slices about ¼ inch thick. Immerse in a sink filled with cold water, then lift out and drain well.

Melt the butter in a large saucepan over medium heat. Add the leeks and cook, stirring often, until tender, about 15 minutes. Add the potatoes and broth, raise the heat to high, and bring to a boil. Turn down the heat to medium-low and simmer until the potatoes are soft, 15 to 20 minutes.

If using the almond cream, remove the soup from the heat and let cool slightly. In batches, combine the soup and the almond cream in a blender and purée until smooth. Transfer to a clean saucepan, place over medium heat, and bring to a simmer. Add the nutmeg and season with salt and pepper.

If not using the almond cream, purée the soup and cream in the blender until smooth, then reheat to a simmer and season with the nutmeg, salt, and pepper. Ladle into bowls and garnish with the almonds and mint.

## *Green Purée for Passover* VELOUTÉ VERT DE PESSAH

I apologize in advance for asking you to shell 5 pounds of fava beans, then peel the beans and then shell 2½ pounds of English peas. But this soup is worth the effort. The recipe is from *Fleur de safran: Images et saveurs du Maroc* by Jacqueline Cohen-Azuelos. The lovely green color doesn't fade in the cooking process because half of the cilantro is added after the soup is cooked.

For a richer soup, use the chicken broth instead of water. You can of course make this soup without the giblet garnish, but I find it to be a flavorful addition that also provides an interesting textural contrast. SERVES 6

| | |
|---|---|
| 5 pounds fresh fava beans | 4 cups water or chicken broth |
| 2½ pounds English peas | Salt and freshly ground black pepper |
| 1 carrot, peeled and chopped | 2 tablespoons peanut or olive oil |
| 1 yellow onion, chopped | 8 ounces chicken or other poultry giblets (hearts and gizzards), cut into small pieces |
| 2 ribs celery, chopped | |
| 1 bunch fresh cilantro, chopped (about ⅓ cup) | 1 cup chicken broth |

Shell the fava beans. Bring a saucepan filled with water to a boil, add the favas, and blanch for about 1 minute. Drain and remove the tough outer skin from each bean. You should have about 4½ cups. Shell the peas. You should have about 2½ cups.

In a soup pot, combine the favas, peas, carrot, onion, celery, half of the cilantro, and the water and bring to a boil over high heat. Turn down the heat to medium-low and simmer, skimming off any foam from the surface, until the vegetables are tender, about 30 minutes.

Remove from the heat and let cool slightly. In batches, transfer the soup to a blender, add the remaining cilantro, and purée until smooth. Season with salt and pepper. Return the soup to the soup pot and set aside.

Warm the oil in a sauté pan over medium-high heat. Add the giblets and cook, stirring occasionally, until golden. Season with salt and pepper. Pour in the broth and deglaze the pan, stirring to dislodge any browned bits from the pan bottom. Turn down the heat to low, cover, and simmer until the giblets are tender, 30 to 40 minutes.

To serve, gently reheat the soup over medium-low heat. (If the giblets have cooled, reheat gently in the broth, as well.) Divide the giblets evenly among the bowls and ladle the hot soup over them.

## *Purim Artichoke Soup*   CREMA DI CARCIOFI ESTER

The repertoire of dishes made with artichokes in the Jewish Italian kitchen is particularly large. In the market in the old Jewish quarter in Rome, I asked a woman why this was the case and she answered, "Well, artichokes are bitter, and that's part of our heritage." This artichoke soup, from the dairy section of *La cucina nella tradizione ebraica,* is named after Esther, Queen of Persia, and is served at Purim, a joyful holiday that commemorates Esther's triumph over the evil minister Haman and her rescue of the Jews. Although it was traditionally thickened with *besciamella,* the classic cream sauce, you can make a less rich version by using rice or potato as a thickening agent and adding only broth, or perhaps a little milk or cream in addition to the broth for thinning. Be patient, as the artichoke flavor needs a few hours to develop. SERVES 6 TO 8

Juice of 1 lemon

12 artichokes

3 tablespoons unsalted butter

2 cloves garlic, minced

12 ounces russet potatoes, peeled and diced, or ½ cup white rice

3 cups vegetable broth, plus more for thinning as needed

Milk or heavy cream as needed for thinning (optional)

Salt and freshly ground black pepper

Chopped toasted hazelnuts or pine nuts or chopped fresh flat-leaf parsley or mint for garnish

Have ready a large bowl of water to which you have added the lemon juice. Working with 1 artichoke at a time, trim the stem to 2 inches if it is tender, then peel away the dark green fibrous outer layer. If the stem is tough, trim it off flush with the bottom. Pull off and discard all of the leaves. Pare away the dark green areas from the base. Cut the artichoke in half lengthwise and carefully remove the choke from each half with a small pointed spoon or a paring knife. Then cut each half lengthwise into ¼-inch-thick slices and slip them into the lemon water.

Melt the butter in a large saucepan over medium heat. Drain the artichokes, add to the pan, and sauté for a few minutes. Add the garlic, potatoes, and about 1½ cups of the broth or enough just to cover the artichokes. Cover the pan and simmer over medium heat until the artichokes are very tender and almost falling apart, 25 to 30 minutes.

Remove from the heat and let cool slightly. In batches, transfer to a food processor and purée until smooth, then return the purée to the saucepan. Add the remaining 1½ cups broth and reheat, adding more broth if needed to achieve a consistency you like. At this point, you can also add a little milk or cream if you prefer a richer soup. Season with salt and pepper. The artichoke flavor intensifies as the soup sits, so it's best to make the soup a few hours ahead of time, or even a day before, and reheat it at serving time. Ladle into bowls and garnish with the hazelnuts.

VARIATION: To make an even richer version of this soup, make a *besciamella* with 2 tablespoons each unsalted butter and all-purpose flour and 1 cup milk and use it in place of the 1½ cups broth added to the purée. You may still need to thin the soup with a little broth.

## *Asparagus Soup with Saffron from the Veneto*
CREMA DI ASPARAGI ALLO ZAFFERANO

One reason this Passover soup is so delicious is because there are no onions to mask the clean asparagus flavor. Use margarine or olive oil for a meat-based meal. SERVES 6

| | |
|---|---|
| 4½ to 5 cups vegetable broth | 1 large russet potato, peeled and diced |
| ¼ teaspoon crumbled saffron threads | Salt and freshly ground black pepper |
| 3½ to 4 pounds asparagus | ¼ cup chopped fresh flat-leaf parsley |
| 4 tablespoons unsalted butter or margarine | ⅓ cup pistachio nuts, toasted and coarsely chopped (optional) |

In a small saucepan, bring ½ cup of the broth to a boil. Remove from the heat, add the saffron, and let steep for 15 minutes.

Have ready an ice-water bath. Trim off the tough stem ends from the asparagus, then cut the spears into 2-inch pieces and reserve the tips. Bring a saucepan filled with salted water to a boil, add the tips, and boil for 3 minutes. Drain, then immerse the tips in the ice-water bath to refresh. Drain and set aside.

Melt the butter in a large saucepan over medium heat. Add the asparagus stalks and cook, stirring, for 3 minutes. Add the potato, saffron infusion, and 4 cups of the broth and bring to a boil, Turn down the heat to low and simmer until the asparagus and potato are very soft, about 20 minutes.

Remove from the heat and let cool slightly. In batches, transfer soup to a blender and purée until smooth, then return the purée to the saucepan. Reheat to a gentle simmer and add the remaining ½ cup broth if needed to achieve the consistency you like. Season with salt and pepper. The asparagus flavor intensifies if the soup is set aside for an hour or so before serving.

To serve, return the soup to medium heat, add the asparagus tips, and reheat until hot. Ladle into bowls and garnish with the parsley and nuts.

## *Turkish Carrot Soup*  HAVUÇ ÇORBASI

Carrot soups can be starchy and overly filling or too pallid to make an impression, unless the carrots are flavorful. This version is wonderfully delicate, light, and creamy and is unusual in that it doesn't have the cooked onions that are used as a flavor base in most soups. Here, success depends on the carrots. SERVES 6

---

4 tablespoons unsalted butter

1 pound sweet carrots, peeled and sliced or chopped

4 cups water or broth

1 teaspoon chopped fresh dill

2 egg yolks

1 tablespoon all-purpose flour

½ cup milk

Salt and freshly ground black pepper

Sugar, if needed

3 tablespoons each chopped fresh dill and finely chopped toasted walnuts, or 3 tablespoons each chopped fresh mint and almonds (optional)

---

Melt 2 tablespoons of the butter in a saucepan over medium heat. Add the carrots and cook, stirring, until well coated with the butter. Add 2 cups of the water and the 1 teaspoon dill, bring to a simmer, and simmer until the carrots are very soft, 25 to 30 minutes.

Remove from the heat and let cool slightly. In batches, transfer to a blender or food processor and purée until smooth, then return the purée to the saucepan. Add the remaining 2 cups water and heat to a gentle simmer over medium-low heat.

Meanwhile, in a bowl, beat the egg yolks until blended. Melt the remaining 2 tablespoons butter in a small saucepan over medium heat, remove from the heat, and stir in the flour. Whisk in the milk, stirring until smooth. Return the pan to medium heat and simmer, stirring constantly, until the mixture thickens, 2 to 3 minutes. Remove from the heat and gradually whisk a little of the hot sauce into the egg yolks to temper and warm them, then whisk the yolks into the milk mixture.

Gradually whisk a little of the hot soup into the milk–egg yolk mixture, then whisk the milk–egg yolk mixture into the remaining soup. Continue to whisk until well blended and piping hot. Do not allow the soup to boil or it will curdle. Season to taste with salt and pepper and with a little sugar if needed to heighten the sweetness. Ladle into bowls and garnish with the dill and walnuts.

## Roasted Eggplant Soup    PATLICAN ÇORBASI

Sephardic Jews in Turkey and those from the Middle East love the smoky flavor of eggplant cooked over a flame, which is why they enjoy this soup. Iranian cooks add 1 teaspoon ground turmeric and ½ teaspoon ground cinnamon to the onions and 1 cup cooked browned lentils to the puréed soup. If you find the smokiness too intense, add some cream to the soup, or roast all of the eggplants in the oven.  SERVES 6 TO 8

| | |
|---|---|
| 4 globe eggplants (12 to 14 ounces each) | ½ cup heavy cream (optional) |
| 3 tablespoons unsalted butter | Salt and freshly ground black pepper |
| 1 yellow onion, sliced | Plain yogurt for garnish (optional) |
| 4 cups vegetable broth, plus more if needed to thin | Chopped fresh mint or flat-leaf parsley for garnish (optional) |

Preheat the oven to 400°F. Prick 2 of the eggplants with a fork in a few places so they don't burst, then put them on a sheet pan and slip the pan into the oven. Roast the eggplants, turning them a few times to ensure even cooking, until they are soft throughout when pierced with a knife, 45 to 60 minutes. Transfer to a colander to drain and cool.

Position a rack several inches from the heat source and preheat the broiler. Place the remaining 2 eggplants on a sheet pan and broil, turning occasionally, until the skin is charred on all sides and the interior is fully tender, about 20 minutes. Alternatively, cook the eggplants on a heavy griddle or grill pan over medium heat on the stove top, turning them occasionally, until charred on all sides and fully tender. This may take a little less time. Transfer the eggplants to a colander to drain and cool. (If you like the smoky flavor of the stove-top eggplant, you can cook all of the eggplants on a griddle or grill pan.)

When all of the eggplants are cool enough to handle, transfer them to a cutting board, cut them in half, scoop out the pulp, and discard the skin. Discard any large seed pockets.

Melt the butter in a saucepan over medium heat. Add the onion and cook, stirring occasionally, until translucent and tender, 8 to 10 minutes. Add the broth and eggplant pulp, raise the heat to medium-high, and bring to a boil. Turn down the heat to medium and simmer the soup for a few minutes.

Remove from the heat and let cool slightly. In batches, purée the soup in a blender or food processor until smooth. Pour the soup into a clean saucepan, reheat over medium-low heat, and thin with broth if needed to achieve the consistency you like. If the eggplant flavor is too smoky for your palate, stir in the cream. Season with salt and pepper. Ladle into bowls and garnish each serving with a dollop of yogurt and some mint.

## *Tomato and Rice Soup* DOMATESLİ PİRİNÇ ÇORBASI

Esin Eden collaborated with Nicholas Stavroulakis on her book *Salonika: A Family Cookbook,* a collection of recipes from the mysterious Ma'min Jewish sect from Turkey that settled in Salonika. They were followers of the renegade rabbi Sabbatai Zevi and eventually became Muslims, so while their basic recipes were of Jewish origin, they showed a casual disregard for following the rule of no dairy with meat. For example, this recipe for tomato soup used butter with chicken broth. I have adjusted it (and any others I have adapted from the book) to stay within the kosher laws. Use margarine or oil if you use chicken broth, or butter if you use vegetable broth. SERVES 4 TO 6

2 tablespoons olive oil or margarine, or butter if using vegetable broth

3 pounds very ripe tomatoes, peeled, seeded, and coarsely chopped

3 to 4 cups chicken or vegetable broth

¼ cup long-grain white rice, rinsed

Salt and freshly ground black pepper

3 tablespoons chopped fresh flat-leaf parsley

Lemon wedges for serving

Warm the oil in a large saucepan over medium heat. Add the tomatoes and cook, stirring often and smashing them down with a wooden spoon, until they break down completely into a purée, 10 to 15 minutes.

In a separate saucepan, bring the broth just to a simmer. Add 3 cups of the hot broth and the rice to the tomatoes, raise the heat to high, and bring to a boil. Turn down the heat to medium-low and simmer until the rice is tender, 15 to 20 minutes.

If the soup is too thick, thin with the remaining broth. Season the soup with salt and pepper and stir in the parsley. Serve hot, accompanied with the lemon wedges.

## *Penny Soup* MANGIR ÇORBASI

A *mangir* was an Ottoman coin of very low value. In Turkey, the homemade pasta used in soup was a small, thin, round egg noodle called *farfur,* which was reminiscent of a coin, thus the English name of this soup. *Mangır çorbası* is a classic avgolemono soup with noodles. You can use broken vermicelli or a small pasta such as orzo in place of the homemade pasta. The use of both the egg-and-lemon mixture and the accompanying lemon wedges makes this soup especially tart.

This Ma'min recipe, like the Tomato and Rice Soup on page 133, is from Esin Eden. This same soup made with rice instead of noodles is called *sopa de huevo y limon* in Salonika and was commonly eaten to break the Yom Kippur fast. Elsewhere in Greece and in Turkey during Passover, a similar soup is made with broken matzo in place of noodles and is called *sodra* by Turks and *sorda* by Moroccans (recipe follows).  SERVES 4 TO 6

---

2 tablespoons margarine

1½ cups orzo, pastina, or other small pasta or broken vermicelli

4 cups meat or poultry broth, plus more if needed, heated

2 eggs

Juice of 2 lemons

Salt and freshly ground black pepper

2 to 3 tablespoons chopped fresh mint or flat-leaf parsley

Lemon wedges for serving (optional)

---

Melt the margarine in a saucepan over medium heat. Add half of the pasta and cook, stirring, until pale gold, about 5 minutes. Add the hot broth and the remaining uncooked pasta, bring to a gentle simmer, and cook until the pasta is tender, 8 to 10 minutes longer. If the soup is too thick, thin with more broth.

In a bowl, beat together the eggs and lemon juice until very frothy. Gradually beat about 1 cup of the hot soup into the egg mixture to temper and warm the eggs, then slowly add the egg mixture to the soup while whisking constantly. Simmer for a minute or two, but do not allow the soup to boil or it will curdle. Season with salt and pepper, then ladle into bowls, garnish with the mint, and serve hot. Pass the lemon wedges at the table.

## Passover Matzo Soup with Meat, Peas, and Favas  SORDA

Here is how the classic Passover matzo soup is prepared in Casablanca and Safi. Some recipes add diced tomatoes and chopped cilantro to the mix, as well.  SERVES 6 TO 8

---

1½ pounds boneless beef, lamb, or chicken, cut into small pieces

8 cups chicken or meat broth

¼ cup olive oil

¼ teaspoon saffron threads

Salt and freshly ground black pepper

1½ cups shelled English peas (from about 1½ pounds)

1½ cups shelled fresh fava beans (from about 1¾ pounds), blanched in boiling water for about 1 minute, drained, and peeled

3 eggs (optional)

3 or 4 matzos

---

In a saucepan, combine the meat, broth, oil, and saffron and season with salt and pepper. Bring to a boil over medium-high heat, turn down the heat to medium-low, cover, and simmer until the meat is half-cooked, 15 to 30 minutes. The timing will depend on the meat. Add the peas and favas, re-cover, and continue to cook until the meat and vegetables are tender, about 15 minutes longer.

In a small bowl, whisk the eggs until very frothy, then gradually add them to the gently simmering soup while stirring constantly. Taste and adjust the seasoning with salt and pepper. To serve, break up the matzos, put them in a soup tureen or individual bowls, and ladle the hot soup over the top.

## *Greek Garlic Soup*   SKORDOZOUMI

*Skordo* is "garlic" in Greek. Unlike the Spanish *sopa de ajo* and the Portuguese *sopa de alho,* both of which add only eggs for thickening, Nicholas Stavroulakis's Greek version adds yogurt and feta cheese along with the eggs to thicken and enrich the basic soup. This soup may be related to the famous *sopa Maimónides* mentioned as a specialty of the Andalusian Jews in Pepita Aris's *A Flavor of Andalusia,* but now with a Middle Eastern addition. In the Sephardic cookbook published by Temple Or VeShalom in Atlanta, this soup is called *pappa,* a term that probably refers more to the bread than to the garlic. In that version, much less garlic is used, milk replaces the yogurt, and lots of croutons are added. SERVES 4

| | |
|---|---|
| 3 cups water | 1 cup plain yogurt, vigorously stirred until creamy |
| 2 tablespoons olive oil | 2 eggs, beaten until very frothy |
| 1 head garlic, cloves separated, peeled, and cut into thin slivers | 2 to 4 slices bread, crusts removed, toasted, and cut into croutons |
| Salt and freshly ground black pepper | Chopped fresh flat-leaf parsley for garnish (optional) |
| 4 ounces feta cheese, finely crumbled | |

In a saucepan, combine the water, oil, and garlic, season with salt and pepper, and bring to a boil over medium-high heat. Turn down the heat to medium and simmer for 10 minutes. Turn down the heat to very low, add the cheese and yogurt, and stir for 2 to 3 minutes. Do not allow the mixture to boil.

Remove from the heat, wait for 1 to 2 minutes, and then gradually add the eggs while whisking constantly. Taste and adjust the seasoning with salt and pepper. Ladle into bowls and garnish generously with the croutons. If you want a bit of color, finish with a little parsley.

# Sephardic Meatball Soup   SOPA DE ALBÓNDIGAS

I found this recipe in *Sefarad Yemekleri,* a book of recipes compiled by the Turkish Jewish community in Istanbul. The word *albóndiga* is Spanish for "meatball" and is Arabic in origin, from *al bundaq,* meaning "round." In this version of *sopa de albóndigas,* the meatballs are cooked directly in the soup and are not browned first. I like to season them with grated onion and a little cinnamon to add intrigue.   SERVES 4 TO 6

1 pound ground beef or lamb

1 large slice coarse country bread, crust removed, soaked in water, and squeezed dry

¼ cup grated yellow onion

½ teaspoon ground cinnamon

Salt and freshly ground black pepper

6 to 7 cups water or meat broth

3 to 4 tablespoons olive oil

4 boiling potatoes, peeled and cut into batons ¼ inch wide and thick and 1½ inches long

3 carrots, peeled and cut into batons ¼ inch wide and thick and 1 ½ inches long

½ cup chopped celery leaves

In a bowl, combine the meat, bread, onion, and cinnamon, season with salt and pepper, and then knead with your hands until it holds together. Fry a nugget in a small sauté pan, taste, and adjust the seasoning if needed. Shape the mixture into tiny meatballs about ¾ inch in diameter. Set aside.

In a saucepan, bring the water and oil to a boil over high heat. Add the potatoes and carrots, turn down the heat to medium, and simmer, uncovered, for 10 minutes. Add the meatballs and continue to simmer until the vegetables are tender and the meatballs are cooked through, about 10 minutes longer. Serve hot, garnished with the celery leaves.

VARIATION:   To thicken and enrich the soup, just before serving, whisk together 2 egg yolks and ¼ cup fresh lemon juice in a bowl until very frothy. Gradually whisk in about ¾ cup of the hot soup to temper the egg yolks, then gradually stir the yolk mixture into the soup over low heat and cook for about 1 minute. Do not allow to boil.

# Italian Passover Soup with Chicken Dumplings and Eggs
## POLPETTE E UOVA PER PESACH

When I was a little girl, my family lived near a kosher chicken market. We would select the chicken and the butcher would kill and clean it while we waited. If we were lucky, inside the bird was a treasure of unborn eggs. I loved those tiny egg yolks, which we poached in chicken soup, because when I bit into them, they popped in my mouth. In days gone by, Italian Jews added these immature eggs to the chicken soup they served at Passover. Rice and little "meatballs" made of chicken and matzo meal went into the soup, as well. I remember those tiny eggs with great nostalgia, for today they are nowhere to be found. To revive the memory, I separate eggs, slide the yolks onto a saucer, slip them into the broth, and poach them gently until barely set, hoping they don't break.

Some Italian Jews prefer to make the much easier *minestra dayenu* (*dayenu* is Hebrew for "that would have been enough"), in which 4 egg yolks and 4 matzos, broken into pieces, are stirred into chicken broth that has been highly flavored with cinnamon. SERVES 8

---

1 large whole boneless chicken breast, ground (about 10 ounces)

1 egg, lightly beaten

⅓ cup matzo meal

Generous pinch of ground cinnamon

Salt and freshly ground black pepper

8 to 10 cups chicken broth

1 cup long-grain white rice

8 hard-boiled egg yolks, chopped, or 8 raw whole eggs (optional)

---

In a bowl, combine the chicken, beaten egg, matzo meal, cinnamon, and a pinch each of salt and pepper and mix well. Cover and refrigerate for about 1 hour, which will make the mixture easier to shape.

To shape the dumplings, dip a spoon into cold water, scoop up a little of the chilled mixture, and, with dampened hands, shape it into a walnut-size ball. Set aside on a platter. Repeat with the remaining mixture, dipping the spoon in cold water before each scoop, then refrigerate the balls until ready to cook.

In a large saucepan, bring the broth to a boil over high heat. Add the rice and chicken balls, turn down the heat to medium-low, cover, and simmer until the rice is tender and the chicken balls are cooked through, about 20 minutes. Ladle into shallow bowls and garnish with the hard-boiled egg yolks. Or, if using the raw eggs, separate them, reserving the whites for a Passover cake, and then carefully poach the yolks in the broth until semifirm and include a yolk in each bowl.

## Persian Chicken Soup with Chicken Dumplings   GONDI

Persian cooks use chickpea flour, rather than matzo meal, to make the dumplings for this soup. Unlike matzo balls, which are first cooked in salted water and then added to soup, these dumplings are cooked directly in the soup. In Iran, dried Omani limes add a pleasant tartness to the soup. SERVES 6 TO 8

## BROTH

one 4-pound stewing chicken, or 4 pounds chicken parts, such as drumsticks and thighs

4 quarts water

2 yellow onions, halved

3 carrots, halved

1 teaspoon ground turmeric

3 dried Omani limes, rinsed and struck with a meat pounder so they crack

## DUMPLINGS

1 large or 2 medium yellow onions, diced

2 cloves garlic, minced

1 pound ground chicken

1 cup toasted chickpea flour

1 egg, lightly beaten

1 teaspoon ground turmeric

1 teaspoon ground cardamom (optional)

2 tablespoons chopped fresh flat-leaf parsley

2 teaspoons salt

½ teaspoon freshly ground black pepper

2 tablespoons olive oil

2 cups drained cooked chickpeas (optional)

2 cups cooked diced carrot (optional)

1 cup chopped fresh dill or flat-leaf parsley, or a mixture

Lemon wedges for serving

To make the broth, if using a whole chicken, cut into parts. Trim off and discard any excess fat from the chicken parts. Put the chicken pieces in a large stockpot and add the water. Place the pot over medium-high heat and bring to a boil, skimming off any foam that forms on the surface. Turn down the heat to medium-low and simmer gently, skimming the surface as needed, for 30 minutes. Add the onions, carrots, turmeric, and limes and continue to simmer gently for 2 hours longer.

Remove from the heat. Have ready a large ice-water bath. Using a slotted spoon or wire skimmer, remove and discard the solids from the broth. Line a fine-mesh sieve with dampened cheesecloth, place over a large bowl, and strain the broth through the sieve. Place the bowl in the ice bath and let the broth cool completely. Then, using a spoon, lift off and discard the fat from the surface. To concentrate the flavor of the broth, transfer the broth to a large saucepan, bring it to a low boil, and boil, skimming if needed, until it has reduced and is more flavorful. Set the broth aside.

To make the dumplings, in a food processor, combine the onions and garlic and process until reduced to a purée. Add the chicken, flour, egg, turmeric, cardamom, parsley, salt, pepper, and oil and pulse just until evenly mixed. If the mixture is dry, add a bit of water. To make shaping the dumplings easier, transfer the mixture to a bowl, cover, and refrigerate for 2 to 4 hours.

To shape the dumplings, dip a spoon into cold water, scoop up a little of the chilled mixture, and, with dampened hands, shape it into a walnut-size ball. Set aside on a platter. Repeat with the remaining mixture, dipping the spoon in cold water before each scoop, then refrigerate the dumplings until ready to cook.

To serve, bring the broth to a boil over high heat. Drop the dumplings into the broth, turn down the heat to a gentle simmer, cover, and cook for 30 minutes. Test a dumpling for doneness. The dumplings are ready when they are tender but still firm in the center. They may take as long as 1 hour to cook. Add the chickpeas and carrots to the broth during the last 15 minutes of cooking. Taste and adjust the seasoning with salt.

Spoon a few dumplings and some chickpeas and carrot into each bowl and ladle the broth on top. Garnish with the dill and pass the lemon wedges at the table.

## Oven-Baked Endive Soup    INDIVIA REHAMINA

In style, this Roman recipe resembles a *panada,* or layered bread soup. Broth, vegetables, and bread are layered in a heavy pan and baked in the oven (the *hamin*) until the bread absorbs most of the broth, creating a cakey mixture that is eaten with a spoon. The pleasantly bitter curly endive (sometimes known as chicory) can be replaced by escarole. SERVES 4 TO 6

---

| | |
|---|---|
| 4 cups meat or vegetable broth | Salt and freshly ground black pepper |
| 2 large heads curly endive, chopped | Grated Parmesan cheese for serving, if using vegetable broth |
| Slices day-old coarse country bread, as needed | |

---

Preheat the oven to 325°F.

In a wide, heavy saucepan with a tight-fitting lid, bring the broth to a boil over high heat. Add the endive and wilt quickly, then cover the greens with the bread slices in a single layer. Remove from the heat, cover the pan, and place in the oven. Bake until almost all of the broth is absorbed, 45 to 60 minutes.

Remove from the oven and season with salt and pepper. To serve, scoop out into shallow bowls. If you have used vegetable broth, sprinkle with Parmesan. If you have used a meat broth, serve as is.

## Passover Matzo Soup    ZUPPA DI AZZIME

This is a cross between a *panada,* an Italian layered bread soup, and a *schacchi* or *mina,* a layered matzo pie served during Passover throughout the Sephardic world. SERVES 6

2 to 3 tablespoons rendered chicken or goose fat or margarine

1 yellow onion, chopped

2 ribs celery, chopped

3 carrots, peeled and chopped

2 or 3 cloves garlic, minced

3 tablespoons chopped fresh flat-leaf parsley

2 tablespoons chopped fresh basil

1 cup tomato sauce

2 cups chopped cooked meat

1 cup cooked English peas

2 cups chopped cooked spinach (about 2 pounds uncooked)

6 to 8 cups meat broth, or as needed

2 teaspoons salt

½ teaspoon freshly ground black pepper

Lots of freshly grated nutmeg

6 matzos

Melt the fat in a saucepan over medium heat. Add the onion, celery, carrots, garlic, parsley, and basil and sauté until the vegetables have softened, about 10 minutes. Add the tomato sauce and meat and simmer for a few minutes. Add the peas and spinach and stir well. If the mixture seems dry, add a bit of the broth. Season with the salt, pepper, and nutmeg and mix well, then taste and adjust the seasoning. Remove from the heat.

Preheat the oven to 350°F.

Place the matzos in a shallow bowl, add broth just to cover, and let soak just until softened, 1 to 2 minutes. Drain the matzos and layer half of them in the bottom of a 3-quart baking dish or in a deep baking pan measuring about 9 by 12 inches. Cover the matzo layer with the vegetable-and-meat mixture, then layer the rest of the matzos on top. Alternatively, make the soup with three layers of matzos: matzo, meat, matzo, meat, matzo. Pour in the broth to cover the layers, place over medium-high heat on the stove top, bring to a boil, cover, and transfer to the oven. Bake until the broth is absorbed, 30 to 45 minutes.

To serve, scoop the soup out into bowls. If you like, heat up additional broth to spoon over each serving.

## Tunisian Fish Soup from Sfax    SFAXIA

A fish soup in Andrée Zana Murat's *La cuisine juive tunisienne: De mère en fille* provided the inspiration for this recipe, which is also known as *soupe de poissons*. Here, the fish is cooked in the broth and then served as a separate course and the broth is served with croutons. A Libyan version uses less fish, cuts it into smaller pieces, and serves the fish in the broth without croutons. In Algeria, cooks make *caldero* (related to the Portuguese *caldeirada*), which calls for simmering pieces of fish in a puréed fish broth lightly scented with tomato and dried sweet peppers (*ñoras*), adding a spoonful of saffron rice to each soup bowl, and then garnishing each serving with *harissa*-seasoned garlic mayonnaise. SERVES 6 TO 8

3 to 4 pounds firm white fish, such as cod, sea bass, or flounder, cut into steaks or thick slices

Salt and freshly ground black pepper

Juice of ½ lemon

2 pounds fish frames (heads, bones, tails, with gills removed)

8 to 10 tablespoons olive oil

1 large yellow onion, coarsely grated

8 cloves garlic, minced

¼ cup tomato purée

1 tablespoon tomato paste

1 tablespoon sweet paprika

1 teaspoon ground cumin (optional)

½ red bell pepper, seeded and diced

1 small bulb fennel, diced

2 pinches of saffron threads

½ bunch fresh flat-leaf parsley, tied in a bundle with kitchen string

3 to 4 slices day-old coarse country bread, crusts removed

Rub the fish pieces with salt and pepper and the lemon juice, place on a plate, cover, and refrigerate until ready to cook.

Rinse the fish frames well, break them up a bit, and place in a large saucepan. Add water to cover by 3 inches, place over medium-high heat, and bring to a boil, skimming off any foam from the surface. Turn down the heat to a steady simmer, cover, and cook for 30 minutes. Remove from the heat. Line a fine-mesh sieve with dampened cheese-cloth, place over a large bowl, and strain the broth through the sieve. Reserve the broth. You should have about 8 cups.

Warm 6 tablespoons of the olive oil in a large saucepan over medium heat. Add the onion and garlic and cook, stirring often, for a few minutes. Off the heat, add the tomato purée, tomato paste, paprika, and cumin and stir well. Return the pan to medium heat and add the bell pepper, fennel, and saffron and mix well. Pour in the fish broth, add the parsley bundle, and bring to a simmer. Cook for 20 minutes to blend the flavors.

Add the fish and simmer gently until it is opaque throughout, 10 to 15 minutes. Do not overcook. Using a slotted spatula or wire skimmer, transfer the fish to a warmed platter and cover to keep warm. Remove and discard the parsley. Keep the broth warm.

Cut the bread into ¾-inch cubes. Warm 2 tablespoons of the remaining oil in a large sauté pan over medium-high heat. Add the bread cubes and fry, turning them to color evenly and adding more oil as needed, until golden on all sides. Using a slotted spoon, transfer to paper towels to drain.

Reheat the broth until piping hot and ladle into bowls. Pass the fish fillets and croutons at the table.

Rice,
Pasta,
and Grains

With the exception of Iran, where rice rules the table, Mediterranean Jewish kitchens do not enjoy a vast repertoire of grain recipes. Grains were—and are—commonly eaten at most meals all over the Mediterranean, but because they were a table staple, recipes for them were not written down. Instead, they were habit. Bulgur and freekeh, for example, appear at the table from time to time, primarily in the Middle East, where they might be served hot as a pilaf or used in salads or in the preparation of *kibbeh,* but written recipes for them are rare.

*Farro,* an early form of emmer wheat cultivated in the Italian regions of Abruzzo, Umbria, and Tuscany, was long ago pushed aside for the more popular and easier to grow semolina wheat used for pasta and bread, so that no recipes for *farro* exist in the classic Italian Jewish kitchen. Its cultivation has experienced a revival in recent decades, however, so that contemporary cooks now prepare it, adding it to soups, cooking it like pilaf or risotto, or using it as a base for salad. Corn arrived in Italy shortly after the voyages of Columbus, and polenta served as a side dish was soon on Italian Jewish menus.

In Greece and Turkey, rice was prepared simply; a few pine nuts, some tomato or spinach, or grated carrot might be added. The need for grain in the diet was typically satisfied by the presence of bread and by the large number of savory pastries served at meals (see chapter 2). Many vegetable dishes were also enriched by the addition of bread. In North Africa, couscous (made from semolina wheat), bread, and savory pastries were the primary grain-based items at the table.

Rice is a star in the Persian Jewish kitchen, where it is traditionally served as a side and, when mixed with meat and poultry, as a main course. For all of the recipes that follow, use basmati rice when long-grain rice is called for, as it is particularly fragrant and holds its shape and texture well. If time allows, after you have rinsed the rice, soak it in lightly salted water for a few hours to achieve more tender kernels once the rice is cooked.

Short-grain rice was mostly used for puddings in the Middle East, and in Italy for risotto. Rice has long been central to the Italian Jewish table. Traditionally, it was made into a simple but elegant *riso del sabato,* rice colored with a pinch of expensive saffron, served on Friday night. Risotto was also made with artichokes, asparagus, eggplant, squash, or peas and, like pasta, was an ideal dish to serve for dairy meals. Any leftover cooked risotto could be formed into a *bomba* (mold) or into *crocchette* (croquettes) stuffed with cheese and baked or fried. Leftover rice pilaf was dressed with oil and lemon juice or vinegar and turned into rice salad, served plain, or adorned with tuna and roasted peppers.

Pasta, along with vegetables, was—and still is—integral to the Italian Jewish diet. In years past, the Italian Jewish menu was largely vegetarian, with meat and fish playing the role of flavor accents to grain and vegetable dishes. Dried commercial pasta was used, but learning to make *pasta all'uovo* (fresh egg noodles) was part of every young cook's training. Sheets of pasta were cut into narrow strips for tagliarini and fettuccine, wide strips for lasagna, or rectangles for *rotoli* (pasta rolls), or they were shaped into ravioli filled with meat, brains, pumpkin, or greens and cheese. Pasta dishes that were prepared before sundown on Friday evening evolved into room-temperature main courses for Saturday lunch, the unintentional forerunners of the now ubiquitous pasta salad sold at nearly every deli counter.

Unlike in Italy, pasta is served only occasionally by the Sephardic Jews in Turkey and Greece and rarely in other parts of the Mediterranean, though it sometimes turns up in soup. Mostly it takes the form of Middle Eastern–style macaroni and cheese or of fried noodles borrowed from the Spanish *fideos* tradition. Some families continue to use the early Arabic name for pasta, *itriya,* but most favor the Ladino name *fidellos,* which is based on the term *fideos,* meaning "overflowing" or "abundant."

## Rice with Pine Nuts   ARROZ CON PIÑONES

A classic of the Sephardic table, this simple pilaf is the traditional accompaniment to Fish with Abraham's Fruit (page 241).  SERVES 6 TO 8

| | |
|---|---|
| ¼ cup olive oil | Scant 1 cup pine nuts |
| 1 small yellow onion, chopped | 4 cups water |
| 2 cups long-grain white rice, rinsed and drained | 1½ teaspoons salt |
| | Pinch of saffron threads (optional) |

Warm the oil in a saucepan over medium heat. Add the onion and cook, stirring occasionally, until translucent, about 5 minutes. Turn down the heat to low, add the rice and pine nuts, and stir to coat them well with the oil for 5 minutes. Add the water, salt, and saffron, increase the heat to medium-high, and bring to a boil. Turn down the heat to low, cover, and cook until the rice is tender and the grains are separate, 18 to 20 minutes.

Remove from the heat. Let rest, covered, for 5 to 10 minutes, then fluff and serve.

# Spinach and Rice Pilaf  ARROZ KON ESPINAKA

This classic pilaf from the Sephardic kitchen is still popular in Greece today, where it is known as *spanakorizo*. It can be served hot or at room temperature. Sometimes it is garnished with chopped hard-boiled eggs, a little crumbled feta cheese, or a dollop of yogurt. For a complete meal, top each serving with a poached egg. If the aesthetics of the dish are important to you, cook the rice and spinach separately and then fold them together just before serving, as the color of the spinach fades when it is cooked for such a long time with the rice. The dish will taste different, of course, but it will look brighter. SERVES 6

6 tablespoons olive oil

2 yellow onions, chopped

1 large clove garlic, minced

1 cup long-grain white rice

8 cups coarsely chopped spinach (about 2 pounds, stemmed)

½ cup chopped fresh dill

2 tomatoes, peeled, seeded, and chopped (optional)

1½ cups water

1½ teaspoons salt

½ teaspoon freshly ground black pepper

2 tablespoons fresh lemon juice

Plain yogurt or plain yogurt seasoned with minced garlic for serving (optional)

Warm 3 tablespoons of the oil in a large sauté pan over medium heat. Add the onions and cook, stirring occasionally, for 5 minutes. Add the garlic and rice and cook, stirring often, for 3 minutes. Add the spinach, dill, tomatoes, water, salt, and pepper and bring to a boil, stirring often and pushing the spinach down into the pan as it wilts. Turn down the heat to low, cover, and simmer until the water is absorbed and the rice is tender, 15 to 18 minutes.

Remove from the heat and let rest, covered, for 5 minutes. In a small bowl, whisk together the remaining 3 tablespoons oil and the lemon juice and drizzle over the rice. Serve hot or at room temperature. At a dairy meal, pass the yogurt for spooning over the rice.

# Syrian Rice with Vermicelli  ROZ ME SHAREYEEH

Rice mixed with noodles is a popular side dish in most Arab countries. If you will be serving this dish at a meat meal, use oil and water or meat or poultry broth. For a dairy meal, use butter and water or vegetable broth. SERVES 4 TO 6

| | |
|---|---|
| 2 tablespoons unsalted butter or olive oil | 1½ cups long-grain white rice, rinsed and drained |
| ½ cup fideos or vermicelli, in 1-inch pieces | 3 cups water or broth |
| | 1 teaspoon salt |

Warm the butter in a saucepan over medium heat. Add the noodles and sauté, stirring often, until golden brown, 3 to 5 minutes. Add the rice and stir until all of the grains are coated with the fat. Add the water and salt and bring to a boil. When some of the water has been absorbed and little holes appear on the surface of the rice, turn down the heat to low, cover, and cook until the rice is tender, about 20 minutes.

Remove from the heat, fluff with a fork, and serve hot.

## *Arabic Rice and Lentils with Caramelized Onions*  MUJADDARA

This is my idea of comfort food. The key ingredients are the lentils and the caramelized onions. The lentils must be cooked perfectly: not too soft, not too crunchy. French or Italian green lentils, which hold their shape when cooked, are best. Black (beluga) lentils are also a good choice. Brown and red lentils will soften too quickly. I have found that red onions caramelize more easily, so I am specifying them here, but you can use yellow or white if you like. Most versions of this recipe call for stirring in the onions, but I prefer to stir in half of them and arrange the remainder on top. At a dairy meal, you can serve this pilaf with a dollop of plain yogurt. A similar dish replaces the rice with bulgur.  SERVES 6

| | |
|---|---|
| 1 cup green or black lentils, picked over and rinsed | Salt and freshly ground black pepper |
| 5 tablespoons olive oil | 1 cup basmati rice, rinsed and drained, then soaked in water to cover for 1 hour |
| 4 large red onions, sliced | |
| ¼ teaspoon ground cinnamon | 1¾ cups water |

In a saucepan, combine the lentils and salted water to cover by about 2 inches and bring to a boil over high heat. Turn down the heat to low and cook until tender but not too soft, 25 to 30 minutes. Check the lentils regularly, as you do not want to overcook them.

Meanwhile, warm the oil in a large sauté pan over medium-high heat. Add the onions and cook, stirring often, until deep golden brown, about 15 minutes. Using a slotted spoon, transfer to paper towels to drain and crisp. Season with the cinnamon and with salt and pepper.

Drain the rice. In a saucepan, bring the water to a boil over high heat. Add the rice, return the liquid to a simmer, then turn down the heat to low, cover, and cook until the rice is tender and the liquid is absorbed, 15 to 20 minutes. Remove from the heat, uncover, fluff with a fork, and let rest for a few minutes.

Drain the lentils, add to the rice in the pot, and toss to mix evenly. Stir in half of the onions, then season with salt and pepper. Transfer to a bowl or serving platter. Top with the remaining onions. Serve warm or at room temperature.

## Egyptian Rice, Lentils, and Noodles  KOSHARI

In Egypt, the combination of lentils and rice, occasionally with the addition of noodles, is served with a spicy tomato sauce or a green chile and garlic condiment.  SERVES 6

---

1 cup green or black lentils, picked over and rinsed

1 cup basmati rice, rinsed and drained, then soaked in water to cover for 1 hour

1¾ cups water

1 cup broken fideos or vermicelli, in 1-inch pieces

3 tablespoons olive oil

2 large yellow onions, chopped

Salt and freshly ground black pepper

SALSA

8 serrano chiles, minced

3 cloves garlic, mashed to a paste with ½ teaspoon salt

Pinch of ground cinnamon

¼ cup white wine vinegar

½ cup olive oil

---

In a saucepan, combine the lentils and salted water to cover by about 2 inches and bring to a boil over high heat. Turn down the heat to low and cook until tender but not too soft, 25 to 30 minutes. Check the lentils regularly, as you do not want to overcook them.

At the same time, cook the rice. In a saucepan, bring the water to a boil over high heat. Add the rice, return the liquid to a simmer, then turn down the heat to low, cover, and cook until the rice is tender and the liquid is absorbed, 15 to 20 minutes. Remove from the heat, uncover, fluff with a fork, and let rest for a few minutes.

While the lentils and rice are cooking, prepare the onions, fideos, and salsa. Bring a saucepan filled with salted water to a boil, add the fideos, and cook until al dente. Drain well and set aside. Warm the oil in a sauté pan over medium-high heat. Add the onions and cook, stirring often, until deep golden brown, 10 to 15 minutes. Using a slotted spoon, transfer to paper towels to drain and crisp, then season with salt and pepper. To make the salsa, combine all of the ingredients, mixing well.

When the lentils are ready, drain them, add them and the noodles to the fluffed rice in the pot, and toss to mix evenly. Stir in half of the onions and season with salt and pepper. Transfer to a bowl or serving platter and top with the remaining onions. Serve warm and pass the salsa at the table.

## Chicken and Rice Pilaf Wrapped in Filo  YUFKALI PİLAV

Both Turkish and Iranian Jews like this spectacular dish, which is often called "veiled pilaf." Some versions call for lining a shallow baking dish with layered filo sheets, allowing them to overhang the sides; adding the pilaf; folding the overhang over the top, and then baking, cutting, and serving similar to how baklava is prepared. In Iran, recipes include ½ cup broken vermicelli, cooked, in the filling. For a more eye-catching presentation at the table, make this pilaf in a large springform pan. SERVES 6 TO 8

**CHICKEN AND BROTH**

2 pounds chicken parts, such as breasts and thighs

1 carrot, peeled and halved

1 yellow onion, halved

6 black peppercorns

Salt

¾ cup olive oil

1 yellow onion, chopped

½ teaspoon ground cinnamon or allspice

¼ teaspoon ground cardamom

Salt and freshly ground black pepper

1½ cups long-grain white rice, rinsed and drained

½ cup slivered blanched almonds, toasted until golden brown in the oven or in a little oil on the stove top

8 to 10 filo sheets

To prepare the chicken and broth, in a large saucepan, combine the chicken, carrot, onion, peppercorns, a generous sprinkle of salt, and water to cover by 2 inches and bring to a boil over medium-high heat, skimming off any foam that forms on the surface. Turn down the heat to low, cover, and simmer gently until the chicken is tender, 25 to 30 minutes. Remove from the heat and, using a wire skimmer, transfer the chicken to a large plate.

When the chicken is cool enough to handle, remove and discard the bones and skin, then cut the meat into bite-size pieces and set aside. Prepare an ice-water bath. Line a fine-mesh sieve with dampened cheesecloth, place over a large bowl, and strain the broth through the sieve. Place the bowl in the ice-water bath and let the broth cool completely; then, using a spoon, lift off and discard the fat from the surface. Measure 3 cups of the broth, bring to a simmer in a clean saucepan, remove from the heat, and cover to keep hot. Reserve the remaining broth for another use.

Warm ¼ cup of the oil in a large saucepan over medium heat. Add the onion and cook, stirring occasionally, until translucent, about 5 minutes. Add the cinnamon and cardamom, season with salt and pepper, and cook, stirring, for a few more minutes. Add the rice and cook, stirring, until the kernels are opaque. Add the reserved chicken and hot broth and bring to a boil. Turn down the heat to low, cover, and cook until the liquid is absorbed and the rice is tender, about 15 minutes. Remove from the heat, uncover, fold in the almonds, and let cool completely.

Preheat the oven to 400°F. Brush a 2-quart baking dish (or a large springform pan) with some of the remaining ½ cup oil. Lay the stack of filo sheets on your work surface and cover with a damp kitchen towel to prevent drying, removing 1 sheet at a time as needed. Layer 8 of the filo sheets in the prepared dish, brushing each sheet with oil once you put it in the dish and allowing the filo to overhang the sides of the dish. Be sure to brush the overhang with oil, and check that the overhang is sufficient to cover the top of the dish once the pilaf is added. Reserve the final 2 filo sheets in case they are needed to ensure coverage. Spoon the cooled cooked pilaf into the filo-lined dish and fold up the overhang to cover the top. Brush the top with oil. You can arrange the remaining 2 filo sheets on top, brushing each with oil and tucking them in around the edges.

Bake until golden, about 25 minutes. Remove from the oven and let rest for 8 to 10 minutes. Invert a serving platter over the baking dish, then invert the platter and dish together and lift off the dish. (If using a springform pan, let rest and then release and lift off the sides and slide the wrapped pilaf onto a platter.) Cut into slices with a sharp serrated knife and serve hot or very warm.

## Persian Rice  CHELO

Once you've made rice this way, you will want it this way every time. The crust that forms on the bottom, called the *tahdig*, is prized by diners. Break it up and put it atop the rice so that everyone can have some. Some cooks add an egg yolk or a spoonful of yogurt to the rice used for the *tahdig*. Others mix the saffron infusion with the egg yolk or yogurt and then mix that with the rice. Still other cooks reserve a few spoonfuls of the loose cooked rice, mix them with the saffron infusion, and then sprinkle the saffron-tinted rice over the cooked rice. All of the options are good, so you may want to experiment to see which one you like best. SERVES 8

2½ cups (1 pound) basmati rice

4 tablespoons salt

4 quarts water

½ cup unsalted butter, or margarine for a meat meal, melted

3 tablespoons hot water

1 egg yolk, lightly beaten, or 1 tablespoon plain yogurt (optional)

½ teaspoon saffron threads, finely crushed and steeped in ¼ cup hot water (optional)

Rinse and drain the rice, then transfer to a bowl. Measure out enough cold water to cover the rice, stir in 1 tablespoon of the salt, and then pour the salted water over the rice. Let soak for 1 to 2 hours or up to overnight.

In a large pot, combine the water and the remaining 3 tablespoons salt and bring to a boil over high heat. Drain the rice, add to the pot, return to a boil, and boil for about 8 minutes, stirring once or twice to prevent the grains from sticking together. Bite a grain. It should be tender on the outside but opaque and uncooked in the center. If not, cook for a minute or two longer. Drain immediately into a colander or sieve and rinse with warm water.

In a heavy saucepan with a tight-fitting lid, stir together ¼ cup of the melted butter and 2 tablespoons of the hot water and place the pan over low heat. Scoop out ½ cup of the rice, mix it with the egg yolk if using, and then add to the pan, mixing it with the butter. Spread it evenly over the bottom of the pan. Add the rest of the rice, piling it on in large spoonfuls and mounding it into a conical shape. Using the handle of a wooden spoon, poke a few holes through the top of the rice. Mix the remaining ¼ cup melted butter with the remaining 1 tablespoon hot water and drizzle over the top. Cover the pan with a dish towel, tie it securely around the pan, and top with the pan lid. Cook the rice over medium heat for 10 minutes to brown and set the crust. Then turn down the heat to very low and steam the rice for 35 minutes longer.

Remove the pan from the heat. Fill the sink with cold water to a depth of about 2 inches, then place the pan in the sink for about 5 minutes to loosen the crust. Remove from the sink, uncover, and spoon the loose cooked rice onto a platter or individual plates, fluffing as you go. Now, turn out the crust, using a spatula to loosen it if it sticks. Place pieces of the crust on top of and around the rice, and then drizzle the rice with the saffron infusion. Serve immediately.

VARIATIONS: *Baked Persian Rice:* If you are nervous about making the classic chelo for fear that the tahdig will remain stuck in the pan, try this oven version. Soak 2 cups basmati rice in salted water to cover for 1 hour and drain. In a large saucepan, bring 4 quarts water and 2 tablespoons salt to a boil, add the drained rice, and boil until a kernel of rice tests done when you bite it, about 8 to 10 minutes. Drain the rice immediately and rinse with warm water. Scoop out 1 cup of the rice and mix it with 1 egg yolk, lightly beaten, and 2 tablespoons melted unsalted butter or olive oil mixed with 1 tablespoon hot water. Oil a shallow 9-by-13-inch baking pan (like a lasagna pan). Spread the buttered rice on the bottom of the prepared pan and press it down with your fingers. Spoon the remaining rice evenly over the top. Season 4 tablespoons melted unsalted butter or olive oil with salt and pepper and mix with ½ teaspoon saffron threads, finely crushed and steeped in ¼ cup hot water (optional), then drizzle the mixture evenly over the rice. Cover with foil and bake in a preheated 350°F oven until the rice is cooked, 25 to 35 minutes. To serve, transfer all of the loose rice to an ovenproof platter and keep warm in a low oven. Raise the oven temperature to 400° or 450°F. Return the rice crust to the oven and bake, uncovered, until the crust is pale golden brown, about 10 minutes. You want the crust to be chewy but not hard. Let the pan sit on a cool surface for about 5 minutes, until the crust is easy to lift out with a spatula. Serve pieces of the browned crust on top of the loose rice.

*Persian Rice with Favas and Dill (Baghali Polo):* Prepare the rice as directed. Fold 1 pound fresh fava beans, shelled, blanched, and peeled, and 2 cups chopped fresh dill into the loose cooked rice.

*Persian Rice with Lentils (Adas Polo):* Cook ⅔ cup green lentils and drain well. Prepare the rice as directed, then fold the warm lentils; ¼ cup raisins, plumped in hot water and drained; 1 teaspoon ground allspice; and ½ teaspoon freshly ground black pepper into the loose cooked rice. Drizzle the finished rice with the saffron infusion if you like.

*Persian Rice with Barberries (Zereshk Polo):* Rinse ½ cup barberries, then soak in warm water for 30 minutes and drain, or fry in 2 tablespoons unsalted butter over medium heat until puffed. Prepare the rice as directed and fold the barberries into the loose cooked rice.

*Persian Rice with Sour Cherries (Albalu Polo):* Soak ½ cup dried cherries in hot water until plumped, then drain. Prepare the rice as directed and fold the cherries and, if you like, ½ cup almonds, toasted, into the loose cooked rice.

# Persian Rice with Carrots and Orange Peel   SHIRIN POLO

This is a glorious and festive dish. Sometimes cooked chicken is added to this pilaf. If you decide to do that, you may want to alternate layers of rice and chicken in the pot. SERVES 6 TO 8

| | |
|---|---|
| Zest of 2 oranges, slivered | 1 teaspoon ground cinnamon |
| 2 cups basmati rice, soaked in salted cold water to cover for 1 hour | 1 teaspoon ground cardamom |
| | ½ teaspoon ground turmeric |
| 4 quarts plus 2 cups water | ½ cup sliced almonds, toasted |
| 2 tablespoons salt | ½ teaspoon saffron threads, finely |
| ½ cup unsalted butter or olive oil | crushed and steeped in ¼ cup hot water |
| 1 cup sugar | ⅓ cup pistachios, chopped |
| 2 cups peeled and coarsely grated carrot | |

Bring a small saucepan filled with water to a boil over high heat, add the orange zest, turn down the heat to medium, and simmer for 5 minutes. Drain into a sieve and rinse with cold water. Repeat this process three times to remove the bitterness from the zest. Set the zest aside.

Drain the rice. In a large saucepan, combine 4 quarts of the water and the salt and bring to a boil over high heat. Add the rice, return to a boil, and boil for about 8 minutes, stirring once or twice to prevent the grains from sticking together. Bite a kernel. It should be tender on the outside but opaque and uncooked in the center. If not, cook for a minute or two longer. Drain immediately into a colander or sieve and rinse with warm water.

To make the traditional crust on the bottom (*tahdig*), warm the butter in a heavy saucepan with a tight-fitting lid over low heat. Pour out half of the melted butter into a small bowl and reserve. Scoop out 2 cups of the cooked rice, mix it with the butter remaining in the pan, and then spread the mixture evenly over the bottom of the pan. Add the rest of the rice, piling it on in large spoonfuls and mounding it into a conical shape. Using the handle of a wooden spoon, poke a few holes in the top of the rice. Drizzle the rice with the reserved butter. Cover the pan with a dish towel, tie it securely around the pan, and top with the pan lid. Cook the rice over medium heat for 10 minutes to brown and set the crust. Then turn down the heat to very low and steam the rice for 35 minutes longer.

While the rice is steaming, in a saucepan, combine the remaining 2 cups water and the sugar and bring to a boil over high heat, stirring to dissolve the sugar. Add the carrot and reserved orange zest, turn down the heat to medium, and cook until the carrot is just tender, about 5 minutes. Drain well, transfer to a bowl, add the cinnamon, cardamom, turmeric, and most of the almonds, and mix well.

When the rice is done, remove the pan from the heat. Fill the sink with cold water to a depth of about 2 inches, then place the pan in the sink for about 5 minutes to loosen the crust. Remove from the sink, uncover, and spoon the loose cooked rice onto a platter, fluffing as you go. Add the carrot and almond mixture to the loose rice and toss to mix well. Drizzle with the saffron infusion. Now, turn out the crust, using a spatula to loosen it if it sticks. Arrange pieces of the crust, the pistachios, and the reserved almonds over and around the rice. Serve immediately.

## *Sabbath Rice*   RISO DEL SABATO

The classic Italian Jewish Friday night rice dish is saffron-flavored rice, which recalls the classic *risotto alla milanese*. Some cooks make it in the manner of a risotto, adding broth in increments, as is done here. Others prepare it as a pilaf, adding the liquid all at once and covering the pan. In *La cucina nella tradizione ebraica,* the rice is sautéed in oil, the hot broth is added, and then the pan is covered and finished in the oven. Once out of the oven, the rice rests, covered, for 10 minutes and then is served with mushrooms, peas, or other seasonal vegetables. For Hanukkah, raisins are added and the dish becomes *riso con l'uvette*. SERVES 4 TO 6

5 to 6 cups chicken or beef broth, or part water and part broth

2 tablespoons olive oil or rendered chicken fat

2 cloves garlic, minced

3 tablespoons chopped fresh flat-leaf parsley

1½ cups Arborio rice

¼ teaspoon saffron threads, finely crushed and steeped in 2 tablespoons hot broth

¾ cup grapes, or sultana raisins, plumped in white wine and drained (optional)

Salt and freshly ground black pepper

Pour the broth into a saucepan and bring to a simmer; adjust the heat to maintain a bare simmer.

Warm the oil in a large sauté pan over medium heat. Add the garlic and parsley and sauté for a few minutes until softened. Add the rice and stir until the kernels are opaque, about 3 minutes. Add a ladleful (about 1 cup) of the simmering broth and stir until the liquid is absorbed, 3 to 4 minutes. Turn down the heat to low and continue adding the broth, a ladleful at a time, stirring until each addition is absorbed before the next is added, until the rice kernels are al dente in the center and creamy on the outside, 20 to 25 minutes in all. Add the saffron infusion about halfway through the cooking, and add the grapes during the last addition of broth. Season with salt and pepper. Serve immediately.

## Butternut Squash Risotto   RISOTTO ALLA ZUCCA GIALLA

Here is Aunt Zita's recipe from Milka Passigli's *Le ricette di casa mia* for a risotto made with *zucca barucca,* the "blessed" and bumpy pumpkin squash of the Veneto. Our butternut squash is the closest to the Italian *zucca,* so it's best to use it instead of pumpkin, which can be watery. I sometimes add 1 cup peeled, cooked, and coarsely chopped chestnuts along with the last addition of broth. SERVES 6

6 cups vegetable broth

3 tablespoons olive oil or part oil and part unsalted butter

2 tablespoons chopped garlic

2 tablespoons chopped fresh sage, plus more for garnish

2½ to 3 cups peeled butternut squash, cut into ½-inch cubes

Salt and freshly ground black pepper

2 cups Arborio rice

½ cup white wine (optional)

6 to 8 tablespoons grated Parmesan cheese

Pour the broth into a saucepan and bring to a simmer; adjust the heat to maintain a bare simmer.

Warm the oil in a deep sauté pan over medium heat. Add the garlic and sage and sauté for a few minutes until softened. Add the squash, sprinkle with salt, and cook, stirring, for 1 minute. Add the rice and stir until the kernels are opaque, about 3 minutes. Add the wine and cook, stirring, for a few minutes just until it evaporates. Add a ladleful of the simmering broth (about 1 cup) and stir until the broth is absorbed, 3 to 4 minutes. Turn down the heat to low and continue adding the broth, a ladleful at a time, stirring until each addition is absorbed before the next is added, until the rice grains are al dente in the center and creamy on the outside, 20 to 25 minutes in all. Stir in 4 tablespoons of the Parmesan cheese, then season with salt and pepper. Serve immediately, sprinkled with the remaining cheese.

VARIATION: For a slightly lighter-tasting dish, make a classic gremolata of 2 tablespoons grated lemon zest, 6 tablespoons chopped fresh flat-leaf parsley, and 1 tablespoon minced garlic and stir it into the risotto during the last few minutes of cooking.

## *Springtime Risotto* RISOTTO MARZOLINO

March (*marzo*) is the month when asparagus and artichokes appear at the market. Inspired by a recipe in Milka Passigli's *Le ricette di casa mia,* this saffron-tinged risotto uses both vegetables. The cream makes the dish very festive and rich and can be omitted if you prefer a lighter risotto. This dish might profit from the addition of a little grated lemon zest with the saffron infusion and a garnish of chopped flat-leaf parsley, basil, or mint. SERVES 6

---

1 pound asparagus, tough stems removed

Juice of 1 lemon

3 large artichokes

6 cups vegetable broth

½ teaspoon saffron threads, lightly crushed

2 to 3 tablespoons oil or unsalted butter

1 small yellow onion, chopped

2 cups Arborio rice

1 cup heavy cream (optional)

½ cup grated Parmesan cheese

---

Bring a saucepan filled with salted water to a boil, add the asparagus, and cook until just tender, about 5 minutes. Drain, immerse in cold water to refresh, then drain again, pat dry, and cut on the diagonal into 1½-inch pieces. Set aside.

Have ready a bowl of water to which you have added the lemon juice. Working with 1 artichoke at a time, trim off the stem flush with the base, then remove all of the leaves until you reach the heart. Pare away the dark green areas from the base. Cut the artichoke heart in half and scoop out and discard the choke from each half with a pointed spoon or a paring knife. Cut each half lengthwise into ¼-inch-thick slices and slip the slices into the lemon water. Bring a saucepan filled with salted water to a boil, drain the artichoke slices, add to the boiling water, and parboil for 8 to 10 minutes, until tender-firm. Drain and set aside.

Pour the broth into a saucepan and bring to a simmer; adjust the heat to maintain a bare simmer. Ladle out 1 cup of the hot broth, place in a bowl, and add the saffron; set aside.

Melt the butter in a large sauté pan over medium heat. Add the onion and cook, stirring occasionally, until translucent and tender, about 8 minutes. Add the rice and stir until the kernels are opaque, about 3 minutes. Add a ladleful of the simmering broth (about 1 cup) and stir until the broth is absorbed, 3 to 4 minutes. Turn down the heat to low and continue adding the broth, a ladleful at a time, stirring until each addition is absorbed before the next is added, until the rice grains are al dente in the center and creamy on the outside, 20 to 25 minutes. For the final cup, add the saffron infusion along with the asparagus and artichokes. Stir in the cream and cheese and heat through. Serve immediately.

## Baked Rice Casserole  BOMBA DI RISO

*Risotto saltato* is a homey Jewish Italian dish of fried leftover risotto. Instead of frying the cooked rice in the classic pancake manner, here it is baked. What you want is a crispy golden exterior and melting cheese inside. In *The Classic Cuisine of the Italian Jews,* Edda Servi Machlin omits the ricotta and adds raisins and grated lemon zest to the rice mixture. I have included directions for cooking the rice in case you don't have leftovers on hand. SERVES 6

---

2½ cups Arborio rice

4 eggs, lightly beaten

⅓ cup grated Parmesan cheese

Salt and freshly ground black pepper

Few gratings nutmeg

1½ cups ricotta cheese

12 ounces fresh mozzarella cheese, cut into ½-inch cubes

---

Preheat the oven to 350°F. Oil a 9-inch ring mold or 1½-to 2-quart soufflé dish.

Bring a saucepan filled with salted water to a boil, add the rice, and cook until al dente, 15 to 18 minutes. Drain well and place in a bowl. Add the eggs and Parmesan cheese and mix well. Season with salt, pepper, and nutmeg.

Pack half of the rice mixture into the prepared mold. Arrange the ricotta and mozzarella cheeses evenly over the rice mixture and then top with the remaining rice mixture.

Bake until golden, about 25 minutes. Remove from the oven, let rest for 10 minutes, and then unmold onto a platter (or scoop out from the baking dish). Serve hot.

VARIATION: *Fried Rice Balls (Crocchette di Riso):* This same mixture of rice, eggs, and Parmesan cheese can be formed into small rice balls with a tiny cube of mozzarella tucked into the center of each one. Coat the balls in fine dried bread crumbs and deep-fry them until golden and the cheese is melted.

## *Farro with Mushrooms and Hazelnuts* FARRO CON FUNGHI E NOCCIOLE

*Farro* is an early variety of wheat, sometimes erroneously labeled spelt, to which it is related. It is primarily cultivated around Lucca in the Garfagnana region of Tuscany, in Umbria, and in the Abruzzo. Lighter in mouthfeel than wheat berries, it has a nutty taste and texture that resembles barley more than wheat. It is now being grown in the United States as well, and I recommend semipearled *farro* from Bob's Red Mill and from Blue-bird Farms in Washington. It can be cooked as you would cook risotto, adding broth by the ladleful; in lots of boiling water; or as a pilaf, which I have done here. SERVES 6

1 ounce (about 1 cup) dried porcini

5 cups water

Salt and freshly ground black pepper

2 cups semipearled farro

5 tablespoons unsalted butter, plus more for finishing (optional)

2 tablespoons olive oil

1½ pounds assorted fresh mushrooms, sliced ¼ inch thick

1 yellow onion, finely chopped (about 1 cup)

½ cup hazelnuts, toasted, skinned, and coarsely chopped

¼ cup chopped fresh flat-leaf parsley, or part parsley and part chopped fresh sage

¾ to 1½ cups vegetable or chicken broth

Rinse the porcini, then soak in hot water to cover until rehydrated, at least 30 minutes.

Meanwhile, bring the water to a boil, add a large pinch or two of salt, and then add the farro. Adjust the heat to maintain a simmer and cook the farro until tender but still chewy at the center. Start checking for doneness after 20 minutes. If it is done but still wet, drain in a sieve. It is fine if a little water remains unabsorbed, as you will need some when you combine the farro with the mushrooms. Set the farro aside.

Drain the porcini, reserving the soaking water, then pass the soaking water through a sieve lined with cheesecloth. Chop the porcini and set aside with the soaking water.

Melt 2 tablespoons of the butter with the oil in a large sauté pan over high heat. Add the fresh mushrooms and sauté until they release some liquid. Stir in the chopped porcini and their soaking water and season with salt and pepper. Remove from the heat.

Melt the remaining 3 tablespoons butter in a large sauté pan over medium heat. Add the onion and cook, stirring occasionally, until translucent and tender, 8 to 10 minutes. Add the cooked mushrooms and all of their pan juices, the hazelnuts, and the parsley and mix well. Fold in the cooked farro, turn down the heat to low, and cook, stirring occasionally and adding ½ to ¾ cup of the broth as needed for a good consistency, until the farro is heated through, 5 to 10 minutes longer Season with salt and pepper. Stir in more butter if you want a richer flavor. If you want a soupier risotto-like consistency, add more broth. Serve hot.

## Bulgur Pilaf

Most recipes for bulgur pilaf call for cooking the grain as if it were rice, steaming it in broth or water to cover. More often than not, this results in a mixture that is heavy and soggy, with the grains sticking together. To keep pilaf light and dry, cook it on the stove top to start and then finish it in the oven.  SERVES 6 TO 8

4 tablespoons unsalted butter or olive oil

1 yellow onion, finely chopped (about 1 cup)

Salt and freshly ground pepper

1½ cups medium-grind bulgur

3 cups chicken broth or water, heated

Chopped green onions, fresh mint, or fresh cilantro; plumped currants; or toasted almonds or pine nuts for garnish (optional)

Preheat the oven to 350°F. Have ready a sheet pan or shallow baking pan.

Melt the butter in a heavy sauté pan over medium heat. Add the onion with a pinch of salt and cook, stirring occasionally, until translucent and tender, about 10 minutes. Add the bulgur and stir until the grains are coated with the butter. Add half of the broth, turn down the heat to low, and stir until the broth is absorbed. Add the rest of the broth, raise the heat to high, and bring to a boil. Turn down the heat to medium-low, cover, and simmer until the broth is absorbed and the bulgur is tender, about 15 minutes.

If the pilaf is soggy, turn it out onto the sheet pan, place in the oven, and bake uncovered for 15 to 20 minutes. Remove from the oven and stir. The pilaf should be ready, but if the grains still seem sticky, return the pan to the oven until the grains are dry and separate, about 10 minutes longer. Transfer to a serving dish. Fold in a garnish, if you like, season with salt and pepper, and serve hot.

## Turkish Bulgur Pilaf with Chickpeas   NOHUTLU BULGUR PİLAVI

There's more to bulgur than the ubiquitous tabbouleh. In Turkey, bulgur is prepared as a pilaf and is served plain, with the addition of toasted pine nuts and plumped currants, or mixed with legumes. Here, chickpeas are added (green lentils can be substituted), resulting in a fine accompaniment to cooked fish, meat, or poultry. Or, you can serve it with a pair of vegetable dishes for a satisfying meal, such as tart spinach and smoky grilled eggplant or sweet roasted tomatoes. To brighten this mild, hearty dish, pass a bowl of *esme* (page 361), the Turkish equivalent of tomato salsa, with the yogurt. SERVES 6

5 tablespoons unsalted butter or olive oil

1 large yellow onion, chopped

1 large tomato, peeled, seeded, and cut into ½-inch cubes

1½ cups drained cooked chickpeas

2 teaspoons salt

3 cups water or vegetable broth

2 cups medium- or coarse-grind bulgur, rinsed

½ teaspoon freshly ground black pepper

¼ teaspoon cayenne pepper, or ½ teaspoon Aleppo pepper flakes

Chopped fresh flat-leaf parsley, dill, or mint for garnish

Plain yogurt for serving

Warm the butter in a saucepan or deep sauté pan over medium heat. Add the onion and cook, stirring occasionally, until translucent and tender, 8 to 10 minutes. Add the tomato and cook, stirring, for 3 minutes longer. Add the chickpeas, salt, and water, raise the heat to high, and bring to a boil. Add the bulgur, stir well, turn down the heat to low, cover, and simmer until the bulgur is tender, about 20 minutes.

Remove from the heat. If liquid is visible even though the bulgur is tender, drain it off, then season the pilaf with the black pepper and cayenne, re-cover the pan, and let the pilaf rest until dry, about 15 minutes (or place the uncovered pan in a low oven for 15 minutes). Garnish with the parsley and pass the yogurt at the table.

## Couscous

Couscous is not a grain but a tiny pasta made from semolina flour and water. The dough is rolled into pellets that are pushed through a screen to make them uniform. Traditionally, the pellets are steamed over a stew in a *couscoussière,* a two-part steamer with a perforated upper pan. Most of us don't have one, of course, but we can easily improvise with a conventional two-part steamer, a colander over a large pot, or a pasta pot with a basket insert. If the holes are too large, you can line the top pan with cheesecloth.

Two sets of instructions follow: the traditional North African steaming method and the quick-and-easy method. The latter will be scorned by purists, but it works, is fast, and produces a respectable result. SERVES 6 TO 8

3 cups couscous (18 to 20 ounces)          Olive oil, as needed

Salt

For the traditional steaming method, spread the couscous in a deep baking pan or dish. Lightly salt 5 to 6 cups hot water and set alongside the pan. Using your fingers, rub the couscous with 2 tablespoons oil, coating the grains evenly. Sprinkle 3 cups of the hot water evenly over the couscous and then let rest until the water is absorbed, about 10 minutes. Rake the couscous with your fingers or a pair of forks to break up the lumps.

Transfer the couscous to a couscoussière or your steamer setup (see headnote) and steam over boiling water until swollen and doubled in size, 15 to 20 minutes. Turn the couscous out into the same baking pan or dish and again rake it to break up the lumps. Sprinkle it with the remaining 2 to 3 cups hot water (the amount depends on how much the pellets swelled on the first steaming), let it absorb the water, and then rake it with your fingers again to break up the lumps. Return the couscous to the couscoussière or steamer setup and steam over boiling water until fully puffed, about 20 minutes longer. Transfer to a platter to serve. This makes a lot of couscous but it can be reheated over boiling water or for a minute or two in a microwave oven if you have leftovers.

For the quick-and-easy method, spread the couscous in a 2-inch deep baking pan or dish. Bring 4½ cups water to a boil and add 1 teaspoon salt and 1 tablespoon olive oil. Pour the boiling water evenly over the couscous, stir gently to moisten every piece, cover the pan with foil, and let rest until the water is absorbed, 15 to 20 minutes. Uncover and rake with a fork to break up lumps. The couscous is now ready to serve. (The yield is smaller than with the traditional method where the repeated steaming makes the couscous swell more.) To hold or for additional swelling, you can steam it over boiling water for 15 to 20 minutes, sprinkling it lightly with hot water. If you have been overly exuberant with the water and the couscous seems too wet, let the couscous sit in a warm place and it will gradually absorb all of the water. As with the traditional method, the couscous can be reheated in a microwave oven.

## Basic Egg Pasta   PASTA ALL'UOVO

Fresh egg pasta is an essential part of the Italian Jewish table. It is easy to make at home with a hand-cranked pasta machine or with the pasta roller attachment for the KitchenAid mixer. Unbleached all-purpose flour or Italian 00 flour can be used for this recipe. Measure the flour by spooning it into a measuring cup and leveling it with a knife. The ingredient amounts are based on using large eggs. If you instead use extra-large eggs, you may not need the water. For the richest pasta, use more egg yolks than whole eggs. Three egg yolks are the equivalent of a single large egg in moisture content.

This recipe makes a stiff, dry-feeling dough, so take the time to knead it well and you will be rewarded with silky, light, tender pasta. It is essential to let the dough rest before rolling it out, giving the gluten in the flour time to relax.

You can buy fresh pasta, of course, but it is rarely as delicate, tender, or thinly rolled as the pasta you make at home. Both Rustichella d'Abruzzo and Fini make high-quality dried egg fettuccine and pappardelle that cook up in minutes and are respectable substitutes for homemade fresh pasta.

---

**MAKES A SCANT 1½ POUNDS (6 MAIN-COURSE OR 8 FIRST-COURSE SERVINGS)**

3 to 3¼ cups unbleached all-purpose or 00 flour

1 teaspoon salt

4 eggs, or 3 eggs and 3 egg yolks, lightly beaten

3 to 4 tablespoons water, if needed

**MAKES 1 POUND (4 MAIN-COURSE OR 6 FIRST-COURSE SERVINGS)**

2¼ to 2½ cups unbleached all-purpose or 00 flour

¾ teaspoon salt

3 eggs, or 2 eggs and 3 egg yolks, lightly beaten

2 to 3 tablespoons water, if needed

**MAKES 8 OUNCES (2 MAIN-COURSE OR 4 FIRST-COURSE SERVINGS)**

1¼ to 1½ cups unbleached all-purpose or 00 flour

½ teaspoon salt

2 eggs, or 1 egg and 3 egg yolks, lightly beaten

1 to 2 tablespoons water, if needed

Semolina flour, fine cornmeal, or Wondra flour for tossing or dusting

---

To make the dough by hand, in a large bowl or on a work surface, stir together the smaller amount of flour and the salt. Make a well in the center and add the eggs to the well. Using a fork, gradually pull the flour into the well until all of it is incorporated and a supple dough forms. If the dough seems too dry, add a bit of water. If it is too wet, add a bit more flour. Turn out the dough onto a lightly floured work surface and knead until smooth, 10 to 15 minutes.

To make the dough in a food processor, combine the smaller amount of flour and the salt in the processor and pulse once or twice to mix. Add the eggs and pulse until the mixture is evenly moistened, adding a bit of water if needed. (Resist the temptation to add too much water or the dough will be too soft and sticky to roll out after it rests.) Gather the dough into a rough ball, transfer to a lightly floured surface, and knead until smooth, 10 to 15 minutes.

Flatten the dough into a thick disk, place in a plastic bag, and let rest for 30 to 60 minutes.

When ready to roll out the pasta, set up the pasta machine or attach the pasta roller to the stand mixer. Divide the dough disk into 2 equal portions for an 8-ounce batch,

4 equal portions for a 1-pound batch, or 6 equal portions for a 1½-pound batch. With a rolling pin, flatten each portion into a piece about the width of the pasta rollers and thin enough to fit through the rollers at their widest setting.

Set the rollers to the widest setting and roll the dough through the rollers. Fold the dough into thirds (like a letter) and pass it through the roller. Repeat this three more times, as which point the dough should be smooth. If the dough begins to stick, lightly dust it with flour. Now, adjust the rollers to the next narrowest setting and pass the dough through the rollers. Continue to pass the dough through progressively narrower settings until you reach the second-to-last setting for lasagna and ravioli. For fettuccine, tagliarini, and pappardelle, proceed to roll the dough through the narrowest setting. If the dough starts to tear, let it rest for 15 minutes so the gluten relaxes and then pass it through the rollers again.

For fettuccine, tagliarini, and pappardelle: Cut the pasta sheets into 9- or 10-inch lengths and let dry on a rack or table for 15 to 20 minutes. If cutting fettuccine or tagliarini by hand, roll up each length into a cylinder and cut crosswise to create strands about ¼ inch wide for fettuccine or about ⅛ inch wide for tagliarini. Or, pass each length through the proper cutter blades on the pasta machine. If making pappardelle, using a pastry wheel, cut the sheets lengthwise into 1-inch-wide noodles. To prevent the strands and noodles from sticking, toss them with semolina flour and then place on sheet pans. You can cook the pasta immediately or cover each pan with a large plastic bag to prevent drying and refrigerate for up to 24 hours.

For ravioli: Roll out the dough into sheets 15 to 18 inches long. Fold each sheet in half lengthwise to mark the midpoint and then unfold. With a long side facing you, place mounds of filling at 2-inch intervals along the lower half of the sheet. Lightly brush or spray with water around each mound, then fold the top half over the lower half, covering the mounds. Press between each mound of filling to seal, but do not seal the bottom edge. Using a pastry wheel, cut between the mounds, pressing out any trapped air. Finally, press the bottom edge to seal, then trim the edge with the pastry wheel. Line sheet pans with parchment paper. Arrange the ravioli, not touching one another, on the prepared pans. Sprinkle lightly with semolina flour. You can cook the ravioli immediately or refrigerate them, uncovered, for a few hours.

## *Stuffed Pasta Rolls*   ROTOLI DI PASTA

Pasta rolls are a specialty of Emilia-Romagna, but they are also found in the *cucina ebraica* of Padua. The pasta dough is rolled out by hand into a large rectangle, which is spread with the filling, rolled up, wrapped in cheesecloth, and simmered in salted water. (A fish poacher or deep roasting pan with a rack is ideal.) The cooked rolls can be sliced and served warm topped with melted butter and grated cheese or with a light sauce, or the slices can be topped with butter and cheese, warmed in the oven, and then served with a light sauce, if desired.

A variety of fillings are used, with spinach and ricotta the most common. The following recipes are interpretations of those found in Giuseppe Maffioli's *La cucina padovana* and a handful of other Italian cookbooks. SERVES 6 TO 8

To shape the rolls, make a 1½-pound batch of Basic Egg Pasta (page 159), shape into a disk, and let rest as directed. Choose a filling and prepare it. Divide the dough in half. On a lightly floured work surface, roll out half of the dough into a 10-by-20-inch rectangle. Spread with half of the filling. Starting on a short side, roll up the pasta sheet to enclose the filling fully. Wrap in cheesecloth, a clean kitchen towel, or plastic wrap, then tie both ends and once in the middle with kitchen string. Repeat with the remaining dough and filling. (At this point, the rolls can be refrigerated for up to 2 hours before continuing.)

To cook the rolls, fill a roasting pan or fish poacher outfitted with a rack with salted water and bring to a simmer. Gently lower the rolls into the water, cover, and simmer for 20 minutes. Carefully remove the rolls from the pan and drain well.

To serve the rolls, allow them to cool for 5 to 8 minutes, then unwrap and cut crosswise into slices ½ to 1 inch thick. Arrange the slices on a serving platter and top with melted unsalted butter and grated Parmesan cheese or with tomato sauce. Alternatively, place the warm slices in a buttered baking dish, or let the rolls cool completely, then slice and arrange in the prepared baking dish. Drizzle with melted butter and sprinkle with grated Parmesan. Place in a preheated 350°F oven for 10 minutes if the rolls were warm when you sliced them. If they were cold, cover the pan with foil or plastic wrap, place in a water bath, and heat in the preheated oven for 30 minutes. Serve with Basic Tomato Sauce (page 328), if desired. If you like, you can thin the tomato sauce with a bit of cream for a lighter tomato flavor.

## Spinach and Ricotta Filling for Pasta Rolls
ROTOLI DI SPINACI E RICOTTA

2 pounds fresh spinach, stemmed and rinsed, or 2 packages (10 ounces each) frozen chopped spinach, thawed

4 tablespoons unsalted butter

1½ cups (12 ounces) ricotta cheese, spooned into a sieve placed over a bowl and drained for 2 hours

2 eggs, lightly beaten

½ teaspoon salt

½ teaspoon freshly ground black pepper

¼ teaspoon freshly grated nutmeg

If using fresh spinach, cook it in the rinsing water clinging to the leaves just until wilted, 3 to 5 minutes. Drain well and chop finely. If using thawed frozen spinach, squeeze dry. Melt the butter in a large sauté pan over medium heat and let it color slightly. Add the spinach and toss it in the butter for a few minutes. Transfer to a bowl, add the ricotta and eggs, season with salt, pepper, and nutmeg, and mix well. Let cool. Shape, poach, and serve the pasta rolls as directed on page 161 with or without the tomato sauce.

## Roman Tuna and Ricotta Filling for Pasta Rolls
ROTOLI DI TONNO E RICOTTA

2 cans (7 ounces each) olive oil–packed tuna, preferably Italian, drained (9 ounces drained)

1 ⅓ cups (11 ounces) ricotta cheese, spooned into a sieve placed over a bowl and drained for 2 hours

2 tablespoons grated Parmesan cheese

3 tablespoons chopped fresh basil

2 cloves garlic, finely minced

½ teaspoon salt

¼ teaspoon freshly ground black pepper

In a bowl, combine all of the ingredients and mix well. Shape, poach, and serve the pasta rolls as directed on page 161 with the tomato sauce.

## Baked Meat-Stuffed Pasta Rolls  ROTOLI DI CARNE AL FORNO

In this recipe the pasta roll is baked, though it can also be poached, sliced, and sauced as described for the pasta rolls on page 161. It is based on a description in *La cucina padovana* by Giuseppe Maffioli, but Mira Sacerdoti, in *Italian Jewish Cooking,* offers a similar recipe called Meat Loaf in a Dressing Gown. It includes the classic additions of pine nuts and raisins. SERVES 6

1½-pound batch Basic Egg Pasta (page 159)

3 tablespoons olive oil

2 yellow onions, chopped

3 cloves garlic, minced

¼ cup chopped fresh flat-leaf parsley

1 pound ground beef or veal

1½ teaspoons salt

¼ teaspoon freshly ground black pepper

¼ teaspoon freshly grated nutmeg

½ teaspoon ground cinnamon

1 cup dry Marsala or dry sherry, such as fino

Grated zest of 1 lemon (optional)

2 eggs

Fine dried bread crumbs, as needed

2 cups Basic Tomato Sauce (page 328), heated (optional)

Make the pasta dough, shape into a disk, and let rest as directed.

Warm the oil in a large sauté pan over medium heat. Add the onions and cook, stirring occasionally, until translucent and tender, 8 to 10 minutes. Add the garlic and parsley and cook for a few minutes longer. Add the beef, salt, pepper, nutmeg, and cinnamon and cook, breaking up any lumps of beef with a wooden spoon, until the meat loses its color, about 8 minutes. Add the wine and the lemon zest, let the wine bubble up, and then continue to cook until the wine has evaporated. Remove from the heat. Lightly beat 1 egg and add to the meat mixture along with enough bread crumbs to bind the mixture. Let cool for 30 minutes.

Preheat the oven to 350°F. Lightly oil a sheet pan or line it with parchment paper.

Divide the dough in half. On a lightly floured work surface, roll out half of the dough into a 10-by-20-inch rectangle. Spread with half of the filling. Starting on a short side, roll up the pasta sheet to enclose the filling fully. Place seam side down on the prepared pan. Repeat with the remaining dough and filling. Lightly beat the remaining egg, then brush both rolls with the beaten egg.

Bake until golden, about 30 minutes. Remove from the oven and let rest for 5 to 8 minutes. Cut the rolls into 1-inch-thick slices and serve warm with the sauce.

## *Meat-Filled Ravioli*   RAVIOLI DI CARNE

Here, I have paired ravioli with tomato sauce, but they are also delicious in a rich meat broth. If you have lots of time on your hands, this filling can be used for tortellini, as well. SERVES 6

1½-pound batch Basic Egg Pasta (page 159)

2 tablespoons olive oil or rendered chicken fat

1 small yellow onion, diced

12 ounces ground lean veal or turkey or chicken breast

2 egg yolks, lightly beaten

Salt and freshly ground black pepper

Few gratings nutmeg

2½ to 3 cups Basic Tomato Sauce (page 328), heated

Make the pasta dough, shape into a disk, and let rest as directed.

Warm the oil in a sauté pan over medium heat. Add the onion and sauté until translucent and tender, about 8 minutes. Add the meat and cook, breaking up any lumps with a wooden spoon, until the meat loses its color, about 8 minutes. Remove from the heat, add the egg yolks, season with salt, pepper, and nutmeg, and mix well. Let cool.

Roll out the pasta dough and fill and shape the ravioli as directed on page 161.

Bring a large pot of salted water to a boil. Add the ravioli and cook until al dente. Using a slotted skimmer, scoop out the ravioli and place in a serving dish. Top with the sauce and serve immediately.

VARIATION: *Ricotta and Spinach Ravioli (Ravioli di Ricotta e Spinaci):* For Purim, substitute Spinach and Ricotta Filling for Pasta Rolls (page 161) for the meat filling, then shape and cook the ravioli as directed. Top with the tomato sauce, or drizzle with melted butter and sprinkle with grated Parmesan cheese.

# Pumpkin-Filled Ravioli from Mantua
## RAVIOLI CON LA ZUCCA BARUCCA

Pumpkin arrived in Italy with the Spanish and Portuguese Jews after the Inquisition. Although popular in Ancona and Ferrara, these much-loved ravioli are a specialty of Mantua, where a sizable Jewish community thrived during the reign of the Gonzaga family. The filling can include the addition of almond macaroons (amaretti); ground toasted almonds; *mostarda di frutta,* a condiment of candied fruit in a mustard-flavored syrup that is a specialty of Cremona; or chopped raisins. None is essential, but each would bring an interesting sweetness to the ravioli. SERVES 6

**FILLING**

1 sugar pumpkin or kabocha or butternut squash (about 2½ pounds)

1 cup grated Parmesan cheese

Freshly grated nutmeg

1 cup crushed almond macaroons (amaretti) or ground toasted almonds (optional)

½ cup chopped raisins (optional)

Fine dried bread crumbs, if needed

1½-pound batch Basic Egg Pasta (page 159)

6 tablespoons unsalted butter, melted

1 tablespoon chopped fresh sage

½ cup chopped toasted hazelnuts or almonds (optional)

To make the filling, roast and purée the squash as directed in Master Recipe for Winter Squash Purée (page 36). Transfer the puréed flesh to a sieve placed over a bowl, cover, and refrigerate overnight to drain off the excess moisture.

The next day, make the pasta dough, shape into a disk, and let rest as directed.

To finish the filling, squeeze the pumpkin flesh to remove any additional moisture, then transfer to a bowl, add the cheese, a generous amount of nutmeg, the macaroons, and the raisins. If the mixture still seems too moist, add bread crumbs as needed to absorb the moisture.

Roll out the pasta dough and fill and shape the ravioli as directed on page 161. Alternatively, cut the pasta sheets into 3- to 4-inch rounds, place a heaping tablespoonful of filling in the center of each round, dampen the edges of the round with water, fold in half, and press the edges to seal.

Bring a large pot of salted water to a boil. Add the ravioli and cook until al dente. Using a slotted skimmer, scoop out the ravioli and place in a serving dish. Drizzle with the butter, sprinkle with the sage, and, if you have not added nuts to the filling, top with the hazelnuts. Serve immediately.

## Sabbath Pasta Dish from Emilia-Romagna   HAMIN PER SABATO

As noted earlier, *hamin* means "oven," but it is also the name for this incredibly rich dish served on *sabato bescialach,* a Sabbath that is special to Italy. This crispy noodle pancake with a tender middle is also known as *ruota di faraone,* or "pharaoh's wheel," or *frisinsal* in Venetian dialect. Originally it was made with goose salami and finely minced rosemary and sage. Today, it's easy to purchase chicken or turkey sausage, which works well in place of the salami, though you will still need some rendered goose or chicken fat. You can substitute store-bought fresh fettuccine for the homemade pasta. SERVES 6

1-pound batch Basic Egg Pasta (page 159)

FILLING

2 to 3 tablespoons rendered goose or chicken fat

2 cups coarsely chopped cooked Beef Sausage (page 350), poultry sausage, or roast chicken

⅔ cup pine nuts, lightly toasted

½ cup raisins, plumped in hot water and drained

1 cup meat juices from a roast or stew or rich meat broth

Make the pasta dough, shape into a disk, let rest, and roll out and cut into fettuccine as directed.

Preheat the oven to 350°F. Oil a 9-by-12-inch gratin dish or, to reflect the image of the pharoah's wheel, a round baking dish of about the same volume.

To make the filling, warm the fat in a sauté pan over medium heat. Add the sausage, pine nuts, and raisins, stir well, and then toss with a little of the meat juices to coat evenly. Remove from the heat and set aside.

Bring a large pot of salted water to a boil. Drop in the pasta, stir well, and cook until al dente. Drain well and toss the warm noodles with the remaining meat juices.

Layer half of the noodles in the prepared baking dish. Top with all of the meat mixture and then with the remaining noodles. Bake until golden and crispy on the outside but still tender in the center, about 30 minutes. Remove from the oven, let cool completely, and serve at room temperature.

# Whole Wheat Pasta with Anchovies and Garlic
## BIGOLI CON SALSA ALLA VENEZIANA

*Bigoli* are whole wheat spaghetti, somewhat thicker and longer than regular packaged spaghetti. They are made with eggs and are extruded through a press called a *bigolaro*. You can make this dish with whole wheat, *farro,* or regular durum wheat packaged pasta. Long, thin shapes are best. Whole wheat pasta cooks quickly and does not hold well, so serve it right away.

This classic Venetian pasta is dressed simply with anchovy, garlic, and olive oil. Salt-packed anchovies are preferred, but olive oil–packed anchovies can be substituted. Don't omit the parsley. It delivers more than just color. Do not chop it too finely, either, or its flavor will be lessened. A little grated lemon zest or a handful of toasted bread crumbs will lighten the fish flavor. SERVES 6

1 pound whole wheat spaghetti

4 to 6 tablespoons extra virgin olive oil

12 salt-packed anchovies, filleted, rinsed, and finely chopped, or 24 olive oil–packed anchovy fillets (about one 3-ounce jar)

3 or 4 cloves garlic, finely minced

6 tablespoons chopped fresh flat-leaf parsley

Freshly ground black pepper

Grated zest of 1 large lemon (optional)

½ cup dried bread crumbs, toasted (optional)

Bring a large pot of salted water to a boil. Drop in the pasta, stir well, and cook until al dente.

Meanwhile, warm the oil in a large sauté pan over low heat. Add the anchovies and cook, stirring, until they start to melt, 1 to 2 minutes. Add the garlic and parsley and cook, stirring, for 2 minutes longer.

Drain the pasta, reserving about ¼ cup of the pasta water. Raise the heat under the sauce to medium and add the pasta and water to the sauté pan. Toss and stir for 1 to 2 minutes to coat and flavor the pasta with the sauce. Sprinkle with some pepper and the lemon zest and bread crumbs and serve immediately.

## Pasta with Tuna Sauce   SPAGHETTI AL TONNO

This recipe takes the *bigoli* recipe on page 167 one step further. It's a bit more filling, as chopped onion is sautéed in olive oil, and canned tuna and capers are tossed into the basic anchovy-garlic sauce at the last minute. Sometimes tomato is added, sometimes not. SERVES 4 OR 5

1 pound long dried pasta, such as spaghetti

5 tablespoons extra virgin olive oil

1 large yellow onion, finely chopped (about 2 cups)

12 salt-packed anchovies, filleted, rinsed, and very finely chopped, or 24 olive oil–packed anchovy fillets (about one 3-ounce jar)

3 cloves garlic, finely minced

6 tablespoons chopped fresh flat-leaf parsley

1 can (6 ounces) olive oil–packed tuna, preferably Italian, drained and broken up

2 tablespoons brined capers, rinsed and chopped

1 to 2 cups chopped canned plum tomatoes (optional)

Grated lemon zest (optional)

Freshly ground black pepper

Bring a large pot of salted water to a boil. Drop in the pasta, stir well, and cook until al dente.

Meanwhile, warm the oil in a large sauté pan over medium heat. Add the onion and cook, stirring occasionally, until translucent, about 6 minutes. Add the anchovies, garlic, and parsley and cook, stirring, until the anchovies melt, about 1 minute. Add the tuna, capers, tomatoes, and lemon zest and cook until all of the ingredients are warmed through, about 2 minutes.

Drain the pasta and add to the sauce in the sauté pan over medium heat. Toss and stir for 1 to 2 minutes to coat and flavor the pasta with the sauce. Sprinkle with pepper and serve immediately.

## Fried Noodles   FIDELLOS TOSTADOS

In Spain, *fideos* is a classic fried noodle dish prepared in the manner of paella. The noodles are sautéed to color them and then they are cooked in broth until the liquid is absorbed. In the Turkish book *Sefarad Yemekleri,* these fried noodles are called *skulaka,* and in some Greek cookbooks they are *fideikos.* The *fidellos* used here is the Ladino term. Coiled vermicelli or *fedelini* are the noodles of choice. If you are using the coils, there is no need to break them up, but if you are using the long pasta, you'll need to break it into 3-inch lengths. If the noodles will be accompanying a meat-based dish, use meat or poultry broth or water; for a dairy meal, use vegetable broth or water. SERVES 4 TO 6

½ cup olive or sunflower oil

1 package (12 ounces) coiled vermicelli, or long fedelini, broken into 3-inch lengths

2 cups peeled, seeded, and diced tomatoes (fresh or canned), optional

3 cups broth or water or part water and part tomato liquid if using canned tomatoes

1 teaspoon salt

Warm the oil in a large sauté pan over medium heat. Add the noodles and fry, turning once, until golden, about 5 minutes total. Add tomatoes, broth, and salt, cover partially, and cook, stirring occasionally, until the liquid is absorbed, 8 to 10 minutes. Remove from the heat and let rest, covered, for 5 minutes. Serve hot.

## *Macaroni and Cheese*  MAKARONIA KON LECHE

Although this seems remarkably familiar and all-American, *makaronia kon leche* was a specialty of the town of Komotini in Thrace and was often served at Shavuot. The Greeks did not use elbow macaroni but the longer version of the noodle. The dish can be cooked on the stove top or in the oven. SERVES 4 TO 6

1 pound macaroni, ziti, or penne

1 cup milk

¼ cup crumbled feta cheese, plus more if baking

¼ cup grated Parmesan cheese, plus more if baking

To cook on the stove top, bring a large pot of salted water to a boil. Drop in the pasta, stir well, and cook until a couple of minutes shy of al dente, about 8 minutes. Drain well.

In a medium-large saucepan, bring the milk just to a boil over medium heat. Add the ¼ cup feta and the ¼ cup Parmesan, turn down the heat to low, and then add the cooked pasta. Cook until all of the liquid has been absorbed and the pasta is quite tender, 5 to 8 minutes. Serve hot.

To cook in the oven, preheat the oven to 350°F. Boil the pasta as directed, transfer to a generously buttered baking dish, stir in the milk and ¼ cup each feta and Parmesan, and sprinkle the top with more feta and Parmesan. Bake until the top is browned, about 20 minutes. Serve hot.

# Syrian Chicken with Macaroni   DJEJ MACARUNI

According to cookbook author Gilda Angel, this is a Sabbath favorite of the Syrian Jews. It is called *treya* in Egypt, and a version of chicken and noodles appears in the Moroccan kitchen as *inetria,* with both names related to *itriya,* the early Arabic term for pasta. In the Moroccan dish, the chicken is simmered in a flavorful broth, skinned, boned, and cut into small pieces, and then tossed with fettuccine-like noodles cooked in the same broth and seasoned with turmeric or saffron. These combos of chicken and noodles are simple and comforting. Certainly this dish would more than please children and any fussy eaters in your family. It's the beloved chicken pasta dish they hunger for and that Italians never serve. SERVES 4 TO 6

2 small broiler chickens, each cut into 8 pieces

Salt and freshly ground black pepper

Sweet paprika

2 to 3 cloves garlic, chopped

1 pound macaroni, shells, farfalle, or other short pasta

2 tablespoons olive oil

⅔ cup tomato sauce

½ cup chicken broth

½ teaspoon ground cinnamon

½ teaspoon ground allspice

Preheat the oven to 375°F.

Season the chicken pieces with salt, pepper, and paprika. Arrange the pieces in a single layer in a baking pan and sprinkle the garlic evenly over them. Cover the dish with foil. Bake until very tender, about 1½ hours.

Meanwhile, bring a large pot of salted water to a boil. Drop in the pasta, stir well, and cook until al dente. Drain, rinse with cold water to stop the cooking, and toss with the oil to prevent sticking.

When the chicken is ready, remove the pieces from the pan, let them cool until they can be handled, and then remove and discard the skin and bones. Cut into bite-size pieces. Add the cooked macaroni to the pan and toss with the pan juices. Add the chicken, tomato sauce, broth, cinnamon, and allspice and mix well.

Bake, uncovered, until the top is browned and crisp, 35 to 45 minutes. Serve hot.

# Pasta and Meat Gratin   TORTINO DE MACCHERONI CON CARNE

In *The Sephardic Kosher Kitchen,* Suzy David also calls this dish *mussaka de macarons.* In keeping with the spirit of a classic moussaka, you can add a layer of cooked eggplant slices to the gratin. In traditional Greek cooking, this dish is known as *pastitsio.* This version of the recipe comes from a Sephardic menu that appears in *Le feste ebràiche,* published in Rome in 1987. SERVE 4 TO 6

---

1 pound macaroni, shells, farfalle, penne rigate, or other short pasta

5 to 6 tablespoons olive oil

1 large yellow onion, chopped

1 pound ground beef or veal, or a combination

Salt and freshly ground black pepper

3 large tomatoes, peeled, seeded, and chopped

5 eggs

¼ cup chopped fresh flat-leaf parsley

1 globe eggplant, peeled, sliced crosswise, and fried in olive oil or baked until soft (optional)

1½ cups Basic Tomato Sauce (page 328)

---

Preheat the oven to 350°F. Oil a 9-by-12-by-2-inch baking dish.

Bring a large pot of salted water to a boil. Drop in the pasta, stir well, and cook until al dente, then drain.

Meanwhile, warm 3 tablespoons of the oil in a large sauté pan over medium heat. Add the onion and cook, stirring occasionally, until translucent and tender, 8 to 10 minutes. Add the beef, season with salt and pepper, and cook, breaking up any lumps with a wooden spoon, until the meat is lightly browned, about 10 minutes. Stir in the tomatoes and remove from the heat. Lightly beat 2 of the eggs and stir into the meat mixture. Stir in the parsley.

Lightly beat the remaining 3 eggs and stir into the drained pasta. Layer half of the pasta in the prepared baking dish. Top with the meat mixture, spreading it evenly, and then with the eggplant slices. Layer the remaining pasta on top. Drizzle with the remaining 2 to 3 tablespoons oil.

Bake until the top is golden, 30 to 40 minutes. Serve hot, accompanied with the sauce.

VARIATION:  Do not add the 3 eggs to the cooked pasta. Make a fake béchamel using 3 tablespoons margarine, 3 tablespoons all-purpose flour, and 1½ cups meat broth. When the sauce has thickened, remove from the heat and gradually whisk in 3 eggs, lightly beaten. To build the gratin, layer half of the pasta in the baking dish, top with one-third of the béchamel, add all of the meat mixture, then add half of the remaining béchamel, all of the remaining pasta, and finish with the remaining béchamel. Bake as directed.

## Polenta

Polenta is a basic accompaniment for many Italian Jewish dishes. It can be served warm, as soft and comforting as porridge, unadorned or enriched with butter or cheese for a dairy meal. Or it can be allowed to firm up and then cut into pieces and sautéed, baked, or deep-fried. Most traditional recipes call for slowly pouring the cornmeal in a fine stream into boiling water and then stirring vigorously to prevent lumps. But I have found that combining the polenta and the cold water in the pot and then gradually bringing the mixture to a boil while whisking occasionally is a foolproof method for preventing lumps. SERVES 4

---

1 cup polenta

4 cups water

Salt

3 to 4 tablespoons unsalted butter and ⅓ cup grated Parmesan cheese if serving soft

Clarified butter or olive oil if sautéing

Grated Parmesan cheese for sprinkling if baking

Olive oil, 1 or 2 eggs, and fine dried bread crumbs for coating, if deep-frying

---

Combine the polenta, water, and 1 teaspoon salt in a heavy saucepan and place over medium-high heat. Bring to a boil, whisking occasionally. Turn down the heat to a simmer and cook, stirring often, until very thick and no longer grainy on the tongue, about 30 minutes. If the polenta thickens too quickly but still feels undercooked and grainy, stir in some hot water and continue to cook until it is cooked through and soft. Taste and adjust the seasoning with salt and then add the butter or cheese if desired.

Serve the polenta warm right out of the pot. You can also hold the polenta over hot water in a double boiler for 30 minutes or so, adding hot water as needed to keep it soft and spoonable.

Or, you can butter or oil a 9-by-12-by-2-inch baking pan, pour the hot polenta into the pan, let cool until just set, and then cover with plastic wrap and refrigerate until chilled and fully set. To serve, cut the polenta into strips, squares, or triangles, or as directed in individual recipes, and then remove from the pan.

To sauté the pieces, place a nonstick or cast-iron frying pan over medium-high heat and add just enough clarified butter to film the bottom. In batches, add the pieces and cook, turning as needed and adding more butter as needed, until golden on both sides, 8 to 10 minutes total. Serve hot.

To bake the pieces, preheat the oven to 400°F and butter 1 or more gratin dishes. Place the polenta pieces in a single layer in the prepared dish(es) and sprinkle with grated Parmesan cheese. Bake until golden and crusty, 20 to 30 minutes. Serve hot.

To deep-fry the pieces, line a sheet pan with paper towels and preheat the oven to 200°F. Pour the oil to a depth of about 1 inch into a wide, deep sauté pan or saucepan and heat to 350°F. Meanwhile, break the egg into a shallow bowl and beat until blended (add the second egg later if needed). Spread the bread crumbs on a plate. Working with a few pieces at a time, dip them into the beaten egg and then into the bread crumbs, tapping off the excess. Slip the pieces into the hot oil and fry, turning once, until golden on both sides, 5 to 7 minutes total. Using a slotted spatula, transfer them to the towel-lined pan to drain and keep warm in the oven until all of the pieces are cooked. Serve hot.

Vegetables

I N GENERATIONS PAST, MEDITERRANEAN JEWISH MEALS were based around grains and vegetables, with only small portions of meat, fish, or poultry. Vegetables were readily available and generally inexpensive, which meant that an extensive repertoire of vegetable recipes evolved. Cooks would take these humble ingredients and make them festive and filling by combining them with bread crumbs and cheese or with *besciamella* in gratins, or by puréeing them and then enriching them with eggs for *sformati* or *quajados* (savory puddings). Such dishes were sometimes the centerpiece of the meal and often rivaled the huge roster of vegetable-based pastas, rice dishes, and savory pies that the Sephardic Jews also favored.

Even though vegetables were plentiful and not costly, there was a constant preoccupation with thrift. Nothing was wasted. Vegetable trimmings became part of a broth. Peas were used in a festive dish one day, and the next day, the reserved pods were turned into a special braised dish called *guscetti* or were simmered and puréed for a pea broth for cooking risotto. Sephardim offered the stems of spinach and Swiss chard in dishes by themselves.

Most vegetables were braised on the stove top. A style of cooking called *sofegae,* in which vegetables were cooked in olive oil with very little water so that they caramelized and their flavor intensified, was popular. It's a wonderful cooking technique, one that I find useful in getting the last bit of sweetness out of vegetables. Of course, such long cooking may sound unappealing to those of us who dwell in the land of al dente, but I encourage you to give it a try. Fennel, carrots, cauliflower, artichokes, and cabbage will take on a sweetness that you've not experienced before.

Now that all of our homes have ovens, we are able to roast vegetables for even deeper flavor, thus adding to the repertoire of gratins and *sformati* that were previously sent to the local bakery to cook in the oven. Roasted vegetables can be sauced with tahini or yogurt sauce, *charmoula,* or a simple vinaigrette and garnished with chopped herbs, crumbled feta, toasted nuts, *za'atar,* or *dukkah.* Many dishes were equally good hot and cold, so that they could be served hot on Friday and then set out at room temperature on the Sabbath.

When choosing a vegetable dish to make, don't overlook the many vegetable recipes in chapter 1 of this book. Room-temperature dishes like caponata (sweet-and-sour eggplant) or roasted peppers marinated in olive oil that are generally part of a meze or antipasto assortment also make a good vegetable course.

## *Crispy Fried Artichokes, Jewish Style*   CARCIOFI ALLA GIUDIA

The first time you eat one of these amazing artichokes in Rome, you will want to cry. They are so beautiful—like crispy chrysanthemums—and so delicious that you will vow to make them at home. Oh, would that it were so simple. *Carciofi alla giudia* are easier to write about than to cook for a few reasons. First, Roman artichokes are picked when they are young and tender. They come to the market with their long stems intact—tender and flexible—and have no wiry central chokes. American artichokes typically have a tough fibrous choke and prickly leaf tips, and the stem is often gone. Then, if you read an Italian recipe for this classic Roman Jewish dish, it appears easy to make: just pound the artichokes open and fry. But if you have tried this at home, you have discovered that many of the leaves crack or fall off! I've found that it is best to parboil medium-size artichokes and then gently poke them open and remove the chokes. For an even greater chance of success, use baby artichokes that have soft, underdeveloped chokes. They are too small to make a dramatic flower on the plate—more like dandelions than chrysanthemums—but you will get the crispy texture of the classic *carciofi alla giudia* and they are easy to work with and will cook in less time (In other words, they're a good start before you tackle medium-size artichokes.) You can also halve or quarter large artichokes, remove and discard the chokes, flatten them a bit, and then fry them. Yes, again you lose the dramatic effect of a big flower, but you do get the correct taste and texture. SERVES 4

---

2 lemons

4 medium artichokes with stems intact, or 8 baby artichokes

At least 4 cups olive oil, or as needed to cover

Salt

Lemon wedges for serving

---

Have ready a large bowl of water to which you have added the juice of 1 lemon. Halve the remaining lemon. Working with 1 artichoke at a time, cut off all but 1½ inches of the stem, then peel away the dark green fibrous outer layer of the stem and the base. Rub the pared areas with a cut lemon half. Using a serrated knife, cut about 1 inch off the tops of the leaves. Remove all of the tough outer leaves and snip off any remaining spines with scissors. As each artichoke is trimmed, slip it into the lemon water. Baby artichokes will need little trimming. Just remove any loose leaves.

When all of the artichokes are trimmed, drain them well and place on a kitchen towel. Carefully open the leaves by poking them open with your fingers, being careful not to crack them at the base. If you can get to the choke without breaking all of the leaves, carefully scoop it out with a melon baller or a small pointed spoon. If not, wait until after the first cooking.

For the first cooking, select a pot that is wide enough and deep enough to hold all of the artichokes side by side. Place them stem end up in the pot and add oil to cover. Bring to a boil over high heat, turn down the heat to medium-low, and simmer until cooked through but not soft, 12 to 16 minutes for medium-size artichokes and 8 to 10 minutes for babies. As the artichokes soften, push down on them gently to open them up. To test for doneness, slide a thin wooden skewer into the base. It should go in easily.

Line a sheet pan with paper towels. Using tongs, transfer the artichokes, stem end up, to the prepared pan and press down gently to keep an open flower shape. If you did not remove the chokes earlier, turn the artichokes over, scoop out each choke with a melon baller or a small pointed spoon, and then turn stem end up again and flatten them a bit more. Baby artichokes will have hardly any choke. The artichokes can be prepared up to this point 2 to 3 hours in advance. (If getting the flower shape does not matter to you, you can cut the medium artichokes in halves or quarters and the baby artichokes in halves to remove the chokes.)

For the second cooking, preheat the oven to 250°F and line a sheet pan with paper towels. Select a deep cast-iron frying pan. Pour in oil from the first cooking to a depth of 2½ to 3 inches and heat to about 350°F (a low boil). Standing back, flick a few drops of water into the hot oil; if it sizzles on contact, the oil is ready. With a long-handled fork, place 2 artichokes, stem end up, in the hot oil. Using tongs to hold them down, press on them to keep the open flower shape. Fry until golden and crisp, about 8 minutes for medium and 5 to 6 minutes for babies. (If you have cut the artichokes into halves or quarters, just fry them in the oil until golden and crisp.)

Transfer the artichokes to the towel-lined pan to drain. Sprinkle with salt and keep warm in the oven. Fry the remaining 2 artichokes the same way (it is impossible to fry 4 artichokes at a time, as you can't hold them down at the same time unless two of you are cooking them or you are an octopus). Serve immediately with the lemon wedges.

# Artichokes with Mint and Garlic, Roman Style
CARCIOFI ALLA ROMANA

Artichokes stuffed with a mixture of mint, parsley, and garlic and braised in olive oil are a Roman specialty. Sometimes bread crumbs or minced anchovies are added to the stuffing mixture. SERVES 4

| | |
|---|---|
| 2 lemons | ¼ cup chopped fresh flat-leaf parsley |
| 4 medium artichokes | ¼ cup chopped fresh mint |
| 2 or 3 cloves garlic, minced | 1 cup fine dried bread crumbs (optional) |

2 tablespoons minced olive oil–packed anchovy fillets (optional)

Salt and freshly ground black pepper

Olive oil, for drizzling and cooking

Lemon wedges for serving

Have ready a large bowl of water to which you have added the juice of 1 lemon. Halve the remaining lemon. Working with 1 artichoke at a time, cut off all but 1½ inches of the stem, then peel away the dark green fibrous outer layer of the stem and the base. If the stem seems tough, trim off flush with the bottom. Rub the pared areas with a cut lemon half. Remove all of the tough outer leaves, keeping the tender inner green leaves and the pale green, pointed core, which should be 1¼ to 1½ inches in diameter at its base. Carefully open the leaves by rapping the artichoke very gently on a tabletop or by poking it open with your fingers. Be careful not to crack the leaves at the base. Using a melon baller or a small pointed spoon, carefully scoop out the choke. Rub the artichoke with a cut lemon half. As each artichoke is trimmed, slip it into the lemon water.

In a small bowl, combine the garlic, parsley, mint, bread crumbs, and anchovies and mix well. Season with salt and pepper and drizzle with oil. Drain the artichokes and pat dry. Tuck the stuffing into the artichokes, both into the cavity left by the choke and between the leaves. Close the leaves tightly over the stuffing.

If you have artichokes without stems, place them stem end down and close together in a Dutch oven or saucepan. Drizzle with 1 part water and 2 parts olive oil to a depth of about 2 inches. Cover the pan, place over very low heat, and cook gently until they test tender when a thin wooden skewer is inserted into the base, 45 to 60 minutes.

If you have artichokes with stems, preheat the oven to 350°F. Tie the leaves closed with kitchen string and put the artichokes, stem end up and snugly packed, in a baking dish or ovenproof pan. Season with salt and add a mixture of 1 part water to 2 parts olive oil to cover completely. Cover, place in the oven, and cook until tender when tested with a thin wooden skewer, 45 to 60 minutes. Alternatively, pack the tied artichokes stem end up in a deep saucepan, cover, place over low heat on the stove top, and cook until they test done, 45 to 60 minutes.

Serve the artichokes warm or at room temperature, accompanied with the lemon wedges.

VARIATION: If you do not want to deal with tucking the stuffing between the leaves, cut off the stems, pare each artichoke down to the heart, fill the centers with the stuffing, place the hearts side by side in a baking dish, drizzle with olive oil, add 1 cup water to the dish, cover, and bake in a preheated 350°F oven until tender, about 40 minutes. Alternatively, braise in a covered pan over low heat on the stove top for the same amount of time. Serve warm or at room temperature with lemon wedges.

# *Spring Vegetable Stew*   CARCIOFATA DI TRIESTE

Please don't let the long list of ingredients scare you away from this wonderful spring vegetable stew from Trieste. It is the ideal dish to serve at Passover, as it includes all of the vegetables of the holiday season. In the old days, the vegetables were cooked together in one pot because flavor was more important than texture and color. But today, they are more appealing if they are cooked separately until almost tender and still colorful and then combined and cooked through at serving time. SERVES 6

Juice of 1 lemon

3 medium artichokes, or 6 small artichokes (about 8 ounces after trimming)

3 tablespoons olive oil

2 teaspoons minced garlic, or more to taste

¼ cup chopped fresh flat-leaf parsley

1 cup shelled English peas, blanched for 1 minute

8 ounces baby carrots, peeled and parboiled for 5 to 7 minutes

8 ounces mushrooms, sliced and sautéed in olive oil for 5 minutes

8 ounces asparagus tips, blanched for 2 minutes

8 ounces little new potatoes, parboiled for 7 to 10 minutes, depending on size, and drained

8 ounces tiny pearl onions, parboiled for 4 to 5 minutes, drained, and peeled

2 cups vegetable broth, or as needed

Salt and freshly ground black pepper

Pinch of sugar (optional)

Chopped fresh mint, flat-leaf parsley, or basil for garnish (optional)

Fill a medium saucepan with lightly salted water and bring to a boil. Meanwhile, have ready a bowl of water to which you have added the lemon juice. Working with 1 artichoke at a time, trim off the stem flush with the bottom, then remove all of the leaves until you reach the heart. Pare away the dark green areas from the base. Cut the artichoke heart in half and scoop out and discard the choke from each half with a small pointed spoon or a paring knife. Cut each half in half again and slip the pieces into the lemon water. When all of the artichokes are trimmed, drain and add to the boiling water. Parboil for 5 minutes and drain.

Warm the oil in a large sauté pan over medium heat. Add the garlic and parsley and stir for a minute or two. Add the artichokes, peas, carrots, mushrooms, asparagus, potatoes, pearl onions, and just enough broth to moisten. Bring to a simmer and cook, uncovered, until all of the vegetables are tender, about 10 minutes. Taste and adjust the seasoning with salt and pepper and add the sugar, if needed for flavor balance. Transfer to a serving dish and garnish with the mint. Serve hot.

VARIATION: *Spring Vegetable Stew with Egg and Lemon (Carciofata con Bagna Brusca):* When the vegetables are tender, whisk together 1 egg and ¼ cup fresh lemon juice until very frothy.

Gradually whisk about ⅓ cup of the hot vegetable cooking liquid into the egg mixture to temper it. Pour the egg mixture into the vegetables, stir well, and remove from the heat. (Once you have added the egg and lemon, you cannot reheat the dish.) Garnish with the mint and serve at once.

## Turkish Sweet-and-Sour Artichokes   ANGINARAS

Artichokes are a Passover specialty all over the Mediterranean, and although this is a Turkish recipe, Sephardic Greeks also serve sweet-and-sour artichokes, as evidenced by a similar recipe called *enginares* in *Cookbook of the Jews of Greece* by Nicholas Stavroulakis. If you like, add the juice of 2 oranges in place of some of the water and a pinch of red pepper flakes to the braising liquid.   SERVES 8

| | |
|---|---|
| 3 large juicy lemons | 2 to 3 tablespoons sugar or honey |
| 8 large artichokes | ¼ cup olive oil |
| 3 cups water | 1 teaspoon salt |

Squeeze the juice from the lemons and set the juice aside. Squeeze any juice remaining in the peels into a large bowl of water and then add the spent peels. Working with 1 artichoke at a time, cut off all but 1 inch or so of the stem. Pull off and discard all of the tough outer leaves until you reach a small cone of pale green, tender leaves. Cut off the top 1 inch of the leaves to remove the thorn-like tips. Pare away the dark green areas from the base and the stem. Cut the artichoke lengthwise into quarters, scoop out and discard the choke from each piece with a small pointed spoon or a paring knife, and slip the quarters into the lemon water.

In a medium saucepan or a large, deep sauté pan, combine the water, lemon juice, sugar, oil, and salt and bring to a boil over high heat. Drain the artichokes, add them to the boiling water, turn down the heat to low, and cook until tender when pierced with the tip of a knife, 20 to 30 minutes.

Remove from the heat and drain off most of the liquid, leaving just enough to cover (about 1 cup). Transfer to a bowl and let cool. Serve at room temperature,

## Braised Artichokes, Favas, and Lettuce
STUFATO DI CARCIOFI, FAVE E LATTUGA ROMANA

Here, the classic Italian Jewish method of cooking vegetables known as *sofegae,* or "suffocated," is used. The vegetables are slowly cooked over very low heat in olive oil or goose or chicken fat and a small amount of water. The recipe, which is often served at Passover, comes from Emma Belforte, whose flavor palate I share, although she cooks her vegetables much longer than I do. I've suggested the contemporary garnish of *gremolata,* a mixture of lemon zest, garlic, and parsley, to bring lightness and sparkle. SERVES 6

Juice of 1 lemon

6 large artichokes

2 small heads romaine or butter lettuce, or 4 heads Little Gem lettuce

¼ cup extra virgin olive oil, or as needed

2 pounds fresh fava beans, shelled, blanched, and peeled (1½ to 2 cups)

¼ cup chopped fresh flat-leaf parsley

¼ cup chopped fresh basil

Salt and freshly ground black pepper

12 ounces asparagus, tough stems removed and cut into 2-inch lengths (optional)

1 cup shelled English peas (optional)

½ cup water or vegetable broth, or as needed

GREMOLATA

Grated zest of 2 lemons

6 tablespoons chopped fresh flat-leaf parsley or basil

1 tablespoon finely minced garlic

Have ready a bowl of water to which you have added the lemon juice. Working with 1 artichoke at a time, trim off the stem flush with the bottom, then remove all of the leaves until you reach the heart. Pare away the dark green areas from the base and then cut the artichoke in half. Scoop out the choke from each half with a small pointed spoon or a paring knife and drop the halves into the lemon water.

Core the lettuces and slice the leaves crosswise into ½-inch-wide strips. Drain the artichoke hearts and cut into small pieces or thin slices.

Warm the oil in a large, deep sauté pan over low heat. Add the artichokes and sauté, stirring often, for about 5 minutes. Add the favas, lettuces, parsley, basil and water to barely cover and season with salt and pepper. Raise the heat to medium and cook, stirring occasionally, until the artichokes are tender and most of the water has evaporated, 10 to 15 minutes. If using the asparagus or peas, add them during the last 5 minutes. Meanwhile, make the gremolata: in a small bowl, stir together the lemon zest, parsley, and garlic, mixing well.

Remove the vegetables from the heat, sprinkle with the gremolata, and stir well. Let rest for 5 minutes—allowing the garlic in the gremolata to soften—then serve.

## *Favas with Cilantro*   AVAS FRESCAS

This Sephardic recipe for favas seasoned with cilantro predates versions cooked in Spain and Portugal that added bacon or sausage. If you cannot find fresh favas, use 2 cups frozen baby lima beans, which are fast and easy because they don't need peeling and cook a little more quickly. SERVES 4 TO 6

2 tablespoons olive oil

1 yellow onion, chopped

3 cloves garlic, finely minced

2½ to 3 pounds fresh fava beans, shelled, blanched, and peeled (about 2 cups)

¾ to 1 cup water

1 small bay leaf

2 teaspoons ground cumin (optional)

Salt and freshly ground black pepper

⅓ cup chopped fresh cilantro

YOGURT-GARLIC SAUCE (OPTIONAL)

1 cup plain Greek yogurt

2 cloves garlic, minced

Warm the oil in a saucepan over medium heat. Add the onion and cook, stirring occasionally, until translucent and tender, 8 to 10 minutes. Add the garlic and cook for a minute or two. Add the favas, ¾ cup of the water, and the bay leaf and simmer, adding more water if the pan begins to dry, until the favas are tender, 10 to 15 minutes. Meanwhile, make the sauce. In a small bowl, combine the yogurt and garlic and mix well.

Remove the pan from the heat, drain off the excess liquid, and transfer the favas to a serving dish. Season the favas with the cumin, salt, and pepper. Add the cilantro and toss gently to mix evenly. Serve hot with the sauce on the side.

## *Slow-Cooked Green Beans*   FASULYAS

In the Mediterranean, vegetables are cooked for taste, not looks. Long, slow cooking brings out sweetness and intensifies flavor. For those who are used to bright-colored, crunchy green beans, this dish will be considered overcooked. But give it a chance to win you over with its own special charm. For the best result, use flat and fleshy romano beans, rather than conventional green beans or haricots verts.  SERVES 6

¼ cup olive oil

1 small yellow onion, minced

2 large tomatoes, peeled and finely chopped or grated

¼ cup water, or as needed

Salt and freshly ground black pepper

2 pounds romano beans, trimmed

Chopped fresh dill, oregano, marjoram, or basil for garnish

Warm the oil in a sauté pan over medium heat. Add the onion and cook, stirring occasionally, until translucent and tender, about 8 minutes. Add the tomatoes and water, season with salt and pepper, and then mix in the beans. Turn down the heat to low, cover, and cook until the beans are very tender, 20 to 30 minutes.

Remove from the heat, transfer to a serving dish, and garnish with the dill. Serve hot.

## Black-Eyed Peas in Tomato Sauce   FIJONES FRESCOS

Beans are traditionally eaten at Rosh Hashanah because they symbolize fertility and abundance and their appearance on the table ensures a fruitful New Year. Black-eyed peas, also called cow peas, are a traditional ingredient in the Sephardic kitchen, where they are turned into this typical holiday dish, which is also known as *lubiya*. In Egypt, a few cloves of minced garlic are added with the onion and a big handful of chopped fresh cilantro is stirred in about 10 minutes before the peas are tender. The peas are most easily purchased frozen or dried.   SERVES 8

3 tablespoons olive oil

1 large yellow onion, chopped

1 can (16 ounces) tomatoes, drained and chopped (about 2 cups)

½ teaspoon ground cinnamon (optional)

3 cups shelled fresh black-eyed peas; 1 package (1 pound) frozen black-eyed peas; or 1¼ cups dried black-eyed peas, picked over, soaked in water for 1 hour, drained, and rinsed

1½ to 2 cups water if cooking fresh or frozen peas, or about 3 cups water if cooking dried peas

Salt and freshly ground black pepper

Warm the oil in a saucepan over medium heat. Add the onion and cook, stirring occasionally, until translucent and tender, 8 to 10 minutes. Add the tomatoes, cinnamon, fresh or frozen peas, and 1½ cups of the water and bring to a simmer. Cover and cook until the peas are tender, about 30 minutes. Check the pan from time to time and add more water if the pan begins to dry. If cooking dried black-eyed peas, use 3 cups water, or as needed to cover, and simmer for about 1½ hours.

Remove from the heat, season with salt and pepper, and serve hot.

## Cabbage Gratin   CAVOLI GRATINATI AL FORNO

This recipe is based on one from Giuseppe Maffioli's *La cucina padovana*. It is a classic gratin in which a precooked vegetable is bound in a béchamel sauce and topped with grated cheese, a cooking technique popular with Sephardic Jews in Italy, Turkey, and Greece. You can use this technique for cooked cauliflower florets, fennel, Belgian endive, and Swiss chard stems (see variations).   SERVES 4 TO 6

1 head green cabbage

1 tablespoon all-purpose flour

BÉCHAMEL SAUCE

3 tablespoons unsalted butter

| | |
|---|---|
| 3 tablespoons all-purpose flour | 2 egg yolks, lightly beaten (optional) |
| 2 cups milk, warmed | |
| Freshly grated nutmeg (optional) | ⅓ cup grated Parmesan cheese |
| Salt and freshly ground black pepper | 2 tablespoons unsalted butter, cut into bits |

Cut the cabbage into quarters through the stem end and cut away the tough core. Fill a large saucepan with salted water and add the flour and cabbage. Bring to a boil over medium-high heat and boil gently until the cabbage is tender but not soft, 5 to 8 minutes. Drain well, then refrigerate the cabbage quarters until chilled.

Preheat the oven to 350°F. Cut each cabbage quarter crosswise into ½-inch-wide slices. Arrange the cabbage slices in a lightly buttered 9-by-12-by-2-inch baking dish.

To make the béchamel, melt the butter in a small saucepan over low heat. Add the flour and stir for a few minutes until smooth and thickened. Gradually stir in the milk, raise the heat to medium, and bring to a gentle boil. Turn down the heat to a gentle simmer and cook, stirring, until thickened, about 5 minutes. Season to taste with nutmeg, salt, and pepper and remove from the heat. If you prefer a richer sauce, gradually whisk in the eggs off the heat, mixing well.

Spoon the béchamel evenly over the cabbage, then sprinkle with the cheese and dot with the butter. Bake until golden, about 30 minutes. Serve warm.

VARIATIONS: *With Cauliflower:* Substitute 1 head cauliflower, broken into florets, for the cabbage. Parboil in salted water for 4 to 6 minutes, drain well, and then proceed as directed.

*With Fennel:* Substitute 6 fennel bulbs, quartered lengthwise, for the cabbage. Parboil in salted water until fork-tender, drain, and arrange in an oiled 2-quart baking dish. Top with the béchamel and then with the cheese, or with the cheese, toasted bread crumbs (see note, page 196), and butter, and then bake until golden, about 25 minutes. Alternatively, add 8 to 10 Medjool dates, chopped, to the dish, scattering them between and around the fennel pieces. The dates nicely accent the sweetness of the fennel. Top with the béchamel, but not the cheese, and then finish with toasted sliced almonds and the butter if you like.

*With Swiss Chard Stems:* Substitute stems from 4 bunches Swiss chard, cut into 2-inch pieces, for the cabbage. Parboil the stems until crisp-tender, drain, and arrange in an oiled 9-by-12-by-2-inch baking dish. Top with the béchamel and cheese (or with toasted bread crumbs; see note, page 196), dot with butter, and bake until golden, 25 to 30 minutes. This dish, known as *coste di bietole gratinati,* comes from the Veneto and is a good illustration of the thriftiness of the Jewish cook.

*With Belgian Endive:* Substitute 4 heads Belgian endive, halved lengthwise, for the cabbage. It is best to cook the endives in the *sofegae* style, as they become waterlogged if parboiled. Film a large sauté pan with olive oil or butter, place over medium heat, and add the endive halves, cut side down, in a single layer. Cook until starting to color, about 5 minutes. Turn the endives over, add ½ cup vegetable broth or water, cover the pan, and cook until tender and the liquid has been mostly absorbed, about 15 minutes. Uncover and transfer the endives, cut side down, to a buttered 9-by-12-by-2-inch baking dish. Top with the béchamel and cheese, and transfer to the oven. Bake until the cheese is bubbly, 15 to 20 minutes longer.

## Braised Carrots, Jewish Style     CAROTE ALLA GIUDIA

In this dish of carrots cooked *sofegae* style from the Veneto, the presence of pine nuts and raisins and the dash of vinegar to balance the sweetness of the raisins are giveaways of its Arab or Levantine origin. Some cooks add a tablespoon or two of sugar, but if the raisins and carrots are sweet enough to suit your palate, the sugar can be omitted. If possible, use chicken fat. It can be a wonderful medium for cooking vegetables, adding flavor as well as rich mouthfeel. SERVES 4 TO 6

¼ to ⅓ cup rendered chicken fat or olive oil

1½ pounds carrots, peeled and sliced (about 5 cups)

¼ cup water

6 tablespoons raisins, plumped in wine

3 tablespoons pine nuts, toasted

Salt and freshly ground black pepper

Dash of red wine vinegar and/or pinch of sugar (optional)

Warm enough of the chicken fat in a sauté pan over medium heat to form a film on the bottom. Add the carrots and sauté until well coated with the fat, 5 to 8 minutes. Add the water, turn down the heat to very low, cover, and simmer until the carrots are tender, about 20 minutes.

Add the raisins with their wine and the pine nuts and season with salt and pepper. Add the vinegar and/or sugar for balance, if you like. Serve warm or at room temperature.

## Cauliflower Pudding     SFORMATO DI CAVOLFIORE

A savory baked pudding that is unmolded onto a plate is called a *sformato*. Its texture is reminiscent of that of a French custard, and it is a popular dish in the Piedmont region of Italy, where Gallic cuisine has a history. Individual *sformati* are easy to unmold. It takes a bit more skill and patience to unmold a large one, however, so if you are nervous about it, you can spoon the *sformato* out of the baking dish. *Sformati* can be served unsauced, as this one is, or they can be topped with a light tomato sauce or a purée of roasted red peppers thinned with cream. Usually served as a first course, *sformati* are rich, so it's wise to keep the portions small. This same basic method can be used for other vegetables (see variations). SERVES 8

| | |
|---|---|
| 1 large head cauliflower, trimmed and divided into florets (4 to 5 cups) | Salt and freshly ground black pepper |
| 1 lemon zest strip (optional) | Freshly grated nutmeg |
| 1¼ cups milk or half-and-half | Pinch of cayenne pepper (optional) |
| 4 tablespoons unsalted butter | 3 eggs, lightly beaten |
| ¼ cup all-purpose flour | ½ cup grated Parmesan cheese |

Bring a large saucepan filled with lightly salted water to a boil. Add the cauliflower and the lemon zest strip (if you want to reduce the strong cabbagey smell) and cook until very tender, about 20 minutes.

Meanwhile, preheat the oven to 350°F. Butter a 1½-quart soufflé dish or other round baking dish or eight 6-ounce custard cups or ramekins. Place the dish or cups in a large baking pan.

When the cauliflower is ready, drain well, spoon into a food processor, and purée until smooth. Transfer the purée to a bowl. (If the mixture seems quite wet, spoon it into a sieve placed over a bowl and set aside to drain for about 1 hour, then transfer to a bowl.) You should have 2½ to 3 cups purée.

In a small saucepan, warm the milk over medium heat until small bubbles appear around the edge of the pan, then remove from the heat. At the same time, in another saucepan, melt the butter over medium heat. When the foam subsides, add the flour to the butter and whisk until smooth. Turn down the heat to low and cook, stirring constantly, for 5 minutes; do not allow the mixture to color. Gradually add the hot milk while whisking constantly, then continue to cook, stirring often, until the mixture thickly coats the back of a spoon, 3 to 5 minutes. Season with salt and black pepper and with a generous amount of nutmeg and add the cayenne if you want a bit of heat. Add the white sauce to the cauliflower purée and then stir in the eggs and cheese.

Pour the mixture into the prepared mold(s) and add hot water to the baking pan to reach halfway up the sides of the mold(s). Cover the pan with aluminum foil. Bake the custard(s) until set when tested with a thin knife blade, 50 to 60 minutes for a single large mold and 25 to 30 minutes for the small molds. Remove the mold(s) from the water bath and place on a dish towel. Let the ramekins rest for 8 to 10 minutes and the large mold for 15 minutes.

Run a knife around the inside edge of the baking dish to loosen the sides of the custard, invert a serving plate over the dish, and invert the plate and dish together. Lift off the dish. Or, loosen the small custards and invert onto individual plates. Serve immediately.

Substitute 2 pounds zucchini, carrots, mushrooms, butternut squash, or spinach or 6 large artichoke hearts for the cauliflower. Once the vegetable is cooked and puréed, or finely chopped in the case of the spinach, you should have 2½ to 3 cups. If you are using butternut squash, purée the squash with 1 tablespoon chopped fresh sage. The artichoke *sformato* tastes great but looks gray, so pair it with a light tomato sauce.

## Roasted Cauliflower with Walnuts KARNABIT AL ORNO

As noted earlier, in the past, many Mediterranean Jewish homes did not have ovens, which meant that braising, steaming, and sautéing were the most common cooking techniques. Because today our stoves have ovens, we can also easily roast vegetables, a method that brings out their sweetness and works especially well with such cabbagey vegetables as cauliflower or Brussels sprouts. SERVES 4

1 large head cauliflower, trimmed and divided into florets

2 tablespoons olive oil

Salt

1 small yellow onion, sliced

Pinch of saffron threads or ground turmeric

½ cup walnuts, toasted and coarsely chopped

¼ cup tahini sauce (page 112)

Ground sumac for garnish

Preheat the oven to 425°F. In a large bowl, toss the cauliflower florets with the oil, coating evenly, then season with salt. Spread on a sheet pan.

Roast the cauliflower until golden and tender when tested with a knife tip, 25 to 30 minutes. Remove from the oven.

About 15 minutes before the cauliflower is ready, warm the oil in a large sauté pan over medium heat. Add the onion and sauté until soft and starting to take on some color, 12 to 15 minutes. When the cauliflower is ready, add it to the sauté pan along with the saffron and walnuts over medium heat, stir to mix well, and warm through. Transfer to a serving dish, spoon on the tahini sauce, and sprinkle with sumac. Serve hot or warm.

VARIATION: *Roasted Butternut Squash with Tahini and Walnuts:* Cut 1 butternut squash (1½ to 2 pounds) in half lengthwise, scoop out the seeds, peel, and then cut crosswise into ½-inch-thick slices. Brush the slices with olive oil, sprinkle with salt, pepper, and a little ground cumin, and arrange in a single layer on 1 or more sheet pans. Bake as directed until tender, 20 to 25 minutes. Transfer to a platter and spoon the tahini sauce over the warm squash. Top with the walnuts or with a sprinkle of dukkah and chopped fresh mint. Roasted beets or carrots can be served this way, too.

## Fried Eggplant with Sugar   PAPEYADA DE BERENJENA

Eggplants were brought to Spain and Italy by the Arabs, and Jewish cooks quickly took to the new food. Initially, they were treated as a fruit and served sweetened with sugar. In the Middle East, cooks have long preserved eggplant in a sugar syrup, and in Morocco, a sweet eggplant condiment is popular (page 369). This Sephardic dish from Turkey, which is ideal for Rosh Hashanah, reveals its Hispano-Arabic origin in its use of double cooking: the eggplant slices are fried, sprinkled with sugar and salt, and then baked. Since the slices are cooked through after the frying step, you could skip the baking step, sprinkle the fried slices with sugar and salt, and eat them as is.   SERVES 6 TO 8

---

2½ pounds globe eggplants

2 eggs

Olive or sunflower oil for frying and drizzling

½ cup sugar

Salt

---

Preheat the oven to 350°F. Oil a 9-by-12-by-2-inch baking dish.

Peel the eggplants and cut them lengthwise into slices about ⅓ inch thick. Soak the slices in a bowl of lightly salted water for 15 minutes, then drain and squeeze dry.

In a shallow bowl, lightly beat the eggs. Pour the oil to a depth of 2 inches into a large, deep sauté pan and heat to 360°F. When the oil is hot, in batches, dip the eggplant slices into the eggs and slip them into the oil. Fry just until golden, 5 to 7 minutes. Using tongs or a slotted spatula, transfer to paper towels to drain briefly, then place in a single layer in the prepared baking dish.

When the bottom of the dish is completely covered, sprinkle the eggplant slices with sugar and salt. Add another layer of eggplant and sprinkle with sugar and salt. Repeat until all the eggplant slices have been used. Drizzle the surface with oil.

Bake until the eggplant is very tender when pierced with a fork, about 25 minutes. Serve hot or warm directly from the dish.

## Moroccan-Inspired Honeyed Eggplant   AUBERGINE AU MIEL

Traditionally served to break the fast at Yom Kippur, this dish, also known as *baraniya,* is so seductive it will convert any eggplant doubters.   SERVES 4

---

4 small or 2 medium Japanese eggplants, halved lengthwise, or 2 globe eggplants, peeled and cut into 1-inch cubes

Olive oil for brushing and frying

2-inch piece fresh ginger, peeled and minced or grated

3 cloves garlic, minced

| | |
|---|---|
| 1 teaspoon ras el hanout | 3 tablespoons fresh lemon juice |
| 2 teaspoons ground toasted cumin | Salt |
| 6 tablespoons honey | ¼ cup water, if needed |

If using Japanese eggplants, score the cut sides of the eggplant halves in a crosshatch pattern with a sharp knife. Brush each half liberally on both sides with oil. Warm a griddle or heavy sauté pan over medium heat and film with a little more oil. In batches, add the eggplant halves and cook, turning a few times and adding more oil if needed to prevent scorching, until softened and golden, 10 to 12 minutes. If using globe eggplants, film a large sauté pan with oil and warm over medium heat. Add the eggplant cubes and sauté, adding more oil as needed to prevent scorching, until golden, 8 to 10 minutes. You may also roast the liberally oiled eggplant halves in a 400°F oven for about 20 minutes.

In a sauté pan large enough to hold the cooked eggplant (preferably in a single layer), warm 3 tablespoons oil over medium heat. Add the ginger and garlic and sauté for a minute or two. Add the ras el hanout and cumin, mix well, and then stir in the honey, lemon juice, and a pinch of salt to make a sauce. Add the water if the sauce is stiff. Simmer for a few minutes, then transfer the eggplant to the pan. Coat the eggplant pieces with the sauce, turn down the heat to low, and cook until the eggplant absorbs most of the sauce and becomes caramelized, 5 to 8 minutes. Transfer to a serving dish and serve hot or warm.

VARIATION:  If you are entertaining and do not want to make this at the last minute, prepare the eggplant and sauce as directed and turn the eggplant pieces in the sauce for a few minutes. Transfer the contents of the sauté pan to a baking dish and bake in a preheated 350°F oven until bubbly, about 25 minutes. If you like, sprinkle with sesame seeds just before serving.

## *Persian Eggplant and Tomatoes with Pomegranate*   NAZHATUN

This delicious little eggplant and tomato stew, seasoned with sweet-tart pomegranate, is perfect for the Rosh Hashanah table. I have roasted the eggplants in the oven, but you can instead peel them, cut them into 1-inch cubes, and then sauté them in olive oil until tender.  SERVES 4 TO 6

| | |
|---|---|
| 2 globe eggplants | Salt |
| 2 tablespoons olive oil | 4 to 6 tablespoons pomegranate molasses |
| 1 yellow onion, chopped | |
| 2 cloves garlic, minced | Fresh lemon juice for seasoning |
| 4 tomatoes, peeled, seeded, and chopped | Pomegranate seeds for garnish (optional) |
| ½ to 1 teaspoon ground cinnamon | |

Roast the eggplants as directed in Master Recipe for Roasted Eggplant (page 27). After draining the pulp, chop it coarsely and set aside.

Warm the oil in a large sauté pan over medium heat. Add the onion and cook, stirring occasionally, until translucent and tender, 8 to 10 minutes. Add the garlic and tomatoes and cook for 5 minutes. Add the eggplant, season to taste with the cinnamon and salt, and add 4 tablespoons of the pomegranate molasses. Stir well, turn down the heat to low, and simmer gently until the tomatoes and eggplant are almost melted, 10 to 15 minutes. Season with lemon juice, then taste and adjust the flavors with salt and more pomegranate molasses if needed. Serve hot or at room temperature, garnished with pomegranate seeds.

## Turkish Eggplants Stuffed with Tomato and Onion  İMAM BAYILDI

Even though it has a Muslim name, this dish is served by Jews in Greece and Turkey and is quite popular in Israel. The most famous of all of the Turkish eggplant dishes, its name means "the imam [priest] fainted," probably because the eggplant was so delicious. Small Japanese eggplants may need only a short cooking time after the initial frying. The small globes will take longer to cook. It's best to prepare the eggplants ahead of time so the flavors have a chance to mellow. Like many Mediterranean vegetable dishes, this is usually served at room temperature, but it is also good warm.  SERVES 4

8 Japanese eggplants, or 4 small globe eggplants (about 2 pounds total weight)

½ cup olive oil, or as needed

3 large yellow onions, halved and thinly sliced

2 cups peeled, seeded, and chopped tomatoes

12 cloves garlic, finely minced or thinly sliced

Pinch of ground cinnamon

Salt and freshly ground black pepper

¼ cup chopped fresh flat-leaf parsley

1 cup hot water

Juice of 1 lemon

2 tablespoons sugar or honey

Peel the skin from the globe eggplants lengthwise in stripes. (Japanese eggplants are too small to stripe.) Warm ¼ cup of the oil in a large sauté pan over medium heat. When the oil is hot, in batches, add the eggplants and cook, turning them a few times and adding oil as needed to prevent scorching, until softened and tender, 5 to 8 minutes for the Japanese eggplants and about 15 minutes for the globe eggplants. Using tongs or a slotted spoon, transfer the eggplants to a baking dish, placing them side by side.

Add the onions to the oil remaining in the pan and cook, stirring occasionally, until translucent and tender, 8 to 10 minutes. Add the tomatoes and garlic and cook, stirring occasionally, for 2 minutes. Add the cinnamon, season with salt and pepper, and stir in the parsley. Remove from the heat.

Preheat the oven to 350°F. Cut a lengthwise slit in each eggplant, stopping 1 inch short of both the stem end and the root end and being careful not to cut all the way through. Pull the sides of the slit apart, forming a pocket. Stuff the eggplants with the onion mixture, dividing it evenly. Mix together the hot water, the remaining ¼ cup olive oil, the lemon juice, and the sugar in a small bowl and then add to the dish. Cover the dish with foil.

Bake until the eggplants are tender and most of the liquid has been absorbed, 20 to 25 minutes for the Japanese eggplants and 30 to 45 minutes for the globe eggplants. Serve at room temperature.

## *Stuffed Eggplant Rolls*   INVOLTINI DI MELANZANE

In his famous 1891 cookbook, *La scienza in cucina e l'arte di mangiare bene,* Pellegrino Artusi observes, "Forty years ago you could hardly find eggplant or fennel in the markets of Florence, because they were considered Jewish food and were abhorred." When the Inquisition banned the Jews from Spain and Spanish settlements in southern Italy, the Italian Jews fled north, bringing with them a repertoire of eggplant dishes. Many of them could be served at room temperature, making it possible to prepare them late on Friday for serving at Sabbath lunch.

Grilled eggplant slices pick up a slight smokiness that adds a second layer of richness to the dish. If you don't want to fire up the grill, you can fry or bake the eggplant. Zucchini can be prepared the same way, cutting it lengthwise into ⅓-inch-thick slices and then grilling or frying. SERVES 4 TO 6

2 globe eggplants, peeled and cut lengthwise into slices ⅓ inch thick (18 to 20 slices)

About ½ cup extra virgin olive oil, or as needed for brushing or frying and drizzling

Salt and freshly ground black pepper

FILLING

½ cup fine dried bread crumbs

½ cup grated pecorino or provolone cheese

¼ cup chopped fresh flat-leaf parsley, or equal parts parsley and basil

2 or 3 cloves garlic, finely minced

1 tablespoon grated lemon zest

Salt and freshly ground black pepper

Lemon wedges for serving

To grill the eggplant slices, prepare a fire in a charcoal grill. Brush the eggplant slices on both sides with oil and sprinkle with salt and pepper. Place the eggplant slices directly over the coals and grill, turning once, until tender but not too soft, about 4 minutes total. Remove from the grill.

To roast the eggplant slices, arrange them in a single layer on sheet pans, brush liberally on both sides with oil, and sprinkle with salt and pepper. Bake in a preheated 400°F oven, turning once, until cooked through and translucent or even slightly golden, 20 to 25 minutes. Remove from the oven.

To fry the eggplant slices, put them in a colander in the sink or over a bowl, sprinkling the layers with salt, and let drain for about 30 minutes. Pat the slices dry with paper towels. Warm the oil in a sauté pan over medium heat. When the oil is hot, in batches, add the eggplant slices and fry, turning once, until translucent and tender but not too soft, 6 to 8 minutes total. Transfer to paper towels to drain.

To make the filling, in a bowl, combine the bread crumbs, cheese, parsley, garlic, and lemon zest and mix well. Season with salt and pepper. (If you do not like the taste of raw garlic, sauté it in a little olive oil over low heat for a minute or two to tame its bite before combining it with the other ingredients.)

Preheat the oven to 400°F or preheat the broiler.

Divide the filling evenly among the eggplant slices, spreading it on the top of each slice. Roll up each slice and then secure with a toothpick if it won't stay rolled. Lightly oil a baking dish (or a flameproof dish if using the broiler) large enough to accommodate the eggplant rolls in a single layer. Arrange the rolls, seam side down, in the dish and then drizzle them with oil.

Place the dish in the oven or slip under the broiler about 4 inches from the heat source and heat the rolls until warmed through, 10 to 15 minutes in the oven or just a few minutes in the broiler. Remove the toothpicks, if used, and arrange the rolls on a platter. Serve warm or at room temperature. Pass the lemon wedges at the table.

VARIATIONS: *Mozzarella Cheese Filling:* Cook the eggplant slices as directed and omit the filling. Dip strips of fresh mozzarella cheese in chopped fresh basil and roll up in the eggplant slices. Arrange the rolls in a baking dish and spoon a little tomato sauce, homemade (page 328) or store-bought, on top of each roll or drizzle a little olive oil on each roll. Bake in a preheated 400°F oven just until the cheese melts, about 15 minutes. Serve warm, while the cheese is still soft.

*Balkan Filling:* Cook the eggplant slices as directed and omit the filling. Combine ½ cup chopped fresh cilantro; 2 cloves garlic, minced; 1 cup finely chopped toasted walnuts; and 2 tablespoons fresh lemon juice and mix well. Spread each slice with a generous tablespoon of the filling and roll and bake as directed. Just before serving, drizzle with more lemon juice or spoon on some tahini sauce (page 112).

# Meatless Moussaka  MELITZANA ASADA

Leave it to creative cooks to come up with a meatless version of moussaka with a dairy topping. It is essentially a gratin or a Greek version of eggplant parmigiana and is so rich and satisfying that you won't even miss the lamb sauce.  SERVES 8

2 large globe eggplants (about 2 pounds total weight)

Salt and freshly ground black pepper

Olive oil for frying

**EGGPLANT SAUCE**

3 large globe eggplants (about 3 pounds total weight)

4 tablespoons unsalted butter or olive oil

2 yellow onions, chopped

5 cloves garlic, finely minced

2 teaspoons ground cinnamon

2 teaspoons dried oregano

1 cup canned tomato purée, or 1½ cups seeded and chopped canned tomatoes

2 tablespoons tomato paste

1 cup dry red wine

¼ cup chopped fresh flat-leaf parsley

Salt and freshly ground black pepper

**CREAM SAUCE**

4 tablespoons unsalted butter

¼ cup all-purpose flour

2 cups milk, warmed

½ teaspoon freshly grated nutmeg, or to taste

Salt and freshly ground black pepper

4 eggs, lightly beaten

1 cup ricotta cheese, or 8 ounces manouri cheese

⅓ cup grated kasseri or Parmesan cheese

⅓ cup fine dried bread crumbs

Peel 2 eggplants, creating a lengthwise-stripe pattern, then cut crosswise into ⅓-inch-thick slices. Spread the slices on a work surface, sprinkle with salt, and let rest for 30 minutes. Pat dry with paper towels.

Pour the oil to a depth of about ⅛ inch into a large sauté pan and warm over medium heat. In batches, add the eggplant slices and fry, turning once and adding more oil as needed to prevent scorching, until translucent and lightly colored on both sides, about 4 minutes on each side. Make sure the eggplant is cooked through and translucent or it will taste bitter. Transfer to paper towels to drain. (Alternatively, arrange the slices on oiled sheet pans, brush them liberally on both sides with oil, sprinkle with pepper, and bake in a preheated 400°F oven, turning once, until translucent and cooked through, about 25 minutes.)

To make the eggplant sauce, roast 3 eggplants as directed in Master Recipe for Roasted Eggplant (page 27). After draining the pulp, chop it coarsely or dice it. You should about 3 cups chunky purée.

Melt the butter in a large sauté pan over medium heat. Add the onions and garlic and cook, stirring occasionally, until translucent and tender, 8 to 10 minutes. Add the cinnamon, oregano, tomato purée, tomato paste, and wine, stir well, and simmer over low heat for about 10 minutes. Add the chopped cooked eggplant and parsley and cook, stirring occasionally, until most of the liquid is absorbed, about 10 minutes. Season liberally with salt and pepper. (The sauce can be made a day in advance and then warmed slightly before assembling the moussaka.)

To make the cream sauce, melt the butter in a saucepan over low heat. Add the flour and stir for a few minutes until smooth and thickened. Gradually stir in the milk, raise the heat to medium, and bring to a gentle boil. Turn down the heat to a gentle simmer and cook, stirring, until thickened, about 5 minutes. Stir in the nutmeg and season with salt and pepper. Don't be cowardly with the nutmeg. You want to taste it. Remove from the heat and gradually whisk in the eggs and ricotta cheese.

Preheat the oven to 375°F. Lightly oil a 9-by-15-by-2½-inch baking dish. In a small bowl, stir together the kasseri cheese and bread crumbs. Sprinkle some of the crumb mixture over the bottom of the prepared baking dish, then top with a layer of eggplant slices followed by a layer of eggplant sauce. Repeat the layers of crumb mixture, eggplant slices, and eggplant sauce. If you have still have eggplant slices, make another layer and top with the crumb mixture. (Even if it is only a partial layer of slices, use what you have, as the custard will cover it.) Pour the cream sauce evenly over the top. Set the baking dish atop a sheet pan in case it bubbles over.

Bake until golden and bubbly, 45 to 60 minutes. If the moussaka is browning too quickly, cover the dish with foil. Remove from the oven and then blot any excess oil that has risen to the top or edges of the dish with paper towels. Let the moussaka rest for 15 minutes before cutting into squares.

## Turkish Eggplant Sandwiches PATLICAN BÖREGİ

Here's another way to enjoy eggplant and cheese, this time fried. These sandwiches make a great appetizer or accompaniment to roasted fish. SERVES 6

2 large or 3 medium globe eggplants

Olive oil for brushing and frying

Salt and freshly ground black pepper

**FILLING**

8 ounces halloumi or Monterey Jack cheese, grated

8 ounces feta cheese, crumbled

2 eggs, lightly beaten

3 tablespoons chopped fresh flat-leaf parsley

2 tablespoons chopped fresh dill

All-purpose flour for coating

2 eggs

Toasted fine dried bread crumbs for coating

Preheat the oven to 400°F. Oil 2 large sheet pans. Peel the eggplants and cut crosswise into slices ½ inch thick. Arrange the slices on the prepared pans, brush them liberally on both sides with oil, and sprinkle with salt and pepper. Bake until almost cooked through and translucent, 15 to 20 minutes. Let cool completely.

To make the filling, in a bowl, combine the cheeses, eggs, parsley, and dill and mix well.

Place a few heaping tablespoons of the filling on half of the cooled eggplant slices and top with a matching slice. You should have about 10 sandwiches. Some will be big and others small. The larger ones can be cut in half after frying for serving.

To fry the sandwiches, line 2 large sheet pans with parchment paper and put a large rack on each pan. Put some flour in a shallow bowl, lightly beat the eggs in a second shallow bowl, and put some bread crumbs in a third bowl. Dip the eggplant sandwiches first in flour, tapping off the excess; then in the eggs, allowing the excess to drip off; and finally in the bread crumbs, coating evenly. As the sandwiches are coated, place them on the racks.

Pour the oil to a depth of 3 inches into a deep, heavy saucepan or deep fryer and heat to 360°F. In batches, add the sandwiches and fry, turning once, until golden, 6 to 7 minutes total. Using tongs or a wire skimmer, transfer the sandwiches to paper towels to drain. Cut any large sandwiches in half, if you like. Serve hot.

## *Baked Fennel*   FINOCCHI AL FORNO

Nearly everyone likes creamy vegetable gratins, but because of their dairy ingredients, they cannot be served at a meat-based meal. Here's another delicious way to get baked vegetables on the table. Donatella Limentani Pavoncello, in her charming family cookbook *Dal 1880 ad oggi: La cucina ebraica della mia famiglia,* boils fennel and then fries it in olive oil before baking it. When cooked this way, it loses some of its pronounced anise flavor and takes on a more intense sweetness. For a dairy meal, add grated Parmesan cheese to the crumb topping. I know that many cooks today use *panko* for bread crumbs, and they are fine in a pinch, but I find that making your own toasted crumbs is much better, so I have included directions for making them. SERVES 6

3 large or 6 small fennel bulbs

¼ cup olive oil

4 cloves garlic, finely minced

¼ cup finely minced fresh flat-leaf parsley

Salt and freshly ground black pepper

6 to 8 tablespoons toasted bread crumbs (see note)

¼ cup grated Parmesan cheese (optional)

Cut off the stalks and feathery tops of the fennel bulbs and reserve for another use. Trim off the rough outside leaves. Cut the bulbs in halves or quarters lengthwise. Remove the tough central core. Bring a saucepan filled with water to a boil, add the fennel pieces, and cook until just fork-tender, 10 to 15 minutes; the timing will depend on the size of the bulbs. Drain well.

Preheat the oven to 375°F.

Warm the oil in a large sauté pan over medium-high heat. Add the fennel, garlic, and parsley and sauté until golden, 5 to 8 minutes. Transfer to a baking dish in which the fennel pieces fit in a single layer and sprinkle with salt and pepper. If serving at a dairy meal, mix together the bread crumbs and cheese and then strew over the top; if serving at a meat meal, sprinkle with just the bread crumbs.

Bake until the crumb topping is golden, 15 to 20 minutes. Serve hot.

NOTE: To make toasted bread crumbs, preheat the oven to 350°F. Put 2 cups crust-free cubed Italian or French bread in a food processor and pulse until reduced to coarse crumbs. Transfer the crumbs to a bowl and toss with ½ cup olive oil and 1 teaspoon each salt and freshly ground black pepper. Spread the crumbs on a sheet pan and bake until golden but not hard, 15 to 20 minutes, stirring occasionally for even browning. Pour onto a plate to cool. Store in an airtight container at room temperature.

## *Braised Okra*  BAMYES

If you have tried okra before but haven't liked it because of the gluey texture, try this recipe. The Greeks have a wonderful technique for ridding okra of its sliminess. They treat it to a vinegar bath before cooking and then rinse away the vinegar and with it the slime. SERVES 4

1½ pounds okra

¾ cup white wine vinegar

Salt and freshly ground black pepper

4 tablespoons olive oil

2 yellow onions, chopped

2 cloves garlic, chopped

1½ teaspoons ground toasted coriander seeds

3 large ripe tomatoes, peeled, seeded, and chopped

2 bay leaves

1 tablespoon honey

Juice of 2 lemons

With a towel, rub the fuzz off of the okra pods. Carefully cut away the stems without cutting into the pods, then place the pods in a bowl. Add the vinegar and a pinch of salt and set aside in a warm place for 30 to 60 minutes. Just before cooking, drain the okra and rinse well. This vinegar bath removes the viscous nature of cooked okra.

Warm 2 tablespoons of the oil in a sauté pan over medium heat. Add the onions and cook, stirring occasionally, until translucent and tender, 8 to 10 minutes. Add the garlic and coriander and stir well. Add the okra and cook, stirring, for 5 minutes. Transfer the contents of the sauté pan to a deeper pan large enough to hold the okra in a single layer.

Wipe out the sauté pan, return it to medium heat, and warm the remaining 2 tablespoons oil. Add the tomatoes and bay leaves and cook, stirring occasionally, until the tomatoes start to soften, 8 to 10 minutes. Add the honey and cook for a few minutes to blend the flavors. Add this sauce to the okra along with just enough water to cover the okra. Add the lemon juice and season with salt and pepper. Simmer gently, uncovered, until the okra is tender, about 30 minutes. Serve hot or warm.

## Braised Peas   PISELLI IN TEGAME

Also called *pisellini alle cegole,* or "peas with onions," in Venetian dialect, this simple braise of sweet spring peas uses wine instead of water. For a dairy meal, you can use butter in place of the oil. SERVES 4

---

2 pounds English peas, shelled (about 2 cups)

2 small yellow onions, finely chopped

6 tablespoons olive oil

¼ cup pine nuts, chopped

¼ cup dry white wine or water

Chopped fresh flat-leaf parsley or mint for garnish

---

Combine the peas, onions, and olive oil in a small saucepan. Place over low heat and cook slowly, stirring occasionally, for 10 minutes. Add the pine nuts and wine and cook until the peas are very tender, 10 to 15 minutes longer. Serve warm, sprinkled with a little parsley.

## Braised Pea Pods   GUSCETTI

Many traditional Italian Jewish recipes demonstrate the thrifty and creative use of "leftovers," using parts of foods that might normally be discarded. This is an old recipe from Ferrara, in the region of Emilia-Romagna. Today we could use a pound of either sugar snap peas or snow peas, but this dish was designed to use every part of the common English pea. SERVES 4

---

2 pounds young English peas

¼ cup olive oil

2 cloves garlic, finely minced

3 tablespoons chopped fresh flat-leaf parsley

---

| | |
|---|---|
| ¼ cup water or vegetable broth | A few tablespoons white wine vinegar (optional) |
| Salt and freshly ground black pepper | Chopped fresh mint or peeled and grated fresh ginger for garnish (optional) |

Shell the peas and use the peas for Double-Crusted Vegetable Pie (page 62) or another recipe. Blanch the pods in boiling water for 2 minutes, refresh in cold water, and peel off the thin membrane covering each pod.

Warm the oil in a sauté pan over medium heat. Add the garlic and parsley and sauté until softened, about 3 minutes. Add the pods and water, turn down the heat to low, cover, and braise until tender, 15 to 20 minutes. Season with salt and pepper.

If you like, sprinkle the pods with the vinegar, which will taste good but will turn them slightly yellow-brown. For a contemporary touch, garnish the pods with mint or ginger. Serve warm or at room temperature.

## Turkish Cheese-Stuffed Peppers   PIPIRIZAS KON KEZO

These peppers are reminiscent of the stuffed *piquillo* peppers served in Spain today and also bear a resemblance to Mexican chiles rellenos. Green bell peppers work well, as they are fleshy and therefore easy to peel and seed without tearing, though you can also use mild poblano chiles or even the elongated and slightly piquant Turkish green peppers. Don't worry if the peppers tear a bit; the flour-and-egg coating acts as a seal. The amount of filling you need varies depending on the size of the peppers. If you have filling left over, spread it on bread and toast it. Although not traditional, the peppers can be served with a light tomato sauce.  SERVES 8

| | |
|---|---|
| 8 large green bell peppers, or 16 smaller green bell peppers or poblano chiles | ¾ cup grated kashkaval or Gruyère cheese |
| 4 eggs | 2 to 3 tablespoons chopped fresh flat-leaf parsley |
| 1½ cups crumbled feta cheese | All-purpose flour for coating |
| 1½ cups farmer or ricotta cheese or fromage blanc | Salt and freshly ground black pepper |
| | Sunflower or canola oil for frying |

To roast the peppers, place them directly over the flame on a gas stove top or on a sheet pan under the broiler and turn them as needed until the skin is blistered and charred on all sides. Transfer to a closed plastic container or a bowl covered with plastic wrap and let stand for 20 minutes. Peel or rub off the skin from each pepper. Carefully cut a lengthwise slit along one side of each pepper and scoop out the seeds.

In a bowl, lightly beat 2 of the eggs. Add all of the cheeses and the parsley and mix well. Stuff each pepper with an equal amount of the mixture and pinch the slit closed.

Spread the flour on a plate, sprinkle with salt and pepper, and mix well. In a shallow bowl, lightly beat the remaining 2 eggs. Pour the oil to a depth of ½ inch into a large sauté pan and place over medium-high heat. When the oil is hot, dip the peppers, one at a time, into the flour, tapping off the excess, and then into the egg, coating evenly, and slip them into the hot oil, being careful not to crowd the pan. Fry, turning as needed to crisp and color on all sides, until golden brown, about 5 minutes total. Using a slotted spoon, transfer the peppers to a platter and keep warm until all are fried. Serve hot.

## *Peppers Stuffed with Eggplant*   PEPERONI RIPIENI

The dairy section of Giuliana Ascoli Vitali-Norsa's *La cucina nella tradizione ebraica* is the source of this delicious adaptation of eggplant-stuffed peppers. It is basically a Sephardo-Italian dolma or a chopped version of eggplant parmigiana slipped inside a pepper. Add the mozzarella after the peppers have cooked a bit or you will lose it in the pan. SERVES 4

---

3 globe eggplants, about 1 pound each, peeled and diced

Salt

Olive oil for sautéing and drizzling

1 egg, lightly beaten

5 tablespoons chopped fresh basil

3 to 4 tablespoons fine dried bread crumbs

Salt and freshly ground black pepper

4 large red bell peppers, halved lengthwise and stems, seeds, and thick ribs removed

3 to 4 tablespoons water

8 to 12 ounces fresh mozzarella cheese, sliced

---

Put the diced eggplants in a colander in the sink or over a bowl, sprinkling them with salt as you go, and let drain for about 1 hour to draw out any bitter juices. Rinse and pat dry.

Warm ¼ cup oil in a sauté pan over low heat. In batches, add the eggplant and sauté, adding more oil as needed to prevent scorching, until tender, about 10 minutes. Transfer to a bowl and mash with a fork, or pulse in a food processor and transfer to a bowl. (A 1-pound eggplant will yield 1 to 1½ cups purée.) Add the egg, basil, and enough bread crumbs to bind and mix well. Season with salt and pepper.

Preheat the oven to 350°F. Arrange the peppers, hollow sides up, in a baking dish. Stuff the eggplant mixture into the peppers, dividing it evenly. Drizzle a little oil into the baking dish, add the water, and cover the dish with foil.

Bake the peppers for 20 to 25 minutes, then remove the foil, top each pepper with a slice of mozzarella, re-cover the dish, and continue baking until the peppers are tender and the cheese has melted, 10 to 15 minutes longer. Serve hot or warm.

## The Widow's Peppers  POIVRONS DE LA VEUVE

Stuffed vegetables are a signature dish of the Mediterranean Jews. Like grape-leaf dolmas, the vegetables are typically filled with a meat, rice, or meat-and-rice mixture. This Tunisian recipe is unusual in that it uses a bread filling. It is named for an apocryphal widow who was too poor to use meat but made a great dish with humble ingredients. SERVES 8

---

8 green bell peppers

2 cups fresh bread crumbs, soaked in water and squeezed dry

3 tablespoons chopped fresh flat-leaf parsley

¼ cup chopped fresh cilantro

4 cloves garlic, minced

1 teaspoon ground caraway

1 teaspoon ground coriander

1 tomato, peeled, seeded, and chopped

2 hard-boiled eggs, peeled and diced

2 eggs, lightly beaten

Salt and freshly ground black pepper

---

Preheat the oven to 350°F. Cut off the stem end of each bell pepper, reserving the caps. Remove and discard the seeds and thick ribs. Boil the shells in lightly salted water for 5 minutes, then drain well.

In a bowl, combine the bread crumbs, parsley, cilantro, garlic, caraway, coriander, tomato, and hard-boiled and raw eggs and mix well. Season with salt and pepper. Stuff the mixture into the peppers, dividing evenly.

Stand the peppers in a baking dish and replace their caps. Pour water to a depth of 1 inch into the dish, then cover the dish with foil. Bake until the peppers are tender, 25 to 30 minutes. Serve warm.

## Braised Sweet-and-Sour Peppers  PEPERONATA

Red and yellow peppers are most commonly used in this typical dish of southern Italy, but green peppers can be used in place of the yellow. I have included tomatoes here, though some recipes omit them. SERVES 6

3 large red bell peppers

3 large yellow or green bell peppers

½ cup olive oil

1 or 2 yellow onions, sliced ¼ inch thick

2 cloves garlic, finely minced

3 ripe tomatoes, peeled, seeded, and diced

¼ cup red wine vinegar

2 tablespoons sugar

¼ cup sliced almonds or pine nuts, toasted

¼ cup raisins, plumped in hot water and drained

Salt and freshly ground black pepper

Cut the bell peppers in half lengthwise and remove the stems, seeds, and thick ribs. Slice lengthwise into ½-inch-wide strips.

Warm the oil in a large sauté pan over medium heat. Add the onions and cook, stirring occasionally, until softened, 5 to 8 minutes. Add the bell peppers and garlic, cover, and cook until the peppers are tender, about 20 minutes.

Add the tomatoes, vinegar, sugar, almonds, and raisins and simmer for a few minutes to allow the flavors to mellow and mingle. Season with salt and pepper. Serve warm or at room temperature.

## Potato and Green Olive Stew   RAGOÛT D'OLIVES VERTES

I discovered this dish in Léone Jaffin's *150 recettes et mille et un souvenirs d'une juive d'Algérie,* where she reports that her Aunt Olga made this delicious stew often for the family. If you find tiny round new potatoes at the market, and like the idea of round potatoes with round olives, you can substitute them here. Parboil them until they are half-cooked and then add them with the olives, along with a bit of water so they will cook through, and cook for about 10 minutes. SERVES 6

3 tablespoons peanut oil

1 large yellow onion, minced

2½ pounds new potatoes, peeled and sliced

1 teaspoon freshly ground black pepper

1 teaspoon sweet paprika

Pinch of cayenne pepper (optional)

1 bay leaf

1⅔ cups green olives, cracked and marinated in fresh lemon juice for a few hours

Warm the oil in a large sauté pan over medium heat. Add the onion and sauté until softened, about 5 minutes. Add the potatoes, black pepper, paprika, cayenne, bay leaf, and enough water to reach about halfway up the sides of the potatoes and cook for 15 minutes. Add the olives and cook until the potatoes are tender and the flavors are blended, about 10 minutes longer. Taste and adjust the seasoning with more black and/or cayenne pepper if needed. Serve hot.

## Potato and Tomato Gratin    PATATE E POMODORI

Although this is an Italian recipe from the city of Ferrara, it is of Spanish Sephardic origin. It was traditionally cooked slowly in a heavy pan on the stove top, but it can also be cooked in the oven. SERVES 6

---

4 or 5 cloves garlic, finely minced

1 cup chopped fresh flat-leaf parsley

1½ to 2 pounds large, ripe tomatoes, sliced ¼ to ⅓ inch thick

Salt and freshly ground black pepper

Olive oil for sprinkling

2 pounds boiling potatoes, such as Yukon Gold, peeled and sliced ¼ inch thick

1 cup water or broth, or as needed (optional)

---

If baking the gratin, preheat the oven to 350°F and oil a large gratin dish. If cooking the gratin on the stove top, oil a large, heavy, deep frying pan, preferably enameled cast iron.

In a small bowl, stir together the garlic and parsley. Layer one-third of the tomato slices in the bottom of the prepared baking dish or frying pan. Sprinkle with salt and pepper, with about one-fourth of the garlic mixture, and with a little oil. Layer half of the potato slices on top, sprinkle with oil, and then top with half of the remaining tomatoes. Sprinkle with salt and pepper, half of the remaining garlic mixture, and a little oil. Top with the remaining potato slices and then the remaining tomato slices. Sprinkle with the remaining garlic mixture, salt and pepper, and some oil. Cover the gratin dish or frying pan.

Place the gratin dish in the oven or place the frying pan on the stove top over medium-low heat. Cook until the potatoes are tender but not falling apart, about 30 minutes. If the potatoes are still undercooked and there is too little liquid in the pan to cook them, add the water as needed. If the tomatoes have given off too much liquid, uncover the dish or pan and cook until the liquids are absorbed. Serve warm or at room temperature.

## Spinach with Pine Nuts and Raisins
SPINACI CON PINOLI E PASSERINE

This Italian Jewish dish is a staple of Genoese and Venetian tables and is also popular in Greece, Turkey, and Spain. It is a perfect accompaniment to delicate fish or poultry dishes. SERVES 6

| 2½ pounds spinach | ¼ cup raisins, plumped in hot water and drained |
| 2 to 3 tablespoons olive oil | |
| 2 small yellow onions or 6 green onions, including green tops, minced | ¼ cup pine nuts, toasted |
| | Salt and freshly ground black pepper |

Rinse the spinach well and remove the stems (reserve the stems for Braised Spinach Stems; recipe follows). Place in a large sauté pan with only the rinsing water clinging to the leaves and cook over medium heat, turning as needed, until wilted, just a few minutes. Do not cover the pan or the spinach will taste metallic. Drain well and set aside.

Warm the oil in the same sauté pan over medium heat. Add the onions and cook, stirring often, until translucent and tender, about 8 minutes. Add the spinach, raisins, and pine nuts and sauté briefly to warm through. Season with salt and pepper and serve warm or at room temperature.

## Braised Spinach Stems   TESTINE DI SPINACI

*Testine* means "little heads." An old Venetian recipe for these spinach stems calls the dish *gambetti de spinasse* in dialect, or "little spinach legs." How thrifty to use the spinach leaves for one dish and then use the stems and inner tiny leaves to make this antipasto or side dish. You will need to start with almost 4 pounds of spinach to yield about 1 pound of stems. The Italians are not the only thrifty cooks. Turkish Jews also cook spinach stems and call the dish *ravikos.* SERVES 3 OR 4

| 1 pound spinach stems and hearts | Dash of red wine vinegar |
| ½ cup olive oil | Salt and freshly ground black pepper |

Trim away any roots and rinse the stems in several changes of water to remove any hidden grit. In a saucepan, combine the stems, oil, and enough water to barely cover. Bring to a boil over high heat and cook uncovered until the water evaporates and the stems are tender, 8 to 10 minutes.

Add the vinegar and continue to cook over high heat until the vinegar evaporates and the stems turn red, just a few minutes. Season with salt and pepper, remove from the heat, and let cool. Serve at room temperature or chilled.

## Spinach Croquettes   POLPETTINE DI SPINACI

My inspiration for this dish comes from a recipe for little spinach dumplings in Giuseppe Maffioli's *La cucina veneziana.* Ideal for either a meat or dairy meal, the little cakes can be fried in butter or oil and served as is, or they can be fried, simmered in broth, and then served with *bagna brusca* (egg-and-lemon sauce) spooned over the top, as they are here. SERVES 4

---

1 pound spinach

6 tablespoons unsalted butter or olive oil

2 cups fresh bread crumbs, soaked in milk or water and squeezed dry

2 whole eggs, lightly beaten, plus 1 egg yolk

½ cup pine nuts, toasted

⅓ cup raisins, plumped in white wine and drained

2 cloves garlic, finely minced

Salt and freshly ground black pepper

1 cup vegetable broth, if using butter, or chicken broth, if using oil

Juice of 1 large lemon

---

Rinse the spinach well and remove the stems. Chop the leaves finely. Warm 3 tablespoons of the butter (for a dairy meal) or oil (for a meat meal) in a large sauté pan over medium heat. Add the spinach and turn it in the pan until wilted, just a few minutes. Transfer to a bowl and add the bread crumbs, whole eggs, pine nuts, raisins, and garlic. Season with salt and pepper. Form into little cakes 2½ to 3 inches in diameter.

Wipe out the pan, return to medium heat, and warm the remaining 3 tablespoons butter or oil. Add the cakes and sauté, turning once, until golden on both sides, about 5 minutes total. Add the broth, turn down the heat to low, and simmer for 5 minutes. Using a slotted spatula, transfer the cakes to a warmed platter. (Or, for a firmer texture, remove the cakes from the pan when golden and place on a warmed serving platter. Deglaze the pan with the broth over high heat, stirring to dislodge any browned bits, and then simmer the broth for 5 minutes.)

In a bowl, whisk together the egg yolk and lemon juice until very frothy, then whisk in a little of the hot broth. Stir the egg yolk mixture into the sauté pan and cook gently, stirring often, until thickened. Spoon over the croquettes and serve at once.

## *Spinach and Ricotta Dumplings* GNOCCHI DI SPINACI E RICOTTA

These spinach-and-ricotta dumplings are affectionately called *ravioli nudi,* or "undressed ravioli." In other words, they are ravioli filling without a pasta coat. The dumplings can be boiled in advance and then placed in a buttered baking dish and reheated later. This is a perfect dish for a dairy meal. If you like, drizzle the dumplings with a little less melted butter, dust with the Parmesan, bake as directed, and then toss with a light tomato sauce. SERVES 4 TO 6

| | |
|---|---|
| 2 cups well-drained, chopped cooked spinach (from 2 pounds fresh) | ⅔ cup all-purpose flour, plus more if needed |
| 1 cup ricotta cheese | 2 teaspoons salt |
| ¾ cup grated Parmesan cheese, plus more for dusting | 1 teaspoon freshly ground black pepper |
| | Few gratings nutmeg |
| 2 eggs, lightly beaten | 4 to 6 tablespoons unsalted butter, melted |

Bring a large pot of salted water to a boil.

While the water is heating, in a bowl, combine the spinach, ricotta, Parmesan, eggs, flour, salt, pepper, and nutmeg and mix well. Form a walnut-size ball of the mixture and then drop it into the boiling water. If it breaks apart, add more flour to the mixture and test again. When the mixture holds together, using a wet spoon and slightly dampened fingers, form the mixture into walnut-size balls.

Preheat the oven to 350°F. Butter a 9-by-12-by-2-inch baking dish.

In batches, drop the balls into the boiling water. They will sink to the bottom of the pot and then eventually rise. When they are floating on the surface, they are ready. Remove them with a slotted skimmer, drain them well, and place in the prepared baking dish. Drizzle them with the butter and then sprinkle with a liberal dusting of Parmesan cheese.

Bake until heated through and lightly golden on top, 10 to 15 minutes. Serve at once.

## *Spinach and Potato Gratin, Izmir Style*   SFONGO DI ESPINAKA

A *sfongo* is a Turkish gratin of vegetables thickened with potatoes, eggs, and cheese. This *sfongo* is unusual in appearance, as little mounds of cheese-and-egg-enriched mashed potato dot the spinach-and-potato gratin base. Some versions of the recipe omit the potato mounds and arrange the spinach and potatoes in alternating layers. In Greece, the Sephardic Jews of Rhodes make this dish with Swiss chard in place of the spinach. SERVES 8

| | |
|---|---|
| 4 pounds spinach | 1½ cups mixed grated cheeses, such as kashkaval, Gruyère, and Parmesan |
| 4 large boiling potatoes, peeled and quartered | 1½ teaspoons salt |
| ¼ cup milk | ½ teaspoon freshly ground black pepper |
| 6 eggs, lightly beaten | Plain yogurt for serving |

Rinse the spinach and remove the stems (reserve the stems for Braised Spinach Stems, page 203). Chop the leaves finely, place in a large sauté pan with only the rinsing water clinging to them, and cook over medium heat, turning as needed, until wilted, just a few minutes. Drain well and squeeze dry. You should have about 4 cups cooked spinach.

Combine the potatoes with lightly salted water to cover generously, bring to a boil over medium-high heat, and boil until the potatoes are tender, about 30 minutes. Drain well, return to the pan, and place over low heat briefly to cook away any remaining moisture. Remove from the heat, add the milk, and mash until smooth. You should have about 4 cups mashed potatoes. Add the eggs, 1 cup of the cheese mixture, the salt, and the pepper and mix well.

Divide the potato mixture in half. Add half of it to the cooked spinach and mix well.

Preheat the oven to 350°F. Brush a 9-by-12-by-2-inch baking dish with warm olive oil and spread the spinach mixture in it. Make ½-inch-deep holes in the mixture at regular intervals, spacing them about 1½ inches apart. Fill with rounded mounds of the remaining mashed potatoes. Top evenly with the remaining cheese mixture.

Bake until golden, 35 to 40 minutes. Serve directly from the dish. Pass a bowl of yogurt at the table.

## *White Beans under Greens*   FAGIOLI COTTI SOTTO LA BIETOLA

Cooking styles have changed dramatically. A recipe of Emma Belforte's in Aldo Santini's *La cucina livornese* recommends stewing white beans and greens for 3 hours and then serving them with couscous for a full meal. I promptly cut the cooking time in half. For fuller flavor, use broth instead of water. Most versions of this recipe ignore garlic, but you would not be remiss in adding some. A Roman version of this recipe, called *fagioli con la lattuga,* includes lettuce and omits the onions. SERVES 6

3 tablespoons olive oil

2 red onions, chopped or thinly sliced

3 cloves garlic, minced (optional)

2 pounds beet greens or Swiss chard, chopped (about 10 cups), blanched, and drained

1¼ cups dried white or borlotti beans, picked over, soaked in water to cover overnight, drained, rinsed, and simmered for 30 minutes in water to cover

3 cups seeded and diced canned plum tomatoes and their juices

Salt and freshly ground black pepper

2 to 3 cups vegetable broth or water, or as needed

Warm the oil in a large, heavy pot over medium heat. Add the onions and garlic and sauté until softened, 5 to 8 minutes. Add the blanched greens, mix well, turn down the heat to low, and cook, stirring occasionally, until tender, 5 to 8 minutes. Remove half of the onions-greens mixture from the pot and then spread the remainder evenly over the bottom of the pot. Top with half of the cooked beans and their cooking liquid. Spread the remaining onions-greens mixture over the beans and top with the remaining beans. Layer the tomatoes and their liquid on top. Season with salt and pepper and pour in enough broth to barely cover.

Place over medium heat and bring slowly to a boil. Cover, turn down the heat to low, and cook very slowly until the beans are tender, 30 to 45 minutes. Taste and adjust the seasoning before serving. Serve hot or warm.

## *Sephardic Swiss Chard and Chickpeas*   PAZI KON GARVANSOS

This Spanish classic made its way into the Sephardic kitchens of Rhodes. It is often used as a base for cooking fish balls or meatballs. Add them uncooked to the cooked chickpeas and chard (before you add the juice of the second lemon) and cook them, basting often with the pan juices, until cooked through. If adding fish balls, use a fish broth for the liquid; if adding meatballs, use chicken or meat broth.   SERVES 4

¼ cup olive oil

1 large yellow onion, chopped

5 cloves garlic, sliced

1 bunch Swiss chard, leaves and stems separated, stems chopped and leaves cut into strips

1 cup cooked chickpeas and their cooking liquid

1 cup peeled, seeded, and diced tomatoes (optional)

1 cup vegetable broth or water

Juice of 2 lemons

Salt and freshly ground black pepper

Chopped fresh dill for garnish (optional)

Warm the oil in a large sauté pan over medium heat. Add the onion and cook, stirring occasionally, until softened, about 5 minutes. Add the garlic and chopped chard stems and cook, stirring often, until softened, about 10 minutes. Add the chickpeas and their liquid, tomatoes, broth, and the juice of 1 lemon and cook, stirring occasionally, for a few minutes. Add the chopped chard leaves and continue to cook until the chard is tender, about 10 minutes longer.

Add the remaining lemon juice and season with salt and pepper. Garnish with the dill and serve hot or warm.

# Moroccan Tagine of Swiss Chard and Chickpeas

MARAK SILK BIL HAMUS

This Moroccan version of beans and greens is livelier in spicing than the Sephardic one on page 207. It can be served with couscous for a vegetarian main course or as a side dish for fish. SERVES 6 TO 8

½ cup olive oil

2 yellow onions, chopped (about 2 cups)

2 cloves garlic, minced

1 tablespoon sweet paprika

1 teaspoon ground coriander

12 cups chopped stemmed Swiss chard leaves (about 3 bunches)

½ cup chopped fresh cilantro

1 cup drained cooked chickpeas

Salt and freshly ground black pepper

2 to 3 tablespoons fresh lemon juice

Peel of 2 preserved lemons, homemade (page 356) or store-bought, rinsed and slivered

Warm the oil in a large, wide saucepan over medium heat. Add the onions and cook, stirring occasionally, until softened, about 5 minutes. Add the garlic, paprika, and coriander and cook for 2 minutes. Add the chard, cover partially, and cook, stirring occasionally, until the chard wilts and is tender, about 10 minutes.

Add the cilantro and chickpeas, stir well, and season with salt and pepper. Cook for a few minutes to heat the chickpeas through. Add the lemon juice as needed to balance the flavor. Stir in the preserved lemon, simmer for a minute or two to heat through, and serve hot.

# Melted Golden Squash     ZUCCA DISFATTA

The yellow-orange squash of the Veneto is often called *zucca barucca*. For Jews, *barucca* is related to *baruch*, the Hebrew word for "blessed." Non-Jewish Italians say it is dialect for *verruca*, meaning bumpy and wart-like, describing the exterior of the squash. What we do know for sure is that there are many Italian Jewish (as well as Spanish and Moroccan Jewish) recipes that call for the pumpkin squash that was brought to Italy by the Sephardim from Spain and Portugal via the New World. The word *disfatta* means "defeated" or "decomposed," in other words, melted and very soft.

This recipe was traditionally served to break the fast at the end of Yom Kippur. It calls for fresh citron, which is sweeter and more aromatic than grated lemon zest. If you cannot find citron at your local market, you can use the exotically shaped Buddha's hand, also known as fingered citron. If you use grated lemon zest instead, you'll find that the sweetness of the squash will help balance any slight bitterness. You might also try substituting sweet potato or yam purée for the squash. SERVES 6

3 tablespoons olive oil or unsalted butter

1 yellow onion, finely chopped (about 1¼ cups)

3 cups squash purée (see master recipe, page 36)

3 tablespoons finely minced citron, or 2 tablespoons grated lemon zest

½ teaspoon ground cinnamon

Salt and freshly ground black pepper

Chopped fresh mint, flat-leaf parsley, or rosemary for garnish (optional)

Warm the oil in a sauté pan over low heat. Add the onion and cook, stirring occasionally, until very soft and sweet, about 15 minutes. Add the puréed squash, citron, and cinnamon and stir well, then season with salt and pepper. Cook over very low heat, stirring often, until the mixture is dry, about 10 minutes. Transfer to a serving dish and sprinkle with mint. Serve hot or warm.

## Moroccan Squash and Apricot Purée   HLOU

*Hlou* is a Rosh Hashanah specialty served as an accompaniment to couscous. Some Moroccan cooks make this sweet squash purée without the apricots, using honey for sweetness and omitting the onions. Kitty Morse, in *Come with Me to the Kasbah,* mentions a similar sweet pumpkin dish that her family called *cassolita,* a specialty of the northern Moroccan city of Tétouan. (The name comes from *cazuela,* a Spanish terracotta cooking pot.) Instead of apricots, she uses raisins and almonds for the note of sweetness. MAKES ABOUT 3 CUPS

½ cup sugar

½ cup olive oil

2 yellow onions, finely chopped

2 cups squash purée (see master recipe, page 36)

8 ounces dried apricots, cut into small pieces, soaked in hot water for 1 hour, and drained

¼ cup fresh lemon juice, or as needed

1 teaspoon ground cinnamon

Salt

Warm together the sugar and oil in a saucepan over medium heat until the sugar has melted and is starting to turn a pale caramel color. (Don't worry if the mixture looks odd and some sugar solidifies. It will melt as the onions cook.) Add the onions and cook over very low heat, stirring occasionally, until tender and sweet, about 20 minutes. Add the squash purée, apricots, lemon juice, and cinnamon and simmer until the apricots are soft, about 10 minutes longer. You may need a pinch of salt and/or a little more lemon juice to round out the flavor. Serve warm or at room temperature.

# Lebanese Pumpkin Kibbeh  KIBBEH BIL SANIYEH LAQTEEN

Here is a delicious version of *kibbeh bil saniyeh* (*saniyeh* means "in a tray"). Instead of using meat, it uses meaty winter squash. It can be assembled hours ahead and baked just before serving time. Some families put the pumpkin and spices in the filling rather than in the outer shell and keep the outer layer just bulgur, onion, flour, salt, and paprika. This version mixes the pumpkin into the outer coating and adds a crunchy onion and walnut filling. SERVES 6

**KIBBEH**

1½ cups coarsely chopped yellow onion

2 cups squash purée (see master recipe, page 36)

1½ to 2 cups fine-grind bulgur

2 teaspoons salt

1 teaspoon ground allspice

1 teaspoon ground cinnamon

½ teaspoon freshly ground black pepper

⅓ cup olive oil

⅓ cup all-purpose flour

**FILLING**

2 tablespoons olive oil

2 to 3 cups chopped yellow onion

½ cup walnuts, toasted and chopped

Salt and freshly ground black pepper

2 tablespoons pomegranate molasses

⅓ cup olive oil

Plain yogurt for serving

To make the kibbeh, pulse the onion in a food processor until finely chopped. Transfer the onion to a bowl, add the squash, bulgur, salt, allspice, cinnamon, pepper, oil, and flour. Cover and refrigerate until the bulgur absorbs all of the moisture, 2 to 3 hours or up to overnight.

To make the filling, warm the oil in a sauté pan over medium heat. Add the onion and cook, stirring occasionally, until translucent and tender, 8 to 10 minutes. Add the walnuts, season with salt and pepper, and remove from the heat. Add the pomegranate molasses and let the filling cool completely.

Preheat the oven to 400°F. Oil a 9-by-12-by-2-inch baking pan or a 9-inch deep-dish pie pan.

Remove the kibbeh from the refrigerator, transfer to the food processor, and process for 20 seconds. Transfer half of the kibbeh to the prepared pan and pat it down into an even layer with wet hands. Spread the filling evenly over the kibbeh, then top with the remaining kibbeh, smoothing the surface with the tines of a fork. Press down again to remove any air pockets. Using a sharp knife, score the layers into diamonds or squares as if scoring baklava, cutting down to the bottom of the pan, and then run the knife around the edge of the pan to loosen the sides. Pour the oil evenly over the top.

Bake until the top is golden brown and crusty, about 40 minutes. Serve warm with the yogurt on the side.

## Sweet-and-Sour Squash    ZUCCA GIALLA IN AGRODOLCE

Sicily is probably the origin of this Sephardic recipe, which I adapted from one that appears in Cia Eramo's *La cucina mantovana.* It is identical to the classic *fegato ai Settecannoli,* named after a quarter in Palermo in which there is a fountain with seven spouts. In the past, few people in that poverty-stricken neighborhood could afford to eat meat. Pumpkin is meaty, however, and when cooked has so much body that it was likened to liver (*fegato*). Note the Arabic touch of sweetness that balances the acidity. Some versions of this dish call for cooking the garlic in the oil, discarding it, and then cooking the squash. Others omit both the vinegar and cinnamon. SERVES 6 TO 8

2-pound piece butternut squash or pumpkin

⅓ cup olive oil, or as needed

Salt and freshly ground black pepper

2 or 3 large cloves garlic, sliced paper-thin

½ cup coarsely chopped fresh mint

½ cup red wine vinegar

½ cup sugar

Pinch of ground cinnamon

Peel the squash, discard any seeds and fibers, and cut the pulp into ⅓-inch-thick slices. Warm half of the oil in a large sauté pan over medium heat. In batches, add the squash slices and sauté, turning to brown both sides and adding more oil as needed to prevent scorching, until tender, 6 to 8 minutes. Using a slotted spatula, transfer the squash to a serving platter. Season with salt and pepper and cover with the garlic and mint.

Add the vinegar, sugar, and cinnamon to the oil remaining in the pan over medium heat. Cook, stirring, until the sugar dissolves and the sauce thickens, about 5 minutes. Season with salt and pepper and pour over the squash. Serve at room temperature.

## Persian Pumpkin Squash Stew    KHORESH-E KADU

This recipe comes from the province of Gilan, near the Caspian Sea, home to walnut and olive orchards. The walnut and pomegranate sauce commonly paired with meat and poultry in the Iranian kitchen also works well with meaty winter squash. Accompany this richly flavored dish with Persian Rice (page 149). SERVES 4 TO 6

1 small butternut squash, about 1½ pounds

5 tablespoons olive oil

1 yellow onion, chopped

1 teaspoon ground turmeric

½ teaspoon ground cinnamon

1½ cups coarsely ground walnuts

1½ cups vegetable broth, or as needed

1 cup pomegranate molasses

3 tablespoons unsalted butter

2 tablespoons sugar

¼ teaspoon saffron threads, finely crushed and steeped in 2 tablespoons hot water

Fresh lemon juice

---

Halve the squash and discard the seeds and fibers. Peel the halves and cut into 1½- or 2-inch pieces.

Warm 2 tablespoons of the oil in a large saucepan over medium heat. Add the onion and cook, stirring occasionally, until softened and starting to take on color, 12 to 15 minutes. Add the turmeric, cinnamon, and walnuts and stir to combine. Add the broth and pomegranate molasses and bring to a boil. Turn down the heat to low and simmer gently.

While the sauce is cooking, warm the remaining 3 tablespoons oil and the butter in a large sauté pan over medium-low heat. Add the sugar and stir until it melts. Add the squash pieces, stir to coat with the fat and sugar, and then cook over medium-low heat until the squash has caramelized and is tender, 10 to 15 minutes.

Add the squash mixture to the walnut-pomegranate sauce and simmer until the flavors are blended, 15 to 20 minutes longer. If the liquid reduces too much, add a little more broth. Add the saffron infusion and stir well. Taste and adjust the seasoning, adding lemon juice or sugar for balance if needed. Serve warm.

## *Pumpkin with Prunes*   KOMIDA DE BALKABAK KON PRUNAS

Cooking dried fruits in savory dishes is typical of Moorish cuisine, as this dish illustrates. It resembles *blou* (page 209), the Moroccan Jewish compote of pumpkin squash and apricots, and would be an ideal accompaniment for roast chicken or grilled lamb. I have reduced the traditional cooking time substantially so that both the squash and prunes hold their shape. I have also used the prune soaking liquid instead of water, as it enriches the flavor of the dish. SERVES 6 TO 8

---

2-pound piece pumpkin or butternut squash

1½ cups pitted prunes, soaked in 2 cups hot water for 1 hour

2 to 3 tablespoons olive oil

Grated zest and juice of 1 lemon

2 tablespoons confectioners' sugar

1½ teaspoons salt

½ teaspoon ground cinnamon (optional)

Peel the pumpkin, discard any seeds and fibers, and cut the pulp into 1½-inch cubes. Put the pumpkin in a large, heavy saucepan and add the prunes and their soaking water, oil, lemon zest and juice, sugar, salt, and cinnamon. Mix well and bring to a boil over high heat. Turn down the heat to low and cook, stirring from time to time and adding water to the pan if the pumpkin threatens to scorch, until the pumpkin is tender and the liquid has been absorbed, 15 to 20 minutes.

Taste and adjust the seasoning and serve warm or at room temperature.

## Moroccan Tagine of Pumpkin and Lentils   ADS BE QAR

Accompany this hearty *tagine* with couscous or rice for a lovely dinner. If you choose to add the greens, they will contribute both color and flavor. I use Swiss chard or escarole. Sometimes *khli,* dried beef preserved in fat, is added to this stew.   SERVES 6

2 tablespoons olive oil

2 yellow onions, chopped

2 fresh hot chiles, thinly sliced

1 tablespoon sweet paprika

2 teaspoons ground toasted cumin

2 teaspoons ground coriander

¼ teaspoon cayenne pepper

1 cup green or black lentils, picked over and rinsed

4 ripe tomatoes, peeled, seeded, and chopped, or 1 can (14 ounces) plum tomatoes, drained, seeded and chopped

¼ cup tomato purée

3 cups water, or as needed

1-pound piece pumpkin or butternut squash, peeled, seeded, and cut into 1-inch dice

1 pound bitter greens, blanched and coarsely chopped (optional)

Warm the oil in a saucepan over medium heat. Add the onions and chiles and cook, stirring occasionally, until the onions are softened, about 8 minutes. Add the paprika, cumin, coriander, and cayenne and continue to cook, stirring occasionally, until the onions are tender, 3 to 5 minutes longer. Add the lentils, tomatoes, and tomato purée, stir well, and add the water to cover. Turn down the heat to low, cover, and simmer for about 20 minutes.

Add the pumpkin and more water if the mixture seems dry, re-cover, and simmer until the squash is tender, about 15 minutes longer. If using the greens, add them during the last 5 minutes of cooking. Serve hot.

## Tomato Halves Two Ways   POMODORI A MEZZO

In this simple and delicious Roman recipe for oven-braised tomatoes, the peeled, seeded tomatoes break down and make a sauce for the unpeeled halves.   SERVES 6

6 firm ripe tomatoes

Extra virgin olive oil, for searing and drizzling

Salt and freshly ground black pepper

1 to 2 tablespoons finely minced garlic

¼ cup chopped fresh flat-leaf parsley

Preheat the oven to 400°F.

Bring a small saucepan of hot water to a boil. One at a time, briefly dip 3 of the tomatoes into the boiling water to loosen their skin. Drain and peel, then cut in half crosswise and gently squeeze out the seeds. Cut the remaining 3 tomatoes in half crosswise and squeeze gently to remove most of the seeds.

Film the bottom of a large sauté pan with oil and warm over high heat. Add the unpeeled tomato halves, cut side down, to the hot oil and sear until golden. Transfer the halves, cut side up, to a heavy ovenproof pot with a lid in which they fit snugly. Sprinkle with salt and pepper. In a small bowl, stir together the garlic and parsley and spread evenly over the tops.

Place the peeled tomato halves, cut sides down, on top of the unpeeled halves. Drizzle with oil and sprinkle with salt and pepper. Cover, place on the stove top over medium heat, and cook for 5 minutes. Uncover, spoon out the excess liquid, and then re-cover and place in the oven. Bake until the top layer of tomatoes breaks down to form a soft sauce atop the bottom halves, 20 to 30 minutes. Sprinkle lightly with salt and serve hot.

## Tomatoes with Grape Juice   POMODORI CON L'UVA

In this traditional Italian Jewish dish, fresh grape juice is poured over fried tomatoes while they are still warm. The original recipe called for tart red wine grapes, but because most of us do not have easy access to a vineyard, we will have to use table grapes. They tend to be sweet rather than tart, so to approximate the acidity, it's best to add a bit of balsamic vinegar to the juices to accentuate the tartness. Look for Zante grapes, dark wine grapes, or any black or red seedless grapes. If grapes are not in season, use about ⅓ cup bottled grape must (*verjus*) mixed with a bit of balsamic vinegar.

Mixing cornmeal with the flour is my addition, as is flavoring the flour with rosemary and the oil with garlic. Traditionally, the garlic and rosemary are fried along with the tomatoes, but I found that they quickly burned and tasted acrid. Green tomatoes are also good prepared this way. SERVES 6

1 small bunch dark grapes (about 1 cup)

1 to 2 tablespoons balsamic vinegar, if needed

All-purpose flour and yellow cornmeal, in equal parts, for coating

1 tablespoon finely chopped fresh rosemary

Salt and freshly ground black pepper

6 firm, almost ripe tomatoes, sliced ½ inch thick

Olive oil for frying

2 cloves garlic, smashed

---

Purée the grapes in a blender, then strain through a fine-mesh sieve, capturing the juice in a bowl. Season the juice with the vinegar if the grapes are too sweet.

Combine the flour, cornmeal, rosemary, and a generous pinch each of salt and pepper on a plate and mix well. One at a time, dip the tomato slices in the flour mixture, coating on both sides and tapping off the excess, and set aside on a plate.

Film the bottom of a large sauté pan with oil, add the garlic, and warm over medium heat. When the oil is hot, in batches, add the tomato slices and cook, turning once, until golden on both sides, about 6 minutes total. Sprinkle with salt and pepper and, using a spatula, transfer to a serving plate. Keep warm until all of the tomato slices are fried. Pour the grape juice over the hot tomatoes and serve immediately.

## Zucchini Peel with Garlic and Pepper
### KACHKARIKAS DE KALAVASA KON AJO I PIMYENTA

Here is the perfect recipe for zucchini that have grown too large to use easily. I adapted it from a recipe for zucchini in Méri Badi's *250 recettes de cuisine juive espagnole* that was unusual in two ways: first, it had lots of garlic, reminiscent of the old days of Spanish cooking, rather than the garlic-reticent Sephardic repertoire as it evolved in Turkey, and second, it used only the outer layer of the zucchini, not the seeds and center. I have shortened the cooking time by quite a bit so that the zucchini does not disintegrate, but it will still seem a bit too soft for anyone who is used to al dente vegetables. You can cook the zucchini even less, but you will have to give the garlic a good head start, as it will take 20 minutes to soften.

Other recipes for braised zucchini peel omit the garlic and pepper and cook the zucchini squares directly in a sauce of fresh or dried greengage plums (also called golden prunes) or sour raisins, using a pinch of sugar, some lemon juice, oil, and water. These recipes with fruit are called *kachkarikas de kalavasa kon avramila* or *kachkarikas de kalavasa kon agras*. SERVES 4 TO 6

---

3 pounds zucchini (about 8 large)

2 small heads garlic, cloves separated, peeled, and halved lengthwise if large

¼ cup extra virgin olive oil

3 cups water

1 teaspoon salt

1 teaspoon freshly ground black pepper

Generous pinch of sugar

---

Cut off both ends of each zucchini and then remove the outer layer of each zucchini in strips about 1 inch wide and about ⅓ inch thick, so that some of the flesh remains attached. Cut the strips crosswise into 1-inch squares. Save the centers for another use or discard.

Combine the garlic, oil, water, salt, pepper, and sugar in a saucepan and bring to a boil over high heat. Turn down the heat to low, cover, and simmer for 10 to 15 minutes. Add the zucchini pieces, mix well, cover partially, and simmer for 10 minutes.

Check the amount of liquid left in the pan. Most of it should have been absorbed. If it is too soupy and the zucchini are tender and the garlic is meltingly tender, using a slotted spoon, transfer the zucchini and garlic to a serving dish and reduce the sauce over high heat. If the zucchini and garlic are still rather firm, uncover the pan and simmer to reduce the excess liquid. Taste and adjust the seasoning with salt and serve warm or cold.

## Turkish Ratatouille    TÜRLÜ

This dish has a Judeo-Spanish origin. It is reminiscent of *pisto* dishes from Murcia or La Mancha but with the Turkish addition of okra. *Pisto* evolved from an ancient stew called *alboronia,* the Moorish name for eggplant. Over time, vegetables from the New World made their entrance into the mix. Although no herbs are traditionally added to this recipe, oregano, marjoram, flat-leaf parsley, or mint would be a good addition.  SERVES 8

6 tablespoons olive oil

2 large yellow onions, chopped

Salt

7 ripe tomatoes, peeled, seeded, and chopped

2 globe eggplants, peeled in a vertically striped fashion, quartered lengthwise, and then cut crosswise into 2-inch pieces

4 small new potatoes, peeled and halved if very small or quartered if larger

2 red or yellow bell peppers, seeded and chopped

2 teaspoons tomato paste

Pinch of sugar (optional)

2 large zucchini, quartered lengthwise and cut crosswise into 1½-inch pieces

8 ounces okra, stems removed, fuzz rubbed off, soaked in ½ cup white wine vinegar for 30 to 60 minutes, drained, and rinsed

1 pound green beans, trimmed and halved crosswise or cut into 2-inch lengths

Few tablespoons chopped fresh herbs (see headnote), optional

Warm the oil in a large, deep sauté pan over medium heat. Add the onions and cook, stirring occasionally, until softened, about 5 minutes. Season with salt, add 4 of the tomatoes, and cook for 3 minutes. Layer the eggplants, potatoes, and peppers on top of the tomatoes and onions. Mix the remaining 3 tomatoes with the tomato paste and scatter over the top. Sprinkle with the sugar, season with salt, and pour in water to a depth of about ½ inch (about 1 cup). Bring to a simmer, turn down the heat to low, cover, and cook until the vegetables are half-cooked, about 20 minutes.

Add the zucchini, okra, and green beans, re-cover, and cook for 20 minutes longer. The dish is ready when the eggplant has absorbed the sauce and is translucent and tender and the potatoes are tender. Add a bit more water and cook longer if needed.

If the vegetables are ready but too much sauce remains, using a slotted spoon, transfer the vegetables to a dish and reduce the sauce over medium-high heat. Then return the vegetables to the sauce, add the herbs, mix well, and taste and adjust the seasoning. Serve warm.

## *Moroccan Vegetable Tagine*   MEHALET

This recipe, which is sometimes called *tajine del sabana,* is a cross between two *tagine* recipes in *La cuisine juive du Maroc de mère en fille* by Maguy Kakon. Similar dishes are found on the Rosh Hashanah table in Fez, Meknes, and Tangier. Almost any combination of vegetables will work for this fragrant stew, which is typically served with couscous. It includes both potatoes and sweet potatoes and the classic addition of preserved lemon and olives, which add salt and tang. If you like, 1 to 1½ pounds butternut squash or pumpkin, peeled and cut into 3-inch chunks, can be used in place of the sweet potatoes. Although not authentic, I sometimes add ½ cup plumped raisins for a note of sweetness. SERVES 8

¼ cup olive oil

2 large yellow onions, chopped

Salt and freshly ground black pepper

2 cloves garlic, minced

1 tablespoon sweet paprika

1 teaspoon ground turmeric

1 teaspoon ground ginger

1 teaspoon Maras pepper flakes

4 ripe tomatoes, peeled, seeded, and chopped

½ cup chopped fresh cilantro

4 cups vegetable broth or water

4 carrots, peeled and cut into 2-inch lengths

2 turnips or rutabagas, peeled and cut into 2-inch pieces

6 small Yukon Gold or new potatoes, cut into 2-inch pieces

3 sweet potatoes, peeled and cut into 3-inch chunks

4 small zucchini, cut into 2-inch lengths

1 cup drained canned chickpeas, rinsed (optional)

Peel of 2 preserved lemons, homemade (page 356) or store-bought, rinsed and cut into fine slivers

1 cup green or violet olives

2 fresh chiles, thinly sliced (optional)

Warm the oil in a large stew pot over medium heat. Add the onions with a pinch of salt and cook, stirring occasionally, until translucent and tender, 8 to 10 minutes. Add the garlic, paprika, turmeric, ginger, pepper flakes, tomatoes, and half of the cilantro and cook, stirring, for a few minutes to bloom the spices. Pour in the broth, stir well, raise the heat to high, and bring to a boil. Turn down the heat to low, cover, and simmer for 30 minutes.

Add the carrots, re-cover, and cook for 15 minutes. Add the turnips, potatoes, and sweet potatoes and simmer for 10 minutes longer. Add the zucchini, chickpeas, preserved lemon, olives, and chiles and simmer until all of the vegetables are tender, about 15 minutes longer. Taste and adjust the seasoning with salt and pepper and add the remaining cilantro. Serve hot.

Fish

FISH HAS A PRESTIGIOUS PLACE on the traditional Mediterranean Jewish table. It is served on Friday night of the Sabbath and might also be the centerpiece of the meatless dinner prepared for Thursday. A whole fish with head intact is traditionally served for Rosh Hashanah, to commemorate the head—that is, the beginning—of the New Year. Fish is important, too, because it is pareve, suitable for both meat and dairy meals.

According to kosher laws, Jews must not eat any fish that does not have scales. These forbidden fish include most swordfish, sturgeon (and its caviar), monkfish, ray, skate, European turbot, shark, and eel, as well as all shellfish, which includes the cephalopods octopus, squid, and cuttlefish. Sole, carp, and mullet are served on special occasions, but many recipes use inexpensive fish, like anchovies and sardines. Sea bass, halibut, cod, and snapper are readily available at most fish markets when fresh anchovies or sardines are not in season. And salmon would be a fine choice, as well.

A wide variety of cooking methods are employed: poaching, frying, baking, braising, and grilling. Because of the laws of the Sabbath, a large repertoire of fish dishes that could be cooked ahead of time and served at room temperature was created, such as the Venetian *pesce in saor,* in which sole or sardines are cooked, treated to a sweet-and-sour onion sauce, and then left to marinate for a day or two before serving.

In the Sephardic community, carp was the first choice for a holiday dinner, especially for Rosh Hashanah, as it represented good luck and longevity. In Salonika, the carp, or *sazan,* came from a lake the Sephardim called Goyvasidi, a Ladino corruption of Agios Vasilios (Saint Basil), the Greek name for the lake. The fish was poached in court bouillon and chilled. Although it could be served very simply, with just the cooking liquid reduced to a shimmering jelly, or with an egg-and-lemon thickener, it was sometimes served with a fragrant nut sauce; with *salsa verde,* a bright mixture of chopped parsley, capers, hard-boiled egg yolks, and vinegar; or with a great homemade mayonnaise.

One of the most common accompanying sauces for fish is the Sephardic *agristada,* an egg-and-lemon mixture (*bagna brusca* in Italian, avgolemono in Greece, and *terbiyeli* in Turkey). This sauce remains popular in Spain, Italy, Greece, and Turkey today, especially for fish and vegetable dishes. (In the kosher kitchen, *agristada* is also used in meat meals, where dairy products are prohibited, in place of béchamel, beurre manié, or cream.) *Agristada* is usually assembled in the pan using the warm fish cooking liquids. However, a version thickened with cornstarch or flour and then chilled like a mayonnaise is also served. *Ajada,* a garlic mayonnaise related to aioli, is another classic sauce for fish, especially for dishes that are served cold, while tahini, left its natural color or tinted green with cilantro and parsley, adds creamy richness primarily to baked fish.

Nut sauces, drawn from the Hispano-Arabic tradition, and sweet-and-sour sauces, often fruit-based with plums or rhubarb or with fruit and tomato, are popular choices, as well. Tomato sauces vary between those that are cooked separately and those prepared in the pan as the fish cooks. The tomatoes are often enhanced with onion, sometimes garlic, and nearly always a good squeeze of lemon juice, a piquant finish consistent with the tart flavors favored by the Sephardic Turkish and Greek palates.

Fish is paired with lemon and olives, bathed in spice marinades like *charmoula,* given a cumin rub, stuffed with almonds and bread crumbs, and baked. Braised fish, cut into thick steaks or ground and shaped into savory fish cakes and fish balls (two thrifty ways to stretch the budget), is served with couscous. Often fish is cooked with greens and other vegetables, with the fish acting as the flavor accent and the vegetables forming the bulk of the dish. During Passover, crumbled matzo replaces couscous as an accompaniment.

In addition to a large fresh fish repertoire, the Italian, Spanish, and Portuguese Sephardic kitchens also boast a big collection of salt cod dishes, with the fish often cooked in a tomato sauce or a sweet-and-sour sauce. Because fish is pareve, many salt cod dishes (and other fish dishes as well) call for simmering in milk or topping with Parmesan cheese in a gratin. Such dishes are then paired with polenta or potatoes, making the meals even more substantial.

## *Spicy Marinated Fish*  ESCABECHE

The word *escabeche* comes from the Arabic *sikbaj,* or "vinegar stew." In Portugal, *escabeche* was originally prepared with meat, poultry, game birds, and only rarely with fish. Today, it is a popular first course made primarily with fish. It resembles the *in saor* dishes of the Veneto, which were probably taken there by the Marrano Jews from Portugal. *Escabeche* even made its way to England via *The Jewish Manual,* a cookbook of Spanish and Portuguese recipes published in 1846 and attributed to Lady Judith Montefiore. This technique for cooking and marinating fish is also used for vegetables, such as eggplants, winter squashes, zucchini, and peppers.

In Italy, Spain, and Portugal, sardines, mackerel, and other small oily fish are traditionally used, as they take to the marinade particularly well and develop a smooth, velvety texture. White fish fillets will work but will not achieve the same voluptuous texture. As it is difficult to find fresh sardines at many fish markets, use Spanish mackerel if your fishmonger carries it. Failing that, use sole fillets. Traditionally, the fish is cooked and then allowed to marinate and mellow for a day or two in a cool place. Given our American fear of foods sitting out of the refrigerator for more than five minutes, and our absence of "cool places," it's likely that you'll put these dishes in the refrigerator. That's no crime, but remember to bring them to room temperature before serving. SERVES 8

---

2 pounds firm white fish fillets or whole fresh sardines or mackerel

Kosher or sea salt

Olive oil for frying

2 to 3 yellow onions, halved and thinly sliced

1 teaspoon red pepper flakes

2 bay leaves, torn into pieces

Pinch of ground allspice

1 teaspoon peeled and grated fresh ginger

½ cup white wine vinegar

---

If using white fish fillets and they are very large, cut them into pieces about 2 to 3 inches wide and 3 to 4 inches long. If using whole sardines or mackerel, fillet them, removing and discarding their head, tail, backbone, and innards, then rinse well and pat dry with paper towels. Sprinkle the fish with salt and refrigerate for 1 hour.

Pour enough oil into a large sauté pan to film the bottom and place over medium-high heat. When the oil is hot, in batches, fry the fish, turning once, until lightly colored on both sides and cooked through, 5 to 6 minutes total. Using a slotted spatula, carefully transfer the fish to paper towels to drain, then place the fish on a shallow platter or other serving dish.

Wipe out the pan, add ¼ cup olive oil to it, and warm over medium heat. Add the onions and pepper flakes and cook, stirring occasionally, until the onions are soft, 8 to 10 minutes. Add the bay leaves, allspice, ginger, and vinegar, turn down the heat to low, and simmer gently for 5 minutes to blend the flavors.

Pour the onion sauce over the fish, cover with plastic wrap, and refrigerate for at least 24 hours or up to 48 hours before serving. Serve at room temperature.

## *Venetian-Style Marinated Fish*   PESCE IN SAOR

*Saor* is Venetian dialect for *sapore,* or "flavor." This typical Venetian Sabbath dish for marinated fish resembles *escabeche,* or *a scapece* in Italian. The wealthy Jews used sole and the less affluent marinated sardines. *Pesce all'ebraica,* another version of *in saor,* adds raisins and pine nuts to the onions, revealing its Sicilian—and thus Arabic—roots (see recipe on page 224). SERVES 6

2 pounds whole fresh sardines (about 12), or 1½ pounds sole fillets

All-purpose flour for coating

Olive oil for frying

Salt

2 pounds white onions, thinly sliced

1½ cups red or white wine vinegar

If using whole sardines, fillet them, removing and discarding their head, tail, backbone, and innards and leaving the fillets attached. Rinse well, dry thoroughly with paper towels, and open them, skin side down, flat like a book. If using sole fillets, cut into pieces 2 to 3 inches wide and about 4 inches long.

Spread some flour on a plate. Dip the sardines or sole pieces, one at a time, into the flour, coating both sides and tapping off the excess, and set aside on a large plate. Pour enough oil into a large sauté pan to film the bottom and place over medium-high heat. When the oil is hot, in batches, add the fish and fry, turning once and adding more oil as needed, until golden on both sides and cooked through, 5 to 6 minutes total. Using a slotted spatula, carefully transfer the fish to paper towels to drain. Sprinkle with salt.

Pour a bit more oil into the pan and warm over low heat. Add the onions and cook, stirring occasionally, until they are soft but have not taken on any color, 15 to 20 minutes. Season with salt, add 1 cup of the vinegar, and raise the heat to medium. Cook until the vinegar is absorbed, 5 to 10 minutes. Remove from the heat.

Layer half of the fish on a platter. Top with half of the onions, followed by the remaining fish, and finally the remaining onions. Sprinkle with the remaining ½ cup vinegar. Cover with plastic wrap and refrigerate for at least 24 hours or up to 48 hours before serving. Serve at room temperature.

## Sweet-and-Sour Fish, Jewish Style   PESCE ALL'EBRAICA

In this version of *in saor,* raisins and pine nuts are added to the onions, revealing the recipe's Sicilian—and thus Arabic—roots. The dish is usually prepared with the wonderful red mullet of the Mediterranean, but a whole rockfish or snapper or fillets of a mild, firm-fleshed white fish can be substituted. In Rome, this dish is often served to break the Yom Kippur fast. SERVES 6

½ cup red wine vinegar

3 tablespoons sugar

½ cup pine nuts, toasted

½ cup raisins, plumped in hot water, drained, and water reserved

¼ cup extra virgin olive oil

Olive oil for frying

1 whole fish, about 2 pounds, cleaned, or 1½ pounds fish fillets (see headnote)

Salt

In a small bowl, stir together the vinegar, sugar, pine nuts, raisins, oil, and a little of the raisin water. Set aside.

Pour enough oil into a large sauté pan to film the bottom and place over medium heat. When the oil is hot, add the fish or fish fillets and sauté briefly on the first side until pale gold. Turn the fish over, sprinkle with salt, and pour in the vinegar mixture. Cover and cook over medium heat until the fish tests done, about 10 minutes for a whole fish or 5 minutes for fillets. Transfer to a platter and serve warm or at room temperature.

## Moroccan Sardines Marinated with Lemon and Cumin
### SARDINES MARINÉES AU CITRON ET CUMIN

This recipe from Simy Danan, whose family moved to Fez from Spain, is a classic Spanish *escabeche* with Moroccan spices. The fish can be arranged on a bed of roasted red and green peppers for a colorful—and tasty—presentation. SERVES 6

| | |
|---|---|
| 2 pounds fresh whole sardines (about 12) | 2 tablespoons sweet paprika |
| 2 to 3 tablespoons plus ½ cup olive oil | All-purpose flour for coating |
| 2 tablespoons chopped fresh cilantro | Juice of 3 lemons |
| 2 teaspoons kosher salt | 1 tablespoon ground toasted cumin |
| 1 teaspoon freshly ground black pepper | ½ cup chopped fresh-flat leaf parsley |

Fillet the sardines, removing and discarding their head, tail, backbone, and innards and leaving the fillets attached. Rinse well, dry thoroughly with paper towels, and open them, skin side down, flat like a book.

On a shallow platter, combine the 2 to 3 tablespoons oil, the cilantro, 1 teaspoon of the salt, ½ teaspoon of the pepper, and 1 tablespoon of the paprika and mix well. Coat the sardines evenly with the mixture.

Spread some flour on a plate. Dip the sardines, one at a time, into the flour, coating both sides and tapping off the excess, and set aside on a large plate. Pour ¼ cup of the oil into a large sauté pan and place over medium-high heat. When the oil is hot, in batches, add the fish and fry, turning once, until golden on both sides, about 6 minutes total. Using a slotted spatula, transfer the fish to paper towels to drain, then place on a serving platter.

In a small bowl, whisk together the remaining ¼ cup oil, the lemon juice, the remaining 1 tablespoon paprika, the cumin, and the remaining 1 teaspoon salt and ½ teaspoon pepper. Pour the marinade evenly over the fish and sprinkle with the parsley.

Cover with plastic wrap and let marinate in a cool place for at least 1 hour or in the refrigerator for up to 1 day. Serve at room temperature.

## Poached Whole Fish

A poached whole fish dressed with a sauce is a centerpiece of many Sabbath meals. A flavorful cooking liquid is critical to the success of this classic, so I have included a versatile court bouillon here that can also be used in other recipes. SERVES 6

COURT BOUILLON

4 cups water

1 cup dry white wine

1 large yellow onion, sliced

2 carrots, peeled and sliced

2 ribs celery with leaves attached, and/or 2 large slices celery root, peeled

3 fresh flat-leaf parsley sprigs

10 to 12 black peppercorns

3 lemon slices

Few fresh ginger slices (optional)

1 whole fish, such as carp, salmon, sea bass, or cod, 5 to 7 pounds, cleaned

In a fish poacher (or, lacking a poacher, a roasting pan), combine all of the ingredients for the court bouillon. Bring to a boil over high heat, turn down the heat to medium, and simmer for 10 minutes.

Measure the thickness of the fish at its widest point. Slip the whole fish into the simmering liquid, cover, reduce the heat to very low so that bubbles barely break on the surface, and poach until the fish tests done when the point of a knife is inserted into the thickest part, about 10 minutes per inch of thickness.

With a pair of slotted spatulas, carefully transfer the fish to a platter. Let it cool and then carefully remove the skin. Clean the platter, removing any extra juices that may have settled on it. Serve the fish at room temperature. The poaching liquid can be used again. Strain it and freeze in an airtight container for up to 2 months.

VARIATION: Fish fillets such as salmon, cod, sea bass, or flounder can be used in place of the whole fish. Use 6 fillets, each 5 to 6 ounces and 1 inch thick. They will cook in 7 to 8 minutes, though keep the rule of 10 minutes per inch in mind.

## Sauces for Poached Fish

Here are five sauces for poached fish. Four of them are Mediterranean nut-thickened sauces of Arabic origin. In Turkey, Syria, and Lebanon, *tarator* is a general name for nut sauces thickened with bread crumbs, flavored with garlic, and thinned with vinegar or lemon. Although walnuts are the most popular choice for *tarator*, hazelnuts, pine nuts, or pistachios can be used. *Teradot* is *tarator* thickened with tahini instead of bread crumbs, making it suitable for Passover. Here, it is made with pistachios, but walnuts can be used in their place. In Greece, the nut sauce *skordalia* is made with almonds and can be thickened with bread or potatoes, the latter also appropriate for Passover. Both versions are included here. Herbs such as parsley or dill are not commonly added to these sauces, though you can choose to stir them into the sauce or sprinkle them on the fish after you have spooned on the sauce. For the fullest flavor, make the nut sauces a few hours ahead of serving. They will thicken as they sit, so you will need to thin them with water and readjust the salt and acidity. The final sauce recipe, which is a version of *salsa verde,* is an herb-based sauce brightened with capers that, like most of the nut sauces, is thickened with bread crumbs.

Each recipe that follows makes enough sauce for 6 fish fillets or 1 large whole fish. If you do not like eating room-temperature fish, all of these sauces can be spooned over warm poached, sautéed, or grilled fish, as well.

## *Tarator Sauce*   MAKES ABOUT 2 CUPS

| | |
|---|---|
| 1 cup walnuts, almonds, hazelnuts, or pistachios, toasted and ground | ½ cup extra virgin olive oil, or as needed |
| 1 cup fresh bread crumbs | ¼ cup fresh lemon juice or white wine vinegar |
| 2 to 3 teaspoons finely minced garlic | |
| 4 to 6 tablespoons chopped fresh flat-leaf parsley or dill (optional) | ¼ cup water, or as needed |
| | Salt and freshly ground black pepper |

In a food processor, combine the nuts, bread crumbs, garlic, and parsley and pulse until well mixed. Transfer to a bowl and stir in the oil, lemon juice, and water, mixing well. Season with salt and pepper. Add more water or oil if needed to create a spoonable sauce. Taste and adjust the seasoning.

## *Pistachio Teradot*   MAKES ABOUT 3½ CUPS

| | |
|---|---|
| 1 cup tahini, stirred well before use | 1 cup pistachios, toasted and finely chopped |
| ½ cup fresh lemon juice | |
| 4 cloves garlic, finely minced | Salt and freshly ground black pepper |
| 1 cup water, or as needed | Pinch of cayenne pepper (optional) |

In a food processor or blender, combine the tahini, lemon juice, and garlic and process until smooth. Add the water as needed to thin to a good sauce consistency, processing until well mixed. You can also add less water and use the mixture as a dip. Add the pistachios and pulse just until mixed. Transfer to a bowl and season with salt, black pepper, and cayenne pepper.

## *Skordalia with Bread*   MAKES ABOUT 2 CUPS

| | |
|---|---|
| **1 cup blanched almonds, toasted** | **Salt** |
| **2 slices day-old white bread, crusts removed, soaked in water, and squeezed dry** | **¼ cup white wine vinegar or fresh lemon juice** |
| **4 to 6 cloves garlic, mashed to a paste with a pinch of salt** | **½ cup extra virgin olive oil, or as needed** |
| | **Freshly ground black pepper** |

In a food processor or blender, combine the almonds, bread, garlic, and a little salt and pulse until very finely ground. Add the vinegar and then, with the motor running, add the oil, a few drops at a time, and process until the mixture is thick, creamy, and holds its shape when dropped from a spoon. Adjust the consistency with a little water as needed. Transfer to a bowl and season with salt and pepper.

## *Skordalia with Potatoes*   MAKES ABOUT 3 CUPS

| | |
|---|---|
| **1 pound boiling or russet potatoes** | **1 cup almonds, toasted and ground** |
| **4 to 6 cloves garlic, finely minced** | **1 egg yolk, lightly beaten (optional)** |
| **Salt** | **¼ cup white wine vinegar** |
| | **¾ to 1 cup extra virgin olive oil** |

Cook the potatoes until tender according to type, boiling the boiling potatoes or baking the russets, then peel them and pass them through a ricer into a bowl. Let cool to lukewarm or room temperature.

In a mortar with a pestle, grind together the garlic and a pinch of salt until a smooth paste forms. Add the garlic paste, almonds, egg yolk, and vinegar to the potatoes and mix well. Gradually beat in the oil, adding it until the mixture is thick, creamy, and holds its shape when dropped from a spoon. Taste and adjust the seasoning with salt. (If you are pressed for time, you can also make this sauce in a food processor or with a handheld mixer.) Serve at room temperature.

## Salsa Verde  MAKES ABOUT 2½ CUPS

1 cup chopped fresh flat-leaf parsley

¼ cup salt-packed capers, rinsed and chopped

2 tablespoons finely chopped olive oil–packed anchovy fillets (4 or 5 fillets)

¼ cup fine dried bread crumbs, or matzo meal during Passover

4 cloves garlic, minced

¼ cup red or white wine vinegar

¼ cup finely minced white or red onion (optional)

1 cup extra virgin olive oil

Salt and freshly ground black pepper

In a bowl, combine the parsley, capers, anchovies, bread crumbs, garlic, vinegar, and onion and mix well. Whisk in the oil and season with salt and pepper.

## Sole with Lemon for the Sabbath  SOGLIOLE AL LIMONE PER IL SABATO

This Italian Sabbath dish traditionally calls for whole fish, but you can use 1½ pounds sole fillets if you cannot find whole fish. With fillets, you will miss some of the delicate flavor that the bones impart, and the fish will cook in 4 to 5 minutes, about half the time of the whole fish. If you have court bouillon left over from poaching fish (page 226), you can use it here. If not, the shortcut I have provided—wine, water, and/or broth—works well. This recipe is rather plain, though it is subtly delicious when the fish is very fresh and of high quality. You can always jazz it up, too, with an egg-and-lemon pan sauce (see variation) or one of the sauces for poached fish on pages 226–229. SERVES 4

4 whole Dover soles, about 1 pound each, cleaned

Kosher or sea salt

3 cups water, dry white wine, or fish broth, or a combination

Few lemon slices

Extra virgin olive oil, fresh lemon juice, and chopped fresh flat-leaf parsley (optional) for dressing

Sprinkle the fish with salt. In a wide saucepan, combine the water and lemon slices and bring to a boil over high heat. Slip the fish into the liquid, cover the pan, adjust the heat to very low so that small bubbles barely break on the surface, and poach until the fish test done when the point of a knife is inserted into the thickest part of each one, about 10 minutes.

Using a slotted spatula, carefully transfer the fish to a platter. One at a time, remove the skin from each fish, then cut along the central bone and carefully remove the top fillet and place it on another platter. Using a fork, lift up and discard the central bone, then transfer the bottom fillet to the platter. In a small bowl, whisk together the oil and lemon juice in a ratio that suits your taste and then whisk in some parsley, if you like. Drizzle the dressing evenly over the fish and serve.

VARIATIONS:   *Fish with Greek-Inspired Dill Sauce:* Poach the fish and fillet as directed. Strain the poaching liquid, then return to the heat and boil until reduced to 1 cup. Add the juice of 1 lemon and 2 cloves garlic, finely minced, to the reduced liquid and simmer for 5 minutes. Season with salt and freshly ground black pepper and stir in 3 tablespoons chopped fresh dill. Pour over the warm fish and serve.

*Fish with Egg-and-Lemon Sauce:* Poach the fish and fillet as directed. Strain the poaching liquid, set aside ½ cup for the sauce, and reserve the remainder for another use. In a small bowl, beat together 2 eggs and the juice of 3 lemons until very frothy. Gradually whisk the ½ cup hot poaching liquid into the eggs to temper them. Pour the egg mixture into the pan used to poach the fish and warm over very low heat. Do not stir the sauce; instead, shake the pan back and forth just until the egg mixture thickens. Spoon the sauce over the warm fish and serve.

## *Fried Fish*   PESHKADO FRITO

In the late fifteenth century, before the Inquisition, a large Jewish community resided in Andalusia, which was known as the "zone of frying" because of the many *freidurías,* or fried-fish shops, in the region. It may be hard to shake the memories of eating at a greasy fish-and-chip emporium, but frying, when done perfectly, can be a wonderful way to capture the natural sweetness of fish. Olive oil was traditionally used in Spain and Turkey, though sunflower oil eventually replaced olive oil in Turkey because of cost.

To fry the fish to a golden crunchiness, you can dip it either in lightly seasoned flour or in lightly beaten eggs and then in flour. At the table, the fish needs only a squeeze of lemon and sometimes a dollop of mayonnaise, though either *ajada,* or Sephardic garlic mayonnaise, or *agristada,* a cold egg-and-lemon sauce, is a welcome accompaniment. SERVES 6 TO 8

2 pounds sole, snapper, or cod fillets or boned smelt

Kosher salt and freshly ground black pepper

All-purpose flour for coating

Sweet paprika

2 eggs

Olive or sunflower oil for frying

Lemon wedges for serving

Mayonnaise or Chilled Egg-and-Lemon Sauce (recipes follow), optional

Sprinkle the fish fillets with salt and refrigerate for 30 minutes.

Spread some flour on a large plate, season it with salt, pepper, and paprika, and mix well. Beat the eggs in a shallow bowl. Pour the oil to a depth of 1 inch into a large, deep sauté pan and place over high heat. When the oil is hot, in batches, dip the fillets first into the eggs, allowing the excess to drip off, and then into the flour, coating both sides and tapping off the excess, and slip them into the oil. Fry, turning once, until golden and crisp, about 6 minutes total.

Serve the fish hot with the lemon wedges and with a sauce, if you like.

# Sauces for Fried Fish

The sauces that follow complement not only fried fish but also fish cakes, fish balls, vegetable fritters, and other dishes.

## Basic Mayonnaise

When garlic is added to this classic sauce, it becomes *ajada* (also called *azada*), a cousin to the Catalan *allioli* and the French aioli (see variation). To ensure greater control when adding the oil, put it into a plastic squeeze bottle. MAKES ABOUT 1½ CUPS

---

2 egg yolks, at room temperature

3 to 4 tablespoons fresh lemon juice

1½ cups sunflower oil or part sunflower oil and olive oil

Kosher salt

---

In a blender or food processor, combine the egg yolks and 1 tablespoon of the lemon juice and pulse to mix. With the motor running, add the oil, drop by drop, until the mixture emulsifies and thickens, then add the remaining oil in a slow, fine, steady stream. When all of the oil is incorporated, add the remaining lemon juice to taste. If the mixture is too thick, thin with a little cold water. Season with salt.

VARIATIONS: For garlic mayonnaise *(ajada)*, halve 5 or 6 garlic cloves lengthwise and remove any green sprouts. Mince the garlic; then, using the side of a broad-bladed knife, mash together the garlic and a pinch of kosher salt to a fine purée. Add the garlic purée to the blender with the egg yolks and proceed as directed.

Some versions add 1 slice coarse country bread, crust removed, soaked in water, and squeezed dry, to the mixture, or ½ cup finely chopped toasted walnuts, which results in a sauce similar to Skordalia with Bread (page 228), though with egg.

For a Moroccan variation of my own invention, add 2 tablespoons rinsed and chopped preserved lemon peel, homemade (page 356) or store-bought, and/or 1 teaspoon or more harissa, homemade (page 355) or store-bought.

## Chilled Egg-and-Lemon Sauce   AGRISTADA

When served warm, this is the classic Sephardic egg-and-lemon sauce called avgole-mono in Greece and *terbiyeli* in Turkey. But when served cold, it has a mayonnaise-like consistency. Cornstarch acts as a stabilizer to hold the sauce in emulsion.   MAKES ABOUT 2½ CUPS

---

2 tablespoons cornstarch

2 cups fish broth or water, or part fish broth and part water

3 eggs

Juice of 2 lemons (⅓ to ½ cup)

Salt

---

In a small saucepan, stir together the cornstarch with a few tablespoons of the broth to make a smooth paste. Add the remaining broth and bring to a boil over high heat, stirring constantly to prevent lumps. Turn down the heat to medium and simmer for 10 minutes.

In a bowl, whisk together the eggs and lemon juice until very frothy. Gradually whisk about ½ cup of the hot broth into the eggs to temper them. Pour the egg mixture into the pan and simmer over very low heat, stirring, until the sauce thickens. Remove from the heat and season with salt. Serve warm or cold.

## "Married" Sardines from Morocco   SARDINES MARIÉES

These fried sardines are "married" with a love potion of spiced potatoes.   SERVES 6

---

1 pound Yukon Gold potatoes, peeled and cut into chunks

3 tablespoons chopped fresh flat-leaf parsley

3 tablespoons chopped fresh cilantro

3 cloves garlic, minced

3 eggs, lightly beaten

1 teaspoon ground toasted cumin

1 tablespoon sweet paprika

½ teaspoon cayenne pepper or Maras pepper flakes (optional)

Salt

2 pounds fresh whole sardines (about 12)

All-purpose flour for coating

Canola or safflower or pure olive oil for frying

Lemon wedges for serving

---

Combine the potatoes with salted water to cover in a saucepan and bring to a boil over high heat. Turn down the heat to medium and simmer until the potatoes are easily pierced with a fork, about 15 minutes. Drain and pass through a ricer into a bowl. Add the parsley, cilantro, garlic, eggs, cumin, paprika, and cayenne and mash together until well mixed. Season with salt.

Fillet the sardines, removing and discarding their head, tail, backbone, and innards and leaving the fillets attached. Rinse well, dry thoroughly with paper towels, and open them, skin side down, flat like a book. Sprinkle lightly with salt.

Scoop up a heaping tablespoon of the potato mixture, flatten it into an oblong patty, and place it on an opened sardine. Top with a second sardine, flesh side down, to make a "sandwich." Repeat with the remaining sardines.

Spread some flour on a plate. Pour the oil to a depth of 1½ inches into a large, deep sauté pan and place over high heat. When the oil is hot, in batches, dip the sandwiched sardines in the flour, coating both sides and tapping off the excess, add to the pan, and fry, turning once, until golden and crisp, about 6 minutes total. Serve hot with lemon wedges.

MOROCCAN VARIATION: In *Fleur de safran,* Jacqueline Cohen-Azuelos replaces the potato filling with a paste of 6 cloves garlic, finely minced; ½ cup each chopped fresh flat-leaf parsley and cilantro; 2 tablespoons sweet paprika; 2 tablespoons ground toasted cumin; juice of 2 lemons; and salt and pepper to taste. If you like, serve with garlic mayonnaise (page 231).

## Baked Whole Fish with Onion Tahini Sauce  SAMAK BIL TAHINEH

Sauces made with tahini have a rich mouthfeel and add creaminess without the use of dairy, a big plus since fish is pareve and can be served at a meat meal. This classic fish recipe from Syrian and Lebanese Jewish kitchens is now quite popular in Israel. A whole fish is baked or grilled, skinned, and placed on a serving platter. It is then coated with a garlic-and-lemon-laced onion tahini sauce and decorated lavishly with cucumbers, radishes, pine nuts, pomegranate seeds, and other garnishes. This dish is usually served at room temperature and would be a good centerpiece for a summer buffet, though it can also be served warm. This onion tahini sauce is good on poached fish (page 226) and on the recipe for fish fillets that follows. SERVES 6

1 whole snapper, sea bass, or cod, 3 to 4 pounds, cleaned

Salt

SAUCE

¼ cup canola, safflower, or olive oil

2 yellow onions, chopped

3 to 5 cloves garlic, finely minced

1 teaspoon salt

½ cup tahini, stirred well before use

6 tablespoons fresh lemon juice

6 tablespoons water or fish broth, plus more if needed

3 tablespoons olive oil

2 tablespoons fresh lemon juice

3 tablespoons coarsely chopped fresh flat-leaf parsley, or handful of pomegranate seeds

¼ cup pine nuts, toasted

Rub the fish inside and out with salt and rinse well. Cut 3 or 4 evenly spaced diagonal slits on both sides of the body, then cover and let rest in the refrigerator for 30 minutes. Preheat the oven to 450°F.

To make the sauce, warm the oil in a sauté pan over medium heat. Add the onions and cook, stirring occasionally, until tender and translucent, about 10 minutes. Add the garlic and salt and cook for a few minutes longer. Transfer the mixture to a food processor and process until a smooth purée forms. Add the tahini and 6 tablespoons lemon juice and process until well mixed, then add the water as needed to achieve a fluffy mixture. Taste and adjust the seasoning with salt and lemon juice if needed.

Place the fish in a baking pan or dish and drizzle with the oil and 2 tablespoons lemon juice. Bake for about 20 minutes. Remove from the oven and peel off the top skin of the fish. Spread the fish with the sauce and return it to the oven. Bake the fish, basting it occasionally with the pan juices, until it tests done when the point of a knife is inserted into the thickest part, about 25 minutes longer.

Transfer the fish to a serving platter. Serve warm or at room temperature. Decorate the fish with parsley and pine nuts just before serving.

## Fish with Green Tahini    SAMAK AL SAHARA

Unlike the recipe for whole fish with tahini sauce on page 227, here fillets are used and the tahini sauce, in keeping with Egyptian and Lebanese tradition, is flavored with cayenne and given a pale green tint with the addition of cilantro and parsley. The tahini crust on the fish keeps it moist throughout the baking. Nuts are the suggested garnish, but you can use both nuts and cilantro, or you can use olives and cilantro. Accompany with rice or Bulgur Pilaf (page 157) and spinach or roasted cauliflower or carrots. If you do not want to bake the fish with the tahini, you can bake, broil, or grill the fish and spoon the sauce on just before serving. SERVES 6

6 snapper, rockfish, or sea bass fillets, each about 6 ounces

SAUCE

½ cup tahini, stirred well before use

1 teaspoon finely minced garlic

¼ teaspoon cayenne pepper

½ teaspoon salt

½ cup tightly packed fresh cilantro leaves

½ cup chopped fresh flat-leaf parsley (optional)

3 to 4 tablespoons fresh lemon juice

½ cup water, or as needed

Chopped walnuts or pine nuts for garnish (optional)

Lemon wedges for serving

Preheat the oven to 450°F. Oil a baking dish large enough to hold the fish fillets in a single layer, then place the fillets in the dish and set aside.

To make the sauce, in a food processor or blender, combine the tahini, garlic, cayenne, salt, cilantro, parsley (if you want a greener, more herbaceous sauce), and 3 tablespoons of the lemon juice and pulse to combine. Add the water as needed to thin, then taste and adjust the seasoning with more lemon juice, cayenne, and salt if needed.

Spread the sauce over the fish. Bake the fish until it flakes when tested with a fork, 8 to 12 minutes, depending on the thickness of the fillets. Transfer to a platter or individual plates, garnish with the nuts, and serve hot, accompanied with lemon wedges.

VARIATIONS: *Yellow Tahini:* Omit the cilantro or the cilantro and parsley and add 1 teaspoon ground turmeric when blending the sauce.

*Red Tahini:* Omit the cilantro or the cilantro and parsley and add ½ cup peeled, seeded, and chopped tomato, 1 to 2 tablespoons tomato paste, or 1 red bell pepper, roasted, peeled, seeded, and chopped, when blending the sauce.

*Pistachio Tahini:* Substitute Pistachio Teradot (page 227) for the sauce.

## Fish with Cilantro  SAMAK HARRAH

Slightly different versions of this recipe appear in books that explore Lebanese and Moroccan traditions. The spices here are a composite of the two kitchens, but the technique is Lebanese. Accompany with rice for soaking up the cilantro sauce. SERVES 8

2 pounds firm white fish steaks or fillets, such as halibut, cod, or sea bass

Kosher salt

½ cup extra virgin olive oil

3 to 4 yellow onions, chopped

1½ cups chopped fresh cilantro

6 to 10 cloves garlic, minced

1 tablespoon ground turmeric

2 teaspoons ground toasted cumin

½ teaspoon freshly ground black pepper

3 or 4 small dried chiles, or ½ teaspoon cayenne pepper

½ cup fresh lemon juice

½ cup tahini, stirred well before use (optional)

Sprinkle the fish with salt and refrigerate for about 1 hour.

Warm 3 to 4 tablespoons of the oil in a large sauté pan over high heat. When the oil is hot, in batches, add the fish and sear quickly, turning once to color both sides. Using a slotted spatula, transfer to paper towels to drain.

Heat the remaining oil in the same pan over medium-high heat. Add the onions and cook, stirring occasionally, until golden, about 15 minutes. Lower the heat to medium, add the cilantro, garlic, turmeric, cumin, black pepper, and chiles and cook for a minute or two. Add the lemon juice and tahini, mix well, turn down the heat to low, and cook, stirring occasionally, until thickened, 5 to 8 minutes.

Arrange the fish on top of the cilantro sauce. Cover the pan and simmer over low heat until the fish flakes when tested with a fork, about 8 minutes. Alternatively, arrange the fish fillets in a single layer in an oiled baking dish, top with the sauce, and bake in a preheated 450°F oven until they test done, 8 to 10 minutes. Serve warm or at room temperature.

# Persian Sweet-and-Sour Fish with Cilantro  GHALIEH MAHI

*Ghalieh* is an ancient term for stew. In this dish from southern Iran, the fish is cooked in a sweet-tart sauce fragrant with tamarind and herbs. The ginger is optional in some versions of this recipe, but because I like ginger, I usually add it. Some cooks add chopped tomatoes to the sauce, which echo the sweet-tart quality of the tamarind, but they can be omitted if you want a green sauce. The fish is usually cut into small pieces, but they can easily overcook, so it is best to use larger fillets. Serve this dish with Persian Rice (page 149). SERVES 6

½ cup olive oil

3 yellow onions, chopped

8 cloves garlic, minced

2 teaspoons peeled and grated fresh ginger (optional)

1 teaspoon hot paprika or Maras or Aleppo pepper flakes

1 teaspoon advieh or mild curry powder (optional)

1 teaspoon salt

⅓ cup tamarind paste or pomegranate molasses

2 to 3 tablespoons fresh lime juice

2 to 3 bunches fresh cilantro, chopped

1 bunch fresh fenugreek leaves, chopped (optional)

2 cups peeled, seeded, and chopped ripe tomatoes (optional)

1½ to 2 pounds fish fillets, such as cod, snapper, halibut, or sea bass

Warm the oil in a large sauté pan over medium heat. Add the onions and cook, stirring occasionally, until translucent and tender, 8 to 10 minutes. Add the garlic, ginger, paprika, advieh, salt, tamarind paste, 2 tablespoons of the lime juice, and most of the cilantro and fenugreek, and the tomatoes and stir well. Simmer the sauce, stirring occasionally, until the flavors have blended, about 20 minutes. Add water if the sauce seems too thick to cook the fish. Taste and adjust with more lime juice and salt if needed.

Add the fish fillets to the sauce and cook until the fish flakes when tested with a fork. The timing will depend on the thickness of the fillets; plan on 8 to 10 minutes per inch. Alternatively, arrange the fish fillets in a single layer in an oiled baking dish, top with the sauce, and bake in a preheated 450°F oven until they test done, about 10 minutes. Sprinkle with the remaining cilantro and fenugreek. Serve warm.

## *Fish with Golden Sauce*   POISSON SAUCE SOLEIL

In Morocco, this dish is served during the Rosh Hashanah holiday. But it looks so gorgeous and is so delicious and easy to prepare that I cook it all year long. The turmeric and saffron in the sauce create the illusion of fish bathed in golden sunlight. Some cooks add a generous handful of green olives at the end of cooking. Although this fish is usually paired with little new potatoes, I often serve it with spinach or with spinach and chickpeas. Swiss chard and chickpeas (page 208) would be good, as well.  SERVES 4

2 large or 3 medium juicy lemons, all peel and pith removed, then sliced paper-thin

1 tablespoon ground turmeric

Salt and freshly ground black pepper

Olive oil for drizzling and frying

4 cloves garlic, any green sprouts removed, chopped

½ teaspoon saffron threads steeped in ⅓ cup hot water

1 bunch fresh cilantro, chopped

4 fish steaks or fillets, such as halibut, sea bass, or cod, each about 6 ounces

1 cup pitted green olives (optional)

Peel of 1 preserved lemon, homemade (page 356) or store-bought, rinsed and cut into thin strips (optional)

Lemon wedges for serving

About 1 hour before cooking, place the lemon slices in a shallow bowl or platter and sprinkle with the turmeric and some salt. Press down on the slices with a fork to extract some juice, then drizzle with a bit of oil. Set aside at room temperature.

Select a sauté pan large enough to hold the fish in a single layer. Warm 1 tablespoon oil in the pan over low heat, add the garlic, and cook, stirring occasionally, for a few minutes. Do not allow to color. Add 3 tablespoons of the saffron infusion and let it bubble up for 1 minute. Arrange the lemon slices on the bottom of the pan, reserving all of the accumulated juices in a bowl. Sprinkle with half of the cilantro, then arrange the fish fillets on the lemon slices. Sprinkle the fish with salt and pepper and top with the remaining saffron infusion, the reserved juices from the lemons, the remaining cilantro, and the olives. Finish with the preserved lemon.

Raise the heat to medium-high, bring the pan juices to a boil, turn down the heat to low, cover, and simmer until the fish flakes when tested with a fork, 8 to 10 minutes. Serve hot or warm.

## *Fish with Cumin*   SAMAK AL KAMOUN

In Lebanon, Syria, Egypt, and North Africa, the spice of choice for fish is cumin. Here, I have bathed the fish in a heady cumin-rich oil-based mixture and then given directions for baking, broiling, or grilling it. Be sure to cut slits on both sides of the fish so the mixture penetrates well and the fish cooks evenly. Serve with rice, bulgur, or roast potatoes and with spinach, zucchini, or eggplant.  SERVES 6

---

**1 whole sea bass, snapper, or cod, 3 to 4 pounds, cleaned**

**3 teaspoons kosher salt**

**6 tablespoons fresh lemon juice**

**2 teaspoons finely minced garlic**

**3 tablespoons ground toasted cumin**

**2 tablespoons sweet paprika**

**½ teaspoon freshly ground black pepper**

**½ cup olive oil**

**½ cup chopped fresh flat-leaf parsley or cilantro (optional)**

---

Rub the fish inside and out with 2 teaspoons of the salt, then rinse with cool water. Cut 3 or 4 evenly spaced diagonal slits on both sides of the body.

In a bowl, combine the lemon juice, garlic, cumin, paprika, the remaining 1 teaspoon salt, and the pepper. Whisk in the oil. Rub the mixture inside and outside of the fish, making sure to get some into the slits on each side.

To bake the fish, preheat the oven to 450°F. Wrap the fish in lightly oiled foil, place in a baking pan, and bake for 25 to 30 minutes. To check for doneness, open the foil and test with a knife tip. The fish should be opaque near the bone and the flesh should flake evenly. To broil or grill the fish, omit the foil and cook for 10 minutes on each side. Serve hot, garnished with the parsley.

VARIATION:   Substitute 6 mild, firm white fish fillets, each 5 to 6 ounces, for the whole fish. Omit the slits and foil. Sprinkle the fillets with salt and cover with the oil mixture. To bake, arrange the fillets in a single layer in a baking dish and bake in a preheated 450°F oven until they test done, 8 to 10 minutes. To broil or grill, cook for about 4 minutes on each side.

# *Fish with Charmoula*   POISSON CHARMOULA

When I was running Square One Restaurant, a few diners called me the Queen of Charmoula because this dish appeared on the menu so often. *Charmoula* is a classic Moroccan herb-and-spice marinade and sauce that is used on poultry and lamb but is especially good on fish. Whether you plan to bake, grill, or broil the fish, marinating it in *charmoula* for a few hours will improve its flavor. Be sure to set aside some *charmoula* for spooning over the fish just before serving. (*Charmoula* is good spooned over simple poached fish, too.) I have called for thick fish fillets here, which can be cubed for making kebabs or left in serving-size pieces, but you can instead use a whole fish, marinate it overnight, and bake it, adjusting the timing as needed. Here are two versions of *charmoula;* the first one is from my Square One days, and the second one calls for saffron and preserved lemon. Serve the fish with couscous or potatoes. SERVES 6

**CHARMOULA I**

3 cloves garlic, finely minced

¼ cup chopped fresh flat-leaf parsley

¼ cup chopped fresh cilantro

1½ teaspoons sweet paprika

¼ teaspoon cayenne pepper

1½ teaspoons ground toasted cumin

½ cup fruity extra virgin olive oil

¼ cup fresh lemon juice

Salt and freshly ground black pepper

**CHARMOULA II**

3 cloves garlic, finely minced

½ cup chopped fresh cilantro

½ cup chopped fresh flat-leaf parsley

Peel of ½ to 1 preserved lemon, homemade (page 356) or store-bought, rinsed and finely minced

1 teaspoon sweet paprika

½ teaspoon cayenne pepper

½ teaspoon saffron threads, finely crushed and steeped in 2 tablespoons water

½ cup plus 1 tablespoon olive oil

¼ cup fresh lemon juice

2 pounds thick fish fillets, such as snapper, sea bass, or halibut

Select a charmoula, then combine all of the ingredients in a bowl and mix well, adding salt and pepper to taste if making version 1.

For kebabs, cut the fillets into 1½-inch cubes and thread onto skewers. For fillets, cut the fillets into serving-size pieces. Arrange the kebabs or fillets in a single layer in a shallow dish and spoon about half of the charmoula over the top. Turn the kebabs or fillets to coat evenly, then cover the dish and refrigerate for 2 to 4 hours.

To broil or grill the kebabs or fillets, preheat the broiler or prepare a fire in a charcoal grill. Cook, turning once, until the fish flakes when tested with a fork, about 4 minutes on each side. To bake the fillets, preheat the oven to 450°F, arrange the fillets in a single layer in a baking dish, and bake until the fish tests done, 8 to 10 minutes. Drizzle the remaining charmoula over the top and serve hot.

## Persian Fish with Green Herb Sauce GHORMEH SABZI BA MAHI

Morocco has *charmoula* and Iran has *ghormeh sabzi,* a fragrant, tart herb mixture. In some spice markets in Iran, you can buy both fresh and dried chopped herb mixtures for this classic green stew. (*Ghormeh sabzi* is also paired with beef; see page 299.) If you live near a store that specializes in Iranian foods, you might find the already-assembled herb mixture and the dried Omani limes that perfume this dish. If you cannot find the limes, add a few tablespoons fresh lime or lemon juice to the final sauce. SERVES 4

⅓ cup dried red kidney beans or black-eyed peas, picked over and rinsed

3 to 4 tablespoons unsalted butter or oil

2 or 3 leeks, white and tender green, chopped

2 cloves garlic, minced

1 bunch fresh cilantro, chopped (about 1 cup)

2 bunches fresh flat-leaf parsley, chopped (about 2 cups)

1 pound spinach, stemmed and chopped

1 cup chopped fresh garlic chives

½ cup fresh fenugreek leaves (optional)

1 teaspoon ground turmeric, or pinch of saffron threads

3 dried Omani limes, rinsed and struck with a meat pounder so they crack (optional)

Fish broth or water to cover

4 thick snapper, halibut, or cod fish fillets

Salt and freshly ground black pepper

Fresh lemon juice

In a saucepan, combine the beans with salted water to cover by 3 inches, bring to a boil over high heat, turn down the heat to low, cover, and simmer until tender, about 2 hours. Check the beans from time to time to make sure they do not overcook or scorch. Add more water if needed. Drain and reserve.

Melt the butter in a large sauté pan over medium heat. Add the leeks, garlic, cilantro, parsley, spinach, garlic chives, and fenugreek and cook, stirring occasionally, for a minute or two. Add the turmeric and stir well. Add the limes and just enough broth to cover and simmer for 10 minutes. Add the fish to the pan in a single layer, turn down the heat to low, cover, and cook until the fish flakes when tested with a fork. The timing will depend on the thickness of the fish; plan on 8 to 10 minutes per inch.

Season with salt and pepper, add the cooked beans, and warm through. Remove and discard the limes and season to taste with the lemon juice and with more salt if needed. Serve hot.

# Fish with Abraham's Fruit   PESHKADO AVRAMILA

According to Sephardic folklore, after Abraham was circumcised, he sat under a sour plum tree, so the plum has come to be called "Abraham's fruit," or *avramila* in Turkish and Ladino. Greek Jews call this dish *peshe con babottes* and use greengage plums for the sauce. The dish is often served for the autumn holiday of Rosh Hashanah, when many different kinds of plums are in the markets. Although green or yellow plums are traditional, if you can't find any, other tart plums or even pluots can be substituted. The amount of moisture the fruit contains varies, so you will have to see how much water you need to add, or conversely, how much you will need to reduce the sauce. If you have a craving for this dish in the dead of winter, dried plums (prunes) can be used along with the same ingredients (see variation). The dish is typically served accompanied with rice with pine nuts. SERVES 6

PLUM SAUCE

2 pounds tart plums, preferably a yellow variety, pitted and cut into pieces

1 cup water

3 tablespoons olive oil or unsalted butter

About ½ cup red wine, a sweet wine like Marsala, or water

Grated zest and juice of 2 lemons

Salt and freshly ground black pepper

Pinch of ground allspice or cloves

Sugar, if needed

Court bouillon (see Poached Whole Fish on page 226)

1 whole salmon, cod, or snapper, 4 to 5 pounds, cleaned

To make the plum sauce, in a saucepan, combine the plums and water and bring to a simmer over low heat. Cook, uncovered, until the plums are quite soft, 15 to 20 minutes. If the skins are not too tough, transfer the contents of the pan to a food processor and purée until smooth. If the skins are tough, pass the mixture through a food mill placed over a bowl. You should have about 1⅓ cups purée.

Return the puréed plums to the saucepan and add the oil and the wine as needed to thin the mixture and some of the lemon zest and juice to balance the plums' sweetness. Place over medium heat, bring to a simmer, and cook, stirring from time to time, until thickened, 15 to 20 minutes. Season with salt, a generous amount of pepper, and the allspice. Taste and add more lemon zest and juice if needed or some sugar if the sauce is too tart. You want a nice sweet-and-sour balance. Cover and keep warm off the heat.

Prepare the court bouillon as directed and have it at a simmer. Measure the thickness of the fish at its widest point, then slip the whole fish into the simmering liquid, cover, reduce the heat to very low so that bubbles barely break on the surface, and poach until the fish tests done when the point of a knife is inserted into the thickest part, about 10 minutes per inch of thickness.

With a pair of slotted spatulas, carefully transfer the fish to a platter. Let it cool until it can be handled, then carefully remove the skin. Clean the platter, removing any extra juices that may have settled on it. Reheat the sauce gently and spoon some of it over the fish. Serve the fish warm or at room temperature. Pass the remaining sauce at the table.

VARIATIONS: *With Fish Fillets:* Arrange 6 fillets, each about 6 ounces, in a single layer in an oiled baking dish, top with the sauce, cover, and bake in a preheated 450°F oven until the fish tests done, 10 to 15 minutes for each inch of thickness. Alternatively, arrange the fillets in a large sauté pan, top with the sauce, cover, and cook on the stove top over low heat following the same timing. Finally, although it is not traditional, you can broil or grill fish fillets and spoon the warm sauce over them.

*Fish with Prune Sauce (Peshe kon Prounes):* For a wintertime version of the plum sauce, in a saucepan, combine 1 pound pitted prunes with water to cover and simmer over medium heat until tender, about 30 minutes. Using a slotted spoon, transfer the prunes to a food processor and purée until smooth. Reserve the cooking water. Pour the purée into a clean saucepan, add the oil, thin with the wine or with the cooking water, and add some of the lemon zest and juice. Simmer for 10 minutes to blend the flavors. Season with the salt, pepper, and allspice as directed, then taste and add more lemon if needed or some sugar if too tart, to create a good sweet-and-sour balance. Serve as directed for the plum sauce.

# Fish with Sephardic Tomato and Rhubarb Sauce
PESCADO CON RUIBARBO

Spring marks the arrival of rhubarb at the farmers' market, just in time for the celebration of Passover. It's no coincidence that in Sephardic homes in Greece and Turkey, fish in sweet-and-sour rhubarb sauce appears on the Seder table. The major sauce difference between the two countries is in the proportion of rhubarb to tomato. In Greece, it is one part rhubarb to two parts tomato; in Turkey, the proportions are reversed. The original version of this recipe from the Jewish community of Rhodes calls for swordfish, but some rabbis forbid its use, as it does not have scales for the first six months of its life. I have suggested other fish here. You can also pair this sauce with a whole poached fish. I like to serve this dish with spinach. SERVES 6

---

**RHUBARB SAUCE**

1½ pounds rhubarb

2 tablespoons olive oil

1½ pounds ripe tomatoes, peeled, seeded and chopped, or 3 cups chopped, seeded canned tomatoes

1 cup dry red wine

1 to 2 tablespoons honey

Grated zest and juice of 1 lemon (optional)

Pinch of ground cinnamon

Salt and freshly ground black pepper

Court bouillon (see Poached Whole Fish on page 226)

2 pounds firm fish fillets, such as cod, sea flounder, bass, or salmon

To make the sauce, clean the rhubarb stalks by pulling off the heavy filaments, much as you would string celery, then cut crosswise into 1½-inch pieces. Place the pieces in a saucepan, add water to barely cover (about 3 cups), and bring to a boil over high heat. Turn down the heat to low and simmer, uncovered, until the rhubarb has melted into a purée and is tender, 8 to 10 minutes. (If you want some crunch in the sauce, set aside some of the rhubarb pieces after a few minutes of cooking, then return them to the sauce when it is ready.)

Warm the oil in a sauté pan over medium heat. Add the tomatoes and cook, stirring occasionally, until the tomatoes are reduced to a thick sauce, about 15 minutes. Add the wine, 1 tablespoon of the honey, and the lemon zest and juice and stir well. Add the tomato sauce to the rhubarb purée, or vice versa, and mix well. Simmer uncovered over low heat until the sauce is thick and rich, about 20 minutes. Season with the cinnamon, salt, and pepper. Taste and adjust the sweet-and-sour balance, adding a bit more honey if needed. Cover and keep warm off the heat.

Prepare the court bouillon as directed and have it at a simmer. Measure the thickness of the fillets at their widest point, then slip the fillets into the simmering liquid, cover, reduce the heat to very low so that bubbles barely break on the surface, and poach until the fillets test done when the point of a knife is inserted into a fillet, about 10 minutes per inch of thickness.

Using a slotted spatula, carefully transfer the fillets to a platter or individual plates. Reheat the sauce gently, then spoon some of the sauce over the fish and serve warm. Pass the remaining sauce at the table.

VARIATION: Arrange the fish fillets in a single layer in an oiled baking dish, top with some of the sauce, cover, and bake in a preheated 450°F oven until the fish tests done, 10 minutes for each inch of thickness. Spoon the remaining sauce over the top before serving. Also, although it is not traditional, you can broil or grill fish fillets and spoon the warm sauce over them.

## Fish Wrapped in Grape Leaves YAPRAKITOS DE PESHE

Sephardic Jews of Spain, Italy, Greece, and Turkey like to enclose fish in grape leaves before grilling or broiling. The leaves protect the fish from charring and add a subtle perfume. This recipe is most often prepared with sardines but is also delicious with salmon. If you like, the fish can be served with a tahini sauce (page 112) in place of the raisin sauce. Serve with rice pilaf and sautéed spinach or grilled or sautéed zucchini. SERVES 6

12 to 24 brine-packed grape leaves (depending on size), well rinsed, patted dry, and stems removed

6 salmon fillets, each 5 to 6 ounces, or 12 whole fresh sardines, cleaned

¾ cup raisins, plumped in hot water, drained, and water reserved

¾ cup extra virgin olive oil

¼ cup fresh lemon juice, plus more if needed

1 cup peeled, seeded, and diced ripe tomatoes (optional)

Salt and freshly ground black pepper

Olive oil for brushing

½ cup pine nuts, toasted

Place the grape leaves shiny side down and wrap each salmon fillet or sardine in 1 or 2 leaves as needed to cover fully. You can secure the leaves with toothpicks, but I find that they adhere well to the fish without additional help.

In a food processor, purée about ¼ cup of the plumped raisins until smooth. In a bowl, whisk together the extra virgin oil, lemon juice, puréed raisins, plumped whole raisins, and some of the raisin soaking water for additional sweetness. For an interesting variation, stir in the tomatoes. Season with salt and pepper, then taste and adjust with more lemon juice if needed.

Prepare a fire in a charcoal grill or preheat the broiler. Brush the fish packets with a little oil and sprinkle lightly with pepper. Place directly over the coals or place on a sheet pan and slip under the broiler. Cook, turning once, for 3 to 4 minutes on each side for salmon or 2 to 3 minutes for sardines. If your broiler does not get very hot, cook the fish for a minute or two longer. Be careful not to overcook, however, as the fish should be moist and juicy when served.

Transfer the fish packets to a platter, spoon the sauce over the top, and sprinkle with the pine nuts. Serve hot.

## Fish in Tomato Sauce   PESHKADO KON SALSA DE TOMAT

When tomatoes were first taken to Europe from the New World, they were thought to be poisonous. It took well over a hundred years before some adventurous people tried cooking with them, at which point they were quickly adopted for all manner of sauces. Fish in tomato sauce soon became a classic Sabbath preparation, as this recipe and the others that follow illustrate.

In this Sephardic recipe, the fish bakes under a blanket of chopped tomatoes that have been enhanced with onion, garlic, and a good squeeze of lemon juice to make the sauce more piquant. The fish can also be simmered on the stove top, in which case the onion, garlic, and tomatoes are sautéed in olive oil for a few minutes, the fish is added to the already-forming sauce, the pan is covered, and the fish cooks until it tests done. If the tomatoes are not as flavorful as you would like, add a few tablespoons of tomato paste dissolved in a small amount of water. SERVES 6

2 pounds firm white fish fillets, such as sea bass, flounder, cod, snapper, or halibut

Salt and freshly ground black pepper

2 yellow onions, finely chopped

2 to 4 cloves garlic, minced

3 cups peeled, seeded, and diced tomatoes

Olive oil for drizzling

Chopped fresh flat-leaf parsley for garnish

Preheat the oven to 450°F. Oil a baking dish large enough to hold the fish fillets in a single layer.

Sprinkle the fillets on both sides with salt and pepper and arrange in the prepared dish. Top with the onions, garlic, tomatoes, and a generous drizzle of olive oil. Bake until the fish flakes when tested with a fork. The timing will depend on the thickness of the fillets; plan on 8 to 10 minutes per inch. Sprinkle with parsley and serve warm.

## Libyan Hot and Spicy Fish    HRAIME

This fish recipe from the Libyan Jews has become a staple in Israel, where it is called *chreime* or *chreimeh*. It is very spicy if you opt for the maximum number of chiles. You can serve it with bread or boiled potatoes to tame the heat. SERVES 4

4 thick fish steaks or thick fillets, such as sea bass, halibut, grouper, or cod, each 5 or 6 ounces

Salt

All-purpose flour for coating (optional)

4 to 6 tablespoons olive oil

7 or 8 cloves garlic, minced

2 to 3 small fresh hot red chiles, chopped, or 1 to 2 teaspoons cayenne pepper

1 tablespoon sweet paprika

2 teaspoons ground toasted cumin

2 teaspoons ground toasted caraway

3 tablespoons tomato paste dissolved in ½ cup water

3 to 4 tablespoons fresh lemon juice

Lemon wedges for serving

3 tablespoons chopped fresh cilantro (optional)

Sprinkle the fish pieces on both sides with salt. If you like, spread some flour on a plate and dip each fish piece in the flour, coating evenly and tapping off the excess. Select a sauté pan large enough to hold the fish in a single layer, add 2 tablespoons of the oil, and place over high heat. When the oil is hot, add the fish and sear quickly, turning once to color both sides. Do not cook the fish through. Set aside. Or, you can skip this step and put the fish directly in the sauce without browning it.

To make the sauce, pour 4 tablespoons oil into a sauté pan large enough to hold the fish in a single layer and place over low heat. Add the garlic, chiles, paprika, cumin, and caraway and sauté for a few minutes. Add the diluted tomato paste and 3 tablespoons of the lemon juice, simmer briefly, and then season with salt and add a little more lemon juice or water if needed to make enough sauce to coat the fish. Add the fish to the pan and turn to coat both sides with the sauce. Cover and cook over gentle heat until the fish flakes when tested with a fork, about 5 minutes if seared or 7 to 10 minutes if uncooked. The timing will depend on the thickness of the fillets.

Remove from the heat and let rest for about 10 minutes so the dish is not piping hot. Serve with lemon wedges (the acidity will tame the heat a bit) and sprinkle with the cilantro for a note of color.

## Egyptian Fried Fish with Tomatoes and Nuts

SAMAK MAGLI KOUSBARIYEH

In this recipe, the fish is fried first to color it and then finished in a sauce of tomatoes, onions, and nuts. Because the fish cooks in two stages, it's best to opt for thick fillets or fish steaks. You could also cook small whole fish this way. SERVES 6 TO 8

1 cup all-purpose flour seasoned with 1 teaspoon salt, ½ teaspoon freshly ground black pepper, 1 teaspoon sweet paprika, and 1 teaspoon ground coriander

2 pounds firm, mild white fish steaks or thick fillets

Olive oil for frying

Salt

SAUCE

2 tablespoons olive oil

2 yellow onions, thinly sliced

2 cups peeled, seeded, and coarsely chopped ripe tomatoes (3 to 4 large)

1 cup hazelnuts or walnuts, toasted, skinned if using hazelnuts, and chopped

⅓ cup pine nuts, toasted

¼ cup chopped fresh flat-leaf parsley

1½ teaspoons salt

½ teaspoon freshly ground black pepper

½ teaspoon ground allspice

Sugar and red wine vinegar for seasoning

Lemon wedges for serving

Spread the seasoned flour on a plate, then dip the fish pieces in the flour, coating both sides and tapping off the excess. To fry the fish, pour the oil to a depth of 1½ inches into a large sauté pan and heat over high heat. When the oil is hot, in batches, add the fish and fry, turning once, until golden and partially cooked, about 2 minutes on each side. Using a slotted spatula, transfer the fish to paper towels to drain, then sprinkle with salt.

To make the sauce, select a sauté pan large enough to hold the fish in a single layer, add the oil, and warm over medium heat. Add the onions and cook, stirring occasionally, until translucent and tender, about 10 minutes. Add the tomatoes and simmer until they break down, 8 to 10 minutes longer. Stir in the hazelnuts and pine nuts and cook, stirring occasionally, for a few minutes. Add just enough water to cover the nuts, then stir in the parsley, salt, pepper, and allspice. Simmer for a few minutes, then taste and adjust seasoning, adding a pinch of sugar and/or a drop or two of vinegar for balance.

Add the fish pieces to the sauce and turn them carefully to coat them well. Simmer for about 5 minutes to finish cooking and heat through. Alternatively, place the fish in a single layer in a baking dish, spoon the sauce over the top, and bake in a preheated 450°F oven for 5 to 8 minutes to finish cooking and heat through. Serve hot or warm accompanied with lemon wedges.

## Tuna with Tomato Sauce and Preserved Lemon  THON À LA TOMATE

This Moroccan recipe for tuna could also be prepared with cod, snapper, sea bass, or another firm white fish. If you do not have preserved lemon on hand, you can use the grated zest of 1 lemon. In the Mediterranean, tuna is not traditionally served rare, which is how it is often cooked in the States nowadays. I have provided instructions for cooking it through, but the choice is yours. Serve with couscous, steamed potatoes, or potatoes and olives.  SERVES 4

---

4 slices tuna fillet, each 5 to 6 inches and about 1 inch thick

½ cup charmoula I or charmoula II (see Fish with Charmoula on page 239), optional

Salt and fresh lemon juice, if not using charmoula

3 cups peeled, seeded, and diced tomatoes (fresh or canned)

2 cloves garlic, finely minced

¼ cup chopped fresh flat-leaf parsley

Peel of 1 preserved lemon, homemade (page 356) or store-bought, rinsed and cut into thin slivers

16 to 20 oil-cured black olives

2 tablespoons brined capers, rinsed (optional)

¼ teaspoon cayenne pepper or Maras pepper flakes (optional)

---

If you have the time, put the fish in a shallow baking dish, pour the charmoula evenly over the top, cover, and refrigerate for 4 hours. This step can be omitted, but it adds a lot of flavor to the fish. If you don't have the time, sprinkle the fish with salt and rub with lemon juice, then let stand for 1 hour.

Put the tomatoes in a saucepan over medium heat and cook, stirring often, until they have been reduced to a thick purée, adding the garlic for the last few minutes. This will take about 15 minutes. Stir in the parsley, preserved lemon, olives, capers, and cayenne and simmer for 5 minutes longer to blend the flavors.

You can cook the fish in the oven or on the stove top. To bake the fish, preheat the oven to 450°F and oil a baking dish large enough to hold the fish in a single layer. Place the fish in the prepared dish, spoon the sauce over the top, cover, and bake until it tests done when a knife point is inserted, 15 to 20 minutes. To cook the fish on the stove top, bring the sauce to a low boil in a large sauté pan, add the fish, turn to coat evenly, turn down the heat to very low, and simmer gently until the fish tests done, about 15 minutes. Serve the fish hot or at room temperature.

## Baked Fish, Plaki Style   PESHKADO PLAKI

In Greece, *plaki* style is one of the most popular ways for preparing baked fish. Layers of onions, tomatoes, and potatoes are arranged in an ovenproof dish to bake along with the fish. Variations of this recipe are found in Italy, France, and Spain, as well.  SERVES 4

---

5 or 6 tablespoons olive oil

3 tablespoons fresh lemon juice

2 teaspoons dried Greek oregano

4 firm white fish fillets, such as cod, flounder, sea bass, or halibut (about 8 ounces each)

Kosher or sea salt and freshly ground black pepper

2 yellow onions, halved and thinly sliced

2 cloves garlic, finely minced

¼ cup chopped fresh flat-leaf parsley

1 pound boiling potatoes, cooked until tender but still firm, peeled, and sliced (optional)

4 large, ripe tomatoes, peeled and sliced

½ cup fish broth or dry white wine, or as needed

---

In a small bowl, mix together 2 tablespoons of the oil, 1 tablespoon of the lemon juice, and the oregano. Rub the fish fillets on both sides with the oil mixture, then sprinkle with salt and pepper. Let stand for about 1 hour.

Warm 3 tablespoons of the oil in a large sauté pan over medium heat. Add the onions and cook, stirring occasionally, until translucent and tender, 8 to 10 minutes. Add the garlic and cook for 1 minute longer. Stir in half of the parsley and season with salt and pepper.

Preheat the oven to 450°F. Oil a baking dish large enough to hold the fillets in a single layer.

If using the potatoes, arrange them on the bottom of the prepared dish and season with salt and pepper. Top with the onions and then the fish. Cover with the tomato slices and pour on any marinade remaining from the fish. Add the broth and, if you are not using the potatoes, drizzle with the remaining 1 tablespoon oil and 2 tablespoons lemon juice. Bake until the fish flakes when tested with a fork, 12 to 18 minutes. If the mixture seems dry, add more broth (or wine or water) during baking. Remove from the oven, sprinkle with the remaining parsley, and serve hot.

# Sephardic Fish and Vegetable Stew   GEWETCH DI PESHKADO

A more baroque version of *plaki* appears in Suzy David's *The Sephardic Kosher Kitchen*. She adds green bell peppers, carrots, celery, peas, and green beans to the tomatoes. The entire dish can be assembled and then baked later. In the cookbook from Atlanta's Temple Or VeShalom, this dish is called *capama,* from the Turkish word for "to cover," and in its English translation, fish creole. Oy! SERVES 8

---

2 large Yukon Gold potatoes

6 tablespoons olive oil

2 yellow onions, sliced

2 ribs celery, sliced

2 carrots, peeled and sliced

2 green bell peppers, seeded and sliced

2 pounds ripe tomatoes, peeled, seeded, and sliced

⅓ cup shelled English peas

2 ounces green beans, trimmed and sliced on the diagonal into 2-inch lengths

Salt

1 teaspoon freshly ground black pepper

½ to 1 teaspoon ground allspice

2 bay leaves

4 tablespoons chopped fresh flat-leaf parsley

3 pounds firm white fish fillets, such as sea bass, halibut, or snapper, cut into slices 2 to 3 inches wide

1 lemon, thinly sliced

---

Bring a saucepan filled with water to a boil, add the potatoes, and parboil for 5 to 7 minutes. Drain the potatoes, let cool until they can be handled, and then peel and thinly slice. Set aside.

Warm 4 tablespoons of the oil in a sauté pan over medium heat. Add the onions, celery, carrots, and bell peppers and cook, stirring occasionally, for about 5 minutes. Using a slotted spoon, transfer to a bowl, leaving the juices in the pan.

Add the tomatoes to the same pan over medium heat and cook for a minute or two. Add the peas and green beans and cook for 3 to 4 minutes. Using the slotted spoon, transfer the vegetables to the bowl holding the onion mixture. Season all of the cooked vegetables with 1½ teaspoons salt, the pepper, and allspice to taste and add the bay leaves and 2 tablespoons of the parsley.

Preheat the oven to 375°F. Oil a deep baking dish.

Spread the vegetables on the bottom of the prepared dish. Insert the potato slices among the vegetables. Arrange the fish pieces on top. Sprinkle the fish with salt and then cover with the lemon slices and the remaining 2 tablespoons parsley. Drizzle with the remaining 2 tablespoons oil. Cover the dish and bake for 20 minutes. Uncover and continue to bake until the fish flakes when tested with a fork, about 10 minutes longer. Serve warm or at room temperature.

# Fish with Red Bell Pepper Sauce
## PESHKADO AHILADO KON SALSA COLORADO

Instead of a red sauce made with tomatoes and lemon, this Turkish recipe from *La table juive* uses roasted red peppers and paprika, a nod to its Spanish origins. The original recipe called for "Arab parsley," a colloquial term for cilantro. To accent the smokiness of the roasted peppers, you may want to use *pimentón de la Vera,* an imported Spanish paprika now widely available in many markets and at specialty spice stores. In another recipe in the same volume, the roasted red peppers are sautéed with 3 large tomatoes, peeled, seeded, and chopped, and then seasoned with salt and pepper and the juice of 4 lemons—a perfect dish for the tart Sephardic palate! SERVES 6

2 pounds firm white fish fillets, such as sea bass, cod, flounder, snapper, or halibut

Kosher or sea salt and freshly ground pepper

3 red bell peppers

6 cloves garlic, minced

½ cup water

1 tablespoon sweet paprika or pimentón de la Vera dulce

1 teaspoon ground toasted cumin (optional)

¼ cup chopped fresh cilantro

Olive oil for drizzling

Sprinkle the fish fillets on both sides with salt and pepper and refrigerate for 1 hour.

To roast the bell peppers, place them directly over the flame on a gas stove top or on a sheet pan under the broiler and turn them as needed until the skin is blistered and charred on all sides. Transfer to a closed plastic container or a bowl covered with plastic wrap and let stand for 20 minutes. Peel or rub off the skin from each pepper, then stem, halve lengthwise, remove and discard the seeds and thick ribs, and chop.

In a food processor or a mortar, combine the peppers, garlic, and water and process or mash with a pestle to make a spoonable sauce, adding more water if needed. You should have about 1½ cups pepper purée. Season with salt, pepper, paprika, and cumin and stir in the cilantro.

Place the fish fillets in a single layer in a large sauté pan, pour the pepper sauce over the top, and drizzle with oil. Place the pan over low heat, cover, and simmer until the fish tests done when the point of a knife is inserted into the thickest part, 10 to 15 minutes. The timing depends on the thickness of the fillets. Alternatively, arrange the fillets in the same manner in an oiled baking dish, top with the sauce and oil, cover the dish, and bake in a preheated 450°F oven until the fish tests done, 10 to 15 minutes. Transfer the fillets and sauce to a platter and serve at once.

# Fish with Chickpeas and Roasted Peppers   POISSON AUX POIS CHICHES

Fish with chickpeas and red peppers is popular in Morocco, especially in the cities of Fez and Rabat. It is often served during the Rosh Hashanah holidays, when bell peppers are at their peak, or on the Sabbath. A firm fish such as sea bass, snapper, halibut, or cod will work well. Mackerel, if you can find it, would be ideal. Some versions of this recipe add a few small hot red chiles, chopped, to the pepper and chickpea mixture in place of the cayenne. This dish is particularly delicious served with braised Swiss chard or a combination of braised greens. If you do not have time to roast the peppers, substitute 8 jarred *piquillo* peppers. SERVES 4

---

1 rounded cup dried chickpeas

4 cloves garlic, halved lengthwise

Kosher salt and freshly ground black pepper

2 red bell peppers

4 tablespoons olive oil, plus more for rubbing if not using charmoula

1½ pounds firm, thick white fish fillets, such as halibut, cod

½ cup charmoula I or charmoula II (see Fish with Charmoula on page 239), optional

Fresh lemon juice for rubbing if not using charmoula

1 small yellow onion, chopped

1 tablespoon minced garlic

1 teaspoon ground turmeric

2 teaspoons sweet paprika

Pinch of cayenne pepper

½ cup chopped fresh cilantro

Peel of 2 small preserved lemons, homemade (page 356) or store-bought, rinsed and cut into narrow strips

---

Pick over the chickpeas, then place in a bowl, add water to cover, and let soak in the refrigerator overnight. Drain, rinse well, and transfer to a saucepan. Add the garlic and water to cover by 3 inches and bring to a boil over high heat. Turn down the heat to low, cover, and simmer until tender, 45 to 60 minutes. After the first 15 minutes of cooking, add 2 teaspoons salt. (The chickpeas can be prepared a day or so ahead. Store them in their cooking liquid in the refrigerator.)

To roast the bell peppers, place them directly over the flame on a gas stove top or on a sheet pan under the broiler and turn them as needed until the skin is blistered and charred on all sides. Transfer to a closed plastic container or a bowl covered with plastic wrap and let stand for 20 minutes. Peel or rub off the skin from each pepper, then stem, halve lengthwise, remove and discard the seeds and thick ribs, and cut lengthwise into ½-inch-wide strips or into ½-inch dice. Transfer to a bowl and toss with 2 tablespoons of the oil. (The peppers can be prepared a day or so ahead. Cover and store in the refrigerator.)

If you have the time, put the fish in a shallow baking dish, pour the charmoula evenly over the top, cover, and refrigerate for 4 hours. This step can be omitted, but it adds a lot of flavor to the fish. If you don't have the time, sprinkle the fish with salt, rub with a little oil and lemon juice, and let stand for 1 hour.

Warm the remaining 2 tablespoons oil in a sauté pan over medium heat. Add the onion and cook, stirring occasionally, until translucent and tender, about 8 minutes. Add the garlic, turmeric, paprika, cayenne, and ¼ cup of the cilantro and cook, stirring occasionally, for a few minutes longer. Add the chickpeas and their liquid and simmer for 5 minutes to blend the flavors. Add the roasted peppers and preserved lemon, stir well, and taste and adjust the seasoning.

Arrange the fish fillets atop the chickpeas and peppers, place over medium heat, and bring to a boil. Turn down the heat to low, cover, and simmer until the fish tests done when the point of a knife is inserted into the thickest part, 15 to 20 minutes.

Using a slotted spatula, transfer the fillets to a platter. Taste and adjust the seasoning of the pan sauce with salt and cayenne. Spoon the sauce over the fish, top with the remaining ¼ cup cilantro, and serve hot or at room temperature.

## *Fish with a Sauce of Artichokes*  PESCE AL SUGO DI CARCIOFI

You would likely be surprised by the many different versions of this dish that appear in both the Italian Jewish kitchen and in Sephardic and Moroccan Jewish cooking. Because Passover is a spring holiday, it is not unusual to find this classic pairing of fish and springtime's tender artichokes on the celebratory table. Sometimes fennel and cardoons are used in place of the artichokes. Serve with roasted potatoes or rice.  SERVES 4

---

4 fish fillets, such as salmon or sea bass, about 6 ounces each

Salt and freshly ground black pepper

Juice of 1 lemon

4 large or 8 medium-size artichokes

8 tablespoons olive oil, or as needed

2 yellow onions, sliced

1 cup peeled, seeded, and diced tomatoes (fresh or canned), or more to taste

Chopped fresh mint or flat-leaf parsley (optional)

---

Sprinkle the fish fillets on both sides with salt and cover and refrigerate until needed.

Have ready a large bowl of water to which you have added the lemon juice. Working with 1 artichoke at a time, trim the stem to about 2 inches, then peel away the fibrous outer layer. Remove all of the leaves until you reach the heart and then remove and discard the choke with a small pointed spoon or a paring knife. Pare away the dark green areas from the base, then cut the heart lengthwise into ⅓-inch-thick slices and slip the slices into the lemon water.

Warm 3 tablespoons of the oil in a large sauté pan over medium heat. Drain the artichokes, reserving some of the lemon water. Add the artichoke slices to the pan and sauté until beginning to soften, about 5 minutes. Add a little of the lemon water and continue to cook the artichokes until almost completely tender, about 5 minutes longer. They should have absorbed all of the liquid in the pan. Transfer to a plate. Add 3 tablespoons of the oil to the same pan and return to medium heat. Add the onions and cook, stirring occasionally, until translucent and tender, about 8 minutes. Add the tomatoes and return the artichokes to the pan. Stir well and season with salt and pepper. Remove from the heat.

Add the remaining 2 tablespoons oil to a saucepan or deep sauté pan wide enough to hold the fish in a single layer and warm over medium heat. Add the fish fillets and sauté for a minute or two on each side, then top with the artichoke mixture, cover the pan, and braise until the fish tests done when the point of a knife is inserted into the thickest part, 8 to 10 minutes. Sprinkle generously with mint and serve hot or warm.

VARIATIONS: *Baked Variation:* Put the fish in a single layer in a baking dish, top with the artichoke mixture, cover the dish, and bake in a preheated 450°F oven until the fish tests done, about 10 minutes.

*Citrus Variation:* Omit the tomatoes. Add the grated zest of 1 orange and 1 large lemon and a generous pinch of red pepper flakes to the onions as they are cooking. Garnish the finished dish with orange segments in addition to the mint.

*Moroccan Variation:* Add 4 cloves garlic, thinly sliced, to the cooked onions and cook for a few minutes, then season to taste with ground coriander, sweet paprika, and cayenne pepper.

*Greek and Turkish Variations:* Add some fresh lemon juice and a pinch of sugar to the finished artichoke mixture to create a sweet-and-sour sauce. Add a pinch of saffron threads steeped in a little hot water at the same time.

## Fish Couscous from Djerba  COUSCOUS DJERBIEN AU POISSON

In Tunisia, fish couscous can be a simple affair or an elaborate presentation. Chickpeas are usually added along with such assorted vegetables as carrots, potatoes, turnips, and zucchini. For Rosh Hashanah, you could prepare this with the classic seven vegetables: onions, tomatoes, potatoes, sweet potatoes or pumpkin, chickpeas, carrots, and turnips. During Passover, serve the fish stew and broth with crumbled matzo.

In Djerba, home to the largest Jewish community in Tunisia, the vegetables are simply onions, garlic, tomatoes or tomato paste, green peppers, and chickpeas. Some cooks purée the sauce and decorate the plate with strips of green bell pepper and chopped fresh mint or basil. Other versions call for serving the couscous and vegetables with the broth and the fish on the side. This recipe is based on one I cooked with Djerba-based chef Abderrazak Haouari at a special dinner in Los Angeles. It is one of his signature dishes, and it received raves and clean plates, the highest compliment of all. SERVES 8

2 to 3 pounds assorted fish steaks or thick fillets, cut into 3-inch-wide pieces

Salt

¼ cup olive oil

2 yellow onions, chopped

2 ribs celery, chopped

6 cloves garlic, minced

1 cup peeled, seeded, and chopped ripe tomatoes

1 tablespoon ground toasted cumin

2 teaspoons sweet paprika

½ to 1 teaspoon cayenne pepper

½ teaspoon freshly ground black pepper

6 cups water or fish broth

1 cup drained cooked chickpeas

3 carrots, peeled and cut into 1-inch-thick rounds (optional)

2 turnips, peeled and cut into 2-inch pieces (optional)

8 to 12 small potatoes, halved (optional)

Couscous made with 3 cups couscous, cooked with water or with part water and part fish broth with a few tablespoons of olive oil or unsalted butter added to the cooking liquid (page 158)

3 to 4 tablespoons chopped fresh mint (optional)

1 tablespoon harissa, homemade (page 355) or store-bought

Fresh lemon juice for diluting harissa

Sprinkle the fish on both sides with salt and cover and refrigerate until needed.

Warm the oil in a large, heavy saucepan or soup pot over medium heat. Add the onions, celery, and garlic and cook, stirring occasionally, for 8 minutes. Stir in the tomatoes, cumin, paprika, cayenne, and black pepper and cook for about 2 minutes. Add the water, chickpeas, carrots, and turnips and simmer for 15 minutes. Add the fish and potatoes and simmer until the fish and potatoes test done when pierced with a knife point, 15 to 20 minutes.

To serve, put a generous spoonful of couscous into each individual soup bowl. Ladle the fish and vegetables around the couscous and then spoon on some of the broth. Or, pile the couscous on a large platter, make a well in the center, place the fish in the well and place the vegetables around the platter. Ladle some of broth over the top of everything. Sprinkle with the mint. Serve the remaining broth separately. Dilute the harissa with some of the broth and a little lemon juice and pass it at the table.

## Venetian Fish Soup   SOPA DI PESCE SPINA ALL'EBRAICA

Despite the name, which literally translates as "soup of fish on the bone," this is more of a fish ragout than a soup. A Jewish-style *zuppa di pesce* from the Veneto, it resembles the famed *cacciucco alla livornese,* but here tomato paste replaces the chopped tomatoes. In an interesting North African–inspired Livornese touch, author Mira Sacerdoti suggests adding a bit of ginger to the *battuto* of garlic, parsley, and chile. You will want to purchase a few small whole fish; a single large fish, which you can cut crosswise into thick slices; or some assorted fish steaks. If you have pesto on hand, add a generous dollop of it for garnish in place of the basil and parsley. SERVES 6

2 ribs celery, chopped

2 carrots, peeled and chopped

1 large yellow onion, chopped

2 cloves garlic

2 teaspoons salt

About 8 cups water

3 pounds assorted firm whole white fish, cleaned and heads removed and reserved (see headnote)

3 tablespoons olive oil

7 tablespoons finely minced fresh flat-leaf parsley

1 tablespoon finely minced garlic

1 teaspoon red pepper flakes (optional)

2 teaspoons peeled and grated fresh ginger (optional)

1 to 2 cups dry white wine

Pinch of saffron threads (optional)

3 tablespoons tomato paste, or 2 cups peeled, seeded, and diced ripe tomatoes (optional)

¼ cup finely minced fresh basil

Small coarse country bread slices fried in olive oil or broken matzos for serving

In a large stockpot, combine the celery, carrots, onion, garlic, salt, and water. Bring to a boil over high heat and cook for 10 minutes. Add the fish, reduce the heat to medium-low, and simmer for about 12 minutes. Using 1 or 2 slotted spatulas, gently remove the fish from the liquid. Carefully remove the skin, bones, and tails from the fish and set the fillets aside. Return the skin and bones to the pot along with the reserved heads. Simmer until the liquid is infused with flavor, about 30 minutes. Strain the broth through a colander lined with dampened cheesecloth and set aside.

Warm the oil in a deep sauté pan over medium heat. Add 3 tablespoons of the parsley and the garlic and sauté until the garlic is pale gold, about 5 minutes. Stir in the pepper flakes and then, if you want that North African–inspired Livornese touch, add the ginger. Add the wine and saffron and let it bubble for a minute or two. Add the reserved fish fillets and the strained broth and bring to a simmer. Add the tomato paste for color, or the tomatoes for a Livornese dish. Warm the fish until heated through. Taste and adjust the seasoning, then stir in the remaining 4 tablespoons parsley and the basil. Ladle into shallow bowls and serve hot, topped with fried bread.

## *Baked Fish with Almond Stuffing*  POISSON FARCI AUX AMANDES

This recipe for fish stuffed with a savory almond filling combines two recipes, one from *Moroccan Jewish Cookery* by Viviane and Nina Moryoussef, who attribute it to the town of Essaouira, and one from *Savoir préparer la cuisine juive d'Afrique du Nord* by Jeanne Ifergan and Marek Lebkowski. SERVES 6

1 whole fish, such as sea bass, snapper, or salmon, about 4 pounds, cleaned

Salt

FILLING

1½ cups blanched almonds, toasted and chopped

1 cup fresh bread crumbs, toasted

½ teaspoon ground mace

½ teaspoon freshly grated nutmeg

3 hard-boiled eggs, peeled and coarsely chopped

3 eggs, lightly beaten

4 tablespoons chopped fresh flat-leaf parsley

Kosher salt and freshly ground black pepper

SAUCE

2 tablespoons olive oil

1 yellow onion, finely chopped

6 cloves garlic, minced

½ teaspoon saffron threads steeped in ¼ cup hot water

1 teaspoon kosher salt

½ teaspoon freshly ground black pepper

2 tomatoes, sliced

1 lemon, all peel and pith removed, then sliced paper-thin

4 tablespoons oilve oil

Rub the fish inside and out with salt and rinse well. Cut 3 or 4 evenly spaced diagonal slits on both sides of the body. Refrigerate the fish until needed.

To make the filling, in a food processor, combine the almonds, bread crumbs, mace, nutmeg, and hard-boiled eggs and pulse briefly to combine. Add the raw eggs and parsley, season with salt and pepper, and pulse briefly to combine. Pack this mixture into the fish and skewer or sew closed. Oil a baking dish large enough to hold the fish, and place the fish in the prepared dish. Preheat the oven to 400°F.

To make the sauce, warm the oil in a small sauté pan over medium heat. Add the onion and cook, stirring occasionally, until translucent and tender, 8 to 10 minutes. Add the garlic, saffron infusion, salt, and pepper, stir well, and cook for 2 minutes longer. Remove from the heat.

Spoon the sauce over the fish. Arrange the tomato and lemon slices over the fish and drizzle with the oil. Bake until the fish tests done when the point of a knife is inserted into the thickest part, about 30 minutes. Serve warm or at room temperature.

## Turkish Stuffed Fish  USKUMRU DOLMASI

In Turkey, this dish is most often prepared with rich, pungent mackerel, though you can use a milder, sweeter trout or salmon trout instead. To shorten your kitchen time, ask the fishmonger to bone the fish. Serve with sautéed spinach or broiled eggplant and zucchini. SERVES 6

3 tablespoons unsalted butter or olive oil

1 cup chopped yellow onion

2 teaspoons ground coriander

1 teaspoon ground allspice or cinnamon (optional)

¼ cup pine nuts, toasted

¼ cup dried currants, plumped in hot water and drained

2 tablespoons chopped fresh flat-leaf parsley

2 tablespoons chopped fresh dill

2 cups fresh bread crumbs, lightly toasted in 3 tablespoons olive oil or unsalted butter

Salt and freshly ground black pepper

6 boneless mackerel, trout, or salmon trout, each 8 to 10 ounces

Olive oil for brushing if baking or broiling, or for sautéing if cooking on the stove top

Lemon wedges for serving

Melt the butter in a small sauté pan over medium heat. Add the onion and cook, stirring occasionally, until translucent and tender, 8 to 10 minutes. Add the coriander and allspice and cook for a minute or two. Remove from the heat and transfer to a bowl. Add the pine nuts, currants, parsley, dill, and bread crumbs and mix well. Season with salt and pepper and let cool completely.

Pack the cooled mixture into the fish and sew or skewer closed. (The fish can be stuffed several hours in advance and refrigerated until needed.) The fish can be broiled, baked, or cooked on the stove top. If broiling, preheat the broiler, or if baking, preheat the oven to 400°F.

If baking or broiling, brush the fish on both sides with a little oil, sprinkle with salt and pepper, and place on a sheet pan. Slip under the broiler and broil, turning once, for about 4 minutes on each side, or place in the oven and bake for about 15 minutes, basting with a little oil once or twice. To cook on the stove top, warm a little oil in 1 or 2 sauté pans over medium heat. Add the fish and cook, turning them once (working carefully so as not to puncture the skin), for 6 to 7 minutes on each side. Serve hot or warm with lemon wedges.

## Fish Kibbeh  KIBBEH SAMAK

*Kibbeh* are torpedo-shaped croquettes traditionally made with meat and bulgur. This is an interesting *saniyeh* version (*saniyeh* means "in a tray") of *kibbeh* that uses fish and is served in Syria and southern Lebanon. The orange zest, cilantro, and pepper provide the needed flavor boost. Season the filling with a heavy hand, as the bulgur tends to absorb and mute the flavors. It is delicious served as is, or you can accompany it with a tahini sauce (page 112) or tahini sauce dressing enriched with a few tablespoons of plain Greek yogurt. SERVES 6

2 cups fine-grind bulgur

1½ pounds firm white fish fillets, such as sole, cod, or halibut, cut into small pieces

1 large yellow onion, chopped

¼ cup chopped fresh cilantro

¼ cup chopped fresh flat-leaf parsley

Grated zest of 2 oranges

2 to 3 teaspoons kosher salt

Freshly ground black pepper

Olive oil for frying

FILLING

¼ cup olive oil

⅓ cup pine nuts

2 large yellow onions, chopped

Salt and freshly ground black pepper

Aleppo pepper flakes

⅓ cup olive oil or melted unsalted butter for topping

In a bowl, combine the bulgur with warm salted water to cover and let stand for 20 minutes. Pour into a sieve and drain well, pushing against the bulgur with the back of a spoon to force out any moisture.

In a food processor, combine the fish and onion and pulse just to mix. One at a time, add the cilantro, parsley, orange zest, and bulgur, pulsing briefly after each addition until incorporated. Season with 2 teaspoons of the salt and lots of pepper, then knead well by hand in a large bowl or in batches in the food processor until smooth. Fry a small patty of the mixture in a little oil to check the seasoning, then adjust with more salt and pepper if needed. Set aside.

Preheat the oven to 350°F. Generously oil a 9-by-12-by-3-inch baking dish.

To make the filling, warm the oil in a sauté pan over medium heat. Add the pine nuts and toast, stirring often, until light brown. Using a slotted spoon, transfer the pine nuts to a bowl. Add the onions to the oil remaining in the pan and cook over medium heat, stirring occasionally, until translucent and tender, 8 to 10 minutes. Season generously with salt, black pepper, and Aleppo pepper. Add the onion mixture to the pine nuts and mix well.

Pat half of the fish-bulgur mixture onto the bottom of the prepared dish. Spread the filling mixture evenly over the fish-bulgur layer. Top with the remaining fish-bulgur mixture, spreading and patting it with a rubber spatula. Using a sharp knife, cut into diamond shapes through the layers to the bottom of the dish. Pour the oil evenly over the top.

Bake until golden brown, 30 to 35 minutes. Serve hot or at room temperature.

# *Fish Cakes* KEFTES DE PESCADO

You will find two kinds of fish croquettes in the Sephardic kitchen, one made with uncooked ground fish and the other with leftover cooked fish. This recipe, which uses raw fish, was inspired by a description in Giuseppe Maffioli's *La cucina veneziana,* a source reflected in the use of the aromatic sweet spices favored by Venetians. The cakes can be bound with bread crumbs or, during Passover, matzo meal. Your fishmonger may be willing to grind the fish for you. If not, cut it into small pieces and pulse it in a food processor.

To soften the raw onion taste, slice the onion, soak the slices in cold water to cover for an hour, and then drain and chop. The seasoned fish mixture can be rolled into small balls, poached in court bouillon (see Whole Poached Fish, page 226) or other fish broth and served with couscous and an egg-and-lemon sauce (*bagna brusca*) made with fish broth (see Fish with Egg-and-Lemon Sauce on page 230). A tomato sauce (page 328) would also be good. Sautéed spinach makes a delicious side dish. SERVES 4 TO 6

---

1½ pounds firm white fish or salmon fillets, ground

1½ to 2 cups finely chopped or grated yellow onion

2 cloves garlic, finely minced

1 cup fresh bread crumbs or matzo meal, moistened with court bouillon (see headnote) or water

½ cup chopped fresh flat-leaf parsley

¼ cup chopped fresh mint

2 teaspoons salt

1 teaspoon freshly ground black pepper

Grated zest of 1 lemon

½ to 1 teaspoon ground cinnamon

⅛ teaspoon ground cloves

Olive oil or clarified butter for frying

1 egg, lightly beaten, if needed, to bind

1 cup fine dried bread crumbs or matzo meal

Lemon wedges for serving

---

In a bowl, combine the fish, onion, garlic, fresh bread crumbs, parsley, mint, salt, pepper, lemon zest, ½ teaspoon cinnamon, and the cloves and mix well. Fry a small patty of the mixture in a little oil to check the seasoning, then adjust with more cinnamon, salt, and pepper if needed. If the mixture seems too crumbly to hold together, mix in the egg. Form the mixture into cakes about 3 inches in diameter and 1½ inches thick.

Spread the dried bread crumbs on a plate. One at time, dip the cakes into the bread crumbs, coating both sides and tapping off the excess. (The cakes can be shaped up to 1 day in advance. Place on 1 or more sheet pans lined with parchment paper, cover, and refrigerate until ready to fry.)

Warm ¼ cup oil in a large sauté pan over medium-high heat. When the oil is hot, in batches, add the fish cakes and fry, turning once, until golden brown on both sides and cooked through, 4 to 5 minutes on each side. Add more oil to the pan as needed with each batch. Transfer to a platter and serve hot with lemon wedges.

## Cooked-Salmon Cakes   POLPETTINE DI PESCE COTTO

As I am a classic Jewish mother, I always poach too large a piece of salmon and have ample leftovers, so this recipe has become a standby. Of course, you don't have to wait until you have leftovers, as salmon is quickly and easily poached or steamed for this dish. You can serve the salmon cakes with lemon wedges, as they are here, or with the walnut-enriched garlic mayonnaise known as *salsa agliata* (see garlic mayonnaise variation on page 231), Chilled Egg-and-Lemon Sauce (page 232), or warm egg-and-lemon sauce (see Fish with Egg-and-Lemon Sauce on page 230).  SERVES 6

2 pounds salmon fillets

Dry white wine to cover if poaching (optional)

4 tablespoons unsalted butter or olive oil

2 cups diced yellow onion

1 teaspoon ground cinnamon

¼ teaspoon ground cloves

¼ teaspoon freshly grated nutmeg

¼ cup finely chopped fresh flat-leaf parsley

1 cup fresh bread crumbs

¾ cup mayonnaise (page 231)

Salt and freshly ground black pepper

6 tablespoons clarified butter or olive oil for frying, plus more for frying sample

1 cup fine dried bread crumbs, toasted

Lemon wedges for serving

Poach the salmon fillets in gently simmering water or wine to cover until cooked through but not dry (see variation accompanying Poached Whole Fish on page 226). Alternatively, steam the fillets over simmering water until they test done. Let the fillets cool, then break them into small pieces with your fingers, discarding any errant bones, and place in a large bowl.

Warm the butter in a saucepan over low heat. Add the onion and cook, stirring occasionally, until translucent and tender, 8 to 10 minutes. Do not allow to color. Add the cinnamon, cloves, and nutmeg and stir well. Cook for 1 to 2 minutes longer and remove from the heat.

Add the onion mixture, parsley, fresh bread crumbs, and mayonnaise to the salmon and mix well. Season with salt and pepper. Fry a small patty of the mixture in a little clarified butter to check the seasoning and adjust if needed. Form the salmon mixture into 12 cakes each about 3 inches in diameter and 1½ inches thick.

Spread the dried bread crumbs on a plate. One at time, dip the cakes into the bread crumbs, coating both sides and tapping off the excess. (The cakes can be shaped up to

6 hours in advance. Place on a 1 or 2 sheet pans lined with parchment paper, cover, and refrigerate until ready to fry.)

Warm 3 tablespoons of the clarified butter in a large sauté pan over medium-high heat. When the butter is hot, in batches, add the fish cakes and fry, turning once and adding more butter to the pan as need with each batch, until golden brown on both sides and warmed through, 4 to 5 minutes on each side. Transfer to a platter and serve hot with lemon wedges.

## Tunisian Fish Ball Tagine   TAGINE KEFTA MN HOOT

In Spain, Sephardic fish balls, called *albóndigas,* were seasoned simply with parsley, maybe a little cheese, and then fried and served with tomato sauce. Those fish balls would bore the Tunisians, however, who like spices! These fish balls can be fried first, if you like, before they are slipped into the poaching liquid. I like to serve them atop Sephardic Swiss Chard and Chickpeas (page 207), though they are delicious served with couscous, as well. The fish mixture can also be formed into cakes, fried until golden brown and cooked through, and served with garlic mayonnaise (page 231). SERVES 6

### FISH BALLS

1½ pounds mild white fish fillets, such as cod, sole, snapper, or sea bass

¼ cup chopped fresh flat-leaf parsley

¼ cup chopped fresh cilantro

3 cloves garlic, finely minced

2 small yellow onions, finely chopped or puréed in a food processor

1½ teaspoons kosher salt

½ to 1 teaspoon harissa, homemade (page 355) or store-bought

2 teaspoons ground toasted cumin

4 ounces day-old bread, crust removed, soaked in water, and squeezed dry, or ½ cup matzo meal

1 egg, lightly beaten

Olive oil for frying (optional)

### SAUCE

3 tablespoons olive oil

2 cloves garlic, minced

6 tablespoons tomato purée; 4 fresh ripe tomatoes, peeled, seeded, and chopped; or 1 can (14 ounces) chopped tomatoes

1½ cups fish broth or water

Salt and freshly ground black pepper

Harissa, homemade (page 355) or store-bought

Peel of preserved lemon, homemade (page 356) or store-bought, rinsed and chopped (optional)

Chopped fresh flat-leaf parsley for garnish

To make the fish balls, finely chop the fish, removing any errant bones. Transfer to a bowl, add the parsley, cilantro, garlic, onions, salt, harissa to taste, cumin, and bread and mix well. Add the egg and knead until smooth. (This mixture can be blended in a food processor.) Dipping a spoon and your fingers in cold water, remove a heaping tablespoon of fish paste and roll into a 1-inch ball. Fry the ball in a little oil to check the seasoning, then adjust if needed. Line a sheet pan with parchment paper. Shape the rest of the fish paste into 1-inch balls, arrange them on the prepared pan, cover, and refrigerate if not cooking right away.

If you like, you can brown the fish balls before you poach them in the sauce. To brown the balls, film a large sauté pan with oil and place over medium heat. In batches, fry the balls, turning them as needed, until lightly browned on all sides. Using a slotted spoon, transfer to paper towels to drain.

To make the sauce, warm the oil in a large saucepan over high heat. Add the garlic, tomato purée, broth, and the salt, pepper, harissa, and preserved lemon to taste and bring to a boil. Add the fish balls, turn down the heat to low, cover, and simmer until cooked through, 15 to 20 minutes. Transfer to a serving dish and garnish with parsley.

## Salt Cod with Tomato Sauce BACCALÀ AL POMODORO

Salt cod cooked in tomato sauce is a Sephardic classic. This recipe comes from Giuseppe Maffioli's *La cucina padovana,* though similar dishes are prepared in Rome, where chopped black olives or pine nuts and raisins are often added. Most old-time Italian Jewish recipes call for simmering the salt cod in the tomato sauce for 3 hours, but I have found that after a day or so of soaking the salt cod I buy in San Francisco, it is perfectly tender within 15 to 20 minutes. Serve this dish with polenta or potatoes. SERVES 4

---

1½ pounds salt cod fillet

All-purpose flour for coating

Salt and freshly ground black pepper

Olive oil for frying

2 yellow onions, chopped

3 cloves garlic, minced

1 cup dry white wine

4 olive oil–packed anchovy fillets, chopped

4 cups Basic Tomato Sauce (page 328)

3 tablespoons chopped fresh flat-leaf parsley

Grated zest of 1 or 2 lemons

---

Soak the salt cod in cold water to cover in the refrigerator for 2 days, changing the water at least 3 times. Drain the salt cod and break it into 2-inch pieces, removing any errant bones or discolored or tough parts. Spread the flour on a plate and season with salt and pepper. Dip the cod pieces in the seasoned flour, coating both sides and tapping off the excess.

Pour the oil to a depth of 1½ inches into a large, deep sauté pan and place over medium-high heat. When the oil is hot, in batches, fry the salt cod, turning once, until golden on both sides, 4 to 5 minutes total. Using a slotted spatula, transfer to paper towels to drain.

In another large sauté pan, warm 2 tablespoons oil over medium-high heat. Add the onions and garlic and cook, stirring often, until soft and pale gold, about 8 minutes. Add the wine and let it bubble up. Then add the anchovies, tomato sauce, and the cod, turn down the heat to medium, and simmer until the cod is almost fully cooked and tender, 15 to 20 minutes. Add the parsley and lemon zest and simmer for 5 minutes longer to blend the flavors. Transfer to a serving platter and serve hot.

## *Jewish-Style Salt Cod*   BACCALÀ ALL'EBRAICA

Because kosher law allows dairy and fish in the same meal, recipes that cook salt cod in milk are most likely of Jewish origin. The milk tames any excessive saltiness that the cod may retain. Hot slices of baked or grilled polenta (page 171) are a delicious accompaniment. SERVES 4

| | |
|---|---|
| 1½ pounds salt cod fillets | 3 to 4 cups milk |
| 3 tablespoons olive oil, plus more if needed | 1 to 2 pinches of ground cinnamon |
| 2 yellow onions, chopped | 3 tablespoons unsalted butter, cut into slivers |
| 3 cloves garlic, finely minced | ½ cup grated Parmesan cheese |
| All-purpose flour for coating | ¼ cup chopped fresh flat-leaf parsley |
| 1 cup dry white wine | |

Soak the salt cod in cold water to cover in the refrigerator for 2 days, changing the water at least 3 times. Drain the salt cod and break it into 2-inch pieces, removing any errant bones or discolored or tough parts.

Warm the oil in a large, deep broiler-proof sauté pan over medium heat. Add the onions and garlic and cook, stirring occasionally, until translucent and tender, about 10 minutes.

Meanwhile, spread the flour on a plate. Dip the cod pieces in the flour, coating both sides and tapping off the excess. When the onions are tender, add the salt cod pieces and continue to cook until the onions are golden, about 5 minutes longer, adding more oil if necessary to prevent scorching. Add the wine and simmer until it has evaporated,

5 to 8 minutes. Add the milk to cover and the cinnamon to taste, turn down the heat to low, and continue to simmer, uncovered, until the cod is meltingly tender, 15 to 20 minutes longer.

Meanwhile, preheat the broiler. Stir the butter, cheese, and parsley into the cod mixture, mixing well. Slip the pan under the broiler and broil until the surface is glazed, just a few minutes. (Alternatively, place in a preheated 400°F oven for 10 minutes.) Serve piping hot.

Poultry

TODAY, WE THINK OF CHICKEN as a relatively inexpensive option for dinner, but years ago in the Mediterranean, chickens were more costly than beef and lamb. Even more important, chickens were valued more for their eggs than for their meat. Thus, poultry recipes are not a large category in the Sephardic and Mediterranean Jewish kitchen, but the number of egg-based or egg-enhanced dishes is impressive.

Chickens were cooked when they were too old to produce eggs. Roast chicken was occasionally served at holiday meals and on the Sabbath. The bird was more often braised, often with peppers, okra, tomatoes, eggplant, or onions. Sauces were sometimes sweetened with the addition of honey or fruits, or made savory with spiced onions, preserved lemons, and briny cured olives. Poultry might also turn up at the center of a spectacular holiday pastry, such as Moroccan *b'stilla* (page 82).

Fried chicken was served at Hanukkah, and chicken dumplings were served in the Passover chicken broth. Odd pieces were ground and formed into little meatballs. Chicken was paired with noodles or rice for a homey family meal, baked as a sturdy meat loaf, or added to omelets and soups to make them more substantial.

Because chickens were older when slaughtered, they took longer to cook than today's quickly raised birds that become tender within minutes. Chicken thighs are my first choice for braising or broiling, as they hold their juiciness better than breasts, which tend to dry out. If you are cutting up a whole bird and cooking the pieces together, watch the breasts carefully as they cook and remove them as soon as they appear done. Cooking them on the bone will also help keep the meat moist. Whether you brown chicken pieces before braising is up to you. The browning will give them better color, but the skin will lose any crispness during the braising.

## Chicken with Apples GAYNA KON MANZANA

Cooking chicken with fruit is a long-established Hispano-Arabic tradition. *La table juive* calls this Turkish recipe "chicken with apples," though apricots should be in the title as well, as they are an integral part of the dish and most assuredly flavor the sauce.

In the original recipe, the chicken and dried fruits are marinated in the same bowl. I prefer to let the fruits soak separately from the bird, as they don't need much time to soften. It is best if the chicken marinates longer—even overnight—to pick up the flavors of the spices and the wine. I imagine that if you made this dish with mixed dried fruits, including dried apples, it would be delicious, as well. SERVES 4 TO 6

1 roasting chicken, 4 to 5 pounds, cut into serving pieces, or 8 to 12 chicken thighs

3 cups white wine, or as needed

1 tablespoon honey

1 teaspoon ground ginger

2 teaspoons ground cinnamon

1 teaspoon freshly ground black pepper

½ teaspoon ground mace

1¾ cups dried apricots

3 pounds tart apples (about 6 large), such as Granny Smith or pippin, peeled, quartered, and cored

2 tablespoons fresh lemon juice

1 tablespoon sugar

1 cinnamon stick

¼ cup olive oil

3 yellow onions, chopped

Salt

½ cup sesame seeds, toasted

Place the chicken pieces in a bowl. In a small bowl, combine 1½ cups of the wine, the honey, ginger, ground cinnamon, pepper, and mace and mix well. Rub the mixture over the chicken pieces and then cover and marinate in the refrigerator for at least a few hours or up to overnight.

In a bowl, combine the apricots with the remaining 1½ cups wine, or as needed to cover, and set aside to soften for a few hours.

In a saucepan, combine the apples, lemon juice, sugar, cinnamon stick, and water to cover. Bring to a simmer over low heat, and simmer for 8 minutes. Drain, reserving the liquid, and set the apples and liquid aside separately.

Warm the oil in a stew pot or other large braising pan over medium heat. Add the onions and sauté, sprinkling them with salt, until golden, about 15 minutes. Add the chicken and its marinade, the soaked apricots and any remaining wine, and the apple poaching liquid to the pan. The chicken should be just covered; if it isn't, add water as needed. Bring to a gentle boil, turn down the heat to low, cover, and cook gently, checking from time to time and adding water if needed to prevent the fruit from scorching, until the chicken is almost cooked, about 30 minutes.

Add the apples and simmer until the chicken and apples are tender, about 5 minutes longer. Remove and discard the cinnamon stick. Serve hot, sprinkled with the sesame seeds.

# Chicken with Apricots and Tomatoes  DJAH MISH MISH

I have seen variations of this recipe in Indian and Syrian cookbooks, even though apricots originated in Iran. The addition of tomatoes makes this an interesting mix of Old World and New World ingredients. The apricot and tomato sauce is sweet, tart, and aromatic and adds a lively tang to simple Cornish hens or chicken. Some Syrian cooks add tamarind to the sauce to heighten the tart-sweet balance. Although I often serve this dish at Passover as part of the Seder meal, I need no special holiday to cook this all year long, as it's a family favorite. Serve with rice, bulgur, or freekeh pilaf and with sautéed spinach. SERVES 6

---

3 tablespoons rendered chicken fat or olive oil, plus more oil if browning the hens

4 cups chopped yellow onions (about 3 medium)

1 tablespoon plus 1 teaspoon ground cinnamon

1 teaspoon ground cloves

3 cups drained diced canned tomatoes (with juices reserved, optional)

3½ cups dried apricots, soaked in warm water to cover (will expand to about 5 cups after soaking)

2 cups chicken broth, water, or a combination of apricot soaking liquid, tomato juices, and water, or as needed

⅓ cup packed brown sugar

Salt and freshly ground black pepper

6 Cornish hens or poussins, each 1 to 1½ pounds, or 12 chicken thighs

---

Warm the chicken fat in a large saucepan over low heat. Add the onions and cook, stirring occasionally, for about 5 minutes. Add 1 tablespoon of the cinnamon and the cloves and cook for about 3 minutes longer. Add about ½ cup of the reserved tomato juices, stir well, and simmer for 5 minutes.

Meanwhile, drain the apricots, reserving the liquid. Purée half of the soaked apricots in a food processor and coarsely chop the remainder.

Add the puréed apricots, diced tomatoes, and 1 cup of the broth to the onions and simmer for 5 minutes. Add the chopped apricots, the brown sugar, and the remaining 1 cup broth and simmer for 5 minutes longer. You should have a medium-thick sauce; add more liquid if needed. Season with salt and pepper and then set aside until serving. (This sauce can be made up to a day in advance, covered, and refrigerated. Reheat just before using.)

This dish can be finished two different ways. Preheat the oven to 450°F. Place the Cornish hens on a rack in a roasting pan. Sprinkle them with salt, pepper, and the remaining 1 teaspoon cinnamon. Roast until the juices run clear when a thigh is pierced, about 45 minutes. Remove from the oven, let cool until they can be handled, cut into quarters, and warm the quarters in the apricot sauce on the stove top and serve hot.

Or preheat the oven to 350°F. Cut the whole birds into quarters, sprinkle them with salt, pepper, and the remaining 1 teaspoon cinnamon, and brown the pieces on all sides in oil in a large sauté pan over medium-high heat. Spoon half of the sauce into a large baking dish, arrange the poultry pieces on top in a single layer, and spoon the remaining sauce over the pieces. Bake until tender, about 30 minutes, and then serve hot.

## Roast Chicken with Orange, Lemon, and Ginger
POLLO ARROSTO ALL'ARANCIA, LIMONE E ZENZERO

This is the old family standby. Everyone loves this Italian Jewish recipe for roast chicken. Ginger arrived in Italy with Arabic traders or North African Jewish immigrants, so it's likely that this is a Sicilian or Livornese recipe. Most Italians would use ground ginger, but since fresh ginger is so plentiful at our markets, I have used it here. SERVES 4 OR 5

---

1 lemon

1 roasting chicken, about 4 pounds

Grated zest of 1 lemon, with remaining lemon cut into quarters

Grated zest of 1 orange, with remaining orange cut into quarters

3 tablespoons peeled and grated fresh ginger

Salt and freshly ground black pepper

5 tablespoons margarine, melted, or olive oil

3 tablespoons honey

¼ cup fresh lemon juice

½ cup fresh orange juice

2 to 4 tablespoons pomegranate molasses, in place of some of the citrus juice (optional)

Orange sections for garnish

---

Preheat the oven to 400°F. Cut the whole lemon into quarters. Rub the outside of the chicken with a lemon quarter and discard it. Reserve the remaining 3 quarters for the cavity.

In a small bowl, stir together the lemon and orange zests and 1 tablespoon of the grated ginger. Rub this mixture evenly in the chicken cavity, then put all of the lemon quarters and the orange quarters in the cavity. Place the chicken on a rack in a roasting pan. Sprinkle it with salt and pepper.

In the same small bowl, combine the margarine, honey, lemon and orange juices (or use pomegranate juice in place of some of the citrus juice), and the remaining 2 tablespoons ginger and mix well.

Place the chicken in the oven and roast, basting with the margarine mixture at least four times during cooking, until the juices run clear when a thigh is pierced with a knife, 1 to 1¼ hours.

Transfer to a serving platter and let rest for about 10 minutes. Carve the chicken and garnish with orange sections.

## Matzo-Stuffed Roast Chicken for Passover    KOTOPOULO PSITO

Here, dried currants, walnuts, and matzo meal combine to make a rich, savory stuffing for the Passover roast chicken. (The same amount of stuffing can be used for two 3-pound birds.) The recipe is based on one from the Greek community of Ioannina as transcribed by Nicholas Stavroulakis in his wonderful *Cookbook of the Jews of Greece.* SERVES 4 TO 6

1 roasting chicken with giblets, about 5 pounds

4 tablespoons olive oil, plus more for rubbing

1 cup matzo meal

1⅔ cups dry white wine, or as needed

3 eggs, lightly beaten

½ cup walnuts, coarsely chopped

2 cups dried currants

Salt and freshly ground black pepper

Juice of 1 lemon

Preheat the oven to 400°F.

Remove the giblets from the chicken cavity. Warm 2 tablespoons of the oil in a small sauté pan over medium-high heat. Add the gizzard and heart and sear well on all sides. Add the liver and cook, turning as needed, for a few minutes longer. Transfer the giblets to a cutting board and chop finely.

In a bowl, combine the matzo meal, ½ to ⅔ cup wine, the eggs, the walnuts, the currants, and the giblets. Add the remaining 2 tablespoons oil, season with salt and pepper, and mix well.

Spoon the stuffing into the chicken cavity loosely and sew or skewer closed. Reserve any extra stuffing. Rub the chicken liberally with oil and the lemon juice and sprinkle with salt and pepper. Place on a rack in a roasting pan.

Roast the chicken, basting occasionally with the remaining wine and with the pan drippings, until the juices run clear when a thigh is pierced with a knife, about 1½ hours. If you have stuffing that did not fit into the bird, put it in the roasting pan for the last 15 minutes of roasting, where it will cook and take on color.

Transfer the chicken to a serving platter and let rest for about 10 minutes. Scoop out the stuffing into a serving bowl and carve the chicken.

# Roast Chicken Stuffed with Rice  DJAJ MIHSHEE BI ROZ

In Syria and Lebanon, chickens are stuffed with a fragrant rice or bulgur pilaf. (If you opt for bulgur, use medium-grind bulgur in the same amount as the rice.) The grain is not fully cooked when the stuffing is made, as it will continue to cook inside the bird, where it will absorb the meat juices. Here, I provide the option of a large roasting chicken or smaller birds. SERVES 6

1 lemon, halved

6 Cornish hens or poussins, each about 1½ pounds, or 1 roasting chicken, about 5 pounds

Kosher salt

STUFFING

2½ cups water, lightly salted

1½ cups basmati rice

4 tablespoons olive oil or margarine

2 yellow onions, diced

1 teaspoon ground allspice

1 teaspoon ground cinnamon

⅔ cup dried currants, plumped in hot water and drained

½ cup pine nuts, toasted

½ cup almonds, toasted

¼ cup chopped fresh flat-leaf parsley

2 tablespoons grated lemon zest (optional)

Salt and freshly ground black pepper

BASTING MIXTURE

4 to 6 tablespoons margarine, melted, or olive oil

1 teaspoon ground allspice or cinnamon

2 cloves garlic, minced

¼ cup fresh lemon juice

Salt and freshly ground black pepper

Rub the cut sides of the lemon over the inside and outside of the birds or roasting chicken, then sprinkle inside and outside with salt. Reserve at room temperature.

To make the stuffing, in a saucepan, bring the salted water to a boil over high heat. Add the rice, stir once, lower the heat to a simmer, and cover the pan. Cook until the liquid is just absorbed, about 15 minutes. Set aside.

Warm the oil in a sauté pan over medium heat. Add the onions and cook, stirring occasionally, until translucent and tender, 8 to 10 minutes. Stir in the allspice and cinnamon and cook for a few minutes longer. Meanwhile, preheat the oven to 400°F.

In a bowl, combine the rice, onion mixture, currants, pine nuts, almonds, parsley, and lemon zest and mix well. Season with salt and pepper. Spoon the stuffing loosely into the birds or chicken and sew or skewer closed.

To make the basting mixture, in small bowl, combine the margarine, allspice, garlic, and lemon juice and mix well. Season with salt and pepper.

Place the birds or chicken on a rack in a shallow roasting pan or in a sheet pan and roast, basting occasionally with the basting mixture, until the juices run clear when a thigh is pierced with a knife, 45 to 60 minutes for the small birds and about 30 minutes longer for the chicken.

Let rest for a few minutes, then serve. For ease of eating, cut the small birds in half and present them on individual plates. Scoop out the stuffing from the large chicken, then carve in the usual fashion and serve on a platter.

IRANIAN VARIATION: Iranian cooks use basmati rice for the stuffing. Prepare the onion mixture as directed, then combine the rice and the onion mixture with 3 tablespoons dried rose petals; ¼ cup each dried cherries and dried barberries or dried cranberries, soaked in hot water to soften; ¼ cup chopped pistachios; and 2 tablespoons grated lemon zest. Stuff and roast the birds or roasting chicken as directed, basting with a mixture of olive oil, orange and lemon juices, and a bit of pomegranate molasses.

## Chicken Tagine with Preserved Lemon and Olives
POULET AUX CITRONS ET OLIVES

This recipe is from *Saveurs de mon enfance* and is a specialty of Fez. Serve with couscous or rice. SERVES 4 TO 6

| | |
|---|---|
| 3 tablespoons olive oil | Peel of 2 preserved lemons, homemade (page 356) or store-bought, rinsed and 1 peel chopped and 1 peel slivered |
| 2 yellow onions, chopped | |
| 2 cloves garlic, minced | 1 fryer chicken, 3½ to 4 pounds, cut into serving pieces |
| ⅓ cup chopped fresh cilantro | |
| 1 teaspoon ground ginger | 1½ cups water |
| 1 teaspoon sweet paprika | 1⅓ cups green olives |
| 1 teaspoon ground toasted cumin | Salt |
| ½ teaspoon freshly ground black pepper | Fresh lemon juice, if needed |
| ¼ teaspoon saffron threads, crushed | |

Warm the oil in a stew pot over medium heat. Add the onions and sauté until pale gold, about 15 minutes. Add the garlic, cilantro, ginger, paprika, cumin, pepper, saffron, and the chopped preserved lemon and mix well. Arrange the chicken pieces on top of the onion mixture, add the water, and bring to a boil. Turn down the heat to low, cover, and simmer for 30 minutes, occasionally turning the chicken in the sauce.

Add the olives and the slivered preserved lemon and continue to cook until the chicken is very tender, about 15 minutes longer. Taste and adjust the seasoning with salt and with lemon juice if needed. If the sauce is too thin, transfer the chicken to a warmed platter and reduce the sauce over high heat until a good consistency is achieved. Spoon the sauce and olives over the chicken and serve.

## *Algerian Tagine of Chicken with Quince*   POULET AUX COINGS

The quince is thought to have been the apple in the Garden of Eden. When they are in season, quinces add an exotic sweetness to any dish and can perfume your entire house if left in a fruit bowl on the dining table. Ideally, they turn a lovely terra-cotta red when cooked. Maybe it's my imagination, but I've noticed that most European quinces turn red more quickly, and ours become tender well before they take on color. To ensure the color, you may want to add a bit of pomegranate molasses to the poaching liquid. When you are making quince jam (page 365), you can cook the fruits for a long time until the color comes up, as texture is not crucial. But if you want the quince slices to retain their shape, as you do here, you cannot cook them too long. That's why I cook the quinces separately and then add them to the chicken stew during the last 15 minutes of braising.

This fragrant stew is the ideal dish for Rosh Hashanah to welcome in the sweet New Year. It is based on a recipe from Léone Jaffin's *150 recettes et mille et un souvenirs d'une juive d'Algérie* and is a favorite of my family. Quince season is short, and because my family loves this stew, I put up several pint jars of preserved quince slices (page 367) each year, which turns this recipe into a quick-and-easy dinner that we can have any time. I cook the chicken thighs and when they are tender I add the preserved slices and heat them through. I steam some couscous and dinner is ready. SERVES 6

---

2 pounds quinces (about 4), peeled, cut into eighths, and cored

Pomegranate molasses, if needed for color

1 large chicken, 4 to 5 pounds; 2 broiler chickens, about 2½ pounds each; or 12 chicken thighs

½ cup olive oil

3 yellow onions, chopped

½ teaspoon freshly grated nutmeg

2 teaspoons ground cinnamon

Salt

---

In a saucepan, combine the quinces with water to barely cover, bring to a simmer over medium heat, and cook until tender, 20 to 30 minutes. Turn off the heat and let the fruit rest for 1 hour. Return the pan to medium heat and continue cooking the quinces until they turn pink or terra-cotta. You can repeat this stop-start method a few times until the quinces turn color, which will take about 30 minutes of active cooking time in all. If you are impatient and the fruits are tender and not yet a rich color, add up to ½ cup pomegranate molasses to the pan. Set the quinces aside in their poaching liquid.

If you are using 1 or 2 whole chickens, cut into serving pieces. Warm the oil in a large sauté pan over high heat. In batches, add the chicken pieces and sear well on all sides. Using tongs, transfer to a plate. Add the onions to the fat remaining in the pan and sauté over medium heat until golden, 15 to 20 minutes. Stir in the nutmeg and cinnamon and cook for 5 minutes longer. Return the chicken pieces and their accumulated juices to the pan, cover, and braise for about 20 minutes. Add the quince pieces and some of their cooking liquid and simmer until the chicken is tender, about 15 minutes longer.

Season with salt, then taste and adjust the seasoning with more nutmeg and cinnamon if you want those flavors to be more intense. Serve hot.

# Persian Chicken with Pomegranate and Walnut Sauce
### KHORESH-E FESENJAN

*Fesenjan* is one of the most revered dishes of Persian cuisine, and deservedly so, because the walnut and pomegranate sauce is exquisite. Traditionally this sauce is used for chicken or duck, so I was surprised to find meatballs cooked in it when I was in Iran. The recipe calls for pomegranate molasses, which you can find in a well-stocked supermarket, at a store specializing in Middle Eastern foods, or online. It is a staple in my pantry. You can instead reduce bottled pomegranate juice, augment it with pomegranate molasses, and then add less chicken broth. In either case, you will need to balance the sweet-tart ratio and cook the sauce until it is thick. In Isfahan, residents prefer their sauce a bit sweeter than in Yazd or Shiraz. The only other variable here is how the walnuts are chopped. Sometimes they are minced almost to the point of a purée; other times, they are chunkier. I like a little texture, but the choice is yours. *Fesenjan* is usually served with *chelo* (page 149). SERVES 4

6 tablespoons olive oil

4 chicken thighs and 4 drumsticks; 8 chicken thighs; or 1 broiler chicken, about 2½ pounds, cut into 8 serving pieces

1½ teaspoons salt

½ teaspoon freshly ground black pepper

2 teaspoons ground cinnamon

3 yellow onions, chopped (about 4 cups)

½ cup pomegranate molasses, or 2 cups pomegranate juice reduced to 1 cup and ¼ cup pomegranate molasses

½ cup tomato sauce

2 cups walnuts, toasted and chopped

1½ cups chicken broth, or 1 cup if using reduced pomegranate juice and molasses, or as needed

Fresh lemon juice and sugar as needed for sweet-tart balance

Pomegranate seeds for garnish (optional)

Warm 4 tablespoons of the oil in a large sauté pan over medium-high heat. Add the chicken pieces and fry, turning as needed and sprinkling with the salt, pepper, and ½ teaspoon of the cinnamon, until lightly colored on all sides. Transfer to a plate and set aside while you make the sauce.

Warm the remaining 2 tablespoons oil in a stew pot over low heat. Add the onions and cook, stirring occasionally, until translucent and tender, about 15 minutes. Add the remaining 1½ teaspoons cinnamon and cook for a minute or two. Add the pomegranate molasses or reduced juice and molasses, tomato sauce, walnuts, and 1½ cups broth if using molasses or 1 cup broth if using reduced juice and molasses. Simmer until thickened, about 20 minutes. If the sauce is too thick, add a bit more broth.

Add the chicken to the sauce, cover, and simmer until the chicken is tender, 25 to 30 minutes. Taste and adjust the seasoning with salt and pepper. If the pomegranate has made the sauce too sweet, add some lemon juice. If the sauce is too tart, balance the flavor with a little sugar. Serve hot, garnished with the pomegranate seeds.

## Moroccan Chicken with Almonds and Raisins
POULET AUX AMANDES ET RAISINS SECS

This recipe can be made with individual birds like *poussins* or Cornish hens, but I think thighs or other chicken pieces are easier to cook, serve, and eat. If you do opt to prepare whole birds, they will need to cook for about an hour. Serve this dish with couscous. SERVES 6

12 chicken thighs (or a few more if small), or 1 large chicken, 4 to 5 pounds, cut into serving pieces

1 lemon, halved

Salt and freshly ground black pepper

1 teaspoon ground coriander

1 teaspoon ground ginger

1 teaspoon ground cinnamon

½ teaspoon ground allspice

½ teaspoon ground cloves

½ teaspoon freshly grated nutmeg

½ cup olive oil, or as needed

4 yellow onions, thinly sliced

½ teaspoon saffron threads steeped in ¼ cup hot water

1½ cups water or chicken broth, or as needed

1 cup raisins

1 cup blanched almonds, toasted

1 cup honey

Preheat the oven to 350°F.

Rub the chicken pieces with the cut sides of the lemon, then sprinkle with salt and pepper. In a small bowl, stir together the coriander, ginger, cinnamon, allspice, cloves, and nutmeg. Rub half of the spice mixture over the chicken pieces.

Select a stew pot large enough to hold all of the chicken pieces, add 3 to 4 tablespoons of the oil, and warm over medium heat. Add the onions and cook, stirring occasionally, until tender and golden, about 15 minutes. Add the remaining spice mixture and stir well. Reserve off the heat.

Warm the remaining 4 or 5 tablespoons oil in a large sauté pan over medium-high heat. In batches, add the chicken pieces and brown well on all sides, adding more oil if needed. As the chicken pieces are ready, add them to the onions. When all of the chicken is in the pot, add the saffron infusion and enough water to come about 1½ inches up the sides of the pot. Bring to a simmer on the stove top, cover, transfer to the oven, and cook for 20 minutes.

Remove from the oven, uncover, and add the raisins and almonds and a little more water if the pot looks dry. Drizzle most of the honey over the chicken pieces to glaze them and let the remainder fall onto the onions. Re-cover the pot, return to the oven, and cook until the chicken is tender, about 20 minutes longer. Taste and adjust the seasoning, then serve.

## *Fried Chicken for Hanukkah*   POLLO FRITTO DI HANUCCA

The dishes served at Hanukkah are fried to remind the Jews of the oil lamp that burned for eight days in the Second Temple in Jerusalem, even though the amount appeared sufficient for only one day. This recipe for fried chicken, Italian style, is rather bland, so I have brined the chicken for added moisture and flavor. I have also added grated lemon and orange zests, garlic powder, onion powder, and nutmeg to the flour. SERVES 4 TO 6

BRINE

1 cup kosher salt

⅓ cup sugar

8 cloves garlic, unpeeled and smashed

2 tablespoons black peppercorns

2 cinnamon sticks

4 allspice berries

5 bay leaves

2 lemons, halved

8 fresh thyme sprigs

8 fresh parsley sprigs

4 quarts water

1 fryer chicken, 3½ to 4 pounds, cut into 8 to 10 serving pieces, or 4 pounds assorted chicken parts

3 eggs

¼ cup fresh lemon juice

Salt and freshly ground black pepper

3 cups all-purpose flour

2 tablespoons grated lemon zest

2 tablespoons grated orange zest

3 tablespoons garlic powder

2 tablespoons onion powder

1 teaspoon freshly grated nutmeg

Canola oil for deep-frying

Lemon wedges for serving

Combine all of the brine ingredients in a large saucepan and bring to a boil over high heat, stirring to dissolve the salt and sugar. Remove from the heat and let cool completely. Place the chicken pieces in a large bowl or plastic container, pour the cooled brine over them, cover tightly, and refrigerate overnight.

Remove the chicken from the brine, rinse, and pat dry. Discard the brine. Place a large rack on a large sheet pan. In a shallow bowl, whisk together the eggs and lemon juice until blended, then season with salt and pepper. In a second bowl, combine the flour, citrus zests, garlic and onion powders, and nutmeg, season with salt and pepper, and mix well. Divide the seasoned flour between 2 shallow bowls or deep platters. One at a time, dip the chicken pieces in the flour, coating both sides and tapping off the excess. Next, dip into the beaten egg, allowing the excess to drip off, and then finally, dip in the second bowl of seasoned flour. As each piece is dipped, set it aside on the rack. Let the pieces stand for 15 to 20 minutes to allow the coating to set.

Pour the oil to a depth of 2 to 3 inches into a large, deep sauté pan and heat to 375°F. Preheat the oven to 250°F. Line a large sheet pan with paper towels. In batches, slip the chicken pieces into the hot oil and fry, turning as needed, until golden on all sides and cooked through, 15 to 20 minutes. Using tongs, transfer to the prepared sheet pan and keep warm in the oven until all of the chicken pieces are fried. Arrange the chicken on a platter and serve hot with lemon wedges.

## My Moroccan-Spiced Fried Chicken for Hanukkah

This chicken is not served in Morocco, but the spices are of the region and the flavor is big and satisfying.  SERVES 8

**Brine (see Fried Chicken for Hanukkah, page 277)**

**6 whole chicken breasts, each about 1 pound, split and then the halves cut in half crosswise; 12 chicken thighs and 12 drumsticks; or any combination of chicken parts totaling about 5 pounds (24 pieces)**

**4 eggs**

**¼ cup fresh lemon juice**

**4 cups all-purpose flour**

**SPICE MIX**

**1 tablespoon ground cumin**

**1 tablespoon ground coriander**

**1 tablespoon ground cinnamon**

**1 tablespoon ground nutmeg**

**1 tablespoon sweet paprika**

**1 tablespoon ground black pepper**

**1 tablespoon ground ginger**

**½ teaspoon cayenne or 1 teaspoon Maras pepper**

**1 tablespoon salt**

**Canola oil for deep-frying**

Make the brine and brine the chicken pieces as directed in Fried Chicken for Hanukkah.

Remove the chicken from the brine, rinse, and pat dry. Discard the brine. Top 2 large sheet pans with racks. In a shallow bowl, whisk together the eggs and lemon juice until blended.

In a second bowl, stir together the flour and all of the spice mix ingredients. Divide the seasoned flour between 2 shallow bowls or deep platters. One at a time, dip the chicken pieces in the flour, coating both sides and tapping off the excess. Next, dip into the beaten egg, allowing the excess to drip off, and then finally, dip in the second bowl of seasoned flour. As each piece is dipped, set it aside on a rack. Let the pieces stand for 15 to 20 minutes to allow the coating to set.

Pour the oil to a depth of 2 to 3 inches into a large, deep sauté pan and heat to 375°F. Preheat the oven to 250°F. Line 1 or 2 large sheet pans with paper towels. In batches, slip the chicken pieces into the hot oil and fry, turning as needed, until golden on all sides and cooked through, 15 to 20 minutes. Using tongs, transfer to the prepared sheet pan(s) and keep warm in the oven until all of the chicken is fried. Arrange the chicken on a platter and serve hot.

NOTE: You may substitute 5 tablespoons prepared ras el hanout (see pantry) for the spice mix, but add ½ teaspoon cayenne or 1 teaspoon Maras pepper.

## *Persian Chicken Kebab*  JUJEH KABAB

Although most recipes for chicken kebabs call for boneless, skinless chicken breasts, the kebabs run the risk of overcooking because the meat is lean. I prefer to use skin-on, boneless chicken thighs. They remain moist and juicy throughout the cooking, and the skin carries the wonderful flavor of the marinade. This marinade can also be used on butterflied *poussins,* small broiler chickens, or Cornish hens or on bone-in chicken breasts, thighs, or other chicken parts.

This recipe was passed on to me by an Iranian friend, but I have seen versions of this dish in cookbooks from the Caucasus, as well. Serve with Persian Rice (page 149) and with sautéed spinach or zucchini with chopped walnuts or toasted pine nuts. SERVES 6

MARINADE

1 yellow onion, cut into chunks (about 1½ cups)

½ cup fresh lemon juice

2 teaspoons sweet paprika

1 teaspoon ground turmeric, or ½ teaspoon saffron threads, finely crushed and steeped in 2 tablespoons hot water

2 teaspoons finely minced garlic

1 cup olive oil

12 large or 18 small skin-on, boneless chicken thighs

Salt and freshly ground black pepper

Ground sumac for sprinkling

Lemon wedges for serving

To make the marinade, in a blender or food processor, combine the onion, lemon juice, paprika, turmeric, and garlic and purée until smooth. Add the oil and process until incorporated.

Place the chicken in a shallow dish, add the marinade, and turn once or twice to coat evenly. Cover and refrigerate for at least 6 hours or up to overnight. (Alternatively, combine the chicken and marinade in a large resealable plastic bag.) Bring the chicken to room temperature before cooking.

Preheat the broiler or prepare a fire in a charcoal grill. Remove the chicken from the marinade and discard the marinade. Thread the thighs onto skewers (if using wooden skewers, soak them in water for 30 minutes before using) and sprinkle with salt and pepper. Broil or grill, turning once, until the juices run clear when a thigh is pierced in the thickest part, about 4 minutes on each side. Sprinkle with sumac and serve with lemon wedges.

MARINADE VARIATIONS:

*Syrian Chicken Kebab (Shish Taouk):* Combine 4 to 6 cloves garlic, finely minced; ½ cup fresh lemon juice; 2 teaspoons chopped fresh thyme; 1 teaspoon sweet paprika; ½ teaspoon cayenne pepper or Aleppo pepper flakes; 1 teaspoon salt; ½ teaspoon freshly ground black pepper; and ½ cup olive oil and mix well. Use only 8 to 12 skin-on, boneless chicken thighs. Marinate and cook as directed. Omit the sumac.

*Persian-Inspired Chicken Kebab with Pomegranate and Orange (Morgh Kabab e Naranj):* Combine ¼ cup pomegranate molasses; ½ cup fresh orange juice; ¼ cup verjus or fresh lemon juice; ¼ cup honey, or to taste; 1 tablespoon grated orange zest; 1 teaspoon each ground cinnamon, ground ginger, and salt; ½ teaspoon ground cardamom; and lots of freshly ground black pepper and mix well. Use only 8 to 12 skin-on, boneless chicken thighs. Marinate and cook as directed. The skin will darken and char a bit because of the honey, but it will still taste delicious. Omit the sumac and lemon wedges. Garnish with orange segments and pomegranate seeds.

*Middle Eastern Chicken Kebab:* Combine 4 cloves garlic, finely minced; 1 tablespoon ground cumin; 1½ teaspoons each ground ginger and allspice; ¼ cup fresh lemon juice; ½ cup olive oil; salt to taste; and lots of freshly ground black pepper and mix well. Use only 8 to 12 skin-on, boneless chicken thighs. Marinate and cook as directed. Omit the sumac.

## Chicken with Onions, Peppers, and Paprika ARMI DO GAYNA

*Armi do gayna* resembles the classic *pollo al chilindrón* from the Rioja and Navarre regions in Spain, both famous for sweet peppers. The addition of allspice is a decidedly Turkish touch. I also like a subtle hint of heat in the background. In *The Sephardic Kosher Kitchen*, Suzy David calls this *gaina kon zarzavat* and adds dill for a leafy touch. Serve with rice and pass lemon wedges to brighten the flavors. SERVES 4 TO 6

3 tablespoons olive oil

1 large chicken, about 4½ pounds, cut into serving pieces

4 or 5 large yellow onions, thinly sliced

3 large red bell peppers, seeded and sliced lengthwise into narrow strips

2½ tablespoons sweet paprika

¾ teaspoon ground allspice

1 bay leaf

Pinch of cayenne pepper or hot paprika (optional)

Salt and freshly ground black pepper

½ cup water or chicken broth, or as needed

Chopped fresh flat-leaf parsley for garnish (optional)

Lemon wedges for serving

Warm the oil in a large, heavy sauté pan over high heat. When the oil is hot, in batches if necessary, add the chicken pieces and fry, turning as needed, until golden on all sides. Using tongs, transfer the chicken to a plate and set aside.

Add the onions to the oil remaining in the pan and sauté over medium heat until tender, about 10 minutes. Add the bell peppers, paprika, allspice, bay leaf, and cayenne, season generously with salt and pepper, and cook, stirring often, until the onions are golden, about 10 minutes longer.

Return the chicken pieces to the pan and add the water. (If the pan is not large enough to hold all of the chicken, transfer the contents of the sauté pan to a stew pot along with the chicken.) Turn down the heat to low, cover tightly, and simmer until the chicken is tender, 30 to 40 minutes. Check the pan from time to time, and if the pan juices have evaporated, add more water.

Taste the pan juices and adjust the seasoning if needed. Transfer the chicken and pan juices to a serving platter and sprinkle with a bit of parsley. Pass the lemon wedges at the table.

## *Chicken with Eggplant*  POLLO KON BERENJENA

The choice of vegetable is the only variable in this Sephardic recipe served in both Greece and Turkey. The chicken is braised in tomato sauce, either eggplant or okra (see variation) is added, and then the chicken and the vegetable are simmered together. The preparation of each vegetable is quite different, however. I have suggested the addition of garlic and oregano to boost the overall flavor of the dish, though they are not traditional. Serve the dish with rice pilaf or olive oil mashed potatoes. SERVES 6 TO 8

2 pounds eggplants

Salt and freshly ground black pepper

Olive oil for frying

2 broiler chickens, each about 2½ pounds, cut into serving pieces, or about 5 pounds chicken thighs

2 yellow onions, chopped

6 cloves garlic, thinly sliced (optional)

6 tomatoes, peeled, seeded, and chopped (fresh or canned)

1 cup dry red wine

½ cup water

Pinch of sugar

1 teaspoon ground cinnamon

½ teaspoon ground cloves

2 teaspoons dried Greek oregano (optional)

Fresh lemon juice or vinegar, if needed to cut the richness

---

Cut the eggplants into 2-inch pieces, put the pieces in a colander in the sink or over a bowl, sprinkle with salt, and let drain for 30 minutes. (Salted eggplant will absorb less oil during frying.) Rinse well and squeeze dry. Warm 3 tablespoons of the oil in a large sauté pan over medium-high heat. In batches, add the eggplant pieces and fry, turning the pieces and adding more oil as needed, until golden. Using a slotted spoon, transfer to paper towels to drain.

Select a large, heavy sauté pan large enough to hold the chicken and eggplant, place over medium heat, and add ¼ cup oil. While the oil is heating, sprinkle the chicken pieces with salt and pepper. In batches, add the chicken pieces to the hot oil and fry, turning as needed, until golden on all sides, 8 to 10 minutes. Using tongs, transfer the chicken to a plate.

Add the onions to the oil remaining in the pan and cook over medium heat, stirring occasionally, until soft and pale gold, 10 to 12 minutes. Add the garlic and cook for a minute or two. Add the tomatoes, wine, water, sugar, cinnamon, cloves, and oregano and simmer, stirring occasionally, until the tomatoes soften, about 5 minutes. Return the chicken to the pan, turn down the heat to low, cover, and cook for 20 minutes. Add the eggplant pieces, re-cover, and cook until the chicken is tender, 15 to 20 minutes longer.

Taste the sauce, adjust with a bit of lemon juice if needed to cut the richness, and then season with salt and pepper. Serve hot.

OKRA VARIATION: Substitute 2 pounds okra in place of the eggplant and omit the frying step. With a towel, rub the fuzz off of the okra pods. Carefully cut away the stem without cutting into the pod, then place the pods in a bowl. Add 1 cup distilled white vinegar and set aside for 30 minutes. Just before cooking, drain the okra and rinse well. This vinegar bath removes the viscous nature of cooked okra. Proceed as directed, adding the okra to the pan after the chicken has cooked for 20 minutes and then cooking the okra and chicken until tender, 15 to 20 minutes longer.

# Chicken with Eggplant Purée  PİLİÇLİ PATLICAN

*Hünkar beğendi* is a classic Turkish dish of roasted eggplant purée enriched with a creamy béchamel sauce and Parmesan cheese. In the non-kosher kitchen, this rich purée is often spread on a platter surrounded by meat or poultry cooked in tomato sauce. Esin Eden's recipe for *piliçli patlıcan* in *A Family Cookbook* shows how to add richness to the eggplant purée without the dairy. She incorporates the braising juices from the chicken with the roasted eggplant, adding body and concentrated flavors while staying kosher. This same eggplant purée can be served surrounded by little meatballs (lamb or chicken) that have been braised in tomato sauce. SERVES 4

---

3 large globe eggplants

3 lemons

5 tablespoons olive oil

1 fryer chicken, 3½ to 4 pounds, cut into serving pieces

Salt and freshly ground black pepper

1 large yellow onion, grated or finely chopped

3 large tomatoes, peeled, seeded, and chopped

1 cup water or chicken broth

4 or 5 cloves garlic, minced (optional)

4 to 6 tablespoons chopped fresh flat-leaf parsley

---

Roast the eggplants as directed in Master Recipe for Roasted Eggplant (page 27). After removing the seed pockets, it is traditional to drop the pulp into a bowl of water to which you have added the juice of 1 lemon to keep the pulp white. Let stand for 15 minutes, then drain well and squeeze dry. Or simply squeeze the juice of the lemon over the pulp to keep it white. Using a fork, mash the pulp to a thick purée. Do not use a food processor as you want some texture here.

While the eggplants are roasting, warm 3 tablespoons of the oil in a large sauté pan over high heat. While the oil is heating, sprinkle the chicken pieces with salt and pepper. In batches if necessary, add the chicken pieces to the hot oil and fry, turning as needed, until golden on all sides, 8 to 10 minutes. Using tongs, transfer the chicken to a plate.

Add the remaining 2 tablespoons oil to the same pan and place over medium heat. Add the onion and cook, stirring occasionally, until soft and pale gold, 10 to 12 minutes. Add the tomatoes, the juice of the remaining 2 lemons, and the water, return the chicken to the pan, and bring to a boil. Turn down the heat to low, cover, and simmer until the chicken is tender, 30 to 40 minutes.

Transfer the chicken to a platter and keep warm. Add the eggplant purée and the garlic to the pan juices and simmer uncovered, stirring occasionally, for 5 minutes. Taste and adjust the seasoning. If the mixture seems dry, add a few tablespoons water.

To serve, spoon the eggplant purée onto a serving platter. Surround with the chicken and top generously with parsley.

# Moroccan Chicken Tagine with Eggplant and Onion Confit

## ESTOFADO

*Estofado* is a very old Maghrebi dish in which chicken is combined with a twice-cooked sweetened eggplant and onion compote. This recipe comes from *Saveurs de mon enfance* and is a specialty of Tangier and Tétouan. *Estofado* is never going to win any food beauty contests. The finished dish is a rather homely dark brown, but its amazing flavor more than makes up for its plain looks. It is served to break the Yom Kippur fast. The slow cooking renders the sauce rich and creamy and keeps the chicken moist. The dish is fully assembled and reheated slowly in the oven, to be served when the family returns from temple. SERVES 4

2 to 3 pounds globe eggplants, cut crosswise into slices about ⅓ inch thick

Salt and freshly ground black pepper

Olive oil for frying

1 fryer chicken, 3 to 4 pounds, cut into 8 serving pieces, or 8 chicken thighs

½ teaspoon ground cinnamon

3 pounds yellow onions, chopped

½ cup sugar

½ cup water

Preheat the oven to 350°F. Oil a rack and place in a large roasting pan.

Put the eggplant slices in a colander in the sink or over a bowl, sprinkle with salt, let drain for 30 minutes, and then pat dry. (Salted eggplant will absorb less oil during frying.) Warm 3 to 4 tablespoons oil in a large sauté pan over medium-high heat. In batches, add the eggplant slices and fry, turning the slices and adding more oil as needed, until golden. Transfer to paper towels to drain.

Meanwhile, sprinkle the chicken pieces with salt, pepper, and the cinnamon. Arrange the pieces on the oiled rack in the roasting pan, place in the oven, and roast until the chicken is almost done, about 25 minutes.

Warm ½ cup oil in a large sauté pan over low heat. Add the onions, sprinkle with the sugar, season with salt and pepper, and cook, stirring from time to time, until the onions are golden and caramelized. This should take about 20 minutes.

When the chicken is ready, remove it from the oven and turn down the oven to 300°F. In a deep baking dish or Dutch oven, make a layer of one-third of the onion confit and top with one-third of the eggplant. Repeat the eggplant and onion layers twice. Arrange the chicken pieces on top, then pour in the water. Cover and bake until the chicken is tender and the flavors have married, 45 to 60 minutes.

Remove from the oven and skim off and discard any excess oil from the surface. Arrange the chicken on a platter and top with the eggplant and onion.

# Moroccan Chicken Tagine with Sweet Tomato Jam
TAGINE DJEJ MATISHA MESLA

This is an especially rich and delicious dish. The tomatoes cook down to a slightly caramelized thick purée, and their sweetness is heightened by the addition of honey and cinnamon. If you prefer to use bone-in thighs or breasts, rather than a cut-up whole chicken, brown them, add a little broth, cover, and cook until the chicken is almost done, and then add the seasoned tomato mixture and simmer, covered, for about 10 minutes longer. Serve this *tagine* with couscous or rice. For a vegetable accompaniment, consider zucchini or Swiss chard. Broiled eggplant also harmonizes with the sweet and hot flavors. SERVES 4

Olive oil for frying

1 fryer chicken, about 3 pounds, cut into 8 serving pieces

Salt and freshly ground black pepper

1 yellow onion, grated

2 cloves garlic, finely minced

½ teaspoon saffron threads, finely crushed

1 teaspoon ground ginger

2 teaspoons ground cinnamon

1½ cups water or chicken broth

1 can (28 ounces) plum tomatoes, puréed in a food processor

2 tablespoons tomato paste

¼ cup dark honey

3 tablespoons sesame seeds, toasted, or ¼ cup sliced almonds, toasted

Chopped fresh cilantro for garnish (optional)

Warm about 3 tablespoons oil in a heavy sauté pan over high heat. When the oil is hot, in batches, add the chicken and fry, turning as needed and sprinkling with salt and pepper as you go, until golden on all sides, 8 to 10 minutes. Using tongs, transfer the chicken to a plate as it is ready.

Combine the chicken, onion, garlic, saffron, ginger, 1 teaspoon of the cinnamon, and the water in a stew pot and bring to a boil over medium heat. Turn down the heat to low, cover, and simmer for 15 minutes. Add the puréed tomatoes, tomato paste, and a little salt and simmer uncovered, turning the chicken pieces often in the sauce, until the chicken is tender, about 15 minutes longer.

Transfer the chicken to a platter and keep warm. Raise the heat to high and reduce the sauce, stirring often to prevent scorching, until it is thick and the oil starts to rise to the surface. Add the honey and the remaining 1 teaspoon cinnamon and cook for a few minutes. Return the chicken to the sauce, turn to coat, and reheat gently. Transfer the chicken and sauce to a platter, sprinkle with the sesame seeds and cilantro, and serve.

## Turkey Scallops with Parsley and Onion
### SCALOPPINE DI TACCHINO DI REBECCA

This dish is named after Rebecca, the ubiquitous Jewish housewife. Economical and low-fat sliced turkey breast and boneless chicken breasts have become the alternative to the more costly veal scaloppine. This authentic Italian turkey scaloppine was way ahead of the trend. A similar dish made with veal is also named after Rebecca. SERVES 3 OR 4

1 pound boneless turkey breast, sliced ⅔ inch thick, or boneless, skinless chicken breast halves

All-purpose flour for coating

Salt and freshly ground black pepper

2 tablespoons olive oil

1 cup dry white wine

3 tablespoons chopped fresh flat-leaf parsley

3 tablespoons chopped green onions, including green tops

Juice of 1 lemon

One at a time, place the turkey slices or chicken breasts between 2 sheets of plastic wrap and pound to a uniform thickness of about ⅓ inch. Do not pound them too thinly or the meat will tear. Spread some flour on a plate and season with salt and pepper. One at a time, dip the pounded slices in the seasoned flour, coating both sides and tapping off the excess.

Warm the oil in a large sauté pan over medium-high heat. Add the scallops and sauté, turning once, until golden and cooked through, about 6 minutes total. Transfer to a platter and keep warm.

Add the wine to the pan over medium-high heat and let it reduce a bit, scraping up any brown bits on the pan bottom. Add the parsley, green onions, and lemon juice and cook for 3 to 4 minutes to let the flavors blend. Pour the sauce over the scallops and serve at once.

## Cooked Chicken on a Bed of Pita Bread   MUSAKHAN

This dish has Palestinian and Arabic roots. It resembles *fatteh,* a dish popular in Lebanon and elsewhere in the Levant, though without the yogurt that traditionally accompanies it. This is a great recipe if you have leftover roast chicken—or even roast turkey after Thanksgiving. You can use any type of flatbread in place of the pita, including naan. Although yogurt is not permitted because of kosher laws, you can drizzle the finished dish with tahini sauce (page 112) just before serving. SERVES 4

| ½ cup olive oil | ½ cup pine nuts, toasted |
|---|---|
| 4 large yellow or red onions, chopped or sliced | 4 pita breads, or enough naan or lavash to line a large sheet pan |
| ½ teaspoon ground allspice | About 6 cups torn cooked chicken meat, in about 2-inch pieces (from a 4- to 5-pound roasted or boiled chicken) |
| ½ teaspoon ground cardamom | |
| 2 to 4 tablespoons ground sumac | |
| Salt and freshly ground black pepper | ½ cup chicken broth |

Warm the oil in a large sauté pan over low heat. Add the onions, season with the allspice, cardamom, 2 tablespoons of the sumac, and salt and pepper to taste and mix well. Cook slowly, stirring occasionally, until the onions are very soft and melting. This will take at least 30 minutes. Stir in half of the pine nuts and more sumac to taste. (The onions can be prepared a day in advance, covered, and refrigerated.)

Preheat the oven to 400°F.

Divide the onion mixture in half. Oil a large sheet pan or baking pan and arrange the pita rounds in a single layer on the prepared pan. Top the breads with half of the onion mixture. Cover the onion mixture evenly with the chicken, then cover the chicken with the remaining onion mixture. Drizzle with the broth. If the onions and chicken are cold when you assemble the dish, cover it with foil and bake for 20 minutes to heat through, then remove the foil so the dish can brown. If the onions and chicken are not cold, bake uncovered until the chicken is heated through and onions are golden brown, 25 to 30 minutes. Top with the remaining pine nuts. Serve hot.

VARIATION: Preheat the oven to 450°F. Tear the bread into small pieces and use two-thirds of it to line the bottom of the oiled sheet pan. Top with half of the onion mixture, followed by the chicken, and then the remaining onion mixture. Scatter the remaining torn bread evenly over the top and drizzle with olive oil. Bake uncovered until crusty and golden, about 30 minutes. If the bread on top darkens too much before everything is heated through, cover the pan with foil.

## *Chicken Meatballs*  KEFTAS DE GAYNA

Although many people think of meatballs as being made only with meat, Sephardic Jews are equally enamored of chicken "meatballs." In Italy, chicken balls made with matzo meal instead of bread are added to chicken broth for Passover. The Turkish touch in this recipe from *La table juive* is the ground almonds, which add a fragrant sweetness to the mild chicken. I like to play up this little exoticism by adding a pinch or two of cinnamon or nutmeg. Nicholas Stavroulakis adds 8 ounces ground beef to the chicken in a Greek Sephardic recipe called *keftikes de poyo*. Serve the meatballs with rice. SERVES 4

MEATBALLS

1 pound ground chicken (breast or thigh meat)

1 cup blanched almonds, ground

1 small slice coarse country bread, crust removed, soaked in water, and squeezed dry, to yield about ¼ cup crumbs (or ¼ cup matzo meal for Passover)

1 egg, lightly beaten

2 teaspoons salt

½ teaspoon freshly ground black pepper

½ teaspoon ground cinnamon or freshly grated nutmeg (optional)

2 to 3 cups chicken broth

2 eggs

Juice of 2 lemons

4 to 6 tablespoons chopped fresh dill or flat-leaf parsley

To make the meatballs, in a bowl, combine the chicken, almonds, bread, egg, salt, pepper, and cinnamon and mix well with your hands.

Bring the broth to a boil in a wide saucepan over medium heat. Turn down the heat until the broth is at a simmer. Form a 1-inch ball of the chicken mixture, add to the broth, and cook through, then taste and adjust the seasoning of the remaining mixture if needed. Form the mixture into 1-inch balls, add to the simmering broth, cover, and poach until cooked through, 10 to 15 minutes.

In a bowl, beat together the eggs and lemon juice until very frothy. Gradually whisk about ½ cup of the hot broth into the eggs to temper them. Pour the egg mixture into the pan, stir well, and simmer over very low heat for 1 to 2 minutes to thicken. Serve hot, sprinkled with the dill.

VARIATION: *Chicken Meatballs with Braised Garlic after Suzy David (Albóndigas kon Ajo):* Make the meatballs as directed, omitting the almonds and adding 2 tablespoons chopped fresh dill. Peel the cloves from 1 large head garlic. In a wide saucepan, bring to a simmer only 1 cup chicken broth (or water) over medium heat, add the garlic cloves, and simmer until tender, 15 to 20 minutes. Add the meatballs, turn down the heat to low, and simmer until the meatballs are cooked through, about 20 minutes. Omit the egg–lemon juice addition. Add 2 tablespoons chopped fresh dill and the juice of 1 lemon to the pan and heat through. Taste and adjust the seasoning.

## *The Bride's Chicken Meatballs* DAR LAARCH

In Tunisia, Daisy Taieb's family served chicken meatballs perfumed with dried rose petals to break the fast after Yom Kippur. These meatballs, also known as *boulettes au poulet dites la mariée,* can be a wonderful weeknight supper. You can even make them a day in advance and reheat them gently. Breast meat is traditional for the balls, but you can use thigh meat. If you cannot find dried rose petals, the chicken balls will still be delicious. Serve with couscous or rice. SERVES 6 TO 8

**MEATBALLS**

2 pounds ground chicken (breast or thigh meat)

2 large yellow onions, minced

¼ cup chopped fresh flat-leaf parsley

6 tablespoons chopped fresh cilantro

2 cloves garlic, minced

4 slices coarse country bread, each 1 inch thick, crusts removed, soaked in water, and squeezed dry

3 to 4 teaspoons crushed dried rose petals (optional)

Big pinch of ground turmeric or saffron threads

Freshly grated nutmeg

2 teaspoons salt

Freshly ground black pepper

2 eggs

**SAUCE**

2 tablespoons olive oil

4 large ripe tomatoes, peeled, seeded, and chopped (about 2 cups; canned tomatoes are acceptable)

2 cloves garlic, chopped

1 bay leaf

½ teaspoon ground turmeric, or ¼ teaspoon saffron threads

Salt and freshly ground black pepper

To make the meatballs, in a large bowl, combine the chicken, onions, parsley, cilantro, garlic, bread, rose petals, turmeric, lots of nutmeg, salt, pepper, and eggs and knead with your hands until the mixture holds together. Shape a small egg-shaped meatball of the mixture, poach it in lightly salted water until cooked through, then taste and adjust the seasoning of the remaining mixture if needed. Shape the mixture into egg-shaped meatballs about 2 inches long and reserve.

To make the sauce, warm the oil in a large sauté pan over medium-high heat. Add the tomatoes, garlic, bay leaf, turmeric, and water to a depth of about 2 inches and cook for 5 minutes. Season with salt and pepper. Add the meatballs, turn down the heat to low, cover, and poach until cooked through, 20 to 30 minutes. If you would like the meatballs to have a little color, you can slip them under a preheated broiler or into a hot oven (make sure the pan is oven-safe). Serve hot.

## Chicken Fricassee with Chicken Meatballs
POLLO CON POLPETTE E SEDANO

When I was growing up in New York, chicken fricassee with little beef meatballs was part of the cooking repertory of many Jewish families. You can imagine my surprise when I found this recipe in Donatella Limentani Pavoncello's charming Roman Jewish cookbook, *Dal 1880 ad oggi: La cucina ebraica della mia famiglia.* It's an Italian fricassee of chicken called *ngozzamodi di pollo con polpette* (the *ngozzamodi* refer to bone-in chicken pieces; *ozza* means "bone"), but the meatballs (*polpette*) are made with ground chicken. For economy, many versions of this recipe omit the chicken pieces and use chicken balls.

You can even use ground turkey in place of the ground chicken. Celery is a favorite vegetable of the Romans, and I've increased it a bit from the original recipe. Serve the chicken and meatballs with rice or olive oil mashed potatoes and peas. SERVES 4 TO 6

MEATBALLS

1 pound ground chicken breast meat

½ to ¾ cup fresh bread crumbs, or as needed to bind, soaked in ½ cup dry white wine

2 eggs, lightly beaten

1 teaspoon ground cinnamon

1 teaspoon salt

½ teaspoon freshly ground black pepper

Chicken broth, as needed

6 to 8 tablespoons olive oil, or as needed

1 broiler chicken, 2½ pounds, cut into 8 serving pieces, or 6 chicken thighs

Salt and freshly ground black pepper

2 yellow onions, chopped

3 cloves garlic, minced

1 large head celery, ribs separated and cut into 2-inch lengths

2 to 3 cups peeled, seeded, and diced ripe tomatoes

¼ cup chopped fresh flat-leaf parsley

To make the meatballs, in a bowl, combine the chicken, bread crumbs and wine, eggs, cinnamon, salt, and pepper and mix gently but thoroughly. Shape a single marble-size meatball of the mixture, poach it in a little broth until cooked through, then taste and adjust the seasoning of the remaining mixture if needed. Shape the mixture into marble-size balls and refrigerate until needed.

Pour the oil to a depth of ¼ inch into a wide, deep sauté pan or Dutch oven and place over high heat. While the oil is heating, season the chicken with salt and pepper. Add the chicken pieces to the hot oil and fry, turning as needed, until browned on all sides. Using tongs, transfer the chicken to a plate.

Add the onions to the fat remaining in the pan, turn down the heat to low, and cook, stirring occasionally, until translucent and tender, 8 to 10 minutes. Add the garlic, celery, and tomatoes and simmer for 5 minutes. Add the browned chicken, cover, and simmer over low heat for 20 minutes.

Carefully distribute the chicken meatballs among the chicken pieces, pushing them down into the pan juices. Add a little broth if the chicken has not given off enough liquid for poaching the meatballs. Re-cover the pan and poach until the chicken balls are cooked through and the chicken is tender, about 15 minutes. Taste the pan juices and adjust the seasoning if needed.

Transfer the chicken pieces, meatballs, celery, and pan juices to a deep platter and sprinkle with the parsley. Serve at once.

VARIATION: *With Egg and Lemon Juice:* Omit the tomatoes and finish the dish with eggs and lemon juice (see Chicken Meatballs, page 287).

# Chicken Meat Loaf   POLPETTONE DI POLLO

This is not exactly a meat loaf. It more closely resembles a giant chicken burger but is served chilled. Some recipes add ground veal to the chicken or use turkey instead of chicken. Another variation stuffs the mixture into a turkey-neck skin. In *La cucina nella tradizione ebraica,* hard-boiled eggs and chopped pistachios are added to the ground chicken mixture, which is stuffed into a boned chicken and then poached in the manner of a galantine. In yet another version, a turkey is deboned and stuffed in the same manner. These are a lot more work and are obviously holiday fare.

Here is my simple everyday version, based on a recipe from Donatella Limentani Pavoncello. She doesn't have pistachios in her version, but they add wonderful texture and another dimension of flavor to what is a rather bland dish. Be sure to test for seasoning by poaching a little of the chicken mixture in simmering water. Any leftover *polpettone* makes a great sandwich with a little lemony mayonnaise and lettuce. SERVES 6 TO 8

---

1 pound ground chicken (breast or thigh meat)

¾ cup fresh bread crumbs, or as needed to bind

2 eggs, lightly beaten

1 teaspoon salt

½ teaspoon white or black pepper, preferably freshly ground

½ teaspoon ground cinnamon or freshly grated nutmeg

¼ cup chopped toasted pistachio nuts (optional)

Olive oil for browning

½ cup dry white wine or Marsala

3 small carrots, peeled and chopped

About 6 cups chicken broth or water, heated

Mayonnaise (page 231), flavored with grated lemon zest and capers or herbs, for serving

---

In a large bowl, combine the chicken, bread crumbs, eggs, salt, pepper, cinnamon, and pistachios and mix gently but thoroughly. Pinch off a small nugget of the mixture, poach in simmering water until cooked through, and taste and adjust the seasoning if needed. Shape the mixture into a single longish loaf or into 2 or 3 small loaf-like patties.

It's a bit tricky to brown the large loaf, but it can be done using wide fish spatulas to turn it. The smaller loaves are easier to work with. Film a large, heavy sauté pan with oil and place over medium-high heat. When the oil is hot, add the single loaf and turn as needed to brown on all sides, shaking the pan from time to time to prevent sticking. If you have made the smaller loaf-like patties, turn them once to brown on both sides. Set the loaf or patties aside on a platter. Pour the wine into the pan and deglaze it, scraping up any brown bits on the pan bottom. Return the loaf or patties to the pan and add the carrots and the broth to cover. Bring to a simmer, cover, adjust the heat to maintain a gentle simmer, and cook until all of the liquid has been absorbed and the chicken is tender, glazed, and golden, about 30 minutes.

Remove from the heat, transfer to a platter, and let cool; then cover and refrigerate until well chilled, about 2 hours. To serve, cut the chilled loaf or patties into thin slices. Serve with the mayonnaise.

Meat

I N KEEPING WITH THE TRADITIONAL MEDITERRANEAN DIET followed by everyone who lived in the region, meat as a main course appeared on Jewish tables only at special-occasion meals, such as the Sabbath, holidays, and family celebrations. Thus, most of the recipes in this chapter were not everyday fare. But because meat was not part of the daily regimen, the recipes for celebratory family favorites were often written down, so that no crucial ingredient would be forgotten.

As described in the introduction, only animals that chew their cud and have cloven hooves can be consumed. That means that pork, rabbit, horse, and game are forbidden. The slaughtering of any animal must always be carried out according to Jewish rituals that prescribe careful bleeding and then, to remove all traces of blood, the meat is soaked in cold water for an hour, sprinkled with kosher salt, left to stand for another hour, and then rinsed three times before cooking. Not surprisingly, these steps tend to dry out the meat, so fattier cuts are generally preferred. Liver can escape this purging if it is broiled or flame-seared.

Following the Jewish tradition of thrift, bits and pieces of cooked meat were used to flavor many different kinds of dishes, such as soups, pastas, and some vegetable stews. A vast assortment of recipes for ground beef and lamb also exists. But hearty braises predominated for Sabbath meals. Because lighting a fire or working on the Sabbath was forbidden, housewives would put a one-pot braise or stew in a very low oven or in the oven of a local baker before sundown on Friday and keep it there until the next day, ensuring a hearty meal in a bowl for Saturday lunch.

Every country seems to have a signature long-simmered one-pot dish of meats and vegetables that is eaten in a big bowl at one time or is enjoyed in courses, with the meats and vegetables following the broth or soup. In Ashkenazi Jewish cooking, it is called *cholent,* probably coming from the Spanish *escallento,* which means "to keep warm." In France, it is cassoulet. For the Sephardim, it can be a *hamin* (the word for "oven"), or, for the Maghrebi and Judeo-Arabic cultures, *adafina* or *d'fina.*

The Spanish and Portuguese *cocido* is based on the Moroccan *adafina,* a dish of beans, meat, and sometimes eggs assembled in a heavy pot and put in a low oven to simmer all night for the Sabbath meal. *Sopa de avikas,* or white beans with beef, is the classic. The importance of *cocido* and beans in the Sephardic kitchen is revealed in the Spanish word *judía,* which means both "bean" and "Jewess." In Spain, the *cocido* was eventually used by the Inquisition as a litmus test of faith for conversos. Confronted with a *cocido* prepared with lard or pork, true conversos would eat it, but those who refused revealed their continued adherence to the Jewish faith.

## BEEF AND VEAL

# The Sabbath One-Pot Stew    D'FINA

The North African *d'fina* is a typical Sabbath stew. Joëlle Bahloul, in her wonderful book *The Architecture of Memory,* tells of Jewish life in Algeria. Of *d'fina* she says, "It is described as the materialization of the slow pace of Sabbath time. Its flavor and thick consistency are presented as the gustatory representation of Sabbath time in abeyance."

The name comes from the Arabic *dfi'ne,* which means "buried"; in this case, the cooking pot was buried in the fireplace ashes. Eggs in their shells are also buried in the stew, much like *hamin* eggs (page 93) and resulting in the same creamy texture. *D'fina* can be served at Passover, as well. In that case, the chickpeas can be replaced with fresh favas or peas, which are just coming into season. And for breaking the fast at Yom Kippur, the *d'fina* is made with chicken, usually stuffed with a meat mixture sweetened with cinnamon and almonds.

In Morocco, this dish is usually called *dafina* or *adafina,* but it becomes a *skhina* (which means "hot") when dates, sweet potatoes, roasted barley or rice, and sometimes a meat loaf seasoned with sweet spices are added to the pot and cooked along with the basic stew of meat, chickpeas, potatoes, and eggs (see variation). Leftovers are eaten at room temperature. On a visit to Morocco, I was invited to a reception given by the American consul. He and his wife, both of them Jewish, served a Moroccan Jewish banquet. The *skhina* with barley was the star. SERVES 8

2 tablespoons olive oil

2 large yellow onions, chopped

6 cloves garlic, minced

3 to 4 pounds well-marbled stewing beef, such as boneless short ribs, chuck, or brisket, cut into 1½- to 2-inch pieces

6 to 8 boiling potatoes, peeled and then halved if large

1½ cups dried chickpeas, picked over, soaked in water to cover overnight in the refrigerator, drained, and rinsed

8 eggs in the shell

1 teaspoon ground ginger

1 teaspoon ground allspice

Salt and freshly ground black pepper

Water or beef broth, to cover

Preheat the oven to 225° to 250°F, or to 300°F for quicker cooking.

Warm the oil in a stew pot over medium heat. Add the onions and cook, stirring occasionally, until pale gold, 15 to 20 minutes. Add the garlic, beef, potatoes, chickpeas, eggs, ginger, and allspice and season with salt and pepper. Pour in water to cover and bring to a boil over medium-high heat. Remove from the heat, cover, and place in the 225° to 250°F oven for 8 hours or in the 300°F oven for 4 to 5 hours. When the stew is ready, the meat, chickpeas, and potatoes will all be tender. (You can also simmer the stew over very low heat on the stove top or in a slow cooker.)

Just before serving, remove the eggs from the stew, peel them, and return them to the stew. Serve hot.

VARIATION:    *Moroccan Skhina:* Add 12 pitted dates or dried apricots to the stew when you add the liquid, then assemble the following cheesecloth packets and place them among the meat and chickpeas:

For the sweet potatoes, peel 1 pound sweet potatoes, cut into large chunks, and rub with a paste of ½ cup ground almonds, 3 tablespoons sugar, ½ teaspoon ground cinnamon, a pinch of ground cloves, and 1 egg, beaten. Wrap in cheesecloth and tie securely.

For the barley, cracked wheat, freekeh, or rice, rinse 2 cups of the grain, then mix with 6 cloves garlic, 1 teaspoon sweet paprika, ½ teaspoon cayenne pepper, 1 teaspoon ground cumin, and ⅓ cup olive oil. Wrap in cheesecloth and tie securely.

For the meat loaf, combine 12 ounces ground beef (not lean), ½ cup fresh bread crumbs, ½ teaspoon ground mace or freshly grated nutmeg, ¼ cup chopped fresh flat-leaf parsley, 2 tablespoons olive oil, and 2 eggs, lightly beaten. Mix well, season with salt and freshly ground black pepper, and form into a long loaf. Wrap in cheesecloth and tie the ends securely.

Cook as directed. One hour before serving, uncover the pot so that the stew can take on some color. To serve, unwrap the sweet potatoes, grain, and meat loaf and serve along with the stew.

# *Sephardic Meat and Bean Stew*    LA LOUBIA

In his book *The Cross and the Pear Tree,* Victor Perera reminisces about a Sabbath dinner cooked by his mother: "Mother had made her traditional hamin, eggs and a shank of beef, all cooked with white beans. The pleasant cooking smells would waft all over the house. . . . After the meal we would all sing the lovely and unusual Sabbath melodies in Spanish."

Called *avikas* in Salonika, this classic Sabbath dish resembles the Spanish *cocido* and the French cassoulet because of its mix of meat and sausage with beans. An Algerian version uses only veal shanks, a whole head of garlic, sometimes with tomatoes, sometimes not, and sweet paprika. In the Algerian city of Constantine, cooks add a meat loaf mixture called *coclo.* The Syrian and Egyptian versions, called *lubiya,* use black-eyed peas or white beans. I added the orange zest, rather than sugar, to sweeten the tomato element. If you like, you can cook the stew in a 300°F oven for the same amount of time. SERVES 4

3 tablespoons olive oil

1 yellow onion, chopped

3 cloves garlic, smashed

2 large ripe tomatoes, peeled, seeded, and chopped (about 1 cup; canned tomatoes are acceptable)

2 tablespoons chopped fresh flat-leaf parsley

1 rounded cup dried white beans, picked over, soaked in water to cover overnight, drained, and rinsed

1½ pounds well-marbled stewing beef,

such as boneless short ribs, chuck, or brisket, cut into 1½- to 2-inch pieces

2 small veal shanks, halved crosswise

Salt and freshly ground black pepper

½ cup tomato purée

Grated zest of 1 orange

2 teaspoons ground toasted cumin seeds

1 teaspoon ground allspice, for a Syrian version (optional)

2 beef or chicken sausages, about 8 ounces total, cut into 1- to 2-inch chunks (optional)

Warm the oil in a stew pot over medium heat. Add the onion and cook, stirring occasionally, until translucent and tender, 8 to 10 minutes. Add the garlic, cook for a few minutes, and then add the tomatoes and parsley and mix well. Add the beans, stir to mix, and arrange the beef pieces and veal shanks on top. Sprinkle with salt and pepper and add just enough water to cover. Cover and cook over low heat until the meat is nearly tender, 1½ to 2 hours.

Add the tomato purée, orange zest, cumin, and allspice, mix well, and then add the sausages. Simmer, uncovered, until all of the fat rises to the surface, about 30 minutes longer. Serve hot.

## Tunisian Bean and Beef Stew with Spinach Essence  T'FINA PKAILA

In Tunisia, *t'fina pkaila,* also known as *t'fina d'épinards,* is served during Rosh Hashanah. This recipe is based on one served at the home of Daisy Taieb, author of *Les fêtes juives à Tunis racontées à mes filles.* After the meat has cooked for an hour, some families add *osbane,* a spicy meat loaf stuffed in an intestine like the Ashkenazi kishka. Others add a meat loaf in the manner of the *skhina* (see variation, page 297). The Taieb family serves this stew with homemade semolina bread rather than couscous or rice. In Claudia Roden's versions of this recipe, she wilts the spinach in oil; other cooks wilt it dry and cook it down without oil. SERVES 6

2½ pounds spinach, stemmed

1 bunch fresh cilantro

1 rounded cup dried white beans, picked over, soaked in water to cover overnight, drained, and rinsed

2 small veal shanks, halved crosswise

1½ pounds well-marbled stewing beef, such as boneless short ribs, chuck, or brisket, cut into 2-inch pieces

4 to 6 cloves garlic

1 yellow onion, minced

1 cinnamon stick

1 teaspoon harissa, homemade (page 355) or store-bought

3 tablespoons chopped fresh dill

3 tablespoons chopped fresh mint, or 1 tablespoon dried mint

Rinse the spinach and cilantro, place in a large saucepan, and wilt over medium-low heat in the rinsing water clinging to the leaves. Drain well, transfer to a stew pot, place over medium heat, and stir with a wooden spoon until dry and browned. Add the beans, veal shanks, beef, garlic, onion, cinnamon stick, harissa, dill, mint, and water to cover. Bring to a boil, turn down the heat to low, cover, and simmer until the liquid has been absorbed and the oil has risen to the top, about 3 hours. If the pot seems too dry before the dish is ready, add a little water. Serve hot.

VARIATION: Rabbi Robert Sternberg in *The Sephardic Kitchen* refers to *pkaila* as a mixture of spinach and herbs that can be prepared ahead of time, like an herb jam. His version contains spinach, cilantro, parsley, mint, and green onions, all of which are chopped and wilted in oil with chopped onion and minced garlic. The mixture is then puréed in a blender or food processor, transferred to a jar, and topped with a thin layer of olive oil before it is capped. It can be stored in the refrigerator for a few weeks and then spooned into a stew as needed.

## *Persian Beef Stew Smothered in Green Herbs* GHORMEH SABZI

This is one of the most famous and also most beloved of all the Persian stews. If you find that the greens turn too dark after cooking for a half hour, add a cup of wilted chopped spinach just before serving to brighten the look of the dish. If you cannot find the Omani limes, add a few tablespoons fresh lime or lemon juice to the final sauce. Serve with Persian Rice (page 149). SERVES 4 TO 6

Olive oil for frying

2 pounds well-marbled stewing beef, such as boneless short ribs, chuck, or brisket, cut into 2-inch pieces

2 large yellow onions, chopped

1 teaspoon ground turmeric

Salt and freshly ground black pepper

½ cup dried red kidney beans, picked over, soaked in water to cover overnight, drained, and rinsed

4 or 5 dried Omani limes, rinsed and struck with a meat pounder so they crack (optional)

5 cups hot water

2 cups chopped fresh flat-leaf parsley

2 cups chopped fresh cilantro

1 cup chopped fresh dill

1 cup chopped celery leaves

1 bunch green onions, including green tops, chopped

1 cup chopped spinach

Fresh lemon juice

Warm 4 tablespoons oil in a large sauté pan over high heat. In batches, add the beef pieces and brown well on all sides. Using tongs, transfer to a plate. Warm 2 tablespoons oil in a stew pot over medium heat. Add the onions and cook, stirring occasionally, until translucent and tender, 8 to 10 minutes. Add the turmeric, season with salt and pepper, and stir well, then add the meat, beans, limes, and water. Bring to a boil, turn down the heat to low, cover, and cook until the meat is almost tender, about 1½ hours.

Wipe out the sauté pan, return it to medium heat, and add 3 to 4 tablespoons oil. Add the parsley, cilantro, dill, celery leaves, green onions, and spinach and cook, stirring and tossing as needed, until everything has wilted and become shiny, 5 to 8 minutes. Season the greens with salt and add to the meat. Mix well, cover, and simmer for 20 to 30 minutes longer. Remove and discard the limes, then taste the pan juices and add lemon juice to taste and more salt if needed. Serve hot.

## *Persian Beef Stew with Prunes and Carrots*  KHORESH-E HAVIJ VA ALU

A Persian *khoresh* is a cross between a stew and a sauce, so sometimes the meat is cut into 1-inch pieces, smaller than for a regular stew. In this dish, the carrots and prunes have equal presence. I often use blood orange juice for its color and perfume, plus blood oranges are one of the joys of our winter season. This dish can be made a day ahead of serving, but the sauce will thicken as it sits. Save the prune soaking liquid to add when reheating, so the prunes don't scorch. Serve with rice pilaf or with Persian Rice (page 149). SERVES 4 TO 6

1 teaspoon ground cinnamon

½ teaspoon ground cardamom

2 teaspoons salt

½ teaspoon freshly ground black pepper

6 tablespoons olive oil

2 pounds stewing beef, such as boneless short ribs, brisket, or chuck, cut into 1-inch pieces

1½ cups beef broth

½ teaspoon saffron threads, finely crushed and steeped in ¼ cup hot water

2 large yellow onions, chopped

1 pound carrots, peeled and cut into 1-inch pieces

1 cup fresh orange juice, or ⅔ cup fresh orange juice and ⅓ cup fresh lemon juice

1 pound pitted prunes, plumped in hot water, drained, and water reserved

2 tablespoons pomegranate molasses, if needed for balance

In a small bowl, combine the cinnamon, cardamom, salt, and pepper and mix well.

Warm 3 tablespoons of the oil in a large sauté pan over medium-high heat. In batches, add the beef pieces and brown well on all sides, sprinkling them with about half of the spice mixture. Using tongs, transfer to a plate. Raise the heat to high, add the broth and the saffron infusion, and deglaze the pan, stirring to dislodge any brown bits on the pan bottom. Set aside off the heat.

Warm the remaining 3 tablespoons oil in a stew pot over medium heat. Add the onions and cook, stirring occasionally, until soft and pale gold, 10 to 15 minutes. Stir the remaining spice mixture into the onions. Add the meat and the contents of the sauté pan to the onions, stir well, and bring to a boil over high heat. Turn down the heat to low, cover, and simmer for 1 hour. Add the carrots, citrus juice, and prunes and simmer until the meat and carrots are tender, about 30 minutes longer.

Taste and adjust the seasoning if needed. It may need a bit of lemon juice or pomegranate molasses for balance or a bit more salt. If the sauce is too thick, add some of the prune soaking water. Serve hot.

## *Imperial Couscous*   COUSCOUS IMPERIAL

Beef, lamb, or chicken can be used for this couscous. This version is a cross between a recipe from Tangier and one from Fez. Algerian cooks prefer beef or chicken for their couscous, but not lamb, and sometimes beef and chicken are used together. You can also replace the meat or poultry with meatballs (see basic recipe on page 333; reduce the initial cooking to a half hour). On Rosh Hashanah, cooked quinces are added along with the raisins to increase the sweetness for the New Year. If served on the night before Passover, fresh favas might be added. When this same stew is served with barley couscous, the dish is called *tchicha,* and when served with new wheat (freekeh), it is called *azenbo.* In other words, if the grain changes, the name changes, too. SERVES 6 TO 8

1 cup dried chickpeas, picked over, soaked in water to cover overnight in the refrigerator, drained, and rinsed

2 pounds stewing beef (such as boneless short ribs, chuck, or brisket) or lamb (such as shoulder), cut into 2-inch pieces, or a mixture of beef or lamb and bone-in chicken pieces

2 large yellow onions, chopped

2 teaspoons salt

2 teaspoons freshly ground black pepper

2 teaspoons ground ginger

½ teaspoon saffron threads, finely crushed and steeped in ¼ cup hot water or meat or poultry broth

¼ cup olive oil

6 large or 12 small carrots, peeled and cut into 1½-inch chunks

3 large or 6 small turnips, peeled and quartered or cut into 1½-inch chunks

1-pound piece winter squash, such as kabocha or butternut, peeled and cut into 1½- to 2-inch chunks

6 small zucchini, cut into 2-inch lengths

3 ripe tomatoes, peeled, seeded, and chopped

½ cup golden raisins

Couscous (page 158)

½ cup almonds, toasted (optional)

Honey (optional)

Harissa, homemade (page 355) or store-bought, for serving

In a saucepan, combine the chickpeas with water to cover by 3 inches and bring to a boil over high heat. Turn down the heat to low, cover, and simmer until tender, 45 to 60 minutes. Drain and reserve.

Put the meat, onions, salt, pepper, ginger, saffron infusion, and oil in a stew pot and turn the ingredients in the oil to coat evenly. Add water to cover and bring to a boil over high heat. Turn down the heat to low, cover, and simmer for 1 hour if using beef or lamb. If you opt for a mixture of meat and chicken, add the chicken after the first 30 minutes. Add the reserved chickpeas, carrots, turnips, and winter squash and cook for 30 minutes longer. Add the zucchini, tomatoes, and raisins, cover, and cook until all of the vegetables and the meat are tender, about 30 minutes longer.

Pile the couscous on a platter. Using a slotted spoon, lift the meat and vegetables from the stew pot and arrange them around the couscous, or make a well in the center of the couscous and put them in the well. Top with the almonds. Taste the pan juices and adjust the seasoning, adding a little honey if you like. Scoop out 1 cup of the pan juices and mix with harissa to taste. Spoon the remaining juices over the meat and vegetables. Serve at once and pass the harissa at the table.

## *Veal and Spinach Stew with Egg and Lemon*
TERNERA Y ESPINACA AVGOLEMONO

Served on the Sabbath, this Sephardic Greek stew from Gilda Angel has a particularly velvety texture. Suzy David has a version of this recipe that uses lamb instead of veal and omits the egg and lemon. Tunisian Jews also pair veal and spinach, but they add white beans and omit the egg and lemon, as well. Serve this stew with rice.

SERVES 8

½ cup olive oil, or as needed

3 pounds boneless veal shoulder or shank meat, cut into 1½-inch pieces

2 yellow onions, chopped

Salt and freshly ground black pepper

Freshly grated nutmeg (optional)

1½ to 2 cups water or meat broth, or as needed

2 pounds spinach, stemmed, blanched, chopped, and squeezed dry, or 2 packages (10 ounces each) frozen chopped spinach, thawed and squeezed dry

3 eggs

Juice of 2 lemons

Select a large stew pot or very wide, deep sauté pan with a tight-fitting lid, add the oil, and place over high heat. In batches, add the veal pieces and brown well on all sides. Using tongs, transfer the veal to a plate.

Add some oil to the pan if none remains (veal does not release any fat and may absorb all of the oil in the pan), turn down the heat to medium, add the onions, and cook, stirring occasionally, until translucent and tender, 8 to 10 minutes. Return the veal to the pan, season with salt, pepper, and nutmeg, and pour in 1½ cups of the water. Bring to a boil, turn down the heat to very low, cover, and simmer for about 1 hour. Check after 35 to 40 minutes and add more water if the liquid has evaporated, shaking or stirring the pan well to dislodge any brown bits and meat juices. (You can prepare the stew up to this point and refrigerate for up to a day and then reheat gently over low heat.) Add the spinach, re-cover, and cook until the meat is tender, 15 to 20 minutes longer.

In a bowl, beat together the eggs and lemon juice until very frothy. Gradually whisk in about ½ cup of the hot stew liquid to temper the eggs. Pour the egg mixture into the pan and stir well over very low heat for a minute or two (or shake the pan back and forth) until the liquid thickens, then serve.

## Sautéed Veal Rolls INVOLTINI DI VITELLO

Sometimes Italian veal rolls are stuffed with the mixture used for meatballs (page 328), but here I have used a milder filling inspired by a recipe in Giuliana Ascoli Vitali-Norsa's *La cucina nella tradizione ebraica*. Potatoes are the usual accompaniment to veal rolls (olive oil mashed potatoes are especially good), but polenta or rice would work, as well. SERVES 4

8 veal scallops (about 1 pound total weight)

8 ounces ground veal

¼ cup fresh bread crumbs, soaked in water and squeezed dry

1 egg, lightly beaten

Salt and freshly ground black pepper

Extra virgin olive oil for frying

1 cup dry white wine

1½ cups beef, veal, or chicken broth, or as needed

Place each veal scallop between 2 sheets of plastic wrap and pound to an even thickness of ⅓ inch. In a bowl, combine the ground veal, bread crumbs, and egg and season with salt and pepper. Spread the ground meat mixture on the veal scallops, dividing it evenly. Roll up each scallop and skewer closed with a toothpick or tie with kitchen string.

Film a large, heavy sauté pan with oil and warm over high heat. Add the veal rolls and brown well on all sides. Add the wine and cook until it evaporates. Add the broth to cover, turn down the heat to low, cover, and simmer until the filling is cooked through, about 20 minutes.

Transfer the rolls to a platter and remove the toothpicks or snip the strings. Keep warm. Raise the heat and reduce the pan juices until slightly thickened. Spoon the pan juices over the veal rolls and serve at once.

## Tongue with Olive Sauce LINGUA DI MANZO CON LE OLIVE

You can use a fresh or a corned tongue here. If you use the latter, bring it to a boil in water to cover, drain, and then re-cover with fresh water to cook. This step will rid the tongue of excess salt. Serve the tongue slices with the olive sauce or with Salsa Verde (page 229). SERVES 6 TO 8

1 beef tongue, about 3 pounds, well scrubbed

2 yellow onions, peeled but left whole

1 large carrot, peeled

3 celery ribs with leaves

12 black peppercorns

1 bay leaf

6 coriander seeds

Boiling water to cover

OLIVE SAUCE

3 tablespoons olive oil

2 cloves garlic, minced

2 to 4 tablespoons chopped fresh herb of choice, such as basil, marjoram, flat-leaf parsley, or mint

1½ cups pitted Mediterranean-style black olives, coarsely chopped

3 tablespoons tomato paste dissolved in ½ cup tongue cooking water

Salt and freshly ground black pepper

Place the tongue in a deep pot and add the onions, carrot, celery, peppercorns, bay leaf, coriander seeds, and boiling water to cover. Place over high heat, bring back to a boil, turn down the heat to low, cover, and simmer until tender, 2½ to 3 hours.

Remove the tongue from the pot. Strain the cooking liquid and reserve. When the tongue is cool enough to handle, peel it and cut away the thick gristle and bones at the large end. Slice the tongue and keep the slices warm.

To make the sauce, warm the oil in a large, deep sauté pan over medium heat. Add the garlic and herb and sauté until the garlic is tender, 1 to 2 minutes. Add the olives and diluted tomato paste, season with salt and pepper, and stir well. Add the tongue slices to the pan, with enough of the strained cooking liquid to cover. Simmer over very low heat for 20 minutes to blend the flavors. Serve hot.

VARIATION: *Sweet-and-Sour Sauce for Tongue (Lingua di Manzo Agrodolce):* Cook the tongue as directed, then peel, trim, slice, and keep warm. To make an agrodolce sauce, warm 3 tablespoons olive oil in a saucepan over medium heat. Add 2 tablespoons all-purpose flour and ½ teaspoon ground ginger and cook, stirring constantly, to form a roux, about 5 minutes. Add 2½ cups meat broth, tongue cooking liquid, or water and 1 cup Basic Tomato Sauce (page 328) and bring to a boil. Turn down the heat to low, whisk in 2 tablespoons red wine vinegar and ½ cup dry Marsala, and simmer for 4 to 5 minutes. Stir in the grated zest of 1 lemon; ½ cup pine nuts, toasted; and ½ cup raisins, plumped in hot water or Marsala. Season with salt and freshly ground black pepper and spoon over the tongue slices. Alternatively, place the tongue slices in the sauce, cover the pan, and simmer gently for about 15 minutes to reheat the tongue and blend the flavors.

# Calf's Liver with Moroccan Spiced Onions   FOIE M'CHERMEL

To alter the number of servings, allow 1 onion and 4 to 5 ounces of liver per person and adjust the spices accordingly. If you are keeping kosher, broil the liver until it is cooked through and then sauce it with the onions. If you are not following the kosher laws, you can sauté the liver to the doneness you prefer. I cannot bring myself to cook it until it is well-done. I like liver rather rare, when it is still tender and not dry. Serve the liver with roast potatoes or couscous. SERVES 6

3 to 6 tablespoons olive oil

4 yellow onions, sliced about ¼ inch thick

1 tablespoon ground cumin

1 tablespoon sweet paprika

¼ teaspoon cayenne pepper

2 tablespoons fresh lemon juice

4 tablespoons chopped fresh cilantro

Salt and freshly ground black pepper

1½ pounds calf's liver, any veins or membrane removed, then cut into slices (not too thin)

All-purpose flour for coating, if sautéing the liver

¾ cup chicken broth, if sautéing the liver

Lemon wedges for serving

Warm 3 tablespoons of the oil in a sauté pan over medium heat. Add the onions and sauté for about 5 minutes. Add the cumin, paprika, and cayenne and sauté until tender, about 5 minutes longer. Add the lemon juice and half of the cilantro, season with salt and pepper, and then taste and adjust the seasoning. Set the onions aside and keep warm.

To broil the liver, preheat the broiler. Brush the broiler pan with oil. Place the liver on the broiler pan, slip the pan under the broiler, and broil the liver, turning once, until cooked to desired doneness. Transfer the liver to a platter and top with the onions. Sprinkle with the remaining cilantro and serve hot or warm, accompanied with lemon wedges.

To sauté the liver, spread some flour on a plate and season with salt and pepper. Dip the liver into the flour, coating both sides and tapping off the excess. Warm the remaining 3 tablespoons oil in a large, heavy sauté pan over medium-high heat. Add the liver and sear briefly on both sides, turning once. The liver should be medium-rare. Transfer the liver to a platter and keep warm. Pour the broth into the pan and deglaze over high heat, stirring to dislodge any brown bits from the pan bottom. Add the onion mixture to the pan and heat through. Pour the onions over the liver and sprinkle with the remaining cilantro. Serve hot or warm, accompanied with lemon wedges.

## *Fried Spiced Liver*  ARNAVUT CİĞERİ

This is known as Albanian liver in Turkey and often appears on the meze table.  SERVES 4

| | |
|---|---|
| 1 pound calf's or lamb's liver, 1 inch thick | 1 teaspoon ground cumin (optional) |
| 2 to 3 tablespoons all-purpose flour | Olive oil for frying |
| 1 tablespoon Maras or Aleppo pepper flakes | Turkish Onion Salad with Sumac (page 45) |

Trim away any veins or membrane from the liver, then cut into 1-inch cubes. In a small bowl, combine the flour, pepper flakes, and cumin and mix well. In batches, coat the liver cubes with the flour mixture, tapping off the excess.

Film a large, heavy sauté pan with oil and warm over high heat. Add the liver cubes and cook quickly, turning to brown on each side, until cooked to desired doneness. Transfer to a plate and, if you like, skewer the cubes with toothpicks. Accompany with the onion salad.

## *Turkish Grilled Liver Kebab*  CİĞER KEBABI

This flavorful liver recipe is acceptable to those keeping kosher, as the liver is broiled or cooked over a fire. Just be careful you do not overcook it or it will be dry. Typically the liver and onion salad are wrapped together in flatbread.  SERVES 4

1 pound calf's liver, 1 inch thick

2 teaspoons ground sumac

1½ teaspoons ground toasted cumin

1 teaspoon Maras or Aleppo pepper flakes

½ teaspoon freshly ground black pepper

Olive oil for marinade and brushing

Turkish Onion Salad with Sumac (page 45)

Flatbread for serving

Lemon wedges for serving

Trim away any veins or membrane from the liver, then cut into 1-inch cubes. In a small bowl, combine the sumac, cumin, pepper flakes, black pepper, and a couple of spoonfuls of oil and mix well. Coat the liver cubes with the spice mixture, cover, and refrigerate for a few hours to marinate.

Prepare a fire in a charcoal grill or preheat the broiler. Thread the liver cubes onto skewers (if using wooden skewers, soak them in water for 30 minutes before using), brush with oil, and place directly over the coals or place on a sheet pan and slip under the broiler. Cook, turning as needed to color all sides, until cooked to desired doneness. Serve with the onion salad, flatbread, and lemon wedges.

## LAMB

A spit-roasted whole baby lamb is a popular centerpiece on special occasions and holidays throughout the Mediterranean. It is often served during Passover, for example, because it is believed that lamb is what the Jews cooked in the wilderness during their exodus from Egypt. Since roasting a whole lamb is not an option for most home cooks, the best and most prestigious cut to use in its place is leg of lamb. But most strictly observant Jews do not cook the hind quarters of an animal in memory of a passage in Genesis in which Jacob battled with the angel, was injured, and became lame. It is not that leg of lamb is forbidden. It's just that for the orthodox to eat the hind quarter of the animal, the sciatic nerve and blood vessels attached to it must be removed, a time-consuming process for the butcher. That's why leg recipes are scarce and shank and shoulder recipes are numerous. Less observant cooks will disregard this arcane stipulation and cook a leg of lamb. But if you do not want to cross that line, you can splurge on lamb racks or on boneless loins, which are the eyes of the chops.

This leads to the question of the degree of doneness. Many of us prefer lamb chops and leg of lamb cooked rare to medium-rare for juiciness, texture, and flavor. As noted earlier, in kosher cooking, all meat must be soaked, salted, and cooked well-done so that no blood is visible. This is fine for stews made with shoulder, lamb shanks, and meatballs, but it poses a dilemma for anyone who likes lamb chops or leg cooked to a lesser degree of doneness. If you are not observant of kosher laws when it comes to cooking meat, you can choose to cook leg of lamb instead of shoulder and to the degree of doneness you prefer. In other words, you can stay with the spirit and flavors of the dish but not cook it in a kosher manner.

If you do shop for lamb shoulder rather than leg, you will find that it is often trimmed carelessly, with lots of outer fat still attached. It may be that you will need to purchase four pounds of lamb shoulder instead of three pounds, to make up for what you will need to trim off. This will not be a problem when you cook a whole shoulder, however, as the outer layer of fat will melt and baste the meat as it cooks.

## Roast Lamb in Moroccan Marinade   MECHOUI

In Morocco, the term *mechoui* refers to a whole lamb cooked on a spit. The dish is served at big parties when the occasion is festive. Here, I have provided a variety of options in place of the whole animal. The spicing is the same as for the traditional *mechoui,* as it is good on any cut you choose. Cooked-vegetable salads are the usual accompaniments, and bowls of cumin salt, thinned *harissa,* and lemon wedges are the traditional condiments. Round out the menu with couscous with almonds and raisins.   SERVES 6

**CHOICE OF MEAT**

3 lamb racks, ends trimmed (24 chops), or

4 lamb tenderloins, each about 8 ounces, cut crosswise into 1½- inch pieces, or

2 pounds lamb from leg, cut into 1½-inch cubes, or

1 bone-in lamb shoulder, 5 to 6 pounds, or

1 boneless leg of lamb, 4 to 5 pounds

**MARINADE (FOR 5 TO 6 POUNDS MEAT)**

2 teaspoons ground toasted cumin seeds

2 teaspoons freshly ground black pepper

1 teaspoon Aleppo or Maras pepper flakes

2 tablespoons minced garlic

½ cup chopped fresh cilantro

¼ cup fresh lemon juice

6 tablespoons extra virgin olive oil

Garlic slivers, if using lamb racks, whole shoulder, or leg (optional)

Olive oil for searing, if using lamb racks

Thin yellow onion slivers for the skewers, if cooking kebabs

About 1½ cups meat broth, if cooking leg of lamb

Lemon wedges for serving (optional)

Cumin salt made from 3 parts ground toasted cumin and 1 part kosher salt (optional)

Harissa, homemade (page 355) or store-bought, thinned with olive oil and fresh lemon juice for serving (optional)

Select the cut of meat. If using lamb racks, a lamb shoulder, or a leg of lamb, you will need to make the whole marinade recipe. If using lamb tenderloins or cubed lamb from leg, you will need to cut the marinade recipe in half. To make the marinade, in a bowl, combine all of the ingredients and mix well.

If using lamb racks: Insert garlic slivers between the chops. Rub the racks with the marinade, coating evenly. Cover and refrigerate for at least 4 hours or up to overnight. Preheat the oven to 450°F. Film a large, heavy sauté pan with oil and warm over high heat. In batches, sear the racks on all sides until nicely browned. Transfer the racks, flesh side up, to a roasting pan and finish in the oven, 15 to 20 minutes. To test for doneness, insert an instant-read thermometer into the thickest part of a rack away from bone; it should read 120° to 130°F for rare, 130° to 140°F for medium-rare, 140° to 150°F for medium, or to desired degree of doneness. Start testing after 12 minutes.

If using tenderloins or meat from leg for kebabs: Rub the meat cubes with the marinade and cover and marinate for 2 hours at room temperature or up to 24 hours in the refrigerator. Prepare a fire in a charcoal grill or preheat the broiler. Thread the meat onto skewers (if using wooden skewers, soak them in water for 30 minutes before using), alternating the cubes with thin slivers of onion, then grill or broil, turning once, to desired degree of doneness.

If using lamb shoulder: Cut slits in the meat and insert a garlic sliver in each slit. Rub the shoulder with the marinade, cover, and refrigerate for at least 4 hours or up to overnight. Bring the shoulder to room temperature. Preheat the oven to 450°F. Put the shoulder in a roasting pan and roast for 30 minutes. Turn down the oven temperature to 350°F and continue to roast, basting occasionally with the pan juices, until cooked through and tender, 2 to 2½ hours longer. Transfer to a carving board, tent with foil, and let rest for 5 to 10 minutes. Cut the lamb into serving pieces and arrange on a platter. Spoon off the fat from the pan juices and serve the defatted juices with the lamb.

If using leg of lamb: Cut slits in the meat and insert a garlic sliver in each slit. If you want to make a spoon sauce for serving with the lamb, reserve a little of the marinade and rub the leg with the remaining marinade. If not, rub all of the marinade on the leg. Cover the leg and refrigerate overnight. The next day, preheat the oven to 450°F. Place the lamb, meatier side up, in a roasting pan and roast for 25 minutes. Lower the heat to 325°F and continue roasting until an instant-read thermometer inserted into the thickest part of the leg reads 120° to 125°F for rare or 130° to 135°F for medium-rare, about 1¼ hours longer. You also can cook the leg well-done, or even meltingly tender, Moroccan style, 2 to 2½ hours longer. Transfer the leg to a carving board, tent with foil, and let rest for 5 to 10 minutes. Spoon off the fat from the pan juices, place the pan over high heat, add the broth, and deglaze the pan, stirring to dislodge any brown bits from the pan bottom. Stir in the reserved marinade, if using. Slice the lamb, arrange the slices on a platter, and spoon the pan sauce over the slices.

Serve the lamb hot. Pass lemon wedges and bowls of cumin salt and thinned harissa at the table.

VARIATIONS: *Mint Variation:* Omit the cilantro in the marinade and add 1 cup chopped fresh mint.

*Sephardic Greek Marinade for Kebabs:* Combine 1 yellow onion, grated; 1 teaspoon bahārāt or ground cumin; ½ teaspoon Aleppo pepper flakes, ½ cup olive oil, and 2 to

4 tablespoons wine vinegar or fresh lemon juice. Marinate the lamb cubes for at least 4 hours or up to overnight, thread onto skewers, and grill or broil as directed.

*Turkish Marinade for Kebabs:* In a food processor, pulse 1 yellow onion, cut into chunks, until grated. Add 2 cloves garlic, 1 teaspoon hot paprika or Aleppo or Maras pepper flakes, 1 teaspoon ground cinnamon, 1 teaspoon freshly ground black pepper, ½ cup olive oil, and 2 to 4 tablespoons fresh lemon juice and pulse to combine. Marinate the lamb cubes overnight, thread onto skewers and grill or broil as directed. Serve with flatbread and Turkish Onion and Sumac Salad (page 45) or with couscous.

## *Braised Lamb Shoulder with Olives*   SPALLA DI MONTONE CON LE OLIVE

In the Roman ghetto, restaurants off the Via Portico d'Ottavio still serve this dish. Traditionally, a shoulder of lamb was boned, rubbed with salt, pepper, cloves, and cinnamon, and then rolled and tied. Here, I have given you the option of cooking a bone-in lamb shoulder, a rolled and tie boneless shoulder, stew-size pieces, or lamb shanks. The rolled and tied shoulder gives you the prettiest servings, as its compact shape ensures nice-looking slices. But it is more important that the meat be meltingly tender than the slices be aesthetically pleasing.  SERVES 6

CHOICE OF MEAT

1 bone-in lamb shoulder, about 5 pounds; or

3½ pounds boneless lamb shoulder, either rolled and tied or cut into 2-inch pieces for stew; or

6 lamb shanks, each about 1 pound

1 teaspoon ground cloves

2 teaspoons ground cinnamon

1 teaspoon freshly ground black pepper

1 teaspoon salt

Olive oil for rubbing and frying

3 yellow onions, sliced

2 cups meat broth, or as needed

½ cup dry white wine (optional)

6 large carrots, peeled and cut into 2-inch chunks

1 tablespoon chopped fresh rosemary

1 to 2 tablespoons grated orange zest (optional)

1 cup Mediterranean-style green olives, pitted and coarsely chopped

Trim the lamb of excess fat. In a small bowl, stir together the cloves, cinnamon, pepper, salt, and a few spoonfuls of oil. Rub the meat with the spice mixture, then cover and let stand at room temperature for 2 hours or up to overnight in the refrigerator.

Film a large, heavy sauté pan with oil and warm over high heat. In batches if necessary, add the meat and brown well on all sides. Transfer the meat to a stew pot, leaving the fat behind in the pan.

Add the onions to the fat remaining in the sauté pan and cook over medium heat, stirring occasionally, until translucent and tender, 8 to 10 minutes. Transfer the onions to the pot. Add about ½ cup of the broth or the wine to the sauté pan, raise the heat to high, and deglaze the pan, stirring to dislodge the brown bits from the pan bottom. Add to the pot. Add broth just to cover the meat and bring to a boil. Cover the pot, reduce the heat to low, and simmer for 1 hour.

Add the carrots and rosemary, re-cover, and cook for 25 minutes. Add the orange zest and olives and continue to simmer until the meat is tender, about 15 minutes longer for stew meat and about 30 minutes longer for the shoulder or shanks. Spoon off the excess fat from the pan juices, then taste the juices and adjust the seasoning if needed. Serve the stew or shanks hot with the juices. If you have cooked a rolled shoulder, let it rest for about 10 minutes, then snip the strings, carve the meat into slices, and serve hot with the juices. If you have cooked a bone-in shoulder, let it rest, then cut into serving pieces and serve hot with the juices.

## *Moroccan Lamb with Preserved Lemon and Olives*  TAGINE MQUALLI

This robust Moroccan stew is flavored with preserved lemon, a pantry staple for any-one who cooks Moroccan food. Lamb shanks can be prepared well ahead of time and reheat beautifully. If you cannot find shanks, or they are too large for your pot, substitute 3 pounds boneless lamb shoulder, cut into 2-inch pieces, and reduce the cooking time by 15 to 30 minutes. Serve the lamb with couscous. SERVES 6

3 tablespoons olive oil, plus more for browning the lamb

6 lamb shanks, each about 1 pound

Salt and freshly ground black pepper

2 yellow onions, finely chopped

3 cloves garlic, finely minced

2 teaspoons sweet paprika

1½ teaspoons ground ginger

1 teaspoon ground toasted cumin

¼ teaspoon saffron threads, finely crushed and steeped in 2 tablespoons hot water

1 to 1½ cups water or meat broth

Peel of 2 to 3 preserved lemons, homemade (page 356) or store-bought, rinsed and cut into narrow strips

⅔ cup Kalamata or other black olives

¼ cup fresh lemon juice

¼ cup chopped fresh cilantro

¼ cup chopped fresh flat-leaf parsley

Film the bottom of a large, heavy sauté pan with oil and warm over high heat. Sprinkle the lamb shanks with salt and pepper. In batches, add the shanks and brown well on all sides. Using tongs, transfer to a plate and set aside.

Warm the 3 tablespoons oil in a stew pot over medium heat. Add the onions, garlic, paprika, ginger, cumin, and saffron infusion and cook, stirring occasionally, until the onions are translucent and tender, 8 to 10 minutes. Add the browned shanks and the water just to cover, bring to a simmer, turn down the heat to low, cover, and cook until tender, about 1½ hours. If the shanks are large, they will take 20 to 30 minutes longer. (Alternatively, transfer the pot to a preheated 350°F oven for the same amount of time.)

Add the preserved lemon, olives, lemon juice, cilantro, and parsley, re-cover, and simmer for 15 minutes longer to blend the flavors. Using tongs, transfer the shanks to individual serving plates, spoon the pan juices, preserved lemon, and olives over the top, and serve.

## Lamb or Kid and Artichokes with Egg and Lemon
AGNELLO O CAPRETTO E CARCIOFI ALL'UOVA E LIMONE

This recipe from Calabria traditionally calls for kid (baby goat), which is starting to appear at our farmers' markets. A similar recipe appears in Roman Jewish kitchens under the name *capretto alla giudia.* Passover lamb recipes of Lazio and Tuscany, *spezzatino d'agnello con salsa di uova per Pasqua* and *agnello brodettato,* respectively, are practically identical, except for their use of lamb. Partially cooked quartered fennel bulbs can be added during the last 10 minutes of cooking. In the spirit of spring, peas, favas, and asparagus can also make their appearance in this stew. Roast potatoes are a good accompaniment. SERVES 6

½ cup olive oil, or as needed

3½ pounds boneless lamb shoulder or kid shoulder, cut into 2-inch pieces

1 large yellow onion, chopped

4 tablespoons chopped fresh flat-leaf parsley

Salt and freshly ground black pepper

2 tablespoons all-purpose flour (optional)

1 cup dry white wine

6 small artichokes

1 lemon, plus juice of 2 large lemons (about ½ cup)

Meat broth or water, if needed

3 egg yolks

1 tablespoon chopped fresh marjoram or mint

Warm the oil in a stew pot or large, heavy sauté pan over high heat. Add the lamb, onion, and 2 tablespoons of the parsley and sauté until the lamb is golden, 8 to 10 minutes. Sprinkle with salt, pepper, and the flour and mix well. Add the wine and bring to a boil. Cook over high heat for about 5 minutes, then turn down the heat to low, cover, and simmer for 35 to 40 minutes.

Meanwhile, prepare the artichokes: Fill a large bowl with water. Cut the lemon in half and squeeze the juice into the water. Working with 1 artichoke at a time, remove all of the leaves until you reach the heart. Trim off the tough base of the stem and then pare away the dark green areas from the base and the tender stem. Cut the artichoke heart in half lengthwise and scoop out and discard the choke from each half with a small pointed spoon or paring knife. Cut each half in half again and slip the pieces into the lemon water.

When the meat has simmered for 50 to 60 minutes, drain the artichokes and add them to the pot along with some broth if needed for moisture, re-cover, and continue to simmer until the meat and artichokes are tender, 20 to 25 minutes longer. Taste and adjust the seasoning.

In a bowl, beat together the egg yolks, lemon juice, the remaining 2 tablespoons parsley, and the marjoram until very frothy. Remove the stew from the heat and beat in the egg-lemon mixture, stirring constantly until fully incorporated. Re-cover and let stand off the heat until the eggs thicken the sauce, about 3 minutes. Serve at once.

## *Tunisian Passover Stew with Spring Vegetables*  MSOKI

For this celebration of spring, Andrée Zana-Murat and Daisy Taieb both offer a varied assortment of vegetables enhanced with the richness of meat juices and bits of cooked meat. Zana-Murat adds a meat loaf called *osbane* (page 351) to the stew after an hour or so of cooking. Crumbled matzos are spread over the top just before serving to absorb the fragrant juices. If you do not want to use lamb shanks, you can use only lamb shoulder, increasing the amount to 4 pounds. But the shanks add wonderful gelatinous juices to thicken the sauce, so I recommend you seek them out. Some people like this dish quite brothy and serve it in soup bowls. Others omit the meat from the vegetable stew and accompany the vegetables with a dish of meatballs in tomato sauce. Serve the stew with couscous. SERVES 10 TO 12

8 carrots, peeled and cut into large dice

4 turnips, peeled and cut into large dice

½ head young celery with leaves, cut into 2-inch pieces

1 small head Savoy cabbage, cored and cut into 2-inch pieces

1 celery root, peeled and cut into large dice

1 or 2 fennel bulbs with leaves, quartered lengthwise

3 white or yellow onions, diced

2 tablespoons ground dried rose petals (optional)

2 teaspoons ground coriander

8 cloves garlic, minced

2 teaspoons salt

2 teaspoons freshly ground black pepper

½ cup chopped fresh cilantro

½ cup chopped fresh dill

½ cup chopped fresh flat-leaf parsley

¼ cup olive or sunflower oil

2 teaspoons harissa, homemade (page 355) or store-bought, or to taste

1 teaspoon ground turmeric

2 large lamb shanks (or veal or beef shanks)

2 pounds boneless lamb shoulder, cut into 1½- to 2-inch pieces

4 artichokes, leaves removed, base and stem trimmed, each heart quartered lengthwise, and choke discarded

2 pounds spinach or young Swiss chard, cut into 1¼-inch pieces

2 pounds fresh fava beans, shelled, blanched, and peeled

⅓ cup chopped fresh mint

4 matzos

In a large bowl, combine the carrots, turnips, celery, cabbage, celery root, and fennel. Add the onions, rose petals, coriander, half of the garlic, 1 teaspoon each of the salt and pepper, 3 tablespoons of the cilantro, and ¼ cup each of the dill and parsley and mix well. Set aside.

Pour the oil into a large stew pot, stir in the harissa, the remaining garlic, the turmeric, and the remaining 1 teaspoon each salt and pepper, and place over medium heat. Add the shanks and shoulder meat and sauté for about 5 minutes, turning the pieces to coat them with the oil and spices. Add water just to cover and simmer for 1 hour.

Add the mixed vegetables, stir well, and simmer for 30 minutes. (Note: if adding osbane do it now.) Add the artichokes and simmer for 20 minutes. Add the spinach, favas, mint, the remaining ¼ cup each dill and parsley, and the remaining 5 tablespoons cilantro. Cover and cook until all of the vegetables and the meats are tender, 15 to 20 minutes longer.

Remove the shanks from the pot, cut off the meat, and return the meat to the pot. (Reserve the shank bones and roast them at high heat for 30 minutes to add to the Passover Seder plate.) Break the matzos into quarters and place them on top of the vegetables and meat. Serve hot or warm.

## *Turkish Lamb with Green Garlic*   KODRERO CON AJO FRESCO

Spring is when green garlic appears at the market. These fragrant green shoots with tiny young bulbs resemble large green onions or baby leeks, and combined with green onions, they make for a delicate and aromatic stew. If you cannot find green garlic at your market, you can use garlic cloves instead. With the slow cooking, the cloves will become mild and creamy. I recommend braising this dish in the oven for even cooking and to eliminate worries about scorching, but if oven space is tight, the stove top will do. This stew was a great favorite at Passover at my restaurant, Square One, and it is usually the centerpiece of my family Seder. Serve with rice or roast potatoes. SERVES 6 TO 8

Olive oil for browning and sautéing

3 to 4 pounds boneless lamb shoulder, cut into 1½- to 2-inch pieces

Salt and freshly ground black pepper

1 cup meat broth or water, or as needed

¼ cup tomato paste

3 tablespoons red wine vinegar

2 teaspoons Maras or Aleppo pepper flakes, or more to taste

1 pound green garlic stalks, or 2 small heads garlic

2 pounds green onions (about 6 large bunches)

2 pounds fresh fava beans, shelled, blanched, and peeled (optional)

Squeeze of fresh lemon juice (optional)

Chopped fresh mint or flat-leaf parsley for garnish

If oven braising, preheat the oven to 350°F.

Film a large, heavy sauté pan with oil and warm over high heat. Season the lamb with salt and pepper. In batches, add the lamb to the pan and brown well on all sides. Using tongs or a slotted spoon, transfer the lamb to a stew pot.

Pour off the excess fat from the sauté pan, add a little of the broth, and deglaze the pan over high heat, stirring to dislodge any brown bits from the pan bottom. Add the pan juices to the stew pot. Combine the tomato paste and vinegar with the remaining broth, stir well, and add to the lamb. The liquid should just cover the lamb; add more if needed. Add the Maras pepper and a sprinkle of salt and bring to a simmer over medium-high heat. Turn down the heat to low, cover, and simmer on the stove top until the lamb is almost tender, about 1 hour. Alternatively, bring to a simmer, cover, and place in the oven for 50 to 60 minutes.

Meanwhile, prepare the green garlic (or garlic) and the green onions. Cut off the root end of the green garlic stalks and slice the stalks into 2-inch lengths, using all of the green. (Or, separate the cloves of the garlic heads and peel the cloves.) Cut off the roots of the green onions, then cut the green onions, including the green tops, into 2-inch lengths. Bring a saucepan filled with salted water to a boil, add the green garlic (or garlic cloves) and green onions, blanch for 2 minutes, drain well, and pat dry.

Warm a few tablespoons oil in a large sauté pan over medium heat. Add the green garlic and green onions and sauté them in batches until they take on a bit of color, about 5 minutes. Season with salt and pepper and reserve.

After the lamb has been cooking for 1 hour, add the green garlic (or blanched garlic cloves) and green onions, re-cover, and continue to simmer until the lamb is tender, 20 to 30 minutes longer. Add the favas during the last 10 minutes of cooking. Taste and adjust the seasoning. Add the lemon juice to brighten the flavors, then spoon into a deep platter, garnish with mint, and serve.

# Turkish Lamb Stew with Rice  TAS KEBAB

When we hear the word *kebab,* we think of a skewer of meat cooked on the grill. In Turkey, however, the word *kebab* usually refers to roasted meat or a dry stew. (A brothy stew is a *yahni.*) Esin Eden's family recipe is a very homey dish, in which rice is cooked along with the meat in the same pan. The flavors are reminiscent of stews prepared *al chilindrón* style from the Navarre and Rioja regions of Spain, though the cinnamon is a Turkish addition. If you want the stew to revert to Spanish roots, replace the cinnamon with 2 teaspoons sweet paprika or a combination of sweet and hot paprika.  SERVES 6

---

4 tablespoons olive oil

3 pounds boneless lamb shoulder, cut into 1½- to 2-inch cubes

2 yellow onions, chopped

3 red bell peppers, seeded and chopped

4 large ripe tomatoes (about 2 pounds), peeled, seeded, and chopped

1 teaspoon ground cinnamon

1 teaspoon ground allspice

2½ cups meat broth, or as needed

Salt and freshly ground black pepper

1 cup basmati or other long-grain white rice, rinsed and then preferably soaked in water to cover for 1 hour and drained

Chopped fresh flat-leaf parsley for garnish

---

Warm 2 tablespoons of the oil in a large, heavy sauté pan over high heat. In batches, add the lamb and brown well on all sides. Using tongs or a slotted spoon, transfer to a plate and set aside.

Warm the remaining 2 tablespoons oil in a stew pot over medium heat. Add the onions and sauté for 5 minutes. Add the bell peppers and sauté for 5 minutes longer. Add the tomatoes, cinnamon, allspice, and 1 cup of the broth and season with salt and pepper. Return the meat to the pot, bring to a simmer, turn down the heat to low, cover, and simmer until the meat is almost tender, about 1¼ hours. Check at the midpoint and add a little more broth if the pan is beginning to dry.

Add the remaining 1½ cups broth, raise the heat to high, and bring to a boil. Add the rice, turn down the heat to low, cover, and cook until the rice is tender, 20 to 25 minutes. If you hear crackling sounds, the pot is likely dry and you need to add a little more broth. Spoon onto a deep platter, garnish with parsley, and serve.

VARIATIONS:  *Upside-Down Stew:* Respected Turkish food writer Nevin Halıcı calls *tas kebab* an "upside-down stew." She cooks the lamb with tomatoes and herbs (no bell peppers), then strains the stewing liquid into a measuring cup and tops it off with enough hot broth to measure 2 cups. She packs the cooked stew meat into an oiled ovenproof bowl, places the bowl upside down in a baking dish, adds 1 cup well-rinsed rice and the hot braising broth to the dish, covers the dish, and then bakes the rice in a preheated 350°F oven for about

25 minutes, or until the rice is tender. The cover comes off, the bowl is removed, and the stew is centered in the middle of the rice for a very dramatic presentation.

*Layered Lamb, Eggplant, Tomato, and Rice (Makloubeh):* This dish is popular in Israel, where it is sometimes prepared with chicken instead of lamb. Oil a deep saucepan or baking dish. Layer sliced tomatoes on the bottom and top with the lamb stew cooked as above, followed by sautéed eggplant slices, and finally the rice, packing the layers well. Add the hot meat broth, cover, and cook on the stove top or in a preheated 350°F oven until the rice is tender, about 20 minutes. Let rest for 10 minutes before unmolding.

*Lamb with Freekeh (Freekeh bel Lahmeh):* Omit the red bell peppers and use freekeh in place of the rice. Garnish with toasted almonds.

## Lamb Stew from Djerba   D'FINA DJERBALIYA

This Sabbath *d'fina* is named for the Tunisian island of Djerba, where a sizable Jewish community once lived. It is also the home to the ancient Ghriba synagogue. The current building dates to the nineteenth century, but the site has been home to synagogues since the sixth century BCE and was the target of a terrorist attack in 2002. Only a few Jewish families remain on the island, but recently the synagogue, protected by government troops, has become the site of a festival that welcomes Jews from other countries to celebrate the holiday of Lag B'Omer. This *d'fina* is an ideal dish for Rosh Hashanah as well as for the Sabbath. Serve with couscous. SERVES 6 TO 8

½ cup dried chickpeas

½ cup dried apricots, soaked in hot water for a few hours

½ cup pitted prunes, soaked in hot water for a few hours

¼ cup olive oil

4 pounds boneless lamb shoulder, cut into 2-inch cubes

2 to 3 yellow onions, diced (about 4 cups)

1 large or 2 small green bell peppers, seeded and diced

4 cloves garlic, finely minced

½ teaspoon ground allspice or cinnamon

1 teaspoon ground toasted cumin

½ teaspoon cayenne pepper

1 teaspoon freshly ground black pepper

2 cups water or lamb broth

1 cup raisins (optional)

Salt

Pick over the chickpeas, then place in a bowl, add water to cover, and let soak in the refrigerator overnight. Drain, rinse well, and transfer to a saucepan. Add water to cover by 3 inches and bring to a boil over high heat. Turn down the heat to low, cover, and simmer until tender, 45 to 60 minutes. Set the chickpeas aside in their cooking liquid.

Drain the apricots and prunes, reserving the soaking water. Coarsely chop the fruit and set aside.

Warm the oil in a large, heavy sauté pan over high heat. In batches, add the meat and brown well on all sides. Using tongs or a slotted spoon, transfer to a stew pot.

Add the onions, bell pepper, and garlic to the fat remaining in the sauté pan and cook over medium heat, stirring occasionally, for 10 minutes. Add the allspice, cumin, cayenne, and black pepper, stir well, and cook for 5 minutes longer. Transfer the contents of the pan to the stew pot, add the water, and bring to a boil over high heat. Turn down the heat to low, cover, and simmer for 1 hour.

Drain the chickpeas and add to the stew pot along with the prunes, apricots, and raisins. If most of the liquid in the pot has been absorbed, add some of the fruit soaking water. Continue to simmer the stew until the meat is tender, about 30 minutes longer. Season with salt, then taste and adjust the seasoning if needed. Spoon into a deep platter and serve.

## Lamb Tagine with Prunes and Honey    MROUZIA

In Algeria, this stew is often served on the second night of Rosh Hashanah as part of the tradition of serving sweet food to celebrate the sweet New Year. It is not served on the first night, as prunes are black and no black food is permitted on the first night. In Morocco, some cooks add a mixture of dried fruits, such as apricots, pears, and raisins, along with the prunes. If you want to follow Algerian tradition, you can serve this on the first night by substituting apricots and golden raisins for the prunes. A cup of toasted blanched almonds can be added in place of the sesame seeds. SERVES 8

---

Olive oil for browning

4 pounds boneless lamb shoulder, cut into 1½- to 2-inch cubes; 4 large lamb shanks, each about 1½ pounds, halved crosswise; or 8 small shanks, each about 12 ounces

3 yellow onions, chopped

1½ teaspoons ground cinnamon

1 teaspoon ground ginger

2 teaspoons ground coriander

½ teaspoon freshly ground black pepper

¼ teaspoon saffron threads, crushed

2 to 3 cups water or lamb broth

1 pound pitted prunes, soaked in hot water for a few hours

⅓ cup dark honey

Salt and freshly ground black pepper

3 tablespoons sesame seeds, toasted

---

Film a large, heavy sauté pan with oil and warm over high heat. In batches, add the lamb and brown well on all sides. Using tongs or a slotted spoon, transfer to a stew pot.

Add the onions to the fat remaining in the sauté pan and cook over medium heat, stirring occasionally, until translucent, about 8 minutes. Add the cinnamon, ginger, coriander, pepper, and saffron and cook for 3 minutes. Transfer the contents of the pan to the stew pot, add the water to barely cover, and bring to a boil over high heat. Turn down the heat to low, cover, and simmer until the meat is almost tender, 1 to 1½ hours.

Drain the prunes and add to the stew. Re-cover and simmer until the meat is tender, about 20 minutes longer. Add the honey and season with salt and pepper. Transfer to a deep platter, sprinkle with the sesame seeds, and serve.

VARIATIONS:  *With Raisins, Almonds, and Honey:* Substitute 2 cups raisins, plumped in hot water and drained, for the prunes and 1 to 1½ cups blanched almonds for the sesame seeds. This is a Passover specialty of Fez and Meknes.

*With Sweet Oranges:* The restaurant at La Maison Arabe hotel in Marrakech adds preserved oranges, rather than prunes or raisins, to their classic lamb tagine. Quarter 4 Candied Oranges (page 370) and add to the stew during the last 20 minutes of cooking instead of the prunes. You may not need to add any honey as the oranges are quite sweet. Garnish with the sesame seeds, if you like.

## Persian Stew with Lamb or Beef, Spinach, and Prunes
KHORESH-E ESFENAJ VA ALU

I use lamb shoulder (or boneless beef short ribs) for this dish, as it has a bit of fat, which will keep the meat juicy. If you have dried Omani limes, use them here. If not, you will need to balance the flavor of the dish with lemon juice just before serving. Iran is known for its golden dried plums, but we can use pitted prunes and still be happy with the results. Some cooks add a bunch of chopped green onions when adding the spinach, but I do not think it is needed as long as the onions are large. Serve with Persian Rice (page 149). SERVES 4

| | |
|---|---|
| 6 tablespoons olive oil | 1 teaspoon ground cinnamon or advieh |
| 1½ pounds boneless lamb shoulder or beef short ribs, cut into 1- to 1½- inch pieces | 3 or 4 dried Omani limes, rinsed and struck with a meat pounder so they crack (optional) |
| Salt | 2 cups chicken or beef broth, or as needed |
| 2 large yellow onions, sliced | 12 prunes, pitted |
| 2 cloves garlic, minced | 1½ pounds spinach, chopped |
| 1 teaspoon ground turmeric | Juice of 2 lemons, if not using limes |

Warm 3 tablespoons of the oil in a heavy sauté pan over medium-high heat. In batches, add the meat and brown well on all sides, sprinkling it with salt. Using a slotted spoon, transfer the meat to a plate and set aside.

Warm the remaining 3 tablespoons oil in a stew pot over medium heat. Add the onions and cook, stirring occasionally, until soft and pale gold, about 15 minutes. Add the garlic, turmeric, cinnamon, and 1½ teaspoons salt and cook for a few minutes. Add the meat, cracked Omani limes (reserve the lemon juice, if using), and the broth to the onion mixture and stir well. Bring to a boil, turn down the heat to low, cover, and cook until the meat is tender, about 1½ hours. Check every 35 or 40 minutes to make sure that the pan is not dry and add more broth if needed. Add the prunes during the last 15 to 20 minutes of cooking.

While the stew cooks, wilt the spinach in a saucepan over medium-low heat in the rinsing water clinging to the leaves just until no liquid remains. If you want the spinach to remain bright green, add it to the stew during the last 10 minutes of cooking; otherwise, add it along with the prunes. When the stew is ready, if you have not used the limes, add the lemon juice. Taste and adjust the seasoning. You may want just a squeeze of lemon juice and a bit more cinnamon and salt. Remove and discard the limes, if used, and serve hot.

## *Lamb Stew with Quince*   ARNAKI ME KYTHONIA

Quinces are greatly prized in Greece and Turkey. During the fall, their unique scent permeates every kitchen. You can stew them along with the meat, or you may cook them separately as a compote (so you can have some for an accompaniment to roast lamb or chicken) and add them during the last 15 minutes the stew cooks. Although this recipe is Greek, the pomegranate juice is a Turkish shortcut to help redden the quinces more quickly. If you have some of my preserved quince slices (page 367) on hand, you can use them instead of the fresh quince, adding them during the last 15 minutes of cooking. If you cannot find fresh quinces and have no preserved quinces, you can use apples or pears, in which case you must cut the sugar to 2 tablespoons. SERVES 6

2½ to 3 pounds lamb shoulder, cut into 2-inch cubes

2 teaspoons ground cinnamon

2 teaspoons ground toasted cumin

Juice of 1 lemon

3 pounds quinces

¼ cup olive oil

2 yellow onions, chopped

Pinch of cayenne pepper (optional)

1 cup water or meat broth

2 tablespoons margarine or olive oil

½ cup sugar

1 cup pomegranate juice or water

Salt and freshly ground black pepper

Rub the meat with 1 teaspoon each of the cinnamon and cumin. Cover and refrigerate for a few hours or preferably overnight.

Have ready a large bowl of water to which you have added the lemon juice. Peel, halve, core, and thickly slice the quinces and slip the slices into the lemon water.

Warm the oil in a large, heavy sauté pan over medium-high heat. In batches, add the meat and brown well on all sides. Using a slotted spoon, transfer the meat to a plate and set aside.

Add the onions to the fat remaining in the pan and cook over medium heat, stirring occasionally, until translucent and tender, 8 to 10 minutes. Add the remaining 1 teaspoon each cinnamon and cumin and the cayenne and cook for a few minutes longer. Add the browned meat and the water, bring to a boil, turn down the heat to low, cover, and simmer for 1 hour.

Meanwhile, drain the quince slices. Warm the margarine in a large sauté pan over medium heat. Add the quince slices, sprinkle with the sugar, and cook, stirring often, for 15 to 20 minutes. Add the pomegranate juice and simmer until the quince slices are translucent, 15 to 20 minutes longer. (You can cook the quince slices up to this point a day in advance and let them rest in their cooking liquid at room temperature until needed. They will redden more with the day's rest.)

When the meat has cooked for 1 hour, add the quince slices and their cooking liquid and simmer until the meat and fruit are tender, about 30 minutes longer. Season with salt and pepper and serve hot.

## Turkish Lamb Stew with Chestnuts  HAMIN DE KASTANYA

The presence of the word *hamin* here implies a Sabbath dish that can be prepared before sundown on Friday. This recipe is adapted from a Turkish cookbook, *Sefarad Yemekleri,* but its origins are Spanish. Most of the work in this dish is peeling the chestnuts. Some say roasting is easier than boiling. I have found that the ease of peeling chestnuts varies from batch to batch; they can be a breeze to peel or maddeningly frustrating. Be patient, have a very sharp knife, and have asbestos-tipped fingers at the ready because the chestnuts must be peeled while hot. Cut a deep cross on the round side of each chestnut. You can then roast them in a 425°F oven, turning them once, for 20 to 30 minutes, or you can boil them in salted water until the shell starts to split. Peel a few at a time and keep them hot. When the chestnuts are fully cooked they lose their white opaque centers.

I have found that the best peeling method for chestnuts is to heat them in the microwave. Cut the cross on all of the chestnuts, soak them in water for a few minutes, drain well, and then, in batches of three or four, put them in the microwave for 50 to 60 seconds. Cut away the outer shell and the thin brown peel that covers each nut. They are not yet cooked but can be cooked through later. If time is short or you cannot find fresh chestnuts, purchase vacuum-packed peeled and cooked chestnuts. Avoid water-packed canned chestnuts. SERVES 6

¼ cup olive or sunflower oil

2 yellow onions, chopped

2 pounds boneless lamb shoulder, cut into 1½-inch cubes

1 teaspoon ground cinnamon

½ teaspoon ground allspice

2 tablespoons tomato paste dissolved in 2 cups meat broth or water, plus more broth or water if needed

Salt and freshly ground black pepper

1 pound chestnuts, peeled (see headnote)

1 pound boiling potatoes, peeled and cut into ½-inch dice

3 to 4 tablespoons chopped fresh flat-leaf parsley

Warm the oil in a stew pot over medium heat. Add the onions and cook, stirring occasionally, until soft and pale gold, about 15 minutes. Add the meat and brown well on all sides. Add the cinnamon, allspice, and the diluted tomato paste to the pot. The liquid should barely cover the meat; add more broth if needed. Season with salt and pepper. Bring to a boil, turn down the heat to low, cover, and simmer until the meat is almost tender, about 1 hour.

If using microwave-peeled chestnuts, add them and the potatoes to the pot and simmer until all of the ingredients are tender, 20 to 30 minutes longer. If using fully cooked vacuum-packed peeled chestnuts or fully cooked oven-roasted or boiled peeled chestnuts, add them during the last 10 minutes of cooking. Transfer the stew to a serving dish, sprinkle with parsley, and serve.

## Eggplant and Lamb Casserole  MOUSSAKA

Moussaka is the ideal cold-weather dish: rich and stick-to-the-ribs hearty. It calls for a lot of eggplant and relatively little meat, for an economical family meal with glorious leftovers. According to culinary historian John Cooper, moussaka was served during Rosh Hashanah. Classic Greek moussaka has a baked topping of cheesy béchamel custard. Because kosher laws do not allow meat and dairy in the same meal, Jewish cooks have come up with inspired alternatives to traditional béchamel. For example, in *La cucina nella tradizione ebraica*, a cookbook compiled by the Italian Jewish women's organization ADEI WIZO, moussaka is topped with a fake béchamel sauce made from flour, fat, and broth. In this Turkish Sephardic moussaka from *La table juive*, moussaka takes on a totally different character. Instead of the richness of cheese and cream, it is rich and smoky from the addition of the chopped roasted eggplant added to the meat filling. Most recipes suggest frying the eggplant slices in oil, but I prefer brushing them with oil and baking them in the oven, as much less oil is used.

In Turkey, moussaka is usually layered in a deep, cylindrical mold, much like a charlotte tin or a soufflé dish, and then unmolded before it is brought to the table. This makes for a dramatic presentation, but it is trickier to serve. If the layers are not compacted well, the mold will collapse after the first cut. I have taken the coward's way out and prepare this recipe in a baking dish and then serve it directly from the dish. Also, although this dish is very tasty when freshly baked, it becomes even tastier when reheated a day later, after the flavors have had a chance to meld and mellow. SERVES 6 TO 8

---

4 globe eggplants (about 1 pound each)

Salt and freshly ground black pepper

Olive oil for brushing and sautéing

1½ pounds lamb shoulder, cut into very small dice, chopped, or coarsely ground

2 large yellow onions, finely chopped

1 pound tomatoes, peeled, seeded, and chopped (canned tomatoes are acceptable)

4 cloves garlic, minced

1 tablespoon dried Greek oregano

1 teaspoon ground cinnamon

4 to 6 tablespoons fine dried bread crumbs

---

Peel the skin lengthwise in stripes from 2 of the eggplants, then cut the eggplants crosswise into slices ⅓ inch thick. Place the slices in a colander in the sink or over a bowl, sprinkling them with salt as you go, and let drain for 30 minutes.

Preheat the oven to 400°F. Oil 1 or 2 sheet pans. Place the eggplant slices on the prepared pan(s), brush the slices with oil, and sprinkle with salt and pepper. Bake, turning once, until soft and translucent, about 15 minutes. Set aside.

Roast the remaining 2 eggplants as directed in Master Recipe for Roasted Eggplant (page 27). After draining the pulp, chop it. You should have about 2 cups coarse purée. Set aside.

Warm a few tablespoons oil in a large, heavy sauté pan over medium heat. Add the lamb and cook, breaking up any lumps with a wooden spoon, until browned, 8 to 10 minutes. Using a slotted spoon, transfer the lamb to a bowl. Add the onions to the fat remaining in the pan and cook over medium heat, stirring occasionally, until translucent, 5 to 8 minutes. Add the tomatoes, garlic, oregano, and cinnamon, season with salt and pepper, and then return the lamb to the pan and mix well. Turn down the heat to low, cover, and simmer until the meat is tender, 20 to 30 minutes. Stir in the chopped eggplant pulp, taste, and adjust the seasoning.

Preheat the oven to 350°F. Brush an 8-by-12-by-2-inch baking dish with oil (or use a large oval gratin dish). Sprinkle the dish lightly with some of the bread crumbs and line the bottom with one-third of the eggplant slices. Evenly spread half of the lamb mixture over the eggplant slices, sprinkle with half of the remaining bread crumbs, and top with half of the remaining eggplant slices. Spread the remaining lamb mixture on top, sprinkle with the remaining bread crumbs, and finish with the remaining eggplant slices. Cover the dish with foil, place in a large baking pan or roasting pan, and add water to the pan to reach halfway up the sides of the baking dish. You may uncover the dish if you want it to take on some color.

Bake until bubbling, about 45 minutes. Let rest for 10 minutes before cutting. Serve very warm. If you feel there is too much oil in the dish, scoop some out with a spoon, though it does contribute to the classic richness of the dish.

# Persian Stew with Eggplant, Tomatoes, and Grapes
## KHORESH-E BADEMJAN BA AB GHUREH

This is sort of a reversed, or deconstructed, moussaka. It is ideal for serving in early fall, when eggplants, tomatoes, and grapes are all in season. Serve the stew with Persian Rice (page 149). SERVES 6 TO 8

---

8 to 10 small round eggplants, or 2 or 3 large globe eggplants (2½ to 3 pounds total)

Salt

Olive oil for frying

2 large yellow onions, sliced

3 cloves garlic, minced

1 pound boneless lamb shoulder, cut into 1-inch pieces

Juice of 1 lemon, plus more if needed

1 teaspoon ground turmeric

2 cups drained chopped canned tomatoes

1 tablespoon tomato paste

1½ to 2 cups hot water or meat broth

4 or 5 cinnamon sticks

4 ripe fresh tomatoes, halved crosswise

1 cup unripe or tart grapes

½ teaspoon saffron threads steeped in 3 tablespoons hot water

---

If using small round eggplants, cut them crosswise into halves or thirds. If using large eggplants, cut them crosswise into 1-inch-thick slices. Place the eggplant pieces in a colander in the sink or over a bowl, sprinkling them with salt as you go, and let drain for 30 minutes. Pat dry with paper towels.

Warm a few tablespoons oil in a large sauté pan over medium-high heat. In batches, fry the eggplant pieces, turning once and adding more oil as needed, until golden brown on both sides. Using a slotted spatula, transfer to paper towels to drain.

Add the onions to the oil remaining in the pan and fry, turning as needed, until lightly browned, 12 to 15 minutes. Add the garlic and 1 teaspoon salt and cook, stirring, for 1 minute. Using a slotted spoon, transfer the onion mixture to a stew pot.

Add the lamb to the oil remaining in the sauté pan over medium heat and brown on all sides. Add the lamb to the onion mixture along with the lemon juice, turmeric, and chopped tomatoes and stir well. Dissolve the tomato paste in 1½ cups of the water and add to the pot. The liquid should barely cover the meat; add more hot water if needed. Raise the heat to high, bring to a boil, turn down the heat to low, place the cinnamon sticks on top, cover, and simmer for 40 minutes. Uncover the pot and arrange the fried eggplant slices on top of the meat. Re-cover and simmer for 20 minutes longer.

Meanwhile, rinse the sauté pan, place over high heat, and add enough oil to film the bottom of the pan. Add the tomato halves and sear briefly on both sides. Place the tomato halves cut side up atop the eggplants, scatter the grapes over the tomatoes, and drizzle the saffron infusion evenly over the top. Re-cover and cook until all of the ingredients are tender, about 20 minutes longer. Taste the pan juices and adjust the seasoning with salt, pepper, and lemon juice if needed. Serve hot.

## GROUND MEAT IN ALL ITS GLORY

This section is a celebration of the thriftiness and creativity of the Mediterranean Jews. You will find recipes for meat loaf, meatballs, *kefta,* sausages, meat fillings for vegetables, and nearly every other dish that uses ground meat. The meat can be beef or lamb and must not be too lean. Ground meat needs some fat if meatballs and meat loaves are to be moist and tender. Fat is a crucial ingredient, and unfortunately, it is getting harder to find anything except extra-lean ground meat at the market.

In Italy and Greece, the same basic mixture can be used for both meatballs and meat loaf. In the spirit of thrift, and according to a long Sephardic tradition, cooked vegetables can be added to extend the meatball mixture and feed a few more hungry diners. In most recipes, tomato sauce is the ubiquitous accompaniment. It can be spicy, sweet-and-sour, fruit enhanced, or laced with herbs.

All of the recipes are prepared in the same general manner. The ground meat is mixed with spices, herbs, and fresh bread crumbs. During Passover, matzo meal is used instead of bread crumbs, and although it works fine, the texture is not as good as it is with bread crumbs. Some meatballs include grated onion or minced garlic. Occasionally, an egg is added to help bind the mixture. It is best to combine the ingredients with your hands, to make sure all of the ingredients are evenly mixed.

The major recipe variations occur in the use of spices. Each country's spice profile is reflected in the seasoning of the meat mixture. That means that Italy might mix in a bit of nutmeg, Greece will use cinnamon, Turkey might add *bahārāt,* Morocco will include a spoonful of *ras el hanout,* Algeria will mix in some *harissa,* and Iran will add *advieh.*

Before shaping any meat mixture into meatballs, fry up a single ball of the mixture to test the seasoning, then adjust the remaining mixture with more salt or spice if needed. When you are happy with the seasoning, shape all of the meatballs and put them on parchment paper–lined sheet pans. You can refrigerate them at this point to cook them later or you can cook them right away. Some meatballs are fried first and others are poached directly in broth or sauce.

Most ground-meat fillings for stuffing vegetables (dolma, *yaprak,* and *sarma*), such as grape leaves and cabbage leaves, call for rice, though a few stay with bread crumbs.

# Sephardic Meat Loaf with Sweet-and-Sour Tomato Sauce
## ROLLO ME HAMINADOS

This recipe comes from the Sephardim of Greece, though similar meat loaf recipes are found in Italian and Iranian Jewish kitchens. This is a Sabbath dish, baked in the *hamin,* or oven, and served at room temperature. But it is especially succulent served hot with a sweet-and-sour tomato sauce.

Meat loaf can be tricky to make correctly, as you want it to set up and be firm enough to slice but not too bready. Achieving this balance is a matter of feel. When you mix the meat, you do not want it to feel too wet, or it won't be sliceable. A bit more bread will help. I have given an option of matzo meal here, too, though bread will absorb the meat juices better. SERVES 6

**SWEET-AND-SOUR TOMATO SAUCE**

2 tablespoons olive oil

4 large ripe tomatoes, peeled, seeded, and chopped (about 2 cups; canned tomatoes are acceptable)

2 tablespoons honey

1 cup dry red wine

½ teaspoon ground cinnamon

Juice of 2 lemons

Salt and freshly ground black pepper

**MEAT LOAF**

1½ pounds ground beef (not too lean)

1 egg, lightly beaten

1 cup fresh bread crumbs, soaked in water and squeezed dry, or matzo meal, or more as needed to bind

1 yellow onion, grated or finely minced

2 cloves garlic, minced

3 tablespoons chopped fresh flat-leaf parsley

3 tablespoons chopped fresh basil

Salt and freshly ground black pepper

3 Long-Cooked Onion Skin Eggs (page 93) or hard-boiled eggs, peeled

To make the sauce, warm 1 tablespoon of the oil in a sauté pan over medium heat. Add the tomatoes and 1 tablespoon of the honey and cook, stirring occasionally, until the tomatoes are reduced to a purée, about 20 minutes. Add the wine and simmer until the sauce thickens. Add the remaining 1 tablespoon each oil and honey and the cinnamon and simmer for a few more minutes to blend the flavors. Add the lemon juice and season with salt and pepper. Remove from the heat and reserve.

Preheat the oven to 350°F. Oil a sheet pan.

To make the meat loaf, in a large bowl, combine the beef, egg, bread crumbs, onion, garlic, parsley, and basil and season with salt and pepper. Mix well with your hands. If the meat mixture feels too wet to hold together, add more bread crumbs to give it structure.

Pat half of the meat mixture into a flattened oval directly on the prepared pan. Arrange the eggs in a lengthwise row down the center. Cover with the remaining meat mixture and then smooth the surface, seal the seams well, and score the loaf with the tines of a fork.

Bake the meat loaf, basting from time to time with some of the sauce, until cooked through, 1 to 1¼ hours. Transfer the meat loaf to a platter and let rest for 10 minutes. Just before serving, gently reheat the remaining sauce. Slice the meat loaf and serve. Pass the sauce at the table.

## *Italian Egg-Stuffed Meat Loaf*   POLPETTONE DI CARNE

Here is the Italian version of the Greek meat loaf with sweet-and-sour tomato sauce on page 326. The ingredients differ, but the method is the same. The nutmeg or cinnamon is the Sephardic touch here. Iraqi cooks also make an egg-stuffed loaf, called "lady's arm" (*zand il khatoon*), which is seasoned with cumin and with the heady spice mixture known as *bahārāt*. The meat mixture is patted flat onto oiled foil, the eggs are placed down the center, the mixture is rolled up into a log around the eggs, and the log is slid off the foil onto an oiled sheet pan, baked, and then served with tomato slices and herbs. SERVES 4 TO 6

1 pound ground beef (not too lean)

1 egg, lightly beaten

1 cup fresh bread crumbs, soaked in beef broth or water and squeezed dry, or more as needed to bind

½ cup grated yellow onion

2 or 3 cloves garlic, minced

Few gratings of nutmeg or pinch of ground cinnamon

Salt and freshly ground black pepper

3 hard-boiled eggs, peeled

½ cup diced roasted red bell pepper

3 tablespoons chopped Mediterranean-style black olives

½ cup tomato purée (optional)

Basic Tomato Sauce for serving (recipe follows)

To make the meat loaf, in a large bowl, combine the beef, egg, bread crumbs, onion, garlic, and nutmeg and season with salt and pepper. Mix well with your hands. If the meat mixture feels too wet to hold together, add more bread crumbs to give it structure.

Preheat the oven to 350°F. Oil a sheet pan. Pat half of the meat mixture into a flattened oval directly on the prepared pan. Arrange the eggs in a row lengthwise down the center. Distribute the red pepper and olives evenly around the eggs. Cover with the remaining meat mixture and then smooth the surface, seal the seams well, and score the loaf with the tines of a fork. If you like, spread the top of the loaf with the tomato purée.

Bake the meat loaf until cooked through, 1 to 1¼ hours. Transfer the meat loaf to a platter and let rest for 10 minutes. Slice the meat loaf and serve. Pass the sauce at the table.

## *Basic Tomato Sauce*   SALSA DI POMODORO

Although this simple sauce is paired with the adjoining meat loaf, it can also be used with many other dishes, from pastas to stuffed vegetables to salt cod braises to other meat loaves and meatballs. MAKES ABOUT 3 CUPS

---

| | |
|---|---|
| 1 can (28 ounces) plum tomatoes, with their juices | 2 to 3 tablespoons extra virgin olive oil (optional) |
| ½ cup tomato purée | Pinch of sugar (optional) |
| Salt and freshly ground black pepper | |

---

Put the tomatoes and their juices in a food processor and process until finely chopped but not liquefied. Transfer to a heavy saucepan. Stir in the tomato purée and place over low heat. Bring to a simmer and cook, stirring often, until the sauce is slightly thickened, about 20 minutes. Season with salt and pepper.

Add the oil and/or sugar to balance the flavors and serve warm. The sauce will keep in an airtight container in the refrigerator for up to 4 days.

## *Meatballs, Jewish Style*   POLPETTE ALLA GIUDIA

Here is a classic recipe for meatballs from the Italian Jewish kitchen. As noted in the introduction to this section, cooked vegetables were often added to extend the number of portions, and three such suggestions for additions follow here. You can add onion to this mixture, but it is more often added only when a vegetable is included in the mixture. SERVES 4 TO 6

---

| | |
|---|---|
| 1 pound ground beef (not too lean) | ¼ cup chopped fresh flat-leaf parsley |
| 1 egg, lightly beaten | Few gratings of nutmeg or pinch of ground cinnamon |
| ¾ cup fresh bread crumbs, soaked in beef broth or water and squeezed dry | |
| ½ yellow onion, grated (optional) | Salt and freshly ground black pepper |
| 2 or 3 cloves garlic, minced | Olive oil for frying |
| | 2 cups Basic Tomato Sauce (above) |

1 tablespoon grated lemon zest (optional)

¼ cup chopped fresh basil (optional)

1 tablespoon sugar dissolved in 2 tablespoons red wine vinegar

In a bowl, combine the beef, egg, bread crumbs, onion, garlic, parsley, and nutmeg and season with salt and pepper. Mix well with your hands. Shape a walnut-size ball of the mixture, fry until cooked through, taste, and adjust the seasoning of the remaining mixture if needed. Form the mixture into walnut-size balls.

Preheat the oven to 350°F. Film the bottom of a large sauté pan with oil and warm over high heat. In batches, fry the meatballs, turning as necessary, until colored on the outside but undercooked in the center, 8 to 10 minutes. Transfer to a baking dish.

In a saucepan, warm the tomato sauce over medium heat and stir in the lemon zest, basil, and the sugar-vinegar mixture. Heat briefly to blend the flavors, then spoon the tomato sauce evenly over the meatballs.

Cover the dish with foil, place in the oven, and bake until the sauce is slightly thickened and bubbly, 15 to 20 minutes. Serve hot.

VARIATION: *Turkish Meatballs (İzmir Köfte):* Add ½ teaspoon each ground cinnamon and sweet paprika to the meat mixture. Shape the meatballs as directed; then, before frying, coat with all-purpose flour, tapping off the excess. Combine the fried meatballs with the tomato sauce in a saucepan, add 1 green bell pepper, seeded and chopped, to the pan, and simmer the meatballs on the stove top until cooked through.

*Vegetable Variations:* To stretch the meat mixture, add one of the following:

1 large eggplant, roasted as directed in Master Recipe for Roasted Eggplant (page 27), peeled, pulp drained, and then mashed with minced garlic to taste, and 2 yellow onions, chopped and sautéed in olive oil until tender, mixed with 2 eggs

12 ounces zucchini, coarsely chopped, and 1 large yellow onion, chopped, sautéed together in olive oil until tender and mixed with 2 eggs

About 2 pounds leeks, white part only, chopped, cooked in water or olive oil until tender, and then chopped again and mixed with 2 eggs

## *Sephardic Leek and Meat Fritters*   ALBÓNDIGAS DE PRASA

The classic combination of leeks and meat is associated with the far western Anatolian city of Izmir. The mixture can be thickened with bread crumbs or mashed potatoes, and I have given both options here. A similar Greek recipe by Nicholas Stavroulakis adds chopped *huevos haminados* and dill to the mixture, and another by Esin Eden adds cinnamon. I like both variations. *Albóndigas de prasa kon muez,* which appears in *Sefarad Yemekleri,* calls for grated walnuts. Pine nuts would be a nice touch, as well. Any leftover fritters can be reheated in tomato sauce. MAKES 36 TO 40 FRITTERS; SERVES 6 TO 8

3 pounds leeks (about 12 small, 8 medium, or 4 large)

1 pound ground beef (not too lean)

3 or 4 slices coarse country bread, crusts removed, soaked in water and squeezed dry (⅔ to ¾ cup), or 2 potatoes, boiled, drained, and mashed (about 1 cup)

2 eggs, lightly beaten

1½ teaspoons salt

¾ teaspoon ground cinnamon (optional)

½ teaspoon freshly ground black pepper

2 to 3 tablespoons grated walnuts (optional)

½ cup chopped fresh dill

2 Long-Cooked Onion Skin Eggs (page 93), peeled and chopped (optional)

Olive oil for frying

All-purpose flour or matzo meal for coating

Lemon wedges for serving

Use the white and only a little of the green of the leeks. Halve the leeks lengthwise, then cut crosswise ½ inch thick. You should have about 6 cups. Immerse in a sink filled with cold water, then lift out and drain. Boil the leeks in lightly salted water in a saucepan until very tender, 20 to 30 minutes. Drain well, let cool, and squeeze dry. You should have about 2½ cups.

In a bowl, combine the leeks, beef, bread, beaten eggs, salt, cinnamon, pepper, walnuts, dill, and chopped eggs and knead with your hands until the mixture holds together well. Fry a nugget of the mixture until cooked through, then taste and adjust the seasoning if needed. Form the mixture into balls about 1¼ inches in diameter. You can keep them round or you can flatten them a bit so they cook more quickly.

Preheat the oven to 200°F. Line a large sheet pan with paper towels. Pour the oil to a depth of 1½ inches into a large, deep sauté pan and heat to 350°F. While the oil is heating, spread some flour on a plate. One at a time, dip the balls in the flour, coating evenly and tapping off the excess. In batches, add the balls to the hot oil and fry, turning as needed, until golden and cooked through, 8 to 10 minutes. Using a slotted spoon, transfer to the towel-lined pan and keep warm in the oven until all the fritters are cooked. Arrange on a platter and sprinkle lightly with salt. Pass the lemon wedges at the table.

VARIATION: *Spinach Fritters from Izmir (Albóndigas de Espinaka):* Omit the leeks. Cook 3 pounds spinach with just the rinsing water clinging to the leaves until wilted and tender, drain well, squeeze dry, and chop finely. Add the spinach to the meat mixture and use bread instead of potatoes. Shape the mixture as directed, then coat with flour, let stand briefly, and then coat with flour again. The mixture is fairly moist and the double coating of flour makes frying the fritters easier. Fry and serve as directed.

# Oven Casserole of White Beans and Meat Loaf from Tuscany

HAMIN TOSCANA DI FAGIOLI CON POLPETTONE

This Sabbath recipe pairs a classic Tuscan bean dish, *fagioli all'uccelletto,* with a typical ground meat mixture that is divided into two loaves, browned, and then cooked atop the beans, either in the oven or on the stove top. You can use the same mixture to make meatballs, shaping it into walnut-size balls, coating the balls with flour, browning them in oil, and then cooking them with the beans for about 10 minutes. SERVES 6

**WHITE BEANS**

1½ cups dried cannellini or other white beans

3 tablespoons olive oil

1 large yellow onion, chopped

2 or 3 cloves garlic, minced

3 or 4 fresh sage leaves

2 cups Basic Tomato Sauce (page 328)

Salt and freshly ground black pepper

**MEAT LOAVES**

1 pound ground beef (not too lean)

1 or 2 eggs, lightly beaten

⅔ cup fresh bread crumbs or matzo meal

½ yellow onion, grated (optional)

¼ cup chopped fresh flat-leaf parsley

Few gratings of nutmeg or pinch of ground cinnamon

Salt and freshly ground black pepper

All-purpose flour for coating

Olive oil for frying

Water, meat broth, or additional tomato sauce, if needed

To prepare the beans, pick over the beans, then place in a bowl, add water to cover, and let soak in the refrigerator overnight. Drain, rinse well, and transfer to a wide saucepan (choose an ovenproof pan if you will be baking the dish). Add water to cover by 2 inches and bring slowly to a boil over medium heat. Meanwhile, warm the oil in a sauté pan over medium heat. Add the onion, garlic, and sage and sauté for a few minutes to soften. Add the onion mixture to the beans along with the tomato sauce and season with salt and pepper. Turn down the heat to low, cover, and cook slowly until the beans are tender, about 1 hour. (The beans can be cooked to this point a day ahead and refrigerated. Reheat gently before continuing.)

Meanwhile, make and shape the meat loaves. In a bowl, combine the beef, 1 egg, bread crumbs, onion, parsley, nutmeg, 2 teaspoons salt, and ½ teaspoon pepper and mix well with your hands. Add the second egg if needed to bind. Shape the mixture into 2 oval meat loaves (or giant meatballs). Spread some flour on a plate and season with salt and pepper. Coat each loaf evenly with the seasoned flour, tapping off the excess.

Preheat the oven to 350°F if you will be cooking the dish in the oven. Pour the oil to a depth of ¼ inch into a large sauté pan and warm over medium-high heat. When the oil is hot, add the meat loaves and brown well on all sides. Transfer the meat loaves to the beans, re-cover the pan, and place in the preheated oven or place over low heat on the stove top and cook until the meat loaves are cooked through, about 30 minutes longer. Check the amount of liquid; if the beans seem dry, add water as needed. The dish should be somewhat brothy.

Carefully remove the meat loaves from the pan and let them rest for about 10 minutes. Slice the meat loaves and serve with the beans.

## Couscous with Meatballs, White Beans, and Greens from Livorno
### CUSCUSSÙ ALLA LIVORNESE

Geographical proximity is always a logical explanation for the migration of foods and recipes. Therefore, we might assume that the famous *cuscussù* of Trapani was carried to Sicily from North Africa, which was quite close by ship. But couscous traveled to Livorno with North African Jews in the 1270s. In fact, so many Jews from Algeria, Tunisia, and Morocco settled in Livorno that the town was nicknamed Little Jerusalem. It is now safe to assume that all the couscous dishes in Italy—in Sicily, in Sardinia, where it took the form of *fregula* or *casca,* and in Liguria and Tuscany—came with the North African Jews. They used lamb, however, while the Italians substituted veal, beef, or fish, often in the form of little meatballs. *Cuscussù* was usually served on Friday nights, and the room-temperature leftovers were eaten at the Sabbath midday meal.

A *cuscussù* meal is quite a bit of work, but all of the parts can be prepared separately and then reheated at serving time. The vegetable stew is not unlike a North African vegetable *tagine,* and the meatballs are common in both an Italian Jewish *cuscussù* and in North Africa. This is a model Mediterranean meal, with grain as the base, lots of vegetables and beans, and meat as a flavor accent—economical and satisfying. SERVES 6 TO 8

Oven Casserole of White Beans and Meat Loaf from Tuscany (page 331)

1 cup chopped cooked vegetable (optional)

**VEGETABLE STEW**

3 tablespoons olive oil

2 yellow onions, chopped

3 carrots, peeled and chopped

3 ribs celery, chopped

2 cups drained chopped canned plum tomatoes

1 small head green cabbage, quartered, cored, and cut crosswise into narrow strips

1 head escarole, cored and cut into narrow strips

1 cup shelled English peas

3 small zucchini, diced

Water or meat broth to cover

Salt and freshly ground black pepper

¼ cup chopped fresh mint or basil

Basic Couscous (page 158)

About 1½ cups meat broth for poaching meatballs (optional)

Spicy Squash Spread (page 37), optional

Cook the white beans and prepare the meat mixture as directed in the white beans and meat loaf recipe, adding the cooked vegetable to the meat mixture to extend it, if you like. Fry a nugget of the meat mixture and taste and adjust the seasoning of the remaining mixture if needed. Shape the meat mixture into marble-size meatballs, cover, and refrigerate until needed. Set the beans aside or refrigerate if made a day in advance.

To make the vegetable stew, warm the oil in a large sauté pan over medium heat. Add the onions, 1 carrot, and 1 celery rib and sauté until tender, about 10 minutes. Add the tomatoes and simmer for 5 minutes to blend the flavors. Add the remaining 2 carrots and 2 celery ribs along with the cabbage, escarole, peas, and zucchini and cook until all of the vegetables are almost tender, about 20 minutes. Add the water to barely cover and continue to simmer until tender, 5 to 8 minutes. Season with salt and pepper. Just before serving, stir in the mint.

To serve, prepare the couscous as directed. About 15 minutes before the couscous is ready, you can brown the meatballs as directed in the oven casserole recipe, or you can poach them gently in a little broth until cooked through. Reheat the beans, add the meatballs, and simmer together for 8 to 10 minutes to blend the flavors.

Place a mound of couscous in the center of a large platter. Top with the bean-and-meatball mixture and surround the couscous with the vegetable stew. Serve hot, accompanied with the squash condiment.

## *Sephardic Meatballs in Seven Styles*   ALBÓNDIGAS

The Spanish word *albóndiga* comes from the Arabic *al bundaq,* meaning "round." *Köfte* are Spanish *albóndigas,* or meatballs, but with a Turkish name. They are called *keftika* in the diminutive. Although the meat mixture is usually formed into balls, it can be shaped into oblongs or flattened patties, as well. Bread crumbs are the common binder, with matzo meal used during Passover. The versatile meatball is simple, and the sauce is the distinguishing feature of each version, as the seven sauces that follow illustrate.   SERVES 4 TO 6

MEATBALLS

1 pound ground beef or lamb (not too lean)

2 slices coarse country bread, crusts removed, soaked in water and squeezed dry, or ¼ cup matzo meal

½ cup grated yellow onion

¼ cup chopped fresh flat-leaf parsley

1 egg, lightly beaten

Salt and freshly ground black pepper

Olive oil for frying

Sauce of choice (recipes follow)

To make the meatballs, in a bowl, combine the meat, bread, onion, parsley, and egg, season with salt and pepper, and mix well with your hands. Shape a walnut-size ball of the mixture, fry until cooked through, taste, and adjust the seasoning of the remaining mixture if needed. Form the mixture into walnut-size balls or 2-inch-long oblong patties.

Film the bottom of a large sauté pan with oil and warm over high heat. In batches, fry the meatballs, turning as necessary, until lightly browned on all sides or until cooked through, depending on the selected sauce.

To make Meatballs in Sweet-and-Sour Sauce (*Albóndigas al Buyor*): Brown the meatballs as directed but do not cook through. Using a slotted spoon, transfer the meatballs to a plate. Add olive oil to the pan as needed to total 2 tablespoons and warm over medium heat. Add 1 small yellow onion, minced, and 2 cloves garlic, minced, and sauté until translucent, about 5 minutes. Add 4 large ripe tomatoes, peeled, seeded, and chopped, then season with salt and pepper and stir well. Add 1 tablespoon honey and ½ teaspoon ground cinnamon and simmer until the tomatoes have broken down and a sauce has formed, about 15 minutes. Add water if needed to thin. Return the meatballs to the pan, turn down the heat to low, cover, and simmer until the meatballs are cooked through, about 20 minutes. Garnish with 2 tablespoons chopped fresh flat-leaf parsley.

To make Meatballs with Egg and Lemon (*Terbiyeli Köfte*): Fry the meatballs as directed, cooking them through. Using a slotted spoon, transfer them to a platter and keep warm. Add ½ cup water to the sauté pan and deglaze the pan over medium-high heat, stirring to dislodge any brown bits on the pan bottom. Dissolve 1 tablespoon all-purpose flour in 3 tablespoons water and gradually add to the pan, stirring constantly. In a bowl, beat together 2 eggs and the juice of 2 lemons until very frothy. Gradually whisk in about half of the hot pan juices to temper the eggs. Pour the egg mixture into the pan and cook over very low heat, stirring constantly, until the mixture thickens and coats a spoon. Pour the sauce over the meatballs. Garnish with chopped fresh flat-leaf parsley.

To make Meatballs with Fruit (*Erikli Köfte*): This dish of Spanish origin dates to the fifteenth century and shows the Moorish influence on the food of the Andalusian Jews. Pit 25 tart plums and boil in water to cover until tender and the fruits have broken down to a sauce-like consistency, about 20 minutes. (Or use 25 pitted prunes or dried apricots, soaked in water to cover overnight, then cooked in their soaking water until tender and starting to break down.) Fry the meatballs as directed, cooking them through. Add the meatballs to the plum sauce along with a squeeze of lemon juice and simmer until the sauce has reduced.

To make Meatballs with Almond Sauce (*Bademli Köfte*): Fry the meatballs as directed but do not cook through. Using a slotted spoon, transfer them to a plate. Add 1 cup water to the sauté pan and deglaze the pan over medium-high heat, stirring to dislodge any brown bits on the pan bottom. Add ½ cup ground almonds and 2 tablespoons chopped fresh flat-leaf parsley, turn down the heat to medium, and simmer for 15 minutes. Return the meatballs to the pan and simmer in the sauce until cooked through, about 15 minutes. Add water if needed to thin the sauce.

To make Meatballs with Walnut Sauce (*Nogada*): Increase the grated onion in the meat mixture to ¾ cup to stand up to the intensity of the walnuts. Fry the meatballs as directed but do not cook through. Using a slotted spoon, transfer the meatballs to a plate. Add ½ cup dry red wine to the sauté pan and deglaze the pan over medium-high heat, stirring to dislodge any brown bits on the pan bottom. Add ½ cup chopped walnuts, turn down the heat to medium, and simmer until the sauce thickens. Return the meatballs to the pan, turn down the heat to low, and simmer in the sauce until cooked through, 15 to 20 minutes.

To make Meatballs with Braised Garlic (*Köfte kon Ajo Sofrito*): Fry the meatballs as directed but do not cook through. Using a slotted spoon, transfer the meatballs to a plate. In a large sauté pan or saucepan, combine the peeled cloves of 2 heads garlic, 2 tablespoons olive oil, the juice of 3 lemons, 1½ cups water, and a pinch of sugar. Bring to a boil over high heat, turn down the heat to low, cover, and simmer until the garlic is tender, about 25 minutes. Add the meatballs to the pan and simmer in the sauce until cooked through, 15 to 20 minutes.

To make Meatballs with Tahini (*Köfte bil Tahini*): This dish is Arabic in origin but has been adopted by the Israelis in a big way. Fry the meatballs as directed but do not cook through. Transfer to a baking dish and top with 2½ cups tahini sauce (page 112). Bake in a preheated 350°F oven until the sauce has thickened to the consistency of heavy cream and the meatballs are cooked through, 10 to 15 minutes. Top with toasted pine nuts.

## *Moroccan Meatball Tagine*   KEFTA MKAOUARA

These tasty Moroccan meatballs are steamed in a fragrant tomato sauce. Traditionally, the meatballs are shaped and added directly to the sauce, but they can be browned first, if you like. For a more filling dish, you can add eggs to the dish just before serving. Serve with couscous. SERVES 4 TO 6

**MEATBALLS**

1 pound ground beef (not too lean)

1 tablespoon sweet paprika

2 teaspoons ground toasted cumin

1½ teaspoons salt

½ teaspoon freshly ground black pepper

½ teaspoon ground cinnamon

¼ teaspoon cayenne pepper

¼ teaspoon ground ginger

3 tablespoons finely minced fresh flat-leaf parsley

2 tablespoons finely minced fresh cilantro

1 small yellow onion, grated or finely chopped (⅓ to ½ cup)

⅓ cup matzo meal, or ½ cup fresh bread crumbs, soaked in water and squeezed dry (optional)

1 egg, lightly beaten, if needed

All-purpose flour for coating (optional)

2 tablespoons olive oil (optional)

SAUCE

2 tablespoons olive oil

2 yellow onions, chopped

4 cloves garlic, minced

2 teaspoons ground toasted cumin

½ teaspoon freshly ground black pepper

Pinch of cayenne pepper

½ cup chopped fresh flat-leaf parsley, mint, or cilantro, or a mixture

2 cups Basic Tomato Sauce (page 328)

1 cup beef broth

1 or 2 eggs per person (optional)

---

To make the meatballs, in a bowl, combine the beef, paprika, cumin, salt, black pepper, cinnamon, cayenne, ginger, parsley, cilantro, onion, and matzo meal and mix well with your hands. If the mixture does not adhere easily, add the egg to bind. Shape a 1-inch ball of the mixture, fry until cooked through, taste, and adjust the seasoning of the remaining mixture if needed. Form the mixture into 1-inch balls.

To brown the meatballs, spread some flour on a plate. Coat the balls evenly with flour, tapping off the excess. Warm the oil in a large sauté pan over high heat. In batches, add the balls and brown well on all sides. Using a slotted spoon, transfer to a plate.

To make the sauce, warm the oil in a large sauté pan over medium heat. Add the onions and cook, stirring occasionally, until translucent and tender, 8 to 10 minutes. Add the garlic, cumin, black pepper, cayenne, and parsley and cook, stirring occasionally, for 5 minutes to blend the flavors. Stir in the tomato sauce and broth and bring to a simmer.

Place the meatballs on top of the sauce, cover the pan, and cook until the meatballs are cooked through, about 15 minutes. To add the eggs, crack them directly on top of the meatballs, re-cover the pan, and cook just until the whites are set and the yolks are done to your liking. Serve hot.

## Meatballs with Saffron Sunset Sauce
### LES BOULETTES SAUCE CREPUSCULE

The Arabic name for this dish, *chems el aachi,* means "setting sun." The golden color of the sauce is reminiscent of a glorious sunset in Morocco. The grated potatoes help stretch the amount of meat needed to make people feel satisfied. Although the seasoning of the meat mixture is mild, the sauce has enough zip to give this dish a good, complex flavor. Interestingly, in *Eat and Be Satisfied,* John Cooper refers to a recipe for *albóndigas* in a saffron sauce that appeared in *Libro novo,* published in Venice in the mid-sixteenth century. It is obviously a dish that arrived in Venice with the Spanish Jews, though, of course, its origin is the Arab kitchen. SERVES 8

**MEATBALLS**

2 pounds ground beef (not too lean)

3 russet potatoes (about 1½ pounds), peeled and grated

2 eggs, lightly beaten

½ cup fine dried bread crumbs or matzo meal

1 tablespoon salt

1 teaspoon freshly ground black pepper

1 teaspoon ground mace or freshly grated nutmeg

½ teaspoon saffron threads, finely crushed and steeped in ¼ cup hot water

**SAUCE**

¼ cup olive oil

4 cloves garlic, minced

1 bunch fresh cilantro, chopped

1 teaspoon sweet paprika

1 teaspoon ground turmeric

1 teaspoon ground toasted cumin

Pinch of cayenne pepper

½ teaspoon saffron threads, finely crushed and steeped in 4 tablespoons hot water

1 cup water or meat broth, or as needed

To make the meatballs, in a large bowl, combine the beef, potatoes, and eggs and mix well with your hands. Add the bread crumbs, salt, pepper, mace, and saffron infusion and mix well with your hands. Shape a walnut-size ball of the mixture, fry until cooked through, taste, and adjust the seasoning of the remaining mixture if needed. Form the mixture into walnut-size balls and set aside.

To make the sauce, warm the oil in a large sauté pan over medium heat. Add the garlic, cilantro, paprika, turmeric, cumin, cayenne, and 2 tablespoons of the saffron infusion and cook, stirring, until the mixture turns yellow. Add the water, which should be at least ½ inch deep so the meatballs will steam; add more as needed. Add the meatballs, preferably in a single layer, cover, and simmer over low heat until cooked through, 25 to 30 minutes. Add the remaining 2 tablespoons saffron infusion and heat through. Taste and adjust the seasoning of the sauce. Serve hot.

## *Prune-Stuffed Persian Meatballs with Green Herbs* KUFTEH-YE SABZI

The abundant use of green herbs (*sabzi*) is prevalent in the Persian kitchen, such as in the popular meat stew, *ghormeh sabzi* (page 299), and fish stew, *ghormeh sabzi ba mahi* (page 240). Here, the herbs are combined with large meatballs, or *kufteh,* a word derived from *kubidan,* which means "to pound." The large meatballs might be stuffed with walnuts, dates, eggs, or prunes. These prune-stuffed meatballs are popular in the city of Tabriz, where they are made with the country's prized golden dried plums. Serve with Persian Rice (page 149). SERVES 8

¼ cup yellow split peas, picked over and soaked in water to cover overnight or for at least a few hours

½ cup basmati rice, soaked in water to cover overnight or for at least a few hours and drained

1 pound ground lamb

2 eggs, lightly beaten

1 cup chopped fresh cilantro

1 cup chopped fresh flat-leaf parsley

½ cup chopped fresh garlic chives

½ cup chopped fresh tarragon

½ cup chopped fresh summer savory

1 teaspoon salt

½ teaspoon freshly ground black pepper

½ teaspoon ground turmeric

8 pitted prunes, plus 4 extra if you want a sweeter sauce

1 large yellow onion, sliced

2 tablespoons olive oil

2 to 3 cups water or broth

Juice of 1 lemon

Coarse country bread for serving

Drain the peas, rinse, place in a small saucepan, and add water to cover by about 2 inches. Bring to a boil over medium-high heat and cook for 20 minutes, adding the rice during the last 10 minutes. Drain and let cool.

In a bowl, combine the cooled peas and rice, lamb, eggs, cilantro, parsley, chives, tarragon, savory, salt, pepper, and turmeric and mix well with your hands. Form the mixture into 8 orange-size balls. Make a hollow in each ball, stuff with 1 prune, and close the meat around it.

Select a deep sauté pan or a Dutch oven large enough to hold the meatballs in a single layer, add the oil, and warm over medium-high heat. Add the onion slices and fry, turning as needed, until browned and caramelized, about 20 minutes. Add the water, bring to a boil, turn down the heat to low, and carefully slide in the meatballs, one at a time. The meatballs should be covered with liquid; if they are not, add water as needed to cover. If you want the sauce to be sweeter, add the 4 extra prunes to the pan. Cover and simmer gently, rolling the meatballs a few times for even cooking, until they are cooked through, 30 to 40 minutes. Add the lemon juice during the last 15 minutes.

Using a slotted spoon, transfer the meatballs to individual soup bowls. If the sauce is thin, boil it until it is reduced to a good consistency, then spoon it over the meatballs and serve. Accompany with bread for sopping up the sauce.

## Cumin-Flavored Meat Patties with Two Sauces
### KEFTA DE VIANDE AU CUMIN ET DEUX SAUCES

In *Marrakech la Rouge*, Hélène Gans Perez describes a Moroccan dish of meat patties served with onion jam, which inspired this recipe. These *kefta* are more like small burgers than meatballs. They can be round or flat, so I have provided both options. In a kosher kitchen, they are grilled until well-done, but you may prefer them medium-rare. You can also opt to fry them rather than grill them.

Some onion jams are seasoned with a mixture of sweet spices, such as ginger, mace, nutmeg, cinnamon, and cloves (page 362), but this is a simpler version, seasoned with only cinnamon and sugar. I have also included a spicy tomato-based sauce here, but you could also serve these meat patties with the Moroccan tomato conserve on page 372. SERVES 4

---

ONION JAM

3 tablespoons olive oil

3 pounds yellow onions, halved and sliced or chopped

1 tablespoon ground cinnamon, or 2 tablespoons ras el hanout

¼ cup sugar or honey

1 teaspoon salt

SPICY TOMATO SAUCE

¼ cup raisins, plumped in hot water and drained

1½ cups tomato purée

1 or 2 cloves garlic

1 tablespoons olive oil

1 tablespoon fresh lemon juice

1 teaspoon Aleppo or Maras pepper flakes, or ½ teaspoon cayenne pepper

Pinch of ground cinnamon

MEAT MIXTURE

1 pound ground beef or lamb (not too lean)

2 to 3 tablespoons olive oil

3 cloves garlic, minced

2 tablespoons chopped fresh flat-leaf parsley

2 tablespoons chopped fresh cilantro

1 tablespoon ground cumin

¼ teaspoon cayenne pepper

1½ teaspoons salt

½ teaspoon freshly ground black pepper

---

Select the onion jam or tomato sauce. To make the onion jam, warm the oil in a large sauté pan over medium heat. Add the onions and cook, stirring often, until translucent and very soft, about 15 minutes. Add the cinnamon, sugar, and salt, turn down the heat to low, and continue to cook and stir until the onions are the consistency of jam, 35 to 45 minutes. The mixture should be dark brown and taste aromatic and sweet. You should have 2½ to 3 cups. Serve warm.

To make the tomato sauce, combine all of the ingredients in a blender or food processor and purée until smooth. Transfer to a small saucepan and simmer over low heat, stirring occasionally, for 20 minutes to blend the flavors. You should have about 1½ cups. Serve warm or at room temperature.

To make the meat mixture, in a bowl, combine all of the ingredients and mix well with your hands. Fry a small nugget of the mixture until cooked through, taste, and adjust the seasoning of the remaining mixture if needed. Divide the mixture into 8 equal portions and shape into oval patties. Alternatively, divide the mixture into 16 equal portions and shape the portions into balls around flat metal skewers.

Prepare a fire in a charcoal grill, then grill the patties or skewers, turning as needed, until cooked to desired doneness. If you do not want to fire up the grill, you can skip the skewers and fry the patties in a cast-iron frying or stove-top griddle filmed with a little oil. Serve hot, accompanied with the onion jam or spicy tomato sauce.

VARIATIONS: *Moroccan:* Combine 1 pound ground beef or lamb; 1 bunch fresh cilantro, chopped; 3 tablespoons chopped fresh mint; 1 teaspoon each ground cumin and sweet paprika; 1½ teaspoons salt; and ½ teaspoon freshly ground black pepper and mix well with your hands. Shape into patties and grill as directed. Serve with harissa, homemade (page 355) or store-bought.

*Syrian:* Combine 1 pound ground beef, ½ cup finely minced yellow onion, 6 tablespoons minced fresh flat-leaf parsley, 3 eggs, ¼ cup fine dried bread crumbs, 1½ teaspoons salt, 1 teaspoon ground allspice, and ½ teaspoon each ground cinnamon and freshly ground black pepper. Shape into small patties, fry in olive oil, and serve with pita bread and the spicy tomato sauce.

*Greek from Rhodes:* Substitute 1 teaspoon *bahārāt* for the cumin in the meat mixture. Shape into patties and grill as directed. Serve with spicy tomato sauce.

*My Lamb Kefta "Burger":* Combine 1 pound ground lamb; ½ yellow onion, grated; 3 cloves garlic, minced; ¼ cup chopped fresh flat-leaf parsley; 1 teaspoon each salt, Aleppo or Maras pepper flakes, ground cumin, and smoked or sweet paprika; ½ teaspoon each freshly ground black pepper and ground cinnamon; ¼ teaspoon ground ginger; and pinch of cayenne pepper. Shape into patties, grill or fry in olive oil, and serve in pita bread with Moroccan-Inspired Sweet-and-Hot Tomato Conserve (page 372).

## Meat-Stuffed Grape Leaves  YAPRAKES

Unlike rice-filled grape leaves, which usually appear as part of a meze assortment, these meat-stuffed leaves, also known as *ojas de parra* and dolmas, are typically served as a main course. In Sephardic kitchens in Greece and Turkey, they are often paired with an egg-and-lemon sauce (see variation). The same filling can be used to stuff vegetables (recipe follows). SERVES 6 TO 8

FILLING

¼ cup olive oil

1 large yellow onion, chopped (about 1½ cups)

3 cloves garlic, minced

2 tablespoons chopped fresh flat-leaf parsley

1 tablespoon salt

1 teaspoon ground allspice

1 teaspoon freshly ground black pepper

1 teaspoon ground cinnamon

½ cup pine nuts, toasted

½ cup dried currants, plumped in hot water and drained

1 pound ground lamb or beef (not too lean)

1 cup water

½ to 1 cup basmati rice, rinsed, soaked in water to cover for 1 hour, and drained

40 to 50 brine-packed grape leaves, well rinsed and patted dry

1½ cups extra virgin olive oil, plus more for drizzling

Juice of 1 to 2 lemons

To make the filling, warm the oil in a very large sauté pan over medium heat. Add the onion and cook, stirring occasionally, until translucent and tender, 8 to 10 minutes. Add the garlic, parsley, salt, allspice, pepper, cinnamon, pine nuts, and currants and cook, stirring, for 3 minutes. Add the meat and cook, breaking up any lumps with a wooden spoon, until it is no longer pink, about 5 minutes. Meanwhile, in a small saucepan, bring the water to a boil, add the rice, and cook for 5 minutes. Drain the rice, add to the meat mixture, mix well, and let the filling cool.

In batches, lay the grape leaves, smooth side up, on a work surface. Snip off the stems with scissors. To stuff each leaf, place a generous teaspoon or so of the mixture near the stem end of a leaf. Fold the stem end over the filling, fold in the sides, and roll up into a cylinder. Do not roll too tightly, as the rice will expand during cooking. Repeat until all of the filling is used.

Select a wide saucepan or a deep, wide sauté pan large enough to hold the stuffed leaves in a single layer. If you have extra leaves, use them to line the bottom of the pan, as they will help prevent the stuffed leaves from sticking. Place the stuffed leaves, seam side down and close to one another, in the pan. Pour in the oil, the lemon juice to taste, and enough very hot water just to cover the stuffed leaves. Top with a heavy ovenproof plate just slightly smaller than the diameter of the pan to prevent the stuffed leaves from moving. Bring the liquid to a boil over medium-high heat, turn down the heat to low, cover, and simmer for 35 to 40 minutes. (Alternatively, transfer the covered pan to a preheated 350°F oven for about 45 minutes.)

Remove from the heat, uncover, and remove the plate. Most of the liquid will have been absorbed by the rice. Let the stuffed leaves rest for 5 minutes, then, using a spatula, carefully transfer them to a platter. (If you will be making the egg-and-lemon sauce variation, reserve about 1 cup of the pan juices.) Drizzle with oil and serve.

VARIATIONS: *Persian Variation with Herbs:* Add ½ cup cooked yellow split peas and 3 cups chopped fresh flat-leaf parsley, cilantro, dill, mint, marjoram, and tarragon, in any combination, to the meat and rice mixture.

*Syrian Variation with Apricots:* Tuck 12 to 14 dried apricots among the stuffed grape leaves before topping with the ovenproof plate and then cook as directed. Serve with the pan juices seasoned with a generous measure of fresh lemon juice and tamarind extract.

*Greek and Turkish Variation with Egg-and-Lemon Sauce:* Reserve 1 cup of the hot pan juices. In a bowl, beat together 2 whole eggs or 3 egg yolks and the juice of 2 small lemons (4 to 5 tablespoons) until very frothy. Gradually whisk in about half of the hot pan juices to temper the eggs. Pour the egg mixture into the pan and cook over very low heat, stirring constantly, until the mixture thickens and coats a spoon. Spoon over the stuffed grape leaves.

## Meat-Stuffed Vegetables   REYNADAS

Also known as *rellenos* and as *legumbres yenos de karne,* these stuffed vegetables use the same fillings as the Meat-Stuffed Grape Leaves. If you are using an assortment of vegetables, select those of a similar size for a nice visual presentation.

---

**About 4 pounds tomatoes, bell peppers, zucchini, onions, or eggplants, or a mixture**

**Filling for Meat-Stuffed Grape Leaves (page 340)**

---

Select a vegetable or an assortment of vegetables to stuff and ready them for stuffing as directed. You need to ready the vegetables first, as the pulp removed from some of them is added to the filling. Then, make the filling as directed, let cool, and stuff and bake the vegetables as directed.

To make stuffed tomatoes (*reynadas de tomat*): Cut off the tops of ripe tomatoes (about 12) and scoop out the pulp. Reserve the pulp, all of the juices, and the tops. Sprinkle the inside of each tomato with salt and a little sugar. Set aside. Put the tomato pulp in a blender or food processor and purée until smooth. Add to the filling. Stuff the filling into the tomatoes. Do not pack the filling too tightly, as the rice will expand. Place the tomatoes in a baking dish and replace the tops. Pour about ⅓ cup hot water into the dish and spoon ½ cup olive oil over the tomatoes. Bake, basting occasionally with the pan juices, until the filling is heated through and the tomatoes are tender, about 30 minutes. Serve hot or cold.

To make stuffed bell peppers (*reynadas de pipirushkas*): Cut off the stem ends of the bell peppers and remove and discard the seeds and any thick ribs. Parboil the shells in boiling water for 4 to 5 minutes, then drain, stuff, and bake as for the tomatoes. Serve warm.

To make stuffed zucchini (*kalavasas yenas de karne*): Cut the zucchini in half lengthwise. If the zucchini are large, using a small melon baller, scoop out and discard the seeds from each half to make a good-size hollow. If using small zucchini, you may need to enlarge the hollow by cutting out some of the pulp, as well. Chop any pulp you remove and sauté it with the onion for the filling. Parboil the shells in boiling water for 3 minutes, then drain, stuff, and bake as directed for the tomatoes. Serve warm.

To make stuffed onions (*reynadas de sevoya*): Bring a large saucepan filled with water to a boil. Add large yellow onions and boil until tender but not soft, about 10 minutes. Drain the onions, let cool until they can be handled, and cut in half crosswise. Scoop out part of the center from each half to make a cavity. Chop the removed onion and use it in the filling. Stuff and bake the onion halves as directed for the tomatoes, reducing the cooking time to about 20 minutes, or until the onions are golden. Serve warm.

To make stuffed eggplants (*kucaras de berenjena*): Halve the eggplants lengthwise and scoop out some of the pulp to make a shell. Chop the pulp, discarding as many seeds as possible, and sauté the pulp with the onion for the filling. Fry the eggplant cases in olive oil for about 5 minutes to soften. Stuff with the filling and bake as directed for the tomatoes. Serve warm.

If you are serving the stuffed vegetables warm, you may want to accompany them with an egg-and-lemon sauce. Follow the directions in the Greek and Turkish Variation with Egg-and-Lemon Sauce that follows the stuffed grape leaves recipe, using 1 cup hot broth for the pan juices.

VARIATION: *Persian Meat-Stuffed Quince (Dolmeh Beh):* You can use the same filling to stuff 6 quinces (or 12 apples). Rub the fuzz off of the quinces and rinse well. Tradition calls for cutting off the top of each quince and scooping out the core and flesh with a sharp melon baller, leaving a shell ½ to ¾ inch thick. But that's hard to do because quinces are so tough. My solution is to bake the fruits whole in a preheated 325°F oven until they feel soft, 1 to 1¼ hours. You can then cut them in half through the stem end or cut off the top and easily scoop out the flesh, leaving a shell ¾ inch thick. Spoon the filling into the quinces and place in a baking pan. Stir together 1 cup water, ½ cup sugar, and ¼ cup fresh lemon juice, dissolving the sugar, and add the mixture to the pan. Bake in a preheated 350°F oven until the quinces are tender, 40 to 60 minutes if you prebaked them and 1½ hours if you have stuffed them without prebaking them. The timing will depend on the size and ripeness of the fruits. Serve warm.

## Braised Meat-Stuffed Artichokes   RAGOÛT D'ARTICHAUTS FARCIS

Braised artichokes stuffed with ground meat are popular throughout the Middle East and North Africa. Léone Jaffin's Algerian recipe adds peas and pearl onions for a very pretty presentation, which I have added here. Some cooks use mashed potato instead of the rice for binding the meat filling. Serve the artichokes with fresh noodles or saffron rice pilaf, or with potatoes during Passover. SERVES 8

Juice of 1 lemon, plus 1 lemon, halved

8 medium artichokes

1 pound ground beef (not too lean)

¼ cup basmati rice, rinsed, soaked in water to cover for 30 minutes, and drained

4 cloves garlic, minced

¼ cup chopped fresh flat-leaf parsley

Spice of choice: 1 teaspoon ground allspice for Arabic version, 1 teaspoon bahārāt for Persian version, 1 teaspoon ground cumin for Moroccan version, or 1 teaspoon each ground cinnamon and allspice for Syrian version

1 egg, lightly beaten

4 tablespoons peanut oil

Salt and freshly ground black pepper

12 to 16 pearl onions, peeled

1½ to 2 cups water

Pinch of saffron threads

1 bay leaf

2½ pounds English peas, shelled (about 2¼ cups shelled)

Pinch of sugar (optional)

Have ready a large bowl of water to which you have added the lemon juice. Working with 1 artichoke at a time, trim off the stem flush with the bottom, then remove all of the leaves until you reach the heart. Remove and discard the choke with a small pointed spoon or a paring knife. Pare away the dark green areas from the base, rub the cut areas of the artichoke heart with the cut lemon, and slip the heart into the lemon water.

To make the filling, in a bowl, combine the beef, rice, garlic, parsley, spice of choice, egg, and 1 tablespoon of the oil and season with salt and pepper. Mix well with your hands. Fry a small nugget of the mixture until cooked through, taste, and adjust the seasoning of the remaining mixture if needed. Divide the mixture into 8 equal portions and shape each portion into a ball. Drain the artichoke hearts, pat dry, and stuff each heart with a ball.

Select a saucepan wide enough to hold all of the artichokes in a single layer. Add the remaining 3 tablespoons oil and warm over medium-high heat. Add the onions and sauté until they take on a bit of color, 5 to 8 minutes. Add 1½ cups of the water along with the saffron, bay leaf, and a pinch of salt. When the water comes to a boil, add the artichoke hearts, base down. The water should be about ½ inch deep; if it isn't, add the remaining water. Turn down the heat to low, cover, and simmer for 25 minutes. Add the peas and the sugar to the pan juices and continue to cook until the artichokes and the peas are tender and the stuffing is cooked through, 8 to 10 minutes longer. Serve warm.

VARIATIONS: *Persian Variation:* Season the meat filling with 1 teaspoon bahārāt, then stuff the artichoke hearts as directed and place them in a baking dish along with a simple tomato sauce (page 328) flavored with lots of fresh lemon juice. Bake in a preheated 350°F oven until the artichokes are tender and the stuffing is cooked through, about 30 minutes.

*Syrian Variation:* Season the meat filling with 1 teaspoon each ground cinnamon and allspice, then stuff the artichoke hearts as directed and place them in a baking dish along with a simple tomato sauce (page 328) flavored with lots of fresh lemon juice and seasoned to taste with tamarind extract, ground cinnamon, and allspice. Bake in a preheated 350°F oven until the artichokes are tender and the stuffing is cooked through, about 30 minutes.

## *Egyptian Meat-Stuffed Artichoke Hearts*   KHARSHOUF MAHSHI

Egyptian cooks stuff artichokes with a mixture of meat, onion, pine nuts, seasonings, and an egg but no rice or bread to bind. SERVES 8

---

Juice of 1 lemon, plus 1 lemon, halved

8 medium artichokes

1 pound ground beef (not too lean)

½ cup grated yellow onion, plus
2 yellow onions, sliced

¼ cup chopped fresh flat-leaf parsley

1 teaspoon ground cinnamon

1 teaspoon ground allspice

¼ cup pine nuts

1 egg, lightly beaten

Salt and freshly ground black pepper

3 or 4 carrots, peeled and sliced

2 cups beef broth, plus more if needed

Fresh lemon juice for serving

---

Have ready a large bowl of water to which you have added the lemon juice. Working with 1 artichoke at a time, trim off the stem flush with the bottom, then remove all of the leaves until you reach the heart. Remove and discard the choke with a small pointed spoon or a paring knife. Pare away the dark green areas from the base, rub the cut areas of the artichoke heart with the cut lemon, and slip the heart into the lemon water.

Preheat the oven to 350°F.

To make the filling, in a bowl, combine the beef, grated onion, parsley, cinnamon, allspice, pine nuts, and egg and season with salt and pepper. Mix well with your hands. Fry a small nugget of the mixture until cooked through, taste, and adjust the seasoning of the remaining mixture if needed. Divide the mixture into 8 equal portions and shape each portion into a ball. Drain the artichoke hearts, pat dry, and stuff each heart with a ball.

Arrange the stuffed artichoke hearts, base down, in a baking dish and surround them with the onion slices and carrots. Add enough broth to come halfway up the sides of the artichokes. Cover the dish with foil and bake until the artichokes are tender and the filling is cooked through, about 30 minutes. (Alternatively, assemble the artichoke hearts, onion slices and carrots, and broth in a deep sauté pan or wide saucepan, cover, and simmer over low heat on the stove top for about 40 minutes.) Just before serving, brighten the dish with a bit of lemon juice. Serve warm.

## *Lebanese Meat-Stuffed Squash with Apricot Sauce* KRA'A

This is an ideal dish for the Rosh Hashanah table. The sweetness of the New Year is echoed in the sweetness of the apricots. There are three ways to stuff zucchini. The most difficult way is to keep them whole and hollow them out with an apple corer. Some Moroccan cooks peel large zucchini in a striped pattern, cut off the ends, cut the zucchini crosswise into 1½- to 2-inch lengths, and then scoop out the pulp, leaving a shell about ⅓ inch thick. I find the third way the easiest: halve the zucchini lengthwise and scoop out the seeds and pulp with a small melon baller. SERVES 6

12 medium zucchini

1 pound ground beef (not too lean)

½ to 1 cup long-grain white rice, preferably basmati, rinsed, soaked in water to cover for 1 hour, and drained

½ teaspoon ground cinnamon

½ teaspoon ground allspice

Salt

2½ cups plus 2 tablespoons water

1 cup dried apricots, soaked in hot water to cover

Juice of 1 lemon

2 tablespoons sugar

2 tablespoons tamarind paste dissolved in ¼ cup water, or 2 tablespoons pomegranate molasses

Cut the zucchini in half lengthwise. Scoop out the pulp with a small melon baller, discarding the seeds and reserving the pulp. Chop the pulp.

In a bowl, combine the beef, rice, cinnamon, allspice, the reserved squash pulp, 1 teaspoon salt, and the 2 tablespoons water and mix well with your hands. Fry a small nugget of the mixture until cooked through, taste, and adjust the seasoning of the remaining mixture if needed. Stuff the mixture into the zucchini shells. If you have leftover meat mixture, shape it into marble-size balls.

Arrange the stuffed zucchini in a single layer in a wide saucepan. Dissolve ½ teaspoon salt in the remaining 2½ cups water and add the water to the pan. If you have made meatballs from leftover filling, tuck them in among the zucchini. Bring the water to a simmer over medium heat, turn down the heat to low, cover, and simmer for 15 minutes.

In a separate saucepan, combine the apricots and their soaking water, the lemon juice, sugar, and tamarind paste, bring to a simmer over medium heat, and simmer for 5 minutes. When the zucchini has cooked for 15 minutes, add the apricot mixture to the pan, re-cover, and cook over low heat until the zucchini is tender and the apricots have formed a sauce. This might take 30 to 40 minutes. Check from time to time to make sure there is enough liquid in the pan and add water if needed. Serve warm.

VARIATION: *Syrian Meat-Stuffed Squash with Tomato (Mahshi Koosa):* Add 1 cup tomato purée to the apricot sauce.

## *Meat-Filled Cabbage Leaves Cooked with Fruit* DOLMAYANI

These cabbage rolls from *Sefarad Yemekleri,* published in Istanbul, are part of a large repertoire of Sephardic dolmas. This recipe is particularly interesting because of the delicious sweet-and-sour sauce that forms after cooking the cabbage packets with seasonal fruit—quinces in fall or winter and plums in summer. SERVES 6

| | |
|---|---|
| 1 large head green cabbage | 2 yellow onions, grated |
| 1 pound ground beef or lamb (not too lean) | 1½ teaspoons salt |
| 3 tablespoons chopped fresh flat-leaf parsley | ½ teaspoon freshly ground black pepper |
| 3 tablespoons chopped fresh dill | 2 or 3 quinces, or 1 pound small plums (about 8) |
| ½ cup long-grain white rice, rinsed, soaked in water to cover for 30 minutes, and drained | Juice of 4 lemons (about 1 cup) |
| | 1 cup tomato juice |

Bring a large pot two-thirds full of salted water to a boil. Cut out the core of the cabbage with a sharp knife. Slip the cabbage into the water, reduce the heat so the water simmers, and cook until the cabbage leaves soften, about 10 minutes. Drain the cabbage carefully and remove the outer large leaves. You should have 12 to 16 leaves. Reserve the remaining cabbage for another use.

In a bowl, combine the meat, parsley, dill, rice, onions, salt, and pepper. Mix well with your hands. Fry a small nugget of the mixture until cooked through, taste, and adjust the seasoning of the remaining mixture if needed.

Spread the cabbage leaves out on a work surface. Place a few tablespoons of the meat mixture on the center of a leaf, fold over the top, fold in the sides, and then fold up the bottom part of the leaf, making a dolma-like packet. Skewer closed with toothpicks. Repeat until all of the filling is used.

If using the quinces, peel, halve, and core them, then cut into ½-inch-thick slices or into ½-inch dice. If using plums, halve or quarter them, discarding the pits.

Place the cabbage packets, seam side down, in a single layer in a large, wide pot or saucepan. Top with the fruit. (If all of the packets will not fit in a single layer, arrange as many as will fit, top with some of the fruit, and then repeat the layers as needed.) Add the lemon juice and tomato juice to the pan and bring to a simmer over low heat. Cover and simmer until tender, 1 to 1½ hours. (Alternatively, place the covered pot in a preheated 300°F oven for 1 to 1½ hours.) Taste the pan juices and adjust the seasoning if needed. Serve hot.

## *Meat-Stuffed Baked Potatoes*  PATATAS KAVAKADAS

This recipe from *Sefarad Yemekleri* uses uncooked boiling potatoes as the shell for a savory meat filling. I have suggested the addition of a little grated onion because it adds a depth of flavor and plays off the starchiness of the potatoes. Although not traditional, swirling a little tomato sauce into the pan juices just before serving is a tasty addition. SERVES 8

3 pounds boiling potatoes (about 8 large)

1 pound ground beef or lamb (not too lean)

2 slices coarse country bread, crusts removed, soaked in water and squeezed dry (about ½ cup)

½ small yellow onion, grated

3 tablespoons chopped fresh flat-leaf parsley (optional)

Salt and freshly ground black pepper

Sunflower oil for frying

1½ cups all-purpose flour

3 eggs

1½ to 2 cups beef broth

Peel the potatoes and cut them in half lengthwise. With a small melon baller or a small, sharp knife, scoop or carve a pocket out of the center of each potato half, leaving an outer shell about ⅓ inch thick.

In a bowl, combine the meat, bread, onion, parsley, 1½ teaspoons salt, and ½ teaspoon pepper and mix well with your hands. Fry a small nugget of the mixture until cooked through, taste, and adjust the seasoning of the remaining mixture if needed. Fill the potatoes with the mixture.

Preheat the oven to 400°F. Pour the oil to a depth of 1 inch into a deep, heavy sauté pan and warm over medium heat. While the oil is heating, put the flour in a shallow bowl and season with salt and pepper. In a second bowl, whisk the eggs until blended.

In batches, dip the potatoes in the seasoned flour, coating them evenly and tapping off the excess, and then in the eggs, allowing the excess to drip off, and slip them into the hot oil. Fry, turning as needed, until golden on all sides, about 5 minutes. Using a slotted spoon, transfer the potatoes to paper towels to drain briefly, then arrange, filling side up, in a baking dish.

Add the broth to a depth of about 1 inch to the baking dish. Sprinkle the potatoes with salt and pepper, cover the dish with foil, and bake until the potatoes are tender, about 20 minutes. Serve hot.

# Baked Layered Kibbeh  KIBBEH BIL SANIYEH

Traditionally *kibbeh* are little football-shaped croquettes made from a mixture of bulgur, meat, and onions and stuffed with a meat mixture. They are time-consuming and require practice to get right. If they are not perfectly kneaded and formed, they can explode when they are fried. This recipe, which is a traditional Lebanese dish that is also popular in Israel, is the way to get the taste of *kibbeh* in an easier and equally traditional format, *bil saniyeh,* or "on a tray." SERVES 6 TO 8

**FILLING**

3 tablespoons olive oil

2 yellow onions, finely chopped

1½ pounds ground lamb or beef (not too lean)

1 teaspoon freshly ground black pepper

½ teaspoon ground cinnamon (optional)

½ teaspoon ground allspice (optional)

Salt

¼ to ½ cup pine nuts, lightly toasted

**KIBBEH**

2 cups fine-grind bulgur

1 pound lean ground lamb or beef

2 yellow onions, finely chopped

1 tablespoon ground cumin

2 teaspoons salt

1 teaspoon freshly ground black pepper

1 teaspoon Aleppo pepper flakes

½ teaspoon ground cinnamon (optional)

Up to ½ cup water

½ cup margarine, melted

To make the filling, warm the oil in a large sauté pan over medium heat. Add the onions and cook, stirring occasionally, until translucent and tender, 8 to 10 minutes. Add the meat and cook, breaking up any lumps with a wooden spoon, until it is no longer pink, about 5 minutes. Add the pepper, cinnamon, and allspice and season with salt. Fold in the pine nuts and set aside.

To make the kibbeh, soak the bulgur in salted water to cover for 15 minutes. Drain, transfer to a bowl, and add the meat, onions, cumin, salt, black pepper, Aleppo pepper, and cinnamon. Mix well with your hands, gradually adding the water as needed to form a paste. Alternatively, combine the ingredients in a food processor and pulse to mix, gradually adding the water as needed to form a paste.

Preheat the oven to 350°F.

Grease a 9-by-12-by-2-inch baking pan with margarine or oil. Place half of the kibbeh mixture on the bottom of the dish, spreading it evenly and patting it down. Spread the meat filling over the kibbeh layer, then top with the remaining kibbeh mixture, smoothing the surface. Pat down again to remove any air pockets. Using a sharp knife, score the layers into diamonds as if scoring baklava, cutting down to the bottom of the pan, and then run the knife around the edge of the pan to loosen the sides. Pour the margarine evenly over the top.

Bake until the top is golden and crusty, 45 to 55 minutes. If the dish is ovenproof, you can also brown the top under the broiler for added color and crunch. Serve hot.

## *Beef Sausage*   LUGANEGA

Forbidden to eat pork, Italian Jews developed a sausage made from beef, which they flavored with sweet spices, revealing an Arabic influence. The flavorful mixture can be stuffed into well-rinsed beef sausage casings purchased from your butcher, but it is just as easy to shape the mixture into long sausages, wrap in aluminum foil or plastic wrap, and refrigerate for up to 5 to 6 days. When you need some sausage, you can just cut off the amount needed. You can also shape this mixture into patties or meatballs for cooking. This recipe is based on a description from *La cucina veneziana* by Giuseppe Maffioli, and it is used for the meatballs in Venetian Bean Soup with Pasta and Meatballs (page 121). SERVES 8 TO 10

---

2½ pounds beef shoulder meat with ample fat, finely ground

6 to 8 cloves garlic, finely minced

1 cup dry white wine

1 tablespoon salt

2 teaspoons freshly ground black pepper

1 tablespoon cracked black peppercorns

1 teaspoon ground cinnamon

¼ teaspoon ground cloves

½ teaspoon freshly grated nutmeg

1 teaspoon ground coriander

2 eggs, lightly beaten, if making patties or meatballs

Olive oil for frying

---

In a bowl, combine the beef, garlic, wine, salt, ground pepper, cracked peppercorns, cinnamon, cloves, and nutmeg and mix well with your hands. Fry a small nugget of the mixture until cooked through, taste, and adjust the seasoning of the remaining mixture if needed. Divide the mixture into 2 or 3 equal portions and shape each portion into a sausage about 1½ inches in diameter. Wrap each sausage well in foil or plastic wrap and refrigerate.

To cook this mixture as patties or meatballs, mix as directed, then work in the eggs to bind and shape into patties or meatballs. Warm a little oil in a large sauté pan over medium heat, add the patties or meatballs, and fry, turning as needed, until golden and cooked through, 8 to 10 minutes. The timing will depend on the thickness of the patties or the size of the meatballs.

If you have stored sausages in the refrigerator, slice off lengths as needed and fry in a little oil until golden and cooked through.

# Spicy Algerian Sausage  MERGUEZ

The meat for *merguez* should not be too lean. It needs fat if it is to remain juicy. These sausages are usually broiled or grilled. Cooks in Tunisia use fewer spices and mince the cloves of almost a head of garlic and add them to the mixture.  MAKES 12 TO 18 SAUSAGES

2 pounds ground lamb

8 ounces beef fat, ground

1 tablespoon ground coriander

1 tablespoon ground cumin

2 teaspoons ground caraway (optional)

1 tablespoon freshly ground black pepper

1 tablespoon sweet paprika

2 teaspoons cayenne pepper, or to taste

2 teaspoons salt

¼ cup olive oil

Lamb casings, well rinsed (optional)

In a bowl, combine the lamb, beef fat, coriander, cumin, caraway, black pepper, paprika, cayenne, salt, and oil and mix well with your hands. Fry a small nugget of the mixture until cooked through, taste, and adjust the seasoning of the remaining mixture if needed. Stuff the mixture into lamb casings and tie off into 3- or 4-inch lengths, or shape into patties.

Prepare a fire in a charcoal grill. If cooking sausages, prick them a couple of times so they do not split. Grill the sausages or patties, turning as needed, until cooked through but still juicy.

# Tunisian Meat Sausage  OSBANE

This mixture is traditionally stuffed into beef intestine or stomach lining (kishka), but you can shape it into a sausage, wrap it in cheesecloth, and secure the ends with kitchen string. Daisy Taieb omits tripe from her version and suggests that the *osbane* go into the *t'fina pkaila* (page 298) after an hour of cooking. If you decide to omit the tripe, double the amount of ground beef. Accompany the sausage with braised lentils or a salad, or add it to *msoki* (page 313) or to *la loubia* (page 297).  SERVES 6

8 ounces ground beef, or 1 pound ground beef if not using tripe

7 ounces veal honeycomb tripe, blanched in salted water and cut into small cubes (optional)

2 yellow onions, chopped

4 cloves garlic, minced

¼ cup chopped fresh cilantro

2 tablespoons chopped fresh mint

8 ounces spinach, stemmed and chopped

2 teaspoons ground coriander

1 egg, lightly beaten

¼ cup long-grain white rice

2 tablespoons olive oil

1 teaspoon harissa, homemade (page 355)
or store-bought

Salt and freshly ground black pepper

1 bay leaf

1 rib celery, halved

In a large bowl, combine the beef, tripe, onions, garlic, cilantro, mint, spinach, coriander, egg, rice, oil, and harissa and season with salt and pepper. Mix well with your hands. Fry a small nugget of the mixture until cooked through, taste, and adjust the seasoning of the remaining mixture if needed. Form the mixture into a sausage shape about 12 inches long and 3½ inches in diameter, wrap in cheesecloth, and tie both ends with kitchen string.

Fill a wide saucepan with salted water to a depth of at least 6 inches. Add the bay leaf and celery and bring to a boil over high heat. Turn down the heat to a simmer, add the sausage, and poach for 1 hour.

Remove the pan from the heat, carefully remove the sausage from the water, and discard the water. Let cool completely, then refrigerate until chilled, 1 to 2 hours. To serve, unwrap and cut into slices.

VARIATION: To make *tebaria*, a similar sausage from neighboring Algeria, add 2 carrots, peeled and diced, to the meat mixture and then shape the mixture around a center of hard-boiled eggs.

Condiments
and
Preserves

HAVING YOUR OWN CONDIMENTS AND PRESERVES on hand enables you to make simple food special and special food even more amazing. I enjoy standing in my preserving cellar and admiring the rows of colorful jars whose delicious contents will give family and friends pleasure all year long. Yes, you can buy condiments and preserves, but the ones you make yourself are seasoned to satisfy your palate. They are not a mass-market concoction that has been tamed to suit the pickiest eater.

Some of the condiments in this chapter need to be stored in the refrigerator, but a number of them can be put up in canning jars and stored for a year or more in a cupboard. Many of them make great gifts when you are invited to dinner.

## CONDIMENTS

## Tunisian Hot-Pepper Condiment    HARISSA

Although *harissa* appears on Moroccan tables, it originated in Tunisia. You can purchase it in paste form in small jars or tubes, but it is easy to make with fresh peppers, roasted peppers, or dried peppers. This recipe, which calls for fresh red peppers and the signature Tunisian seasoning mixture of caraway, coriander, chile, and garlic known as *tābil*, was taught to me by Baroui Karoui, a visiting Tunisian chef who cooked with me at Square One Restaurant during a Mediterranean food conference sponsored by the American Institute of Wine and Food. In Morocco, *harissa* is seasoned with cumin, chile, and garlic. You can extend either recipe with a small amount of canned tomato paste or tomato purée. MAKES ABOUT 1 CUP

4 large red bell peppers or pimiento peppers, seeded

5 to 8 large cloves garlic, finely minced

1 tablespoon ground coriander

1 tablespoon ground toasted caraway

1½ to 2 teaspoons cayenne pepper

Salt

Extra virgin olive oil, for storing and
thinning to a sauce

Pass the bell peppers through a meat grinder or purée them in a food processor or blender. Transfer the purée to a sieve placed over a bowl and let drain for several minutes to rid the purée of excess water. You should have about ¾ cup purée.

Transfer to a small bowl, stir in the garlic, coriander, caraway, and 1½ teaspoons cayenne pepper, and season to taste with salt. Taste and adjust the seasoning with cayenne if needed. To store, transfer to a jar, film the surface with oil, cap tightly, and refrigerate for up to 3 weeks. To serve as a sauce, add oil as needed until fluid.

VARIATION: *Harissa with Dried Peppers:* Soak 2 ounces ancho chiles, stemmed and seeded, in hot water for 1 hour and drain. Combine the rehydrated chiles, 3 or 4 cloves garlic, chopped; 2 teaspoons ground toasted cumin; 1 teaspoon sweet or smoked paprika; 1 teaspoon cayenne pepper; and ½ teaspoon ground coriander (optional) in a small food processor and process until a purée forms. Season to taste with salt and with more cayenne if needed. Transfer to a jar, film the surface with extra virgin olive oil, cap tightly, and refrigerate for up to 6 weeks.

## Moroccan Preserved Lemons   CITRONS CONFITS

A signature condiment in the North African kitchen, preserved lemons are unique in flavor and texture. Once you have prepared them, they must sit for a few weeks before they can be used, so try to put up a new jar as soon as you see you are running low. You will also probably find ways to use them in dishes that are not North African. I like to add them to vinaigrettes, fish recipes, and vegetable dishes. Because Eureka and Lisbon lemons have thick peels, they are the best choice for preserving. Meyer lemons can be preserved as well, but their peels are so thin that their shelf life is only about half that of lemons with thicker peels. MAKES 8 PRESERVED LEMONS

8 juicy lemons (about 2 pounds total
weight)

About 1¼ cups kosher salt, or as needed

Fresh lemon juice to cover

Scrub the lemons well with a brush under running cold water. Place the lemons in a bowl, add water to cover, and let soak for 3 days, changing the water at least once a day. (If you are short of time, soak for at least a few hours.)

Drain the lemons and dry well. Have ready a few sterilized pint canning jars. (You only use 1 or 2 lemons at a time, so pint jars, rather than quart jars, are best, as they take up less room in the refrigerator once opened.) Using a sharp knife, cut each lemon lengthwise into quarters, stopping just short of the bottom. The cut lemon should resemble a tulip. Push a heaping tablespoon of kosher salt into the center of each lemon. Place a heaping tablespoon of salt at the bottom of each jar and pack the salted lemons tightly in the jars. Pour lemon juice into each jar to cover the lemons. Seal the jars.

Turn the jars occasionally for a few days, then store in a cool, dry place for 3 to 4 weeks before using. Unopened jars will keep for a year or a bit longer. The color of the lemons will fade over time. Once a jar has been opened, store it in the refrigerator, where it will keep for 3 to 4 months. If a white film forms on the lemons, just rinse it off. The lemons are still good.

To use the lemons, rinse briefly under running cool water and pat dry. Cut away and discard the pulp. Cut the peel as directed in individual recipes.

VARIATION:  *Quick Brine for Lemons:* Dissolve ⅓ cup kosher salt in 1 cup boiling water, then let cool. Scrub and cut 4 lemons as directed, put the lemons in sterilized pint canning jars, pour the brine over the lemons to cover, and seal the jars. Store the jars in a cool cupboard, turning them occasionally, for 2 weeks before using the lemons.

# Passover Seder Fruit Condiment  HAROSET

*Haroset* is an essential part of the Passover Seder. This sweet fruit condiment symbolizes the mortar enslaved Israelites used to build the pyramids. It is typically a paste that combines finely chopped dried fruits, nuts, wine, and occasionally fresh fruits like apples, pears, or bananas and can be cooked or uncooked. North African *haroset* is usually rolled into little balls rather than served as a spread. In Iran, the fruit-and-nut paste is sometimes shaped into a log and sliced.

All of the recipes that follow can be stored for several weeks, even months, in the refrigerator. Pack them into an airtight container unless otherwise noted. Long after Passover is past, you can still enjoy these condiments with roast chicken and lamb chops. Always bring *haroset* to room temperature before serving.

## Uncooked Haroset from Algeria  MAKES ABOUT 4 CUPS

| | |
|---|---|
| 1¾ cups chopped pitted dates | 1 teaspoon ground cinnamon |
| 1¾ cups chopped dried figs | ¼ teaspoon freshly grated nutmeg |
| ¼ cup red wine | 2 tablespoons confectioners' sugar |

Combine all of the ingredients in a food processor and pulse to reduce to a paste. Roll into walnut-size balls.

## Uncooked Haroset from Iran  MAKES ABOUT 6 CUPS

1 cup pitted Medjool dates, chopped

1 cup raisins

2 tablespoons honey

2 tablespoons pomegranate molasses

1 teaspoon ground cinnamon

1 teaspoon ground cardamom

½ teaspoon salt

¾ cup almonds

1 cup pistachios

1 cup walnuts

2 apples, peeled, halved, cored, and diced

1 to 2 cups pomegranate juice or sweet wine, as needed to bind

Combine the dates, raisins, honey, pomegranate molasses, cinnamon, cardamom, salt, all of the nuts, the apples, and 1 cup of the pomegranate juice in a food processor and pulse to reduce to a paste, adding more pomegranate juice if needed to bind. Shape the paste into a log and wrap in plastic wrap and then in foil to store. Cut into slices to serve.

## Uncooked Haroset from Ancona  MAKES ABOUT 5 CUPS

3 cups chopped pitted dates

1⅔ cups chopped almonds

⅓ cup raisins

2 apples, peeled, halved, cored, and grated

Juice of 2 large oranges

Combine all of the ingredients in a bowl and stir well.

## Uncooked Haroset from the Veneto  MAKES 6 CUPS

1 cup unsweetened chestnut purée

8 ounces dates, pitted and coarsely chopped

8 ounces dried figs, coarsely chopped

½ cup walnuts, coarsely chopped

½ cup almonds, coarsely chopped

½ cup golden raisins

2 tablespoons poppy seeds

Grated zest and juice of 1 orange

½ cup sweet wine

Honey

Combine the chestnut purée, dates, figs, walnuts, almonds, raisins, poppy seeds, orange zest and juice, and wine in a food processor and pulse a few times to reduce to a coarse paste. Mix in honey to taste. The mixture should be thick but spoonable.

## *Cooked Haroset from Morocco*  MAKES 7 TO 8 CUPS

1 pear, peeled, halved, cored, and diced

3 apples, peeled, halved, cored, and diced

3 bananas, peeled and mashed

1 pound pitted dates

8 ounces blanched almonds

2 tablespoons ground cinnamon

1 cup sweet wine, or as needed

Combine all of the ingredients in a food processor and process until puréed. Transfer to a saucepan, place over low heat, and simmer gently, stirring often and adding more wine or water as needed to prevent scorching, until thickened, about 20 minutes. Let cool to room temperature before serving.

## *Sephardic Cooked Haroset*  MAKES ABOUT 4 CUPS

1¾ cups pitted dates, chopped

2 apples (about 8 ounces total weight), peeled, halved, cored, and grated

½ cup finely chopped walnuts

1 orange, unpeeled, gently boiled in water to cover for 1 hour until soft and then ground in a blender

½ cup sugar

1 teaspoon ground cinnamon

Pinch of ground cloves

½ cup water, or as needed

2 tablespoons fresh lemon juice

In a saucepan, combine the dates, apples, walnuts, ground orange, sugar, cinnamon, cloves, and water and bring to a boil over high heat, stirring often. Turn down the heat to low and simmer, stirring occasionally, until a smooth paste forms, 10 to 15 minutes, adding a little more water if the mixture is too stiff. Stir in the lemon juice and simmer for 2 minutes longer. Let cool to room temperature before serving.

## Cooked Haroset from Greece  MAKES ABOUT 4 CUPS

1¼ cups pitted dates, chopped

¾ cup dried currants

¾ cup raisins, coarsely chopped

Sweet red wine, as needed to moisten

½ cup almonds, chopped

½ cup walnuts, chopped

3 tablespoons honey

In a bowl, combine the dates, currants, raisins, and water to cover generously and let soak overnight.

The next day, transfer the rehydrated fruits and their soaking water to a saucepan, place over medium heat, bring to a simmer, and simmer until very soft, about 25 minutes. Drain the fruits, reserving the liquid. Mash the fruits well in a bowl or pulse in a food processor. Add the reserved liquid and the wine as needed to moisten. Stir in the almonds, walnuts, and honey. Let cool to room temperature before serving.

## Cooked Haroset from Padua  MAKES ABOUT 6 CUPS

1 cup dried chestnuts, cooked in water to soften, or 1 cup freshly cooked shelled chestnuts

1½ cups chopped apples

¾ cup chopped walnuts

⅔ cup chopped pitted dates

⅔ cup chopped pitted prunes

⅔ cup raisins

½ cup fresh orange juice

½ cup sweet wine

½ teaspoon ground cinnamon

Combine all of the ingredients in a saucepan and bring just to a boil over medium-high heat, stirring often. Turn down the heat to low and simmer, stirring occasionally, until thickened, 15 to 20 minutes. Taste and adjust the seasoning with cinnamon if needed. Let cool before serving.

## Cooked Haroset from Livorno  MAKES ABOUT 4 CUPS

1 cup pitted dates

1⅓ cups raisins

¾ cup walnuts

¼ cup sugar

Grated zest and juice of 1 large orange

½ cup sweet wine

In a bowl, combine the dates and raisins with warm water to cover generously and let stand until softened, about 30 minutes. Drain, reserving the soaking water.

Transfer the rehydrated fruits to a food processor and pulse to chop. Transfer to a saucepan, add the walnuts, sugar, orange zest and juice, and about 1 cup of the soaking water, and bring just to a boil over medium-high heat, stirring to dissolve the sugar. Turn down the heat to low and simmer, stirring occasionally, until the liquid is absorbed, about 10 minutes. Let cool to room temperature and stir in the wine.

## Turkish Roasted Tomato Condiment   ESME

I first tasted this wonderful tart and spicy tomato relish at a small restaurant in Kadikoy, on the Asian side of Istanbul. The restaurant specialized in the regional food of Gazantiep (near the Syrian border), and this *esme* was part of an extensive meze course. It was served with flatbread and also used as a condiment for lamb sausage. Once the host realized that I was a chef, he dared me to guess the ingredients in the sauce and was surprised when I mentioned that there might be pomegranate as well as lemon juice in it. He said he preferred the tartness of pomegranate over lemon juice and offered me a taste of his home brew.

If you cannot find pomegranate molasses, use vinegar or lemon juice for tartness with a pinch of sugar for balance. If you cannot find poblano chiles, use long green Anaheims and increase the amount of cayenne pepper. Serve with pita bread or as a condiment for lamb, chicken, or fish. MAKES ABOUT 1½ CUPS

1 pound ripe tomatoes

1 large or 2 small poblano chiles

1 tablespoon minced garlic

4 to 6 green onions, mostly white part, chopped, or ¼ cup grated yellow onion

1 teaspoon sweet paprika

½ teaspoon cayenne pepper

2 tablespoon pomegranate molasses, or more to taste

Wine vinegar or fresh lemon juice

Honey

Salt

Very coarsely chopped fresh flat-leaf parsley for serving

Heat a large cast-iron frying pan or griddle over medium-high heat. Place the tomatoes and chile(s) on the hot surface and roast, turning them as needed, until the skins are blistered and charred on all sides. Transfer the chile(s) to a small closed plastic container or a small bowl covered with plastic wrap and let stand for 20 minutes. Peel or rub off the skin, then stem, halve lengthwise, remove and discard the seeds, and finely chop. Transfer the tomatoes to a work surface, let cool until they can be handled, then peel, core, halve lengthwise, squeeze out most of the seeds, and chop coarsely. If the tomatoes are watery, transfer to a sieve placed over a bowl and let drain for several minutes.

In a bowl, combine the tomatoes, chile(s), garlic, green onions, paprika, and cayenne and mix well. Season to taste with the pomegranate molasses, vinegar, honey, salt, and with more cayenne if needed. Serve immediately, or store in an airtight container in the refrigerator for up to 1 week, then bring to room temperature before serving. To serve, spoon into a shallow bowl and top with parsley.

## North African Onion and Honey Condiment  MZGALDI

This savory onion jam is seasoned with *ras el hanout,* which is Moroccan in origin but used throughout North Africa. Serve with lamb or with meatballs. MAKES ABOUT 3 CUPS

| | |
|---|---|
| 3 tablespoons olive oil | 2 tablespoons ras el hanout |
| 1 pound red or white onions, thinly sliced (about 6 cups) | 1 teaspoon salt |
| | ¼ cup honey |

Warm the oil in a large sauté pan over medium heat. Add the onions and cook, stirring often, until very soft and translucent, about 15 minutes. Add the ras el hanout and salt, turn down the heat to low, and cook, stirring occasionally, until the onions are golden and have a jam-like consistency, 25 to 35 minutes longer. Stir in the honey and cook for a few more minutes to blend the flavors. Remove from the heat and let cool. Serve immediately, or store in an airtight container in the refrigerator for up to 1 week, then bring to room temperature before serving.

## PRESERVES

Preserving is science, but not rocket science. Here are some tips to make the job easier and more efficient.

During preserving season, keep some small plates in the freezer at all times. You will need them to test when a preserve has cooked long enough and can be ladled into jars, sometimes called the plate test. A preserve is ready if a small spoonful of it dropped onto a frozen plate sets up within a minute or two. If it is too loose and runny, continue to cook for several minutes and then test again.

You will need canning jars and lids. Jars can be reused from season to season and wide-mouthed jars are easier to fill. Look them over before each use to make sure the rims are free of chips or cracks. The ring band of a two-part lid can be reused as well, but the flat top with the rubber gasket must always be new.

Sterilize canning jars in a dishwasher, immerse them in boiling water for 15 minutes, or put them on a sheet pan in a 350°F oven for 20 minutes. Jars need to be only mildly hot, rather that scorching hot, when you fill them. Boil the lids just before you are ready to fill the jars.

Use a heavy, nonreactive pot for cooking preserves. Enameled cast iron is a good choice. Have on hand a widemouthed funnel for filling the jars and a clamp-like gadget called a jar lifter for gently depositing the jars in the water bath and then removing them. A pair of tweezers or a magnet on a stick is handy for removing the lids from the boiling water and placing them on the filled jars.

Processing preserves in a water bath ensures that molds, yeasts, and bacteria will not grow, which can cause spoilage. To set up a water bath, you need a large pot with a lid (or use two pots if all of the jars won't fit comfortably in one pot). A rack that fits in the bottom of the pot is handy for holding the jars, but if you don't have one, that's okay. Just be sure that when it is time to put the jars in the pot, you lower them gently into the hot water and rest them carefully on the bottom of the pot and that you keep the water at a simmer. The jars rarely ever break in my experience. Fill the pot one-half to two-thirds full of water (when the jars are put in the pot, they should be covered by at least 1 inch of water), bring to a boil over high heat, and cover the pot.

Ladle the hot preserves into the hot jars, leaving about ½-inch headspace, then wipe the rim of each jar clean with a damp paper towel, as any drips will prevent a good seal. Top each jar with a lid and a ring band and tighten the ring band. Carefully lower the jars into the water bath, making sure they are not touching one another. Turn down the heat to a simmer, cover the pot, and set the timer for 10 to 12 minutes. When the timer rings, transfer the jars to a sheet pan to cool. Listen for the cheerful popping sound as each jar cools down and seals itself. It can happen immediately or hours later, so be patient.

When all of the jars have cooled, check the lids. If the lid is depressed and does not pop up when pressed with a fingertip, the seal is good. Store any jars that failed to seal properly in the refrigerator. Label each jar with its contents and date and store in a cool, dark place. Most preserves will keep for up to a year or two; once opened, they will keep in the refrigerator for up to several weeks. I have noted any differences from this general rule in the recipes.

Predicting the yield of a recipe is an educated guess, as every batch of fruit behaves slightly differently. For example, some fruits shrink more than others or contain more water and take longer to thicken. Yields for the same recipes will vary from season to season, too, so sterilize more jars and lids than you think you will need.

## *Pumpkin Sweet* BALKABAĞI TATLISI

In the Sephardic kitchen, pumpkin is enjoyed as both a savory and a sweet. After the Inquisition, the Hispano-Arabic pumpkin sweets made their way to Turkey, where chopped walnuts or pine nuts were added to the already rich mixture. This recipe offers two different options. You can prepare it as is done in Turkey, where the cooked pumpkin is served as a dessert compote, topped with a spoonful of *kaymak*. Or you can continue to cook it down to a preserve or spoon sweet. In Sicily, Greece, and Spain, the pumpkin for this confection is cooked first in water until tender and then drained and cooked in sugar syrup until it becomes a spoonable jam. MAKES ABOUT 5 CUPS COMPOTE OR 5 OR 6 HALF-PINTS PRESERVE

---

2-pound piece pumpkin or butternut squash

3 cups sugar

1 cup water, plus more if needed

2 lemon zest strips

A few whole cloves, or 1 cinnamon stick (optional)

½ cup chopped toasted walnuts or pine nuts, if making compote

Kaymak, labneh, or clotted cream for serving, if making compote

4 to 6 tablespoons fresh lemon juice, if making preserve

1 to 2 teaspoons ground cinnamon, if making preserve (optional)

Vanilla extract and/or orange flower water, if making preserve (optional)

---

Peel the pumpkin and discard any seeds and fibers. For the compote, cut the pulp into 1-inch cubes or into strips 2 inches long and 1/2 inch wide and thick. The style choice is yours. For the preserve, cut the pulp into 1/2-inch dice.

To make the compote, place the pumpkin pieces in a shallow, heavy saucepan, add the sugar, and mix well. Add the water, lemon zest, and cloves, cover, place over low heat, and cook, stirring occasionally, until the pumpkin has absorbed almost all of the water and is tender, about 30 minutes. If all of the water is absorbed and the pumpkin is not yet tender, add a little more water and continue to cook until tender. Remove from the heat and let cool. Serve sprinkled with the nuts and topped with kaymak.

To make the preserve, combine the sugar, water, lemon zest, and 2 tablespoons of the lemon juice in a heavy, nonreactive pot large enough to accommodate the pumpkin, place over high heat, and bring to a boil, stirring until the sugar dissolves. Add the pumpkin and enough additional water just to cover, bring back to a boil, turn down the heat to low, and cook until the pumpkin has softened, 20 to 30 minutes. Remove from the heat and let the pumpkin sit in the syrup for at least 3 hours or up to overnight to absorb more of the syrup.

The next day, return the pan to the stove top and bring the pumpkin preserve to a boil over medium-high heat. Add the remaining lemon juice and cinnamon to taste. Cook over medium-high heat, stirring often, until the syrup is thick and the pumpkin is translucent, 10 to 15 minutes. Remove and discard the zest strips. Following the directions on page 362, test the preserve using the plate test, and if it passes the test, add the vanilla, ladle into jars, cap, and process in a water bath.

# Persian Carrot Jam   MORABA-YE HAVIJ

Many of the carrot jams I ate in Iran were too sweet for me. I have found that selecting highly flavorful carrots is the key to making this traditional jam with less sugar. If you want a bit more punch, you can stir in some freshly grated ginger, though the addition is not authentic. In Iran, carrot jam is usually served for breakfast on flatbread with a soft, creamy white cheese like *labneh* or with clotted cream. For toast, I think pairing the jam with the clotted cream makes the jam taste even better. It is also delicious slightly warmed and spooned over rice pudding, yogurt, or vanilla ice cream.   MAKES 6 OR 7 HALF-PINTS

2½ pounds full-flavored carrots (about 2 pounds after trimming)

3 oranges

5 cups sugar

3 cups water or part water and part fresh orange juice

4 tablespoons fresh lemon juice, plus more if needed

2 teaspoons ground cardamom

½ cup pistachio nuts or almonds (optional)

2 tablespoons orange flower water (optional)

Peel the carrots and grate in a food processor using the shredding disk or on the medium holes of a box grater. You should have 6 to 7 cups.

Grate the zest of the oranges and set aside. Pare away the white pith from the pulp, then halve the fruits, remove the seeds, and coarsely chop the pulp.

In a heavy, nonreactive pot, combine the sugar and water and bring to a boil over high heat, stirring to dissolve the sugar. Cook until the syrup is slightly thickened, about 5 minutes. Add the carrots, orange zest and pulp, and 2 tablespoons of the lemon juice and cook over medium heat, stirring occasionally, until thickened, 20 to 30 minutes. Add the cardamom and the remaining 2 tablespoons lemon juice, stir well, and then taste and add more lemon juice if needed. Simmer for a few minutes longer.

Following the directions on page 362, test the jam using the plate test—it should be thick and a bit runny but not loose—then ladle into jars, cap, and process in a water bath.

# Quince Conserve   BIMBRIYO

Quinces made their way from Iran via the Moors to Andalusia in southern Spain, where the very large Jewish community soon incorporated them into their repertoire. *Bimbriyo* is a Ladino corruption of the word *membrillo,* which is used for both "quince" and "quince paste" in Spanish. In Portugal, the fruit is known as *marmelo* and the paste made from it is called *marmelada* (the origin of the word *marmalade*). Quinces and the Jews made their way into Greece, where this conserve, or jam, became *kythoni glyko,* and into Turkey, where it is called *ayva reçli.* Today, the conserve is still eaten as a sweetmeat, often with a soft fresh white cheese. A bowl of stewed quinces or quince conserve is a traditional finale to the Rosh Hashanah repast. What follows is the traditional way to make the conserve. For an easier technique, see Membrillo My Way on page 368. MAKES ABOUT 4 HALF-PINTS

---

2 pounds quinces

About 3½ cups sugar

2 to 4 tablespoons fresh lemon juice

1 teaspoon ground cinnamon or cardamom (optional)

2 to 3 tablespoons rose water (optional)

---

Wipe the fuzz off of the quinces, rinse well, and then peel, halve, and remove the cores and seeds. Place the peels, cores, and seeds on a piece of cheesecloth, gather the corners together, and tie securely with kitchen string. Slice the quinces, place in a heavy, non-reactive pot, and add water to cover and the cheesecloth bundle. Bring to a boil over high heat, turn down the heat to low, and simmer for 30 minutes. Let sit overnight and bring back to a boil the next day. Cook slowly for another 30 minutes. You may want to stop the cooking a few times for an hour or two, to allow the quince slices to rest and redden, then continue simmering. Add water if needed to keep the fruit submerged. (This process can be extended to a day or two, and there is no need to refrigerate the quince slices when they are resting.) If the quince is not red, let it rest for a few hours and resume simmering until red and very tender, another 30 minutes. Remove and discard the cheesecloth bundle.

Drain the quince slices, reserving the cooking liquid. Purée the quince slices in a food processor, then combine with enough of the cooking liquid to measure 3 to 3½ cups and return to the pot. Measure an equal amount of sugar and add to the pot along with 2 tablespoons of the lemon juice and the cinnamon. Place over low heat and cook very slowly, stirring occasionally, until thickened, 20 to 30 minutes. Taste and add more lemon juice if desired. Following the directions on page 362, test the conserve using the plate test, and if it passes the test, add the rose water, ladle into jars, cap, and process in a water bath.

VARIATIONS: *Quince Conserve with Rose Petals and Cardamom:* Omit the rose water and use the cardamom instead of cinnamon. Add 2 cups of the sugar and 1 cup dried rose petals to a food processor and purée until the rose petals are ground. Add the rose sugar to the pot along with the remaining 1½ cups sugar, the lemon juice, and the cardamom.

*Quince Candy:* Proceed as directed for the conserve, but continue to simmer the quince purée, stirring often to prevent sticking and scorching, until it is very, very thick and starting to bubble madly like a volcano. Put on a long oven mitt and use a long-handled wooden spoon or long-handled silicone spatula to guard against burns. Line a sheet pan with parchment paper and very lightly spray the paper with nonstick cooking spray. Ladle the purée into the prepared pan and spread it evenly. It should be about ¾ inch thick. Let dry for a few days in a clean, warm, dust-free place. Cut the sheet into squares or lozenges and roll the pieces in sugar, or in shredded dried coconut, as they do in Morocco. If the sheet is not firm enough to cut, roll it into small balls. Top each piece with an almond or walnut. Store in an airtight container at room temperature.

## Sliced Preserved Quince

I have a quince tree in my garden that produces about half a dozen quinces each year. That's not much to brag about, but they are special to me. I use them to make this preserve, buying additional fruits from local farmers. Peeling quinces, cutting out the tough cores, and making even slices is a brutal task, so try to enlist help from a friend or family member. Use these slices in the chicken and lamb recipes on pages 274 and 320, respectively, or add them to your own chicken or lamb stews during the last 10 minutes of cooking. MAKES ABOUT 6 PINTS

4 pounds quinces

8 cups water

4 cups sugar

1 tablespoon fresh lemon juice

1 lemon, thinly sliced on a mandoline and then slices quartered or halved

3 to 4 tablespoons peeled and thinly sliced fresh ginger, cut into julienne

1 teaspoon cardamom seeds

1 teaspoon ras el hanout

½ teaspoon ground cinnamon, or 1 cinnamon stick

1 star anise pod

½ teaspoon whole cloves

Peel, halve, and core the quinces, then cut into ½-inch-thick slices. You should have about 3 pounds after trimming. Set aside.

In a heavy, nonreactive pot, combine the water, sugar, lemon juice and slices, ginger, cardamom, ras el hanout, cinnamon, star anise, and cloves and bring to a boil over high heat, stirring to dissolve the sugar. Turn down the heat to medium-high and cook for 15 to 20 minutes to thicken the syrup. Add the quince slices, turn down the heat to medium, and cook, stirring often, until the slices are translucent, about 20 minutes.

Stop the cooking for 2 to 3 hours to allow the quince slices to rest and redden. Return the pot to high heat, bring back to a boil, and then turn down the heat to low and simmer until the quince slices turn red, 20 to 30 minutes longer.

Following the directions on page 362, ladle the slices and syrup into jars, cap, and process in a water bath.

# Membrillo My Way

I have always liked to make my own *membrillo* (quince paste) for serving with cheese for dessert, but I never looked forward to the traditional ordeal of peeling, coring, and slicing the quinces. Then I found a solution in *Bitter Almonds,* Maria Grammatico's Sicilian dessert book, which she wrote with the help of Mary Taylor Simeti. Grammatico boils the quinces whole, then cuts them, cores them, and purées them. Her recipe is for quince jam, but it works perfectly for quince paste, too. I added the cardamom and love the way it accents the lemony sweetness of the fruit. This cooking method is also how I make my quince conserve now, as it is faster than the traditional method on page 365. MAKES ABOUT 12 CUPS OR 6 POUNDS

6 pounds Pineapple or Smyrna quinces (10 to 12 fruits)

3 lemons

About 8 cups sugar

1½ teaspoons ground cardamom, or 1 teaspoon ground cinnamon (optional)

Wipe the fuzz off of the quinces and rinse well. Put the whole fruits in a deep, heavy, nonreactive pot, packing them in well. Cut 1 lemon into slices and tuck the slices among the quinces. Add water to cover and top with a heatproof weight if needed to keep the fruits submerged. Bring to a boil over high heat, turn down the heat to low, cover, and simmer until very tender, about 1 hour.

Using a slotted spoon, transfer the quinces to a sheet pan. Cut away the cores and seeds and discard. Scoop the lemon pieces out of the cooking liquid and set aside with the quinces. Reserve the cooking liquid for cooking other batches of quinces. I call this quince tea. It can be refrigerated or frozen and is rich in pectin.

In batches, combine the quinces and lemon pieces in a food processor and purée until very smooth.

Measure the purée, transfer to a heavy, nonreactive pot, and add an equal amount of sugar. Juice the remaining lemons and add the juice to the pot along with the cardamom. Place over medium heat and cook, stirring almost constantly, until very thick, about 20 minutes. The mixture will bubble up like molten lava, so put on a long oven mitt and use a long-handled wooden spoon or long-handled silicone spatula to guard against burns. (If making quince conserve, add 1 cup quince tea when combining all of the ingredients in the pot and cook over medium heat, stirring often, until the jam passes the plate test on page 362, then ladle into jars, cap, and process in a water bath as directed.)

Meanwhile, line a sheet pan or jelly-roll pan with parchment paper and spray it lightly with nonstick cooking spray. When the mixture is very thick, carefully ladle it onto the prepared pan and spread it evenly. It should be ¾ to 1 inch thick. Set the paste aside in a clean, warm, dust-free place, like an oven with a pilot light. After 3 days, if the top feels firm, line a second pan with parchment paper, flip the quince sheet over onto the second pan, and place the pan in the same spot for 2 to 3 days longer.

Cut into squares or rectangles and transfer to 1 or more airtight plastic containers. Store in a cool place (like a cellar) for up to 9 months. Do not refrigerate or the texture will stiffen.

## Fig Preserve   DULSE DE IGO

This rich Sephardic spoon sweet, also known as *dulse de fijos,* is traditionally served after dinner, with silver spoons for scooping up each small bite and glasses of ice water for sipping. It's also pretty yummy spread on toast or used as a filling for cookies. I make this preserve every summer, sometimes adding a bit of grated fresh ginger along with the spices. During the last half hour of cooking, you must stay by the stove to stir so the figs do not scorch or stick.   MAKES 6 HALF-PINTS

3 pounds ripe Black Mission figs

3½ cups sugar

Grated zest of 2 lemons

Grated zest of 1 orange

Juice of 2 oranges (about ⅔ cup)

1 teaspoon ground cinnamon, or ½ teaspoon each ground cinnamon and ground cloves

Juice of 2 lemons (about ½ cup or a bit more)

Trim off the stem from each fig. Cut the figs lengthwise into halves, or into quarters if large. Put them in a heavy, nonreactive pot, cover with the sugar, and let stand at room temperature overnight.

The next day, add the lemon zest, orange zest and juice, and water just to cover. Add the cinnamon and stir well. Place over medium heat, bring to a simmer, and cook, stirring occasionally to prevent scorching and sticking, for 20 minutes. Remove from the heat and let rest for an hour or two to plump up a bit.

Return the pot to medium heat, bring to a simmer, and cook, stirring often, until the jam is thick and large bubbles appear on the surface, 20 to 30 minutes. Following the directions on page 362, test the preserve using the plate test, then ladle into jars, cap, and process in a water bath.

## Candied Eggplant   CONFIT D'AUBERGINES

Sweet eggplant conserve likely sounds a bit strange to some people. But preserving eggplants in a sugar syrup—eggplant is, in fact, a fruit—is a time-honored practice in the

Sephardic kitchen. To break the fast after Yom Kippur, Moroccan Jews in Essaouira serve golden slices of fried eggplant dressed with sugar or a mixture of sugar and honey and generously topped with roasted sesame seeds and cinnamon. MAKES ABOUT 4 PINTS

---

2 pounds small round Italian eggplants or Japanese eggplants, 3 to 4 inches long

1 cup water

2 pounds sugar (about 4 cups)

2 cinnamon sticks

12 whole cloves

1 tablespoon ground ginger, or ¼ cup peeled and julienned fresh ginger

1 cup fresh lemon juice

---

Prick the eggplants all over with the tines of a fork. Do not remove the stems. Place in a large bowl with water to cover and let stand overnight.

The next day, drain the eggplants. Bring a large saucepan of water to a boil over high heat, add the eggplants, and cook for about 5 minutes. Drain, let cool until they can be handled, and then squeeze them a bit with your hands to rid them of excess water.

In a saucepan, combine the water, sugar, cinnamon sticks, cloves, and ginger and bring to a gentle boil over medium heat, stirring to dissolve the sugar. Turn down the heat to low and simmer, stirring often, until the syrup is as thick as honey, about 30 minutes. Add the eggplants and lemon juice and cook over low heat, turning the eggplants occasionally, until most of the syrup has been absorbed, 30 to 40 minutes.

Remove from the heat and discard the whole spices. Using a slotted spoon, transfer the eggplants to sterilized jars, then cap and process in a water bath as directed on page 362.

MOROCCAN VARIATION: This eggplant spread from Tangier is Hispano-Arabic in origin. Slice 2 or 3 globe eggplants, fry in oil until tender, and then chop the slices. In a heavy, nonreactive pot, combine the chopped eggplant, about ½ cup honey, and ½ teaspoon ground ginger or cinnamon and cook over medium-low heat, stirring often, until reduced to a jam-like consistency. Taste and adjust with more honey if needed. Remove from the heat, fold in ½ cup chopped toasted almonds, and sprinkle with sesame seeds. Serve as a spread for bread both before and after the Yom Kippur fast.

## *Candied Oranges*  ORANGES CONFITES

This recipe is from Hélène Gans Perez's *Marrakech la Rouge.* Clementines or tangerines can be substituted for the oranges. I have sometimes added a few of these oranges to a lamb *tagine* in place of prunes or raisins. MAKES 4 TO 5 PINTS

4 pounds oranges

Juice of 1 to 2 lemons

9 cups (4 pounds) sugar

Lightly scratch the skin of each orange with a grater, then rinse, place in a large pot, and add water to cover. Bring to a boil over high heat, turn down the heat to medium, and simmer until the oranges are tender. This can take as long as 1 hour. Drain, reserve the cooking liquid, and let the oranges cool until they can be handled. Cut the oranges through the stem end into quarters and remove and discard the seeds.

Pour the reserved cooking liquid into a large saucepan. Add the lemon juice and sugar, place over medium heat, and heat, stirring, until the sugar dissolves. Add the quartered oranges to the syrup, raise the heat to high, and bring to a rolling boil. Skim off any foam from the surface, turn down the heat to medium, and cook, uncovered, until the syrup thickens to the consistency of corn syrup or honey (thread stage, or 220°F). This can take as long as 1½ hours. The oranges will have absorbed lots of syrup, the centers will be soft, and the skins will be translucent but firm.

Using a slotted spoon, transfer the oranges to sterilized jars, then cap and process in a water bath as directed on page 362.

## *Persian Sour Cherry Preserve with Cardamom*  MORABA-YE ALBALU

In Iran, sour cherries are prized for use in rice pilafs and preserves. For cooks in the United States, the challenge is to locate fresh sour cherries. They are grown in abundance in Michigan but not widely cultivated elsewhere. The cherries are also small, which makes them tedious to pit. If you cannot find sour cherries, you can make this with regular cherries. This preserve tastes great spooned over thick yogurt, *panna cotta,* or vanilla or honey ice cream. Or serve it with Greek Yogurt Cake (page 398) or Spanish Cake (page 396). Turkish Jews make a similar sour cherry preserve called *vişne reçeli,* which omits the cardamom and grinds 2 cups of the sugar with 1 cup dried rose petals. MAKES 8 HALF-PINTS

3 pounds sour cherries

4 cups sugar

Juice of 1 lemon

1 teaspoon ground cardamom

Pit the cherries and drain well. You should have about 7 cups. Place the cherries in a heavy, nonreactive pot, add the sugar, and let stand overnight.

The next morning, add the lemon juice and cardamom, place over high heat, and bring to a boil, stirring to dissolve the sugar. Let boil for 2 minutes, then remove from the heat and let rest for a few hours. Using a slotted spoon, transfer the cherries to a bowl and reserve.

Return the syrup to high heat, bring to a boil, and boil until thickened to the consistency of thin honey, 15 to 20 minutes. Return the cherries to the syrup and boil until the mixture is thick, 3 to 5 minutes. Following the directions on page 362, test the preserve using the plate test, then ladle into jars, cap, and process in a water bath.

## Moroccan-Inspired Sweet-and-Hot Tomato Conserve

I started making a cherry tomato conserve in 1968. The original recipe was inspired by Catherine Plagemann's *Fine Preserving*. I added the Moroccan seasoning in 1985, so I could serve it with Moroccan mixed grills at Square One. It is a good accompaniment to grilled or roast chicken, roast turkey, lamb chops or kebabs, lamb *kefta,* and even grilled eggplant. Toasted walnut bread or matzo spread with fresh goat cheese and topped with a dollop of this jam is also a treat. MAKES 4 TO 5 PINTS

8 ounces fresh ginger, peeled and thinly sliced across the grain

1 cup cider vinegar

1 tablespoon ground cinnamon

1 teaspoon ground cloves

1 tablespoon ground toasted cumin

1 teaspoon cayenne pepper

1 teaspoon salt

½ teaspoon freshly ground black pepper

2 quarts cherry tomatoes (4 pint containers), stemmed

4 cups sugar

2 large juicy lemons, sliced paper-thin on a mandoline, slices cut into eighths

¾ cup water

In a food processor or blender, combine the ginger, vinegar, cinnamon, cloves, cumin, cayenne, salt, and black pepper and process until the ginger is ground. Transfer to a heavy, nonreactive pot. Add the tomatoes, sugar, lemons, and water, bring to a boil over high heat, and cook for 15 minutes. Lower the heat to medium and cook, stirring often to prevent scorching, until the mixture is thick, 30 to 40 minutes.

Following the directions on page 362, test the conserve using the plate test, then ladle into jars, cap, and process in a water bath. The conserve will keep for up to 2 years. Alternatively, pack into sterilized jars, cap, and store in the refrigerator for up to 1 year.

Desserts

SOON AFTER THE MOORS PLANTED RICE, sugarcane, and almonds in Spain and Portugal, Sephardic Jews in Spain and Portugal came under the seductive culinary influence of the Moorish Arabs who lived there. They developed a sweet tooth and created an array of recipes to satisfy it. But these rich, sweet desserts were not an everyday occurrence. Served on holidays and special occasions, they were ceremonial and symbolic of hospitality. Daily meals might end with fresh fruit, a cookie, or occasionally a pudding.

Mediterranean Jewish desserts followed the same pattern as Muslim sweets except for the use of margarine or oil for pastry served at a meat meal. Signature flavor ingredients included citrus; nuts such as almonds, walnuts, hazelnuts, pistachios, and pine nuts; dried fruits such as raisins, apricots, figs, and dates; and preserved and candied fruits. Sugar syrups enhanced with rose water or orange flower water and spices such as cinnamon, cloves, ginger, and cardamom perfumed pastries and compotes. Eggs and especially egg yolks were used with abandon in cakes and puddings, along with rice and rice flour, cornstarch, and semolina. Sweets were also flavored with vanilla, coconut, sesame seeds, rose geranium water, and honey, though less often. Chocolate appeared occasionally in the desserts of Spain, Portugal, and Italy because of long-standing connections with Sephardic Jews who had set up chocolate factories in the Netherlands.

In years past, many homes did not have ovens, so rich custards, puddings thickened with rice flour or cornstarch, and fried desserts such as doughnuts, fritters, and pancakes were prepared at home on the stove top. Cakes and sweet breads were taken to the village oven for baking or were purchased at a bakery. Although some desserts were simple sponge cakes or nut tortes, they were often bathed or dipped in syrup after baking or frying, a practice that echoes the Arabic style of double cooking. *Ouarka* or filo pastries like baklava or *bougatsa* were also popular, as were tarts and cookies filled with fruits and nuts.

Not surprisingly, dessert chapters in Sephardic and Mediterranean Jewish cookbooks are typically large and varied, and this chapter, with recipes that draw from all of the classic categories—fruits and puddings, cakes and tarts, pastries and cookies—maintains that tradition. Simply put, temptation abounds in the following pages.

# Greek Baked Quince Filled with Walnuts    KYDONI STO FOURNOU

A bowl of quinces can perfume an entire house, but resist the temptation to bite into a raw one. Uncooked quinces are astringent and tough. They must be cooked for their magic flavor to emerge.

In late fall and winter, baked and poached quinces are especially popular in Iran, Greece, Turkey, and the Balkans. Most quince varieties turn a delightful shade of Venetian red when cooked. If you cannot find quinces, you can use apples for this recipe. SERVES 6

---

6 small or 3 large Pineapple or Smyrna quinces (about 2 pounds total weight)

4 tablespoons unsalted butter, at room temperature

½ cup chopped walnuts

6 tablespoons plus ⅔ cup sugar

1 teaspoon ground cinnamon

1¼ cups water

Clotted cream, kaymak, mascarpone, labneh, or plain Greek yogurt for serving

---

Preheat the oven to 350°F. Butter a baking dish large enough to accommodate the quinces once they are halved.

Wipe the fuzz off of the quinces, rinse well, and cut in half lengthwise. Using a sharp melon baller or paring knife, remove and discard the core and seeds from each half. Place the halves, hollow side up, in the prepared baking dish. In a food processor, pulse together the butter, walnuts, 6 tablespoons of the sugar, and the cinnamon until evenly mixed. Place a spoonful of the nut mixture in the center of each quince half.

In a small saucepan, combine the water and the remaining ⅔ cup sugar over medium heat and heat, stirring, just until the sugar dissolves. Pour this mixture into the bottom of the baking dish. The liquid should be about ¾ inch deep. Bake the quince halves, basting frequently with the liquid, until tender, 1 to 1½ hours.

Because quince are so hard to core when they are raw, I have devised another method that I think works well. Bake the fruits whole in a preheated 325°F oven until they feel soft, about an hour. Cut them in half through the stem end, remove the core, and fill each hollow with the nut mixture. Arrange the halves, filled side up, in the baking dish, add the syrup to the pan, return to the oven, and bake, basting occasionally, until the halves turn red and are tender, about 30 minutes longer.

Serve the quinces warm with the clotted cream.

# Turkish Poached Quince in Syrup    AYVA TATLISI

In Italy, Greece, and Turkey, quinces poached in a clove-and-cinnamon-scented syrup are often served at Rosh Hashanah and to break the fast at Yom Kippur. Most quince recipes suggest peeling the fruits before poaching, but because raw quinces are so difficult to peel and core, some recipes call for partially cooking the unpeeled fruits in water and then peeling and coring them and cooking them in syrup, as I have done here. If you make the *membrillo* on page 368, you can use some of the "quince tea" that remains from cooking whole quinces in water for the syrup here. SERVES 6

| | |
|---|---|
| 2 pounds Pineapple or Smyrna quinces | Juice of 1 lemon |
| 2 cups sugar | 2 whole cloves |
| 1 cup water, or as needed | 2 cinnamon sticks |
| 1 lemon zest strip | Kaymak, clotted cream, mascarpone, labneh, or plain Greek yogurt for serving |

In a large saucepan, combine the quinces with water to cover. Bring to a boil over high heat and cook, uncovered, until barely tender, about 20 minutes. Drain the quinces and, when cool enough to handle, peel, halve or quarter, and core them.

To make the syrup, in a saucepan large enough to accommodate the quince, combine the sugar, water, lemon zest and juice, cloves, and cinnamon sticks, place over medium heat, and bring to a simmer, stirring to dissolve the sugar. Add the quince pieces and additional water if needed to cover and cook over medium heat for 5 minutes, then turn off the heat. Over the next 12 hours, bring the pan to a boil three times, boiling the fruit for 5 to 10 minutes each time. This helps to bring up the rich red color of the quinces and helps the fruit absorb the syrup.

If after the third boiling, a lot of syrup still remains in the pan, using a slotted spoon, transfer the quince pieces to a serving dish, reduce the syrup over high heat, and pour the syrup over the quince. Serve at room temperature or chilled. The chilled syrup may set up a bit like jelly. Top each serving with a dollop of kaymak.

## *Fresh Apricot Compote*   KAYISI KOMPOSTOSU

Apricot season is fleeting, so when apricots appear at the market, I jump at the chance to buy them. This Turkish compote is a fine way to dress up a simple cake or is delicious just eaten with a spoon. SERVES 6 TO 8

| | |
|---|---|
| ½ cup sugar | 24 large firm apricots, halved and pitted |
| 1 cup water or white wine | 1 to 2 tablespoons orange flower water |
| 3 or 4 lemon zest strips | Chopped pistachio nuts for garnish (optional) |

In a saucepan, combine the sugar, water, and lemon zest and bring to a simmer over medium heat, stirring to dissolve the sugar. Simmer until slightly thickened, about 10 minutes.

Add the apricot halves and simmer gently until tender, 5 to 10 minutes. They get soft very quickly. Using a slotted spoon, transfer the apricots to a serving bowl. If the syrup seems too thin, reduce it over medium-high heat until it has thickened to a nice consistency, then remove from the heat and stir in the orange flower water to taste. Spoon the syrup over the fruit. Serve the compote chilled, garnished with the pistachios.

VARIATION: *Baked Fresh Apricots:* Preheat the oven to 350°F. Omit the lemon zest and orange flower water. Halve and pit the apricots as directed. Arrange the halves, skin side up, in a single layer, or slightly overlapping, in a baking dish. Cut 1 vanilla bean into several pieces and tuck the pieces among the apricots. Scatter several cardamom seeds among the apricots, if you like. Pour the water into the dish, then sprinkle the sugar evenly over the top. Bake until tender, about 25 minutes. Serve warm, sprinkled with the pistachios, if you like.

## *Cream-Filled Apricots*   KAYMAKLI KAYISI TATLISI

To make this sweet treat, you must seek out Turkish dried apricots, which are dried whole. When they are cooked, they plump up and reveal a seam where the pit was removed. You can pull apart that seam to create a pocket for holding thick clotted cream. In Turkey, this special cream is called *kaymak,* the best of which is made with buffalo milk. In the absence of real *kaymak* in the States, I have found mascarpone is the best substitute, though thick crème fraîche or *labneh* can also be used. SERVES 4 TO 6

8 ounces dried Turkish apricots

1½ cups sugar

2 cups water

2 teaspoons fresh lemon juice

1 cup kaymak, mascarpone, thick crème fraîche, or labneh

½ cup chopped pistachio nuts

In a bowl, combine the apricots with water to cover and let stand overnight.

The next day, drain the apricots. In a saucepan, combine the sugar and water and bring to a simmer over medium heat, stirring to dissolve the sugar. Simmer until slightly thickened, about 10 minutes. Add the apricots and cook until tender, 15 to 20 minutes. Add the lemon juice and simmer for 1 minute.

Using a slotted spoon, transfer the apricots to a sheet pan or large plate and let cool. The syrup should be the consistency of thick honey. If it is not thick enough, reduce it over medium-high heat as needed, then set aside to cool.

Gently pull open the seam on each apricot to reveal a pocket, being careful not to separate the fruit into halves. Using a small spoon, slip a spoonful of the kaymak into each pocket.

Arrange the apricots side by side on a serving platter. Spoon the syrup over the stuffed apricots, cover, and refrigerate for about 2 hours to set the syrup. Before serving, bring the apricots to room temperature and sprinkle with the pistachios.

## Persian Melon and Peach Compote   KOMPOT-E HULU VA TALEBI

This colorful compote, which is also known as *kharpouzeh ve hulu makhlut,* is refreshing after a filling Sabbath meal. Iran gets unbearably hot in the summer months, so sometimes the fruit is topped with crushed ice or the melons and peaches are chopped and mixed with shaved ice. SERVES 8

| | |
|---|---|
| 1 large ripe honeydew melon | ½ cup sugar |
| 1 ripe cantaloupe | Pinch of salt |
| 4 peaches, peeled, halved, pitted, and sliced | ¼ cup fresh lemon juice |
| | 2 to 3 tablespoons rose water |

Halve the melons. Place a sieve over a large bowl and spoon the seeds from each melon into the sieve. Let stand until the juice stops dripping, then discard the seeds. Using a melon baller, scoop the flesh from the melon halves and add the balls to the bowl holding the juice. Add the peaches, sugar, and salt and stir gently to mix well. Add the lemon juice and the rose water to taste and stir again. Cover and chill well before serving.

## Caramelized Fresh Fruit   FRUTTA CARAMELLATA

These crisp, crunchy sugar-coated fruits are refreshing and festive after a filling meal. They are also known as *golosezzi veneziani,* but because I first read about them in Donatella Limentani Pavoncello's book of Roman Jewish recipes, I have given them the Roman name. She uses apples, pears, and oranges, but I have found that strawberries make a nice addition to the mix. SERVES 8 TO 10

| | |
|---|---|
| 2 tablespoons unsalted butter or margarine, melted (optional) | 24 strawberries, hulled |
| 4 cups sugar | Navel orange or mandarin orange segments (optional) |
| 4 tart apples, halved, cored, and each half quartered | |

Brush a sheet pan with the butter. (Alternatively, set a wire rack on the sheet pan.)

Place the sugar in a wide, heavy saucepan. Place over medium heat, stir once, and heat without stirring, until the sugar melts and caramelizes to golden amber. Stir away any lumps with a wooden spoon, being careful that the sugar doesn't spatter and burn you. Have a bowl of ice water nearby in case you burn your hands. While the sugar melts, make sure the fruits are dry.

Thread the fruits onto wooden skewers, or use tongs or chopsticks for each piece. *Carefully* dip the fruit skewers, one at a time, or the individual fruits, into the hot caramel, coating evenly, and then place on the prepared sheet pan. When all of the fruits have been coated, let stand until cool and set, 10 to 15 minutes. Once the fruits have set, serve them as soon as possible so they are crisp when eaten.

## Caramelized Figs   FICHI CARAMELLATI

Unlike the recipe for caramelized fruit on page 379, in which the fresh fruit is dipped into caramel, here the figs caramelize in the pan. Look for ripe Black Mission or Turkey figs that are slightly cracked and oozing juice. Thin strips of lemon zest tucked into the figs permeate the fruits with their subtle perfume. Meyer lemons are especially fragrant and a good choice for this dessert. If serving a dairy meal, accompany each serving with a scoop of ice cream. SERVES 8

| | |
|---|---|
| 2 pounds ripe figs (2 or 3 per person) | 2 cups sugar |
| 16 to 24 lemon zest strips, 1 inch long and ¼ inch wide (1 strip per fig) | Dark rum, as needed (optional) |
| | Vanilla bean, cut into 3 or 4 pieces |

Trim off the stem from each fig, then cut a small slit at the top of each fig. Insert a lemon zest strip into each slit. Arrange the figs in a single layer in a deep, wide saucepan. Sprinkle the sugar over the figs and add water or part water and part rum to a depth of ¼ inch to the pan. Tuck the vanilla bean pieces in among the figs.

Place the pan over high heat and bring to a boil. Turn down the heat to medium and simmer until the sugar caramelizes, 15 to 20 minutes. Serve warm.

## Spiced Dried Fig Compote   İZMİR KOMPOSTOSU

When summer is over and you still crave figs, use the dried Black Mission variety for this compote. I have taken a few liberties with this recipe, which is a specialty of Izmir. I have tried both red and white wine and found that both were good, and I have added bay leaves and a pinch of black pepper. This compote is lovely when spooned over cheesecake or a simple sponge cake. SERVES 4

| | |
|---|---|
| 1 pound dried Black Mission figs | 2 cinnamon sticks |
| 2 cups water or white wine, or a combination of water or wine and fresh orange juice, or as needed to cover | 2 star anise pods |
| | 1 wide orange zest strip |
| | 1 wide lemon zest strip |
| ½ cup sugar | Pinch of freshly ground black pepper |
| ¼ cup honey | ½ cup chopped hazelnuts or pistachio nuts (optional) |
| 2 bay leaves | |

Trim off the stem and blossom end from each fig. If you have time, in a bowl, combine the figs with the water or wine or part juice to cover and set aside to soften for at least 6 hours or up to overnight.

If you have soaked the figs, drain them, reserving the soaking liquid. Pour 2 cups of the soaking liquid into a saucepan and add the sugar, honey, bay leaves, cinnamon sticks, star anise, citrus zests, and pepper and bring to a boil over medium-high heat, stirring to dissolve the sugar. Turn down the heat to medium and simmer until slightly thickened, about 10 minutes. Add the figs, turn down the heat to low, and cook, stirring occasionally, until the figs have softened and are perfumed with the spices, 10 to 15 minutes. Using a slotted spoon, transfer the figs to a serving bowl, then check the consistency of the syrup and, if you like, reduce the syrup over medium-high heat until it coats a spoon. Pour the syrup over the figs and serve the compote warm or at room temperature, sprinkled with the nuts.

## Orange Compote with Fragrant Syrup   KOMPOSTO DE PORTOKAL

Portuguese traders were the first to bring oranges to Europe from China. *Portokal* is the Ladino name for "orange," thus giving credit to the Portuguese. This refreshing Sephardic dessert compote, which is perfumed with orange flower water and cinnamon and is served well chilled, would also be at home in Greece, North Africa, or Israel. The compote is also delicious served on a slice of pound cake or Spanish Cake (page 396) and will keep for a few days in the refrigerator. SERVES 6

| | |
|---|---|
| 6 large navel oranges | 2 to 3 tablespoons orange flower water |
| ½ cup water | ¼ cup Grand Marnier (optional) |
| 1¼ cups sugar | 2 tablespoons chopped fresh mint, or ¼ cup chopped toasted pistachio nuts or almonds (optional) |
| 2-inch piece cinnamon stick | |
| ¼ cup fragrant honey | |

Using a vegetable peeler, remove the zest from the oranges and then cut the zest into narrow julienne strips. Have ready a bowl of cold water. Bring a saucepan filled with water to a boil, add the zest strips, and blanch for 3 to 5 minutes. Drain, immerse in the cold water until cool, then drain again. Repeat the blanching and cooling down twice to remove any bitterness, then set the zest aside.

Trim away all of the white pith from the oranges. Then, working with 1 orange at a time, hold the orange over a bowl and cut along both sides of each segment to release it from the membrane, letting the segments drop into the bowl.

In a saucepan, combine the water, sugar, cinnamon stick, and honey and bring to a boil over high heat, stirring until the sugar dissolves. Cook briskly until the syrup has thickened to the thread stage, about 230°F on a candy thermometer. It could take 20 to 25 minutes. Remove from the heat, let cool for a few minutes, and remove and discard the cinnamon stick. Add the reserved zest, stir well, and pour all of the warm syrup over the orange segments. Add the orange flower water to taste and stir gently. Let cool completely, cover, and chill well before serving. If you like, finish the compote by stirring in the Grand Marnier or by garnishing with the mint or nuts.

## Lebanese Apricot Pudding CRÈME D'AMARDINE

This Lebanese pudding was traditionally prepared with sheets of dried apricots called *amardine,* or apricot leather, but it can also be made with dried apricots, which are more readily available. Dried apricots vary in tartness, so you may have to adjust the amount of sugar or add some lemon juice. A similar dairy version of this pudding omits the cornstarch thickener and folds whipped cream and stiffly beaten egg whites into the apricot purée to lighten it, making it reminiscent of a mousse. SERVES 6 TO 8

1 pound dried apricots

4 cups water or as needed

½ cup sugar, or to taste

2 tablespoons cornstarch dissolved in ¼ cup water

Fresh lemon juice, if needed

1 tablespoon orange flower water

1 cup heavy cream whipped to soft peaks with 2 tablespoons sugar, or 1 cup mascarpone, if serving a dairy meal

2 tablespoons chopped toasted pistachio nuts

In a bowl, combine the apricots and water and let stand overnight.

The next day, transfer the apricots and their soaking water to a saucepan, adding a little more water if needed to cover the fruit, place over medium-high heat, and bring to a boil. Turn down the heat to a gentle simmer, and cook, stirring occasionally, until the apricots are very soft, about 30 minutes. Remove from the heat, let cool slightly, and then purée in a food processor or blender.

Return the purée to the saucepan and bring to a simmer over medium heat. Stir in the sugar and dissolved cornstarch, turn down the heat to low, and cook, stirring occasionally, until thickened, about 3 minutes. Taste and add more sugar or, if the mixture is too sweet, stir in lemon juice. Stir in the orange flour water. Transfer to 6 to 8 individual serving bowls, cover, and refrigerate until well chilled.

If serving a dairy meal, top the pudding with a dollop of whipped cream. Garnish each serving with the pistachios.

## *Almond Pudding*   SCODELLINE

Portuguese Jews brought this pudding to Italy. It is reminiscent of their classic sweet egg custards, such as *ovos moles* ("soft eggs"), but with the addition of almonds at the end of cooking. (There was always a surfeit of egg yolks in Portugal, as the whites were used in the "fining," or clarification, of wine.) The Portuguese used this pudding as a pastry filling or spooned it over cake. It has a soft texture, and because it is very rich, it should be served in tiny ramekins or *pot de crème* cups. (The name tells you what to do: *scodelline* means "small plates.") You can also spoon this pudding onto individual plates and serve alongside fresh fruit, or take a hint from the Portuguese and serve it with a slice of sponge cake (page 396). In the Veneto, this same sweet dish is known as *rosada con le mandorle* and is a Purim specialty. SERVES 12

---

10 egg yolks

1½ cups sugar

½ cup water

1½ cups blanched almonds, toasted and ground or grated

1 tablespoon orange flower water

2 teaspoons grated lemon zest (optional)

1 teaspoon ground cinnamon

---

In a heatproof bowl, using an electric mixer, beat the egg yolks on medium speed just until blended. In a heavy saucepan, combine the sugar and water over low heat and stir until the sugar dissolves. Raise the heat to medium and cook until the mixture reaches the soft-ball stage, 235° to 240°F on a candy thermometer. Do not allow the mixture to color. (If you lack a thermometer, test the mixture by dropping a tiny bit into ice water; it should form a pliable ball when pressed between your fingers.)

With the mixer on medium-high speed, gradually pour the hot syrup into the egg yolks and beat until the mixture is thick and holds a 3-second slowly dissolving ribbon when the beaters are lifted, about 5 minutes. Return the mixture to the saucepan and warm over low heat, stirring occasionally, until thickened, about 5 minutes. Do not allow it to boil. Add the almonds, orange flower water, and lemon zest and stir well.

Pour the custard into twelve 3-ounce ramekins and refrigerate until cool, about 1 hour. (Or, cover and refrigerate for up to 2 days before serving.) Sprinkle with the cinnamon just before serving.

## Almond and Chocolate Pudding    BUDINO DI MANDORLE E CIOCCOLATA

According to cookbook author and cultural anthropologist Claudia Roden, the use of chocolate in Livornese desserts came about because of trade between Jews in Livorno and Marrano Jews in Amsterdam who had started a chocolate factory. Emma Belforte's original recipe, as reproduced in Aldo Santini's *La cucina livornese,* did not advise baking this pudding in a bain-marie, but I found that it turned out dry and more like an overcooked brownie than a pudding. The bain-marie ensures a creamier, more appealing texture. This is a good dessert for a dairy meal. SERVES 8

---

½ cup plus 1 tablespoon unsalted butter

4½ ounces bittersweet chocolate

1¼ cups chopped blanched almonds

½ cup plus 1 tablespoon sugar

4 eggs, separated

Whipped cream for serving (optional)

---

Preheat the oven to 300°F. Butter a 9-inch round cake pan or eight 6-ounce ramekins.

Combine the butter and chocolate in the top pan of a double boiler placed over (not touching) barely simmering water in the lower pan and heat, stirring occasionally, until melted and smooth. Remove from the heat. In a food processor, combine the almonds and sugar and process until the almonds are finely ground. Transfer the almond mixture to a bowl and whisk in the chocolate mixture and the egg yolks.

In another bowl, using a whisk or an electric mixer, beat the egg whites until medium-firm peaks form. Stir one-third of the egg whites into the chocolate mixture to lighten it, then fold in the remaining egg whites just until no white streaks remain.

Spoon the mixture into the prepared pan or ramekins. Place in a baking pan, pour hot water into the baking pan to come halfway up the sides of the cake pan or ramekins, and cover the baking pan with foil.

Bake until the center appears just set and is no longer wet, 35 to 45 minutes for the large pudding or about 25 minutes for the small puddings.

Carefully transfer the cake pan or ramekins to a rack and let cool completely. To unmold, invert a serving plate over the cake pan or an individual serving plate over each ramekin, invert the mold and plate together, and lift off the mold. Serve with whipped cream.

# Ricotta Soufflé Pudding  TIMBALLO DI RICOTTA

Be sure to use fresh, moist ricotta for this classic Roman Jewish cheese dessert. The original recipe from *La cucina nella tradizione ebraica* by Giuliana Ascoli Vitali-Norsa tasted flat, so I've increased the sugar and citrus zest, and I added a little flour for a smoother texture. You might want to try dark rum or Marsala as an alternative to Cognac. Serve the pudding with berries or other fresh fruit. Another version of this recipe, called *cassola* or *channa,* calls for cooking the same mixture in an oiled sauté pan on the stove top and then glazes it under the broiler (see variation). SERVES 8 TO 12

| | |
|---|---|
| **2 cups (1 pound) ricotta cheese** | **2 tablespoons Cognac** |
| **4 eggs, separated** | **Grated zest of 2 lemons** |
| **1 cup sugar** | **½ teaspoon ground cinnamon** |
| **1 tablespoon all-purpose flour** | |

Spoon the ricotta into a sieve placed over a bowl and let drain in the refrigerator for 1 to 2 hours.

Preheat the oven to 300°F. Butter twelve 6-ounce ramekins or one 2-quart soufflé dish.

In a bowl, using an electric mixer, beat together the egg yolks and sugar until very thick and pale. Add the drained ricotta, flour, Cognac, lemon zest, and cinnamon and mix gently with a rubber spatula until well combined. In another bowl, using clean beaters, beat the egg whites until stiff peaks form. Stir about one-fourth of the egg whites into the ricotta mixture to lighten it, then fold in the remaining egg whites just until no white streaks remain.

Pour the mixture into the prepared ramekins or soufflé dish. Place in a baking pan, pour hot water into the baking pan to come halfway up the sides of the ramekins or soufflé dish, and cover the baking pan with foil. Bake until set but still a little jiggly, 25 to 30 minutes for the ramekins or about 40 minutes for the large soufflé dish.

Carefully transfer the ramekins or soufflé dish to a rack and let cool for at least 30 minutes for the large dish and 20 minutes for the small dishes. Serve warm.

VARIATION: *Stove-Top Ricotta Pancake:* Prepare the ricotta mixture as directed. In a broiler-proof 9-inch nonstick frying pan, warm 2 tablespoons olive oil over medium heat. Add the ricotta mixture, turn down the heat to low, and cook until the bottom has set, 15 to 20 minutes. Slip under the broiler until glazed and golden, about 5 minutes. Serve warm.

# Rice and Milk Pudding   ARROZ CON LECHE

In earlier times, milk was so valuable that Sephardic cooks mixed ground almonds with boiling water to make almond milk as a substitute. Today, everyone has milk, and rice pudding is a popular family dessert, especially for dairy meals. To serve this pudding at a meat meal, substitute almond milk for the cow's milk and omit the butter. This pudding, like rice puddings in Spain and Portugal, is simmered on the stove top rather than baked. Cooking the rice in water and then in milk, in the Portuguese manner, is more economical as it uses much less milk. You can use 1 teaspoon vanilla extract in place of the vanilla bean, adding it just as the pudding is removed from the heat.   SERVES 8

---

4 cups milk

⅔ cup sugar

1 tablespoon unsalted butter

1 lemon or orange zest strip, 3 inches long

1 cinnamon stick

1 vanilla bean

3 cups water

½ cup to ⅔ cup short-grain white rice

Pinch of salt

Chopped toasted almonds for garnish

Ground cinnamon for garnish

---

In a saucepan, combine the milk, sugar, butter, lemon zest, cinnamon stick, and vanilla bean over medium-high heat and bring to a boil, stirring to dissolve the sugar. Remove from the heat and let steep for 30 minutes to develop the flavors.

In a second saucepan, bring the water to a boil over high heat. Add the rice and salt, turn down the heat to low, and cook, stirring occasionally, until the rice has swelled, 10 to 15 minutes. Drain the rice.

Return the saucepan holding the milk mixture to medium heat, add the rice, and simmer over low heat, stirring often, until thickened. This should take about 30 minutes or even a bit longer. Remove the lemon zest, cinnamon stick, and vanilla bean and discard. Spoon the pudding into custard cups or into a single serving bowl. Sprinkle with almonds and cinnamon and serve at room temperature or chilled.

VARIATIONS: *Syrian or Lebanese Rice Pudding (Roz bi Haleeb):* Syrian cooks prefer the perfume of rose water; add 2 tablespoons at the end of cooking. For a Lebanese version, add 2 tablespoons orange flower water at the end of cooking.

*Iranian Rice Pudding (Shir Berenj):* Flavor the rice and milk mixture with 1 teaspoon ground cardamom and add ¼ to ½ cup rose water during the last 20 minutes of cooking. Top with rose petals and chopped pistachio nuts instead of almonds and cinnamon.

## Cream of Rice Pudding   SUTLATCH

This creamy and delicate Sephardic Greek pudding, which calls for rice flour instead of rice, was served to break the fast after Yom Kippur. It was also served at Shabbat *desayuno* after morning services. Although it is usually prepared with milk, the cooking liquid can also be *pipitada* (see variation), a refreshing beverage made from melon seeds that was drunk to restore body fluids lost while fasting on Yom Kippur. Gilda Angel's version of this recipe in *Sephardic Holiday Cooking* uses vanilla as the aromatic flavoring for a milk-based pudding, but Nicholas Stavroulakis suggests either grated orange zest or rose water. Other names for this pudding are the Turkish *muhallebi,* which translates as "made with milk," and the Greek Christian *rizogalo.*   SERVES 8

| | |
|---|---|
| 6 tablespoons rice flour | 4 cups milk |
| 6 tablespoons sugar | 2 tablespoons grated orange zest or rose water |
| 5 to 6 tablespoons water | Ground cinnamon for garnish |

In a bowl, combine the rice flour and sugar. Gradually add the water, stirring constantly to create a thick, lump-free paste.

In a saucepan, bring the milk to a boil over medium-high heat. Gradually add the rice flour paste, whisking constantly to prevent lumps. Turn down the heat to medium and cook, whisking constantly, until the pudding thickens, 4 to 5 minutes. Remove from the heat and stir in the orange zest. Pour the pudding into eight 4-ounce custard cups. Sprinkle with cinnamon, cover, and refrigerate until well chilled before serving.

PIPITADA VARIATION: Spread the seeds from 4 or 5 cantaloupes on paper towels and leave to dry until they are free of moisture, at least 2 days or up to 1 week. If necessary, you can dry them in a 200°F oven. Grind the seeds in a blender or food processor, tie them in a cheesecloth bundle, immerse the bundle in 8 cups water, and leave to steep at room temperature for 24 hours. Squeeze the cheesecloth package from time to time to extract the flavor from the seeds into the water. The water will look milky. Discard the seed packet. Add 2 to 4 tablespoons sugar, to taste, and 2 drops rose water or orange flower water. Substitute 4 cups of the pipitada for the milk in the pudding recipe. Cover and chill the remainder for drinking.

## Syrian Cream Pudding   MAHALABIA

This creamy pudding—*mahalabia* means "made with milk"—is popular all over the Middle East. In Syria, it is flavored with rose water, but in other parts of the

Middle East, orange flower water is used. Some versions add finely ground almonds. It is always served chilled and can be garnished with chopped nuts or a drizzle of honey. SERVES 6

| | |
|---|---|
| 3 cups milk | 1 cup water |
| ¾ cup sugar | 1 cup heavy cream |
| 2 or 3 cardamom pods, crushed | 1 tablespoon rose water |
| 6 tablespoons cornstarch, or 4 tablespoons rice flour and 2 tablespoons cornstarch | Chopped toasted pistachio nuts for garnish |

In a saucepan, combine the milk, sugar, and cardamom over medium heat and gradually bring to a boil, stirring to dissolve the sugar. Meanwhile, in a small bowl, whisk together the cornstarch and water until smooth. When the milk mixture is boiling, gradually add the cornstarch mixture while stirring constantly. Continue to cook over medium heat, stirring often, until thickened, about 5 minutes. Remove from the heat and stir in the cream and rose water.

Spoon the pudding into 6 serving dishes, let cool, cover, and refrigerate until well chilled. Serve chilled, topped with pistachios.

## *Saffron Rice Pudding* ZERDE

*Zerde* is a classic Turkish dessert that came to the Jews via the followers of Sabbatai Zevi, a charismatic rabbi and kabbalist who was born in Izmir in 1626. He attracted numerous adherents as he traveled to Istanbul, Salonika, Cairo, and Jerusalem and soon declared himself the Messiah. He was excommunicated but continued to gain power and a greater following. To survive, he became a Muslim, as did thousands of his followers. Rather than follow the strict tenets of the Talmud and other paths to asceticism, Zevi's followers relied on ecstasy achieved through wild dancing to free the spirit to find God. Feasts instead of fasts were their way of worship. This sect of Muslimized Jews of Sephardic origin was initially called Dönme (which translates to "converts" or "turncoats," depending on what text you read). Sect members who later moved to Salonika renamed themselves Ma'min, or the "faithful."

Saffron is a costly spice, so this golden-hued rice pudding was served only on special occasions, such as weddings and circumcisions. All of the ingredients in the pudding—rice, pine nuts, raisins, pomegranate seeds, saffron—symbolize good fortune and fertility. SERVES 6 TO 8

½ cup short-grain white rice, well rinsed

1½ cups sugar

6 cups cold water

2 large pinches of saffron threads, finely crushed

½ cup warm water

1 tablespoon arrowroot or cornstarch dissolved in 3 tablespoons water

⅓ cup golden raisins

½ cup pine nuts, toasted

Pomegranate seeds for garnish (optional)

In a saucepan, combine the rice, sugar, and cold water and bring to a boil over medium heat, stirring to dissolve the sugar. Turn down the heat to low and simmer, uncovered, stirring often, until the rice is quite plump but some liquid still remains in the pan, about 30 minutes.

Meanwhile, toast the saffron in a small, dry frying pan over low heat just until fragrant. Be careful it does not burn. Transfer to a small bowl, add the warm water, and let steep for 15 minutes.

When the rice mixture is ready, stir in the dissolved arrowroot and then the saffron infusion and raisins. Continue to simmer over low heat, stirring often, until the mixture is thick, about 15 minutes longer. Spoon the pudding into individual bowls or a single large bowl. Serve at room temperature or chilled. Top with the pine nuts and pomegranate seeds just before serving.

VARIATION: *Persian Rice Pudding with Saffron (Sholeh Zard):* The Persian name translates as "yellow fire." One version of this recipe doubles the sugar but that is too sweet for me. Increase the sugar to 2 cups. Omit the raisins and add 1 to 3 teaspoons ground cardamom, to taste, and ½ cup rose water along with the saffron infusion. Garnish with chopped pistachio nuts and almonds and a sprinkle of ground cinnamon in place of the pine nuts and pomegranate seeds.

## *Turkish Grain and Fruit Pudding* AŞURE

When I first tasted this dessert in Turkey, I thought it was odd. White beans, chickpeas, and grain are mixed with dried fruits and topped with nuts to make a sort of cooked granola deluxe but with legumes. That said, I can imagine that if you have been fasting all day for Yom Kippur, a bowl of the pudding would be both comforting and filling. The name *aşure* comes from the Arabic *ashura,* the tenth day of Muharram, the first month on the Islamic calendar. According to author Nicholas Stavroulakis, *aşure* goes back to ancient Greece, where it was offered as a placating gift to the gods of the underworld: Pluto, Persephone, and Poseidon. It became part of Greek Christian liturgical ceremonies as a ritual sweet associated with mourning, symbolizing death and rebirth.

Stavroulakis believes that the Jews probably adopted it because of its close resemblance to the fruits of Tu B'Shevat, when bowls of wheat kernels, pomegranate seeds, raisins, and carob are blessed. It is most likely that the recipe came to the Turkish table with the Muslimized Ottoman Jews known as the Dönme (see headnote for *zerde,* page 388). Some versions use long-grain rice, and others add 1 to 2 cups milk along with the sugar, which moves the pudding to a dairy menu. SERVES 8 TO 10

---

¼ cup wheat berries, soaked in water overnight

¼ cup dried white beans, picked over and soaked in water overnight

¼ cup chickpeas, picked over and soaked in water overnight

8½ cups water

¼ cup short-grain white rice

Grated zest of 1 orange

¼ cup raisins

½ cup dried figs, cut into pieces

¼ cup dried apricots, cut into pieces

1½ cups sugar

2 tablespoons rice flour dissolved in 2 tablespoons water, if needed

1 tablespoon rose water or orange flower water

¼ cup chopped toasted walnuts

¼ cup toasted almonds

¼ cup pomegranate seeds (optional)

---

Drain the wheat berries, beans, and chickpeas, place in a saucepan, add 8 cups of the water, and bring to a boil over high heat. Turn down the heat to low and simmer until everything is tender, about 1¼ hours. Do not drain.

Meanwhile, in a small saucepan, combine the rice, orange zest, and the remaining ½ cup water and bring to a boil over high heat. Turn down the heat to low, cover, and cook until the water is absorbed and the rice is tender, about 20 minutes. In a second small saucepan, combine the figs and apricots with water to cover, bring to a simmer over medium heat, and cook until the fruits are soft and have absorbed most of the water, 15 to 20 minutes.

When the wheat berries and beans are ready, add the rice, cooked fruits, and sugar and simmer, stirring often to dissolve the sugar and prevent scorching, until the mixture has thickened, 15 to 20 minutes. If the mixture is still quite soupy, add the dissolved rice flour, stir well, and simmer for 10 to 15 minutes longer. If the mixture seems too thick, add water as needed to thin.

Remove from the heat and stir in the rose water. You should have about 5 cups pudding. Divide it among custard cups or transfer to a single large bowl. Let cool, cover, and chill well. Serve chilled, topped with the nuts and pomegranate seeds.

VARIATIONS: *Egyptian Variation:* Egyptians call the pudding *ashura* and omit the chickpeas and white beans. They cook the wheat berries in milk and use nuts and raisins for topping.

*Syrian Variation:* Syrians make a similar pudding called *sliha* that combines cooked wheat berries, walnuts, pistachios, pine nuts, cinnamon, aniseeds, and pomegranate seeds and serve it to celebrate a baby's first tooth.

## Orange Custard  FLAN D'ARANCIA

Flan is the classic Spanish dessert custard prepared with cream or milk, eggs, and flavoring. This Sephardic version, however, uses orange juice instead of milk or cream, so it can be served after a meat-based meal. The texture may seem a bit odd at first, especially if you are partial to richer cream-based custards. Author Claudia Roden adds 1 cup ground almonds to the custard mixture in the Portuguese tradition. The nuts rise to the top in baking and then end up on the bottom after the custard is unmolded. The almonds add another dimension of sweetness, though their strong flavor cuts the presence of the orange.  SERVES 6

1½ cups sugar

2 tablespoons water

1 cup blanched almonds (optional)

6 eggs, or 8 egg yolks

1 cup fresh orange juice

Grated zest of 2 oranges

Orange segments for garnish (optional)

In a small, heavy saucepan, combine ½ cup of the sugar and the water and melt the sugar over high heat. Cook, without stirring, until the mixture is a caramel color and fragrant. Do not let it get too dark or it will taste bitter. Carefully pour the caramel into the bottom of a 1-quart flan mold or 6 custard cups. Swirl quickly to coat the bottom(s) and sides.

Preheat the oven to 350°F.

If using the almonds, in a food processor, combine ¼ cup of the sugar and the almonds and process until the almonds are finely ground. Set aside.

In a bowl, whisk together the eggs and the remaining sugar (¾ cup if using the almonds or 1 cup if not). Add the orange juice and zest and mix well. Whisk in the almonds, if using.

Pour the mixture into the prepared custard cups or mold. Place in a baking pan, pour hot water into the baking pan to come halfway up the sides of the cups or mold, and cover the baking pan with foil. Bake the flan until a knife inserted into the center emerges clean, 35 to 40 minutes for the custard cups or about 1 hour for the flan mold. Transfer the custard cups or mold to a heatproof work surface and let cool for a few minutes. Cover with foil or plastic wrap and refrigerate until well chilled.

To serve, run a thin knife blade around the inside edge of each custard cup or the mold. If using custard cups, invert each flan onto an individual plate. If serving a large mold, invert a large serving plate on top of the mold, invert the mold and plate together, and then lift off the mold. Spoon the caramel that flows onto the plate(s) over the top(s). Garnish with orange segments.

## Passover Hazelnut Sponge Cake   PAN DI SPAGNA ALLE NOCCIOLE

A family favorite, this light, flourless Italian Passover cake is fragrant with sweet toasted hazelnuts—a specialty of the Piedmont region—and with subtle hints of citrus.  SERVES 10 TO 12

10 eggs, separated

1 cup sugar

Grated zest and juice of 1 orange (3 to 4 tablespoons juice)

Grated zest and juice of 1 lemon (2 to 3 tablespoons juice)

1½ cups finely ground toasted and peeled hazelnuts

6 tablespoons Passover cake meal, sifted

2 tablespoons potato starch

Pinch of salt

1 teaspoon vanilla extract

Preheat the oven to 350°F. Have ready an ungreased 10-inch tube pan.

In a bowl, combine the egg yolks, ½ cup of the sugar, and the citrus zests and juices. Using an electric mixer, beat on high speed until the mixture is thick and pale and holds a 3-second slowly dissolving ribbon when the beaters are lifted.

In a second bowl, using clean beaters, beat the egg whites on medium speed until foamy. On medium-high speed, gradually add the remaining ½ cup sugar and continue to beat until stiff peaks form. Gently fold the egg whites into the egg mixture just until combined, then fold in the hazelnuts, Passover cake meal, potato starch, salt, and vanilla.

Pour the batter into the tube pan and smooth the top. Bake until a toothpick inserted into the center of the cake comes out clean, 45 to 50 minutes. Invert the cake still in the pan onto a wire rack and let cool completely. Lift off the pan and transfer the cake to a serving plate. Cut into slices and serve.

## Sephardic Walnut Cake   TISHPISHTI

*Tishpishti* is a classic Turkish walnut cake of Sephardic origin. Even though it is bathed in syrup, it has an unctuous texture and, surprisingly, is not too sweet. In *Sephardic Holiday Cooking*, Gilda Angel uses honey syrup, but most recipes for this cake use lemon-scented sugar syrup, which is lighter. Some cooks pour cooled syrup over the hot cake. Others pour warm syrup over a cooled cake. Although one recipe I discovered used walnuts and almonds and another used walnuts and hazelnuts, walnuts are the signature flavor. If you are serving the cake at a dairy meal, a dollop of whipped cream would be a nice enhancement. SERVES 8 TO 10

SYRUP

2 cups sugar

1 cup water

2 to 4 tablespoons fresh lemon juice

1 tablespoon orange flower or rose water (optional)

CAKE

10 eggs, separated

⅔ cup sugar

1 teaspoon vanilla extract

1½ teaspoons ground cinnamon

Pinch of ground cloves

2 teaspoons baking soda dissolved in 2 tablespoons fresh orange juice or water

2 cups ground toasted walnuts

Grated zest of 1 orange

Grated zest of 1 lemon

To make the syrup, in a saucepan, combine the sugar, water, and lemon juice (use the larger amount if you like a bolder lemon flavor) over medium-high heat and bring to a boil, stirring to dissolve the sugar. Turn down the heat to low and simmer until slightly thickened, about 10 minutes. Do not allow the syrup to get too thick. Remove from the heat, let cool, and stir in the orange flower water.

Preheat the oven to 350°F. Butter a 10-by-14-by-3-inch baking pan.

To make the cake, in a bowl, using an electric mixer, beat the egg yolks on high speed until pale yellow. Gradually add the sugar and continue to beat until the mixture is quite thick. Add the vanilla, cinnamon, cloves, and dissolved baking soda and beat until combined. Stir in the walnuts and citrus zests.

In a separate bowl, using clean beaters, beat the egg whites on medium-high speed until stiff peaks form. Stir one-third of the beaten egg whites into the egg yolk mixture to lighten it and then fold in the remaining whites just until no white streaks remain.

Pour the batter into the prepared pan. Bake the cake until a toothpick inserted into the center comes out clean, 25 to 35 minutes. Let cool in the pan on a wire rack for about 15 minutes. Using a toothpick or a small wooden skewer, poke holes into the surface of the cake, spacing them about 1 inch apart. Pour the cooled syrup evenly over the warm cake and then let the cake cool completely. It will absorb all of the syrup. Cut into squares or rectangles to serve.

VARIATION: *Greek Passover Walnut Cake from Ioannina (Korydato):* Omit the baking soda. Replace ½ cup of the walnuts with ½ cup Passover cake meal. Or, for a lighter cake, replace 1 cup of the walnuts with 1 cup Passover cake meal. Proceed as directed.

# Sephardic Orange and Almond Cake for Passover  GÂTEAU D'ORANGE

The theme of orange and almonds is pervasive in Sephardic desserts. This recipe is a variation on a classic Judeo-Spanish cake that Claudia Roden recorded in her *Book of Jewish Food.* Because of the ground cooked fruit, the cake is very moist and dense. The good news is that the cake keeps well at room temperature for a few days and tastes best on the second and third days, which makes it ideal for entertaining, as you can make it in advance.

I tried making this recipe with many different citrus fruits and have discovered that it can also be made with 5 Meyer lemons or with 5 or 6 mandarin oranges. Meyer lemons will become completely soft in about 30 minutes. If you want to use a different citrus fruit, make sure you do not exceed 2¼ cups citrus purée or the cake will be soggy. If you cannot find almond flour, substitute 2 cups blanched almonds ground in a food processor with ¼ cup of the sugar. You can also make this cake with ground pistachio nuts in place of the almonds.  SERVES 12

| | |
|---|---|
| 3 Valencia oranges | 2 teaspoons baking powder (optional) |
| 9 eggs, separated | ½ teaspoon almond extract, if needed |
| 1½ cups granulated sugar | ½ to 1 cup Passover cake meal |
| 2 cups almond flour | Confectioners' sugar for dusting |

Scrub the oranges, then place in a saucepan, add water to cover, and bring to a boil over medium-high heat. Turn down the heat to medium and simmer, adding more water as needed to keep the fruits submerged, until soft, 1 to 1½ hours. You may have to weight the oranges down with a heatproof plate or pan, as they have a tendency to float.

Drain the oranges and transfer to a bowl. When they are cool enough to handle, cut them open and pick out and discard any seeds. Transfer the oranges to a food processor and pulse until puréed. You should have 2 to 2¼ cups purée. (This step can be done a day or two in advance. Cover and refrigerate until needed.)

Preheat the oven to 350°F. Butter or oil a 10-inch springform pan, then coat with Passover cake meal and tap out the excess.

In a bowl, using an electric mixer, beat the egg yolks and 1 cup of the granulated sugar on medium-high speed until thick and pale. Stir in the orange purée, almond flour, and baking powder. If the almond flour is not very fragrant, stir in the almond extract. Fold in ½ cup of the Passover cake meal. If the mixture still seems very wet, fold in up to ½ cup more cake meal.

In a second bowl, using clean beaters, beat the egg whites on medium speed until foamy. On medium-high speed, gradually add the remaining ½ cup granulated sugar and beat until stiff peaks form. Stir one-third of the whites into the yolk mixture to lighten it, then fold in the remaining whites just until no white streaks remain.

Pour the batter into the prepared pan. Bake until golden brown and springy and a toothpick inserted into the center comes out clean, 50 to 60 minutes. Let cool completely in the pan on a wire rack. Remove the pan sides and slide the cake onto a serving plate. Dust with confectioners' sugar and serve.

## Olive Oil, Orange, and Pistachio Cake

This recipe from Anne Walker of Bi-Rite Creamery in San Francisco is a variation on the cake with cooked oranges. It uses pistachios instead of almonds and contains flour, so it cannot be served at Passover. It is an ideal choice for a meat-based meal, as olive oil replaces butter. SERVES 8

| | |
|---|---|
| 2 oranges | 1 cup all-purpose flour |
| 1 lemon | 1 tablespoon baking powder |
| 3⅓ cups sugar, plus more if needed | 4 eggs |
| 2 cups water | ½ teaspoon salt |
| 1½ cups pistachios or almonds, toasted | ⅔ cup mild, fruity olive oil |

Scrub the oranges and lemon. In a deep saucepan, combine 2 cups of the sugar and the water and bring to a boil over medium heat, stirring until the sugar dissolves. Add the oranges and lemon, which should be submerged in the liquid. If they are not, add equal amounts of additional sugar and water until the fruits are covered. Cook the fruits, turning them from time to time, until very soft, 45 to 60 minutes or longer, depending on their size. Using a slotted spoon, transfer the fruits to a bowl. When cool enough to handle, cut them open and pick out and discard any seeds. Transfer the fruits to a food processor and pulse until puréed. Reserve the syrup for another use.

Rinse and dry the processor bowl. Add the nuts and ⅓ cup of the sugar to the food processor and process until the nuts are finely ground. Transfer the nuts to a large bowl, add the flour and baking powder, and whisk to combine.

Preheat the oven to 350°F. Oil a 9-inch springform pan, then line the bottom with parchment paper and oil the parchment.

In a bowl, using an electric mixer, beat together the eggs and salt on medium speed until light and foamy. On high speed, gradually beat in the remaining 1 cup sugar until thick and pale. On medium speed, beat in the oil and then add the puréed fruit, mixing for 1 minute to combine. Stir one-third of the flour-nut mixture into the egg mixture and mix well. Fold in the remaining flour-nut mixture just until combined.

Pour the batter into the prepared pan. Bake the cake until the top is golden brown, about 1 hour and 10 minutes. Let cool in the pan on a wire rack for about 30 minutes, then run a knife around the inside edge of the pan to loosen the cake sides. Remove the pan sides, slide the cake onto the rack, peel off the parchment, and let cool completely. The cake will keep in an airtight container at room temperature for 3 to 4 days.

## Spanish Cake   PANDESPANYA

According to John Cooper in *Eat and Be Satisfied: A Social History of Jewish Food,* this classic orange-scented sponge cake, called *pandespanya* by Sephardim and *panaspana* by the Romaniote Greeks, goes back to Spanish medieval traditions. The non-Passover version uses flour. For Passover, omit the flour and use 1½ cups Passover cake meal, 1 cup ground nuts and ½ cup Passover cake meal, or 1½ cups potato flour. You can also increase the egg whites to 10 to 12, as they will be the only leavening.  SERVES 10

8 eggs, separated

1 cup sugar

1½ cups all-purpose flour

½ teaspoon baking soda

Grated zest of 2 oranges

¼ cup fresh orange juice

½ teaspoon vanilla extract

4 tablespoons unsalted butter, melted and cooled, or mild, fruity olive oil if serving with a meat meal

Preheat the oven to 350°F. Butter or oil a 10-inch springform pan, then dust with flour and tap out the excess.

In a bowl, using an electric mixer, beat together the egg yolks and ½ cup sugar on high speed until thick and pale. Add the flour, baking soda, orange zest and juice, and vanilla and mix well.

In a second bowl, using clean beaters, beat the egg whites on medium speed until foamy. On medium-high speed, gradually beat in the remaining ½ cup sugar until stiff peaks form. Fold the butter into the batter until combined, then fold the egg whites into the batter just until no white streaks remain.

Pour the batter into the prepared pan. Bake the cake until the top is golden and springs back when pressed gently with a fingertip, about 45 minutes. Let cool completely in the pan on a wire rack. Remove the pan sides and slide the cooled cake onto a plate to serve.

## Turkish Hazelnut Tea Cakes   GÂTEAUX DES NOISETTES

The Black Sea region of Turkey is known for its excellent hazelnuts. These small cakes, which are traditionally served at Purim, have a delicate, not-too-sweet flavor and are a bit chewy. Although not traditional, you may want to glaze them with some confectioners' sugar diluted with a bit of lemon or orange juice. However, I suspect that they were meant to be dunked in coffee or tea. My grandson says that one of them fits nicely in his pocket. MAKES 24 SMALL CAKES

1 vanilla bean, cut into small pieces

¾ cup granulated sugar

1¾ cups all-purpose flour

2 teaspoons baking powder

1½ teaspoons ground cinnamon

¼ teaspoon ground cloves

¼ teaspoon salt

¼ teaspoon freshly ground black pepper

6 eggs

1 cup plus 3 tablespoons unsalted butter, at room temperature

½ cup confectioners' sugar

Grated zest of 2 lemons or 1 lemon and 1 orange

1⅓ cups toasted, peeled, and ground hazelnuts

Butter 24 muffin-pan cups, then dust with flour and tap out the excess.

In a spice mill or food processor, grind the vanilla bean with the granulated sugar until the bean is ground to a powder. In a small bowl, sift together the flour, baking powder, cinnamon, cloves, salt, and pepper.

In a bowl, using an electric mixer, beat the eggs on medium-high speed until thick and pale. In a separate bowl, using the mixer and clean beaters, beat together the butter, confectioners' sugar, and the vanilla sugar on medium-high speed until creamy and pale. On medium speed, add the eggs and lemon zest to the butter mixture and beat until incorporated. Fold in the hazelnuts and the flour mixture just until combined.

Spoon the batter into the prepared muffin cups, filling them two-thirds full. Let rest for 1 hour.

Preheat the oven to 400°F. Bake the cakes until a toothpick inserted into the center of a cake emerges dry, about 15 minutes. Remove from the oven and turn out of the pans onto racks. Let cool completely. The cakes will keep in an airtight container at room temperature for up to 2 days.

## *Crunchy Semolina Cake*   REVANI

*Revani* was named after a sixteenth-century Turkish poet who wrote about the delights of food. Both Greek and Turkish Jews are fond of this dessert. It is also popular in Israel, where orange marmalade is added to the mix. The texture of this cake is a bit crunchy because of its use of semolina flour. Some versions use 1 cup all-purpose flour and 1 cup semolina flour, some mix ¼ cup ground dried coconut or ground nuts into the batter, and some use as many as 10 eggs. The syrup must be cold when it is poured over the cake, so you can make it well ahead of time. Surprisingly, even with the syrup, *revani* is not overly sweet. If you like, dust the cake with confectioners' sugar just before serving, or serve with *kaymak*.  SERVES 8 TO 10

**SYRUP**

2 cups sugar

2 cups water

4 teaspoons fresh lemon juice

Orange flower water to taste, if using orange zest in the cake batter

**CAKE**

2 cups semolina flour

1 tablespoon baking powder

8 eggs, separated

1 cup sugar

Grated zest of 2 lemons or 1 large orange

4 tablespoons unsalted butter (or margarine), melted

Preheat the oven to 350°F. Butter or oil a 9-by-12-by-2-inch baking pan.

To make the syrup, in a saucepan, combine the sugar and water and bring to a simmer over medium heat, stirring until the sugar dissolves. Turn down the heat to low and simmer until slightly thickened, 10 to 15 minutes. The syrup should not be too thick. Remove from the heat, stir in the lemon juice and the orange flower water to taste, if using, and let cool completely.

To make the cake, in a bowl, whisk together the flour and baking powder. In a separate bowl, using an electric mixer, beat together the egg yolks, ¾ cup of the sugar, and the lemon zest on high speed until the mixture is very thick and pale and holds a 3-second slowly dissolving ribbon when the beaters are lifted. Fold the flour mixture into the yolk mixture, mixing well.

In another bowl, using clean beaters, beat together the egg whites and the remaining ¼ cup sugar on medium speed until soft peaks form. Fold the butter into the yolk mixture, then stir in one-third of the whites to lighten the mixture. Fold in the remaining whites just until no white streaks remain.

Pour the batter into the prepared pan. Bake the cake until the top is golden, 35 to 45 minutes. Transfer the pan to a wire rack. Using a sharp knife, cut the cake into diamonds and then immediately pour the cooled syrup evenly over the top. Let cool completely before serving.

## *Greek Yogurt Cake*  YAOURTOPITA

Many of us are familiar with cake recipes that use sour cream for richness. (The classic sour cream pecan coffee cake made by many Jewish bakers comes to mind.) But you can use yogurt instead for a lovely moist cake. I like the perfume of cardamom, so if you do too, add it along with the flour and nuts. If you are not a fan of cardamom, you can add 3 tablespoons Grand Marnier to the batter to enhance the citrus flavor of the cake. This cake is delicious served plain, or you can dust it with confectioners' sugar and accompany each slice with berries or fruit compote. SERVES 8 TO 10

---

½ cup unsalted butter, at room temperature

1 cup sugar

2 eggs

3 tablespoons grated orange zest

1⅔ cups all-purpose flour, or 1½ cups if using ground almonds

2 teaspoons baking powder

¼ teaspoon salt

½ cup finely ground almonds (optional)

1 cup plain Greek yogurt

½ teaspoon baking soda

---

Preheat the oven to 350°F. Lightly butter a 9-inch Bundt pan or a deep 9-inch springform pan, then coat with flour, tapping out the excess.

In a bowl, using an electric mixer, beat the butter on medium speed until light and fluffy. Gradually add the sugar, beating until incorporated, and then continue to beat for 5 minutes longer. Add the eggs, one at a time, beating well after each addition. Add the orange zest and beat until combined.

In a separate bowl, sift together the flour, baking powder, salt, and almonds. In a small bowl, stir together the yogurt and baking soda. Add the flour mixture to the butter-egg mixture in three batches alternately with the yogurt in two batches, beginning and ending with the flour mixture and mixing well after each addition.

Pour the batter into the prepared pan. Bake the cake until the top is pale gold and a toothpick inserted into the center comes out clean or the center springs back when lightly pressed with a fingertip, about 40 minutes. Let cool in the pan on a wire rack for 10 minutes. Then, if using a Bundt pan, turn the cake out onto the rack. If using a springform pan, remove the pan sides and slide the cake onto the rack. Let cool completely before serving.

## Carrot Cake from the Veneto    TORTA DI CAROTE DEL VENETO

This carrot cake is a combination of three recipes from the Veneto, all of which had something good and something not quite right about them. Two were from Fernanda Gosetti's *I dolci della cucina regionale italiana,* and one was from Giovanni Capnist's *I dolci del Veneto.* I also found one in Milka Passigli's *Le ricette di casa mia.* I tried all of them a few times, but there were problems of dryness and texture. You will find this version to be problem-free. The only caveat is that you must use the sweetest, most flavorful organic carrots—not starchy giants. Otherwise, this cake will be a big "so what." SERVES 8

| | |
|---|---|
| 2 cups all-purpose flour | 2 eggs |
| 2 teaspoons baking soda | ½ teaspoon almond extract |
| 1 teaspoon ground cinnamon | 1 teaspoon vanilla extract |
| ½ teaspoon freshly grated nutmeg | Grated zest of 1 large lemon |
| Pinch of salt | 4 cups finely grated carrots (from about 1 pound) |
| ½ cup unsalted butter, at room temperature | ½ cup ground toasted almonds |
| 1 cup granulated sugar | Confectioner's sugar for dusting |

Preheat the oven to 350°F. Butter a 9-inch cake pan, line it with parchment paper, and butter the parchment.

In a bowl, sift together the flour, baking soda, cinnamon, nutmeg, and salt. In another bowl, using an electric mixer, beat together the butter and granulated sugar on medium-high speed until light and fluffy. Add the eggs, almond and vanilla extracts, and lemon zest and beat until thoroughly incorporated. Fold the flour mixture into the butter mixture, mixing well, then fold in the carrots and almonds. Pour into the prepared cake pan.

Bake until golden and the top springs back when lightly pressed with a fingertip, 45 to 60 minutes. Remove from the oven and cool on a wire rack. When cool, invert the cake, lift off the pan, peel off the parchment, and turn upright on a serving platter. Sift a light dusting of confectioners' sugar over the top.

*Passover Variation:* For Passover, omit the flour. Increase the ground almonds to 2 cups and stir together the almonds and 4 tablespoons potato starch or Passover cake meal with the baking soda, spices, and salt. Beat 4 egg whites until stiff peaks form and fold the whites into the batter just before pouring it into the pan.

## *Pumpkin Cake from the Veneto*  TORTA DI ZUCCA BARUCCA

Dense and creamy at the same time, this cake comes from the town of Treviso in the Veneto. The use of pumpkin and citron indicates a Sephardic origin. SERVES 8

| | |
|---|---|
| 1 sugar pumpkin or butternut squash, about 2 pounds | ½ cup ground almonds |
| ¾ cup unsalted butter | ½ cup candied citron, minced |
| ¾ cup plus 2 tablespoons sugar | ⅓ cup raisins, plumped in 3 tablespoons plum grappa or wine |

| Grated zest of 2 large lemons | 1 teaspoon ground cinnamon |
| ½ cup all-purpose flour | Pinch of salt |
| 2 teaspoons baking powder | 3 eggs, separated |

Halve the pumpkin, scoop out and discard the seeds and fibers, and peel the halves. Cut the flesh into ½-inch dice. You should have about 4 cups.

Melt the butter in a large sauté pan over low heat. Add the pumpkin, cover, and cook until it is falling-apart tender and lump-free, about 25 minutes. Meanwhile, preheat the oven to 325°F. Butter a 9-inch round cake pan, line the bottom with parchment paper, and butter the parchment.

Remove the sauté pan from the heat and empty its contents into a bowl. Mash the pumpkin with a potato masher until smooth. Whisk the sugar, almonds, citron, raisins and any remaining grappa, and the lemon zest into the pumpkin.

In a small bowl, sift together the flour, baking powder, cinnamon, and salt. Add the flour mixture to the pumpkin mixture and mix well, then beat in the egg yolks until thoroughly combined. In another bowl, using an electric mixer, beat the egg whites on medium-high speed until stiff peaks form. Fold the egg whites into the pumpkin mixture just until no white streaks remain.

Pour the batter into the prepared pan. Bake the cake until a toothpick inserted into the center comes out clean, 45 to 60 minutes. Let cool completely in the pan on a wire rack. Invert the cooled cake onto the rack, lift off the pan, and peel off the parchment. Turn the cake upright onto a serving platter to serve.

## Double-Crusted Carrot and Ginger Tart
TORTA DI CAROTE E ZENZERO

Sephardic Jews like desserts and confections made with sweetened squash and even carrots. This double-crusted tart filled with carrot purée perfumed with ginger is inspired by a description in Giuseppe Maffioli's *La cucina padovana*. The top crust is decorated with a Star of David, inscribed with the tines of a fork. SERVES 6 TO 8

| PASTRY | 1 teaspoon vanilla extract |
| 2¼ cups all-purpose flour | 1 teaspoon fresh lemon juice |
| ½ cup sugar | 2 to 3 tablespoons ice water |
| Pinch of salt | FILLING |
| ¾ cup plus 2 tablespoons cold unsalted butter, cut into cubes | 2 pounds sweet carrots, peeled and coarsely grated (7 to 8 cups) |
| 1 egg, lightly beaten | 1½ cups sugar |

2 to 4 tablespoons water

6 tablespoons finely chopped candied ginger

1 egg beaten with 2 tablespoons water, for egg wash

---

To make the pastry, in a bowl, stir together the flour, sugar, and salt. Scatter the butter over the flour mixture and, using a pastry blender, cut in the butter until the mixture resembles coarse meal. Add the egg, vanilla, lemon juice, and 2 tablespoons of the water and stir and toss with a fork until the mixture is evenly moist. If the dough seems too crumbly, drizzle in more water and toss to mix. Alternatively, combine the flour, sugar, and salt in a food processor and pulse briefly to mix. Scatter the butter over the flour mixture and pulse until most of the butter is the size of peas. Add the egg, vanilla, lemon juice, and 2 tablespoons of the water and pulse until the mixture comes together in a rough mass, adding more water, a little at a time, if the mixture is too crumbly. Gather the dough into a rough ball and divide into 2 pieces, one slightly larger than the other. Flatten each piece into a disk, wrap in plastic wrap, and refrigerate for 1 hour.

To make the filling, in an enameled cast-iron or similar heavy pot, combine the carrots, sugar, and 2 tablespoons of the water and place over medium heat. Cook, stirring often and adding another tablespoon or two of water if the mixture begins to scorch, until the mixture cooks down to a thick conserve, 18 to 20 minutes. Stir in the ginger, remove from the heat, and let cool. (The filling can be made up to 1 day in advance, covered, and refrigerated.)

Preheat the oven to 375°F.

On a lightly floured work surface, roll out the larger pastry disk into an 11-inch round about ⅛ inch thick. Carefully transfer the dough round to a 9-inch pie pan, pressing it gently onto the bottom and up the sides of the pan. Spoon the filling into the pastry-lined pan.

Roll out the second disk into a 10-inch round about ⅛ inch thick. Carefully place the second round over the filling, trim the overhang to about ¾ inch, turn under the pastry edges to form a slight rim, and press to seal. Press the edges with the tines of a fork to create an attractive rim. Inscribe the Star of David in the center of the tart with fork tines. Brush the top with the egg wash.

Bake until golden brown, 20 to 25 minutes. Let cool completely in the pan on a wire rack before serving.

## *Rice Pudding Tart*   TORTA TURCHESCA

It was rice and *not* pasta that was introduced to Italy by Marco Polo, and it became popular in the sixteenth century. In those days, anything exotic was credited to Turkey (including that bird from the New World!), thus the name of this tart. The filling is a heady mix of raisins, dates, rose water, cinnamon, and orange. Some versions add almonds or pine nuts, as well, and you can, too. The Turks would serve this mixture as a pudding, in the manner of *aşure* (page 389), but the Italians bake it in a crust. SERVES 6 TO 8

PASTRY

1⅓ cups all-purpose flour

4 teaspoons sugar

¾ teaspoon grated lemon zest

5½ tablespoons well-chilled lightly salted butter, cut into cubes

5½ tablespoons well-chilled unsalted butter, cut into cubes

4 teaspoons water

¾ teaspoon vanilla extract

FILLING

2¾ cups milk

½ cup Arborio or other short-grain rice

½ cup heavy cream

⅓ cup sugar

¼ cup golden raisins, plumped in hot water and drained

¼ cup chopped pitted dates

¼ cup pine nuts or almonds, toasted and coarsely chopped (optional)

1 tablespoon grated orange zest

½ teaspoon ground cinnamon

4 egg yolks

¾ teaspoon vanilla extract

½ teaspoon rose water

Whipped cream flavored with rose water or ground cinnamon for serving

To make the pastry, in a food processor, combine the flour, sugar, and lemon zest and process briefly to mix. Add the lightly salted butter and pulse until the mixture resembles coarse meal. Add the unsalted butter and process until the mixture begins to come together in a rough mass. Add the water and vanilla and pulse twice. Gather the dough into a ball and then allow it to rest for 10 minutes. Flatten the ball into a thick disk, wrap in plastic wrap, and refrigerate for 1 hour. (The dough can be made up to 1 day in advance.)

Preheat the oven to 350°F. Place the dough disk between 2 sheets of plastic wrap and roll out into an 11-inch round about ⅛ inch thick. Peel off the top sheet of plastic wrap. Using the bottom sheet, invert the dough round over a 9-inch tart pan with a removable bottom. Peel off the bottom sheet and press the dough onto the bottom and into the fluted sides of the pan. Using a rolling pin, roll it over the top of the pan to trim away the excess dough even with the rim. Line the pastry with foil, allowing it to overhang the sides, and fill with pie weights or dried beans.

Bake for 15 minutes. Remove from the oven, remove the pie weights and foil, and return the crust to the oven. Continue baking until golden brown, about 14 minutes longer. Let cool completely on a wire rack. Leave the oven on.

To make the filling, in a heavy saucepan, combine 2 cups of the milk and the rice, place over medium heat, bring to a boil, reduce the heat to low, cover, and simmer until the rice is tender, about 15 minutes. Add the remaining ¾ cup milk, the cream, sugar, raisins, dates, nuts, orange zest, and cinnamon and bring to a gentle simmer over low heat, stirring occasionally. In a small bowl, whisk together the egg yolks, vanilla, and rose water. Gradually whisk ½ cup of the warm rice mixture into the egg yolk mixture to temper the yolks, then gradually whisk the warmed yolk mixture into the rice mixture, mixing well.

Pour the filling into the cooled pastry shell and smooth the top. Bake the tart until the top is lightly browned, about 25 minutes. Let cool in the pan on a wire rack for 15 minutes, then remove the sides and slide the tart onto a serving plate. Cut into slices and serve warm with a dollop of whipped cream.

## Double-Crusted Fruit-and-Nut Tart  SPONGATA DI BRESCELLO

*Spongata* is said to have been brought to Italy by the Spanish Jews at the end of the fifteenth century. From 1867 to 1990, four generations of the Jewish Muggia family of Brescia made this rich tart their specialty. Ironically, it is now a Christmas classic in many cities of Emilia-Romagna, especially Parma and Brescia. Sometimes it's called *spongata di Busseto,* as Busseto is the birthplace of Giuseppe Verdi, whose picture appears on packages of the commercially made pastries. Some versions use *mostarda di frutta* (candied fruit in mustard syrup), others use marmalade, and still others use fresh fruit cooked down into a jam. Lynne Rossetto Kasper, in her fine book *The Splendid Table,* has a version of the tart filled with dried fruits and nuts, but no jam. SERVES 8 TO 10

PASTRY

2½ cups all-purpose flour

½ cup plus 2 tablespoons superfine sugar

Pinch of salt

¾ cup cold unsalted butter, cut into cubes

1 whole egg plus 2 egg yolks, lightly beaten

Grated zest of 1 lemon

¼ cup water or sweet wine

FILLING

⅔ cup pine nuts, toasted and coarsely chopped

1 cup almonds, toasted and coarsely chopped

¼ cup candied citron, chopped

¼ cup candied orange peel, chopped

1¼ cups apricot jam

¾ cup toasted bread crumbs

½ cup raisins, plumped in hot water and drained

1 cup honey

½ cup water

1 teaspoon ground cinnamon

Confectioners' sugar for dusting

To make the pastry, in a bowl, stir together the flour, sugar, and salt. Scatter the butter over the flour mixture and, using a pastry blender, cut in the butter until the mixture resembles coarse meal. Add the egg and egg yolks, lemon zest, and water and stir and toss with a fork until the mixture is evenly moist and just holds together. Alternatively, combine the flour, sugar, and salt in a food processor and pulse briefly to mix. Scatter the butter over the flour mixture and pulse until most of the butter is the size of peas. Add the egg and egg yolks, lemon zest, and water and pulse until the mixture comes together in a rough mass. Gather the dough into a rough ball. Divide the dough in half, flatten each half into a disk, wrap in plastic wrap, and refrigerate for 1 to 2 hours.

To make the filling, in a heatproof bowl, combine the pine nuts, almonds, citron, orange peel, jam, bread crumbs, and raisins and mix well. In a small saucepan, combine the honey and water over medium heat and bring slowly to a boil, stirring from time to time. When the mixture is boiling, remove from the heat, pour over the fruit-and-nut mixture, and stir well. Season with the cinnamon, then taste and add more cinnamon if needed. Let cool until warm. (This mixture can be made several days in advance. Before assembling the tart, warm it slightly until spreadable.)

Preheat the oven to 375°F. Line a sheet pan with parchment paper.

On a lightly floured work surface, roll out 1 dough disk into a round 10 inches in diameter and ¼ inch thick. Carefully transfer the dough round to the prepared sheet pan. Spread the fruit-and-nut mixture over the round, leaving a 1-inch border uncovered. Roll out the second dough disk the same way. Dampen the uncovered border of the filled round with water and carefully cover the filling with the second round. Trim away any excess pastry and press the edges together well to seal.

Bake until golden, about 20 minutes. Remove from the oven and, keeping the tart on the parchment, slide them together onto a wire rack. Let cool completely. Transfer the tart to a serving platter and dust the top with confectioners' sugar.

## Moroccan Raisin and Walnut Tart  TARTE AUX RAISINS ET NOIX

Here, a classic Moroccan raisin and walnut conserve called *mroziya* or *mrozilla* is used as a filling for a dessert tart. This recipe is inspired by one in Fortunée Hazan-Arama's *Saveurs de mon enfance.* SERVES 6 TO 8

CONSERVE

12 ounces raisins, preferably large Malaga type (generous 1½ cups)

1 cup sugar

1 cup water

½ teaspoon ground cinnamon

¼ teaspoon ground cloves

1 tablespoon grated orange or lemon zest

1¼ cups walnut halves, toasted

PASTRY

2 cups all-purpose flour, or as needed

¼ cup sugar

½ teaspoon baking powder (optional)

½ cup mild olive or canola oil,
or cold unsalted butter, cut into
bits

1 egg yolk, lightly beaten

1 teaspoon vanilla extract

To make the conserve, rinse the raisins well, breaking them apart, and then set aside. In a saucepan, combine the sugar and water and bring to a boil over medium heat, stirring until the sugar dissolves. Add the raisins, cinnamon, cloves, and orange zest and simmer until the raisins are puffed, 10 to 15 minutes. Add the walnuts and simmer just until the nuts are slightly caramelized. This should take 10 to 15 minutes longer. Do not let the conserve become too thick or it will set up like glue. Remove from the heat and set aside.

To make the pastry, in a bowl, stir together the flour, sugar, and baking powder. Add the oil or butter, egg yolk, and vanilla and toss together with a fork to combine. Knead the mixture in the bowl until it comes together in a soft dough, adding a little more flour if needed to achieve the correct consistency. Alternatively, combine the flour, sugar, and baking powder in a food processor and pulse briefly to mix. Add the oil or butter, egg yolk, and vanilla and pulse until the mixture comes together in a soft dough, adding a little more flour if needed to achieve the correct consistency. Gather the dough into a ball and then flatten into a disk. If you have used butter, wrap in plastic wrap and chill for 30 minutes.

Preheat the oven to 375°F.

Place the dough disk between 2 sheets of parchment paper and roll out into an 11-inch round about ⅛ inch thick. Peel off the top sheet of parchment. Using the bottom sheet, invert the dough round over an 8- or 9-inch tart pan with a removable bottom. Peel off the bottom sheet and press the dough onto the bottom and into the fluted sides of the pan. Using a rolling pin, roll it over the top of the pan to trim away the excess dough even with the rim. Spoon the conserve into the pastry shell and spread it smoothly over the bottom.

Bake the tart until the crust is golden and the filling is set, 18 to 25 minutes. Let cool completely in the pan on a wire rack. Remove the pan sides and slide the tart onto a serving plate.

## Layered Filo and Nut Pastry   BAKLAVA

The Turkish town of Gaziantep is reputed to be the home of the country's best baklava. But many other Middle Eastern countries claim they are home to the best version of this sweet masterpiece, and who can blame them? Greeks, Syrians, Lebanese, Iranians, and Iraqis also all serve this festive pastry, which can be made with walnuts, almonds, hazelnuts, pistachios, or a combination of walnuts and almonds. These pastries can also turn up filled with oranges, cherries, apples, chocolate, or coconut.

A 1-pound package of filo usually holds about 24 sheets. Trim them to fit your baking pan. You can create layered stacks of 6 filo sheets and add the nuts in three parts, or layered stacks of 8 filo sheets and add the nuts in two parts. Some recipes stack half of the filo sheets, add all of the nuts in a single layer, and then layer the remaining filo sheets on top. I prefer at least a couple of nut layers, but each family has a different tradition.

All versions are bathed in syrup. Honey syrups are not part of the Greek, Turkish, Iranian, or Syrian tradition. Cooks in those countries prefer sugar syrup flavored with lemon juice and zest, which they pour over the baklava after baking. Some cooks pour hot syrup on hot baklava, and others let the syrup cool before pouring it on the hot pastry.

Because baklava is so rich, it is difficult to judge the number of servings from a whole pan. However, a 9-by-14-by-2-inch baking pan will yield about 36 small pieces. I like to serve baklava warm, as it tastes lighter than when it is cold and has settled. You can reheat it in a 300°F oven for about 10 minutes.

Baklava can be frozen unbaked for up to 2 months and then put in the oven straight from the freezer, allowing an extra half hour of baking time. MAKES 36 PIECES

---

1 pound (about 4 cups) blanched almonds or walnuts, coarsely chopped

½ cup sugar

2 teaspoons ground cinnamon

½ teaspoon ground cardamom (optional)

1-pound box filo sheets (24 sheets)

1 cup unsalted butter, melted and clarified, or margarine, melted

SYRUP

2 cups water

2 cups sugar

2 lemon zest strips, each 3 inches long

2 tablespoons fresh lemon juice

---

In a bowl, combine the nuts, sugar, cinnamon, and cardamom and mix well. Have ready a 9-by-14-by-2-inch baking pan. Remove the filo sheets from the box, place on a work surface, and cut the stack to fit the dimensions of your pan with a large, sharp knife. Immediately cover the sheets with a damp kitchen towel or plastic wrap to prevent drying, removing 1 sheet at a time as needed.

Brush the bottom of the pan with butter. Lay a filo sheet on the bottom of the pan and brush it with butter. Repeat, brushing each sheet with butter, until you have built up 6 layers. Spread one-third of the nut mixture evenly over the stack of buttered filo. Layer 6 more filo sheets on top of the nut mixture, brushing each sheet with butter as you go. Top with half of the remaining nut mixture. Layer 6 more filo sheets on top of the nut mixture, brushing each sheet with butter. Top with the remaining nut mixture, followed by the remaining 6 filo sheets, brushing each sheet with butter, including the final one. Cover the pan and refrigerate for about 30 minutes to firm up the butter.

Preheat the oven to 350°F. With a sharp knife, cut the baklava on the diagonal to create about 36 diamonds, cutting all the way through to the bottom of the pan. Bake until golden, 40 to 50 minutes.

While the baklava is baking, make the syrup. In a deep saucepan, combine the water, sugar, and lemon zest and bring to a boil over medium-high heat, stirring to dissolve the sugar. Turn down the heat to a simmer and simmer the syrup until it thickens, 10 to 15 minutes. Remove from the heat, remove and discard the zest strips, and stir in the lemon juice. You can pour the hot syrup over the hot pastry or you can let the syrup cool before pouring it over the hot pastry.

When the baklava is ready, transfer the pan to a wire rack and pour the syrup evenly over the top.

To serve, recut the pieces with the sharp knife. Serve slightly warm or at room temperature.

VARIATIONS: *Syrian Variation:* For the filling, use 3 cups pistachios, ½ cup sugar, 3 tablespoons rose water, and 2½ teaspoons ground cinnamon. For the syrup, use 2 cups sugar and 1 cup water and add 1 tablespoon fresh lemon juice and 2 tablespoons rose water when the syrup is removed from the heat.

*Persian Variation:* For the filling, use 4 cups chopped blanched almonds, 1 cup sugar, and 2 to 3 teaspoons ground cardamom. For the syrup, use 2 cups sugar and 1 cup water and add 3 to 4 tablespoons rose water when the syrup is removed from the heat.

*Lebanese Variation:* For the filling, use 3½ cups chopped blanched almonds, ½ cup sesame seeds, and ½ cup sugar. For the syrup, use 2 cups honey and 1 cup water and add 2 tablespoons fresh lemon juice and 2 tablespoons rose water or orange flower water when the syrup is removed from the heat.

## *Orange Baklava*   PORTOKALI BAKLAVA

Cooked oranges, a signature ingredient in Sephardic Jewish desserts, make an appearance in this Turkish baklava, where their bitterness cuts some of the sweetness of the rich, sweet dessert. This specialty of Istanbul has eight layers of buttered filo, a layer of orange purée, and then eight more layers of buttered filo, resulting in a baklava with an intense fruit flavor that is uncut by nuts. MAKES 24 PIECES

| | |
|---|---|
| 4 or 5 Valencia oranges (about 1 pound) | 16 filo sheets |
| 2 to 4 tablespoons orange marmalade (optional) | ½ cup unsalted butter, melted and clarified |

SYRUP

2 cups sugar

½ cup water

½ cup fresh orange juice

1 tablespoon orange flower water

---

Scrub the oranges, then place them in a large saucepan with water to cover and bring to a boil over medium-high heat. Turn down the heat to medium and simmer until the oranges are soft, 1 to 1½ hours. You may have to weight down the oranges with a heat-proof plate or pan, as they have a tendency to float. Drain the oranges well, let cool until they can be handled, then cut into thick slices and remove and discard the seeds. Transfer the oranges to a food processor or blender and pulse until puréed. Pour into a sieve placed over a bowl and let drain for several minutes to remove any excess liquid. Some cooks add a few tablespoons of orange marmalade to the purée.

Have ready a 7-by-12-by-2-inch or 8-by-11-by-2-inch baking pan. Place the filo sheets on a work surface and cut the stack to fit the dimensions of your pan with a large, sharp knife. Immediately cover the sheets with a damp kitchen towel or plastic wrap to prevent drying, removing 1 sheet at a time as needed. Brush the bottom of the pan with butter. Lay a filo sheet on the bottom of the pan and brush it with butter. Repeat, brushing each sheet with butter, until you have built up 8 layers. Spread the orange purée evenly over the stack of buttered filo. Layer the remaining 8 filo sheets on top of the orange purée, brushing each sheet with butter as you go, including the final one. Cover the pan and refrigerate for about 30 minutes to firm up the butter.

Preheat the oven to 350°F. With a sharp knife, cut the baklava on the diagonal to create 24 diamonds, cutting all the way through to the bottom of the pan. Bake for 30 minutes. Turn down the oven temperature to 300°F and continue to bake until the top is golden, about 15 minutes longer.

While the baklava is baking, make the syrup. In a deep saucepan, combine the sugar, water, and orange juice and bring to a boil over medium-high heat, stirring to dissolve the sugar. Turn down the heat to medium and simmer the syrup until it thickens, 15 to 20 minutes. Remove from the heat and stir in the orange flower water. Let cool.

When the baklava is ready, transfer the pan to a wire rack and pour the cooled syrup evenly over the top. To serve, recut the pieces with the sharp knife. Serve slightly warm or at room temperature.

VARIATION: *Orange Baklava with Nuts:* Cook and purée the oranges as directed. To make the nut filling, combine 2 cups blanched pistachio nuts, lightly toasted and coarsely chopped; ½ cup sugar; and 1 teaspoon ground cardamom and mix well. Use a 1-pound box of filo sheets (24 sheets) and 1 cup unsalted butter, melted and clarified. Butter the baking pan as directed. Layer 6 filo sheets in the pan, brushing each sheet with butter. Spread with half of the nut mixture. Top the nut mixture with 6 filo sheets, brushing each sheet with butter. Spread the orange purée evenly over the stack of buttered filo. Top with 6 filo sheets, brushing each sheet with butter. Top with the remaining nut mixture, followed by the remaining 6 filo sheets, brushing each sheet with butter, including the final one. Refrigerate, cut, bake, and make and use the syrup as directed.

## *Creamy Cheese-Filled Filo Pastry* BOUGATSA

After I ate my first piece of *bougatsa* in Salonika, I immediately went back for seconds. When you taste this dessert, you will understand why. I have adapted Nicholas Stavroulakis's Sephardic *bougatsa* recipe from the Greek town of Ioannina. In earlier times, *staka,* a thick cream made from the milk of water buffalo or sheep, was used for the filling, but I have used mascarpone or cream cheese with good results. Some recipes douse the pastry with a sugar syrup, though I favor a simple dusting of confectioners' sugar, sometimes with a pinch of ground cinnamon. Although this pastry is typically served at room temperature or cold, I prefer to serve it warm. To make that possible, I assemble the pastry up to 8 hours in advance, refrigerate it until 1½ hours before serving time, and then bake it and serve it warm. SERVES 10

1 pound mascarpone or cream cheese, at room temperature

1½ cups sugar

6 eggs

1 teaspoon vanilla extract

10 filo sheets if using a rectangular pan, or 12 to 14 filo sheets if using a round pie dish

½ cup unsalted butter, melted

Confectioners' sugar for dusting

In a bowl, combine the mascarpone, sugar, eggs, and vanilla and beat until creamy.

Have ready a 9-by-14-by-2-inch baking pan. Place the 10 filo sheets on a work surface and cut the stack to fit the dimensions of your pan with a large, sharp knife. Immediately cover the sheets with a damp kitchen towel or plastic wrap to prevent drying, removing 1 sheet at a time as needed. Brush the bottom of the pan with butter. Lay a filo sheet on the bottom of the pan and brush it with butter. Repeat, brushing each sheet with butter as you go, until you have built up 5 layers. Spoon the cheese filling over the stack of buttered filo and spread evenly. Layer the remaining 5 filo sheets on top of the cheese filling, brushing each sheet with butter as you go, including the final one. Cover the pan and refrigerate for about 30 minutes to firm up the butter.

Alternatively, have ready a 10- or 12-inch round pie dish or a 14-inch pizza pan. Place the 12 filo sheets on a work surface and cover as directed to prevent drying. Brush the bottom of the pie dish with butter. Arrange 6 filo sheets in the pie dish, brushing each sheet with butter as you go, arranging the sheets like the spokes of a wheel, and overlapping the sheets so the pie dish is completely covered and the filo is overhanging the sides. Be sure to brush the overhang with butter. Spoon the cheese filling into the dish and spread evenly, then fold the overhanging filo over the cheese filling. Top with 6 to 8 more filo sheets, again brushing each one with butter, arranging them like the spokes of a wheel, and being careful to brush the overhang. Carefully tuck the overhang under the pastry. Cover the pie dish and refrigerate for about 30 minutes to firm up the butter.

Preheat the oven to 375°F. If you have used a rectangular pan, use a sharp knife to score the surface of the pastry into 10 to 12 diamonds or rectangles. If you have used a round dish, do not score the pastry. Bake the pastry until golden brown, 40 to 50 minutes. Transfer to a wire rack. Let the rectangular pastry cool for several minutes, then cut along the score marks, cutting down to the bottom of the pan. Do not cut the round pastry into wedges until just before serving. Let the pastry cool until warm or at room temperature, then dust with confectioners' sugar and serve.

*Custard-Filled Variation:* You can fill the *bougatsa* with the semolina custard used with *galataboreko,* a custard-filled baklava. Combine 3 cups milk and ½ cup sugar in a saucepan and bring to a boil over medium heat, stirring to dissolve the sugar. Put ½ to ⅔ cup semolina in a small bowl and stir in enough of the hot milk mixture to make a smooth, fluid paste. Gradually stir the paste into the hot milk mixture. Whisk 3 eggs until blended and then whisk in a small amount of the hot milk mixture to temper the eggs. Pour the egg mixture into the saucepan while whisking constantly. Turn down the heat to low and cook, stirring constantly, until the mixture thickens, about 5 minutes. Stir in 2 teaspoons vanilla extract or 1 tablespoon rose water or orange flower water, if you like, and let cool completely.

## Syrian Cream-Filled Konafa Pastry    KUNAFEH MIN JIBN

*Konafa* pastry, called *kadaif* in Greece, resembles shredded wheat or vermicelli and is sold in 1-pound packages. It dries out quickly, so keep it covered until you toss it with butter. It can be filled with nuts, like baklava; with sweetened cheese, like *bougatsa;* or with semolina custard. Some Turkish versions fill the pastry with a thinly sliced or shredded string or mozzarella-like cheese. I don't like the contrast of a rubbery cheese and the crunchy crust, however, so I have created a filling that combines ricotta and soft fresh mozzarella or *burrata* (see variation). SERVES 16 TO 20

**SYRUP**

3 cups sugar

2 cups water

1 tablespoon fresh lemon juice

1 tablespoon orange flower water or rose water (optional)

**CREAM FILLING**

2 cups milk

3 tablespoons sugar

¼ cup semolina

1 tablespoons rose water or orange flower water

1 pound konafa pastry

1 cup unsalted butter, melted and clarified, or as needed

To make the syrup, in a saucepan, combine the sugar, water, and lemon juice and bring to a boil over medium-high heat, stirring to dissolve the sugar. Turn down the heat to medium and simmer until the syrup thickens slightly, about 10 minutes. Remove from the heat, stir in the orange flower water or rose water, depending on which flavoring you are using in the filling, and let cool completely.

To make the filling, in a small saucepan, combine the milk and sugar and bring to a boil over medium heat, stirring to dissolve the sugar. Place the semolina in a small bowl and stir in enough of the hot milk mixture to make a smooth, fluid paste. Gradually stir the paste into the hot milk mixture, turn down the heat to low, and cook, stirring occasionally, until the mixture thickens to the consistency of Cream of Wheat cereal, about 10 minutes. Remove from the heat, stir in the flower water of choice, and let cool completely.

Preheat the oven to 350°F. Brush a 9-by-12-by-3-inch baking pan or a 9-inch round baking pan with 3-inch sides with butter. Pull the konafa strands apart with your fingers and place in a bowl. Drizzle the konafa with the butter and then toss to coat the strands evenly. Lay half of the konafa in an even layer in the prepared pan. Top with the filling and then cover with the remaining konafa.

Bake the pastry until golden on top, 50 to 60 minutes. Transfer to a wire rack and immediately pour the cold syrup evenly over the hot pastry. Let cool completely. Cut into pieces to serve.

VARIATIONS: *Semolina Custard and Ricotta Cheese Filling:* Make the cream filling as directed and let cool. Stir in 2 cups (1 pound) ricotta cheese.

*Cream and Ricotta Cheese Filling:* In a saucepan, combine 2 cups heavy cream, ½ cup milk, and 2 tablespoons each sugar and cornstarch and bring to a boil over high heat, stirring to dissolve the sugar and cornstarch. Turn down the heat to low and cook, stirring constantly, until smooth and thickened to the consistency of crème fraîche, about 15 minutes. Remove from the heat, stir in 2 teaspoons rose water, and let cool. Stir in 3 cups (1½ pounds) ricotta cheese.

*Rice Custard Filling:* Measure 5½ cups milk. In a small bowl, combine ½ cup rice flour with enough of the milk to make a smooth, fluid paste. Pour the remaining milk into a saucepan and bring to a boil over high heat. Gradually stir the paste into the hot milk, mixing well. Turn down the heat to low and simmer, stirring constantly to prevent scorching, until the mixture thickens to the consistency of Cream of Wheat cereal,

15 to 20 minutes. Add ¼ cup sugar and stir to dissolve. Remove from the heat, let cool, and mix in ½ cup heavy cream.

*Soft Cheese Filling:* In a bowl, stir together 2 cups (1 pound) ricotta cheese; 1 pound burrata or fresh mozzarella cheese, chopped; and ½ cup sugar.

*Traditional Turkish Cheese Filling:* Make the cream filling as directed and let cool. Stir in 12 ounces mozzarella cheese, shredded.

## Almond Macaroons MARUCHINOS

This is a Passover cookie from the Sephardim of Turkey. MAKES ABOUT 36 COOKIES

3 egg whites

Pinch of salt

1½ cups sugar

3 cups finely ground blanched almonds (from about 12 ounces whole nuts)

1½ cups sugar

Preheat the oven to 325°F. Line 2 sheet pans with parchment paper.

In a bowl, using an electric mixer, combine the egg whites and salt and beat on medium speed until foamy. On medium-high speed, gradually add the sugar and beat until stiff peaks form. Fold in the almonds just until incorporated.

Drop the mixture by heaping spoonfuls onto the prepared sheet pans, spacing them about 1 inch apart. Bake the cookies until lightly browned, 10 to 15 minutes. Let cool on the pans on wire racks for 10 minutes, then transfer to the racks and let cool completely. The cookies will keep in an airtight container at room temperature for up to 1 week.

## Passover Coconut Cookies PASTICCINI DE COCO

I found this recipe in *Dolci ebraici della tradizione veneziana* by Maria Agostini, a little book sold at the Jewish Museum of Venice. It includes Sephardic and Ashkenazi recipes representing the various synagogues in the ghetto that are near the museum. MAKES ABOUT 36 COOKIES

4 cups grated dried coconut

2 cups sugar

4 eggs, separated

Grated zest of 1 lemon

Grated zest of 1 orange

Preheat the oven to 400°F. Line 2 sheet pans with parchment paper.

In a bowl, combine the coconut, 1 cup of the sugar, the egg yolks, and the orange and lemon zests and mix well. In a bowl, using an electric mixer, beat the egg whites on medium speed until foamy. On medium-high speed, gradually add the remaining 1 cup sugar and beat until stiff peaks form. Fold the egg whites into the coconut mixture just until no white streaks are visible.

Drop the mixture by heaping spoonfuls onto the prepared sheet pans, spacing them about 1 inch apart. Bake the cookies until lightly golden, about 15 minutes. Let cool on the pans on wire racks for 10 minutes, then transfer to the racks and let cool completely. The cookies will keep in an airtight container at room temperature for up to 1 week.

## Purim Butter Cookies    GHORAYEBAH

Very fragile and rich, these butter cookies are easy to assemble. Although they are a Purim treat in Morocco, they are also quite nice with mint tea any day of the week. In Syria, the same dough is used to make cookies known as lovers' pastries. The dough is rolled into narrow ropes, each rope is shaped into a heart, and an almond is placed where the two ends of the rope meet. MAKES 30 TO 36 COOKIES

| | |
|---|---|
| 1½ to 2 cups unsalted butter, at room temperature | 2 tablespoons orange flower water |
| 1 cup superfine or confectioners' sugar | 3 cups sifted all-purpose flour |
| | 30 to 36 blanched almonds |

Preheat the oven to 300°F. Line 2 sheet pans with parchment paper.

In a bowl, using an electric mixer, beat the butter on medium speed until creamy and pale. Add the sugar and continue to beat until light and fluffy. Beat in the orange flower water, then gradually add the flour, continuing to beat until fully incorporated and the mixture is stiff. Knead the dough in the bowl until it holds together, adding a little additional flour if needed.

Shape the dough into walnut-size balls and place on the prepared sheet pans, spacing them 2 inches apart (they spread quite a bit in the oven). Top each ball with an almond. Bake until firm to the touch, 15 to 20 minutes. Do not allow to color. Transfer to wire racks and let cool completely. The cookies will keep in an airtight container at room temperature for up to 1 week.

## Greek Shortbread    KOURABIEDES

Although these Greek butter cookies are popular with Christians, this almond-enhanced version comes from the Jewish community in Volos. MAKES ABOUT 30 COOKIES

2 cups unsalted butter, at room
temperature

1 cup superfine sugar

½ cup finely ground blanched almonds
(from about 2 ounces whole nuts)

2 cups all-purpose flour

2 cups confectioners' sugar

Preheat the oven to 350°F. Line 2 sheet pans with parchment paper.

In a bowl, using an electric mixer, beat the butter on medium speed until creamy and pale. Add the superfine sugar and continue to beat until light and fluffy. Fold in the almonds and flour and mix until a supple but firm dough forms.

Shape the dough into walnut-size balls and place on the prepared sheet pans, spacing them 1 inch apart. Bake until very lightly colored, about 20 minutes. Do not allow to brown. Transfer to wire racks and let cool for 10 minutes, then generously dust the warm cookies with confectioners' sugar or roll them in a bowl of the sugar. Let cool completely before serving. The cookies will keep in an airtight container at room temperature for up to 1 week.

## *Stuffed Butter Cookies*   MA'AMOUL

These simple Sephardic cookies are common in the Levant and beyond, where they are also traditionally eaten by Muslims around Ramadan and by Christians around Easter. Once you master folding the dough over the filling, the cookies are easy to prepare. Some bakers inscribe the dough with intricate patterns or use a mold to decorate them. I have kept these plain. MAKES ABOUT 30 COOKIES

1 cup unsalted butter, at room
temperature

2 tablespoons granulated sugar

3½ cups sifted all-purpose
flour

2 to 4 tablespoons milk or water

1 tablespoon orange flower water

NUT FILLING

2 cups finely chopped walnuts, blanched
almonds, or pistachio nuts

1 cup sugar

1 tablespoon orange flower water

2 teaspoons ground cinnamon

Confectioners' sugar for dusting

Preheat the oven to 300°F. Line 2 sheet pans with parchment paper.

In a bowl, using an electric mixer, beat the butter on medium speed until creamy and pale. Add the sugar and continue to beat until light and fluffy. Gradually add the flour and continue to beat until fully incorporated. Beat in 2 tablespoons of the milk and the orange flower water. Knead in the bowl until the dough holds together and it is easy to shape, adding the remaining 2 tablespoons milk if the dough is a bit dry.

To make the filling, combine all of the ingredients and mix well.

To form each cookie, roll a walnut-size piece of dough into a ball, hollow it out with your thumb, and then pinch the sides up to form a pot shape. Place a small spoonful of the filling into the hollow and pinch the sides of the dough closed over the filling, sealing well and then shaping into a smooth ball. As the cookies are shaped, place them on the prepared sheet pans, spacing them 1 inch apart and flattening them slightly with your palm. If you like, you can lightly score each cookie decoratively with fork tines, but be careful not to puncture the dough.

Bake the cookies until set, about 20 minutes. Do not allow to brown. Carefully transfer the cookies to a wire rack and let cool for 10 minutes, then generously dust the warm cookies with confectioners' sugar. Let cool completely. The cookies can be stored in an airtight container at room temperature for up to 1 week.

VARIATIONS: *Almond and Fruit Filling:* Combine 2½ cups chopped blanched almonds, ¾ cup granulated sugar, ¼ cup chopped candied citron and/or candied lemon or orange peel, grated zest of 1 large lemon, ½ teaspoon vanilla extract, ½ teaspoon ground cinnamon, and 1 egg, lightly beaten, and mix well.

*Date Filling:* In a small saucepan, combine 1 pound pitted dates, chopped, and ½ cup water and simmer over low heat, stirring often, until the dates are reduced to a paste, about 15 minutes. Remove from the heat and stir in the grated zest of 1 orange and ½ teaspoon ground cinnamon, mixing well. Let cool before using.

## *Marzipan-Filled Cookies*  KNEDETTES

There are many affectionate names for these egg yolk and almond cookies, which are reminiscent of Spanish and Portuguese sweets. Algerian cook Emma Bensaid calls them *knedettes,* and *knadels* and *kneglets* appear in Fortunée Hazan-Arama's *Saveurs de mon enfance* and in Maguy Kakon's *La cuisine juive du Maroc de mère en fille.* Moroccan cooks sometimes call them *massapane* and use special molds that look like fluted tartlet molds. I think using tartlet molds (see variation) is a good idea, as forming the cookies by hand into stars is tricky, and the dough has to set up properly to hold the star shape during baking. MAKES 24 TO 30 COOKIES, DEPENDING ON YOUR ROLLING SKILLS

DOUGH

4 cups sifted all-purpose flour

2 whole eggs or 4 egg yolks

¼ cup sunflower or canola oil

3 tablespoons sugar

⅓ cup fresh orange juice

1 to 2 tablespoons orange flower water

1 teaspoon vanilla extract (optional)

ALMOND FILLING

3½ cups blanched almonds

1½ cups sugar

4 egg yolks plus 1 whole egg

Grated zest of 1 lemon

1 egg white, if needed

Plain or colored sanding sugar for sprinkling

To make the dough, in a bowl, combine the flour, eggs, oil, sugar, orange juice, orange flower water (use the larger amount if you prefer a bolder flavor), and vanilla and stir until a rough dough forms. Knead in the bowl until the dough is firm yet workable.

On a lightly floured work surface, roll out the dough ⅛ inch thick. Using a 2½- to 3-inch round cookie cutter or an overturned glass, cut out as many rounds as possible. Transfer the rounds to a clean kitchen towel, then reroll the dough scraps, cut out more rounds, and transfer them to the towel. Let the dough rounds rest for about 1 hour.

To make the filling, in a food processor, combine the almonds and ½ cup of the sugar and pulse until the almonds are ground. Transfer the almond mixture to a bowl, add the remaining 1 cup sugar, the egg yolks and whole egg, and the lemon zest and mix until you have a homogenous but not too stiff paste. If it is too firm, mix in the egg white.

Preheat the oven to 350°F. Line 2 sheet pans with parchment paper.

To form each cookie, place a generous spoonful of the filling on the center of a dough round. Or, if the filling is firm enough to roll, shape it into a 1-inch ball and place the ball in the center of the dough round. Pull up the sides of the dough and make small pleats to form a six-sided star around the filling. As the cookies are formed, transfer them to the prepared pans, spacing them 1 inch apart. Sprinkle the cookies with sanding sugar.

Bake the cookies until golden, 25 to 30 minutes. Transfer to wire racks to cool completely. The cookies will keep in an airtight container at room temperature for up to 2 weeks.

VARIATION: Using 3-inch oval tartlet molds, place a small ball of the dough in each mold and press the dough gently against the bottom and sides of the mold, lining it evenly. Fill the center of each mold with a ball of almond paste. Bake as directed.

## Nut-and-Honey-Filled Cookies SFRATTI

These cookies, which are shaped like sticks, are called *sfratti,* which means "evicted." The name comes from Italian landlords of long ago who used sticks to chase away poor tenants who had not paid their rent, some of them probably poor Jews. Jewish cooks have turned the origin of these cookies around, making them into sweet symbols of eviction (much like Passover *haroset* is the sweet symbol of the mortar used to build the pyramids.) These honey-and-nut-filled cookies are served at Rosh Hashanah. Butter or margarine is used, depending on whether the rest of the meal is dairy or not. My family thinks these are better than *rugelach!* MAKES 36 TO 42 COOKIES

PASTRY

3 cups all-purpose flour

1 cup sugar

Pinch of salt

⅓ cup cold margarine or unsalted butter, cut into cubes

⅔ cup sweet wine, such as Marsala or sweet sherry

FILLING

⅔ cup honey

1 teaspoon ground cinnamon

¼ teaspoon ground cloves

2 cups walnuts, coarsely chopped

1 tablespoon grated lemon zest

1 tablespoon grated orange zest

Pinch of freshly ground black pepper

All-purpose flour or fine dried bread crumbs for dusting

1 egg yolk beaten with 2 tablespoons water, for egg wash

Chill a pastry board. To make the pastry, in a bowl, stir together the flour, sugar, and salt. Scatter the margarine over the flour mixture and, using a pastry blender, cut in the margarine until the mixture resembles coarse meal. Add the wine and stir and toss with a fork until the mixture is evenly moist and just holds together. Alternatively, combine the flour, sugar, and salt in a food processor and pulse briefly to mix. Scatter the margarine over the flour mixture and pulse until most of the butter is the size of peas. Add the wine and pulse until the mixture comes together in a rough mass. Gather the dough into a rough ball. Divide the dough in half, flatten each half into a disk, wrap in plastic wrap, and refrigerate for 1 to 2 hours.

To make the filling, pour the honey into a heavy saucepan, place over medium-high heat, and bring to a boil. Add the cinnamon and cloves and boil until the honey forms a ribbon when a spoon is lifted, about 10 minutes. Add the walnuts, citrus zests, and pepper and simmer for 10 minutes. Remove from the heat and let cool until you can touch the mixture without burning yourself.

Dust the chilled pastry board with flour, then pour the hot filling onto the board. Using your hands, roll the filling into 6 thin ropes each 12 to 14 inches long. Act quickly as the mixture sets up fast!

Preheat the oven to 375°F. Butter 1 or 2 sheet pans or line with parchment paper.

On a lightly floured work surface, divide each pastry disk into 3 equal pieces. Roll out each piece of dough into a rectangle 4 inches wide and 12 to 14 inches long. Place a strip of nut paste near the long edge of each rectangle and roll up the dough around the paste, fully enclosing it. Cut each roll crosswise into 2-inch lengths.

Place the cookies, seam side down, on the prepared pan(s), spacing them 1½ inches apart. Brush them with the egg wash. Bake until golden, about 20 minutes. Transfer the cookies to wire racks and let cool completely. The cookies will keep in an airtight container at room temperature for up to 1 week.

## Walnut-Filled Cookies   BOREKAS DE MUEZ

This Turkish walnut-filled *boreka* is served at Purim. The same filling can be used in filo dough and formed into triangles or into cylinders.   MAKES ABOUT 36 COOKIES

**FILLING**

2 cups ground walnuts or blanched almonds (from about 8 ounces whole nuts)

2 teaspoons ground cinnamon

6 tablespoons confectioners' sugar

Grated zest of 2 large oranges

1 egg, lightly beaten

¼ cup orange marmalade, or as needed

1 apple, peeled, halved, cored, and grated (optional)

**PASTRY**

3½ cups all-purpose flour

¼ cup granulated sugar

Pinch of salt

¾ cup canola oil

½ cup margarine, melted

½ cup water or sweet white wine

All-purpose flour for shaping cookies

1 egg yolk beaten with 2 tablespoons water, for egg wash

Confectioners' sugar for dusting

To make the filling, in a bowl, combine all of the ingredients and mix well, adding more marmalade if needed to moisten. The filling should be moist enough to hold together.

To make the pastry, in a bowl, stir together the flour, granulated sugar, and salt. Add the oil, margarine, and water and beat with a wooden spoon until the mixture comes together in a rough dough. Turn the dough out onto a lightly floured work surface and knead until smooth and cohesive.

Preheat the oven to 350°F. Line 2 sheet pans with parchment paper.

Roll the dough into walnut-size balls. Spread some flour on a plate and dip the balls in the flour, coating evenly and tapping off the excess. Roll out each ball into a 2½- to 3-inch round. To shape each cookie, place 1 tablespoon filling in the center of a dough round. Moisten the edges of the round with water, fold the round in half, encasing the filling, and then pinch the edges to seal securely. As the cookies are formed, transfer them to the prepared pans, spacing them about 1½ inches apart.

Brush the cookies with the egg wash. Bake until golden, about 20 minutes. Transfer to wire racks, let cool completely, and then dust with confectioners' sugar. The cookies will keep in an airtight container at room temperature for up to 1 week.

## Almond Filo Cigars   LES CIGARES AUX AMANDES

Moroccans and Tunisians are fond of these flaky nut-filled sweets, which are sometimes filled with walnuts instead of almonds and are also known as *briks aux amandes* and *briouats aux amandes.* In Algeria, where the filling does not include ginger, cloves, or flower water, they are served after the Yom Kippur fast. The raisin and walnut conserve for the tart on page 405 would also make a good filling. These pastries can also be baked in a preheated 350°F oven until golden, about 25 minutes. MAKES 24 PASTRIES

| | |
|---|---|
| 1 pound blanched almonds, toasted and coarsely chopped (about 4 cups) | 2 eggs, separated |
| 1½ cups sugar | 1 tablespoon orange flower water |
| 1 teaspoon ground ginger | 12 feuilles de brik, or 24 filo sheets |
| 1 teaspoon cloves | ¾ cup unsalted butter or margarine, melted, if using filo |
| 1 teaspoon cinnamon | Canola oil for deep-frying |
| | ¾ cup orange blossom honey |

Combine the almonds and sugar in a food processor and pulse until a paste forms. Add the ginger, cloves, cinnamon, egg yolks, and orange flower water and pulse until well mixed. If the paste is too dry to hold together, add 1 egg white and pulse to mix. Divide the paste into 24 equal portions and shape each portion into a strip about 4 inches long.

In a small bowl, lightly beat the remaining egg white. If using feuilles de brik, cut the circles in half. Position a half circle vertically, place a strip of filling horizontally along the edge closest to you, fold the edge over the filling, fold in the sides, and then roll up into a cigar shape. Dampen the edge with a little egg white and press to seal.

If using filo, cut the filo sheets into rectangles measuring about 6 by 12 inches. You should have 48 rectangles. Brush 1 strip with melted butter, top with another strip, and brush with butter. (Keep the rectangles you are not immediately using covered with a damp kitchen towel or plastic wrap to prevent drying.) Place a strip of filling along the 6-inch side, tuck in the sides, and roll up like a cigar.

Pour the oil to a depth of 3 inches into a deep, heavy saucepan or a deep fryer and heat to 365°F. While the oil is heating, warm the honey in a small saucepan over low heat. In batches, add the pastries to the hot oil and fry, turning once, until golden, 3 to 4 minutes total. Using a slotted spoon or tongs, transfer the pastries to paper towels to drain briefly. Then gently lift each pastry with tongs, dip it into the warm honey, and place on a platter. Serve immediately.

VARIATION: *Honey-Lemon Syrup:* Omit the honey for dipping. In a saucepan, combine ¼ cup each honey and sugar, grated zest and juice of 1 lemon, and ½ cup water and bring to a boil over medium heat, stirring to dissolve the sugar. Simmer until thickened to a nice syrup consistency and then remove from the heat. Arrange the hot pastries on a platter and spoon the hot syrup over the pastries.

## Haman's Ears   ORECCHIE DI AMMAN

These cookies, which are served at Purim, represent the ears of the wicked minister Haman. A strip of dough is formed into a circle or a butterfly to resemble an ear and then fried in oil.  MAKES ABOUT 24 COOKIES

3 whole eggs, or 2 whole eggs and 2 egg yolks

¼ cup granulated sugar

½ teaspoon salt

2 teaspoons grated lemon zest or orange zest

½ teaspoon vanilla extract

3 tablespoons olive oil

3 tablespoons brandy

2½ to 3 cups all-purpose flour

Canola oil for frying

Confectioners' sugar for dusting

In a bowl, using a whisk or a wooden spoon, beat together the eggs, granulated sugar, salt, lemon zest, vanilla, oil, and brandy until well combined. Gradually add the flour, stirring until the mixture comes together in a soft dough. Turn the dough out onto a lightly floured work surface and knead until smooth, about 5 minutes.

Clean the work surface, dust again lightly with flour, and then roll out the dough into a thin sheet. Using a pastry wheel, cut the sheet into strips about 1½ inches wide. Cut the strips either 4 inches long or 6 inches long, depending on how many circles or butterflies you want. Pinch together the ends of the longer strips to form circles, and pinch the centers of the shorter strips to form butterflies.

Pour the oil to a depth of 3 inches into a deep, heavy saucepan or a deep fryer and heat to 365°F. In batches, slip the pastries into the hot oil and fry until golden, about 3 minutes. Using a slotted spoon or wire skimmer, transfer the cookies to paper towels to drain and keep them warm until all of the cookies are fried. Arrange the cookies on a platter, dust with confectioners' sugar, and eat while warm.

## Squash Fritters from the Veneto   FRITTELLE DI ZUCCA

Crisp and citrusy, these Venetian squash fritters are the perfect Hanukkah dessert. A few words about measurements: It's hard to find a squash that weighs exactly 1¼ pounds. Just be sure the cubed squash is covered with milk, and then add enough flour to make a mixture that is as thick as sour cream. You will need to adjust the sugar to taste, as squashes vary in sweetness. Butternut is usually sweeter than kabocha or pumpkin. This recipe is an adaptation of two recipes, one from Giovanni Capnist's *I dolci del Veneto* and the other from Milka Passigli's *Le ricette di casa mia.*  SERVES 6

1 butternut or kabocha squash or pumpkin, about 1¼ pounds

2 cups milk, or as needed

1½ cups all-purpose flour, or as needed

2 teaspoons baking soda dissolved in 2 teaspoons water

Pinch of salt

2 eggs

⅔ cup granulated sugar

Grated zest of 1 or 2 oranges

½ cup candied citron, cut into small dice

⅓ cup golden raisins

½ cup pine nuts, toasted

Canola oil for deep-frying

Confectioners' sugar for dusting

Halve the squash, scoop out and discard the seeds and fibers, and cut into ½-inch dice. You should have 3 to 3½ cups. Place in a saucepan, add milk to cover, and place over medium heat. Bring to a simmer and cook until the squash breaks down into a smooth purée, about 30 minutes. Don't worry if the mixture looks curdled; it will smooth out. Stir in the flour and continue to stir until the mixture is thick, about 5 minutes, adding more flour as needed to bind. Beat in the dissolved baking soda and the salt and then beat in the eggs, one at a time, mixing well after each addition. Add the granulated sugar, orange zest, citron, raisins, and pine nuts. Remove from the heat and let stand until most of the moisture has been absorbed, about 15 minutes.

Pour the oil to a depth of 3 inches into a deep, heavy saucepan or a deep fryer and heat to 365°F. In batches, drop the batter by small spoonfuls (about 1 inch in diameter) into the hot oil and fry until golden, 3 to 5 minutes. (The fritters must not be too large or the center will not cook.) Using a slotted spoon, transfer the fritters to paper towels to drain and keep them warm until all of the fritters are fried. Arrange the fritters on a platter, dust generously with confectioners' sugar, and eat while hot or very warm.

## Moroccan Hanukkah Doughnuts   SFENJ

Although these Moroccan doughnuts are usually dipped in warm honey, you can use granulated sugar instead. A similar fritter, called *yoyo,* is made next door in Tunisia, though it relies on baking powder for leavening, has eggs in the dough, and is perfumed with vanilla and orange zest. I have found that this dough is easier to work with if you add the eggs and a bit of oil or melted margarine or butter. Some *sfenj* are scented with orange zest and orange juice (both optional here), and they add bright flavor to what would otherwise be a somewhat boring doughnut. MAKES ABOUT 20 DOUGHNUTS

2 envelopes (2½ teaspoons each) active dry yeast

¼ cup sugar

1½ to 2 cups warm water or part water and part fresh orange juice

4 cups all-purpose flour, plus more if needed

½ teaspoon salt

2 eggs, lightly beaten (optional)

Grated zest of 1 orange (optional)

4 tablespoons canola oil, or margarine or unsalted butter, melted (optional)

Canola oil for deep-frying

Warmed honey for dipping or sugar for sprinkling

In a small bowl, sprinkle the yeast and sugar over ½ cup of the warm water and let stand until bubbling and foamy, 5 to 10 minutes. Pour the yeast mixture into a large bowl and add the flour, salt, eggs, orange zest, and oil. Stir to mix well, then stir in just enough of the remaining water to form a soft dough. Knead the dough in the bowl until it is elastic, shiny, and no longer sticks to your hands or the bowl, adding a little more flour if needed to reduce the stickiness. (Alternatively, use a stand mixer fitted with the paddle attachment to mix the dough and then use the dough hook to knead the dough.) Shape the dough into a ball, place in a large oiled bowl, and turn the dough to coat it evenly with the oil. Cover the bowl with a kitchen towel and let the dough rise in a warm place until doubled in bulk, 1½ to 2 hours.

Oil your hands. Punch down the dough and then divide it into balls about the size of a plum (about 2 inches in diameter).

Pour the oil to a depth of 3 inches into a deep, heavy saucepan or a deep fryer and heat to 365°F. Oil your hands to shape the doughnuts. Use your index finger to make a hole in the center of each ball and then gently pull the sides outward to make a doughnut shape. When the oil is ready, in batches, add the doughnuts to the hot oil and fry, turning them as needed to color evenly, until puffed and golden, 3 to 4 minutes. Using a slotted spoon or wire skimmer, transfer the doughnuts to paper towels to drain and keep them warm until all of the doughnuts are fried. Dip the warm doughnuts in honey or sprinkle with sugar and then arrange on a platter. Serve at once.

VARIATION: *Israeli Hanukkah Doughnuts (Sufganiyot):* Make the dough and shape into balls as directed, then fry in the hot oil and drain briefly. Using a pastry bag fitted with a small plain tip, pipe 1 tablespoon raspberry or cherry jam into the center of each fried ball. Coat with granulated sugar and serve hot.

## Dates Stuffed with Almond Paste
### DATTES FARCIES À LA PÂTE D'AMANDES

In Morocco, these stuffed dates are served with a platter of fresh fruit at the end of a meal. Prunes may be stuffed the same way. Sometimes a bit of red food coloring is added to the almond paste to make it pink. And to be even more festive, you can dip the stuffed dates into colored sanding sugar. If time is short, substitute softened store-bought almond paste for the almond filling here. MAKES 24 STUFFED DATES

---

2 cups blanched almonds

⅔ cup confectioners' sugar

2 tablespoons light or dark rum, Grand Marnier, or orange flower water

1 teaspoon almond extract

24 large Medjool dates, sliced open partway and pitted

Sanding sugar for coating

---

In a food processor, combine the almonds and confectioners' sugar and pulse until the almonds are finely ground. Add the rum and almond extract and process until the mixture comes together. Turn the mixture out onto a work surface and knead it just until it holds together.

To stuff each date, break off a piece of the almond paste, roll it into a small oval, and stuff it into the pocket left by the pit. When all of the dates are stuffed, roll them in the sanding sugar to coat lightly. The dates can be served right away or kept in an airtight container at room temperature for up to 2 days.

## *Lemon Marzipan*   MANZAPADES

This recipe for marzipan, a favorite Passover sweet, is from the Jewish community of Volos. The Greeks seem to add lemon juice to almost everything, and they also don't discard the peels, as this recipe illustrates. The origin of marzipan is widely debated, but the most accepted theory is that it was carried to Spain by the Arabs. Some believe its name comes from *mautaban,* the Arabic term for the sweet, which itself comes from the Arabic word *uataba,* or "white." However, marzipan also has been associated with Saint Mark's bread, the *panis martis,* or March bread, of Roman antiquity that was a common offering during the rites of spring and was later adopted by the Catholic church. Marzipan is still a popular confection in Spain and Portugal (a tradition kept alive today by the convents) and certainly would have been adapted in Greece and Turkey by Jews from Sicily where the marzipan tradition was entrenched. MAKES ABOUT 20 PIECES

---

Peels of 10 to 12 lemons (reserve the juice for another use)

1 cup blanched almonds, finely ground

2 cups granulated sugar

1 cup confectioners' sugar

---

Put the lemon peels in a bowl, add water to cover, and let soak for 2 days, changing the water every 3 to 4 hours. On the third day, rinse the peels, transfer them to a saucepan, and add water to cover. Place over low heat, bring to a simmer, and simmer until very soft, 45 to 60 minutes. Drain well and mash to a pulp or pulse in a food processor. You should have about 1 cup pulp.

For each cup of lemon pulp, you need 1 cup ground almonds and 2 cups granulated sugar. If you have more or less pulp, adjust the almond and sugar as needed. Put the lemon pulp, almonds, and granulated sugar in a saucepan and mix well. Place over low heat, bring to a gentle simmer, and simmer, stirring often with a wooden spoon, until the mixture thickens and pulls away from the sides of the pan, 20 to 30 minutes. Remove the pan from the heat, pour the mixture onto a marble slab or cold platter, and let cool.

Spread some of the confectioners' sugar on a plate. Knead the cooled lemon mixture a bit until it is pliable and then pinch off pieces the size of hazelnuts and roll each piece into a ball. One at a time, roll the balls in the sugar, coating evenly, and place on a platter. Dust the balls with the remaining confectioners' sugar. Cover and let rest in a cool place for 24 hours before serving.

# Pantry Ingredients

## THE MEDITERRANEAN MASALA

Today, many of the traditional spice mixtures of the Mediterranean Jewish kitchen, such as *ras el hanout* and *za'atar, advieh,* and *bahārāt,* can be purchased at specialty food stores or online. Other once hard-to-find ingredients, such as freekeh, pomegranate molasses, tamarind paste, and tahini, are now commonly found in well-stocked grocery stores as well as online.

**ADVIEH.** This Iranian spice mix, which is also popular in Iraq, varies from region to region, from family to family, and even from dish to dish, with pilafs using a different combination of spices than is used for stews. A typical blend would be 2 tablespoons each ground turmeric and cinnamon; 1 tablespoon ground cardamom; 1 teaspoon each ground coriander, ginger, and saffron; ½ teaspoon each freshly ground black pepper and freshly grated nutmeg; and a pinch of cayenne pepper. Some blends add dried rose petals.

**ALEPPO, MARAS, AND URFA PEPPER FLAKES.** These three mildly hot red pepper varieties are from the Syrian town of Aleppo and from Kahramanmaraş and Şanlıurfa in northeastern Turkey, respectively. Aleppo lies less than 30 miles from the Syrian-Turkish border and all three cities are within 150 miles of one another. Brick red and fruity, Maras pepper (also known as Marash and Turkish red pepper) and Aleppo pepper are nearly interchangeable, with Maras a bit hotter, though neither pepper is very hot. Blackish purple Urfa peppers are molasses sweet with a bit of bitterness like coffee and have a smoky, raisiny, earthy flavor.

Both Turkish peppers are processed with salt (the US Food and Drug Administration allows packagers to include up to 8 percent salt with these pepper flakes). The producers insist that if they did not add salt, the pepper flakes would quickly spoil.

**BAHĀRĀT.** This spice blend—*bahārāt* is the Arabic word for "spices"—is used in many countries of the Middle East. Its composition varies, however, with different spices, ratios, and degrees of sweetness. It is usually composed of allspice, cardamom, black pepper, cinnamon, cloves, coriander, cumin, nutmeg, and paprika. The Turks may add some dried mint, and the Tunisians favor a simple mixture of cinnamon, black pepper, and dried rose petals. *Bahārāt* is used to flavor meat, fish, and poultry. Here are three common blends:

1½ tablespoons each allspice, coriander, cinnamon, and cumin; 1 tablespoon each black pepper and paprika; 2 teaspoons nutmeg; and 1 teaspoon each cardamom and cloves

2 tablespoons each paprika and black pepper; 1½ tablespoons cumin; 1 tablespoon each coriander, cinnamon, and cloves; 1½ teaspoons cardamom; and ½ teaspoon nutmeg

2 tablespoons each allspice and cinnamon, 1 tablespoon black pepper, 1 teaspoon each cloves and cardamom, and ½ teaspoon each nutmeg and ginger (Iraqis call this seven spices)

BARBERRIES. These tart, dark crimson dried fruits are about the size of a currant or small raisin and are used in Iranian cooking, often mixed with rice. Before adding them to a dish, they must be plumped in hot water or quickly sautéed in butter to soften.

BULGUR. A staple grain of the Lebanese, Jordanian, Syrian, and Turkish kitchens, bulgur is durum wheat berries that have been partially hulled and then steamed, dried, and ground. Bulgur, which is considered a whole grain because its exterior is only lightly abraded, comes in four grinds. Fine is used for tabbouleh and is easily reconstituted by soaking, medium is used mainly for pilafs and *kibbeh* and cooks in 15 to 20 minutes, and coarse and extra coarse are also used for pilafs and take longer to cook. Bulgur is not to be confused with cracked wheat, which is ground raw wheat berries.

CHARMOULA. A specialty of Morocco but popular throughout North Africa, this spice-and-herb mixture, sometimes spelled *chermoula,* is used as a marinade and finishing sauce primarily for fish and less often for vegetables and meats (see page 239).

COUSCOUS. These small, fine pasta pellets made from semolina (durum wheat) are the signature starch of North Africa (see page 158).

DRIED OMANI LIMES. These sour fruits originated in the Persian Gulf, thus their name. They are used in kitchens throughout the region and have been cultivated in Iran for centuries, where they are added to soups and stews to impart a tart flavor. Available whole and powdered, they range in color from cream to almost black and will impart some of their color to the dish in which they are cooked. If using whole limes, rinse them well and then give them a gentle thwack with a meat pounder so they crack, allowing their flavor to diffuse throughout the dish.

DUKKAH. Also spelled *duqqa,* this Egyptian seasoning mixture, which is now used elsewhere in the Middle East, as well, is typically made up of nuts, seeds, spices, and herbs that are toasted separately and then pounded together (the word *dukkah* comes from the Arabic word for "to pound"). Some mixtures include toasted chickpeas, as well. *Dukkah* is primarily eaten on bread that has first been dipped in olive oil and is also good on raw and cooked vegetables and rice. Here are two suggested combinations:

¾ cup hazelnuts, toasted, skinned, and finely chopped; ¼ cup coriander seeds, toasted and ground; 3 tablespoons cumin seeds, toasted and ground; ½ cup sesame seeds, toasted; 1 teaspoon salt; ½ teaspoon freshly ground black pepper; and a pinch of paprika or nigella seeds (optional)

½ cup almonds or hazelnuts, toasted, skinned, and finely chopped; 3 tablespoons coriander seeds, toasted and ground; 2 tablespoons cumin seeds, toasted and ground; 1 teaspoon Aleppo or Urfa pepper flakes; 3 tablespoons sesame seeds, toasted; 1 teaspoon nigella seeds; 2 teaspoons salt; and 1 teaspoon dried mint

FREEKEH. Popular in Syria, Lebanon, Jordan, Egypt, and to a lesser degree in Turkey and North Africa, freekeh is green wheat that has been roasted and cracked. The wheat is harvested when the seeds are still soft, and the stalks are stacked and left to dry in the sun. The stacks are carefully set on fire to burn off only the chaff and straw, leaving behind the roasted kernels, which are then thrashed and dried again in the sun. Sold both whole and cracked, freekeh is used in soups, pilafs, and stuffings and is easy to cook: allow a ratio of three parts water to one part wheat and start checking for doneness after 15 minutes if using cracked freekeh or after 45 minutes if using whole freekeh.

HARISSA. This North African hot sauce is used primarily in Tunisia and Morocco. Moroccan *harissa* is typically a mixture of chiles, garlic, cumin, and olive oil. The Tunisian version is a bit more distinctive, as it infuses sweet red peppers with *tābil* (see entry), a mixture of caraway, coriander, and garlic. Although you can buy *harissa* paste in a tube or jar, it will never be as good as when you make it yourself. I have included two recipes for *harissa* on page 355.

KAYMAK. Similar to clotted cream, creamy, rich Turkish *kaymak* is made by gently simmering milk (traditionally water buffalo's milk) until a thick, creamy layer forms on the surface, which is then removed and left to firm up and ferment slightly before using. Similar preparations are found in Iran and Iraq and throughout Central Asia. *Kaymak* is a common breakfast food and a popular accompaniment to desserts. It is difficult to find outside the region, however. Clotted cream, *labneh* (see entry), mascarpone, or Greek yogurt can be used in its place in recipes in this book.

LABNEH. This Middle Eastern fresh cheese, which is becoming more commonly available in the dairy case of US markets, is traditionally made by hanging yogurt in cheesecloth until most of the moisture has dripped away and a soft cheese has formed. It is delicious drizzled with olive oil and sprinkled with *za'atar* as an accompaniment for pita bread and is a good substitute for *kaymak* in recipes in this book.

NIGELLA SEEDS. These tiny black seeds, sometimes called black cumin or black caraway, have a slightly oniony taste. They are sprinkled atop pastries for both a color accent and the aroma they impart.

ORANGE FLOWER WATER. Sold in bottles, this is the clear liquid that results from distilling orange blossoms. It is a popular addition to desserts in the Mediterranean, North Africa, and the Middle East.

POMEGRANATE MOLASSES. Sometimes labeled "pomegranate juice concentrate," pomegranate molasses is a thick syrup made by reducing pomegranate juice. Tart and sweet, it is used in the Middle East in dressings, as a marinade, and as a sauce enhancement where a sweet-and-sour flavor is desired. The best-known brands are Cortas and Carlo, imported from Lebanon.

PRESERVED LEMONS. A staple in every Moroccan kitchen, preserved lemons are a signature flavor in many of the country's dishes. See page 356 for directions on putting them up.

RAS EL HANOUT. The name of this Moroccan spice mixture means "top of the shop." *Ras el hanout* can contain as many as thirty spices and is added to stews and other meat dishes, vegetable dishes, marinades and brines, and condiments. Because commercial *ras el hanout* in years past often included cantharides beetle in the mix, making the spice blend non-kosher, observant Jews traditionally prepared their own blend.

To make your own *ras el hanout,* combine equal parts ground cinnamon, ground cardamom, ground mace, ground nutmeg, ground sweet paprika, ground black pepper, ground turmeric, and ground ginger. Toast the spices in a dry pan until fragrant, and store in a tightly sealed jar.

ROSE WATER. Made from fresh petals by the process known as steam distillation, rose water was first mass-produced by Persians in medieval times. Today it is widely used in desserts throughout the Middle East.

SAFFRON. Introduced to Spain and Portugal from Asia Minor by the Moors, and planted in Andalusia, Valencia, and southern Castile, saffron is best when bought in threads or filaments rather than in powder form. To release the maximum flavor, the threads are ideally warmed in a dry pan on the stove top until fragrant or on a plate in a microwave oven for 30 seconds. The warmed threads are then typically crushed in a mortar and steeped in warm liquid (wine, broth, or water) to develop their flavor and color. Saffron imparts a lovely golden hue and an intriguing sweet-bitter accent to food. The best Spanish brand is La Mancha, which packages deep red threads. Superb saffron also comes from Iran.

SUMAC. The dried fruits (drupes) of a shrub native to the Middle East, sumac is a dark reddish purple spice with a tart, lemony taste. It is sold both whole and ground and is used to garnish meze and to flavor salads like *fattoush*. In Iran, where a shaker of sumac sits on the table alongside salt and pepper, it is sprinkled over rice, kebabs, and anything else that needs a tangy accent. Sumac is also one of the components of *za'atar* (see entry).

TĀBIL. A signature spice mixture in Tunisian cooking—*tābil* means "seasoning" in Tunisian Arabic—*tābil* is a combination of caraway, coriander, garlic, and lots of hot pepper. It is a common addition to soups and stews.

TAHINI. A pantry staple in the Arab nations of the Middle East, Turkey, and Israel, tahini is a thick paste made from grinding toasted sesame seeds and oil. It comes to the market in cans, jars, and plastic containers. Not all tahini is of equal quality, so I advise sampling a few different brands to find one that has a rich flavor and no bitterness. (Some of the natural foods brands are not mellow enough for my palate, and a few have a nasty aftertaste.) My favorite brand, Al Wadi, is produced in Lebanon. Once the tahini is packed, the sesame paste settles to the bottom of the container in a dense lump, with the oil floating on top. You will have to stir it vigorously, using a strong wrist and a fork, before using it. A whirl in a blender or food processor will also work, after which you can put what you don't use back in the original container. Every time you return to the container, however, you will have to repeat the stirring process, as the paste will always settle to the bottom, topped with the oil layer.

Tahini becomes a salad dressing by blending it with fresh lemon juice and thinning the purée with water. It can be thick or quite thin. Garlic is usually added, as well as such spices as cumin and cayenne pepper. Creamy tahini dressing can be served as a dip for pita bread, cucumber spears, carrot batons, radishes, or green onions, or it can be spooned over cooked fish. When thinned with additional water, it is delicious drizzled over sliced tomatoes, beets and greens, or a simple salad of romaine lettuce, sliced cucumbers, and sliced radishes. It is superb spooned over sautéed or grilled eggplant or zucchini or roasted carrots or beets. You can also stir tahini into mashed roasted eggplant to make baba ghanouj (page 29) or into mashed chickpeas to create hummus (page 38).

TAMARIND. The tart-sweet pulp found inside the pods that grow on trees of the same name, tamarind (from the Arabic *tamr-hindī*, meaning "date of India") is used in Turkey, Iran, Syria, Lebanon, and elsewhere in the Middle East in sauces and marinades and in meat, fish, and poultry dishes. It can be purchased as a paste or extract and diluted as needed.

ZA'ATAR. Popular all over the Middle East, *za'atar* is an aromatic dry mixture typically made up of hyssop or oregano, thyme, sumac, and sesame seeds. It is commonly eaten with pita bread that has first been dipped in olive oil and is also good sprinkled on top of cooked vegetables, soft goat cheese, or hummus or other spreads. Although *za'atar* is traditionally made with dried herbs, I sometimes use fresh herbs for their fragrance. Here is a simple recipe: ¼ cup sesame seeds, 2 tablespoons ground sumac, ½ teaspoon salt, and about ½ cup chopped fresh thyme, hyssop, or marjoram.

# Bibliography

Abadi, Jennifer Felicia. *A Fistful of Lentils: Syrian-Jewish Recipes from Grandma Fritzie's Kitchen.* Boston: Harvard Common, 2002.

Abdennour, Samia. *Egyptian Cooking: A Practical Guide.* New York: Hippocrene Books, 1998.

Admony, Einat. *Balaboosta: Bold Mediterranean Recipes to Feed the People You Love.* New York: Artisan Books, 2013.

Agostini, Maria. *Dolci ebraici della tradizione veneziana.* Venice: Filippi Editore, 1995.

Algar, Ayla Esen. *Classical Turkish Cooking: Traditional Turkish Food for the American Kitchen.* New York: HarperCollins, 1991.

Alhadeff, Nora Pinto. *Quaderno di cucina: Profumi, sapori e ricordi di una vita di viaggi.* Verona: Arnoldo Mondadori, 1993.

Altabé, David Fintz. *Spanish and Portuguese Jewry before and after 1492.* Brooklyn, NY: Sepher Hermon, 1993.

Anderson, Jean. *The Food of Portugal.* New York: William Morrow, 1986.

Andrews, Colman. *Catalan Cuisine: Europe's Last Great Culinary Secret.* New York: Atheneum, 1988.

Angel, Gilda. *Sephardic Holiday Cooking: Recipes and Traditions.* Mount Vernon, NY: Decalogue Books, 1986.

Aris, Pepita. *A Flavor of Andalusia.* Edison, NJ: Chartwell Books, 1996.

Ascoli Vitali-Norsa, Giuliana. *La cucina nella tradizione ebraica: Ricette di cucina ebraica, italiana, askenazita e sefardita.* Florence: ADEI WIZO-La Giuntina, 1987.

Badi, Méri. *250 recettes de cuisine juive espagnole.* Paris: Jacques Grancher, 1984.

Bahloul, Joëlle. *The Architecture of Memory: A Jewish-Muslim Household in Colonial Algeria, 1937–1962.* Cambridge: Cambridge University Press, 1996.

——. *Le culte de la table dressée: Rites et traditions de la table juive algérienne.* Paris: A.-M. Métailié, 1983.

Bassani, Giorgio. *The Garden of the Finzi-Continis.* Translated by William Weaver. New York: Harcourt Brace Jovanovich, 1977.

Batman, Najmieh. *Ma cuisine d'Iran.* Paris: Jacques Grancher, 1984.

Batmanglij, Najmieh. *Food of Life: A Book of Ancient Persian and Modern Iranian Cooking and Ceremonies.* Washington, DC: Mage, 1986.

Baysal, Ayşe. *Samples from Turkish Cuisine.* Ankara: Turkish Historical Society, 1993.

Belgrado Passigli, Milka. *Le ricette di casa mia: La cucina casher in una famiglia ebraica italiana.* Florence: La Giuntina, 1993.

Bishara, Rawia. *Olives, Lemons & Zaatar: The Best Middle Eastern Home Cooking.* Lanham, MD: Kyle Books, 2014.

Blady, Ken. *Jewish Communities in Exotic Places.* Northvale, NJ: Jason Aronson, 2000.

Bundy, Ariana. *Pomegranate and Roses: My Persian Family Recipes.* London: Simon & Schuster, 2012.

Calimani, Riccardo, and Katherine Silberblatt Wolfthal. *The Ghetto of Venice.* Milan: Rusconi, 1988.

Capnist, Giovanni. *I dolci del Veneto.* Padua: Franco Muzzio, 1983.

Chiche-Yana, Martine. *La table juive: Tome 1, Traditions des fêtes de l'année juive, coutumes et recettes.* Aix en Provence: Édisud, 1992.

———. *La table juive: Tome 2, Recettes et traditions du cycle de vie.* Aix en Provence: Édisud, 1994.

Cohen, Stella. *Stella's Sephardic Table: Jewish Family Recipes from the Mediterranean Island of Rhodes.* Capetown: Hoberman Collection, 2012.

Cohen-Azuelos, Jacqueline. *Fleur de safran: Images et saveurs du Maroc.* Aix-en-Provence: Édisud, 1999.

Congregation Or VeShalom Sisterhood. *The Sephardic Cooks.* Rev. ed. Atlanta: Congregation Or VeShalom Sisterhood, 1981.

Cooper, John. *Eat and Be Satisfied: A Social History of Jewish Food.* Northvale, NJ: Jason Aronson, 1993.

Corey, Helen. *The Art of Syrian Cookery.* Garden City, NY: Doubleday, 1962.

Craig, Lisa Elmaleh. *Grandma Elmaleh's Moroccan Cookbook.* London: Hesperus, 2012.

Dana-Haeri, Jila. *From a Persian Kitchen: Fresh Discoveries in Iranian Cooking.* London: I. B. Tauris, 2014.

Danan, Simy. *La nouvelle cuisine judéo-marocaine: Authentique et allégée.* Paris: ACR Edition, 1994.

David, Suzy. *The Sephardic Kosher Kitchen.* Middle Village, NY: Jonathan David, 1984.

Dweck, Poopa. *Aromas of Aleppo: The Legendary Cuisine of Syrian Jews.* New York: Ecco, 2007.

Eden, Esin, and Nicholas Stavroulakis. *Salonika: A Family Cookbook.* Athens: Talos, 1997.

Eramo, Cia. *La cucina mantovana.* Padua: Franco Muzzio, 1987.

Farah, Madelain. *Lebanese Cuisine: Over Two Hundred Authentic Recipes Designed for the Gourmet, the Vegetarian, the Healthfood Enthusiast.* Portland, OR: Lebanese Cuisine, 1991.

Field, Carol. *Celebrating Italy.* New York: William Morrow, 1990.

———. *Italy in Small Bites.* New York: William Morrow, 1993.

Fortis, Umberto. *Jews and Synagogues: Venice, Florence, Rome, Leghorn; a Practical Guide.* Venice: Edizioni Storti, 1973.

Fromer, Rebecca Camhi. *The House by the Sea: A Portrait of the Holocaust in Greece.* San Francisco: Mercury House, 1998.

Galluzzi, Maria Alessandra Iori, Narsete Iori, and Marco Inotta. *La cucina ferrarese.* Padua: Franco Muzzio, 1987.

Gans Perez, Hélène. *Marrakech la Rouge: Les juifs de la Médina.* Geneva: Métropolis, 1996.

Gerber, Jane. *The Jews of Spain: A History of the Sephardic Experience.* New York: Free Press, 1992.

Ghanoonparvar, M. R. *Persian Cuisine.* 2 vols. Lexington, KY: Mazdâ, 1982–1984.

Gitlitz, David, and Linda Kay Davidson. *A Drizzle of Honey: The Lives and Recipes of Spain's Secret Jews.* New York: St. Martin's, 1999.

Gosetti, Fernanda. *I dolci della cucina regionale italiana.* Milan: Fabbri, 1993.

Gosetti della Salda, Anna. *Le ricette regionali italiane.* Milan: Casa Editrice Solares, 1967.

Greene, Gloria Kaufer. *The Jewish Holiday Cookbook: An International Collection of Recipes and Customs.* New York: Times Books, 1950.

Guinaudeau, Zette. *Traditional Moroccan Cooking: Recipes from Fez.* London: Serif, 1994.

Gur, Janna. *The Book of New Israeli Food: A Culinary Journey.* New York: Schocken Books, 2007.

Halıcı, Nevin. *Nevin Halici's Turkish Cookbook.* London: Dorling Kindersley, 1989.

Haroutunian, Arto der. *Middle Eastern Cookery.* London: Century, 1982.

——. *North African Cookery.* London: Century, 1985.

——. *Sweets and Desserts from the Middle East.* London: Century, 1984.

Hazan-Arama, Fortunée. *Saveurs de mon enfance: La cuisine juive du Maroc.* Paris: Robert Laffont, 1987.

Helou, Anissa. *Lebanese Cuisine.* London: Grub Street, 1994.

Ifergan, Jeanne, and Marek Lebkowski. *Savoir préparer la cuisine juive d'Afrique du Nord.* Paris: Créalivres, 1990.

Jaffin, Léone. *150 recettes et mille et un souvenirs d'une juive d'Algérie.* Paris: Editions Encre, 1996.

Kaak, Zeineb. *La sofra: Cuisine tunisienne traditionnelle.* Tunis: Cérès, 1995.

Kakon, Maguy. *La cuisine juive du Maroc de mère en fille.* Paris: Daniel Briand, 1996.

Kasper, Lynne Rossetto. *The Splendid Table: Recipes from Emilia-Romagna, the Heartland of Northern Italian Food.* New York: William Morrow, 1992.

Kaufman, Sheilah. *Sephardic Israeli Cuisine: A Mediterranean Mosaic.* New York: Hippocrene Books, 2002.

Kochilas, Diane. *The Food and Wine of Greece.* New York: St. Martin's, 1990.

——. *The Greek Vegetarian: More Than 100 Recipes Inspired by the Traditional Dishes and Flavors of Greece.* New York: St. Martin's, 1996.

Koronyo, Viki, and Sima Ovadya, eds. *Sefarad Yemekleri: Sephardic Cooking Book.* Istanbul: Subat (Society of Assistance to Old People), 1990.

Kouki, Mohamed. *Cuisine et pâtisserie tunisiennes: Ommok sanafa, 650 recettes.* Tunis: La Société d'Arts Graphiques, d'Édition et de Presse, Tunis, 1987.

Laasri, Ahmed. *240 recettes de cuisine marocaine.* Paris: Jacques Grancher, 1982.

Lahlou, Mourad. *Mourad: New Moroccan.* New York: Artisan Books, 2011.

Latemendía, Ana de, Lourdes Plana, and Gonzalo Sol. *The Different Flavours of Spain.* Madrid: Ministerio de Agricultura Pesca y Alimentacion, Ediciones El Viso, 1991.

Luzzatto, Amos. *Midor ledor, de generazione in generazione: Vita e cultura ebraica nel Veneto.* Bresseo di Teolo, Padua: Edizioni Scritti Monastici, Abbazia di Praglia, 1989.

Machlin, Edda Servi. *The Classic Cuisine of the Italian Jews.* 2 vols. New York: Dodd, Mead, 1981 (vol. 1). Croton on Hudson, NY: Giro Press, 1993 (vol. 2).

Maffioli, Giuseppe. *La cucina padovana: Dal cinquecento ad oggi.* Padua: Franco Muzzio, 1981.

——. *La cucina veneziana.* Padua: Franco Muzzio, 1987.

Manjón, Maite. *The Gastronomy of Spain and Portugal.* New York: Prentice Hall, 1990.

Marks, Copeland. *Sephardic Cooking: 600 Recipes Created in Exotic Sephardic Kitchens from Morocco to India.* New York: Donald I. Fine, 1992.

Marks, Gil. *The World of Jewish Cooking.* New York: Simon & Schuster, 1996.

Mazda, Maideh. *In a Persian Kitchen: Favorite Recipes from the Near East.* Rutland, VT: Charles Tuttle, 1960.

Mendel, Janet. *Traditional Spanish Cooking.* Reading, UK: Garnet, 1996.

Milano, Attilo. *Storia degli ebrei in Italia.* Turin: Einaudi, 1963.

Morse, Kitty. *Come with Me to the Kasbah: A Cook's Tour of Morocco.* Casablanca: Éditions Serar, 1989.

Moryoussef, Viviane, and Nina Moryoussef. *Moroccan Jewish Cookery*. Paris: J. P. Taillandier/
Sochepress, 1983.

NAJDA (Women Concerned about the Middle East). *Arabic Cook Book*. Berkeley: NAJDA,
1961.

Nathan, Joan. *The Foods of Israel Today*. New York: Alfred A. Knopf, 2001.

——. *Jewish Cooking in America*. New York: Alfred A. Knopf, 1994.

——. *The Jewish Holiday Kitchen*. New York: Schocken Books, 1988.

Ottolenghi, Yotam, and Sami Tamimi. *Jerusalem: A Cookbook*. Berkeley: Ten Speed Press,
2012.

Passigli, Milka Belgrado. *Le ricette di casa mia: La cucina casher in una famiglia ebraica italiana*.
Florence: Giuntina, 1993.

Passmore, Jacki. *The Complete Spanish Cookbook*. Boston: C. E. Tuttle, 1993.

Pavoncello, Donatella Limentani. *Dal 1880 ad oggi: La cucina ebraica della mia famiglia*. Rome:
Carucci, 1982.

Perera, Victor. *The Cross and the Pear Tree: A Sephardic Journey*. Berkeley: University of California
Press, 1996.

Plagemann, Catherine. *Fine Preserving*. New York: Simon and Schuster, 1967.

Ramazani, Nesta. *Persian Cooking: A Table of Exotic Delights*. Charlottesville: University Press of
Virginia, 1974.

Rayess, George N. *Rayess' Art of Lebanese Cooking*. Beirut: Librairie du Liban, 1966.

Ríos, Alicia, and Lourdes March. *The Heritage of Spanish Cooking*. New York: Random House, 1992.

Roden, Claudia. *The Book of Jewish Food: An Odyssey from Samarkand to New York*. New York: Alfred
A. Knopf, 1996.

Rodrigue, Aron. *Images of Sephardi and Eastern Jewries in Transition: The Teachers of the Alliance
Israélite Universelle, 1860–1939*. Seattle: University of Washington Press, 1993.

Roth, Cecil. *Doña Gracia of the House of Nasi*. Philadelphia: The Jewish Publication Society of
America, 1977.

——. *The History of the Jews of Italy*. Philadelphia: Jewish Publication Society of America,
1946.

——. *The Spanish Inquisition*. New York: W. W. Norton, 1964.

Saban, Giacomo, and Elio Toaff. *Le feste ebràiche: Tradizioni canti e ricètte da tutto il mondo*. Rome:
Logart, 1987.

Sacerdoti, Annie, and Francesca Brandes. *Veneto: Itinerari ebraici: I luoghi, la storia, l'arte*. Venice:
Marsilio, 1996.

Sacerdoti, Annie, Annamarcella Tedeschi Falco, and Vincenza Maugeri. *Emilia-Romagna: itinerari
ebraici: i luoghi, la storia, l'arte*. Venice: Marsilio, 1992.

Sacerdoti, Annie, and Luca Fiorentino. *Italy: Jewish Travel Guide*. Brooklyn, NY: Israelowitz,
1993.

Sacerdoti, Mira. *Italian Jewish Cooking*. London: Robert Hale, 1993.

Salloum, Habeeb, and James Peters. *From the Lands of Figs and Olives: Over 300 Delicious and Unusual
Recipes from the Middle East and North Africa*. New York: Interlink Books, 1995.

Santini, Aldo. *La cucina livornese*. Padua: Franco Muzzio, 1988.

——. *La cucina maremmana*. Padua: Franco Muzzio, 1991.

Scheindlin, Raymond P. *A Short History of the Jewish People: From Legendary Times to Modern
Statehood*. New York: Macmillan, 1998.

Scicolone, Michele. *La Dolce Vita: Enjoy Life's Pleasures with 170 Recipes for Biscotti, Torte, Crostate,
Gelati, and other Italian Desserts*. New York: William Morrow, 1993.

Seal, Rebecca. *Istanbul: Recipes from the Heart of Turkey.* Melbourne: Hardie Grant, 2013.

Segre, Bruno. *Gli ebrei in Italia.* Milan: Fenice, 2000, 1993.

Sephardic Temple Bikur Holim Congregation Ladies Auxiliary. *Sephardic Cooking.* Rev. ed. Seattle: The Auxiliary, 1993.

Shafia, Louisa. *The New Persian Kitchen.* Berkeley: Ten Speed Press, 2013.

Shaida, Margaret. *The Legendary Cuisine of Persia.* New York: Interlink Books, 2002.

Shaw, Stanford J. *The Jews of the Ottoman Empire and the Turkish Republic.* New York: New York University Press, 1991.

Simnegar, Reyna. *Persian Food from the Non-Persian Bride: And Other Kosher Sephardic Recipes You Will Love.* Brookline, MA: Exotic Kosher, 2013.

Stavroulakis, Nicholas. *Cookbook of the Jews of Greece.* Port Jefferson, NY: Cadmus Press, 1986.

———. *The Jews of Greece.* Athens: Talos, 1990.

Sternberg, Rabbi Robert. *The Sephardic Kitchen: The Healthful Food and Rich Culture of the Mediterranean Jews.* New York: HarperCollins, 1996.

Stille, Alexander. *Benevolence and Betrayal: Five Italian Jewish Families under Facism.* New York: Summit Books, 1991.

Taieb, Daisy. *Les fêtes juives à Tunis racontées à mes filles.* Nice: Association Epsilon, 1998.

Taieb, Jacques. *Être juif au Maghreb à la veille de la colonisation.* Paris: Albin Michel, 1994.

Tamzali, Haydée. *La cuisine en Afrique du Nord.* Paris: Vilo Press, 1986.

Tas, Luciano. *Storia degli ebrei italiani.* Rome: Newton Compton, 1987.

Valero, Rina. *Delights of Jerusalem: A Treasury of Cooking and Folklore.* Tel Aviv: Nahar, 1985.

Vincent, Mary, and R. A. Stradling. *Cultural Atlas of Spain & Portugal.* Oxford: Andromeda Oxford, 1994.

Wolfert, Paula. *Mediterranean Cooking: Revised with 75 New Recipes.* Rev. ed. New York: HarperPerennial, 1994.

———. *Mediterranean Greens and Grains: A Book of Savory, Sun-Drenched Recipes.* New York: HarperCollins, 1998.

———. *The Cooking of the Eastern Mediterranean: 215 Healthy, Vibrant, and Inspired Recipes.* New York: HarperCollins, 1994.

Wright, Clifford. *A Mediterranean Feast: The Story of the Birth of the Celebrated Cuisines of the Mediterranean, from the Merchants of Venice to the Barbary Corsairs, with More than 500 Recipes.* New York: William Morrow, 1999.

Zana-Murat, Andrée. *La cuisine juive tunisienne: De mère en fille.* Paris: Albin Michel, 1998.

Zanini de Vita, Oretta. *Il Lazio a tavola: Guida gastronomica tra storia e tradizioni.* Rome: Alphabyte Books, 1994.

Zeitoun, Edmond. *250 recettes de cuisine tunisienne.* Paris: Jacques Grancher, 1977.

# Acknowledgments

Thanks to:

Dore Brown, editor, friend, and excellent guide to what is possible, probable, and meaningful—plus an avid cook who not only edited but also cooked the recipes!

Kate Marshall, for directing this project to a successful conclusion at UC Press and for testing cake recipes for fun

Sharon Silva, copyediting goddess extraordinaire, who gets more thorough with every book

Artist Hugh d'Andrade, for his creative illustrations inspired by traditional Jewish woodcuts

Book designer Lia Tjandra, for her elegant choice of type and layout

Publicist Alex Dahne, for going to bat for this book

Bill LeBlond, who had the foresight to recognize a growing interest in Jewish cooking and published my early Jewish cookbooks while he was food editor at Chronicle Books

Staffan Terje and Umberto Gibin, for cooking my recipes every Passover for the past seven years at Perbacco restaurant and making the diners happy

Paula Wolfert, for turning Americans on to the amazing food of the Mediterranean

Oldways Preservation Trust, for educating chefs and the dining public about the health benefits of the Mediterranean diet

CUESA and the farmers and purveyors at the Ferry Plaza Farmers' Market

My family, for eating all of the test recipes and asking for more. I still love cooking for you.

# Index

Designer: Lia Tjandra
Text: 10/14 Hoefler Txt Roman
Display: Hoefler Txt, Hoefler Titling
Compositor: IDS Infotech Limited
Indexer: Thérèse Shere
Illustrator: Hugh D'Andrade
Printer and binder: Jostens USA, represented by Qualibre, Inc.